σ Unknown, $n_{A_1} \neq n_{A_2}$

$$s_{\overline{X}_{A_1} - \overline{X}_{A_2}} =$$

$$\sqrt{\left[\frac{(n_{A_1} - 1)s_{A_1}^2 + (n_{A_2} - 1)s_{A_2}^2}{n_{A_1} + n_{A_2} - 2}\right]\left[\frac{1}{n_{A_1}} + \frac{1}{n_{A_2}}\right]}$$

PROBABILITY

Probability (p) of Occurrence of an Event

$$p(\text{event}) = \frac{\text{number of occurrences of the event in a population}}{\text{total number of events in a population}}$$

z SCORES AND STANDARD SCORES

Single Score

$$z = (X_i - \mu)/\sigma$$

$$\text{Standard score} = (X_i - \overline{X})/S$$

$$= (X_i - \overline{X})\bigg/\sqrt{\sum_{i=1}^{N}(X_i - \overline{X})^2/N}\,.$$

Sample Mean

$$z = (\overline{X} - \mu)/\sigma_{\overline{X}}$$

t TESTS

One-Sample t Test

$$t = (\overline{X} - \mu)/s_{\overline{X}} = (\overline{X} - \mu)/(s/\sqrt{N})$$

$$df = N - 1$$

t Test for Independent Groups

$$t = (\overline{X}_{A_1} - \overline{X}_{A_2})/(s_{\overline{X}_{A_1} - \overline{X}_{A_2}})$$

$$df = N - 2$$

t Test for Related Groups

$$t_{rel} = (\overline{X}_{A_1} - \overline{X}_{A_2})\bigg/\sqrt{\frac{\left[\sum D^2 - \left(\sum D\right)^2\big/N\right]}{[N(N-1)]}}$$

$$df = N - 1$$

ANALYSIS OF VARIANCE

One-Factor Between-Subjects Design

Sums of Squares

$$SS_{Total} = \sum_{j=1}^{a}\sum_{i=1}^{n_a}(X_{ij} - \overline{X}_G)^2$$

$$SS_A = \sum_{j=1}^{a}\sum_{i=1}^{n_a}(X_A - \overline{X}_G)^2$$

$$SS_{Error} = \sum_{j=1}^{a}\sum_{i=1}^{n_A}(X_{ij} - \overline{X}_A)^2$$

Degrees of Freedom

$$df_{Total} = N - 1$$

$$df_A = a - 1$$

$$df_{Error} = a(n_A - 1) = N - a$$

Mean Squares

$$MS_A = SS_A/df_A$$

$$MS_{Error} = SS_{Error}/df_{Error}$$

F Statistic

$$F = MS_A/MS_{Error}$$

Two-Factor Between-Subjects Design

Sums of Squares

$$SS_{Total} = \sum_{k=1}^{b}\sum_{j=1}^{a}\sum_{i=1}^{n_{AB}}(X_{ijk} - \overline{X}_G)^2$$

$$SS_A = \sum_{k=1}^{b}\sum_{j=1}^{a}\sum_{i=1}^{n_{AB}}(\overline{X}_A - \overline{X}_G)^2$$

$$SS_B = \sum_{k=1}^{b}\sum_{j=1}^{a}\sum_{i=1}^{n_{AB}}(\overline{X}_B - \overline{X}_G)^2$$

$$SS_{A \times B} = \sum_{k=1}^{b}\sum_{j=1}^{a}\sum_{i=1}^{n_{AB}}(\overline{X}_{AB} - \overline{X}_A - \overline{X}_B + \overline{X}_G)^2$$

$$SS_{Error} = \sum_{k=1}^{b}\sum_{j=1}^{a}\sum_{i=1}^{n_{AB}}(X_{ijk} - \overline{X}_{AB})^2$$

Degrees of Freedom

$$df_{Total} = N - 1$$

$$df_A = a - 1$$

$$df_B = b - 1$$

$$df_{A \times B} = (a - 1)(b - 1)$$

$$df_{Error} = ab(n_{AB} - 1)$$

Statistical Concepts for the Behavioral Sciences

Statistical Concepts for the Behavioral Sciences

Harold O. Kiess
Framingham State College

Allyn and Bacon
Boston • London • Sydney • Toronto

Series editor: John-Paul Lenney
Production/design service: York Production Services
Series editorial assistant: Susan S. Brody
Cover administrator: Linda Dickinson
Manufacturing buyer: Bill Alberti
Composition buyer: Linda Cox

Library of Congress Cataloging-in-Publication Data

Kiess, Harold O., 1940–
    Statistical concepts for the behavioral sciences/Harold O. Kiess.
       p.   cm.
    Bibliography: p.
    Includes index.
    ISBN 0–205–11883–6
    1. Social sciences—Statistical methods. 2. Statistics.
I. Title.
HA29.K4857 1989
519.5—dc19
                                                     88-28173
                                                      CIP

Printed in the United States of America
10 9 8 7 6 5 4 3 2   93 92 91 90 89

Brief Contents

Contents

Chapter 6
The Normal Distribution   119

Part

Chapter 10
Elementary Research Methods and the *t* Test for Two Independent Groups   225

Chapter 12
Multiple Comparison Procedures for the One-Factor Between-Subjects Analysis of Variance   319

Chapter 13
Two-Factor Between-Subjects Analysis of Variance   351

Chapter 16
Errors, Power, and Strength of Effect   491

Part

III

Preface

An understanding of statistical concepts is vital to the behavioral science student, for statistical thinking permeates current behavioral science research. It is difficult, however, for the student of introductory statistics to see the relevance of the many statistical methods to the search for knowledge in the behavioral sciences. My goal is to help the student see this relevance by presenting a conceptual development of basic statistical methods in the context of their use in behavioral science. To achieve this, I have placed a strong emphasis on utilizing contemporary research problems in the behavioral sciences. I believe that real problems clearly illustrate the immediate relevance of statistical analysis in scientific research.

I have tried to be mindful of problems encountered by students attempting to grasp the sometimes difficult conceptual basis of statistics. A variety of special features are employed to keep the material strongly tied to actual research problems and to permit students to assess their understanding of the material as they proceed through a chapter. The organization of the text also is designed for continuity in the concepts presented.

ORGANIZATION OF THE TEXT

The text is divided into three parts:
Part I: Summarizing and Describing Data. The seven chapters in this part deal with measuring behavior, organizing data with frequency distributions, summarizing data with measures of central tendency and variability, an introduction to the normal distribution, and using statistics for inference and estimation. A strong emphasis is placed upon the information contained in the various descriptive measures and techniques. In addition, the chapters set the stage for the need for statistical hypothesis testing.

Part II: Statistical Hypothesis Testing. The nine chapters in this part begin with a discussion of the z test. The one-sample t test is then introduced, followed by the t test for independent groups. Four chapters devoted to the analysis of variance follow. Analysis of variance is currently the most widely used statistical test in the behavioral sciences, and students need to be familiar with its use. Thus, a thorough introduction is provided for the one-factor between-subjects, one-factor within-subjects, and the factorial between-subjects analysis of variance. Considerable attention is given to the interpretation of an interaction in a factorial design. One chapter of this part presents nonparametric statistics. The final chapter presents an overview of issues dealing with the power of statistical tests and the use of strength of association measures.

Part III: Correlation and Regression. The first chapter in this part introduces both the Pearson and Spearman correlation coefficients. Statistical hypothesis testing with each correlation coefficient is also introduced. The second chapter provides an overview of the basics of simple linear regression. The placement of these chapters at the end of the text is somewhat unusual for a statistics text. Many texts include these chapters following a discussion of descriptive statistics. But I believe this common placement poses conceptual difficulties for students. Descriptive statistics, such as the mean and standard deviation, lead naturally to a discussion of statistical tests for the difference between sample means. Interposition of correlation and regression between descriptive statistics and statistical hypothesis testing interrupts this continuity of thought. I thus elected to maintain the continuity of conceptual development and place the correlation and regression material at the end of the text.

SPECIAL FEATURES

Realistic Problems

All statistical methods are introduced in the context of a problem from behavioral research. Many of the problems are based on studies drawn from contemporary published research. The studies on which these problems are based are referenced fully so the interested student may read the original research.

Conceptual Development of Statistics

The various statistics are introduced conceptually, often by use of a definitional formula. A problem is then worked using this conceptual approach so that students may see what the statistic does with the data. After the conceptual introduction, computational formulas are presented and the problem worked step-by-step using these formulas. Some instructors may wish to omit the computational formulas and have their students utilize one of the many statistics programs available for computer analysis. The computational formulas may be omitted easily without loss of continuity in the conceptual development.

I have tried not to overwhelm students mathematically when introducing a statistic. The mathematics required for elementary statistics is simple, yet many students are deterred in their study of statistics by a first chapter that reviews basic mathematics. Thus I have introduced and explained the necessary mathematical concepts when they are needed rather than putting the review in one chapter.

Testing Your Knowledge Sections

Each chapter contains interspersed *Testing Your Knowledge* sections. These learning aids provide an opportunity for students to review and test their understanding of the text material. Many of the questions asked focus on actual research problems. Thus, not only do these questions provide a review, they also give examples of the uses of the various statistical methods. I strongly encourage students to complete these exercises whenever they are encountered before continuing on in the chapter.

Statistics in Use

After a statistical method has been introduced, its use in actual research is described in a *Statistics in Use* section. Each Statistics in Use presents a brief summary of recently published research and a description of how the statistical method was employed in that research.

Sample Journal Formats

For many statistical tests, a sample journal report of a statistical analysis is presented with an explanation of the information contained in the report. The sample is followed by exercises on extracting information from journal presentations of the results of a study.

Readability

The text is written so that it may be read and studied without interruption by boxed features or optional reading. Each section of the text follows from the previous material. The flow of ideas is cumulative and continuous.

I hope that you will find that this text leads to an interesting and rewarding study of statistics. If you have any comments or suggestions on the text, please write me at the Department of Psychology, Framingham State College, Box 2000, Framingham, MA 01701.

Acknowledgments

A number of individuals contributed to the development of this text. The idea for the text came from Allen Workman of Allyn and Bacon, who suggested that I use the approach taken in a psychological research methods text, *Psychological Research Methods, A Conceptual Approach,* I coauthored with my colleague, Dr. Douglas W. Bloomquist, and extend it to a statistics text. John-Paul Lenney, Senior Editor at Allyn and Bacon, enthusiastically endorsed the idea and provided the impetus for carrying the project to completion. John-Paul's ideas and visions for the text have strongly shaped this book. I would also like to thank Diane L. McOscar, who, upon becoming Senior Editor, gave wholehearted support to the development of many of the ancillary materials for the text. Bill Barke, Editor in Chief at Allyn and Bacon, also deserves acknowledgment; it was his encouragement and confidence seven years ago that led me to even attempt to write a college-level text.

Many of the conceptual ideas used in this text are similar to those developed in *Psychological Research Methods, A Conceptual Approach.* I thank Doug Bloomquist for his contributions to the development of those ideas and material, and for his willingness to let me use that material in this text. I also thank Doug, and another of my colleagues, Len Flynn, for their presentation of the supplementary materials for the text.

Various professors were also involved in the development of this text. Some responded to a detailed questionnaire offering suggestions regarding content and approach. Others reviewed part or all of the manuscript; their careful scrutiny helped me immensely in clarifying the presentation and avoiding conceptual and mathematical errors. Of course, any inaccuracies or conceptual inadequacies remaining are my responsibility alone. I am extremely grateful to the following for their assistance: Mike Brown, Pacific Lutheran University; William H. Calhoun, The University of Tennessee at Knoxville; David Campbell, Humboldt State University; Donna Cruse, Syan, Inc., Corvallis, Oregon; Ernest Dahl, American River College; Lambert Deckers, Ball State University; Richard J. Harris, University of New Mexico; William D. Kalberer, California State University, Chico; William McDaniel, Georgia College; Jim McMartin, California State University, Northridge; George Parrott, California State University, Sacramento; Glen Sizemore, Northeastern State University; W. Newton Suter, University of Arkansas at Little Rock; and Eric F. Ward, Western Illinois University.

At Framingham State College, members of the Department of Computing Services, Karin Steinbrenner, Director; Alice Doyle, Susan Hovencamp, Joe McCaul, and Sarah McEwen helped to convert material from one word processing system to another. Without their willing assistance the text would be a jumble of ASCII codes.

A number of other individuals at Allyn and Bacon also made important contributions to the fruition of this book. Leslie Goldberg served as a very capable developmental editor, providing quick and helpful answers to my many questions and problems. Susan Brody shepherded the many manuscript pages into the maze of production. And, Peter Petraitis served as a most capable production editor.

Mary Jo Gregory, production supervisor at York Graphic Services, made everything come together in the form of a textbook.

I also thank CRC Press, Inc. for their gracious permission to use many of the statistical tables in the Appendix.

A final acknowledgment is to those who have been affected most by the work required to write a book—the members of my family, Sandra, Kimberley, and Jeffrey. They have been most understanding of my involvement in this project; I could not have completed it without their understanding and encouragement.

Summarizing and Describing Data

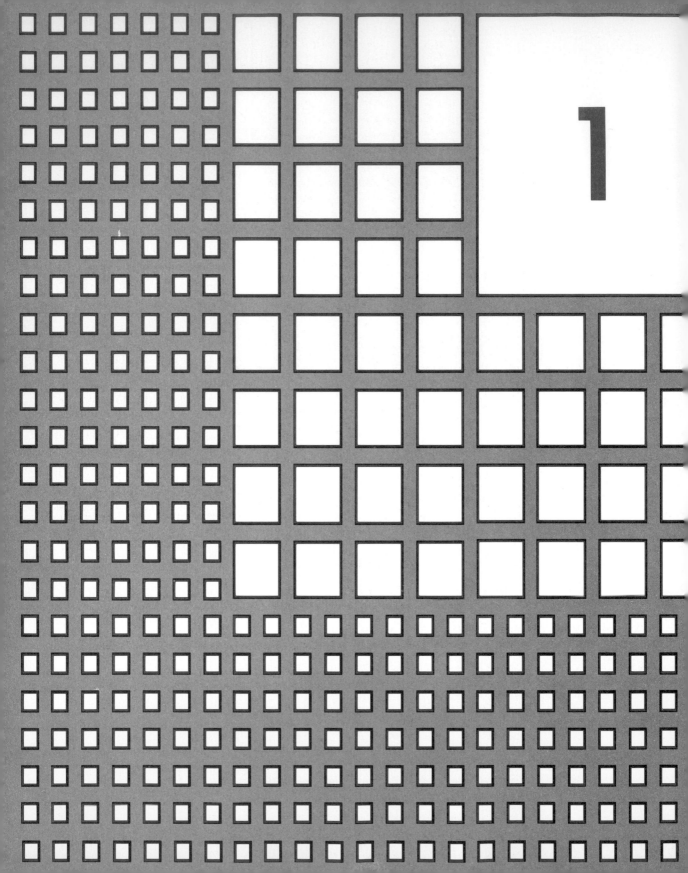

1

Behavioral Research and the Need for Statistics

What Are Statistics?

Using Statistics: An Overview
    Description and Inference
    Experimentation and Statistical Hypothesis Testing
    Correlation and Regression

Why Are Statistics Necessary?

WHAT ARE STATISTICS?

Behavioral scientists attempt to understand and explain human and animal behavior. Their research frequently involves obtaining numerical measurements of behavior or characteristics from samples of people or animals. To aid in describing and analyzing these measurements, behavioral scientists often apply a set of procedures called **statistics** to the measurements they have obtained. The study of statistics refers to the methods or procedures that are used to summarize, analyze, and draw inferences from the numerical measurements that have been obtained. A **statistic** is a single number that may be used to describe the collection of numerical measurements from a sample or to analyze those measurements more fully.

USING STATISTICS: AN OVERVIEW

Statistical procedures are used in many different ways by behavioral scientists. We provide several examples in this chapter and then discuss the procedures more fully in following chapters. These examples also introduce some of the fundamental terms used in statistical methods.

Description and Inference

From our everyday reading, all of us are familiar with statistical descriptions of large sets of measurements. For example, the national newspaper, *USA Today*, offered a description of the activities of typical individuals in the United States in the mid–1980s ("The Way," 1985). One characterization offered was that the average household watches 7.12 hours of television per day. This numerical value illustrates two important uses of statistical methods: description and inference. Although the value of 7.12 hours is intended to characterize the population of all U.S. households, it was not obtained by observing and measuring all the households in the country. Rather, only a portion, or sample, of all households was observed and measured. The number of hours that each household included in the sample watched television in a day was recorded. The measurements from the different households in the sample were then summarized by calculating a single number, a statistic, 7.12 hours. This statistic is intended to describe the daily amount of time that a typical household in the sample watched television. The number of hours of television watched per day by a typical household in the population of all households in the United States was then inferred, or estimated, from this statistic.

Behavioral scientists and statisticians often refer to populations and samples. A **population** is some set of measurements of people, animals, objects, or events, that in principle can be identified. The members of a specified population share a common characteristic that is measured. For example, all the households in the United States constitute a population. So, too, do all the college students in the United States, all the adult females in North Carolina, the farmers in Nebraska, individuals who commute on a daily basis to New York City, or all the people who have one or more bank credit cards. Any group of individuals may be thought of as a population as long as all those possessing the characteristic or characteristics being measured are included in the group.

Behavioral scientists often want to be able to characterize entire populations with statements such as, "the typical American household watches 7.12 hours of television per day" or "the average U.S. male earns $19,438 per year whereas a female earns only $9,584 per year" ("The Way," *USA Today*, 1985). But it should be obvious to you that in most instances these characterizations cannot be obtained from measuring all members of the population. Rather, the behavioral scientist employs only a sample of the population.

A **sample** is a group of individuals selected from the population, often following a set of rules to ensure that the individuals selected are representative of the population. A characteristic of the members of the sample is then measured (e.g., the amount of time each watched television is observed, or his or her yearly income is recorded). A statistic is calculated to describe these measurements. This descriptive statistic may then be used to infer a characteristic of the population. The word *infer* implies reasoning from something known to something unknown. Translated into the activity of the behavioral scientist, **statistical inference** is the process of reaching conclusions about unknown population values (e.g., the number of hours that the typical U.S. household watches TV per day) called *parameters*, from statistics obtained from measurements made on members of a sample. We discuss the procedures involved in description of samples and inference to a population primarily in Chapters 3 to 7.

Statistics in Use 1–1

Health Seeking Behaviors: Estimation and Inference

We are often urged by the popular media to change our behavior to improve our health. For example, public service announcements suggest that we should not smoke, or that we should drink alcoholic beverages only in moderation, or that we should have our blood pressure checked regularly. But how does the general public perceive the importance of such behaviors to the maintenance of good health? Bausell (1986), as part of a larger study, sampled 1254 adults in the United States and asked them to rate the perceived importance of a variety of potential health-improving behaviors. For example, individuals were asked how important they believed not driving after drinking is to good health. They rated each behavior on a scale similar to the one illustrated below.

1	2	3	4	5	6	7	8	9	10
low				moderate					utmost
importance				importance					importance

Bausell reports that, on the average, individuals in the sample rated "not driving after drinking" as 9.3, "exercising regularly" as 8.3, and "drinking in moderation" as 6.6. Each of these values is a descriptive statistic, a number describing the typical response of members of the sample. Because each person in the sample did not give the same rating to an item, Bausell also presented other descriptive statistics, called *measures of variability*. These measures indicate the amount of variation in the ratings given. From these descriptive statistics, we are able to infer that, among the general public, not driving after drinking is perceived as more important in maintaining good health than is exercising regularly; and exercising regularly is rated as more important than drinking in moderation. Because Bausell used a stratified random sample from the population, we can be confident that the inferences made from the sample to the general public are correct. We discuss this method of selecting a sample and other problems of inference more fully in Chapter 7. ▪

Testing Your Knowledge 1–1

On a separate sheet of paper, test your knowledge of the material in this section by answering the following questions.

1. Define: statistics, statistic, population, sample, statistical inference.
2. In a recent election, 600 potential voters of a congressional district were polled to discover who they planned to vote for in an upcoming election. The results indicated that 312 voters, or 52 percent of the sample, planned to vote for candidate A; 240 voters, or 40 percent, planned to vote for candidate B; and 48 voters, or 8 percent, said they did not plan to vote or had no preference among the candidates. Based upon the results of the poll, the researchers estimated that candidate A would win the election with about 52 percent of the total vote.
   a. Explain why descriptive statistics are necessary to summarize the results of this research.
   b. What inferences to a population were made from the statistics obtained? ▪

Experimentation and Statistical Hypothesis Testing

Behavioral scientists are not only interested in describing and characterizing samples and populations; they also desire to find the *causes* of behavior for individuals or groups. A number of scientific approaches are available for this task. One approach is to perform an experiment. To conduct an experiment, a researcher identifies a variable, called an **independent variable,** that he or she thinks affects a person's behavior. The behavior that is expected to be affected by this independent variable is called the **dependent variable.**

For example, a behavioral scientist might expect alcohol consumption to affect a person's response to violence: People under the influence of alcohol are expected to be more accepting of violence than people who are not under the influence of alcohol (Gustafson, 1987a). In this instance, alcohol consumption is the independent variable. The experimenter has control over whether a person does or does not consume alcohol, and he or she expects it to affect the acceptance of violence. A measure of the person's acceptance of violence is the dependent variable. Acceptance of violence is presumed to depend upon whether or not a person has consumed alcohol. The statement of the researcher's expectation that alcohol consumption will affect the acceptance of violence is called a research hypothesis. A **research hypothesis** is a statement of an expected or predicted relationship between two or more variables. In an experiment, a research hypothesis is a statement of a predicted relationship between an independent variable and a dependent variable.

The simplest experiment that a researcher could perform to test the research hypothesis relating alcohol consumption to acceptance of violence begins by creating two equivalent groups of people. We often refer to the people who participate in research studies as **subjects** or **participants. Equivalent groups,** then, are groups of subjects that are not expected to differ in any consistent or systematic way prior to receiving the treatment conditions of the experiment. An experiment in which two or more groups are created is often called a **between-subjects design.** After the equivalent groups are created, the researcher manipulates or varies the independent variable and measures the dependent variable. In our example, the experimenter might give subjects in the first group 0.8 milliliters of alcohol per kilogram of body weight mixed with an equal amount of orange juice. Subjects in the second group might be given 1.6 milliliters of plain orange juice per kilogram of body weight. The dependent variable might be measured by having the subjects watch a violent movie and then rate the movie on the acceptability of the violence shown. For each subject, then, a score on the rating task is obtained. This score is the dependent variable, for we expect it to depend upon whether or not the subject had consumed alcohol prior to watching the movie. A **score** is simply the measurement obtained on the subject's performance of a task.

The scores obtained from all the subjects provide the **raw data** for the experiment. From these raw data, the researcher must decide if the independent variable of consumption of alcohol affected the subjects' rating of the acceptability of violence in the movie.

The process by which the experimenter decides if the independent variable had an effect or not involves several steps. The first step is to describe the ratings of each of the two groups. This description involves calculating descriptive statistics that indicate the typical ratings of subjects in each group. This step is identical to the process of description of data discussed earlier in this chapter. Moreover, you are familiar with some common descriptive statistics such as the mode, the median, or the arithmetic mean.

The second step involves deciding if any observed difference in the descriptive statistics for the two groups of scores is large enough to be attributed to the effect of the independent variable. This step requires the use of **statistical hypothesis testing.** Why is statistical hypothesis testing necessary to make this decision? The answer to this question is simple. Whether or not the independent variable has an effect, the scores of subjects within each group and the typical scores of the two groups will differ from each other. Indeed, it is a fact of life that on almost any behavior you can imagine, individuals differ from each other. Suppose you were to form two equivalent groups without manipulating an independent variable, such as the consumption of alcohol. You could be assured that the typical ratings of the two groups would differ by chance alone. A statistical test allows the researcher to estimate the possibility of these chance differences. The difference actually observed between the two groups in the experiment is then compared to the possibility of obtaining a chance difference as large as the one obtained. If the possibility of obtaining a chance difference as large as the actual difference found is sufficiently small, then the researcher decides that the observed difference does not reflect a chance difference. Rather, it is attributed to the effect of the independent variable.

Statistical testing is used widely in the behavioral sciences. To understand fully the concepts involved, however, requires building upon a knowledge base of descriptive statistics and statistical inference and estimation: topics discussed in Chapters 2 to 7. We discuss statistical testing and its application to several different research designs in Chapters 8 to 16.

Statistics in Use 1–2

Errors in Perception: Statistical Hypothesis Testing

Scientists have long been interested in the question of how we perceive our world. Our common experience indicates that we do not perceive the environment exactly as it physically exists. For example, when asked to judge the size of an object that is a considerable distance away from us, we may let the expected or familiar size of the object affect our perception of it. To gain a greater understanding of how experience affects our perception, Predebon (1987) conducted an experiment that required individuals to estimate the size of an object. The independent variable manipulated was the type of object viewed. Two different objects were used. The first was a 7.1 centimeters (cm) high reproduction of a "nine of spades" playing card. This reproduced card was only 0.8 the size of a regular playing card, which is 8.9 cm high. The other object was a blank white card that was the same size as the reproduced nine of spades card (i.e., 7.1 cm). Two equivalent groups of 12 subjects each were formed; one group (identified as the experimental group) estimated the height of the reproduced nine of spades card, the other group (identified as the control group) estimated the height of the blank white card. For these size estimates, the card was placed about 27 feet from the subject in a black visual alley so that common distance cues could not be used to aid the size judgments. The estimated size of the card was the dependent variable. Predebon hypothesized that the reproduced card would be estimated to be larger than the blank white card. He expected this relationship to occur because the familiar size of a playing card would influence a subject's perception of the reproduced playing card but not the blank white card.

The mean height estimates were 6.8 cm for the control group and 8.6 cm for the experimental group. To determine if these observed estimates differed by more than would be expected by chance, Predebon employed a statistical test called the *t*. This test indicated that the estimates of the two groups differed by an amount larger than that expected from chance differences alone. Although the stimuli were actually the same physical size, the subjects in the experimental group judged the stimulus to be larger than did the subjects in the control group. These results agreed with the research hypothesis and indicate that thought processes do indeed influence our visual perception. ▪

Testing Your Knowledge 1–2

On a separate sheet of paper, test your knowledge of the material in this section by answering the following questions.

1. Define: independent variable, dependent variable, research hypothesis, subjects, equivalent groups, between-subjects design, score, raw data, statistical hypothesis test.
2. Students learning the basic positions of ballet often have difficulty assuming the correct foot positions. One problem is that of foot pronation, letting the feet roll in when the heels are placed together and the toes pointed laterally outward. To help students overcome this problem, Clarkson, James, Watkins, and Foley (1986) formed two equivalent

groups of females who had not previously had ballet training. For one group, electrodes were attached to the feet; and, when the students allowed their feet to pronate, a buzzer was sounded. The other group of subjects also had electrodes placed on their feet, but they were not given any feedback about foot pronation. Both groups were then taught basic ballet positions, and the amount of time the feet pronated was measured. For one test period, the researchers found that subjects given auditory feedback had 3.1 seconds of foot pronation, whereas the subjects in the no-feedback group had 21.8 seconds of foot pronation. A statistical test confirmed that the difference in foot pronation time between the groups was a real and not a chance difference.

a. Identify the independent variable manipulated by Clarkson *et al.*
b. Identify the dependent variable measured.
c. Explain why this study is an experiment.
d. Explain why statistical hypothesis testing is necessary in this experiment. ▮

Correlation and Regression

In many instances of behavioral science research, an experimenter may be interested in whether two or more characteristics of individuals are related to each other, or covary. Two variables are said to **covary** if they consistently vary in relation to each other. For example, is a person's typical level of anxiety related to his or her self-esteem? That is, do anxiety and self-esteem co-relate? Are high levels of anxiety related to high levels of self-esteem? Or, conversely, are high levels of anxiety related to low levels of self-esteem? Or, are the two measures not at all related?

To answer these questions the scientist may obtain a sample of individuals and obtain two scores from each person—a measurement of each person's anxiety level and a measurement of self-esteem. Then, to determine whether or not the scores on these two measures are related, the researcher will calculate a correlation coefficient. A **correlation coefficient** is a statistic that provides a numerical description of the extent of the relatedness of two sets of scores and the direction of the relationship. Values of this coefficient may range from -1.00 to $+1.00$.

Statistical hypothesis testing also enters into use with the correlation coefficient. There will always be some chance relationship among scores. Thus, is the observed relation, given by the numerical value of the correlation coefficient, greater than would be expected from chance alone? A statistical test on the correlation coefficient provides an answer for this question.

If the two sets of scores are related, then the scientist may be interested in attempting to predict one score from the other. If you knew a person's anxiety score, could you predict his or her self-esteem score?

And, if you could predict the self-esteem score, how accurate would your prediction be? The problem of prediction of one set of scores from a different set of scores is approached by using *regression statistics.*

Correlation and regression techniques are used widely in many areas of behavioral science. One prominent use is in the area of standardized test construction, for the purpose of many standardized tests is to predict future behaviors in school or on the job. We discuss and develop correlation and regression in Chapters 17 and 18.

Statistics in Use 1–3

Are Lonely People Also Depressed? Using Correlational Statistics

Are any of your friends lonely people? Do they appear depressed also? Loneliness and depression among individuals seem to be related characteristics. But, are these characteristics related? And, if they are related, how strong is the relationship? Ouellet and Joshi (1986) attempted to provide answers to these questions by using paper-and-pencil rating scales to measure the loneliness and depression of 81 college undergraduates. Each student thus provided two numerical scores: a loneliness score and a depression score. To determine if the two scores were related, Ouellet and Joshi calculated a correlation coefficient on the two scores and obtained a value of +0.41. A statistical test indicated that this correlation is not simply a chance relationship. Loneliness and depression tend to vary together. Lonely people typically are also depressed, and nonlonely individuals usually are not depressed. Consequently, Ouellet and Joshi confirmed with actual measurements the relationship between depression and loneliness that many of us have observed casually. ■

Testing Your Knowledge 1–3

On a separate sheet of paper, test your knowledge of the material in this section by answering the following questions.

1. Define: covary, correlation coefficient.
2. Many people believe in paranormal phenomena, such as precognition, extrasensory perception, and psychokinesis. Is the extent of belief in such phenomena related to the type of high school courses taken by such individuals? Tobacyk, Miller, and Jones (1984) measured the belief in paranormal phenomena of 193 eleventh-grade high school students. They also recorded the total number of science courses each student had taken. When relating the number of science courses to belief in paranormal phenomena, they discovered an inverse relationship. The more

science courses a student had taken, the weaker the belief in paranormal phenomena.
a. Explain why correlational statistics are needed in this study.
b. What are the two sets of measures that are employed in this study? ▪

WHY ARE STATISTICS NECESSARY?

We have presented three common uses of statistical analysis in behavioral science research. Nagging at you, however, may be the discomforting question of why statistical methods are necessary in the behavioral sciences in the first place. The answer is straightforward and the same for each of the statistical procedures we have presented: It is a delightful fact of life that we are all different from each other on almost every characteristic that can be measured. It would certainly be a tiresome world if every person were identical to every other person, but such an environment would possess the advantage of requiring no need for statistical techniques. Why? Consider the various uses of statistics that we have introduced.

The first deals with describing numerical measurements obtained from individuals. But if all people were alike, then a measurement taken on any one person would describe all other people. Everyone, for example, would earn exactly $19,438 per year. To make an inference to a population, then, only one person would need to be measured. Accordingly, there would be no need for descriptive statistics to represent a typical score for members of the sample.

The second use deals with statistical hypothesis testing to answer questions of whether an independent variable has an effect on behavior. Think how easy it would be to decide if an independent variable has an effect on behavior if every person's behavior were identical to every other person's. Suppose, for example, that you wanted to know if a particular drug lowers heart rate. Without the drug, everyone's heart rate is 60 beats per minute; and, with the drug, everyone's heart rate is 55 beats per minute. Is there any question of whether the drug lowers heart rate? Because there is no chance variation from person to person, there would be no doubt that the drug lowered heart rate. Statistical hypothesis testing would be unnecessary.

Finally, the third use deals with the problem of correlation and regression. Are two behaviors related and, if so, can we predict the occurrence of one behavior from the occurrence of the other? This question only arises because people are different from one another and behave differently in the same situation. If every person were identical to every other person on all behaviors, then all behaviors would be perfectly predictable. Because there would be no variability in behaviors among people, we could predict all behaviors perfectly without using correlation and regression statistics.

An environment with no variability among people and animals would eliminate the need for statistical analysis, but what a dreadful place it would be. Fortunately, we do not have such a world. But a life with variability among its peoples requires the need for statistical techniques in order to conduct research.

SUMMARY

- A statistic is a number used to describe the scores from a sample.
- A statistic also may be used to infer the value of a population parameter.
- Statistical hypothesis testing is used to determine whether an observed difference between two groups in an experiment is large enough to be attributed to the effect of an independent variable rather than to chance.

- Correlational statistics are used to determine if two sets of scores are related.
- Regression statistics are used to predict one set of scores from another set of scores.

KEY TERMS

between-subjects design
correlation coefficient
covary
dependent variable
equivalent groups
independent variable

population
raw data
research hypothesis
sample
score
statistic

statistical hypothesis testing
statistical inference
statistics
subjects

REVIEW QUESTIONS

On a separate sheet of paper, test your knowledge of the material in this chapter by answering the following questions.

For each of the studies described briefly below, identify which uses of statistics discussed in this chapter are employed. Then answer the questions following each description.

1. Crews, Shirreffs, Thomas, Krahenbuhl, and Helfrich (1986) measured the percentage of body fat in 23 professional female golfers. They related this measure to the golfer's average score for a year of competitive play and found they could predict golf scores from percentage of body fat. A low percentage of body fat was related to a low average golf score, whereas higher percentages of body fat were associated with higher average golf scores.
   a. Explain why correlational statistics are needed in this study.
   b. What are the two sets of measures that are employed in this study?

2. Kawasaki syndrome is a disease of childhood characterized by fever, fissured lips, a bright red tongue, redness of the palms and soles, and a rash. Typical therapy has involved taking aspirin. Recent research, however, has suggested that gamma globulin plus aspirin may be more effective than aspirin alone. To test this research hypothesis, Newburger *et al.* (1986) randomly assigned 168 children suffering Kawasaki syndrome to one of two treatment conditions: aspirin or aspirin plus gamma globulin. They found that, after one day of treatment, the temperature of children in the aspirin-plus-gamma globulin treatment group fell an average of 2.3°F, whereas the temperature of the children in the aspirin-only treatment group fell 0.8°F. A statistical test indicated that the difference in the temperature decreases was not a chance difference between the two groups and that the aspirin-plus-gamma globulin group had a greater temperature decrease than the aspirin-alone group.
   a. Identify the independent variable manipulated by Newburger *et al.*
   b. Identify the dependent variable measured.
   c. Explain why this study is an experiment.
   d. Explain why statistical hypothesis testing is necessary in this experiment.

3. Gurnack and Werbie (1985) analyzed the court records of 3,941 individuals arrested for drunken driving in Wisconsin. They discovered that about 40 percent of the individuals were under 25 years old, about 40 percent were between 26 to 44 years old, and about 20 percent were older than 44 years. They also found that about 50 percent of those arrested were unskilled workers.

   a. Explain why descriptive statistics are necessary to summarize the results of this research.

   b. What descriptive statistic was used in this study?

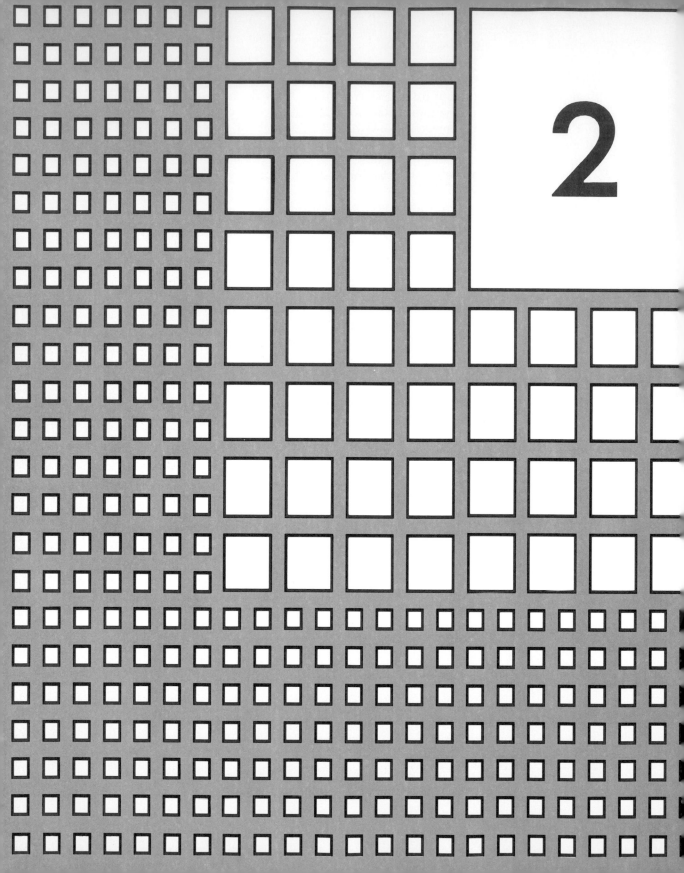

2

Measuring Behavior

Statistics is built upon a foundation of measurement. Indeed, statistical methods are necessary because scientists are able to measure behaviors and events. **Measurement** is a process of assigning numbers to variables according to a set of rules. A **variable** is any environmental condition or event, stimulus, personal characteristic or attribute, or behavior that can take on different values at different times or with different people. A person's height, weight, anxiety level, intelligence, or marital satisfaction are examples of variables, for they may take on different values at different times. It is assumed that the variable being measured exists in some true amount. The actual measurements made by a behavioral scientist will measure this true amount only imperfectly. This conceptualization of measurement is illustrated in Figure 2–1. A true amount of a variable (e.g., anxiety) is assumed to exist. A rule of measurement is applied and an observable scale of measurement for the variable is obtained. Most typically the observed measurements are classified into one of four scales: nominal, ordinal, interval, or ratio measurements.

SCALES OF MEASUREMENT

Nominal Measurement

Nominal measurement is a classification of the measured variable into different categories. As an example, with a nominal measurement of

FIGURE 2–1.
Schematic illustration of the concept of measurement.

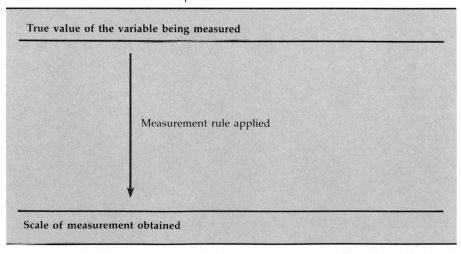

True value of the variable being measured

Measurement rule applied

Scale of measurement obtained

ethnic origin, people may be categorized as American Indian, Asian, Black, Caucasian, or Hispanic. People within a category may vary on the true nature of their ethnic origin, but the rule of nominal measurement places individuals possessing differing amounts of the characteristic into the same category. That is, once people have been categorized by a nominal measurement rule, all people in the same category (e.g., those categorized as Caucasian) are equated on the measurement obtained, even though they may not possess the same amount of the characteristic. If numbers are assigned to describe the categories, the numbers are used only to name the category (hence the term *nominal*, which means *to name*); each individual assigned to the same category will be assigned the same number. A schematic illustration of nominal measurement is shown in Figure 2–2a.

Many behavioral scientists do not regard nominal scales as actual measurements because there is no quantitative information. The numbers assigned in nominal measurement serve the purpose of identification only. However nominal scales are viewed, they represent the lowest scale of measurement.

Statistics in Use 2–1

First Class Attendance and Academic Performance: The Use of Nominal Measurement

Is attendance on the first day of class related to course grades? Assuming the more motivated the students, the more likely they would attend the first class meeting and would also do well in the course, Buckalew, Daly, and Coffield (1986) investigated this relationship. Students who attended the first class day were assigned a category of "1" and those who were absent on this day assigned a category of "0." Notice the scale of measurement of class attendance was nominal; attendance was recorded as one of two categories: present—1, or absent—0. The assigned number is used only to identify the category of the person's behavior. No mathematical operations can be performed on the numbers beyond tabulating frequencies of responses. It would have been just as reasonable to assign a 0 to a student present on the first class day and a 1 to a student absent on the first class day. In fact, numbers need not be assigned to the response categories at all for nominal measurement. One can simply tabulate the behaviors as present or absent.

(You might be interested in knowing that the course grades of students attending the first class day were higher than the course grades of those not attending.) ■

Ordinal Measurement

When variables can be differentiated and placed in an ordered set along some dimension, then an **ordinal measurement scale** is employed. For

FIGURE 2–2.
Schematic illustration of scales of measurement.

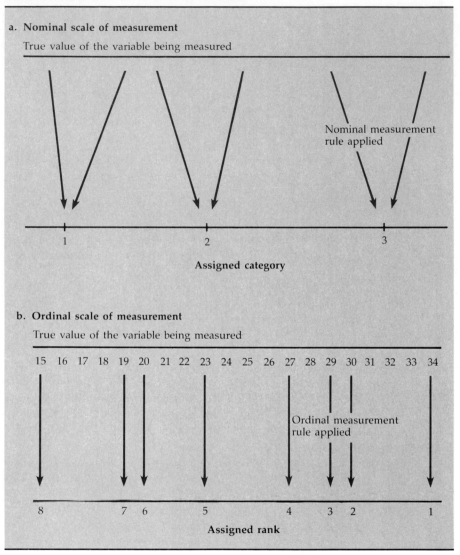

a. Nominal scale of measurement

True value of the variable being measured

Nominal measurement rule applied

Assigned category

b. Ordinal scale of measurement

True value of the variable being measured

Ordinal measurement rule applied

Assigned rank

example, people may be asked to rank order a series of cartoons on a funniness scale from most to least funny. Or, the pecking order for a flock of hens can be determined by ordering the chickens on the variable of dominance from most dominant to least dominant. Typically a rank of 1 is assigned to the stimulus or individual possessing the greatest amount of the characteristic being measured, a rank of 2 to that person or stimulus that exhibits the next greatest amount, and so forth. If, for example, anxiety is

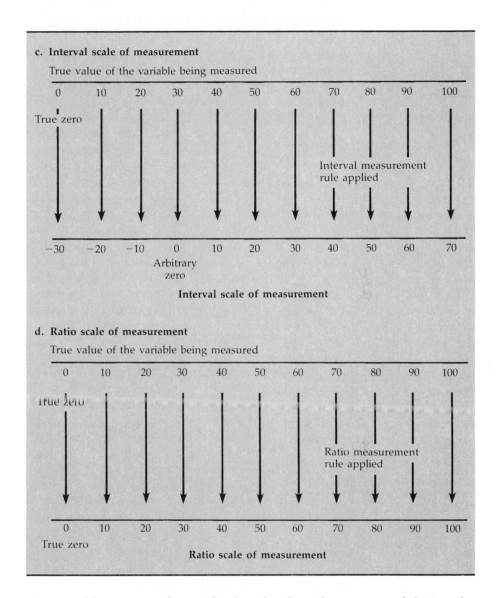

c. Interval scale of measurement

True value of the variable being measured

| 0 | 10 | 20 | 30 | 40 | 50 | 60 | 70 | 80 | 90 | 100 |

True zero

Interval measurement
rule applied

| −30 | −20 | −10 | 0 | 10 | 20 | 30 | 40 | 50 | 60 | 70 |

Arbitrary
zero

Interval scale of measurement

d. Ratio scale of measurement

True value of the variable being measured

| 0 | 10 | 20 | 30 | 40 | 50 | 60 | 70 | 80 | 90 | 100 |

True zero

Ratio measurement
rule applied

| 0 | 10 | 20 | 30 | 40 | 50 | 60 | 70 | 80 | 90 | 100 |

True zero

Ratio scale of measurement

measured by means of an ordinal scale, then the person exhibiting the most anxiety is assigned a 1, the person showing the next largest amount of anxiety a 2, the next a 3, and so on. Although there may be a true zero amount of the variable being measured, no zero will appear in the ranking. The value of 0 typically is not used in ranking scores.

An ordinal scale permits one to differentiate among objects, individuals, or behaviors on the variable being measured and to determine the direction of the differences. Someone or something assigned a rank of 1 possesses more of the characteristic than one given a rank of 2. Ordinal measures do not, however, permit determination of how much of a real difference exists in the measured variable between ranks. A large difference in the true characteristic being measured may exist between ranks 1 and 2, but only a small difference may exist between ranks 2 and 3. Therefore, even though there is an apparent equal numeric difference between rank values of 1 and 2, and between the rank values 2 and 3, one cannot determine how much of a real difference in the measured variable exists between adjacent ranks. This problem is illustrated in the rankings and their relation to the true amount of the attribute being measured shown in Figure 2–2b. In this figure the difference between ranks 1 and 2 on the true value of the variable being measured is $34 - 30 = 4$. The difference between ranks 2 and 3, however, is $30 - 29 = 1$. As an example, the times for the first three runners of a marathon may be 3 hours 19 minutes, 3 hours 24 minutes, and 3 hours 36 minutes, respectively. The rank order of the finish of these marathoners is 1, 2, and 3. But the time difference between the first and second finisher is 5 minutes, whereas it is 12 minutes between the second- and third-place contestants.

Another limitation of ordinal scales should be noted. Rank ordering is merely a procedure in which the stimuli, individuals, or behaviors are placed along a continuum from "most" to "least" and must be assigned a rank. Thus, one cannot assume that a rank of 1 necessarily corresponds to a large amount of the variable being measured. Nor can one assume that the lowest-ranked object or person possesses little of the property being measured. A person who is asked to rank order cartoons from most to least funny may find no humor in any of them. Yet, a rank of 1 assigned to a cartoon by this individual conveys the same information as a rank of 1 assigned a cartoon by another person who may regard all the cartoons as funny. Here, the same measured numerical value (e.g., a rank of 1) from both individuals represents true characteristics that actually differ considerably in magnitude. Ordinal scales do not indicate how much of the measured variable exists; they provide information only about the order of individuals or objects on the variable measured.

Statistics in Use 2–2

"Who Are You?": Using Ordinal Measurement

As we have suggested, measurement rules may be applied to characteristics or behaviors of individuals, or they may be applied to objects or stimuli in the environment. A study by Gottesfeld and Burke (1986) illustrates ordinal measurement of a characteristic of an individual. These researchers were interested in finding how important personal self-fulfillment is for current college undergraduates. As part of the study students were given the "Who Are You" test. This test asks a series of "who are you" questions, and the individual responds by describing him- or herself with statements such as "a female," "a daughter," "a sister," "a student," "a potential biologist," "assertive," "strong," "creative," "intelligent," and so forth. The number of responses emphasizing self-fulfillment (e.g., "a female," "a daughter," "a potential biologist," etc.) were then tabulated. Based on the number of responses, the students were rank-ordered on an emphasis on self-fulfillment in their lives. Assume that five individuals were measured; the outcome of the rank-ordering from most to least self-fulfillment may then appear as:

Rank	Person
1	Gordon
2	Elizabeth
3	Marisa
4	Rivka
5	Michael

Notice in this example that Gordon was ranked as having the most emphasis on self-fulfillment in his life and Michael the least emphasis. But the ranking does not indicate whether Gordon's emphasis on self-fulfillment is large or small; it indicates that he has the most of this characteristic among the individuals measured. The ranking indicates also that Gordon has more emphasis on self-fulfillment in his life than does Elizabeth. We cannot tell, however, how much more emphasis Gordon has on self-fulfillment compared to Elizabeth or any of the other individuals. Further, from the ranking we cannot determine if the difference in emphasis on self-fulfillment between Gordon and Elizabeth is the same as the difference between Elizabeth and Marisa, or between Rivka and Michael. From the rank orders, a scientist can be confident that one person has greater emphasis on self-fulfillment in his or her life than another. But he or she cannot know if the differences between individuals ranking adjacently correspond to equal differences in amount of emphasis on self-fulfillment. ■

Statistics in Use 2–3

Rank Ordering Values of Medical Students

The use of ordinal measurement to rank stimuli is illustrated by research of DiRenzo (1986). Interested in the question of the values of medical practitioner, DiRenzo had medical students rank order 18 values in order of their importance to them. For example, one individual may rank the values in order of importance as:

Rank	Value
1	self-respect
2	mature love
3	wisdom
4	true friendship
5	happiness
6	family security
7	inner harmony
8	equality
9	sense of accomplishment
10	social recognition
11	comfortable life
12	world at peace
13	national security
14	world of beauty
15	exciting life
16	freedom
17	pleasure
18	salvation

This ranking indicates the order of importance of these values to this individual. But we cannot tell if any of these values are really important to this person. In addition, we do not know how much more self-respect is valued than is wisdom, or if the difference in importance between happiness and family security is the same as the difference between comfortable life and world at peace. ▪

Testing Your Knowledge 2–1

On a separate sheet of paper, test your knowledge of the material in this section by answering the following questions.

1. Define: measurement, variable, ordinal scale of measurement, nominal measurement.
2. Identify four characteristics of people other than those given in the text that may be considered variables.
3. Identify the four scales of measurement.
4. Identify one deficiency of nominal measurements.
5. What information is provided by a rank of 2 assigned to an individual on a ranking of motivation to achieve?
6. On a rank-ordering of depression proneness from most to least of 13 people, Jennifer was ranked 1, Debbi 2, Ena 12, and Marty 13.
   a. Explain why you cannot conclude that Jennifer is very prone to depression and Marty is not at all depression prone.

b. Is it appropriate to conclude that the difference in depression proneness between Jennifer and Debbi is the same as the difference in depression proneness between Ena and Marty? Explain your answer. ▪

Interval Measurement

If the requirements for an ordinal scale are met, and in addition the differences between the assigned numbers represent equal increments in the magnitude of the variable measured, then an **interval scale** is created. An interval scale, however, has no true zero point for which a value of zero represents the complete absence of the characteristic measured. A zero value on an interval scale is merely an arbitrary starting point that could be replaced by any other value as a starting point. Interval scale measurement is illustrated in Figure 2–2c. Notice in the figure that equal differences in the observed measurement correspond to equal differences in the true value of the variable measured. For example, on the obtained measure, the difference between a 60 and a 40 is 20, as is the difference between a $+10$ and a -10. These equal differences on the observed measurement correspond to equal differences in the true value of the variable. For the true value of the variable, the difference between a 60 and a 40 is $90 - 70 = 20$ and the difference between a $+10$ and a -10 is $40 - 20 = 20$. Assigning a 0 to a true value of 18 is arbitrary; we could assign the 0 point to any value of the variable and not change the properties of our measurement.

The most typical examples of an interval scale are those used to measure temperature. Both the Fahrenheit and centigrade scales, which measure temperature in degrees, are examples of interval scales. With neither of these scales, though, does 0° represent an absence of temperature; neither contains a true zero point because measured temperatures may fall below 0°. Thus, with such scales, it is accurate to state that the difference in temperature between 20° and 40° is equivalent to the difference in temperature between 40° and 60°, but it is not appropriate to say that 40° is twice as high a temperature as 20°. We can see why this difficulty arises by comparing several equivalent centigrade and Fahrenheit temperatures as shown below.

Equivalent Temperatures

°C	°F
20	68
40	104
60	140

Notice that a difference of 20° C is always equal to a difference of 36° F. But because each scale starts with an arbitrary zero point, adjacent scores on one scale do not form ratios equal to adjacent scores on the other scale. For example, a ratio of 40° C/20° C = 2.0; whereas a ratio of 104° F/ 68° F = 1.5.

Examples of psychological scales that achieve true interval measurement are rare. Although some behavioral scientists argue that scores on well standardized tests, such as intelligence tests, represent interval measurement, others take issue with such a view. If intelligence-test scores do represent interval scale measurement (but notice, that we are not arguing that they do), then it would be correct to state that the difference in intelligence between individuals who have intelligence scores of 100 and 105 is equal to the difference in intelligence between persons with scores of 75 and 80. It would not be correct, however, to say that a person with an intelligence-test score of 100 is twice as intelligent as a person with a score of 50, for scales of intelligence tests do not have a true zero that represents the complete absence of intelligence.

Statistics in Use 2–4

Rating Scales Treated as Interval Measurements

As we have observed, it is often unclear whether any psychological scales actually meet the requirements for interval scale measurement. But, one type of measurement technique, the use of rating scales, is often treated as yielding interval scale scores. Rating scales are frequently used in behavioral science research to measure attributes of people such as personality characteristics, attitudes, marital happiness, fear of objects, motivation to achieve, or leadership ability. These scales take on many forms, but generally they involve a statement and then a response scale with two extremes and several points between the extremes. For example, in attitude measurement a person may be asked to respond to a statement, such as "Welfare payments to the poor reduce crime," by making a checkmark on the scale

Strongly Agree	Agree	Uncertain	Disagree	Strongly Disagree

Other forms of rating scales may ask you to rate another person on a set of bipolar adjectives such as:

Dishonest ____ : ____ : ____ : ____ : ____ : ____ : ____ Honest

Unattractive ____ : ____ : ____ : ____ : ____ : ____ : ____ Attractive

Cold ____ : ____ : ____ : ____ : ____ : ____ : ____ Warm

The response scales may have any number of categories between the extremes; and the scales may be referred to as 5-point, 7-point, or 9-point scales, depending upon the number of categories provided. Often the adjectives anchoring the end points of the scale are reversed for half the items. Thus half the favorable adjectives are at the left of the scale and half at the right. This reversal avoids problems of response set, such as checking only the items on the right side of the scale.

After a person has responded on the scale, a numerical weight is assigned to each category on the scale, such as

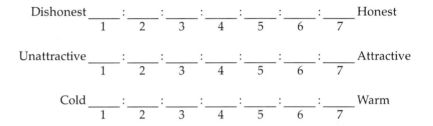

In many instances, a series of scales is presented, and the scores on the separate scales are added or averaged to yield a score for a person. Such scales are called *summated rating scales.* As an illustration of a summated rating scale, Rotton and Kelly (1985) developed a scale for assessing one's belief in the effect of a full moon on behavior — the Belief in Lunar Effects Scale. The scale consists of nine statements. For each statement the respondent indicates his or her agreement with the statement by choosing a number between 1 (*strong disagreement*) to 9 (*strong agreement*). For example, one statement on the scale is[1]

It is a good idea to stay at home when the moon is full.

1	2	3	4	5	6	7	8	9
Strongly Disagree				Neither Agree Nor Disagree				Strongly Agree

An individual's score is obtained by summing over the nine statements to yield a total score for the rating scale. The possible range of scores is from 9 (obtained by responding with a 1 to all nine statements) to 81 (obtained by responding with a 9 to all nine statements).

[1]Reprinted with permission of authors and publisher from J. Rotton and I. W. Kelly. A scale for assessing belief in lunar effects: Reliability and concurrent validity. *Psychological Reports*, 1985, *57*, 239–245. Table 1, adapted.

What scale of measurement is represented by scores on the Belief in Lunar Effects Scale and other similar rating scales? It should be clear that the value obtained from the rating for each statement represents at least ordinal scale measurement. A score of 4 indicates more of a particular characteristic described by the statement than does a 3, and a 3 reflects more than a 2; however, one cannot be certain that the difference between a 4 and 3 represents the same difference in a characteristic as that between a 3 and 2. In other words, one cannot assume that equal increments in numerical values along the rating correspond to equal increments in the true characteristic being measured as needed for an interval scale.

Such rating scores do seem to provide more than merely ordinal information, however. We might expect that the person, in selecting one of the categories to respond to, somehow subjectively divides the categories into roughly equal intervals between the ends of the scale. Moreover, if the values obtained from an individual on a number of separate scales are totaled or averaged, then it seems reasonable to assume that the resulting scores provide more than just rank-order information. Indeed, Gardner (1975) argues that scores from such summated scales are elevated to a scale of measurement in a gray region between ordinal and interval. Gardner adds that this category of measurement "obviously includes a large proportion of all the instruments used in educational and psychological research. The category occupies an intermediate position on the ordinal/interval continuum" (p. 53). Consequently, many researchers treat summated rating scales as representing interval scale measurement.

We have devoted attention to scores derived from rating scales for several reasons. They are used widely in behavioral science research, and we think it is useful for you to gain some understanding of them. In addition, we do not wish to convey the impression that any measurement necessarily fits neatly into one of the four major categories of measurement scales. Many measurements employed in research, including rating scales and standardized test scores, probably represent a scale of measurement between ordinal and interval.

Ratio Measurement

A **ratio scale** replaces the arbitrary zero point of the interval scale with a true zero starting point that corresponds to the absence of the variable being measured. Thus, with a ratio scale it is possible to state that one thing (e.g., a stimulus, an event, or an individual) has twice, or half, or three times as much of the variable measured than another. Figure 2–2d illustrates the characteristics of ratio scales. Notice that there is a one-to-one correspondence of the observed measure with the true value of the variable.

Ratio scales are used frequently in behavioral science research when measurements such as time (e.g., reaction time in milliseconds), length (e.g., in millimeters) or weight (e.g., in grams) are employed. Notice that such measurements have a true zero point (zero length or zero weight) and the intervals between the units of measurement are equal. The difference between 1 gram and 2 grams is equal to the difference between 5 grams and 6 grams, and 6 grams is twice as heavy as 3 grams.

Statistics in Use 2–5

Which Line Is Longer? Using Ratio Scales

The magnitude of perceptual illusions may often be measured with a ratio scale. An illusion occurs when the perceived characteristics of a stimulus do not correspond to the physical characteristics of the stimulus; one misperceives what actually exists. A familiar example is the Müller-Lyer illusion, which is illustrated in Figure 2–3. Here you perceive (or are most likely to perceive) line A to be longer than line B. Both lines are physically equal in length, however. Your perception is in error. The magnitude of this illusion can be measured by determining how much the perceived length of the stimulus differs from the actual length of the stimulus. An individual's perceptual error measured in millimeters (mm) represents ratio scale measurement. It is possible for a person to have an error of 0 mm (i.e., no error) when the perceived length of the stimulus does not differ from the actual length. The difference between an error of 5 mm and an error of 8 mm is the same as the difference between errors of 10 mm and 13 mm; in each case the difference is 3 mm. Moreover, an error of 10 mm represents an illusion magnitude that is twice as great as an error of 5 mm.

As an example of the use of such a measurement, LeTourneau (1976) hypothesized that the extent to which a person perceives an illusion depends upon the person's spatial abilities and specialized training. To test this hypothesis, he compared architectural-design students with optometry students

FIGURE 2–3.
The Müller-Lyer illusion.

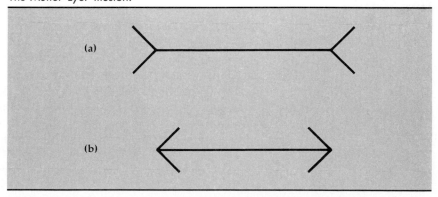

on their perception of the Müller-Lyer illusion. Presumably, architectural-design students possess greater spatial visualization skills and also have had more training employing these skills than optometry students. He found, in agreement with his hypothesis, that architectural-design students typically were about 13.1 mm in error in their perception of the illusion, whereas optometry students perceived the illusion with a typical error of 24.2 mm. ▪

The Choice of a Scale of Measurement

Whenever possible, behavioral scientists prefer to employ interval and ratio scales in their measurements, for these scales allow more precise measurement of the underlying attribute or characteristic being measured than do nominal or ordinal scale measurements. Further, because interval and ratio measures permit the use of common mathematical procedures, such as addition, subtraction, multiplication, and division, they allow the development of more versatile statistical techniques. To a large extent, then, many of the statistical techniques presented in this text are for scores measured at the interval or ratio scale.

Testing Your Knowledge 2–2

On a separate sheet of paper, test your knowledge of the material in this section by answering the following questions.

1. Define: interval scale of measurement, ratio scale of measurement.
2. The following scores were obtained on an interval scale measure of leadership ability: Rosana, 84; Eva, 78; Pierce, 71; Victoria, 65; Nancy, 42; and William, 0.
   a. Is it accurate to conclude that the difference in leadership ability between Rosana and Eva is the same as the difference between Pierce and Victoria? Explain your answer.
   b. Is it accurate to conclude that Rosana possesses twice as much leadership ability as Nancy? Explain your answer.
   c. Is it accurate to conclude that, because of his score of 0, William totally lacks leadership ability? Explain your answer.
3. Several college students participated in a study on sleep, in which the amount of time (in minutes) spent in rapid-eye-movement sleep (REM sleep, the dream sleep stage) was measured using an electroencephalograph. On one night, the durations of REM sleep were: Dominic, 204 minutes; Greta, 194 minutes; Andre, 175 minutes; Jody, 165 minutes; and Carmen, 102 minutes.
   a. Is it appropriate to conclude that the difference in the amount of REM sleep between Dominic and Greta is the same as the difference between Andre and Jody? Explain your answer.

b. Is it appropriate to conclude that Dominic spent twice as much time in REM sleep as Carmen? Explain your answer.

c. Suppose Cory spent 0 minutes in REM sleep. Is it appropriate to conclude that she had no REM sleep that night? Explain your answer. ■

DISCRETE AND CONTINUOUS VARIABLES

In Figure 2–1 we conceptualized measurement as a process of attempting to quantify the amount of an underlying variable. We need now to make a distinction between discrete and continuous variables.

Discrete Variables

A **discrete variable** is one that can take on only a finite or potentially countable set of values. The word *finite* in this instance means a definite set of possible values. The number of students at your college is a discrete variable: there may be 5,652 students or 5,653 students, but not 5,652-1/2 students. The number of students may increase or decrease by one whole student, not one-half or one-third student. Thus, the number of students takes on a definite countable set of values. Typically, variables whose possible values can be counted are discrete variables: the number of people living in a city, the number of children in a family, the number of burglaries in a year, the number of automobiles registered in a state, and so forth.

Continuous Variables

A **continuous variable** is one that can take on an infinite set of values between any two levels of the variable. A continuous variable has thus an unlimited set of values in the range within which it varies. For example, the true amount of anxiety in individuals may take on an unlimited number of values among different people. Intelligence, too, varies on a continuous dimension. Weight is another example, for you may weigh 135.6 pounds or 135.64 pounds. Your weight is not limited to discrete values such as 135 pounds or 136 pounds. Notice that we are referring to the underlying variable that is being measured when we identify discrete and continuous variables. It is possible that you may have a scale that indicates your weight only in whole pounds, such as 135 or 136 pounds. Yet, your true weight is not limited to these specific values. It may indeed take on any value between 135 and 136 pounds.

REAL LIMITS OF A MEASUREMENT

Many variables measured by behavioral scientists are continuous in nature. When measurements are made of such variables, specific numerical values are assigned to the amount of the variable present. But the observable measures only approximate the true underlying amount of the variable. Consequently, we must be aware of the accuracy attained by measurements, regardless of the scale of measurement that we are using. And, the accuracy of measurement of a continuous variable is contained in the real limits of the number assigned.

Real limits of a measurement are easily understood using measurements of the variable of time. Suppose we are measuring the amount of time that a person can hold his or her hand in a tub of 40° F water. This task is often used to induce pain safely in individuals in experiments dealing with relaxation strategies to increase pain tolerance. Consider an obtained duration of 37 seconds measured by observing the seconds hand on a stopwatch. How accurate is this measurement? Because we measured to the nearest whole second, the duration could not have been 36 or 38 seconds. But might the actual duration have been 37.2 seconds or 36.7 seconds? The answer to this question is, of course, yes; for we would have rounded either 36.7 seconds or 37.2 seconds to 37 seconds. The accuracy of this measurement of 37 seconds is given by the real limits of this number. The **real limits of a number** are the points that are exactly midway between the number and the next lower and the next higher numbers on the scale used to make the measurements. For a measured value of 37 seconds, then, the **real lower limit** is 36.5 seconds and the **real upper limit** is 37.5 seconds. The real lower limit of 36.5 seconds is midway between 36 seconds, the next lower measured value on the scale used, and 37 seconds. The real upper limit of 37.5 seconds is midway between 37 seconds and 38 seconds, the next higher measured value on the scale used.

Suppose now that you had measured the duration with an electronic stopwatch that provided measurements to the nearest 1/100 of a second, such as 37.21 seconds. What are the real upper and lower limits of this measurement? Again, the rule is to find the midpoint between the next lower and the next higher value on the measuring scale used. Thus the real lower limit is the midpoint between 37.20 (the next lower number) and 37.21 seconds, or 37.205 seconds. The real upper limit is the midpoint between 37.21 seconds and 37.22 seconds (the next upper value), or 37.215 seconds.

Every numerical measurement of a continuous variable has real upper and lower limits associated with it. For example, rating scales are often used to measure variables. Suppose we are using the rating scale illustrated in Figure 2–4, with seven points and behavioral anchors at each end of the scale. Assume a person checked a response of 3 on this scale.

FIGURE 2–4.

Real upper and lower limits for a response (indicated by the X) on a seven-point rating scale.

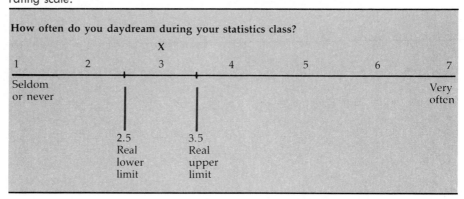

Following the rules presented earlier, the real lower and upper limits for this score are 2.5 and 3.5, respectively.

The real limits of a measurement become important when plotting frequency distributions of scores and when rounding values in statistical computations. We discuss frequency distributions in Chapter 3.

Rounding

Answers to Computations

Suppose you asked three friends to complete the scale shown in Figure 2–4, and you obtained the following responses: 4, 4, and 3. To describe the typical response, you found the sum of these numbers, 11, and divided it by 3, or, $11/3 = 3.666\overline{6}$. The bar (¯) over the last 6 indicates that the 6s continue endlessly. How many decimal places should you present in your answer?

One convention is that the final value of a computation should be rounded to one decimal place beyond the value to which the original scores were measured. In our example, the scores were given to the ones (or units) place, so a person could check 3 or 4, but not 3.2 or 4.6. Following this rule, then, the final value of the computation is rounded to one decimal place beyond the ones place, or to 3.7. To carry the value of the computation to a greater number of decimals, such as 3.67 or 3.667, implies that the raw scores were measured more accurately than to a whole number.

Not all behavioral scientists follow this convention, however. When reading the results of research studies, you may find final values of computations carried to two decimal places. Following this convention, the result of the computation is given as 3.67.

In this text we follow the convention of rounding answers to one decimal place beyond the value to which the scores were measured.

Intermediate Steps in Computations

If computations require a number of steps prior to obtaining the final answer, then intermediate numerical values should be carried to two decimal places beyond the number of decimal places needed for the final answer. For example, if the value of 11/3 were to enter into further computations, we would not round its value to 3.7. Rather, we carry it to two additional places, 3.667, for the additional computations. Following this convention minimizes rounding error in computations. If you use a pocket calculator for computations, this suggestion is easily followed. Most pocket calculators carry computations to a minimum of four or five decimal places.

Rounding Rules

Suppose we have an answer to a computation such as 3.6*AB*, where the *A* and *B* are symbols for possible numerical values. For example, if *A* = 2 and *B* = 9, then 3.6*AB* = 3.629. We wish to round this number to two decimal places. There are several rules typically followed when rounding numbers:

- If the number represented by the letter *B* is greater than 5, increase *A* by one and drop the *B* value. Following this rule, 3.629 (here *A* = 2, *B* = 9) is rounded to 3.63.
- If the number represented by the letter *B* is less than 5, leave the *A* value as is and drop the *B* value. Following this rule, 3.623 (here *A* = 2, *B* = 3) is rounded to 3.62.
- If the number represented by the letter *B* is exactly 5, increase *A* by one if *A* is an odd number, but leave its value as is if it is an even number; then drop *B*. Following this rule, 3.635 (here *A* = 3, *B* = 5) is rounded to 3.64, but 3.625 (here *A* = 2, *B* = 5) is rounded to 3.62. Notice, however, if the number is 3.6251 it is rounded to 3.63, not 3.62.

Testing Your Knowledge 2–3

On a separate sheet of paper, test your knowledge of the material in this section by answering the following questions.

1. Define: discrete variable, continuous variable, real limits of a number, real upper limit, real lower limit.
2. Identify each of the following variables being measured as discrete or continuous.
   a. A person's hand-grip strength.
   b. The eye contact of an accuser with a defendant in a courtroom.

    c. The number of stotts (leaping vertically with four legs off the ground simultaneously) made by a Thompson's gazelle in a one-hour period.

    d. The length of a song by a male songbird during courtship.

    e. The funniness of a set of cartoons.

    f. The number of altruistic behaviors observed in nursery school children.

3. Provide the real lower and real upper limits for each of the scores presented.

    a. A height of 152.4 centimeters.

    b. A duration of eye contact of 17.3 seconds.

    c. An assigned rating of 4 on a 7-point scale.

    d. A reaction time of 0.437 seconds.

    e. An error of 6.9 mm on the Müller-Lyer illusion.

    f. A hand-grip strength of 67.81 kilograms.

4. Round the following values to the number of decimal places indicated.

    a. 27.436 (one decimal place)

    b. 119.0276 (three decimal places)

    c. 1.445 (two decimal places)

    d. 1263.75915 (four decimal places)

    e. 0.352 (one decimal place)

SUMMARY

- Measurement is a process of assigning numbers to variables according to a set of rules.
- Nominal measurement is a classification of the measured variable into different categories.
- Ordinal measurement scales place a variable in an ordered set along a dimension.
- Interval scales create equal increments in the magnitude of the variable measured, but they do not have a true zero.
- Ratio scales possess the properties of the interval scale plus a true zero point.
- A discrete variable can take on only a finite or potentially countable set of values.
- A continuous variable can take on an infinite set of values between any two levels of the variable.
- The real limits of a number are the points that are exactly midway between the number and the next lower and the next higher numbers on the scale used to make the measurements.

KEY TERMS

continuous variable	nominal measurement	real lower limit of a number
discrete variable	ordinal measurement scale	real upper limit of a number
interval scale	ratio scale	variable
measurement	real limits of a number	

REVIEW QUESTIONS

On a separate sheet of paper, test your knowledge of the material in this chapter by answering the following questions.

For each of the following descriptions, identify the underlying variable being measured and the scale of measurement attained by the measure employed. Then answer any additional questions asked.

1. The career orientation of police officers was measured by having police officers order four paragraphs describing various career orientations from 1—the paragraph closest to the individual's career orientation to 4—the paragraph furthest from the individual's career orientation.

2. Professional female golfers were weighed to determine if body weight was related to their game.
   a. The weight of one golfer was reported as 134.6 pounds. What are the real upper and lower limits of this measurement?
   b. Six golfers were weighed to the nearest pound. Their average weight was 127.648 pounds. Round this computation following the convention discussed in the text.

3. Parents of hemophilic children were measured on a personality trait of emotional stability using a summated rating scale.
   a. Suppose a person assigned a rating of 8 on a 9-point rating scale for agreement or disagreement with a statement. What are the real upper and lower limits of this measurement?
   b. Suppose you measured six people on this statement and found their typical rating to be 5.833. Is this result correctly reported with respect to the number of decimal places given? Explain your answer.

4. The amount of motivation of an individual was measured by the time the person spent working at the task during a two-hour period.
   a. Suppose a person was measured as having spent 97.21 minutes at the task. What are the real upper and lower limits of this measurement?
   b. The scores of four people on this task are 97.21, 67.44, 83.94, and 103.62 minutes, respectively. You find the average of these four scores by finding their total and then dividing by 4, or 352.21/4. To how many decimal places should you carry your answer?
5. Interpersonal values of an individual were measured by having the person order 12 value statements from most to least important.
6. The behavioral interactions of children at a nursery school with other children at the school were categorized as agonistic (i.e., argumentive or fighting), neutral (i.e., not interacting), or altruistic (i.e., helpful).

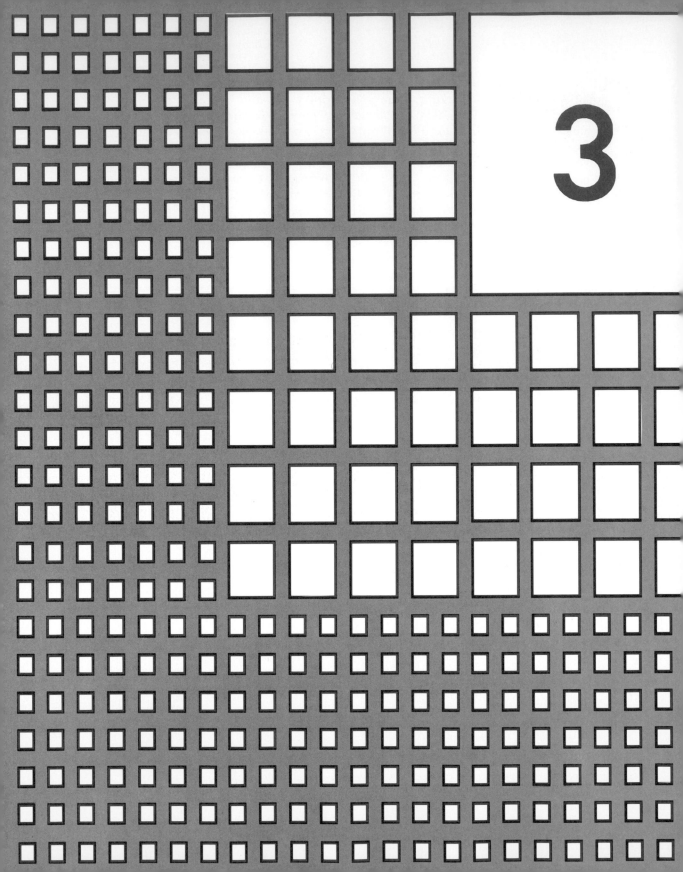

3

Organizing Data: Distributions of Scores

OVERVIEW

As discussed in Chapter 1, behavioral scientists often collect a large number of scores in a set of measurements. Their goal is to extract information from these scores. In order to do this, they must summarize and describe the measurements obtained. The first step is to arrange these raw data as frequency distributions and graphs of frequency distributions. This process of organizing data is the topic of this chapter.

MEASURING TEST ANXIETY: AN EXAMPLE PROBLEM

Have you ever thought, "If only I could get my anxiety under control I could do much better on examinations"? If so, you are not alone. In recent years, counselors and psychologists have identified test anxiety as a contributor to poor performance for many students. To measure and quantify test anxiety, Spielberger (1980) developed the *Test Anxiety Inventory* (TAI). The TAI is composed of 20 statements similar to "I become very uneasy and upset before a big examination." For each statement, the student completing the inventory chooses one of the alternatives—*almost never, sometimes, often, almost always*—that best applies to him or her. After the inventory is completed, a numerical value is assigned to each alternative: *almost never* = 1, *sometimes* = 2, *often* = 3, *almost always* = 4. An individual's score is obtained by adding the numerical values of the alternatives selected. This inventory is thus a summated rating scale (see Statistics in Use 2–4) with a score ranging from 20 to 80. A score of 20 indicates the minimum level of anxiety possible on the TAI and a score of 80 the maximum level. As observed in Chapter 2, summated rating scales probably are in a gray area of measurement. Yet, for statistical purposes, scores from rating scales often are treated as representing interval level of measurement. We follow this custom with our example problem.

Suppose that a counselor is interested in the level of test anxiety in students at her college. Accordingly, she administers the Test Anxiety Inventory to a sample of 100 sophomore and junior females. The scores obtained are portrayed in Table 3–1. Such scores are called **raw data** or **raw scores,** for they are exactly as collected and have not been subjected to statistical analysis. The letter N is used to indicate the total number of scores obtained; thus N for this example is 100.

WHAT DO THE RAW DATA TELL US?

Suppose you met this counselor and found yourselves discussing her research on test anxiety. After she described the inventory, you might ask,

TABLE 3–1.

Test Anxiety Inventory scores from 100 students.

42	44	41	36	39	50
28	38	44	34	40	46
37	41	22	48	39	37
45	41	32	43	36	60
58	38	35	46	25	60
41	37	41	43	31	47
39	50	38	42	40	36
52	40	47	28	39	73
40	31	52	41	38	43
34	50	48	38	45	46
25	41	55	41	70	37
43	46	41	65	36	46
49	37	28	42	44	34
45	40	36	46	39	29
48	38	41	34	42	40
42	26	44	38	44	37
44	41	55	40		

"What were your results?" She might respond by showing you the raw data (i.e., Table 3–1) and say, "The results were interesting. Take a look." Inspection of the scores in the table quickly reveals how difficult it is to make sense of raw data.

Look at the scores in Table 3–1. Can you make sense of this information? In scanning the scores you will notice considerable variation among them. Many of the scores are in the 30s to 50s range. It may appear that scores in the 40s are listed more often than scores in the 30s and 50s, but you cannot be confident of this conclusion without counting the numbers of each score. Despite the obvious variation among the scores, it also seems that the "typical" anxiety score is somewhere in the 40s. What sense, then, are we to make of these data? Coming to a conclusion about either typical test anxiety level or the extent of differences among individuals is difficult. This inability to see the forest for the trees in raw data is especially acute when there is a large number of scores. Consider how much more complicated the task would be if there were 500 or even 1,000 scores. It becomes an impossible task to reach conclusions by mere visual inspection of the raw data.

ORGANIZING RAW DATA: FREQUENCY DISTRIBUTIONS WITH UNGROUPED SCORES

A much clearer picture of the information in the scores emerges when the raw data are organized as a frequency distribution. A **frequency** distribution is a table showing each score obtained by a group of individuals and how frequently each score occurred. Table 3–2 illustrates an ungrouped frequency distribution for the Test Anxiety Inventory scores presented in Table 3–1. An **ungrouped frequency distribution** may be constructed by listing all obtained score values from highest to lowest (column *a* of Table 3–2) and then placing a tally mark (/) beside each score every time it occurs (shown in column *b* of Table 3–2). The simple frequency of occurrence of each score (symbolized by *f*) is then tabulated and recorded as illustrated in column *c* of the table.

The frequency of occurrence of scores in an ungrouped frequency distribution also may be presented as other than a simple count of the scores. Ungrouped frequency distributions are also presented as relative frequencies, percentage frequencies, cumulative frequencies, cumulative relative frequencies, or cumulative percentage frequencies.

Relative Frequency Distributions

A **relative frequency distribution** is obtained by dividing the frequency of each score by the total number of scores. Thus, a **relative frequency** (symbolized by *rf*) is expressed as a proportion of the frequency of a score out of the total number of scores obtained, or

$$rf \text{ of a score} = f \text{ of a score}/N.$$

As an example, the relative frequency of occurrence of the score of 42 in Table 3–2 is obtained by dividing its frequency (i.e., 5) by the total number of scores ($N = 100$), which equals 0.05. The relative frequency of TAI scores is presented in column *d* of Table 3–2.

Percentage Frequency Distribution

A **percentage frequency distribution** expresses the frequency of occurrence of a score as a percentage of the total number of scores obtained. The **percentage frequency of a score** (symbolized by %*f*) may be obtained by multiplying the relative frequency of a score by 100, or

$$\%f \text{ of a score} = [(f \text{ of a score})/N] \times 100.$$

When using this formula, you complete the steps inside the brackets before multiplying by 100.

The percentage frequency may also be found by substituting the *rf* of a score for (*f* of a score/*N*), or

$$\%f \text{ of a score} = (rf \text{ of a score}) \times 100.$$

The percentage frequency of scores in Table 3–2 is presented in column *e*. Notice that columns *c*, *d*, and *e* of this table present equivalent

TABLE 3–2. Ungrouped frequency distribution for Test Anxiety Inventory scores of Table 3–1.

(a)	(b)	(c)	(d)	(e)	(f)	(g)	(h)
Score	Tally	Frequency (f)	Relative Frequency (rf)	Percentage Frequency (%f)	Cumulative Frequency (cf)	Cumulative Relative Frequency (crf)	Cumulative Percentage Frequency (c%f)
73	/	1	.01	1	100	1.0	100
72		0	0	0	99	.99	99
71		0	0	0	99	.99	99
70	/	1	.01	1	99	.99	99
69		0	0	0	98	.98	98
68		0	0	0	98	.98	98
67		0	0	0	98	.98	98
66		0	0	0	98	.98	98
65	/	1	.01	1	98	.98	98
64		0	0	0	97	.97	97
63		0	0	0	97	.97	97
62		0	0	0	97	.97	97
61		0	0	0	97	.97	97
60	/ /	2	.02	2	97	.97	97
59		0	0	0	95	.95	95
58	/	1	.01	1	95	.95	95
57		0	0	0	94	.94	94
56		0	0	0	94	.94	94
55	/ /	2	.02	2	94	.94	94
54		0	0	0	92	.92	92
53		0	0	0	92	.92	92
52	/ /	2	.02	2	92	.92	92
51		0	0	0	90	.90	90
50	/ / /	3	.03	3	90	.90	90
49	/	1	.01	1	87	.87	87
48	/ / /	3	.03	3	86	.86	86
47	/ /	2	.02	2	83	.83	83
46	/ / / / / /	6	.06	6	81	.81	81
45	/ / /	3	.03	3	75	.75	75
44	/ / / / / /	6	.06	6	72	.72	72
43	/ / / /	4	.04	4	66	.66	66
42	/ / / / /	5	.05	5	62	.62	62
41	/ / / / / / / / / / /	11	.11	11	57	.57	57
40	/ / / / / / /	7	.07	7	46	.46	46
39	/ / / / /	5	.05	5	39	.39	39
38	/ / / / / / /	7	.07	7	34	.34	34
37	/ / / / / /	6	.06	6	27	.27	27
36	/ / / / /	5	.05	5	21	.21	21
35	/	1	.01	1	16	.16	16
34	/ / / /	4	.04	4	15	.15	15
33		0	0	0	11	.11	11
32	/	1	.01	1	11	.11	11
31	/ /	2	.02	2	10	.10	10
30		0	0	0	8	.08	8
29	/	1	.01	1	8	.08	8
28	/ / /	3	.03	3	7	.07	7
27		0	0	0	4	.04	4
26	/	1	.01	1	4	.04	4
25	/ /	2	.02	2	3	.03	3
24		0	0	0	1	.01	1
23		0	0	0	1	.01	1
22	/	1	.01	1	1	.01	1

information about the distribution of scores in Table 3–1. The advantage of having frequencies presented as relative or percentage frequencies is that these values are independent of the total number of scores obtained. Thus, if you had a second sample of 180 scores ($N = 180$) from another group of students, it would be easier to compare the frequency distributions from the two different size samples if the frequency distributions were expressed as either relative or percentage frequencies rather than as simple frequencies alone.

Obtaining Information from a Frequency Distribution

At a glance, the simple frequencies, relative frequencies, or percentage frequencies presented in Table 3–2 produce several impressions of the Test Anxiety Inventory scores that are not readily apparent from the unorganized raw data of Table 3–1. For example, from each distribution you can easily notice that

- The lowest score obtained is 22,
- The highest score obtained is 73,
- The most frequently occurring score is 41,
- The majority of the scores are between 34 and 50.

Obviously, organizing raw data in a frequency distribution makes it easier to see certain important characteristics of these data.

Cumulative Distributions of Scores

Cumulative Frequency Distribution
Each form of frequency distribution discussed—a simple frequency, relative frequency, and percentage frequency—also may be presented as a cumulative frequency distribution. The **cumulative frequency of a score** (symbolized as *cum f* or *cf*) is the frequency of occurrence of that score plus the sum of the frequencies of all the scores of lower value. For example, the cumulative frequency of a score of 32 in Table 3–2 is 11, because 11 scores were either 32 or less than 32. The cumulative frequency distribution of scores in Table 3–2 is presented in column *f*.

Cumulative Relative Frequency Distributions
Relative frequencies and percentage frequencies also may be presented as cumulative frequencies. The **cumulative relative frequency of a score** (symbolized as *cum rf* or *crf*) is the relative frequency of that score plus the sum of the relative frequencies of all scores of lower value. For example, the cumulative relative frequency of a score of 32 in Table 3–2 is 0.11. The cumulative relative frequencies of scores in Table 3–2 are presented in column *g*.

Cumulative Percentage Frequency Distribution

The **cumulative percentage frequency of a score** (symbolized as *cum %f* or *c%f*) is the percentage frequency of that score plus the sum of the percentage frequencies of all the scores of lower value. The cumulative percentage frequency of a score of 32 in Table 3–2 is 11 percent. Cumulative percentage frequencies of the scores in Table 3–2 are presented in column *h*. Cumulative distributions of scores become useful when we discuss percentile ranks later in this chapter and standard scores in Chapter 6.

Example Problem 3–1
Constructing ungrouped frequency distributions

Problem:

Psychologists are interested in the perception of ambiguous figures. They believe that full understanding of how we perceive these figures will provide insights applicable to our perception of the everyday world. The Mach pyramid shown below is an example of an ambiguous figure, for it is reversible in perspective.

You may see this figure either as a pyramid with the small square appearing to project out of the page toward you or as a room in perspective with the small square being the far wall. Riani, Tuccio, Borsellino, Radilová, and Radil (1986) employed several variations of this figure and timed how long an individual maintained each perspective. Suppose they employed 25 subjects and found that these individuals could see the figure as a pyramid for the following durations (to the nearest whole second):

2, 7, 10, 5, 5, 3, 9, 11, 5, 8, 2, 4, 7, 6, 10, 7, 3, 9, 7, 11, 4, 6, 3, 1, and 8 .

The Mach Pyramid

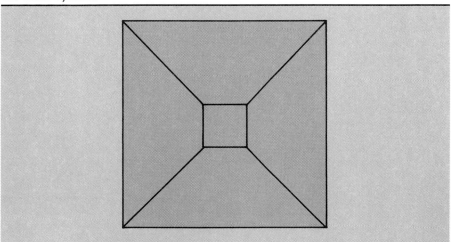

Construct the following ungrouped frequency distributions for these scores: simple frequency distribution, relative frequency distribution, percentage frequency distribution, cumulative frequency distribution, cumulative relative frequency distribution, and cumulative percentage frequency distribution. What conclusions about the scores may you reach from these distributions?

Solution:

The requested frequency distributions are shown in the table below.

Score	Tally	f	rf	$\%f$	cf	crf	$c\%f$
11	/ /	2	.08	8	25	1.00	100
10	/ /	2	.08	8	23	.92	92
9	/ /	2	.08	8	21	.84	84
8	/ /	2	.08	8	19	.76	76
7	/ / / /	4	.16	16	17	.68	68
6	/ /	2	.08	8	13	.52	52
5	/ / /	3	.12	12	11	.44	44
4	/ /	2	.08	8	8	.32	32
3	/ / /	3	.12	12	6	.24	24
2	/ /	2	.08	8	3	.12	12
1	/	1	.04	4	1	.04	4

Conclusions:

From the simple, relative, and percentage frequency distributions we can easily determine that the scores range from 1 to 11 seconds and the most frequently occurring score is 7 seconds. From the several cumulative frequency distributions you can notice, for example, that 52 percent of the scores fell in the range from 1 to 6 seconds and that 76 percent of the scores were 8 seconds or less. ■

Testing Your Knowledge 3–1

On a separate sheet of paper, test your knowledge of the material in this section by answering the following questions.

1. Define: raw data, raw scores, frequency distribution, ungrouped frequency distribution, relative frequency distribution, percentage frequency distribution, rf, $\%f$, cumulative frequency of a score, cumulative relative frequency, cumulative percentage frequency, cf, *cum f*, *crf*, *cum rf*, $c\%f$, *cum %f*.

2. Good and Good (1973) developed a scale to measure fear of success. Individuals high in the fear of success are thought to avoid being too successful in their endeavors for fear of antagonizing others. Scores on the fear of success scale may range from 0, indicating no measured fear of

success, to 29, indicating the greatest fear of success measurable on this scale. Suppose you administered the scale to 20 people and obtained the scores: 6, 13, 4, 19, 3, 12, 9, 8, 5, 11, 6, 8, 15, 5, 8, 10, 9, 14, 4, and 8.

a. Construct the following ungrouped frequency distributions for these scores: simple frequency distribution, relative frequency distribution, percentage frequency distribution, cumulative frequency distribution, cumulative relative frequency distribution, and cumulative percentage frequency distribution.

b. What are the lowest and highest scores obtained?

c. What is the most frequently occurring score?

d. What percentage of scores is equal to or less than 8?

e. What scores constitute the lowest 25 percent of the scores? ■

ORGANIZING RAW DATA: GROUPED FREQUENCY DISTRIBUTIONS

If there is a wide range of score values in the data collected, then an ungrouped frequency distribution as illustrated in Table 3–2 can become spread out, making it difficult to see clear patterns in the data. Often, then, it is useful to construct a **grouped frequency distribution** in which scores are grouped together in **class intervals.** The class intervals then are arranged from highest to lowest, and the frequency of scores occurring within each class is tallied and tabulated. Table 3–3 presents grouped

TABLE 3–3.

Grouped simple, relative, and percentage frequency distributions for the Test Anxiety Inventory scores of Table 3–1.

(a) Class Interval	(b) Tally	(c) f	(d) rf	(e) %f
70–74	/ /	2	.02	2
65–69	/	1	.01	1
60–64	/ /	2	.02	2
55–59	/ / /	3	.03	3
50–54	/ / / / /	5	.05	5
45–49	/ / / / / / / / / / / / / / /	15	.15	15
40–44	/ /	33	.33	33
35–39	/ /	24	.24	24
30–34	/ / / / / / /	7	.07	7
25–29	/ / / / / / /	7	.07	7
20–24	/	1	.01	1

simple, relative, and percentage frequency distributions using a class interval of size 5 for the Test Anxiety Inventory scores of Table 3–1. For the
data in Table 3–1, this frequency distribution using grouped data and
class intervals probably is more informative than one constructed on the
ungrouped data such as that shown in Table 3–2. By collapsing the scores
into class intervals a more compact distribution emerges, providing a
clearer picture of the distribution's shape and the most commonly occurring scores. We now explain how we constructed the distributions illustrated in Table 3–3.

Constructing Grouped Frequency Distributions

Constructing grouped frequency distributions requires two decisions:
(a) the number of class intervals to be used, and (b) the size (or width) of
the class interval.

Number of Class Intervals

The number of class intervals to be used is determined by the range of the
scores: 10 to 20 class intervals ordinarily are used. The number of intervals is chosen so that the class interval is 2, 3, 5, or a multiple of 5. The
range of scores in Table 3–1 is from 22 to 73, or 51. With this range of
scores 10 to 12 intervals are sufficient to group the data. We choose
12 class intervals to continue the example.

Size of Class Intervals

After the number of intervals is determined, the size of the interval is
found by dividing the difference between the largest and smallest score
by the number of class intervals to be used. Hence, the size of the class
interval, where the letter X represents a score, is obtained by

$$\text{Size of class interval} = \frac{X_{\text{highest}} - X_{\text{lowest}}}{\text{number of intervals}}.$$

Here, X_{highest} indicates the highest score and X_{lowest} the lowest score in
the distribution. Using the raw data of Table 3–1 with $X_{\text{highest}} = 73$ and
$X_{\text{lowest}} = 22$, and employing 12 class intervals, the size of the class interval
for the Test Anxiety Scores equals

$$\frac{73 - 22}{12} = \frac{51}{12} = 4.25.$$

If the obtained size of the interval is a decimal, such as the 4.25 we obtained, then we round up to the next larger whole number, 5.0 for example. Should scores be decimals less than 1.0, then, of course, we do

not round the interval to a whole number. Rather, a convenient decimal interval (such as .2, .3, .5, or .02, .03, .05) is employed.

Constructing the Distribution

After finding the size of the class interval, we construct the grouped distribution. Generally, there are two guidelines used to construct such distributions:

- The lowest interval must contain the lowest score.
- The lower limit of the first interval, that is, the lowest possible score value in the first interval, should be evenly divisible by the size of the class interval.

In Table 3–3 the class interval is 5.0 and the lowest score to be included is 22. Accordingly, the lowest class interval begins with a limit of 20 because 20 is the first score less than 22 that is evenly divisible by the class interval of 5.0. The first class interval is then from 20 to 24. Notice that it is possible for five score values to fall into this interval: 20, 21, 22, 23, and 24.

After the limits of the class intervals are determined (see column *a* of Table 3–3), scores are tallied in the interval into which they fall (see column *b* of Table 3–3). For example, a score of 35 is tallied into the class interval of 35 to 39. The tallies in an interval are then summed to obtain the frequency for that interval (given in column *c* of Table 3–3).

Grouped Relative Frequency and Percentage Frequency Distributions

Relative frequency distributions and percentage frequency distributions also may be obtained for grouped frequency distributions. The procedures are similar to those used for the ungrouped frequency distributions.

Grouped Relative Frequency Distributions. A **grouped relative frequency distribution** is obtained by dividing the frequency of scores in an interval by the total number of scores. Thus,

$$rf \text{ of scores in an interval} = \frac{f \text{ of scores in interval}}{N}.$$

A grouped relative frequency distribution for the scores of Table 3–1 is presented in column *d* of Table 3–3.

Grouped Percentage Frequency Distributions. A **grouped percentage frequency distribution** is obtained by

$$\%f \text{ of scores in an interval} = \left[\frac{f \text{ of scores in interval}}{N} \right] \times 100.$$

A grouped percentage frequency distribution for the scores of Table 3–1 is presented in column *e* of Table 3–3.

Obtaining Information from a Grouped Frequency Distribution

The several grouped frequency distributions in Table 3–3 indicate that the majority of scores are in the range from 30 to 54. Further, the distributions let us determine that almost one-third of the anxiety scores are in the interval from 40 to 44. Some information is lost with a grouped frequency distribution, however. For example, the exact numerical value of scores is lost in Table 3–3. Thus we can no longer determine the exact range of scores or the most frequently occurring score. But this loss of information often is offset by the greater ease with which we can perceive the general shape of the distribution.

Cumulative Grouped Frequency Distributions

The various cumulative frequency distributions may also be constructed from grouped frequency distributions. Because such cumulative distributions are frequently used to plot histograms or to determine percentile points and percentile ranks, it is often necessary to distinguish between the stated and real limits of the class intervals of a grouped frequency distribution.

Stated Limits of a Class Interval

Look at the intervals shown in Table 3–3. Each interval has upper and lower stated limits (also called *nominal limits* or *score limits*). The **upper and lower stated limits of a class interval** are the highest and lowest scores that could fall into that class interval. Thus, for the class interval of 40 to 44 the lower stated limit is 40 and the upper stated limit is 44. A numerical score of 40 is the lowest score that may be contained in the interval and a score of 44 the highest that may be placed in the interval. Figure 3–1 illustrates the lower and upper stated limits for the class interval of 40 to 44.

Real Limits of a Class Interval

In Chapter 2 we introduced the real limits of a number and defined the real limits as the points that are midway between the number and the next lower and higher numbers on the scale used to make the measurements. Real limits exist for the intervals of a grouped frequency distribution also, and these real limits are found similarly to the real limits of a number. The **lower real limit of a class interval** is the point that is midway between the lower stated limit of the class interval and the upper stated limit of the next lower class interval. For example, we find the lower real limit of the class interval of 40 to 44 in Table 3–3. The lower

FIGURE 3–1.

Illustration of upper and lower stated limits, upper and lower real limits, and the midpoint of a class interval of a grouped frequency distribution.

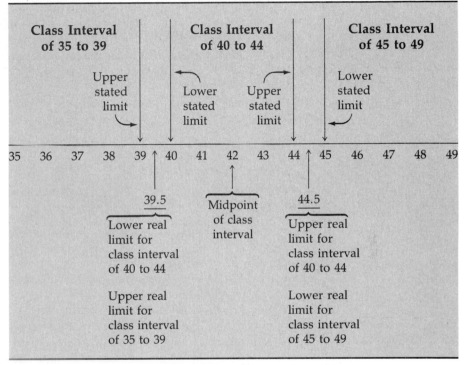

stated limit of this interval is 40. The upper stated limit of the next lower class interval (i.e., the interval of 35 to 39) is 39. Accordingly, the real lower limit of the class interval of 40 to 44 is the midpoint between 39 and 40, or 39.5. This lower real limit is also illustrated in Figure 3–1.

The **upper real limit of a class interval** is the point that is exactly midway between the upper stated limit of that class interval and the lower stated limit of the next higher class interval. The upper real limit of the class interval of 40 to 44 is thus 44.5. This upper real limit is found by obtaining the midpoint of the upper stated limit of the interval of 40 to 44 (i.e., 44) and the lower stated limit of the next higher class interval, the interval of 45 to 49. The lower stated limit of this interval is 45; thus the upper real limit of the class interval of 40 to 44 is the midpoint of 44 and 45, or 44.5. This upper real limit is shown in Figure 3–1. Notice that this upper real limit for the class interval of 40 to 44 is also the lower real limit for the next class interval of 45 to 49. The upper and lower real limits of the class intervals in the grouped frequency distribution of Table 3–3 are presented in column *b* of Table 3–4.

TABLE 3–4.

Cumulative grouped frequency distribution of Test Anxiety Inventory scores of Table 3–1 with upper and lower real limits for each class interval.

(a)	(b)	(c)	(d)	(e)	(f)	(g)
Class Interval	Real Limits Lower–Upper	Midpoint of Class	f	cf	crf	c%f
70–74	69.5–74.5	72	2	100	1.00	100
65–69	64.5–69.5	67	1	98	.98	98
60–64	59.5–64.5	62	2	97	.97	97
55–59	54.5–59.5	57	3	95	.95	95
50–54	49.5–54.5	52	5	92	.92	92
45–49	44.5–49.5	47	15	87	.87	87
40–44	39.5–44.5	42	33	72	.72	72
35–39	34.5–39.5	37	24	39	.39	39
30–34	29.5–34.5	32	7	15	.15	15
25–29	24.5–29.5	27	7	8	.08	8
20–24	19.5–24.5	22	1	1	.01	1

Midpoints of Class Intervals

Each class interval also has a midpoint. The **midpoint of a class interval** is the point midway between the real limits of the class interval. The midpoint of the class interval 40 to 44 is 42, because 42 is the midpoint between 39.5 and 44.5. Midpoints of a class interval can be found by adding the values of the real limits of a class interval and dividing the sum by 2. For the class interval of 40 to 44, then, the midpoint is found by:

$$\frac{(39.5 + 44.5)}{2} = 42 .$$

The midpoints of each class interval for the grouped frequency distribution of Table 3–3 are shown in column c of Table 3–4.

Simple Cumulative Grouped Frequency Distributions

The **cumulative frequency of a class interval** is the frequency of occurrence of scores in that interval plus the sum of the frequencies of scores of lower class intervals. The simple frequency distribution of scores falling into each class interval of Table 3–3 is presented again in column d of Table 3–4. The simple cumulative frequency of each class interval is then shown in column e of Table 3–4.

Cumulative Grouped Relative and Percentage Frequency Distributions

The cumulative grouped relative frequencies and percentage frequencies for each class interval of Table 3–4 are presented in columns f and g, respectively. These cumulative frequency distributions are obtained just as we obtained the cumulative relative and cumulative percentage frequencies of an ungrouped distribution. The only difference is that we use the frequencies associated with a class interval instead of the frequencies of individual scores.

PERCENTILES AND PERCENTILE RANKS

Cumulative frequency distributions are often used to find percentiles and percentile ranks. A **percentile** is the score at or below which a specified percentage of scores in a distribution fall. For example, if the 35th percentile on an examination is 70, 35 percent of the scores on the examination are equal to or less than 70. The **percentile rank** of a score indicates the percentage of scores in the distribution that are equal to or less than that score. Thus, in our example, the percentile rank of a test score of 70 is 35. Thirty-five percent of the scores are equal to or less than 70.

The benefit of providing the percentile rank for a score or a percentile point is that it provides information about the location of the scores with respect to the other scores in the distribution. Suppose you were one of the 100 students who took the TAI and your score was 41. Simply knowing your score does not give you any information about your test anxiety level. Is 41 high or low compared to other students? But if you were told that your score was the 49th percentile point or the percentile rank for a score of 41 was 49, then you would know that 49 percent of the scores were equal to or less than 41. Your score is about in the middle of the distribution.

Finding the Percentile Rank of a Score

We wish to find the percentile rank of a score of 41 in the distribution portrayed in Table 3–4. This score falls into the class interval of 40 to 44. The cumulative percentage frequency of scores up to the lower real limit of this interval is 39 (from column g) and the cumulative percentage frequency of scores to the upper real limit of this interval is 72 (from column g). Thus, the percentile rank of 41 will be somewhere between 39 and 72. To find the exact percentile rank, we use the following formula:

$$PR_X = \left[\frac{cf_L + [(X - X_L)/i]f_i}{N} \right] \times 100 \, ,$$

where
PR_X = percentile rank of a score of X.
cf_L = cumulative frequency of scores up to the lower real limit of the interval containing X, the score of interest.

X = the score for which the percentile rank is being found.
X_L = the lower real limit of the interval containing X.
i = size of the class interval.
f_i = frequency of scores in the interval containing X.
N = the total number of scores in the distribution.

For a score of 41 in Table 3–4 these values are

$$PR_X = PR_{41}.$$
$$cf_L = 39 \text{ (from column } e \text{ of Table 3–4)}.$$
$$X = 41.$$
$$X_L = 39.5 \text{ (from column } b \text{ of Table 3–4)}.$$
$$i = 5.$$
$$f_i = 33 \text{ (from column } d \text{ of Table 3–4)}.$$
$$N = 100.$$

Substituting these values into the formula for percentile rank, we obtain

$$PR_{41} = \left[\frac{39 + [(41 - 39.5)/5]33}{100} \right] \times 100,$$
$$PR_{41} = [(39 + 9.9)/100] \times 100,$$
$$PR_{41} = 48.9.$$

The percentile rank of a score of 41 is 48.9; 48.9 percent of the scores in Table 3–4 are equal to or less than 41. Typically this percentile rank is rounded to a whole number and reported as 49.

Finding a Percentile Point of a Distribution

A second problem is finding a score that corresponds to a specified percentile point in a distribution. For example, suppose we wish to find the 49th percentile point of the distribution in Table 3–4. We notice that this percentile point is a score in the class interval of 40 to 44, for 39 percent of the scores fall below the lower real limit of this interval and 72 percent of the scores fall below the upper real limit. We can find the exact score corresponding to a specified percentile point in a distribution by using the formula

$$X_P = X_L + \left(\frac{P(N) - cf_L}{f_i} \right) i$$

where

X_P = the score at a specified percentile point.

X_L = the lower real limit of the interval containing the specified percentile point.

P = the required percentile given as a proportion between 0 to 1.00.

N = the total number of scores in the distribution.

cf_L = cumulative frequency of scores up to the lower real limit of the interval containing X, the score of interest.

f_i = frequency of scores in the interval containing X.

i = size of the class interval.

For the 49th percentile these values are

$$X_P = X_{49}.$$

$$X_L = 39.5 \text{ (from column } b \text{ of Table 3–4)}.$$

$$P = 0.49.$$

$$N = 100.$$

$$cf_L = 39 \text{ (from column } e \text{ of Table 3–4)}.$$

$$f_i = 33 \text{ (from column } d \text{ of Table 3–4)}.$$

$$i = 5.$$

Substituting these values into the formula, we obtain

$$X_{49} = 39.5 + \left(\frac{0.49(100) - 39}{33} \right) 5,$$

$$X_{49} = 39.5 + 1.52,$$

$$X_{49} = 41.02.$$

Rounding this value to a whole number, $X_{49} = 41$. Forty-nine percent of the scores in the distribution are equal to or less than 41.

Example Problem 3–2
Grouped frequency distributions

Problem:

Suppose we investigated the problem of perception of ambiguous figures discussed in Example Problem 3–1 and measured the duration that subjects could see the pyramid in the Mach pyramid figure. Suppose further, however, that we had used 50 subjects and obtained the following scores (to the nearest whole second): 18, 2, 7, 23, 16, 10, 5, 30, 5, 15, 17, 3, 31, 9, 11, 13, 5, 13, 8, 19, 16, 2, 14, 4, 7, 7, 6, 2, 10, 6, 7, 24, 3, 8, 9, 7, 19, 7, 11, 9, 4, 7, 6, 1, 3, 10, 1, 26, 8, and 5.

a. Construct the following grouped frequency distributions for these scores: simple frequency distribution, relative frequency distribution, percentage frequency distribution, simple cumulative frequency distribution, cumulative relative frequency distribution, and cumulative percentage frequency distribution. Include the real lower and upper limits of the class intervals, and the midpoint of each class interval. What conclusions about the scores may you reach from these distributions?

b. Find the percentile rank of a score of 16 seconds.

c. What is the 25th percentile point for this distribution?

Solution:

a. The solution requires choosing the number of class intervals to be used, finding the size of the class interval, and then constructing a grouped frequency distribution using these class intervals.

Number of class intervals. The range of scores is from 1 to 31 seconds, or 30 seconds. Ten class intervals seem sufficient to group the data.

Size of class intervals: $(31 - 1)/10 = 3.0$.

Constructing the distribution. The lowest score obtained is 1 second and the class interval to be used is 3 seconds. The first class interval then is 0 to 2. This interval contains the lowest score and the lower stated limit of this interval (i.e., 0) is divisible evenly by the size of the class interval (i.e., 3). The class intervals of the grouped frequency distribution are presented in column a of the table below. The upper and lower real limits for each interval are obtained by finding the points midway between adjacent class intervals. For example, upper and lower real limits for the class interval of 24 to 26 are the points midway between 23 and

(a)	(b)	(c)	(d)	(e)	(f)	(g)	(h)	(i)	(j)
Class Interval	Real Limits Lower–Upper	Midpoint of Interval	Tally	f	rf	$\%f$	cf	crf	$c\%f$
30–32	29.5–32.5	31	/ /	2	.04	4	50	1.00	100
27–29	26.5–29.5	28		0	.00	0	48	.96	96
24–26	23.5–26.5	25	/ /	2	.04	4	48	.96	96
21–23	20.5–23.5	22	/	1	.02	2	46	.92	92
18–20	17.5–20.5	19	/ / /	3	.06	6	45	.90	90
15–17	14.5–17.5	16	/ / / /	4	.08	8	42	.84	84
12–14	11.5–14.5	13	/ / /	3	.06	6	38	.76	76
9–11	8.5–11.5	10	/ / / / / / / /	8	.16	16	35	.70	70
6– 8	5.5– 8.5	7	/ / / / / / / / / / / / /	13	.26	26	27	.54	54
3– 5	2.5– 5.5	4	/ / / / / / / / /	9	.18	18	14	.28	28
0– 2	−0.5– 2.5	1	/ / / / /	5	.10	10	5	.10	10

24 (lower real limit), and midway between 26 and 27 (upper real limit), respectively. The real limits of each class interval are shown in column *b* of the table. Midpoints for each class interval are presented in column *c*. The scores are tallied in column *d*, and the grouped frequency distributions obtained following the procedures described in this chapter. The frequency distributions requested are presented in columns *e* through *j* of the table.

Conclusions:
From the simple frequencies (column *e*), relative frequencies (column *f*), or percentage frequencies (column *g*) we see that scores in the interval of 6 to 8 seconds occurred most frequently. The cumulative frequency distributions indicate that .70 or 70 percent of the scores were durations of 11 seconds or less.

b. Percentile rank of a score is found using the formula

$$PR_X = \left[\frac{cf_L + [(X - X_L)/i]f_i}{N} \right] \times 100.$$

The values needed to find the percentile rank of a score of 16 are

$$PR_X = PR_{16}$$
$$cf_L = 38$$
$$X = 16$$
$$X_L = 14.5$$
$$i = 3$$
$$f_i = 4$$
$$N = 50.$$

Substituting these values, we obtain

$$PR_{16} = \left[\frac{38 + [(16 - 14.5)/3]4}{50} \right] \times 100,$$
$$PR_{16} = [(38 + 2)/50] \times 100,$$
$$PR_{16} = 80.$$

The precentile rank of a score of 16 seconds is 80. Eighty percent of the durations are equal to or less than 16 seconds.

c. The 25th percentile point is found using the formula

$$X_P = X_L + \left(\frac{P(N) - cf_L}{f_i} \right) i.$$

The numerical values needed to find the 25th percentile point are

$$X_P = X_{25}$$
$$X_L = 2.5$$
$$P = 0.25$$
$$N = 50$$
$$cf_L = 5$$
$$f_i = 9$$
$$i = 3$$

Substituting these values, we obtain

$$X_{25} = 2.5 + \left(\frac{0.25(50) - 5}{9}\right)3,$$
$$X_{25} = 2.5 + 2.5,$$
$$X_{25} = 5.0.$$

A score of 5 seconds is the 25th percentile point. ▪

Testing Your Knowledge 3–2

On a separate sheet of paper, test your knowledge of the material in this section by answering the following questions.

1. Define: grouped frequency distribution, class interval, lower stated limit of a class interval, upper stated limit of a class interval, lower real limit of a class interval, upper real limit of a class interval, midpoint of a class interval, cumulative frequency of a class interval, percentile, percentile rank.
2. What is the recommended number of class intervals to use when constructing a grouped frequency distribution?
3. What is the formula for finding the size of the class interval?
4. The largest score in a distribution is 88, the smallest 14. You plan to construct a grouped distribution employing 14 intervals. What will be the size of your class interval?
5. The largest score in a distribution is 95, the smallest 62. You want the class interval to be 2. How many intervals will you use?
6. What are the two guidelines for constructing grouped distributions?
7. Write the formula for finding the f of scores in an interval of a grouped frequency distribution.
8. Write the formula for finding the $\%f$ of scores in an interval of a grouped percentage frequency distribution.

9. A grouped frequency distribution has class intervals of 120–122, 123–125, 126–128, 129–131, and 132–134.
   a. Identify the lower stated limit for the class interval of 123–125.
   b. Identify the upper stated limit for the class interval of 129–131.
   c. Identify the lower real limit for the class interval of 123–125.
   d. Identify the upper real limit for the class interval of 129–131.
   e. Identify the lower and upper real limits for the class interval of 126–128.
   f. Find the midpoint of the class interval 120–122.

10. Animals appear to do strange things. When approached by a predator, for example, Thompson's gazelles leap straight up with all four feet simultaneously off the ground. This behavior, known as stotting, appears costly to the gazelle, for it delays the onset of flight from the predator. To learn more about stotting, Caro (1986) studied gazelles in Serengeti National Park, Tanzania. One measure obtained was the estimated distance of a predator, such as a cheetah, from a gazelle before the first stott occurred. Suppose Caro observed 50 instances of a cheetah approaching a gazelle and recorded the following estimated distances (in meters) between the cheetah and the gazelle before the first stott occurred: 47, 61, 72, 63, 56, 54, 67, 75, 91, 72, 83, 140, 31, 37, 25, 38, 57, 62, 49, 205, 66, 39, 43, 81, 66, 72, 42, 29, 190, 64, 76, 54, 38, 67, 61, 33, 48, 55, 59, 68, 18, 49, 37, 83, 70, 154, 91, 50, 58, and 66.
   a. Construct the following grouped frequency distributions for these scores: simple frequency distribution, relative frequency distribution, percentage frequency distribution, cumulative simple frequency distribution, cumulative relative frequency distribution, and cumulative percentage frequency distribution. Include the lower and upper real limits of the class intervals, and the midpoint of each class interval. Use 20 class intervals.
   b. What conclusions about stotting distances are you able to reach from the information in the grouped frequency distributions?
   c. Find the percentile rank of a score of 68.
   d. What is the 50th percentile point for this distribution? ■

PRESENTING FREQUENCY DISTRIBUTIONS GRAPHICALLY

The purpose of finding a frequency distribution is to provide a systematic way of "looking at" and understanding our data. To further this understanding, the information contained in a frequency distribution often is displayed in more graphic or pictorial forms. We consider three general forms of graphic presentation of frequency distributions: histograms, frequency polygons, and stem-and-leaf displays. First, however, we review some of the common rules of constructing graphs.

- Graphs are most easily and accurately drawn on graph paper.
- The two axes of the graph are drawn at right (90°) angles to each other. The horizontal axis is identified as the *X axis* or the *abscissa*. The vertical axis is called the *Y axis* or *ordinate*.
- The scores obtained, or the class intervals of the scores in a grouped frequency distribution, are located along the *X* axis. A measure of frequency (e.g., simple frequency, relative frequency, percentage frequency, cumulative frequency, etc.) is located along the *Y* axis. Each axis is labeled so that the reader knows what information is being graphed.
- The origin of each axis is normally at zero. If a part of the scale between the zero origin and the first recorded score or frequency of a score is left off the axis, then a break, indicated by – / /–, is inserted into the axis.
- A scale should be chosen for the *Y* axis such that the maximum graphed height of the frequency measure is about two-thirds to three-fourths of the width of the *X* axis.

The Histogram

Histograms usually are drawn only for grouped frequency distributions and the measure of frequency used is the simple frequency tabulation for a class interval (e.g., column *c* of Table 3–3). A histogram of the grouped frequency distribution of the Test Anxiety Inventory scores is presented in Figure 3–2. The size of each class interval is represented by the width of the bar on the abscissa. The frequency of occurrence of scores in the interval is given by the height of the bar. Notice that the bar is centered on the midpoint of the class interval and the vertical sides of each bar are drawn at the real limits of each class interval. In most instances, scores on the abscissa are indicated only by the numerical value of the midpoint of each class interval as we have illustrated in Figure 3–2. On occasion, however, you will find the stated limits of each class interval also listed on the abscissa.

Frequency Polygon

A **frequency polygon** may be constructed by placing the midpoints of each class interval on the abscissa and indicating the frequency of a class interval by placing a dot at the appropriate frequency above the midpoint. The dots are then connected by straight lines. Figure 3–3 portrays a frequency polygon of the grouped Test Anxiety scores of Table 3–3. The frequency measure used is the simple frequency tabulation in column *c* of the table. Notice on Figure 3–3 that we have included one extra class interval containing no scores at each end of the distribution, and that we

FIGURE 3–2.

Histogram of frequency of Test Anxiety Inventory (TAI) scores.

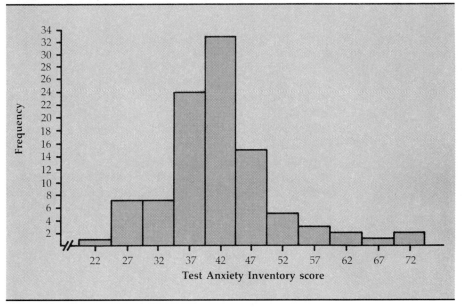

FIGURE 3–3.

Frequency polygon of Test Anxiety Inventory (TAI) scores.

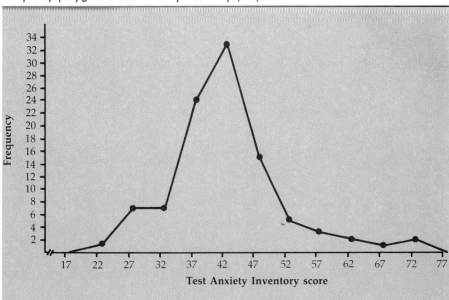

have brought the frequency polygon to a zero frequency at each end of the graph. This practice commonly is followed in the construction of frequency polygons.

Relative Frequency Histograms and Polygons

Histograms and frequency polygons may be constructed using relative frequencies in place of the simple frequencies used in Figures 3–2 and 3–3. A histogram and a frequency polygon of the Test Anxiety Inventory scores employing relative frequencies (from column *d* of Table 3–3) are presented in Figures 3–4 and 3–5, respectively.

The benefit of employing relative frequencies to plot the histogram or frequency polygon is that the relative frequency values indicate the proportion of scores falling in the various class intervals. Thus two frequency polygons presenting relative frequencies can more easily be compared with each other than can frequency polygons employing simple frequencies.

Obtaining Information from a Histogram or a Frequency Polygon

The histogram and frequency polygon present the same information as does a frequency distribution. The advantage of histograms and frequency polygons is that the information presented is often more easily

FIGURE 3–4.

Relative frequency histogram of Test Anxiety Inventory (TAI) scores.

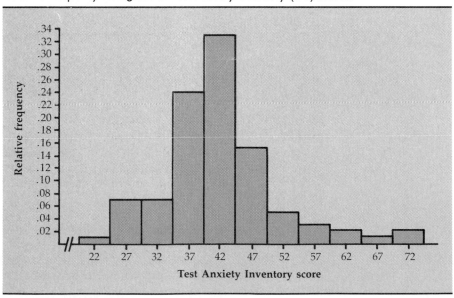

FIGURE 3–5.

Relative frequency polygon of Test Anxiety Inventory (TAI) scores.

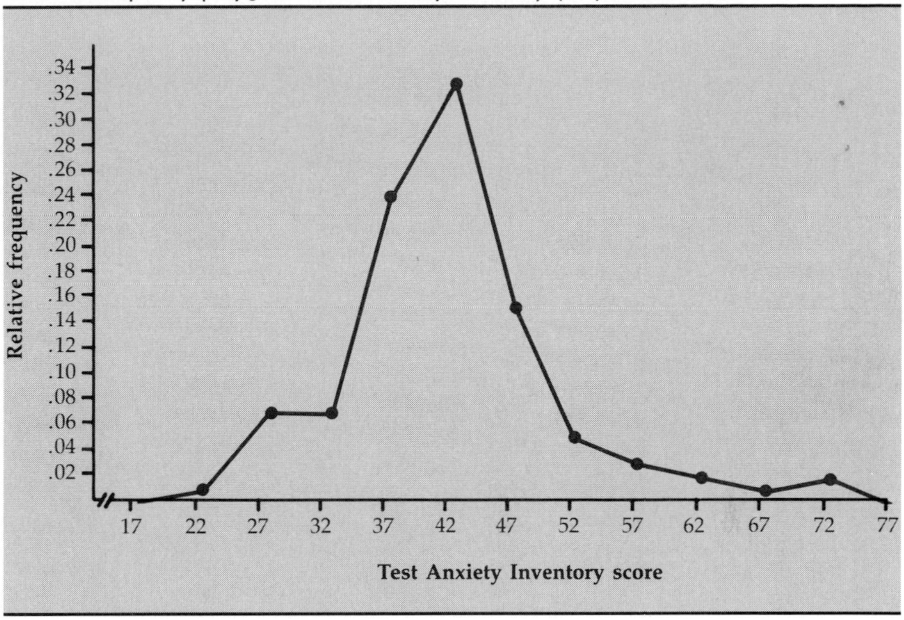

grasped visually. Notice that from any of Figures 3–2, 3–3, 3–4, or 3–5, you can see that the peak of the distribution of the anxiety scores is in the low 40s and more scores are closer to the bottom of the anxiety scale score (i.e., 20) than to the top (i.e., 80). A few scores, however, tail off in the direction of high test anxiety.

Statistics in Use 3–1

Using Frequency Distributions to Find Birthday–Deathday Relationships

Some behavioral scientists have hypothesized that dying individuals may attempt to delay their death until after an approaching birthday. To investigate this suggested hypothesis, Zusne (1986–87) tabulated the birthday and deathday records of 3306 individuals, 1646 males and 1660 females. For each person he obtained the difference, in days, between the deathdate and birthdate. Thus, a score of −10 days indicates that an individual died 10 days before his or her birthday; whereas a score of +47 days indicates that a person died 47 days after his or her birthday. If the hypothesis of deathday–birthday relationship is correct, then as the birthdate approaches, the frequency of scores should decrease. We expect to see a low frequency of scores of 0 and an increase after the birthdate.

In order to see if this pattern appeared in the scores, Zusne plotted frequency polygons employing four different class intervals for the scores: 1 day, 10 days, 30 days, and 90 days. These frequency polygons are shown below. Notice that with a class interval of 1 day there are many dips and rises in the frequency of the scores. And, although there appears to be a dip

Frequency polygons showing frequency of deaths as a function of birthday–deathday difference (BD = birthday, N = 3306). (a) Class interval of 1 day, (b) Class interval of 10 days, (c) Class interval of 30 days, (d) Class interval of 90 days. Reprinted with permission of author and publisher from L. Zusne, Some factors affecting the birthday–deathday phenomenon, *Omega*, 1986–87, *17*, pp. 9–26. © 1986 Baywood Publishing Co., Inc.

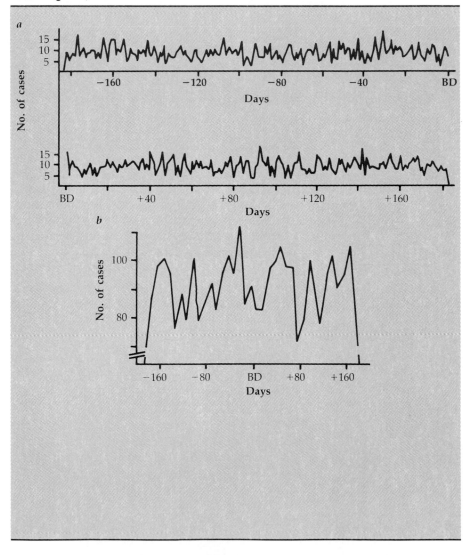

on the birthday followed by a rise, there are many similar dips and rises throughout the range of scores. The frequency polygon based on a class interval of 10 days shows a more definite dip as the birthdate approaches followed by a rise for 50 or so days. The dip prior to the birthday followed by a rise also appears in the frequency polygon employing 30-day class intervals. The apparent dip and rise about the birthday do not appear when the class interval of 90 days.

Based upon these four frequency distributions, Zusne decided that if a dip in scores prior to the birthday followed by a rise actually occurred, it was most likely to be seen employing a class interval of 10 days. He then plotted similar frequency polygons using a class interval of 10 days for individuals

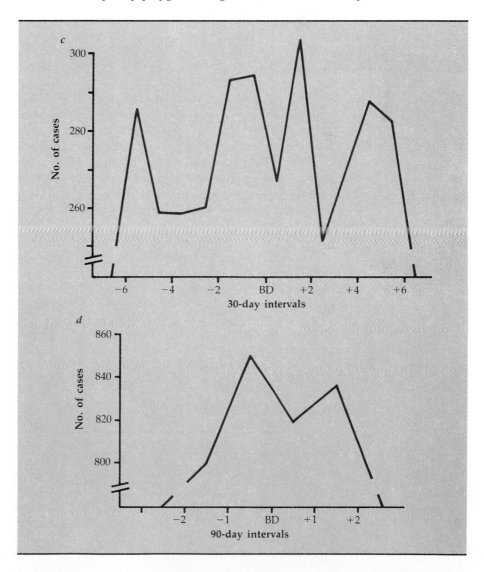

dying at different ages, and for males and females. He found that there appears to be a relationship of birthdate and deathdate, but the relationship differs for males and females. For males there is a dip in the death rate at the time of the birthdate, followed by an increase in the following month. For females, however, there appears to be a rise in the death rate as the birthdate approaches, followed by a dip after the birthday.

This work demonstrates the value of carefully analyzing frequency distributions. It illustrates also that the size of a class interval in a grouped frequency distribution may be important for allowing trends in the data to appear. And, to determine the most appropriate class interval, you may have to construct several frequency distributions, each distribution employing a class interval of different size. ■

STEM-AND-LEAF DISPLAYS

The **stem-and-leaf display** is a technique for displaying raw data that combines the qualities of a frequency distribution and a graphic display of the data (Tukey, 1977). Table 3–5 presents a stem-and-leaf display of the Test Anxiety Inventory scores of Table 3–1. In this display, the numbers to the left of the vertical line are the *stems* and represent the first digit of a score. For example, for a score of 35, the 3 is the stem. Stems are usually ordered with the lowest stem (in our example, 2) at the bottom of the display and the largest stem (in our example, 7) at the top. The numbers to the right of the vertical line are the *leaves* and represent the second digit of the score, in the example of 35, a 5.

Stem-and-leaf displays are constructed easily from the raw data, and no information is lost in the process as occurs in a grouped frequency distribution; all the raw scores can be reconstructed from the display. From an examination of Table 3–5 and simply counting the number of scores, you can quickly determine that the scores vary from 22 to 73, and that scores in the 40s occur most frequently with 41 the most frequent score with 11 occurrences.

TABLE 3–5.

Stem-and-leaf display of Test Anxiety Inventory scores presented in Table 3–1.

Stem	Leaf
7	03
6	005
5	00022558
4	00000001111111111122222333344444455566666677889
3	1124444566666777777888888899999
2	25568889

Statistics in Use 3–2

Belief in Lunar Effects: Using a Stem-and-Leaf Display

We offered the example of a summated rating scale called the Belief in Lunar Effects Scale in Statistics in Use 2–4. This scale was developed by Rotton and Kelly (1985) to measure belief in the effect of a full moon on behavior. Recall that the minimum score on this scale is 9—indicating minimal or no belief in lunar effects and the maximum score is 81—indicating maximum belief in lunar effects. Rotton and Kelly administered this scale to 157 undergraduate college students, and the scores they obtained are portrayed in the stem-and-leaf display below.[1]

Stem		Leaf
7	.	12
	*	59
6	.	0011114
	*	5666668999
5	.	000111111222334
	*	5555555555666678888899
4	.	0011112233333344444
	*	56666677788899999
3	.	0000112223344444
	*	55667777899999
2	.	00001122234444
	*	5566667788888899
1	.	122334

For this stem-and-leaf display the stem represents the 10s value of the score and the leaf the 1s value of the score. Thus, a stem of 3 and a leaf of 7 is a score of 37. Rotton and Kelly added several refinements to their stem-and-leaf plot. Notice the column of periods (.) and asterisks (*) next to the stem column. For a particular stem value the period is used to denote leaf values from 0 through 4 and the asterisk is used to indicate leaf values from 5 through 9. For example, scores with a stem of 1 are given in the table as

	*	556666778888899
1	.	122334

The leaf values in the row preceded by the period range from 1 to 4. When preceded by their stem of 1, these values become scores of 11, 12, 12, 13, 13, and 14, respectively. The leaf values in the row preceded by the asterisk (*)

[1]Reprinted with permission of authors and publisher from: Rotton, J., & Kelly, I. W. A scale for assessing belief in lunar effects: Reliability and concurrent validity. *Psychological Reports*, 1985, *57*, 239–245. Table 2, adapted.

also have a stem of 1, but they are leaf values from 5 through 9. When preceded by their stem of 1, these values become 15, 15, 16, 16, 16, 16, 17, 17, 18, 18, 18, 18, 18, 19, and 19, respectively. The use of the periods to indicate leaf values from 0 through 4 and asterisks to denote leaf values from 5 through 9 provides for a more compact table. This compactness is especially useful when a large number of scores are being placed in a stem-and-leaf display.

From this stem-and-leaf display we can see that the range of scores obtained was from 11 to 72, and the single most frequently occurring score was 45 with nine occurrences. No information is lost in this plot, for each of the 157 scores may be reconstructed from the display. ■

Testing Your Knowledge 3–3

On a separate sheet of paper, test your knowledge of the material in this section by answering the following questions.

1. Assume, as in question 10 of Testing Your Knowledge 3–2, that you estimated the distance of a predator from a gazelle when the gazelle first stotted and you obtained the following distances (in meters): 47, 61, 72, 63, 56, 54, 67, 75, 91, 72, 83, 140, 31, 37, 25, 38, 57, 62, 49, 205, 66, 39, 43, 81, 66, 72, 42, 29, 190, 64, 76, 54, 38, 67, 61, 33, 48, 55, 59, 68, 18, 49, 37, 83, 70, 154, 91, 50, 58, and 66.
   a. Construct a histogram and a frequency polygon for these scores employing the simple frequencies of a grouped distribution with a class interval of 10 meters.
   b. Construct a relative frequency histogram and a relative frequency polygon from the grouped distribution of question 1a.
   c. What conclusions do you reach about stotting distances from the graphs you have constructed?
2. Construct a stem-and-leaf plot of the 50 distance estimates given in question 1.
   a. What is the shortest distance recorded?
   b. What is the longest distance recorded?
   c. What is the most frequently occurring distance? ■

SHAPES OF FREQUENCY DISTRIBUTIONS

A distribution of scores may take on any one of an endless variety of shapes. Thus, there usually is no simple way to describe precisely the shape of a frequency distribution in a word or two. There are, however, some general descriptive terms that apply to the shape of a distribution and that help to describe a distribution in words. To illustrate, Figure 3–6 presents examples of idealized frequency polygons.

FIGURE 3–6.
Shapes of hypothetical frequency distributions.

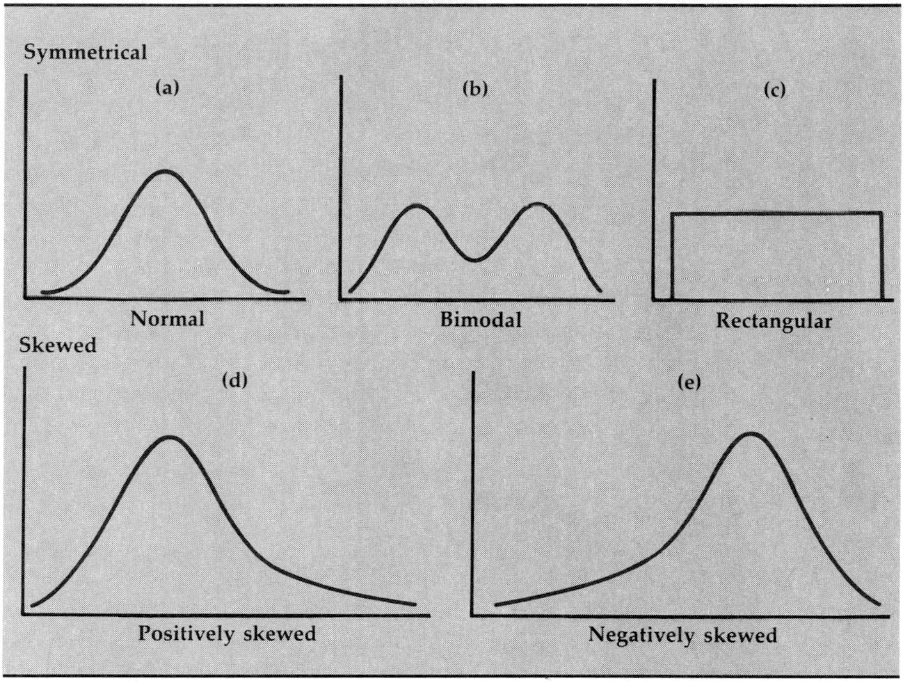

Symmetrical Distributions

A **symmetrical distribution** is one that, if it were to be folded in half about a midpoint, would produce two halves identical in shape. One side of the distribution is a mirror image of the other. The distributions *a*, *b*, and *c* in Figure 3–6 are symmetrical distributions, but distributions *d* and *e* are not symmetrical; they are **asymmetrical**. The symmetrical bell-shaped or *normal distribution* shown in Figure 3–6a is of special interest and importance in the behavioral sciences. Because this distribution has properties that permit use of powerful data analysis techniques, researchers often hope that their data conform closely to a normal distribution. We discuss the normal distribution more fully in Chapter 6.

Skewness

In practice, it is rare to obtain a distribution that is perfectly symmetrical. Instead, frequency distributions are likely to be somewhat asymmetrical; that is, they have some skewness. In a **skewed distribution** scores are clustered at one end of the distribution with scores occurring infrequently at the other end (or tail) of the distribution. A distribution is described as **positively skewed** if the tail occurs for the high scores at the right of the distribution (Figure 3–6*d*) or **negatively skewed** if the tail occurs for the low scores at the left of the distribution (Figure 3–6*e*).

Modality

Distributions also are described in terms of their modality. The **mode** is the most frequently occurring score in a group of scores. In an ungrouped frequency distribution the mode is given by the peak of the distribution. A **unimodal distribution** (see Figures 3–6*a*, *d*, and *e*) has just one peak or "hump" corresponding to the most frequently occurring score. A frequency distribution that has two peaks (illustrated in Figure 3–6*b*) is described as **bimodal**. A **multimodal distribution** has three or more peaks, thus indicating there are three or more score values that are the most frequently occurring scores. There is no mode in the flat rectangular distribution illustrated in Figure 3–6*c*; in such distributions each score occurs an equal number of times or nearly so.

Testing Your Knowledge 3–4

On a separate sheet of paper, test your knowledge of the material in this section by answering the following questions.

1. Define: symmetrical distribution, asymmetrical distribution, skewed distribution, positively skewed distribution, negatively skewed distribution, unimodal distribution, bimodal distribution, multimodal distribution.
2. Describe the frequency distributions below with respect to symmetry, skewness and modality. ▧

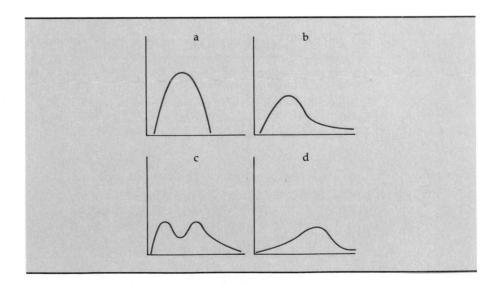

SUMMARY

- A frequency distribution is a table showing each score obtained by a group of individuals and how frequently each score occurred.
- Frequency distributions are used to organize raw data.
- An ungrouped frequency distribution may be used when there is not a large number of scores in the data set.
- Grouped frequency distributions are used when the number of scores becomes large or the scores extend over a wide range of values.
- Either ungrouped or grouped frequency distributions may be portrayed as simple, relative, or percentage frequencies.

- A percentile is the score at or below which a specified percentage of scores in a distribution fall.
- The percentile rank of a score indicates the percentage of scores in the distribution that are equal to or less than that score.
- Frequency distributions may be presented graphically as histograms, frequency polygons, or stem-and-leaf displays.
- Shapes of frequency distributions are described in terms or their symmetry, skewness, and modality.

KEY TERMS

asymmetrical distribution
bimodal distribution
class intervals
cumulative frequency of a class interval
cumulative frequency of a score
cumulative percentage frequency
cumulative relative frequency of a score
cf
$cum\ f$
crf
$cum\ rf$
$c\%f$
$cum\%f$
frequency distribution

frequency polygon
grouped frequency distribution
grouped percentage frequency distribution
grouped relative frequency distribution
histogram
lower real limit of a class interval
lower stated limit of a class interval
midpoint of a class interval
mode
multimodal distribution
negatively skewed distribution

percentage frequency distribution
percentile
percentile rank
positively skewed distribution
$\%f$
raw data
raw scores
relative frequency distribution
rf
skewed distribution
stem-and-leaf display
symmetrical distribution
ungrouped frequency distribution
unimodal distribution
upper real limit of a class interval
upper stated limit of a class interval

REVIEW QUESTIONS

On a separate sheet of paper, test your knowledge of the material in this chapter by answering the following questions.

1. One survey ("The Way", 1985) found that the average man of the 1980s sleeps for 7 hours and 43 minutes (or 463 minutes) per night. You are curious if this figure holds also for male college students. Hence, you ask 50 college males to record how long they slept for one night. The sleeping times you obtained, in minutes, were 440, 223, 309, 427, 463, 275, 315, 290, 356, 407, 399, 263, 417, 328, 377, 406, 275, 316, 391, 350, 422, 431, 382, 350, 371, 410, 295, 305, 327, 400, 227, 275, 340, 364, 279, 300, 412, 388, 296, 320, 342, 371, 258, 470, 496, 384, 439, 284, 351, 417.

   a. Construct a grouped percentage frequency distribution and grouped cumulative percentage frequency distribution for these scores. Use 14 class intervals.

   b. Which class interval contains the most scores? Is the midpoint of this interval in agreement with the 463 minutes reported in the survey?

   c. Estimate from the grouped cumulative frequency distribution the amount of time that divides the distribution in half, that is, the amount of time that places 25 people above it and 25 people below it.

   d. Find the 50th percentile point of this distribution. Does it agree with your estimate from question 1c?

   e. What is the percentile rank of a score of 431 minutes?

2. Male bowerbirds build elaborate nests decorated with shells, colorful leaves, and blue feathers from parrots. Apparently, success in mating is related to the number of decorations on the bower. It often has been observed that male bowerbirds will steal decorations from the bowers of other birds and use them to decorate their own nest. Borgia and Gore (1986) observed this stealing behavior among 59 bowerbirds in New South Wales, Australia. They marked feathers in a bower and recorded which feathers had been stolen from other bowers. Suppose that over the duration of their observation period they recorded the following number of feathers stolen by each bird: 0, 8, 17, 0, 21, 2, 6, 14, 1, 10, 3, 0, 26, 37, 47, 4, 0, 6, 21, 3, 6, 6, 51, 8, 11, 0, 0, 4, 2, 5, 9, 4, 6, 24, 4, 1, 18, 63, 1, 5, 6, 4, 7, 12, 5, 3, 4, 3, 15, 46, 0, 5, 0, 26, 5, 17, 1, 58, 9.

   a. Construct a grouped relative frequency distribution and a cumulative grouped relative frequency distribution for these scores. Use 12 class intervals.

b. Which class interval contains the most scores?

c. Find the 50th percentile point of this distribution.

d. Construct a stem-and-leaf plot for this distribution. What are the lowest and highest scores in this distribution? What is the most frequently occurring score?

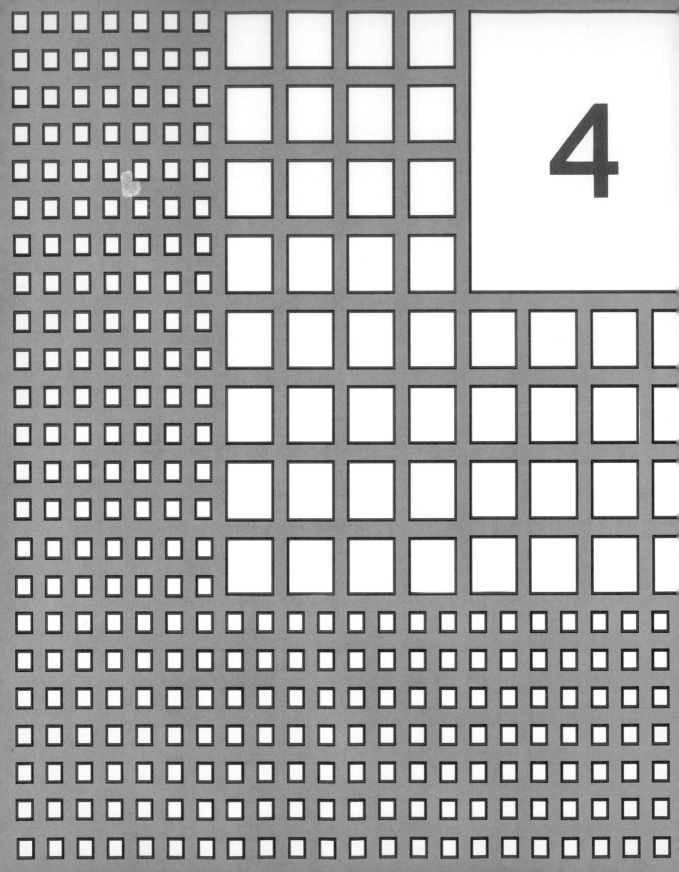

4

Describing Data: Measures of Central Tendency

OVERVIEW: DESCRIPTIVE STATISTICS AND THE NEED FOR MEASURES OF CENTRAL TENDENCY

Reliable conclusions cannot be reached by visual examination of frequency distributions alone. Behavioral scientists need to describe the scores obtained in their research in only one or two numbers. These numbers are called descriptive statistics. **Descriptive statistics** are numbers that are used to summarize and describe the raw data obtained from a sample of individuals. Descriptive statistics reduce the raw data into one or two numbers that summarize the scores in the sample. Some descriptive statistics, called *measures of central tendency*, describe the typical score obtained, and others, called *measures of variability*, indicate the amount of dispersion or variation around the typical score.

Descriptive statistics serve two functions. Their first use is to describe the scores of a sample. Their second use is to estimate or infer characteristics of a population from the sample. For example, our researcher of Chapter 3 may be interested in estimating the level of test anxiety in the population of females at her college. She would base this estimate on the descriptive statistics obtained from the scores of her sample of 100 females.

The remainder of this chapter is concerned with the descriptive use of measures of central tendency. The descriptive uses of measures of variability and the use of descriptive statistics for inferring population characteristics are introduced in Chapters 5 and 7, respectively.

Measures of central tendency are numbers that represent the average or typical score obtained from measurement of a sample of individuals. There are three measures of central tendency in common use: the mode, median, and arithmetic mean.

THE MODE

The **mode** is the most frequently occurring score in a set of scores. The mode is readily determined by inspecting a simple ungrouped frequency distribution and observing which score was tallied most often. As we pointed out in Chapter 3, the most frequently occurring score on the Test Anxiety Inventory was 41. Accordingly, the *modal* Test Anxiety Inventory score for the distribution of scores in Table 3–2 is 41. Because there is only one modal score for this set of scores, this distribution is said to be **unimodal**. But, a set of scores may possess more than one mode. A distribution of scores may be **bimodal** (i.e., having two modes) or even **multimodal** (i.e., having more than two modes). Recall from Chapter 3 that one way of describing the shape of a frequency distribution is on the basis of modality and unimodal and bimodal distributions are shown in Figure 3–6.

Although the mode is computed readily from a simple ungrouped frequency distribution, it is rarely used or reported as a measure of central tendency in behavioral science research. One reason for this rarity of use is that a distribution may have more than one mode. And, if more than one mode exists, which is a more typical score? Thus, the mode may not provide one typical score to characterize a distribution.

A second reason for the infrequent use of the mode is that a change in only one score may change the mode of a distribution quite dramatically. Suppose, for example, you gave individuals a test of short-term memory, saying to a person a list of 10 digits. After you have finished the list, you ask the person to repeat back as many digits of the list as possible. Assume you gave this task to six people and obtained the following numbers of digits given back:

Person	Number of Digits
1	5
2	6
3	7
4	7
5	8
6	9

The mode of this distribution is 7, for two people repeated back 7 digits. Suppose, however, that person 4 repeated back only 5 digits instead of 7. Now the mode of the distribution is 5 rather than 7. The change of only one score shifted the mode considerably. As another instance, suppose person 3 had recalled 10 digits instead of 7. Now the distribution possesses no mode, for each of the scores occurs an equal number of times. Because the mode may be so dependent on only a few scores, scientists often do not view it as a useful measure of central tendency.

As we have suggested, the mode is not used widely to characterize behavioral science data. But, Senders (1958) gives examples of two instances where the mode proves useful. Her first instance is a distribution of scores that is distinctively bimodal (or multimodal). Such a distribution might occur with measures of political attitudes on the eve of an important election. People are likely to have decided on either the Republican or Democratic candidate and would not likely be neutral at this time. The distribution of their attitudes would be bimodal.

Senders' second example concerns the instance when a score is needed that exactly characterizes or "fits" the most people.

If a shoe salesman can take only one demonstration pair with him, he will do better to take a pair of the modal size than a pair of the median or mean size. Nobody may have feet that are fitted by either of the latter, and a shoe that almost *fits is not much better than a shoe that is much too big or too small. What the salesman wants is the shoe that will fit perfectly the largest number of people, and a shoe of the modal size is just what he needs (Senders, 1958, p. 161).*

Example Problem 4–1
Finding the mode

Problem:

Studies investigating visual perception of real-world scenes sometimes present individuals with a picture of a scene for study and then ask the individuals to recall details of the scene. Suppose you followed this procedure with 18 subjects and found the following number of details recalled for each person.

Person	Details Recalled
1	7
2	3
3	7
4	9
5	6
6	10
7	14
8	3
9	6
10	9
11	14
12	9
13	8
14	5
15	4
16	6
17	9
18	13

What is the number of details most frequently recalled?

Statistic to be used: Mode

Solution:

Finding the mode requires finding the most frequently occurring score. If the distribution involves only a small number of scores, then visual examination will reveal the mode. If the distribution involves a larger number of scores, you may have to arrange them in a frequency distribution, such as the ungrouped distribution below, to find the mode.

Score	Tally	f
14	/ /	2
13	/	1
12		0
11		0
10	/	1
9	/ / / /	4
8	/	1
7	/ /	2
6	/ / /	3
5	/	1
4	/	1
3	/ /	2
2		0
1		0

The score of 9 occurs four times in this distribution; no other score occurs as frequently. Consequently, the modal number of details recalled is 9.

Placing the scores in a stem-and-leaf display also reveals the modal score as 9:

Stem	Leaf
1	0344
0	33456667789999. ▪

The Modal Song of a Fruitfly

Most of us probably are not aware that fruitflies can sing, but they do. When courting, male fruitflies produce a "song" by repeating a pattern of wing vibrations. To investigate the function of this song in mating, Lee (1986) measured the duration needed for a single, complete vibration of the wings in a song. He observed the following durations in milliseconds (a millisecond, abbreviated ms, is 1/1000 of a second), for 17 male fruitflies:

Song Period (ms)	Number of Fruitflies
14	2
15	4
16	6
17	1
18	4

The modal song period for these fruitflies was 16 ms, for a song 16 ms in length occurred in six fruitflies. ▪

On a separate sheet of paper, test your knowledge of the material in this section by answering the following questions.

1. Define: descriptive statistics, measures of central tendency, mode, unimodal distribution, bimodal distribution, multimodal distribution.
2. Identify two uses of descriptive statistics.
3. Identify two problems that may occur with the use of the mode as a measure of central tendency.
4. A researcher measured self-esteem in 25 seventh-grade girls. The girls rated their self-esteem on a summated rating scale. Scores on the scale can range from 10 (lowest self-esteem) to 70 (highest self-esteem). The scores obtained were: 49, 53, 67, 20, 27, 36, 49, 27, 61, 17, 49, 50, 29, 56, 65, 27, 48, 24, 49, 15, 32, 66, 46, 24, and 38.
   a. Find the mode for this distribution.
   b. Is this distribution unimodal, bimodal, or multimodal?
5. Assume that one of the individuals measured in question 4 with a score of 49 had instead obtained a score of 27.
   a. Find the mode for this distribution.
   b. Is this distribution unimodal, bimodal, or multimodal?
6. Assume that one of the individuals measured in question 4 with a score of 49 had instead obtained a score of 24.
   a. Find the mode for this distribution.
   b. Is this distribution unimodal, bimodal, or multimodal?
7. What limitation of the mode as a descriptive statistic is illustrated by your answers to questions 5 and 6?

THE MEDIAN

The **median** (abbreviated *Md*) corresponds to a score value in the distribution so that an equal number of scores are above and below it. The median thus corresponds to the *50th percentile point* in a distribution. Recall from Chapter 3 that a percentile point represents the value below which a certain percentage of scores in a distribution lie. For a median, then, 50 percent of the scores fall below its value. Accordingly, the median may be obtained from a grouped frequency distribution using the formula

$$Md = X_{.50} = X_L + \left(\frac{.50(N) - cf_L}{f_i} \right) i,$$

where

X_L = the lower real limit of the interval containing the 50th percentile point.

N = the total number of scores in the distribution.

cf_L = cumulative frequency of scores up to the lower real limit of the interval containing the median.

f_i = frequency of scores in the interval containing the median.

i = size of the class interval.

In many instances you may want to calculate the median on a small number of scores. If so, there are several quick ways of obtaining the median that do not require the computations of this formula.

Calculating the Median: Odd Number of Untied Scores

With an odd number of untied scores (i.e., there are no duplicate scores), the median usually is determined by finding the middle score in the frequency distribution. For example, for the seven untied Test Anxiety Inventory scores: 22, 34, 35, 37, 38, 44, 72, the median is 37. This value is the fourth score and falls in the middle of the distribution of the seven scores. There are three scores less than 37 and three scores greater than 37. Notice, essentially, that a counting procedure is used to determine a median. The numerical values of the scores that go into the "count" are not utilized in determining the value of the median.

Calculating the Median: Even Number of Untied Scores

With an even number of untied scores, the median is conventionally taken as the value that lies midway between the two middle scores in the frequency distribution. Consider, for example, six untied Test Anxiety Inventory scores: 34, 35, 37, 38, 44, 72. The median for these scores is 37.5, a value that falls halfway between 37 (the third score) and 38 (the fourth score); therefore, one-half of the six scores lie below a value of 37.5 and one-half lie above it.

Calculating the Median When Tied Scores Occur near the Median

In most instances of research there will not be as few as six or seven untied scores in a distribution. Typically, the number of scores will be large and several scores in the region of the median will have the same value; that is, they will be tied. For example, in Table 3–2, the simple ungrouped frequency distribution of 100 Test Anxiety Inventory scores, 46 scores fall below a value of 41 and 37 scores fall above 41. The score of 41 is obtained 11 times. Thus, because the score value of 41 was tied among 11 people, there are 57 of 100 individuals who had a score of 41 or less and 43 people who had a score of 42 or more. There is no obtained score value (for example, 41) that exactly divides the distribution in half. What shall we use as the median for this distribution? One procedure is to use the formula for the median to find a median value that does not actually exist as an obtained score. Using the formula, the median of this set of scores is 40.9. When this value is rounded to the nearest whole number it becomes 41, the value of the median obtained simply by counting the scores. It is only rarely that the precise value of the median (e.g., 40.9) is needed to characterize a distribution. For most practical purposes the median can be found quickly from counting scores in the frequency distribution, and, if scores are tied at the median, using tied scores as the median.

Characteristics of the Median

The median is obtained essentially by counting scores, ignoring numerical values except for the score that is the median. Therefore the median is not influenced by deviant or extreme scores in the tails of a distribution. As an example, the median for all the distributions below is 37:

Distribution		
A	B	C
22	34	22
34	34	34
35	35	35
37	37	37
39	39	39
44	44	44
44	109	117

The median ignores the extreme scores in the tails of distributions B and C.

 Example Problem 4–2
Finding the median

Problem:
Suppose you had the distribution of details recalled in the picture recall task presented in Example Problem 4–1. Find the median.

Statistic to be used: Median

Solution:
Eighteen scores are given in the distribution; thus the median is the score with nine scores on either side of it. Accordingly, the median is

midway between the ninth and tenth score when the scores are placed in a frequency distribution as portrayed below.

Score	f
14	2
13	1
12	0
11	0
10	1
9	4
8	1
7	2
6	3
5	1
4	1
3	2
2	0
1	0

The ninth score is 7 and the tenth score is 8; thus, the median is 7.5, midway between the scores of 7 and 8. ▪

Statistics in Use 4–2

Median Reaction Times

Psychologists frequently measure reaction times to a variety of stimuli and situations. Reaction time to a stimulus is the duration from the appearance of the stimulus to the beginning of your response. It is commonly noted, for example, that when driving, your reaction time to beginning to apply the brakes after you see a child dart into the street is on the order of a half-second or more.

To understand how we process visual information, Peterson, Simon, and Wang (1986) visually presented subjects with either two vowels (for example, *EI*) or two consonants (for example, *DG*). After the presentation of the stimuli, the subjects had to indicate as quickly as possible whether the letters were the same (for example, *EE, II, DD,* or *GG* pairs) or different (for example, *EI, IE, DG,* or *GD* pairs). They hypothesized that vowel pairs would be recognized more quickly than consonant pairs. The duration that it took individuals to respond was their reaction time. A frequency distribution of such reaction times is likely to be positively skewed. A lower bound exists on the reaction time; a person cannot respond before the stimulus occurs. Most reaction times are likely to be about a half-second in length; but a few may be quite long, perhaps even 2 seconds or more. Because the median is not affected by a few such extreme scores, Peterson et al. used it as the measure of central tendency for the reaction times obtained from a person. Using a statistical test, they found the median reaction time to vowel pairs, 496 milliseconds, to be faster than the median reaction time to consonant pairs, 503 milliseconds. Vowels, then, are more quickly found in memory than are consonants. ▪

Statistics in Use 4–3

Life in 2020: Using the Median

What do adolescents think about the future? To find out, Tismer (1985), told 247 adolescents to suppose that a seer who can foretell the future exists. They were then asked to state what year in the future they would like the seer to tell them about. The subjects replied with a year, such as 1998 or 2010. Such a score offers the possibility of a positively skewed distribution. The lower bound of a response is provided by the year that has just passed, a year already known about. On the other hand, there is no upper bound to the year someone may want to know about—for example, 3076 or 4121. Realistically, most adolescents will choose a future year in which they expect to be alive, such as 2015 or 2023. To describe his results, Tismer chose the median as a measure of central tendency; the median is not affected by a few large scores. With regard to knowing about the world as a whole, the median year named by males was 2003, whereas the median year named by females was 2000. These results concur with others indicating that boys have a more distant future orientation than girls. ▪

Testing Your Knowledge 4–2

On a separate sheet of paper, test your knowledge of the material in this section by answering the following questions.

1. Define: median
2. Is the value of the median typically affected by a few large scores in a tail of a distribution? Explain your answer.
3. A researcher measured self-esteem in 25 seventh-grade girls and obtained the scores: 49, 53, 67, 20, 27, 36, 49, 27, 61, 17, 49, 50, 29, 56, 65, 27, 48, 24, 49, 15, 32, 66, 46, 24, and 38.
   a. Find the median for this distribution.
   b. Assume the experimenter measured one additional seventh-grader and obtained a score of 28. Include this score in the distribution given above and find the median of the distribution.
   c. Assume the original distribution of 25 scores. Suppose, however, that the scores of 61, 65, 66, and 67 were changed to 51, 55, 56, and 57, respectively. What is the median of this new distribution of scores?

d. Compare your answers to questions 3a and 3b, and to 3a and 3c. What limitations of the median as a measure of central tendency are illustrated by your answers? ■

THE SAMPLE MEAN

The most familiar measure of central tendency, the one most people think of as the "average" score, is the sample mean. The sample mean is often called the *arithmetic mean,* or simply the *mean,* and is abbreviated by the symbol $\overline{X}$ (pronounced "X bar" or "bar X"). The **sample mean** is defined as the sum of a set of scores divided by the number of scores that were summed. In statistical notation, this definition is represented as

$$\overline{X} = \sum_{i=1}^{N} \frac{X_i}{N}.$$

The letter X represents a score for any individual. The subscripted i is used to indicate a particular person. Thus X_1 indicates person 1, X_2 person 2, X_{10} person 10, and so on. The upper limit to i is given by N, the number of individuals or scores in the sample. Accordingly, if $N = 10$, then the upper value of i is 10, or X_{10}. The symbol Σ (the Greek capital letter *sigma*) is a summation sign; it indicates summing or adding up a set of numbers. The limits over which the scores are added is indicated by the $i = 1$ and the N in the summation. These limits indicate that the summation should be over all scores, from the first person ($i = 1$) to the last person (the Nth person). When it is clear that the summation is over all N scores in a sample, then the limits are often not included on the summation symbol and the formula is written as

$$\overline{X} = \sum \frac{X_i}{N},$$

or even as

$$\overline{X} = \sum \frac{X}{N}.$$

Calculating the Sample Mean

Assume we have obtained the following six Test Anxiety Inventory scores: $X_1 = 34$, $X_2 = 35$, $X_3 = 37$, $X_4 = 38$, $X_5 = 44$, and $X_6 = 72$. The sample mean for this set of scores is obtained as follows:

$$\sum_{i=1}^{N} X_i = 34 + 35 + 37 + 38 + 44 + 72 = 260,$$

and thus

$$\overline{X} = \sum_{i=1}^{N} \frac{X_i}{N} = \frac{260}{6} = 43.3,$$

rounded to one decimal place. The mean of all 100 Test Anxiety Inventory scores in Table 3–1 is found by summing the 100 scores and then dividing the sum by 100. In notation, this mean is found by:

$$\overline{X} = \frac{42 + 28 + 37 + \cdots + 29 + 40 + 37}{100},$$

or,

$$\overline{X} = \frac{4164}{100} = 41.64,$$

or rounded to one decimal place, 41.6.

Characteristics of the Sample Mean

Computation of the mean utilizes the numerical value of every score in the distribution in contrast to the mode or the median. Hence, any change in the value of a score in a distribution will necessarily change the value of the mean for that distribution. For example, consider seven Test Anxiety Inventory scores: 26, 26, 26, 30, 34, 40, 42. The mode of this distribution is 26, the median 30, and the mean 32. If only one score, 40, for example, changes, it will not affect the mode, it may change the median, but it definitely will affect the mean. Suppose the 40 changes to a 43. The mode of the distribution remains 26 and the median 30, but the mean is now 32.4. Because the mean depends upon the magnitude of each score, extreme scores in the tail of a distribution will affect the value of the mean and distort its value as a measure of central tendency. Employing the distribution of seven Test Anxiety Inventory scores given originally, suppose the 40 changes not to a 43, but to a 78. The mode and the median of the distribution remain 26 and 30, respectively. But the mean has increased to 37.4. Thus, we see that if a distribution includes a few extreme scores, the mean may not be a representative typical score.

A second characteristic of the mean is that the deviations of the scores about the mean of those scores sum to zero. Notationally,

$$\sum_{i=1}^{N} (X_i - \overline{X}) = 0.$$

This notation indicates that if we subtract the mean from each score in a distribution, the sum of the differences will be zero. We use Table 4–1 to help explain this concept.

Column a of Table 4–1 portrays seven Test Anxiety Inventory scores with a mean of 35.0 (i.e., $\overline{X} = 35.0$). The numerical value of the mean is subtracted from each of the seven scores in column b of the table. The sum of column b, $\Sigma(X_i - \overline{X})$, is zero.

The value of $\Sigma(X_i - \overline{X})$ will always be zero. However, the value of $\Sigma(X_i - \overline{X})^2$ will not be zero. This value is calculated in column c of the table.

TABLE 4–1.

A set of seven scores with a mean of 35.0
Column b shows the value of $X_i - \overline{X}$ for
each score. In column c the $X_i - \overline{X}$
deviation is squared for each score.

(a)	(b)	(c)
X_i	$X_i - \overline{X}$	$(X_i - \overline{X})^2$
22	$22 - 35 = -13$	169
34	$34 - 35 = -1$	1
35	$35 - 35 = 0$	0
35	$35 - 35 = 0$	0
37	$37 - 35 = +2$	4
38	$38 - 35 = +3$	9
44	$44 - 35 = +9$	81
Sums	0	264

In column c each deviation of a score from the mean is squared (i.e., multiplied by itself). For example, the score of 22 differs from $\overline{X}$ by -13, and $(-13)^2 = 169$. The total of the scores in column c, or $\Sigma(X_i - \overline{X})^2$, is 264. Mathematically, it can be demonstrated that the sum of the squared deviations of the scores from the mean [i.e., $\Sigma(X_i - \overline{X})^2$] is smaller than the squared deviation of the scores from any other statistic such as the median or the mode. This property is a third characteristic of the mean and allows the mean to be used in several very important statistical techniques. Because of this property, the sample mean is perhaps the most commonly used measure of central tendency in research.

Example Problem 4–3
Calculating the mean

Problem:
Suppose you had the same distribution of scores in a picture recall task as presented in Example Problem 4–1. Find the mean of these scores.

Statistic to be used: $\overline{X} = \Sigma X_i / N$.

Solution:
The first step is to obtain ΣX_i, where the Σ symbol indicates to sum the scores of all subjects. Thus, ΣX_i equals

$$7 + 3 + 7 + 9 + 6 + 10 + 14 + 3 + 6 + 9 +$$
$$14 + 9 + 8 + 5 + 4 + 6 + 9 + 13 = 142 .$$

The value of N is the number of scores added, or 18 in this example. Accordingly,

$$\overline{X} = \Sigma \, \frac{X_i}{N} = \frac{142}{18} = 7.9. \quad \blacksquare$$

Statistics in Use 4–3

Self-Touching: Using the Sample Mean

A great deal of communication between individuals is of a nonverbal nature, and part of nonverbal communication involves touching parts of our own body. How does self-touching behavior develop? In an attempt to answer this question, D'Alessio and Zazzetta (1986) observed four different age groups of children and recorded each time that a child touched him- or herself. The mean number of self-touches of different body areas during the observation periods were then calculated. For example, they found that for children of about age 3 years the mean number of touches to the head was about the same for boys (20.9 touches) and girls (22.7 touches). The mean number of total touches decreased considerably with age, however. For example, girls of about age 3 years had a mean total of 66.3 self-touches, whereas girls of about age 5 years 8 months had a mean of only 25.5 self-touches.   ▪

Statistics in Use 4–4

Does Caffeine Keep You Awake? Describing Scores with the Mean

Is caffeine consumption related to sleep duration? To find out, Hicks, Hicks, Reyes, and Cheers (1983), asked subjects to estimate how many caffeinated beverages they drank each day and the number of hours of sleep they obtained each night. For people who drank one or fewer caffeine drinks per day the mean number of hours of sleep per night was 7.5. For individuals who drank more than eight caffeinated beverages per day the mean was 5.8 hours per night. A statistical test revealed the difference between the means was larger than expected by chance. Greater caffeine usage is related to shorter amounts of sleep.   ▪

Testing Your Knowledge 4–3

On a separate sheet of paper, test your knowledge of the material in this section by answering the following questions.

1. Define: $\Sigma_{i=1}^{N} X_i, \Sigma X_i, \overline{X}, \Sigma$.
2. Write the formula for the arithmetic mean.

3. Is the value of the mean typically affected by a few large scores in a tail of a distribution? Explain your answer.

4. Find the sample mean for the following scores: 97, 90, 86, 93, 76, and 86.
   a. Demonstrate that $\sum_{i=1}^{N}(X_i - \overline{X}) = 0$ for these scores.
   b. Find the value of $\sum_{i=1}^{N}(X_i - \overline{X})^2$ for these scores.

5. Assume again that a researcher measured self-esteem in seventh-grade girls and obtained the scores: 49, 53, 67, 20, 27, 36, 49, 27, 61, 17, 49, 50, 29, 56, 65, 27, 48, 24, 49, 15, 32, 66, 46, 24, and 38.
   a. Find the mean of these scores.
   b. Suppose the experimenter measured one additional seventh-grader and obtained a score of 28. Include this score in the distribution given above and find the mean of the distribution.
   c. Assume the original 25 scores. Suppose, however, that the scores of 61, 65, 66, and 67 were changed to 51, 55, 56, and 57, respectively. What is the mean of this new set of scores?
   d. Compare your answers for questions 5a, 5b, and 5c. What strength of the mean is illustrated by your answers? ◾

COMPARING MEASURES OF CENTRAL TENDENCY

Which is the "best" average score? There is no single answer to this question. Which measure of central tendency is best depends upon the use for which the statistic was computed. Measures of central tendency have both descriptive and inferential uses.

Descriptive Uses of Measures of Central Tendency

The choice of which measure of central tendency to use as a descriptive statistic depends upon the scale of measurement realized in the scores and the shape of the frequency distribution of the scores.

Scale of Measurement of the Scores

Nominal Scale. A nominal scale merely places responses into categories; a response occurred or it did not occur. The only measure of central tendency that may be used with a nominal scale then is the mode — the category that occurs most frequently.

Ordinal Scale. Ordinal scales place scores in order of magnitude, but there is no assurance that on the underlying variable being measured the intervals between adjacent scores are equal. Consequently, a median score may be obtained. The median divides the distribution of scores into two equal halves. Of course, a modal score, should one occur, also may be obtained.

Interval and Ratio Scales.   In both interval and ratio scales the intervals between adjacent scores are assumed to represent equal intervals on the conceptual variable being measured. Thus, it is appropriate to compute a mean on scores that reach either interval or ratio measurement. It also is appropriate to find the median and the mode for scores at this level.

Shape of the Distribution of Scores

Figure 3–6 presented shapes of several typical distributions of scores. There are, of course, many other possible shapes that distributions may assume. How well a measure of central tendency characterizes a distribution depends upon the shape of the distribution. If a distribution is unimodal and symmetric, such as the normal distribution of Figure 3–6a, then the mode, median, and mean are identical values. Each statistic characterizes the distribution of scores equally well. Often, however, obtained distributions are not unimodal and symmetric—they may be either positively or negatively skewed. In a skewed distribution, the mode, median, and mean will be different from each other. Because the mean is responsive to the extreme scores of a skewed distribution, usually it will move more in the direction of the skew than either the mode or the median. And, the direction of the difference in the mean and median will reveal whether the distribution is positively or negatively skewed. In a negatively skewed distribution the mean will have a lower value than the median; similarly, a few extreme high scores in a positively skewed distribution will inflate the mean with respect to the median. Figure 4–1 illustrates the relative locations of the median and mean in positively and negatively skewed distributions. As you can see from this figure, if a distribution is seriously skewed, with a large difference between the mean and median values, then the median usually provides a better measure of central tendency than does the mean.

Whenever description is important, we recommend presentation of all three measures of central tendency for any distribution of scores that you may obtain. As you read behavioral sciences literature, however, you will discover that the mean is the most widely presented descriptive measure of central tendency and the mode is rarely provided. This choice of the mean is not based upon its superior descriptive characteristics; rather the mean is the most useful of the three measures of central tendency as an inferential statistic. And, as we will find, inference is an important aspect of statistical analysis.

Do Some Distributions Not Have a Central Tendency?

Distributions that are bimodal cannot be described adequately by a single measure of central tendency, especially when the modal scores are widely separated. Suppose, for example, that a researcher had obtained a distri-

FIGURE 4–1.

The relative locations of the median and mean in positively and negatively skewed distributions.

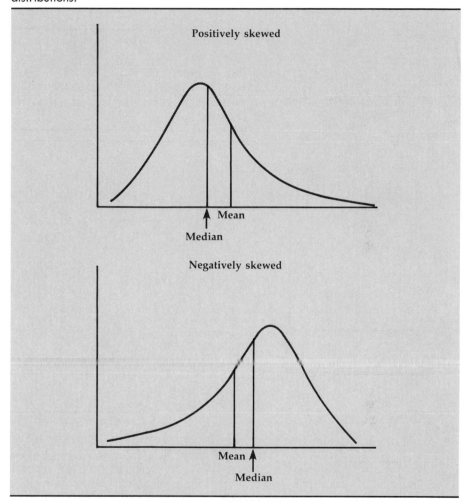

bution of Test Anxiety Inventory scores such as that shown in Table 4–2. This distribution is clearly bimodal with a mode at 34 and another at 58. The median of the distribution is 45.5 and the mean 48.5. But notice that no individuals obtained scores near either the median or the mean. Clearly, neither the median nor the mean represents the test anxiety of a typical person in this sample. In this instance, the two modal scores present the best description of typical scores.

Consider another example. For a recent year the Department of Agriculture reported that the per capita consumption of chewing tobacco in the United States was 1.33 pounds per person. Does this statistic describe

TABLE 4–2.

A bimodal distribution of 26 Test Anxiety Inventory scores.

Score	Tally	f	
61	/	1	
60			
59	/ /	2	
58	/ / / / /	5	Mode
57	/ / /	3	
56	/	1	
55	/	1	
54			
53			
52			
51			
50			
49			
48			
47			
46			$\overline{X} = 45.8, \quad Md = 45.5$
45			
44			
43			
42			
41			
40			
39			
38			
37			
36	/	1	
35	/ / /	3	
34	/ / / / /	5	Mode
33	/ /	2	
32	/	1	
31	/	1	

you? We suspect not. If you do not chew tobacco, then this number is much too high. But if you do chew tobacco, then the value is likely far too low. The distribution of use of chewing tobacco is skewed severely and not symmetrical. A minority of the population uses chewing tobacco and their consumption is considerably in excess of 1.33 pounds per year. The majority of the population does not chew tobacco and their mean use is exactly 0 pounds per year. Glass and Stanley (1970) point out that "some groups of scores simply do not 'tend centrally' in any meaningful way, and it is often misleading to calculate one measure of central tendency" (p. 68). We think their point is clearly illustrated by this example.

Inferential Uses of Measures of Central Tendency

The choice of a measure of central tendency is determined in part by whether the statistic is to be used for subsequent inferential purposes. For reasons that we discuss in Chapter 7, the mean is the most useful of the three measures of central tendency for inferential purposes. Consequently, the mean enters into a number of important statistical tests. Because the mean is so useful for inference, then, behavioral scientists often use the mean to describe their data when considerations of level of measurement and shape of the frequency distribution might dictate against it.

Testing Your Knowledge 4–4

On a separate sheet of paper, test your knowledge of the material in this section by answering the following questions.

1. Identify the factors involved in choosing a measure of central tendency.
2. Which measure of central tendency would you choose to achieve each of the following?
   a. Provide a value that is the 50th percentile point in a distribution.
   b. Minimize the sum of the squared error deviation of each score in the distribution from the measure of central tendency.
   c. Describe the most frequently occurring score in a distribution.
   d. Utilize the numerical value of each score in its computation.
3. A distribution is severely negatively skewed. Would you expect the mean to be smaller than, equal to, or larger than the median? Explain your answer.
4. The mean of a distribution is considerably larger than the median. Do you expect the distribution to be symmetrical, negatively skewed, or positively skewed? Why?

SUMMARY

- Measures of central tendency may be used for both descriptive and inferential purposes.
- The mode, median, and sample mean are the three commonly used measures of central tendency.
- The mode is the most frequently occurring score in a distribution of scores.
- The median is a value corresponding to a score in the distribution so that an equal number of scores are above and below it.

- The sample mean is found from $\sum_{i=1}^{N} X_i / N$.
- The appropriate use of each statistic for descriptive purposes depends upon the scale of measurement realized and the shape of the frequency distribution of the scores.
- The mean is the most used measure of central tendency for inferential purposes.

KEY TERMS

bimodal distribution   median $\overline{X}$
descriptive statistics   mode $\Sigma_{i=1}^{N} X_i$
Md   multimodal distribution ΣX_i
mean   sample mean
measures of central tendency   unimodal distribution

REVIEW QUESTIONS

On a separate sheet of paper, test your knowledge of the material in this chapter by answering the following questions.

1. In Chapters 2 and 3 we reported research by Rotton and Kelly (1985) employing the Belief in Lunar Effects Scale. Scores on this scale may range from 9 to 81. For one sample of individuals they report a mean of 37.9 and a median of 39. From this information, would you judge the distribution of scores to be approximately symmetrical or skewed? Why?

2. Davidson and Templin (1986) gathered data on a sample of professional golfers. For 119 top money-winning golfers, they reported mean winnings of $118,016 and median winnings of $93,021. Is the distribution of winnings skewed? If so, in which direction? Why?

3. Egli and Meyers (1984) surveyed 151 teenagers at a video-game arcade. The results revealed that the individuals played a mean of 5.2 hours per week, with a median of 2.5 hours per week. Is the distribution of hours played per week skewed? Why?

4. Researchers in behavioral medicine often are interested in psychological methods of controlling pain. To induce pain safely in their subjects they may use the cold pressor task. One form of this task involves having subjects immerse a hand in cold water. Suppose a scientist studying pain had 17 individuals place a hand in a tub of 40°F water. She then timed how long the subjects could hold their hand in the water before the pain became too intense to endure. The following scores (in seconds) were obtained: 35, 39, 38, 30, 37, 43, 30, 38, 41, 52, 25, 44, 33, 41, 38, 56, and 37.
   a. Calculate the three measures of central tendency for this set of scores.
   b. Compare the measures of central tendency. Is the distribution skewed? Explain your answer.
   c. Do you think one of the measures of central tendency describes the scores better than the others? If so, which measure and why?

5. Suppose an experimenter again employed the cold pressor task and obtained the following durations (in seconds) that subjects were able

to hold their hand in the water: 20, 28, 26, 29, 60, 21, 37, 30, 28, 57, 29, 25, 63, 26, 32, 30, and 28.

a. Calculate the three measures of central tendency for this set of scores.

b. Compare the measures of central tendency. Is the distribution skewed? Explain your answer.

c. Do you think one of the measures of central tendency describes the scores better than the others? If so, which measure and why?

6. Once again, suppose an experimenter employed the cold pressor task and obtained the following durations (in seconds) that subjects were able to hold their hand in the water: 45, 23, 57, 50, 47, 52, 20, 53, 50, 30, 52, 60, 52, 49, 52, 49, and 53.

a. Calculate the three measures of central tendency for this set of scores.

b. Compare the measures of central tendency. Is the distribution skewed? Explain your answer.

c. Do you think one of the measures of central tendency describes the scores better than the others? If so, which measure and why?

7. A scientist again employed the cold pressor task described in question 4 and obtained the following times (in seconds) that subjects were able to hold their hand in the water: 52, 23, 40, 60, 52, 21, 20, 52, 50, 23, 55, 26, 28, 53, 26, 49, and 26.

a. Calculate the three measures of central tendency for this set of scores.

b. Compare the measures of central tendency. Is the distribution skewed? Explain your answer.

c. Notice that the distribution is bimodal. Does this distribution tend centrally about a single number? Explain your answer.

d. Do you think the median adequately describes the typical amount of time that a subject held his or her hand in the water? Explain your answer.

e. Do you think the mean adequately describes the typical amount of time that a subject held his or her hand in the water? Explain your answer.

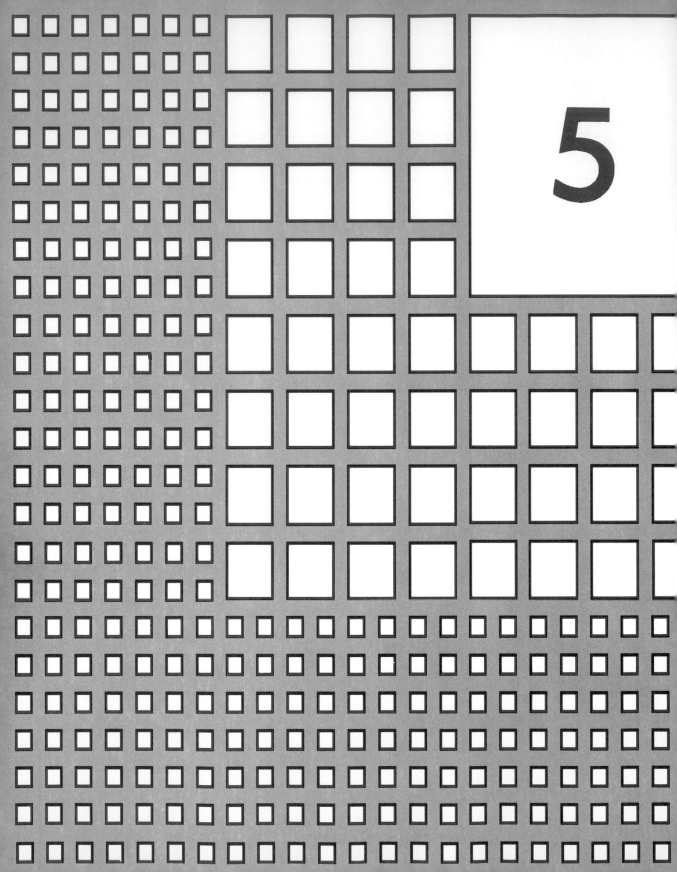

5

Describing Data: Measures of Variability

A measure of central tendency tells only part of the "story" about the scores obtained from a sample of individuals. From only this measure we cannot tell whether the scores are dispersed widely or clustered closely about that typical score. The mode, median, or mean alone does not give any indication of how much dispersion or variability there is among the scores used to calculate that statistic. Thus, in order to know how well the measure of central tendency represents a typical score, we also must know the variability of the scores. Measures of variability also are important to the use of descriptive statistics as estimates of population characteristics. In this chapter we introduce several measures of variability.

Variability refers to how much scores are spread out or dispersed in a distribution. The more the scores are clustered around the measure of central tendency, the better a particular measure of central tendency represents all the scores in a group. Conversely, the more dispersion there is among scores within a group, the less accurately an average score depicts the typical score of an individual.

To illustrate the concept of variability, suppose a researcher measures three different groups of people, Groups 1, 2, and 3, on the amount of time that individuals laugh while reading a book of cartoons. The scores she obtained, in seconds, are portrayed in Table 5–1. The mode, median,

TABLE 5–1.

Duration of laughter scores in seconds for three groups of nine people each.

	Group		
	1	2	3
	X_i	X_i	X_i
	41	38	21
	41	39	26
	41	40	33
	41	41	41
	41	41	41
	41	41	41
	41	42	50
	41	43	51
	41	44	65
Mode	41	41	41
Md	41	41	41
$\overline{X}$	41	41	41

and mean for each set of scores is 41.0. But it should be apparent that the measures of central tendency are not equally representative of the scores in each group. In Group 1 each score is equal to 41; there is no variability among the scores. Consequently, each measure of central tendency perfectly represents the scores in the distribution. But the scores in Group 1 would be an exceedingly rare outcome if actual duration of laughter scores were obtained from nine people. In Group 2 the scores are clustered closely around the measure of central tendency; no score deviates more than 3 seconds from 41 seconds. Each of the measures of central tendency appears representative of all individuals in this group, for there is little variability among the individual scores.

The situation is different in Group 3. Here you can see that there is a considerable amount of variability in the amount of laughter. In comparison to Group 2, no scores are within 3 seconds of 41 seconds in this set. Clearly, any measure of central tendency for this set of scores is not as representative of the scores as are the measures of central tendency for the scores in Groups 1 and 2. As with measures of central tendency, the variability of scores must be quantified. Accordingly, there are several statistics to describe the dispersion of scores in a distribution.

RANGE MEASURES OF VARIABILITY

One form of a measure of variability provides an interval containing a certain percentage of the scores in a distribution. Three such measures commonly are used: the range, the interquartile range, and the semi-interquartile range.

The Range

The simplest measure of variability for a set of scores is called the range. The **range** is found by

$$\text{Range} = X_{\text{highest}} - X_{\text{lowest}},$$

where X_{highest} represents the highest score and X_{lowest} the lowest score in a distribution. For Group 3 of Table 5–1, $X_{\text{highest}} = 65$ and $X_{\text{lowest}} = 21$; thus the range for this group is $65 - 21$, or 44. The range for scores in Group 2 is $44 - 38$, or 6, and the range of scores for Group 1 is $41 - 41$, or 0. The highest and lowest scores in the three groups are found easily by visual inspection of the data. If a larger number of scores is obtained, then it may be necessary to construct a frequency distribution to identify the highest and lowest scores. For the 100 Test Anxiety Inventory (TAI) scores given in Table 3–1, the highest and lowest scores are determined easily from the frequency distribution presented in Table 3–2. The highest score is 73 and the lowest score is 22; thus the range for this distribution is 73 − 22, or 51 rating scale points.

Characteristics of the Range

The range describes the overall spread between the highest and lowest scores in a distribution. But because it depends upon only these two scores, the range is a relatively unstable measure of variability. Any change in either the highest or lowest score will affect the range, even though all other scores may remain unchanged. Moreover, the larger the size of the sample, the more likely it is that one deviant score may be obtained to inflate the value of the range. The major virtue of the range is its easy computation, but because of its lack of stability, it is not a frequently reported measure of variability

The Interquartile Range

A more informative measure of variability is the interquartile range. The **interquartile range (IQR)** describes the range of values for the middle 50 percent of the scores in a distribution. It is obtained by subtracting the score corresponding to the 25th percentile (or first quartile, Q_1) from the score that falls at the 75th percentile (or third quartile, Q_3). In notation, the interquartile range is defined as

$$IQR = Q_3 - Q_1 .$$

Values of Q_1 and Q_3 may be obtained using the formula in Chapter 3 for finding a specified percentile point of a distribution (p. 54).

Characteristics of the IQR

The interquartile range provides useful information about the variability of scores in a distribution, for it reveals the range of scores typical for the middle 50 percent of the individuals grouped around the median. Because the interquartile range excludes the top 25 percent and the bottom 25 percent of the scores in a distribution, its value is unaffected by few extreme scores. Obviously, the interquartile range will be smaller than the range for a set of scores. For example, for the TAI scores of Table 3–1, $Q_3 = 45$ and $Q_1 = 37$ (rounded to the nearest whole number). Thus the IQR is

$$IQR = Q_3 - Q_1 = 45 - 37 = 8 ,$$

whereas the range for these scores is 51. Although the full range of the TAI scores of Table 3–1 is large, the range for the middle 50 percent of the scores is relatively small.

The Semi-Interquartile Range

The **semi-interquartile range (*SIQR*)** is one-half of the interquartile range, or

$$SIQR = \frac{IQR}{2} = \frac{(Q_3 - Q_1)}{2}.$$

Characteristics of the *SIQR*

The *SIQR* describes the average spread of scores for 25 percent of the scores above and below the median. Only when the distribution is perfectly symmetrical, however, will the *SIQR* represent exactly the range of scores for the 25 percent of the scores above the median and the 25 percent of scores below the median. As an example, for the TAI scores in Table 3–1, the *SIQR* is 8/2, or 4. This *SIQR* indicates that the middle 50 percent of the scores in the distribution did not extend more than about 4 rating points above or 4 rating points below the median. Notice that we qualified the preceding statement with the word *about*. Because the frequency distribution for the TAI scores is somewhat skewed, this semi-interquartile range does not include exactly 25 percent of the scores on each side of the median.

Statistics in Use 5–1

Belief in Lunar Effects: Describing a Distribution of Scores

Most scientists, when reporting the results of their research, present measures of variability as well as measures of central tendency. As an example, in Statistics in Use 3–2 we presented the stem-and-leaf display of 157 Belief in Lunar Effects Scale scores obtained by Rotton and Kelly (1985). In addition to the stem-and-leaf display, Rotton and Kelly provided a complete description in terms of measures of central tendency and variability. The median of the 157 scores is 39; the largest score is 72, the smallest is 11, and thus the range is 61; Q_3 is 48, Q_1 is 26.5, and thus the *IQR* is 21.5; and the *SIQR* is 10.75. From these measures of variability, we know that the middle 50 percent of the scores fall into the range between 26.5 to 48, and that about 50 percent of the scores fall within 10.75 rating points of the median of 39. ■

Statistics in Use 5–2

Average Salaries: Using the *SIQR*

The United States Bureau of Labor Statistics maintains statistics on average salaries for a variety of jobs. One report for service-type jobs in the Boston, Massachusetts, area indicated a mean weekly salary for drafters of $486.00

with an *IQR* of \$395.00 to \$562.50 (Adams, 1986, November 11). For registered industrial nurses the mean weekly salary was \$490.50 with an *IQR* of \$447.00 to \$528.00. Although both jobs pay about the same mean salary, they differ considerably in variability of salary. The middle 50 percent of salaries for registered industrial nurses are more closely clustered about the mean of \$490.50 than are the middle 50 percent of salaries for drafters about the mean of \$486.00. ▪

Testing Your Knowledge 5–1

On a separate sheet of paper, test your knowledge of the material in this section by answering the following questions.

1. Define: variability, range, interquartile range, semi-interquartile range, Q_1, Q_3.
2. The highest score on a class test is 98 and the lowest is 54. The 75th percentile score on the test is 92 and the 25th percentile score is 74. Find the range, *IQR*, and *SIQR* for these scores.
3. On a test of complex reaction time, the longest score is 929 milliseconds (ms), and the shortest score is 642 ms. The 75th percentile score is 809 ms and the 25th percentile score is 724 ms. Find the range, *IQR*, and *SIQR* for these scores.
   a. What information about the scores in this distribution is given by the *IQR*?
   b. What information about the scores in this distribution is given by the *SIQR*?
4. Explain why the range is a relatively unstable measure of variability.
5. Explain why the *IQR* is a more stable measure of variability than is the range. ▪

MEASURES OF VARIABILITY ABOUT THE SAMPLE MEAN

The range, interquartile range, and semi-interquartile range each provide an interval containing a certain percentage of the scores (e.g., 100 percent for the range) around the central location in a distribution. None of these statistics, however, utilizes all the scores in the distribution for its computation. There are instances, however, when a single number, based on all the scores in a distribution and describing the typical amount of variability in the scores, is needed. Two very important statistics use the mean as the measure of central tendency: the variance and the standard deviation.

The Sample Variance

The arithmetic mean is obtained by adding together all the scores in a sample and dividing by the number of scores, or $\overline{X} = \Sigma X_i / N$. It is an obvious step to take a similar approach to deriving a measure of variability of the scores around the mean. To do so, we could subtract the mean from each score, add up all the resulting deviations, and then divide the sum by the number of scores. In notation this measure of variability would be $\Sigma(X_i - \overline{X})/N$. But there is a problem with this proposed measure of variability. As illustrated in column b of Table 4–1 (see p. 87), the sum of $X_i - \overline{X}$ deviations for a distribution of scores will always equal zero; that is, $\Sigma(X_i - \overline{X}) = 0$. To avoid this dead end we could square each deviation value, i.e., $(X_i - \overline{X})^2$, before summing and dividing. The value of $\Sigma(X_i - \overline{X})^2$ usually would not be zero. In fact, it will be zero only if each $X_i - \overline{X}$ value is zero. This procedure is used to derive the sample variance and, subsequently, the sample standard deviation.

To obtain the **variance** (represented in notation as S^2) the squared deviations are summed and divided by the number of scores. In notation, this definition of the variance is written as:

$$S^2 = \sum_{i=1}^{N} \frac{(X_i - \overline{X})^2}{N}.$$

This formula for the variance is appropriate when the distribution of scores represents an entire population of interest. Seldom is an entire population measured; however, more typically a researcher needs to estimate the population variance from the variance obtained on a sample from the population. The sample variance given by the formula above consistently underestimates the actual value of the population variance. It provides a biased estimate of the population variance. This bias may be corrected, however, by employing $N - 1$, instead of simply N, as the denominator. This form of the variance is represented in notation as s^2. Thus, the definitional formula for the most typically used form of the variance is

$$s^2 = \sum_{i=1}^{N} \frac{(X_i - \overline{X})^2}{(N - 1)}.$$

Except for the discussion of standard scores in Chapter 6, we use this definition of the variance from this point on. The formula employing N in the denominator is reserved for instances when the variance is calculated on a population of scores.

The sum of squared deviations, $\Sigma(X_i - \overline{X})^2$, in the numerator of the formula for s is often called the **sum of squares** and represented by the symbol **SS**. Thus, the sample variance may also be defined as

$$s^2 = \frac{SS}{(N - 1)}.$$

The variance is an important concept in the statistical analysis of data, and we discuss it much more fully in Chapter 11. Because the variance shares characteristics with the standard deviation, we discuss these characteristics in a later seaction of this chapter.

Example Problem 5–1
Calculating the sample variance from the definitional formula

Problem:
Find the sample variance of the nine duration of laughter scores of Group 2 in Table 5–1, using the definitional formula for s^2.

Statistic to be used: $s^2 = \Sigma(X_i - \overline{X})^2/(N - 1)$.

Solution:
The steps necessary in the calculation of s^2 are illustrated in the table below. The definitional formula requires us first to obtain the sum of squared deviations, SS or $\Sigma(X_i - \overline{X})^2$, by subtracting the mean from each score. The nine scores are given in column a. The mean for these scores is 41, and this value is presented in column b. This mean is then subtracted from each score as illustrated in column c. The resulting deviation for each score is squared as shown in column d. The squared deviations are then summed and this sum, given at the bottom of column d, is 28. This value is the $\Sigma(X_i - \overline{X})^2$, or SS, needed for the numerator of s^2. To obtain s^2, the SS is divided by $N - 1$. Because nine scores were used, $N = 9$ and $N - 1 = 8$. Accordingly, $s^2 = 28/8 = 3.5$.

(a)	(b)	(c)	(d)
X_i	$\overline{X}$	$(X_i - \overline{X})$	$(X_i - \overline{X})^2$
38	41	−3	9
39	41	−2	4
40	41	−1	1
41	41	0	0
41	41	0	0
41	41	0	0
42	41	+1	1
43	41	+2	4
44	41	+3	9
	Sums	0	28

Raw-Score Computational Formula for the Sample Variance
The definitional formula for the sample variance best conveys conceptually what s^2 is. The formula is easy to use when relatively few scores are involved and the scores and the mean of the scores are whole numbers.

When decimal values are obtained with either the scores or the mean, or if a large number of scores is involved, then the computations become more cumbersome. Therefore, it is easier to calculate s^2 with a raw-score formula that is equivalent algebraically to the definitional formula. The raw-score computational formula for s^2 is

$$s^2 = \frac{\sum\limits_{i=1}^{N} X_i^2 - \left[\left(\sum\limits_{i=1}^{N} X_i\right)^2 / N\right]}{N - 1}.$$

Example Problem 5–2
Calculating the sample variance from the raw-score formula

Problem:
Find the sample variance of the nine duration of laughter scores of Group 2 in Table 5–1 using the raw-score computational formula for s^2.

Statistic to be used:

$$s^2 = \frac{\sum\limits_{i=1}^{N} X_i^2 - \left[\left(\sum\limits_{i=1}^{N} X_i\right)^2 / N\right]}{N - 1}.$$

Solution:
The steps necessary in calculating s^2 using the raw-score formula are illustrated in the table below. The nine scores are presented in column a. The sum of these scores, $\sum X_i$, is 369, and is presented at the bottom of column a. The procedure requires each raw score to be squared as illustrated in column b [e.g., $(38)^2 = 1{,}444$]. The sum of the squared raw scores, $\sum X_i^2$, is 15,157 and is shown at the bottom of column b. Nine scores were used; thus $N = 9$ and $N - 1 = 8$.

	(a)	(b)
	X_i	X_i^2
	38	1,444
	39	1,521
	40	1,600
	41	1,681
	41	1,681
	41	1,681
	42	1,764
	43	1,849
	44	1,936
Sums	369	15,157

We now have found all the values needed to calculate s^2. Substituting these values into the computational formula, we obtain:

$$s^2 = \frac{\sum_{i=1}^{N} X_i^2 - \left[\left(\sum_{i=1}^{N} X_i\right)^2 / N\right]}{N - 1}$$

$$s^2 = \frac{15{,}157 - [(369)^2 / 9]}{9 - 1}$$

$$s^2 = \frac{15{,}157 - (136{,}161 / 9)}{8}$$

$$s^2 = \frac{15{,}157 - 15{,}129}{8} = \frac{28}{8} = 3.5.$$

Notice that this value of s^2, 3.5, is identical to that obtained in Example Problem 5–1 using the definitional formula of s^2. ■

The Sample Standard Deviation

The **sample standard deviation** (identified in notation as s) is obtained by taking the square root of the variance. In notation, the sample standard deviation is defined as

$$s = \sqrt{s^2} = \sqrt{\frac{\sum_{i=1}^{N} (X_i - \overline{X})^2}{(N - 1)}},$$

or, in sums of squares notation,

$$s = \sqrt{\frac{SS}{(N - 1)}}.$$

Example Problem 5–3
Calculating the standard deviation

Problem:
Find the sample standard deviation of the nine duration of laughter scores of Group 2 in Table 5–1.

Statistic to be used: $s = \sqrt{s^2}$.

Solution:
To obtain s, the value of s^2 must first be found. This value was calculated for the scores of Group 2 in Example Problem 5–1 using the

definitional formula for s^2 and in Example Problem 5–2 using the raw-score computational formula for s^2. Using either formula, the value of s^2 is 3.5. Thus,

$$s = \sqrt{s^2} = \sqrt{3.5} = 1.87 \text{ seconds.} \quad \blacksquare$$

Characteristics of the Sample Variance and the Standard Deviation

There are several characteristics common to the variance and the standard deviation. Notice that $\Sigma(X_i - \overline{X})^2$ is used for the numerator of both. If all the scores in a distribution are equal to the mean, such as those of Group 1 of Table 5–1, then $\Sigma(X_i - \overline{X})^2$ will be equal to zero. Therefore, s^2 and s also will equal zero. If you see a value of s^2 or s equal to zero, then you know that all scores in the distribution are equal to the sample mean.

On the other hand, if any of the scores in the distribution are not equal to the mean, then the value of $\Sigma(X_i - \overline{X})^2$ will become positive. Consequently, the values of s^2 and s also will take on a positive value greater than zero. Further, the value of each will increase as the variability of the scores increases. You can see this increase in size of s^2 and s with increasing variability of scores by comparing the distributions of Groups 2 and 3 of Table 5–1. Notice that the scores of Group 3 are more variable about the mean of 41 than are the scores in Group 2. For scores in Group 2, $s^2 = 3.5$ and $s = 1.87$, whereas in Group 3, s^2 and s are 180.7 and 13.44, respectively.

Another characteristic of s^2 and s is that scores that differ considerably from the mean will contribute more to s^2 or s than will scores that differ less from the mean. For example, in Group 2 of Table 5–1 the scores of 42 and 43 differ from the mean of 41 by 1 and 2 seconds, respectively. Yet, in terms of their contribution to the value of s^2 or s, the 43 is weighted four times as much as the 42. This unequal contribution of scores occurs because $(X_i - \overline{X})^2$ for 42 is equal to 1, but for 43 it is equal to 4.

The standard deviation is more often presented in reports of research than is the variance. One reason for this greater use is that because the standard deviation is the square root of the variance, it provides a measure of the variability of scores in the original scale units of the scores. Thus, in Example Problem 5–3, the s was given as 1.87 seconds, for the raw scores were measured in seconds.

Review of Formulas

The variance and the standard deviation are important statistics for the analysis of data and we use them frequently in following chapters. Consequently, it is useful to review the formulas for them. Table 5–2 presents the definitional, raw-score computation, and sum of squares notation formulas for both s^2 and s. Each formula provides the same numerical value of the statistic when applied to a set of data.

TABLE 5–2.

Definitional, computational, and sum of squares notation formulas for the sample variance and standard deviation.

	Formula		
	Definitional	*Computational*	*Sum of Squares*
Variance s^2	$\dfrac{\Sigma(X_i - \overline{X})^2}{N - 1}$	$\dfrac{\Sigma X_i^2 - [(\Sigma X_i)^2/N]}{N - 1}$	$\dfrac{SS}{N - 1}$
Standard deviation $s = \sqrt{s^2}$	$\sqrt{\dfrac{\Sigma(X_i - \overline{X})^2}{N - 1}}$	$\sqrt{\dfrac{\Sigma X_i^2 - [(\Sigma X_i)^2/N]}{N - 1}}$	$\sqrt{\dfrac{SS}{N - 1}}$

Statistics in Use 5–3

Hyperactivity and Reaction Time: Using the Standard Deviation to Describe Variability

The sample standard deviation is a measure of variability about the sample mean. Thus, when the arithmetic mean is taken as a measure of central tendency, the standard deviation often is used as a measure of variability in the scores, as we illustrate in this example.

Reaction time is the length of time required to respond to the onset of a stimulus. Children who are diagnosed clinically as hyperactive have certain reaction times that are longer than children characterized as normal. Alberts-Corush, Firestone, and Goodman (1986) examined whether this relationship holds also for the biological parents of hyperactive and normal children. As part of their research they found a mean reaction time for fathers of hyperactive children of 328.57 milliseconds (a millisecond, abbreviated ms, equals 1/1000 of a second) with a standard deviation of 65.07 ms. The corresponding mean and standard deviation for fathers of normal children were 270.62 ms and 33.18 ms, respectively. They used these measures of central tendency and variability along with a statistical test to be discussed in Chapter 11 to conclude that the fathers of hyperactive children had longer reaction times than fathers of normal children. Not only is the mean reaction time of fathers of normal children shorter than the mean of fathers of hyperactive children, there is also less variability in the reaction times of fathers of normal children. The smaller standard deviation for the fathers of normal children indicates a distribution of scores clustered more tightly around the mean than the scores for the fathers of hyperactive children. ■

Statistics in Use 5—4

Describing a Bee's Busyness with the Mean and Standard Deviation

Industrious individuals often are described as being "busy as a bee." Indeed, bees are busy, but do they ever tire? To answer this question, Schmid-Hempel (1986) attached tiny weights to the thorax of honeybees that had been trained to collect nectar from a patch of artificial flowers. The purpose of the weights was to simulate the additional weight on a honeybee from a load of nectar. Without weights, the bees visited a mean of 36.6 flowers with a standard deviation of 6.5 flowers. With the weights added, the bees visited a mean of 23.3 flowers with a standard deviation of 3.0 flowers. The effect of the weights appears twofold: the bees made fewer visits with weights added and the variability in the number of trips made among the bees decreased. It seems that bees, too, become tired. ■

Statistics in Use 5—5

Describing Assaultive Husbands

Spouse abuse is a real problem in society. To understand more fully the nature of such abuse, Browning and Dutton (1986) investigated reports of assaultive behavior by husbands in 30 couples who had been referred for therapy. To describe the sample of assaultive husbands studied, they reported the mean age of these husbands as 34.3 years, $s = 6.8$ years; the mean years married as 8.2 with $s = 5.4$ years; and the mean number of years of schooling as 11.0, $s = 2.2$ years. From these descriptive statistics, we see that the typical assaultive husband studied in this research was a man in his late 20s or in his 30s. Because $s = 6.8$ years of age, it is unlikely that any husbands were in their 50s or 60s. If husbands had been this old, then such large differences from the mean would have increased the value of the standard deviation. On the other hand, the standard deviation of 5.4 for years of marriage is quite large in comparison to the mean of 8.2 years of marriage. Hence there must be considerable variability in this measure—some couples were married for only a short time, others for a number of years. ■

Testing Your Knowledge 5—2

On a separate sheet of paper, test your knowledge of the material in this section by answering the following questions.

1. Define: s^2, s, SS, variance, standard deviation, sum of squares.
2. Homan, Topping, and Hall (1986) investigated the effect on test scores of a teacher's oral reading of a test to students. Suppose you, too, were

interested in this problem and created two different groups of students. One group of students read the test by themselves, whereas you read the test out loud to the other group of students. Suppose you obtained the following two sets of scores on the test (minimum score is 0, the maximum is 100):

Group	
Read by Themselves	*Read by Teacher*
60	51
50	74
64	64
53	63
61	52
65	45
60	50

   a. Find $\overline{X}$, s^2, and s for each group using the definitional formula for s^2 as illustrated in Example Problem 5–1.

   b. Find $\overline{X}$, s^2, and s for each group using the raw-score formula for s^2 as illustrated in Example Problem 5–2.

   c. From the values of s and s^2 obtained, which group has more variable scores?

3. Many psychologists have been intrigued with the concept of personal space, the idea that each of us has an invisible boundary or space around us that we do not want strangers to encroach upon. One approach to the investigation of this phenomenon has been to invade a person's personal space in a public place, such as a college library or cafeteria, by having an experimenter sit in an empty chair next to the person. An accomplice of the experimenter then covertly times how long the person remains seated next to the experimenter who invaded his or her personal space. Suppose a male experimenter invaded the personal space of two groups of individuals in this fashion. One group was composed of 8 college-aged males, the other group of 8 college-aged females. Both groups of individuals were invaded while seated in a library. The amount of time (in minutes) that each person stayed seated next to the experimenter was recorded as follows:

Gender of Person	
Male	*Female*
10.6	8.6
19.8	4.7
4.3	9.1
21.6	6.3
15.7	2.4
8.1	7.0
26.4	7.8
17.9	10.5

    a. Find $\overline{X}$, s^2, and s for each group. Use the raw-score formula for s^2 as illustrated in Example Problem 5–2.

    b. From the values of s and s^2 obtained, which group has more variable scores? ▨

WHAT IS A LARGE AMOUNT OF VARIABILITY?

No one rule of thumb is used to determine whether a particular value for any measure of variability reflects a reasonable or an excessive amount of dispersion in the scores. Whether the variability in a set of scores is extensive or not is relative to the magnitude of the units used in measuring the dependent variable and to the possible range of scores that can be obtained on the measure. Senders (1958) illustrates this relation for the standard deviation:

> *A standard deviation of 3 inches in a set of 100 telegraph poles would not be alarming, but the same standard deviation in a set of 100 noses would be, quite literally, out of this world! Noses are, in general, shorter than telegraph poles (p. 318).*

Practicing researchers often get a sense of the relative amount of variability in an experiment by comparing it to prior research by others on the topic. This approach is recommended to gain a sense of the amount of variability to be expected in research.

A COMPARISON OF MEASURES OF VARIABILITY

To aid in comparing measures of variability, we have calculated each measure of variability for the TAI scores of Table 3–1. Table 5–3 presents a summary of these measures. It is evident that the values differ from each other considerably. Because each measure conveys different information

TABLE 5–3.

Comparison of measures of variability for the 100 Test Anxiety Inventory Scores of Table 3–1.

Measure of Variability	Value
Range	51
Interquartile range (*IQR*)	8
Semi-interquartile range (*SIQR*)	4
Standard deviation (*s*)	8.66
Variance (*s*)^2	74.92

about the scores, the numerical values of different measures are not directly comparable to each other. The range, *IQR*, and the *SIQR* provide intervals containing a certain percentage of participants' scores; 100 percent for the range, the middle 50 percent for the interquartile range, and 25 percent on each side of the median for the semi-interquartile range. The variance and standard deviation provide an index of the average amount by which scores deviate from the mean. For all measures of variability, however, the smaller the value, the less dispersion there is among the scores. If there were no variability at all, that is, if all individuals had the same scores, then the value for all measures of variability would be zero.

THE CHOICE OF DESCRIPTIVE STATISTICS

We have discussed a variety of descriptive statistics that are used to describe the average score and the variability of scores from a sample. In Chapter 4 we made recommendations concerning the choice and use of measurements of central tendency. We now expand those recommendations to include measures of variability.

Researchers usually select only one measure of central tendency and one measure of variability to summarize their data from a study. How does the researcher decide which descriptive statistic to use to summarize his or her data? The selection is not arbitrary. Instead, the choice depends principally upon three considerations: (1) the scale of measurement realized by the scores; (2) the shape of the frequency distribution of the scores; and (3) the intended use of the descriptive statistics for further statistical analysis. Table 5–4 summarizes the recommended measures depending on the scale of measurement and the shape of the distribution.

TABLE 5–4.

Recommended measures of central tendency and variability given scales of measurement of the scores and the shape of the frequency distribution.

	Shape of the Frequency Distribution				
	Approximately Symmetrical Unimodal			Skewed Unimodal	
Scale of Measurement	Measure of Central Tendency	Measure of Variability		Measure of Central Tendency	Measure of Variability
Ordinal	Md	SIQR		Md	SIQR
Interval or ratio	$\overline{X}$	s		Md	SIQR

Scale of Measurement

Nominal Measurement

In Chapter 2 we indicated that some measurement scales provide greater precision in measuring behavior than others. We noted then that nominal measurement is the lowest form of measurement. Individuals' responses are classified into categories and all individuals within a category are equated behaviorally. Consequently, nominal data usually are described only in terms of frequencies (i.e., how many individuals in a group were assigned to one category or another) or percentages. Thus, we have not included nominal measurement in Table 5–4.

Ordinal Measurement

With ordinal data the median is the most appropriate measure of central tendency regardless of the shape of the frequency distribution or what further statistical analyses are intended. When the median is taken as the measure of central tendency, then typically the range, the interquartile range, or the semi-interquartile range is used as a measure of variability.

Interval and Ratio Measurement

When the frequency distribution of scores is approximately symmetric, the mean is the preferred measure of central tendency for interval and ratio measures. Typically, the mean offers the potential of providing the most representative value of the scores, for all the scores in a sample are involved in its computation. The standard deviation is the measure of variability commonly employed with the mean.

Rating Scales

Scores from rating scales lie within a gray area, in that such scores seem to possess properties beyond the ordinal scale of measurement, but do not attain interval measurement. For purposes of statistical analysis, then, should an ordinal or interval scale of measurement be assumed in treating rating scores? Gardner (1975) suggests that it is appropriate to treat rating scores as interval data. This recommendation is consistent with the practice of many behavioral scientists who utilize rating scales. The issue is not without controversy, however. Labovitz (1967) agrees with Gardner, but Champion (1968) and Black and Champion (1976) argue that rating scales cannot be defended as representing more than an ordinal scale of measurement.

One resolution to this controversy is for the researcher to provide a complete description of rating scale scores using descriptive statistics appropriate for ordinal measurement scales and statistics appropriate for interval and ratio measurement scales. Rotton and Kelly (1985) followed this approach in presenting descriptive statistics for the *Belief in Lunar Effects Scale* (see Statistics in Use 2–4 and 3–2). They presented the median, range, and interquartile range as well as the mean and standard deviation.

Shape of the Frequency Distribution

The shape of the frequency distribution usually is a determinant in the choice of the descriptive statistics only when the dependent variable is measured with an interval or ratio scale of measurement. If the distribution of scores is approximately symmetric, then the sample mean and standard deviation are the preferred statistics. But if the distribution of scores is considerably skewed, then the median and *SIQR* may be the descriptive statistics of choice.

Further Data Analysis

The choice of measures of central tendency and variability also is determined in part by whether the descriptive statistics are to be used for subsequent inferential purposes. For inferential purposes the mean, standard deviation, and variance are used often because they are related to the known characteristics of the normal distribution. These relationships are discussed in Chapter 6. Hence, behavioral scientists may use the sample mean and standard deviation to summarize their data when considerations of level of measurement and shape of the frequency distribution might dictate against it. The issue of making inferences from the data sometimes overrides these other considerations. For this reason, you will find that the mean and standard deviation are the most frequently utilized descriptive statistics in behavioral research.

Testing Your Knowledge 5–3

On a separate sheet of paper, test your knowledge of the material in this chapter by answering the following questions.

1. For each of the following distributions of scores, indicate the measure of central tendency and variability that would provide the most appropriate description of the scores.
   a. The scores achieve an interval scale of measurement and the distribution is heavily negatively skewed.
   b. The scores achieve an ordinal scale of measurement and the distribution is approximately symmetric.

    c. The scores achieve a ratio scale of measurement and the distribution is approximately symmetric.

    d. The scores achieve an ordinal scale of measurement and the distribution is heavily positively skewed.

    e. The scores achieve an interval scale of measurement and the distribution is approximately symmetric.

    f. The scores achieve a ratio scale of measurement and the distribution is heavily positively skewed. ▪

SUMMARY

- Measures of variability quantify how much scores of a sample are spread out or dispersed in a distribution.
- The range is found by $X_{highest} - X_{lowest}$.
- The interquartile range is the interval between the first and third quartiles of a distribution.
- The semi-interquartile range is one-half the interquartile range.
- The variance, s^2, is defined as $\Sigma(X_i - \overline{X})^2/(N - 1)$.
- The square root of the variance provides the standard deviation, s.
- The variance and the standard deviation are the most frequently used measures of variability.

- The choice of a measure of variability depends upon the scale of measurement achieved in the scores, the shape of the frequency distribution of the scores, and what further data analysis is intended.

KEY TERMS

interquartile range	s^2	standard deviation
IQR	s	sum of squares
Q_1	semi-interquartile range	variability
Q_3	SIQR	variance
range	SS	

REVIEW QUESTIONS

On a separate sheet of paper, test your knowledge of the material in this chapter by answering the following questions.

1. Is student perception of the expertness of a professor related to the professor's gender? Suppose that to answer this question, you had 20 male college juniors rate the expertness of a male professor giving a lecture. To rate expertness, you used the Teacher Rating Form, a summated rating scale (McCarthy & Schmeck, 1982). Scores on this scale may range from 12 (perceived as very inexpert) to 84 (perceived as very expert). The 20 scores you obtained were: 50, 65, 44, 47, 52, 55, 35, 43, 43, 50, 60, 40, 45, 50, 45, 57, 47, 53, 54, 57.
   a. Find the Md, $\overline{X}$, IQR, and s for this distribution.
   b. From a purely descriptive view, does the Md or $\overline{X}$ appear to be a better measure of central tendency for these scores? Explain your answer.
2. Suppose now that you had 20 male college juniors rate the expertness of a female professor giving the same lecture as the male professor of question 1, and obtained the following expertness scores: 50, 80, 44, 47, 52, 55, 17, 43, 43, 50, 60, 40, 45, 50, 45, 57, 47, 53, 54, 57.
   a. Find the Md, $\overline{X}$, IQR, and s for this distribution.
   b. From a purely descriptive view, does the Md or $\overline{X}$ appear to be a better measure of central tendency for these scores? Explain your answer.
   c. The value of s increased considerably in this example compared with the value of s for question 1. The IQR did not change, however. Explain this outcome.
3. For each of the following statements, which measure of variability is described?
   a. It provides an interval that contains 100 percent of the scores.
   b. Its value is found by subtracting the 25th percentile score from the 75th percentile score.
   c. It provides an interval that contains about 25 percent of the scores above and below the median.
   d. It provides the average squared deviation of a score from the mean of the distribution.
   e. It provides the square root of average squared deviation of a score from the mean of the distribution.
   f. It provides an interval that contains the middle 50 percent of the scores in a distribution.
   g. Its value depends upon only two scores in the distribution.

h. Its value is found by the formula

$$\frac{\Sigma(X_i - \overline{X})^2}{(N - 1)}.$$

i. Its value is found by the formula

$$\sqrt{\frac{\Sigma(X_i - \overline{X})^2}{(N - 1)}}.$$

j. Its value is found by the formula

$$\frac{(Q_3 - Q_1)}{2}.$$

6

The Normal Distribution

OVERVIEW: POPULATIONS AND SAMPLES

To this point, we have discussed description of scores from a sample. We now turn to a discussion of the normal distribution, a theoretical distribution of considerable importance to behavioral scientists. Because the normal distribution is a population distribution, we briefly review the distinction between a sample and a population.

In Chapter 1 we defined a **population** as a set of measurements of people animals, objects, or events that are identified as possessing a common characteristic. For behavioral scientists, the populations of interest are scores or measurements obtained from people or animals. A **sample** is some subset or group selected from a population. In Chapters 4 and 5 we learned how to describe the scores obtained from a sample by using descriptive statistics such as the Md, $\overline{X}$, $SIQR$, and s.

The scores of a population, too, may be described by measures of central tendency and variability. Suppose that we could measure all the individuals in some population of interest. Following procedures developed in Chapters 4 and 5, we could summarize the scores by computing, for example, a mean and a standard deviation on the scores. Now, however, we no longer identify the mean as $\overline{X}$ and the standard deviation as s, but, because we measured an entire population, we identify the mean as μ (mu, the 12*th* letter of the Greek alphabet) and the standard deviation as σ (sigma, the 18*th* letter of the Greek alphabet). Moreover, we no longer identify the numerical values obtained as statistics; rather we call them parameters. A **parameter** is a number or a characteristic of the population, such as the mean or standard deviation. As statistics describe the scores in a sample, parameters describe the scores of a population. The purpose of this change in terminology is to ensure that it is clear whether we are discussing a sample or a population. This terminology is summarized in Table 6–1. It is important to understand this distinction, for the normal distribution is characterized by μ and σ, rather than by $\overline{X}$ and s.

TABLE 6–1.

Notation for samples and populations.

	Sample	Population
Descriptive characteristics	Statistics	Parameters
Mean	$\overline{X}$	μ
Standard deviation	s	σ
Variance	s^2	σ^2

THE NORMAL DISTRIBUTION

The **normal distribution** is a theoretical mathematical distribution that specifies the relative frequency of occurrence of Y for any value of X. For a normally distributed set of scores, the frequency distribution can be described completely by knowledge of only two parameters of the population: the mean (μ) and the standard deviation (σ). A normal distribution with $\mu = 70$ and $\sigma = 10$ is illustrated in Figure 6–1. The distribution shown in Figure 6–1 is a mathematical distribution that does not represent any specific population of scores. No actual measured population of scores is distributed so precisely that it will be exactly normal. But it will be useful later to assume that some populations of scores are approximately normally distributed. In this chapter, however, we focus on the normal distribution as a theoretical mathematical distribution.

Properties of the Normal Distribution

The normal distribution possess the properties of being symmetrical, asymptotic, and continuous.

FIGURE 6–1.

A normal distribution with $\mu = 70$ and $\sigma = 10$.

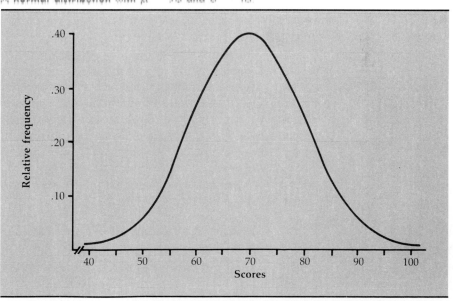

Symmetrical

A theoretical normal distribution is symmetrical about its mode, median, and mean. In a normal distribution, then, the mode, median, and mean are equal to each other.

Asymptotic

Notice from Figure 6–1 that the tails of the normal distribution approach closer to the baseline, or abscissa, as they get farther away from μ. The distribution, however, is *asymptotic*—the tails never touch the baseline, regardless of the distance from μ.

Continuous

The normal distribution is continuous for all values of X between plus and minus infinity. This means that for any two values of X, we can always find another value of X that lies between them.

The Normal Distribution and the Behavioral Sciences

The normal distribution was not discovered by behavioral scientists; rather it arose from the work of James Bernoulli (1654–1705), Abraham de Moivre (1667–1754), Pierre Rémond de Montmort (1678–1719), Carl Friedrich Gauss (1777–1855), and others. Their interests were in developing mathematical approximations for probabilities encountered in various games of chance or in the distribution of errors to be expected in observations, such as in astronomy or physics. The normal distribution soon became an important distribution to statisticians, because many inferential problems in statistics can be solved only if a normal distribution is assumed.

The normal distribution gained importance for behavioral scientists because it is reasonable to assume that any behavioral measures determined by a large number of independent variables will be approximately normally distributed for a population. Many human capabilities, such as mathematical ability or verbal skills, are determined by a number of independent factors—genetic heritage, parental encouragement, schooling, a particular teacher, social class, cultural forces, and so forth. Consequently, measurements of such abilities are likely to be approximately normally distributed in a population. We stress the word *approximately*, for Glass and Stanley (1970) state:

> *Somehow the misapprehension arises in the minds of many students that there is a necessary link between the normal distribution—an idealized description of some frequency distributions—and practically any data they might collect. The normal curve is a mathematician's invention that is a reasonably good description of the frequency polygon of measurements on several different variables. A collection of scores that are exactly normally*

distributed has never been gathered and never will be. But much is gained if we can tolerate the slight error in the statement and claim from time to time that scores on a variable are "normally distributed." (p. 104)

Area Under the Normal Distribution

The normal distribution is a theoretical relative frequency distribution. Recall from Chapter 3 that the relative frequency of a score is the frequency of occurrence of a particular score divided by the total number of scores obtained. Thus, relative frequencies are expressed as proportions and the total cumulative relative frequency in a distribution is 1.0 (see, column g of Table 3–2). Because the normal distribution is a relative frequency distribution, the total area under the distribution is equal to 1.0. That is, the relative frequencies of the scores in a normal distribution cumulate to 1.0.

In all normal distributions specific proportions of scores will fall within certain intervals about the mean. In any normally distributed population of scores, 0.3413 of the scores will fall in an interval between μ and $\mu + 1\sigma$. Because the distribution is symmetrical, the same proportion of scores will fall within an interval of scores between μ and $\mu - 1\sigma$. This relationship is shown in Figure 6–2. The interval from one to two

FIGURE 6–2.

Relative frequencies of scores in certain intervals of a normal distribution.

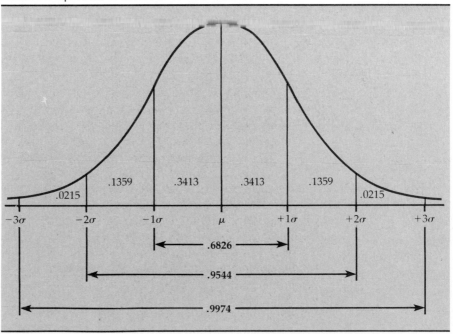

standard deviations above the mean ($\mu + 1\sigma$ to $\mu + 2\sigma$) contains 0.1359 of the scores. Similarly, an interval from one to two standard deviations below the mean ($\mu - 1\sigma$ to $\mu - 2\sigma$) also contains 0.1359 of the scores. Because the normal distribution is symmetrical, corresponding intervals above and below the mean always contain equal areas. Scores more than two standard deviations above μ occur only 0.0228 of the time, as do scores more than two standard deviations below μ.

The areas under the curve may also be added so that, for example, the interval from $\mu - 1\sigma$ to $\mu + 1\sigma$ contains 0.6826 (0.3413 + 0.3413) of the scores. Similarly within plus or minus two standard deviations around the mean, the interval from $\mu - 2\sigma$ to $\mu + 2\sigma$, 0.9544 of the scores occur. Extending the range to three standard deviations around the mean (the interval from $\mu - 3\sigma$ to $\mu + 3\sigma$) encompasses 0.9974 of the scores. You should note that these proportions remain the same regardless of the values of μ and σ.

To illustrate these relationships, suppose a population of scores is normally distributed with $\mu = 100$ and $\sigma = 15$. A score of 85 lies one standard deviation below the mean ($\mu - 1\sigma$) and a score of 115 is one standard deviation above the mean ($\mu + 1\sigma$) in this distribution. Accordingly, 0.6826 of the scores fall within the interval of 85 to 115. Similarly, 0.9544 of the scores will have values between 70 and 130 (the interval from $\mu - 2\sigma$ to $\mu + 2\sigma$), and 0.9974 of the scores will have values from 55 to 145 (the interval from $\mu - 3\sigma$ to $\mu + 3\sigma$).

As another example, suppose that we have a second normally distributed population of scores with $\mu = 50$ and $\sigma = 5$. In this instance, 0.6826 of the scores fall into the interval from 45 to 55 (the interval from $\mu - 1\sigma$ to $\mu + 1\sigma$), 0.9544 into the interval 40 to 60 (the interval from $\mu - 2\sigma$ to $\mu + 2\sigma$), and 0.9974 into the interval 35 to 65 (the interval from $\mu - 3\sigma$ to $\mu + 3\sigma$).

To summarize, in a normal distribution the following relations hold between μ, σ, and the proportion of scores contained in certain intervals about the mean:

Interval	Proportion of Scores Contained
$\mu \pm 1\sigma$	0.6826
$\mu \pm 2\sigma$	0.9544
$\mu \pm 3\sigma$	0.9974.

Testing Your Knowledge 6–1

On a separate sheet of paper, test your knowledge of the material in this section by answering the following questions.

1. Define: population, sample, statistic parameter, μ, σ, $\overline{X}$, s, normal distribution.

2. Identify three properties of the normal distribution.

3. Why may scores obtained from an actual population of people never be exactly normally distributed? Hint: Think of the properties of the normal distribution.

4. Assume that you have a normally distributed population of scores with $\mu = 200$ and $\sigma = 20$. Indicate the proportion of scores that will be contained within each of the following intervals (use Figure 6–2).

Interval	
a.	200 to 220
b.	200 to 240
c.	200 to 260
d.	180 to 200
e.	160 to 200
f.	140 to 200
g.	180 to 260
h.	160 to 240
i.	140 to 260
j.	220 to 240
k.	220 to 260
l.	140 to 160

THE STANDARD NORMAL DISTRIBUTION

The specification of the mean and standard deviation of a normal distribution provides very precise information concerning the proportion of scores contained within certain intervals on that distribution. Because the normal distribution is defined by a mathematical equation, we can determine the exact relative frequency for any interval of scores on the distribution. A problem we face, however, is that we have to utilize a complex mathematical equation for the normal distribution employing the value of μ and σ for the distribution of scores of interest. Fortunately, there is a simple way around this problem. The solution is to transform a normal distribution with mean μ and standard deviation σ (e.g., $\mu = 20$, $\sigma = 2$) into a standard form with $\mu = 0$ and $\sigma = 1$. Then, if we use only one standard normal distribution, with $\mu = 0$ and $\sigma = 1$, we can solve the equation for score values on the X axis of the distribution and table the relative frequencies found. Subsequently, we could simply look up the relative frequency or cumulative relative frequency of scores in a table rather than utilizing the equation of the normal distribution.

The **standard normal distribution** (also called the *unit normal distribution*) has a mean of zero ($\mu = 0$) and a standard deviation of one ($\sigma = 1$). A score (e.g., X_i) from a normally distributed variable with any μ and σ

may be transformed into a score on the standard normal distribution simply by employing the relation

$$z = \frac{(X_i - \mu)}{\sigma},$$

where X_i is the original score, and μ is the mean and σ the standard deviation of the normal distribution from which the score X_i arose. The
value of z is the value of the score on the standard normal distribution;
hence, it is often called a *standard normal deviate*. A standard normal distribution is illustrated in Figure 6–3. To demonstrate its use, suppose a score
of 115 ($X_i = 115$) is obtained from a normally distributed set of scores with
$\mu = 100$ and $\sigma = 15$. This score is converted to a score on the standard
normal distribution by

$$z = \frac{(X_i - \mu)}{\sigma} = \frac{(115 - 100)}{15} = \frac{15}{15} = +1.0.$$

Thus for the original score of 115, the transformed standard normal score
is +1.0. The z score of +1.0 indicates that the original score (i.e., 115) is
one standard deviation (i.e., 15) above the mean (i.e., 100) of the normal
distribution from which it was obtained.
    The transformation of a score to a z score on the standard normal dis-
tribution locates the original score in terms of how many σ units the score

FIGURE 6–3.
The standard normal distribution with $\mu = 0$ and $\sigma = 1$.

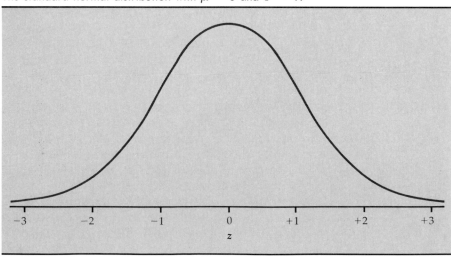

TABLE 6–2.

Transformation of scores from a normal distribution with $\mu = 75$ and $\sigma = 10$ to z scores on a standard normal distribution.

Score (X_i)	z	Score (X_i)	z
105	+3.0	70	−.5
100	+2.5	65	−1.0
95	+2.0	60	−1.5
90	+1.5	55	−2.0
85	+1.0	50	−2.5
80	+.5	45	−3.0
75	0		

is away from the mean. The score that we used (i.e., 115) is +1.0 σ units away from the mean of its distribution. Consider the scores in Table 6–2 and their corresponding z values. These scores were obtained from a normal distribution with $\mu = 75$ and $\sigma = 10$. Attempt to calculate some of the z scores given. Notice the z value for any score is simply how many standard deviation units the score is above or below the mean of zero on the standard normal distribution.

A note of caution is in order here. A transformation of a score, X_i, into a z score will precisely locate the original score (i.e., X_i) on the standard normal distribution only if the score arose originally from a normally distributed set of scores. If the score originated from a non-normal distribution, for example, the rectangular distribution or the bimodal distribution of Figure 3–6, then the use of the transformation $z = (X_i - \mu)/\sigma$ does not make the original score normally distributed. The score is located on the standard normal distribution only if it originated in a normally distributed set of scores.

Using a Table of the Standard Normal Distribution

The advantage of transforming scores into z scores on a standard normal distribution is that the proportion of scores occurring between various values of z is known and tabled precisely. These proportions are presented in Table A–1 of the Appendix. A portion of Table A–1 is illustrated in Table 6–3. This table provides the proportions of area under the standard normal distribution between $z = 0$ and z, and between z and infinity. Column a lists values of z obtained when numerical values are substituted into the formula

$$z = \frac{(X_i - \mu)}{\sigma}.$$

TABLE 6–3.
Proportions of area under the normal distribution.

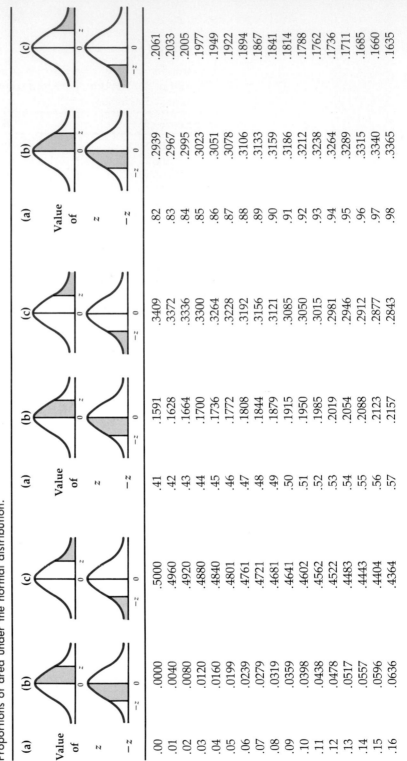

(a) Value of z / −z	(b)	(c)	(a) Value of z / −z	(b)	(c)	(a) Value of z / −z	(b)	(c)
.00	.0000	.5000	.41	.1591	.3409	.82	.2939	.2061
.01	.0040	.4960	.42	.1628	.3372	.83	.2967	.2033
.02	.0080	.4920	.43	.1664	.3336	.84	.2995	.2005
.03	.0120	.4880	.44	.1700	.3300	.85	.3023	.1977
.04	.0160	.4840	.45	.1736	.3264	.86	.3051	.1949
.05	.0199	.4801	.46	.1772	.3228	.87	.3078	.1922
.06	.0239	.4761	.47	.1808	.3192	.88	.3106	.1894
.07	.0279	.4721	.48	.1844	.3156	.89	.3133	.1867
.08	.0319	.4681	.49	.1879	.3121	.90	.3159	.1841
.09	.0359	.4641	.50	.1915	.3085	.91	.3186	.1814
.10	.0398	.4602	.51	.1950	.3050	.92	.3212	.1788
.11	.0438	.4562	.52	.1985	.3015	.93	.3238	.1762
.12	.0478	.4522	.53	.2019	.2981	.94	.3264	.1736
.13	.0517	.4483	.54	.2054	.2946	.95	.3289	.1711
.14	.0557	.4443	.55	.2088	.2912	.96	.3315	.1685
.15	.0596	.4404	.56	.2123	.2877	.97	.3340	.1660
.16	.0636	.4364	.57	.2157	.2843	.98	.3365	.1635

.17	.0675	.4325	.58	.2190	.2810	.99	.3389	.1611
.18	.0714	.4286	.59	.2224	.2776	1.00	.3413	.1587
.19	.0753	.4247	.60	.2257	.2743	1.01	.3438	.1562
.20	.0793	.4207	.61	.2291	.2709	1.02	.3461	.1539
.21	.0832	.4168	.62	.2324	.2676	1.03	.3485	.1515
.22	.0871	.4129	.63	.2357	.2643	1.04	.3508	.1492
.23	.0910	.4090	.64	.2389	.2611	1.05	.3531	.1469
.24	.0948	.4052	.65	.2422	.2578	1.06	.3554	.1446
.25	.0987	.4013	.66	.2454	.2546	1.07	.3577	.1423
.26	.1026	.3974	.67	.2486	.2514	1.08	.3599	.1401
.27	.1064	.3936	.68	.2517	.2483	1.09	.3621	.1379
.28	.1103	.3897	.69	.2549	.2451	1.10	.3643	.1357
.29	.1141	.3859	.70	.2580	.2420	1.11	.3665	.1335
.30	.1179	.3821	.71	.2611	.2389	1.12	.3686	.1314
.31	.1217	.3783	.72	.2642	.2358	1.13	.3708	.1292
.32	.1255	.3745	.73	.2673	.2327	1.14	.3729	.1271
.33	.1293	.3707	.74	.2704	.2296	1.15	.3749	.1251
.34	.1331	.3669	.75	.2734	.2266	1.16	.3770	.1230
.35	.1368	.3632	.76	.2764	.2236	1.17	.3790	.1210
.36	.1406	.3594	.77	.2794	.2206	1.18	.3810	.1190
.37	.1443	.3557	.78	.2823	.2177	1.19	.3830	.1170
.38	.1480	.3520	.79	.2852	.2148	1.20	.3849	.1151
.39	.1517	.3483	.80	.2881	.2119	1.21	.3869	.1131
.40	.1554	.3446	.81	.2910	.2090	1.22	.3888	.1112

Excerpted and Adapted from Table II.1 The Normal Probability Function .nd Related Functions. CRC *Handbook of Tables for Probability and Statistics* (2nd ed.). Copyright 1968, CRC Press, Inc., Boca Raton, Florida. Used by Permission.

Column *b* presents the area between $z = 0$ and the value of z obtained from the formula above. The shaded area in the small figure at the top of the column illustrates this area. Column *c* provides the area between the obtained value of z and infinity, that is, the area beyond z. Again, the small figure at the top of the column illustrates this area. Because the normal distribution is symmetrical, negative values of z encompass areas identical to positive values of z. Thus negative values of z are not tabled.

To demonstrate the use of this table, consider again a normally distributed set of scores with $\mu = 100$ and $\sigma = 15$. Suppose a score of 115 is obtained from this distribution. What proportion of scores is equal to or greater than 115? To solve this problem we convert the score of 115 to a z score by

$$z = \frac{(X_i - \mu)}{\sigma}.$$

Accordingly, $z = (115 - 100)/15 = +1.00$. Using Table 6–3 we next find the value of $z = 1.00$ in column *a*. We then read across to column *c*, which presents the proportion of scores beyond z. This value is 0.1587. Thus, 0.1587 of the scores are equal to or greater than 115.

Consider another problem. What proportion of scores is equal to or less than 82? Again we convert this score to a z score, $z = (82 - 100)/15 = -1.20$. The question can then be answered by finding the proportion of scores beyond z equal to -1.20. Because the standard normal distribution is symmetrical, as many scores lie beyond -1.20 as lie beyond $+1.20$. Therefore, we find a value of $z = 1.20$ in column *a* and read across to column *c*. The value in column *c* is 0.1151; thus 0.1151 of the scores are equal to or less than 82. Other uses of the standard normal distribution are given in the example problems that follow.

Example Problem 6–1
Using the standard normal distribution

Assume that you have a population of 1,000 scores that are normally distributed with $\mu = 81.4$ and $\sigma = 4.7$.

Problem:
What proportion of scores is equal to or greater than 88.8?

Statistic to be used: $z = (X_i - \mu)/\sigma$.

Solution:
The score of 88.8 must be converted into a score on the standard normal distribution. Then Table A–1 may be used to find the proportion of

scores equal to or greater than the z value obtained. Substituting numerical values in the formula for z, we obtain

$$z = \frac{(88.8 - 81.4)}{4.7} = \frac{7.4}{4.7} = +1.57 \, .$$

Column c of Table A–1 indicates that the area of the standard normal distribution equal to or greater than z = +1.57 is 0.0582. Hence the proportion of scores equal to or greater than 88.8 is 0.0582. Thus, out of 1,000 scores in the population, 58.2 are equal to or greater than 88.8.

Problem:
What proportion of scores fall between 81.4 and 84.8?

Solution:
Both scores must be converted to z scores. Then we must find the area of the standard normal distribution between the values of z for the two scores. Substituting numerical values, we find

$$z \text{ for } 81.4 = \frac{(81.4 - 81.4)}{4.7} = \frac{0}{4.7} = 0.00, \quad \text{and}$$

$$z \text{ for } 84.8 = \frac{(84.8 - 81.4)}{4.7} = \frac{3.4}{4.7} = +0.72$$

From Column b of Table A–1, we see that for z = 0.00, the proportion of scores between 0 and z = 0 is 0.0000. For z = +0.72, the proportion of scores between 0 and z is 0.2642. To find the proportion of scores between z = 0.00 and z = +0.72, then, we subtract 0.0000 from 0.2642. The result is 0.2642. Thus, the proportion of scores that fall into the interval from 81.4 to 84.8 is 0.2642. For a population of 1,000 scores, 264.2 fall between scores of 81.4 to 84.8.

Problem:
What proportion of scores falls between 75.7 and 79.8?

Solution:
This problem is solved identically to the previous problem. Both scores must be converted to z scores. Then we must find the area of the standard normal distribution between the values of z for the two scores. Substituting numerical values, we find

$$z \text{ for } 75.7 = \frac{(75.7 - 81.4)}{4.7} = -\frac{5.7}{4.7} = -1.21, \quad \text{and}$$

$$z \text{ for } 79.8 = \frac{(79.8 - 81.4)}{4.7} = -\frac{1.6}{4.7} = -0.34.$$

Because the standard normal distribution is symmetrical, the same relations hold for negative z scores as for positive z scores. Thus, we find from Column b of Table A–1 that 0.3869 of the scores fall between 0 and $z = -1.21$. For $z = -0.34$, 0.1331 of the scores fall between 0 and z. Accordingly, we find the proportion of scores between $z = -1.21$ and $z = -0.34$ by subtracting 0.1331 from 0.3869. This value is 0.2538. The figure below helps to visualize the steps in this problem. The answer is provided by the shaded area between the two values of z. This area is 0.2538.

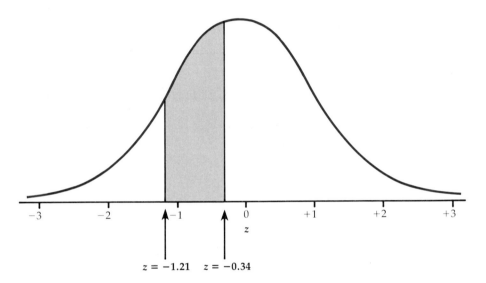

The proportion of scores that falls into the interval from 75.7 to 79.8 is 0.2538. For a population of 1,000 scores, 253.8 fall between scores of 75.7 to 79.8.

Problem:
What range of scores includes the middle 80 percent of the scores on the distribution?

Solution:
This problem may be solved by finding areas in Table A–1 that include a proportion of 0.40, or 40 percent of the scores on each side of the mean, determining the z value for these scores, and then solving the formula for z to find values of X_i. Consulting Table A–1, we read down Column b until we find the proportion closest to 0.40. This area is 0.3997, which corresponds to a z of 1.28. Thus scores that result in z values between 0 to $+1.28$ will occur with a relative frequency of 0.3997 and scores that result in z values between 0 to -1.28 will also occur with

a relative frequency of 0.3997. The total area encompassed by scores between $z = -1.28$ to $z = +1.28$ is $0.3997 + 0.3997 = 0.7994$, or approximately 0.8. The last step is to find the values of X_i that correspond to $z = -1.28$ and $z = +1.28$. To find these values, we subtitute values of z, μ, and σ into the formula

$$z = \frac{(X_i - \mu)}{\sigma}.$$

For $z = +1.28$, then $1.28 = (X_i - 81.4)/4.7$. Solving this equation for X_i, we find $X_i = 87.4$. For $z = -1.28$, $-1.28 = (X_i - 81.4)/4.7$. Solving this equation for X_i, we find $X_i = 75.4$. Hence, the middle 80 percent of the scores fall between 75.4 to 87.4. ■

Statistics in Use 6–1

Type A and Type B Behavior Patterns: Using the Standard Normal Distribution

Scores on tests standardized on a large number of individuals are often considered as approximately normally distributed. Thus scores on the test may be expressed as z scores. The knowedgeable reader then knows exactly where a particular score falls with respect to the rest of the scores in the distribution. As an example, Yarnold, Grimm, and Mueser (1986) investigated whether Type A and Type B behavior patterns are related to social conformity. Individuals characterized as Type A are thought of as extremely competitive, aggressive, impatient, and quickly irritated. Type B individuals, on the other hand, are characterized as noncompetitive, nonaggressive, patient, and calm in the face of delays and frustrations. One measure of Type A–Type B behavioral patterns is the Jenkins Activity Survey (Jenkins, Zyzanski, & Rosenman, 1979). This survey is a paper-and-pencil questionnaire about typical activities of an individual. The survey contains questions similar to:

When stuck in a traffic jam in your car, do you ever blow the horn to express your frustration?

Never   *Occasionally*   *Frequently*   *Almost always*

Type A individuals are expected to answer with "frequently" or "almost always," whereas Type Bs are expected to answer with "occasionally" or never."

Yarnold et al. hypothesized that Type A individuals would conform less to group consensus than Type B individuals. To test this research hypothesis, they selected two groups of people—extreme Type A individuals and extreme Type B individuals based upon Jenkins Activity Survey Scores.

They report the mean z score on the Jenkins Activity Survey for the Type A individuals was +1.22 (positive z scores indicate Type A behavior) and the mean z score for Type B individuals was −1.38 (negative z scores indicate Type B behavior). This information on the mean z scores for each group permits us to precisely locate each group on the Type A–Type B dimension of the Jenkins Activity Survey. From column c of Table A–1 we determine that only about 0.11 of the values of z on a standard normal distribution are equal to or exceed z = +1.22. Thus a z of +1.22 places the group mean at the 89th percentile of scores in Type A behavior. Likewise, for a z of −1.38, we note that only about 0.08 of the scores are below this value on the Type B dimension. The goal of achieving groups extreme in either Type A or Type B behavior was met. When tested on a task of judging line lengths, Type B individuals conformed to a group consensus twice as often as Type A subjects. ■

Testing Your Knowledge 6–2

On a separate sheet of paper, test your knowledge of the material in this section by answering the following questions.

1. Define: standard normal distribution, standard normal deviate, z.
2. For each of the following values of X_i, μ, and σ, find the value of z. Then use Table A–1 to find the area between 0 and z and the area beyond z.

	μ	σ	X_i
a.	73	4.2	81
b.	127	11.6	121
c.	17	1.3	18
d.	50	6.0	39
e.	5	0.4	5.7
f.	256	35.0	212

3. Solve the following problems using the approach illustrated in Example Problem 6–1. You have conducted a large scale testing project measuring 6,000 students on a test of reasoning with verbal analogies. Assume that the distribution of test scores is normally distributed with $\mu = 72.6$ and $\sigma = 7.8$.
   a. What proportion of scores is equal to or greater than 85.0?
   b. What proportion of scores falls between 80.0 and 90.0?
   c. What proportion of scores falls between 60.0 and 70.0?
   d. What range of scores includes the middle 90 percent of scores on the test? ■

THE NORMAL DISTRIBUTION AND PROBABILITY

We have discussed the normal distribution as theoretical relative frequency distribution. A theoretical relative frequency distribution also is a probability density function. Most of us have some intuitive understanding of probability, but to understand its importance in statistical analysis we need to develop more fully what is meant by probability and a probability density function.

The Probability of Discrete Events

Many of us frequently receive letters proclaiming:

Urgent Notification — Reply Immediately. You are the lucky winner of one of the following prizes:

- *A Brand New Cadillac Town Car, Value $27,000*
- *A Two Week All Expenses Paid Vacation in Hawaii, Value $5,500*
- *A Wide–Screen TV with Stereo Sound, Value $1995*
- *An Easy-Use Microwave Oven, Value $375*
- *A Top Quality 35mm Camera, Value $75*
- *A Whiz-Bang Home Computer, Value $549.*

All you need to do to claim your prize is visit Beautiful Lazy Acres Vacation Resort *and see the* magnificent *homesites available for your purchase. You will definitely win one of the above prizes when you visit our* stunning *resort.*

Visions of a luxurious town car or a delightful two-week vacation begin to fill our thoughts. All those beautiful visions are shattered, however, when we read the small print on the second page of the letter. Here we find our chances of winning each gift and often they are expressed as

	Gift	Number of Awards/ 1,000,000 Visitors
1	Car	6
2	Vacation	20
3	TV	34
4	Oven	66
5	Camera	999,840
6	Computer	34

Which prize do you think it is most likely we will win? Which prize do you think it is least likely that we will win? Forget that town car, prize 1—take a picture of it instead with your camera, prize 5. The promoters of the contest have provided us with the frequencies of award of the various prizes per one million visitors. From this information, we may determine the probability that we may win any one of the prizes. Assuming that each visitor has an equal chance of winning one prize, this probability is found simply by dividing the numbers of that prize to be awarded by the total number of prizes to be given, or

$$\text{Probability of a specific prize} = \frac{\text{Number of specific prizes to be awarded}}{\text{Total number of prizes awarded}}.$$

Applying this formula to prize 3, for example, we obtain the probability of prize 3 as 34/1,000,000, or 0.000034. If we calculate the probability of each prize, we obtain the following results:

Gift	Number of Awards/ 1,000,000 Visitors	Probability of Winning
1	6	0.000006
2	20	0.000020
3	34	0.000034
4	66	0.000066
5	999,840	0.999840
6	34	0.000034

You may have noted that this formula for the probability of a prize looks much like the formula for relative frequency given in Chapter 3. Indeed, this formula simply is a specific application of the relative frequency formula. In a more general sense, if the occurrence of an event in a population is independent of the occurrence of other events in that population, then the **probability (p) of occurrence of an event** is defined as

$$p(\text{event}) = \frac{\text{Number of occurrences of the event in a population}}{\text{Total number of events in a population}}.$$

This definition is that of a relative frequency except that it is based upon all the events in a population, and not only those that may occur in a sample of the population. Notice that this formula provides the probability for **discrete events,** events that have a countable set of values, such as the number of cars to be awarded per one million visitors. Thus, the probabilities associated with the awarding of each prize constitute a discrete probability distribution.

The Standard Normal Distribution as a Probability Density Function

The normal distribution is a theoretical relative frequency distribution. Because the relative frequencies specified in the normal distribution are based upon a population, the normal distribution also is a probability distribution. But it is a slightly different probability distribution than the discrete probability distribution just introduced. A score, X_i, in a normal distribution is a continuous variable, one that can take on an infinite set of values in the range within which it varies. Suppose that the scores to which a theoretical normal distribution is being applied are body weights. We wonder what the probability is of finding an individual who weighs exactly 123 pounds. But weight is a continuous variable, and presumably some individuals may weigh 123.3, or perhaps 123.36, or even 123.364 pounds. Conceptually, we might even find someone weighing 123.3642193 pounds. Is a weight of 123.3 pounds to be considered 123 pounds? What of a weight of 123.00001 pounds? We can never obtain a weight of exactly 123 pounds, for presumably we could always measure weight to a greater degree of accuracy.

Consequently, the probability of occurrence of an exact value of a continuous score is zero. But the probability of the score falling within a certain interval is not zero. Although it is impossible to obtain a weight of exactly 123 pounds, it is not impossible to obtain a weight in the interval between 122.5 and 123.5 pounds. For example, regardless of the number of decimal places to which we may carry our measurements, a score of 123.36 (or 123.3642193) will always fall into the interval between 122.5 and 123.5. Thus, the probability function specified by the normal distribution does not provide probabilities for discrete values of X_i; rather it provides probabilities that the value of X_i will fall within a certain interval. Such a probability distribution is known as a probability density function. A **probability density function** specifies the probabilities associated with scores falling into a certain interval of the distribution. The probability is provided by the area under the distribution encompassed by the interval. Because the density function contains all scores that may occur, the area under a probability density function is equal to 1.00.

As an example of the normal distribution used as a probability density function, consider the following problem. Suppose you know that a set of scores is normally distributed with $\mu = 150$ and $\sigma = 8$. If you were to randomly select a score from this distribution, what is the probability of obtaining a score between 150 and 158? To answer this question we first transform the distribution into the standard normal distribution with $\mu = 0$ and $\sigma = 1$. When we do this step, the score of 150 becomes $z = 0.00$, and the score of 158 becomes $z = +1.00$. Thus, the question resolves to what is the probability of obtaining a score with a value between $z = 0.00$ and $z = +1.00$? The answer is the area under the standard normal distribution between $z = 0.00$ and $z = +1.00$, or 0.3413 (obtained from Column *b* of Table A–1). Accordingly, the probability of obtaining a score between 150 and 158 is 0.3413. We may phrase this conclusion in probability terms as $p(150 \le X_i \le 158) = 0.3413$. This statement is read "the probability that X_i is equal to or greater than 150 and equal to or less than 158 is 0.3413."

Example Problem 6–2
Using the standard normal distribution as a probability density function

Assume that you have the population of 1000 scores described in Example Problem 6–1 that are normally distributed with $\mu = 81.4$ and $\sigma = 4.7$.

Problem:
What is the probability of a score being equal to or greater than 88.8?

Statistic to be used: $z = (X_i - \mu)/\sigma$

Solution:
The score of 88.8 must first be converted into a score on the standard normal distribution. Then Table A–1 may be used to find the proportion of scores equal to or greater than the z value obtained. This proportion represents the probability requested. Substituting numerical values into the formula for z we obtain,

$$z = \frac{(88.8 - 81.4)}{4.7} = \frac{7.4}{4.7} = +1.57$$

Table A–1 indicates that the area of the standard normal distribution equal to or greater than $z = +1.57$ is 0.0582. Thus, the probability of a score being equal to or greater than 88.8 is 0.0582, or as a probability statement, $p(X_i \ge 88.8) = 0.0582$.

Problem:
What is the probability of a score being between 82.7 and 85.6?

Solution:
Both scores must be converted to z scores. Then we must find the area of the standard normal distribution between the values of z for the two scores. Substituting numerical values, we find

$$z \text{ for } 82.7 = \frac{(82.7 - 81.4)}{4.7} = \frac{1.3}{4.7} = +0.28 \, ;$$

$$z \text{ for } 85.6 = \frac{(85.6 - 81.4)}{4.7} = \frac{4.2}{4.7} = +0.89 \, .$$

From column b of Table A–1, we see that for $z = +0.28$, the proportion of scores between 0 and z is 0.1103 For $z = +0.89$, the proportion of scores between 0 and z is 0.3133. To find the proportion of scores between $z = +0.28$ and $z = +0.89$, we subtract 0.1103 from 0.3133. The result is 0.2030. This proportion represents the probability requested. Thus, the probability of a score falling into the interval from 82.7 to 85.6 is 0.2030. In probability terms, $p(82.7 \leq X_i \leq 85.6) = 0.2030$.

Problem:
What is the probability of a score falling between 72.5 and 77.3?

Solution:
This problem is solved identically to the problem above. First, both scores must be converted to z scores. Then we must find the area of the standard normal distribution between the values of z for the two scores. Substituting numerical values, we find

$$z \text{ for } 72.5 = \frac{(72.5 - 81.4)}{4.7} = -\frac{8.9}{4.7} = -1.89;$$

$$z \text{ for } 77.3 = \frac{(77.3 - 81.4)}{4.7} = -\frac{4.1}{4.7} = -0.87.$$

Consulting Table A–1 and recalling that because the standard normal distribution is symmetrical, the same relations hold for negative z scores as for positive z scores, we find from column b that 0.4706 of the scores fall between 0 and $z = -1.89$. For $z = -0.87$, 0.3078 of the scores fall between 0 and z. Accordingly, we find the proportion of scores between $z = -1.89$ and $z = -0.87$ by subtracting 0.3078 from 0.4706, which equals 0.1628. This proportion represents the probability requested; hence $p(72.5 \leq X_i \leq 77.3) = 0.1628$. ∎

Statistics in Use 6–2

Playing the Lottery

Millions of people play state lotteries on a daily or weekly basis. One popular form of the lottery is the "million dollar" lottery where only a few winners share a very large lottery prize, often as large as several million dollars. But, the probability of winning such a lottery with one ticket is exceedingly small. Probabilities of winning as small as 0.0000005 or even smaller often exist in these lotteries. A probability of 0.0000005 represents 5 chances out of 10,000,000 of winning the lottery. It seems clear that such a probability is so small that no rational person would purchase a lottery ticket; there is virtually no chance of winning. Yet people continue to buy lottery tickets in record numbers. Why? Many behavioral scientists believe that people play these lotteries because they cannot conceptualize the probabilities involved.

In our opening to the section on probability we indicated that most of us have an intuitive notion of probability. Indeed, this is likely the case for probabilities that we commonly encounter—the probability of 0.3 that rain will fall on a certain day or the probability of 0.5 that a flipped coin will land as a head. Typically, we don't encounter probabilities as small as 0.0000005. What does it mean to say that our chances of winning are 5 in ten million? Can you visualize this probability? We doubt it. You can visualize a coin being flipped and coming up heads or tails, but how can you visualize the occurrence of 5 events out of a possible ten million events? Unless you are very unusual, we suggest that you can't visualize this very small probability.

One behavioral scientist, David Bell, suggests that this probability could be visualized by imagining 10,000,000 playing cards placed face down, side-by-side, and top-to-bottom on an open field (Mehegan, 1985, October 17). To accommodate this many cards, the field would have to be approximately 1,000 feet long and 700 feet wide (approximately the size of two and one-half football fields). Five of the cards are marked with an X on the face. Your task is to pick out the five cards with the X on the first try. If you visualize the probability of winning in a lottery this way, would you still continue to play? ■

Testing Your Knowledge 6–3

On a separate sheet of paper, test your knowledge of the material in this section by answering the following questions.

1. Define: discrete event, probability density function.
2. What is the formula for the probability of occurrence of a discrete event?
3. You have purchased a ticket for a raffle of a bicycle. The ticket states that one bicycle will be raffled off for every 700 tickets sold. What is the probability that you will win a bicycle in this raffle?
4. A recent survey based on a large random sample of adults in the United States indicated that 19 percent of American men report sleeping in the nude. If you were to ask a randomly chosen man about his sleeping attire, what is the probability he would report sleeping in the nude?
5. For each of the following values of X_i, μ, and σ, find the value of z. Then use Table A–1 to find the probability of a score being equal to or larger than the score given.

	μ	σ	X_i
a.	73	4.2	81
b.	127	11.6	121
c.	17	1.3	18
d.	50	6.0	39
e.	5	0.4	5.7
f.	256	35.0	212

6. You have conducted a large scale testing project measuring 6000 students on a test of reasoning with verbal analogies. Assume that the distribution of test scores is normally distributed with $\mu = 72.6$ and $\sigma = 7.8$.

   a. What is the probability of a score being equal to or greater than 83.6?
   b. What is the probability of a score falling between 78.4 and 86.2?
   c. What is the probability of a score falling between 64.7 and 71.1?

STANDARD SCORES

We have seen that we can take a normally distributed raw score and transform it into a score on the standard normal distribution by using the formula

$$z = \frac{(X_i - \mu)}{\sigma}.$$

The z is a standard score that can be used for comparing scores from two different normal distributions. For example, suppose that a person obtained a score of 75 on a test with $\mu = 70$ and $\sigma = 5$ and a score of 110 on a second test with $\mu = 100$ and $\sigma = 10$. Assume scores on both tests are normally distributed. For both scores the z score is +1.00. On both tests the individual scored one standard deviation above the mean. Accordingly, the person's standing in relation to other scores on the tests is identical for both tests; he or she has obtained a score equal to or larger than 84 percent of the scores.

It would be useful to be able to make a similar transformation on any set of scores, even if the scores were not normally distributed and we did not know μ or σ. We may make such a transformation using the formula[1]

$$\text{Standard score} = \frac{(X_i - \overline{X})}{S},$$

where
X_i = the score of interest,
$\overline{X}$ = the mean of the set of scores, and
S = the standard deviation using the formula

$$S = \sqrt{\frac{\Sigma(X_i - \overline{X})^2}{N}}.$$

[1]Some statisticians identify this formula as a z score also. To avoid confusion with the formula for finding the value of a score, z, on the standard normal distribution, we will use the notation *standard score* in this chapter. This formula is used again in Chapter 17. There we will utilize the z notation for the formula.

This formula transforms a score into a number indicating how far away from the mean the score is in standard deviation units. To illustrate, suppose we gave a statistics test and a history test to five students and obtained the following raw and standard scores.

		Test		
	Statistics		*History*	
Person	*Raw Score*	*Standard Score*	*Raw Score*	*Standard Score*
Amalia	91	+1.34	93	+1.18
Denise	62	−0.70	79	0.00
Jeff	87	+1.06	73	−0.50
Hans	56	−1.13	90	+0.92
Matt	64	−0.56	60	−1.60
$\overline{X}$	72		79	
S	14.2		11.9	

Standard scores were obtained using the formula given above. For example, Amalia's raw score on the statistics test was 91. The mean on the test was 72 and S was 14.2. Thus Amalia's standard score is found as

$$\text{Standard score} = \frac{(X_i - \overline{X})}{S}$$

$$\text{Standard score} = \frac{(91 - 72)}{14.2}$$

$$\text{Standard score} = \frac{19}{14.2} = +1.34.$$

By knowing the standard score we know Amalia's relative score with relation to the class mean; it is 1.34 standard deviations above the mean.

We can also compare scores from one test to the other, something we cannot do from the raw scores alone without knowing $\overline{X}$ and S. For example, Jeff is 1.06 standard deviation units above the mean on his statistics test, but 0.50 standard deviation units below the mean on his history test. Positive standard scores indicate scores above the sample mean, scores of 0.00 (such as the history score of Denise) are equal to the sample mean, and negative standard scores are below the sample mean.

Standard scores often are used when reporting test results, for the score provides the person's relative standing with respect to others taking the same test. The standard score conversion does not change the shape of the distribution of scores, however. If the distribution of raw scores was skewed, then the distribution of standard scores will be skewed similarly.

SUMMARY

- The normal distribution is a theoretical relative frequency distribution; no measured scores are exactly normally distributed. It is useful, however, to assume that some behavioral measures are approximately normally distributed.
- A normal distribution can be transformed into a standard normal distribution with $\mu = 0$ and $\sigma = 1$ by the relation $z = (X_i - \mu)/\sigma$.
- The standard normal distribution is a probability density function. It can be used with normally distributed scores to either find the proportion of scores that will fall within specified intervals, or to find the probability of scores occurring within specified intervals.

- Raw scores may be transformed into standard scores using the formula

$$\text{Standard score} = \frac{(X_i - \overline{X})}{S}.$$

This formula transforms a score into a number indicating how far away from the mean the score is in standard deviation units. It does not change the shape of the distribution of the raw scores.

KEY TERMS

discrete event	probability of a discrete event	standard score
μ	sample	statistic
normal distribution	σ	$\overline{X}$
parameter	s	z
population	standard normal deviate	
probability density function	standard normal distribution	

REVIEW QUESTIONS

On a separate sheet of paper, test your knowledge of the material in this chapter by answering the following questions.

1. Intelligence tests often involve measures of digit span, ability to follow instructions, vocabulary, analogy completion, picture completion, logical reasoning, and mathematical calculation. Explain why you would expect the overall score of individuals on intelligence tests to be approximately normally distributed in the population.
2. Measures of reaction time, the amount of time that it takes to initiate a response after the onset of a stimulus, typically are not normally distributed. Rather, they often demonstrate a reverse *J* function; that

is, the distribution of obtained scores looks like a reversed letter J (⌐). Explain why you expect these scores to be distributed as they are.

3. Over the years, thousands of scores have been collected for the Wechsler Adult Intelligence Scale. Assume that the distribution of these scores is normal with $\mu = 100$ and $\sigma = 15$.
   a. What proportion of intelligence scores is equal to or greater than 115?
   b. What proportion of intelligence scores is less than 70?
   c. What proportion of intelligence scores is less than 60?
   d. What proportion of scores falls between 100 to 120?
   e. What proportion of scores falls between 75 to 100?
   f. What interval of scores includes the middle 80 percent of scores on the test?
   g. If you select a person at random, what is the probability that his or her intelligence score will be between 90 to 120?
   h. If you select a person at random, what is the probability that his or her intelligence score will be less than 80?
   i. If you select a person at random, what is the probability that his or her intelligence score will be greater than 125?
   j. If you select a person at random, what is the probability that his or her intelligence score will be greater than 140?

4. You have been summoned, along with 64 other people, to a court-house as a prospective jury member. To choose members of the jury, the names are put in a box and drawn one at a time. What is the probability that your name will be the first chosen?

5. The national newspaper, *USA Today*, published a column entitled "Chances" (1985, December 31) presenting the odds that certain events might happen to an individual in a year. For each of the following events, find the probability of the event occurring for an individual.
   a. Many firms often run sweepstakes contests. For one recent contest, one prize was given for every 3000 entries. What is the probability of an entrant winning a prize in this contest?
   b. Times have been difficult for farmers in recent years. One farmer out of every 5314 went out of business in one year. What is the probability of a farmer going out of business in a year?
   c. Many of us dream about writing a best-selling novel. But for every 4637 book-length fiction manuscripts submitted to publish-ers in a year, only one is published. You have written a novel. What is the probability it will be published this year?

6. We discussed the research of Yarnold et al. (1986) employing Type A and Type B individuals in Statistics in Use 6–1. To obtain Type A or Type B individuals, Yarnold et al. chose people based upon their scores on the Jenkins Activity Survey. The population mean for the Jenkins Activity Survey is 0 and population standard deviation is 10.

Suppose you were interested in following up on Yarnold's work. To obtain Type A individuals you want to select people with Jenkins Activity Survey scores greater than +13.0 and to obtain Type B individuals you want to select people with Jenkins Activity Survey scores less than −13.0. Assume that scores on the Jenkins Activity Survey are normally distributed.

a. What is the probability of selecting a person with a Jenkins Activity Survey score of +13.0 or more?

b. What is the probability of selecting a person with a Jenkins Activity Survey score of −13.0 or less?

c. What is the probability of choosing a person with a score between −13 and +13?

7. Suppose you observed six students on the mean amount of time spent playing video games per week (in hours) and their semester grade point average (GPA) and found the following values:

Student	Video Games	GPA
Alex	6	2.5
Lauren	8	2.0
Yvonne	0	3.9
Laval	15	3.4
Bonnie	3	3.1
Jason	16	1.3

a. Transform each set of scores into standard scores.

b. Lauren has a standard score of 0 for time spent playing video games. What does this score tell you about the time she spends playing video games each week?

c. What information does Yvonne's standard score for GPA tell you about her GPA?

d. What does a negative standard score for GPA indicate?

e. What does a positive standard score for video game playing time indicate?

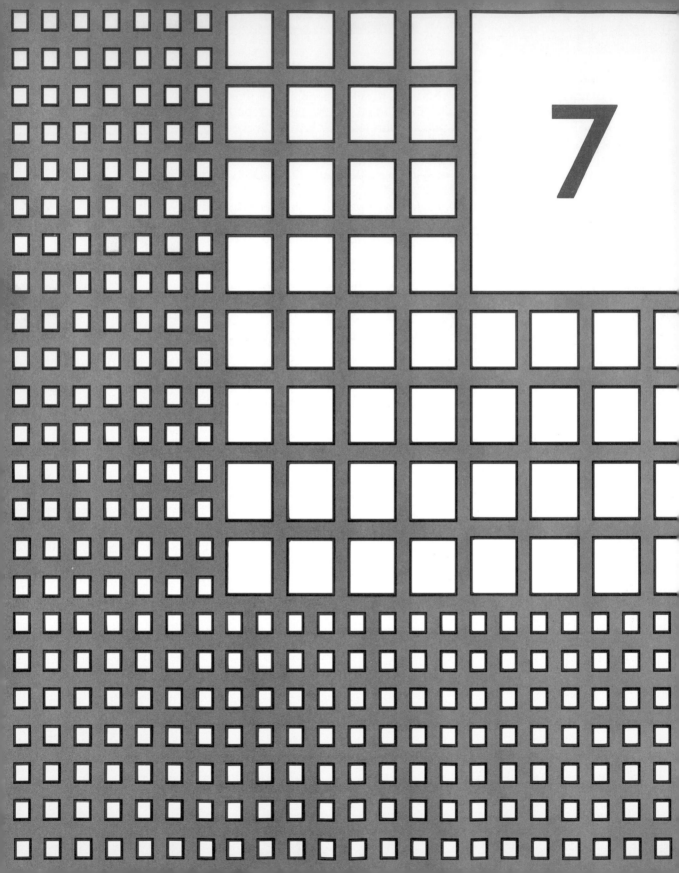

7

Using Statistics for Inference and Estimation

OVERVIEW: STATISTICAL INFERENCE

In Chapters 1 through 6, we emphasized the use of statistics to describe the scores in a sample. Summarizing scores with measures of central tendency and variability is, however, only one step in the process of analyzing data. Behavioral scientists also are interested in estimating population parameters from the descriptive statistics of a sample. There are two reasons for this interest. First, researchers wish to generalize their results beyond the observations in the sample. Our researcher of test anxiety would like to generalize her results beyond the 100 students in her sample. As we have suggested, however, it is not possible for our researcher to measure all the members of a population that she wishes to generalize. Moreover, her situation is not unique.

Marketing researchers cannot identify or test all potential consumers. They must generalize from sample data. Political pollsters cannot possibly evaluate opinions of all registered voters. Here again, sampling and generalizing to the voter population is the only feasible methodology. Similarly, it is not possible to measure the amount of alcohol consumption, attitudes toward birth control, frequency of sexual activity, or any other behaviors among all members of a large population. It is necessary for behavioral researchers to estimate population values from sample descriptive statistics.

A second need for estimating population parameters occurs when a researcher makes decisions about the effect of an independent variable in an experiment. In Chapter 1 we discussed the importance of conducting experiments in behavioral science research. The purpose of an experiment is to find whether an independent variable affects behavior. And, one aspect of experimentation is statistical hypothesis testing. Statistical testing determines if a particular outcome in sample data is a probable or an improbable event given a hypothesis about population parameters. In these tests, sample statistics are used to estimate various population parameters. Statistical hypothesis testing is developed in Chapter 8. In this chapter we discuss the principles of estimation and inference needed to understand statistical hypothesis testing.

THE SAMPLE MEAN AS AN ESTIMATOR OF THE POPULATION MEAN

Estimating population parameters from descriptive statistics requires making inferences from sample data. **Inference** is the process of reasoning from something known to something unknown. As a task for the behavioral scientist, **statistical inference** is the process of drawing conclusions about unknown population values from sample statistics. Statistical inference, then, is estimating unknown population parameters from known sample statistics. Our first interest is in using the sample mean ($\overline{X}$) to estimate the population mean (μ). Then we discuss the sample variance (s^2) as an estimate of the population variance (σ^2).

Characteristics of $\overline{X}$ as an Estimate of μ

The sample mean ($\overline{X}$) often is used to estimate a population mean (μ). For example, the sample mean of 41.6 from the Test Anxiety Inventory scores of Table 3–1 may be used to estimate the mean test anxiety of a population of college females. Using this sample mean would lead to an estimate of 41.6 for the population mean. This sample mean is an unbiased and consistent estimator of the population mean.

Unbiased Estimator
An **unbiased estimator** is one which, if we were to obtain an infinite number of random samples of a certain size, the mean of the statistic would equal the parameter. The sample mean, $\overline{X}$, is an unbiased estimate of μ, because if we took all possible random samples of size N from a population, then the mean of the sample means would be equal to μ.

Consistent Estimator
A **consistent estimator** is one that as the sample size increases, the probability that the estimate has a value close to the parameter also increases. Because it is a consistent estimator, a sample mean based on 25 scores has a greater probability of being closer to μ than does a sample mean based upon only five scores. To generate an intuitive understanding of why the mean is a consistent estimator, consider two extremes in sample size. If one were to sample the whole population of interest so that the sample consists of an entire population, then the mean of the sample would be the same as that of the population and there would be no error in the sample estimate. On the other hand, consider a sample of only one randomly selected member from a population. The resulting sample mean (equal to the one score divided by 1) would be as variable from one sample to another as the scores in the population. It is not surprising, then, that better estimates of a population mean should be more probable from larger samples.

Accuracy of Estimation

The sample mean is an unbiased and consistent estimator of μ. But, we should not overlook the fact that an estimate is just a rough or approximate calculation. It is unlikely in any estimate that $\overline{X}$ will be exactly equal to μ. Whether or not $\overline{X}$ is a good estimate of μ depends upon the representativeness of the sample, the sample size, and the variability of scores in the population.

Representativeness and Sampling

Any sample from a population will provide some idea about characteristics of that population. Indeed, in the absence of any other information, a single sample mean provides the "best guess" about the value of the corresponding population mean. To ensure that the sample mean is a good estimate of the population mean, however, the characteristics of the sample should be similar to those of the population of interest. The distribution of attributes such as sex, age, intelligence, socioeconomic status, religion, political affiliation, anxiety, height, weight, and so forth should occur in the sample much as they do in the population. In other words, the sample should be representative of the population to which we wish to generalize. A number of sampling methods have thus been developed in an attempt to ensure representativeness of a sample.

Simple Random Sampling.   **Simple random sampling** (often called **random sampling**) is defined as the process of selecting members from a population in such a way that:

1. Each member of the population has an equal chance of being selected for the sample; and
2. The selection of one member is independent of the selection of any other member of the population.

A random sample is one selected without bias; therefore, the characteristics of the sample should not differ in any systematic or consistent way from the population from which the sample was drawn. But random sampling does not guarantee that a particular sample will be exactly representative of a population. Because samples are usually much smaller than a population, we cannot expect the characteristics of the sample to be distributed exactly the same as in the population. Moreover, because characteristics of a population are distributed by chance, some random samples will be more representative than others. Random sampling does ensure, however, that in the long run (i.e., over an infinitely large number of samples) such samples will be representative of the population.

Stratified Random Sampling.   Simple random sampling is one of several methods of sampling from a population. Another approach is the **stratified random sample.** Assume there are subgroups within the population whose members are relatively homogeneous on some characteristic. Consider, for example, a population of females at a university. There are various subgroups within this population, for example the subgrouping of year in college. The population may be stratified, or put into levels, on the basis of year in college—freshman, sophomore, junior, senior. The members of each college-year subgroup are homogeneous, or alike, on the characteristic of year in college. Obviously, there are many possible subgroupings, such as academic major, possessing a part-time job, and so forth.

Suppose we stratify the population of females at a college on college-year and find the following percentage of females in each stratum (i.e., level or subgroup): freshmen — 40 percent, sophomores — 25 percent, juniors — 20 percent, and seniors — 15 percent. Simple random sampling from this population ensures that if we draw many, many samples, the proportion of females in the population for each class-year would be represented in similar proportions in the sample. But such proportionality would be unlikely to exist in any single sample. This possible imbalance is illustrated in part A of Table 7–1. Column a of this table represents the proportion of students in each stratum, or class-year level in the population. Column b presents the proportion of students selected from each class level if a large number of simple random samples were to be drawn from the population. Column c illustrates the proportion that might occur in any single random sample.

A stratified random sample, however, selects individuals in proportion to the frequency of the stratum in the population. If sophomores represent 25 percent of the population, then they will be 25 percent of the

TABLE 7–1.

Illustration of simple random sampling and stratified random sampling for a population of college females stratified by class level.

	A. Simple Random Sampling		
	(a)	*(b)*	*(c)*
Class Level	*Proportion in Population*	*Proportion over Many Random Samples*	*Possible Proportion in a Single Random Sample*
1	.40	.40	.46
2	.25	.25	.18
3	.20	.20	.15
4	.15	.15	.21

	B. Stratified Random Sampling	
	(a)	*(b)*
Class Level	*Proportion in Population*	*Proportion in Stratified Random Sample*
1	.40	.40
2	.25	.25
3	.20	.20
4	.15	.15

sample. Part *B* of Table 7–1 illustrates the relation of the stratified random sample to the characteristics of the population. Column *a* of this table represents the proportion of students in each class-year level in the population. Column *b* presents the proportion of students in each class-year level in the stratified random sample. When strata can be identified in a population and when membership in a particular stratum is related to the behavior being measured, then a stratified random sample likely will provide a more representative sample than will simple random sampling.

Sample Size

We have seen in our discussion of consistency that larger samples are more likely to produce an estimate that is closer to the value of μ than are estimates from smaller samples. Thus, sample size is related to the accuracy of the estimate obtained.

Variability in Population Measures

Consider the unlikely possibility that the scores for all members of a population are exactly the same. Thus, every score is equal to the mean of the population. Under these conditions, it is evident that the $\overline{X}$ obtained from a sample of any size will exactly equal μ. There will be no error in the sample estimate. On the other hand, consider a population that has extensive variation among the scores measured. Although it should occur infrequently, by chance alone the scores in one random sample may consist principally of low values. The resulting sample mean, then, would differ considerably from the population mean. Similarly, a relatively poor estimate of the population mean would be obtained if primarily high scores were randomly sampled from a population. Thus, the accuracy of a particular sample estimate will be related to the amount of variability in the population. The more extensive the variability in the scores of the population, the less likely a particular sample mean will be an accurate estimate of the population mean.

Statistics in Use 7–1

Sampling for Surveys and Polls

Scientists conducting survey research (e.g., political polling) often estimate population parameters from a small sample. In Statistics in Use 1–1, we discussed the survey research of Bausell (1986), who was interested in the importance individuals attributed to certain behaviors in maintaining good health. Bausell selected one of his samples from the telephone-owning population of the continental United States. This sample involved 1254 adults who were contacted by telephone. To ensure proportional geographic representation, the sample was stratified by geographical regions and metropolitan and nonmetropolitan residence. Within a stratum, the sampling of individuals was done by simple random sampling. Because of this careful attention to sampling procedure, Bausell can be confident that this sample of individuals is representative of the larger population of the telephone-owning adults in the United States.

Surveys that are done in the popular media may not pay such careful attention to sampling procedures as did Bausell. As an example, one popular weekly tabloid reported that an "overwhelming majority" of their readers believe that nonviolent criminals should be whipped or agonizingly shocked instead of being sent to jail (Levy, 1983, June 7). This conclusion was based on the responses of 470 readers to a poll published in a previous issue. Of the 470 respondents, 84 percent (or 394 readers) stated that nonviolent criminals should be punished by beatings and shock. The author implied that the responses of these 470 readers were typical of the approximate 4.5 million readers of this tabloid. Is this inference reasonable? We think not. This sample was not selected by any procedure that would ensure representativeness of the population of readers. Rather, the respondents were likely those people sufficiently interested in the question to send in a response to the poll. And, it seems obvious that the people most motivated to respond were those individuals who believe in beating and shocking nonviolent criminals. Individuals who recognize that such punishments are unconstitutional, or who regard the idea as absurd, did not respond. Thus, it may be that out of the readership of about 4.5 million, only 394 people believe in beating and shocking criminals and they are the individuals who sent responses to this poll. It is perhaps an understatement to say that such a poll is scientifically useless. ▪

Testing Your Knowledge 7–1

On a separate sheet of paper, test your knowledge of the material in this section by answering the following questions.

1. Define: statistical inference, unbiased estimator, consistent estimator, simple random sampling, stratified random sampling.
2. Suppose a population of individuals with anxiety disorders contains 27 percent generalized anxiety disorder, 23 percent agoraphobia, 19 percent simple phobia, 22 percent panic disorders, and 9 percent obsessive-compulsive disorder. You plan to draw a stratified random sample from this population using the types of disorders as strata.
   a. What proportion of your sample would be in each stratum?
   b. If you drew a sample of 100 individuals, how many people would be in each stratum? ▪

DETERMINING THE ACCURACY OF AN ESTIMATE: THE SAMPLING DISTRIBUTION OF THE MEAN

Our discussion has indicated that the accuracy of a sample estimate for a parameter depends upon both sample size and the variability of scores in the population. Unless the sample encompasses all the scores in the population or there is no variability of scores in the population, the sample statistic likely will be in error in estimating the value of the population parameter.

A researcher never knows for sure just how accurate a particular estimate of a population parameter is. He or she cannot determine precisely how much the sample estimate may deviate from the population parameter. But we can determine the amount of error that can be expected in the estimate. To understand the basis for quantifying the expected error in estimating population parameters from sample statistics, we must understand sampling distributions. The concept of a sampling distribution is crucial to understanding inferential statistics, and we introduce a number of sampling distributions later. This section introduces the sampling distribution of the mean.

To help conceptualize the sampling distribution of the mean, suppose we select 1000 independent, random samples from the same population. For each sample a score is obtained from each individual in the sample, and the sample mean is calculated. Thus, we calculate a thousand sample means, each sample mean estimating the same population mean, μ.

What could we do with a thousand sample means? Recalling Chapter 3, we might organize them into a frequency distribution in which the values of the sample means are arranged from low to high. The number of times each mean occurs is tallied. The resulting frequency distribution of sample means is called the **sampling distribution of the mean.** You will easily be able to remember what a sampling distribution of the mean is if you realize that it is simply a distribution of sample means. More generally, a frequency distribution for any statistic derived from sample data is called a **sampling distribution for that statistic.**

Empirical and Theoretical Sampling Distributions

Sampling distributions may be generated in two ways—empirically and theoretically. The word *empirical* means observable or observed. Empirical sampling distributions may be obtained by doing what we have just described—actually drawing a number of samples from a population and then plotting a frequency distribution of the means obtained.

A theoretical sampling distribution is obtained from use of a mathematical equation. Each of the statistical tests introduced in following chapters requires a knowledge of the sampling distribution for the statistic employed. These sampling distributions are theoretical sampling distributions obtained from mathematical equations.

An Example of an Empirical Sampling Distribution of the Mean

To illustrate this discussion, we now generate three different empirical sampling distributions of the mean. We do so by an actual sampling from a population in which μ and σ are known. The population of interest has 100 scores. A frequency polygon of the 100 scores is shown in Figure 7–1. As you can see, the distribution of scores in the population is symmetrical and unimodal. The scores range from 8 to 20 with a mean, μ, of 14.0 and a standard deviation, σ, of 2.14.

Empirical sampling distributions of the mean were obtained for three different sample sizes by drawing simple random samples from this population with the aid of a computer. First, 100 random samples of two scores in each sample ($N = 2$) were obtained and the mean of each sample was calculated. Then, 100 random samples of five scores in each sample ($N = 5$) were drawn and the mean of each sample found. Finally, 100 random samples of 10 scores in each sample ($N = 10$) were obtained and the mean of each sample determined. The set of means for each of

FIGURE 7–1.

Frequency distribution for a population of 100 scores with $\mu = 14.0$ and $\sigma = 2.14$.

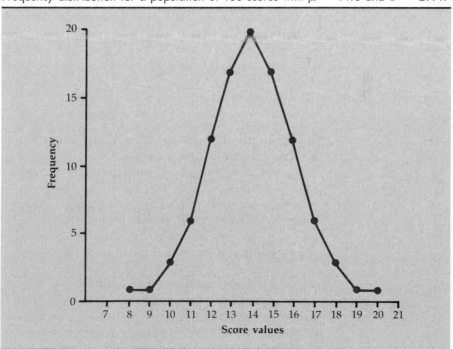

FIGURE 7–2.
Three empirical sampling distributions of the mean for 100 samples drawn from the population of scores presented in Figure 7–1. The sample sizes are (a) $N = 2$, (b) $N = 5$, (c) $N = 10$.

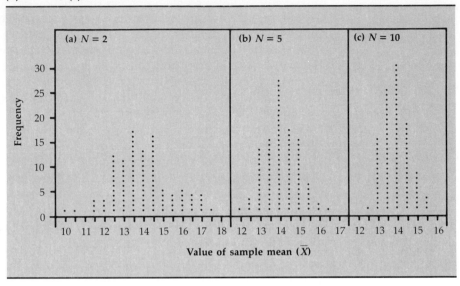

the three samples was then placed on a grouped frequency distribution. Frequency polygons of the grouped frequency distributions for each set of 100 means are presented in Figure 7–2. Each distribution (*a*, *b*, and *c*) represents a sampling distribution of the mean for a particular sample size ($N = 2$, 5, and 10, respectively).

Characteristics of the Sampling Distribution of the Mean

Recall from Chapter 3 that a frequency distribution can be summarized in terms of its shape, measure of central tendency, and measure of variability. Because the sampling distribution of the mean is a frequency distribution, it, too, can be described in terms of its shape, mean, and standard deviation.

Shape of a Sampling Distribution of the Mean

Observe that the three sampling distributions in Figure 7–2 are relatively symmetrical and unimodal. Any variations from symmetry are simply chance variation in the values of the sample means obtained in sampling. Notice also that the distribution becomes more peaked and less spread out as the sample size increases (compare $N = 2$ to $N = 10$). A general principle applies to the shape of the sampling distribution of the mean: *As sample size increases, any sampling distribution of the mean will be approximately normally distributed.* This approximation of the normal distribution occurs whether the shape of the distribution of individual scores in the population is symmetrical or skewed. This characteristic of the sampling distribution of the mean is known as the **central limit theorem** and can be proven mathematically. For our purposes, however, it is sufficient to realize that regardless of the shape of the distribution of the underlying population of scores, the sampling distribution of the mean for that set of scores will approach a normal distribution as sample size increases.

How large must N be before the sampling distribution of the mean becomes approximately normally distributed? The answer to this question depends upon the shape of the distribution of scores in the population. The population that we sampled from is not normally distributed, but is unimodal and symmetrical (see Figure 7–1). From such a distribution, the sampling distribution of the mean for sample sizes as small as $N = 5$ or $N = 10$ begins to approach the shape of a normal distribution (see Figures 7–2b and 7–2c). If the population distribution is skewed, then the sample size must be larger for the sampling distribution of the mean to approximate a normal distribution. For population distributions that are not heavily skewed, many statisticians consider a sample size of 30 ($N = 30$) to lead to a sampling distribution of the mean that will be approximately normally distributed. Because many characteristics of humans and animals are symmetrically distributed in the population and often approach normality, behavioral scientists may consider sample sizes as small as even $N = 10$ or $N = 15$ as having sampling distributions of the mean that are approximately normally distributed.

A theoretical sampling distribution of the mean based upon the central limit theorem is depicted in Figure 7–3. Observe that this distribution is symmetrical, unimodal, and normal. Notice that this distribution is

FIGURE 7–3.

Theoretical sampling distribution of the mean with mean μ and standard error $\sigma_{\overline{X}}$.

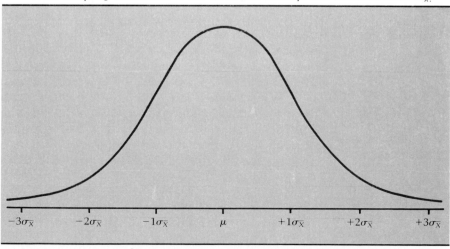

considered to be a population distribution. Rather than a distribution of individual scores in the population, however, it is a distribution of sample means drawn from the population. This idealized sampling distribution is a statistician's invention; it would occur only in the long run with an infinite number of samples. In developing inferential statistical tests in following chapters, however, we will use theoretical sampling distributions rather than empirical sampling distributions such as those presented in Figure 7–2. Because we know that the sampling distribution of the mean will always approach normality, there is no need to generate empirical sampling distributions in actual practice.

Mean of a Sampling Distribution of the Mean

As one might expect, the mean of the sample means (represented by $\mu_{\overline{X}}$) in a theoretical sampling distribution will be equal to the population mean (μ) of the scores in question. In an empirical sampling distribution of the mean, however, the mean of the sample means (represented by $\overline{X}_{\overline{X}}$) will not be exactly equal to the population mean. This point is illustrated by the empirical sampling distributions of Figure 7–2. The means of the sample means in the three sampling distributions are not exactly equal to 14.0, the mean of the parent population. The mean values are $\overline{X}_{\overline{X}} = 13.96$, $\overline{X}_{\overline{X}} = 14.14$, and $\overline{X}_{\overline{X}} = 13.99$ for distributions a, b, and c, respectively.

Sampling Error and the Standard Error of the Mean

Sampling Error.   As you can see from Figure 7–2, some sample means in a sampling distribution of the mean provide more accurate estimates of the population mean than do other means. The error in an estimate due to chance factors is called sampling error. **Sampling error** is the amount by which a particular sample mean differs from the population mean (i.e., $\overline{X} - \mu$). If the sample mean is exactly the same as the population mean, that is, if $\overline{X} = \mu$ and thus, $\overline{X} - \mu = 0$, then there is no sampling error in the estimate. Figure 7–2 illustrates that sampling error is related to sample size. The values of the 100 sample means in Figure 7–2a, with each mean based on two scores, are clearly more dispersed than the sample means in Figures 7–2b and c, which were derived from either five or 10 scores, respectively. Thus, there is more sampling error evident in Figure 7–2a than in either Figure 7–2b or c. The sample means most deviant from μ (those with the greatest sampling error) occur in the smaller sample sizes. Conversely, the sample mean values are less variable with the larger sample sizes and the sampling error typically is smaller.

Standard Error of the Mean.   The amount of sampling error in a sampling distribution of the mean is measured by the standard error of the mean. To understand the standard error of the mean, consider a simple frequency distribution of raw scores obtained from a sample (such as the frequency distribution shown in column c of Table 3–2). The amount of variability among the scores in this distribution can be described by the standard deviation (s). Similarly, the amount of variability among the sample means in a sampling distribution of the mean can be described by the standard deviation computed upon the values of the sample means. This type of standard deviation is not called a standard deviation, however, but rather a **standard error of the mean** or simply a **standard error.** Specifically, the true standard error of the mean, $\sigma_{\overline{X}}$, is equal to the standard deviation of the population divided by the square root of the size of the sample. In notation, $\sigma_{\overline{X}} = \sigma/\sqrt{N}$, where σ represents the standard deviation of scores in the population and N is the size of the sample. The standard error of the mean, $\sigma_{\overline{X}}$, is a standard deviation, just as σ is a standard deviation. But $\sigma_{\overline{X}}$ is a standard deviation of a distribution of sample means, rather than being a standard deviation of the raw scores in a population as is σ.

Look at Figure 7–3, the theoretical sampling distribution of the mean. Remember that this theoretical sampling distribution is normally distributed. In Chapter 6 we discussed the area under the normal distribution and explained how we may find the proportion of scores that fall within certain areas of the distribution. Because the sampling distribution of the mean is a normal distribution, the same relationships hold for this distribution also. In this instance, however, it is not raw scores that are contained in the intervals, but sample means. Thus, for example, the interval from $\mu - 1\sigma_{\overline{X}}$ to $\mu + 1\sigma_{\overline{X}}$ will contain 0.6826 of the sample means, the interval from $\mu - 2\sigma_{\overline{X}}$ to $\mu + 2\sigma_{\overline{X}}$ will contain 0.9544 of the sample means, and the interval from $\mu - 3\sigma_{\overline{X}}$ to $\mu + 3\sigma_{\overline{X}}$ will contain 0.9974 of the sample means.

As an example of the use of this relationship, suppose that a population of scores has a mean of $\mu = 50$ and $\sigma = 6.0$. If samples of $N = 9$ are drawn from this population, then $\sigma_{\overline{X}} = 6/\sqrt{9}$, which equals 6/3 or 2.0. This value, $\sigma_{\overline{X}} = 2.0$, is the standard deviation of the sampling distribution of the mean for samples of size $N = 9$ from the population. Thus, in the theoretical sampling distribution of the mean for samples of $N = 9$, 0.6826 of the sample means will fall into the interval of $\mu \pm 1\sigma_{\overline{X}}$, or the interval from 48 to 52. The interval $\mu \pm 2\sigma_{\overline{X}}$, or 46 to 54, will contain 0.9544 of the sample means, and 0.9974 of the values of X will be in the interval defined by $\mu \pm 3\sigma_{\overline{X}}$, or from 44 to 56. This knowledge will be useful to us as we develop an approach to estimating the accuracy with which a sample mean estimates μ.

Using the Standard Normal Deviate with the Sampling Distribution of the Mean

The sampling distribution of the mean is normally distributed with mean $\mu_{\overline{X}}$ and a standard error $\sigma_{\overline{X}}$. Thus we may convert a value of $\overline{X}$ in such a distribution to a score on the standard normal distribution by

$$z = \frac{(\overline{X} - \mu_{\overline{X}})}{\sigma_{\overline{X}}}.$$

This z score may be used with the sample mean just as it was for an individual score in Chapter 6. Example Problem 7–1 illustrates its use.

 Example Problem 7–1
Using the Sampling Distribution of the Mean

Problem:
Suppose we have a normally distributed population of scores with $\mu = 80$ and $\sigma = 12$. We plan to draw a large number of samples of size 16 ($N = 16$) from this population and compute the mean for each sample. What proportion of the sample means will be equal to or greater than 82?

Solution:
The solution to this problem requires recognizing that the sampling distribution of the mean is normally distributed, with $\mu_{\overline{X}} = 80$ and $\sigma_{\overline{X}} = 12/\sqrt{16} = 3.0$. The proportion of sample means in any interval on the theoretical sampling distribution may be found by converting the value of the sample mean (i.e., 82) to a value on the standard normal distribution and looking up the appropriate proportion in the standard normal table, Table A–1. The sample mean may be converted to a z value by

$$z = \frac{(\overline{X} - \mu_{\overline{X}})}{\sigma_{\overline{X}}}.$$

Substituting numerical values,

$$z = \frac{(82 - 80)}{3.0} = +0.67.$$

Column c of Table A–1 indicates that the area beyond $z = +0.67$ is 0.2514. Thus, 0.2514 of the sample means are expected to be equal to or greater than 82. We may phrase this conclusion in probability terms as

$$p(\overline{X} \geq 82) = 0.2514. \quad ∎$$

Testing Your Knowledge 7–2

On a separate sheet of paper, test your knowledge of the material in this section by answering the following questions.

1. Define: sampling distribution of the mean, standard error of the mean, $\mu_{\overline{X}}, \sigma_{\overline{X}}$.
2. Distinguish between an empirical and a theoretical sampling distribution of the mean.
3. State the central limit theorem.

4. Suppose you plan to draw 100 random samples of size 25 ($N = 25$) from a population of intelligence test scores with $\mu = 100$ and $\sigma = 15$.
   a. What proportion of the sample means do you expect to be between 97 and 103?
   b. What proportion of the sample means do you expect to be greater than 103?
   c. What proportion of the sample means do you expect to be less than 94?
   d. What proportion of the sample means do you expect to be greater than 105?
   e. What proportion of the sample means do you expect to be between 100 and 105? ▨

ESTIMATING THE STANDARD ERROR OF THE MEAN

The sampling distribution of the mean provides a method of assessing variability expected among sample means. But there is an apparent road-block to our use of this knowledge. As you recognize, σ is a population parameter, and we have said that any population parameter typically is unknown to the researcher (which is why estimates are made from samples to begin with). Therefore, how can we determine the standard error of the mean, $\sigma_{\bar{X}}$, which requires knowing σ?

Perhaps you have anticipated that the answer to this question lies in estimating σ from the data of a sample just as we have estimated μ from $\bar{X}$. In this instance the sample standard deviation (s) is used as an estimate of the population standard deviation (σ). Therefore, although it is only rarely possible to determine the true standard error of a population, $\sigma_{\bar{X}}$, it is possible to estimate its value. This **estimated standard error of the mean,** identified as $s_{\bar{X}}$, is based on the sample standard deviation and is expressed in notation as

$$s_{\bar{X}} = \frac{s}{\sqrt{N}},$$

where s is the standard deviation of the scores in a sample and N is the sample size. Thus, $s_{\bar{X}}$ is the estimated standard deviation of the sampling distribution of the mean.

It is important to understand the distinction between $\sigma_{\bar{X}}$ and $s_{\bar{X}}$. The $\sigma_{\bar{X}}$ is a fixed value that can be determined when the population standard deviation, σ, is known. Because we seldom know σ, however, we typically must estimate the value of $\sigma_{\bar{X}}$ by $s_{\bar{X}}$. The $s_{\bar{X}}$, though, because it is an estimate based upon the value of s from a sample, will vary from sample to sample. Different random samples from the same population can be expected to produce different standard deviations because of the chance differences in scores that will occur from one sample to another. Nevertheless, the scores of the sample provide the only basis for estimating the standard error of the mean, $\sigma_{\overline{X}}$.

Factors Affecting the Value of $s_{\overline{X}}$

The formula for the standard error, $s/\sqrt{N}$, shows how the variability of sample means in a sampling distribution is related to (a) the variability of scores in the population, and (b) to the size of the sample used to estimate the population mean. The more variable the scores in the population, the larger the standard deviation (s) of scores in the sample. And, as s increases, the standard error does also. However, increasing sample size (N) increases the denominator of the formula for $s_{\overline{X}}$, which contributes to making the standard error smaller. Thus, we can expect to obtain a smaller $s_{\overline{X}}$ with large random samples from populations in which the variability of scores is small. Although an investigator can control sample size, often little can be done to reduce the variation of scores in the population other than attempting to reduce errors of measurement. Thus, to decrease the value of $s_{\overline{X}}$, behavioral scientists often resort to using larger sample sizes.

Use of $s_{\overline{X}}$

The standard error is used to measure the amount of sampling error in the sampling distribution of the mean. Therefore $s_{\overline{X}}$ may be used to determine how well an obtained sample mean estimates a population mean. The smaller the obtained standard error the better the sample mean estimates μ, in the sense that the smaller the $s_{\overline{X}}$, the more confident one can be that the sample mean does not differ substantially from the population mean. We will use our knowledge of $s_{\overline{X}}$ to make precise statements about the accuracy with which $\overline{X}$ estimates μ in Chapter 8. To simplify our discussion in the remainder of this chapter, however, we assume that $\sigma_{\overline{X}}$ is known to us. You should remember, however, that in actual practice $\sigma_{\overline{X}}$ will not be known and $s_{\overline{X}}$ must be used in its place.

Review of Types of Distributions

Table 7–2 summarizes the several types of distributions we have discussed in this and previous chapters. Distributions may be composed of either the raw scores or the means of samples drawn from a population. Population distributions of raw scores typically are unknown to the researcher and their parameters must be estimated by statistics obtained from a sample.

TABLE 7–2.

Summary of types of distributions and their characteristics.

Type of Distribution Raw Scores	Obtained by	Mean	Standard Deviation	Variance
Population	Measuring all members of the population	μ	σ	σ^2
Sample	Drawing and measuring a sample from a population	$\overline{X}$	s	s^2
Sampling Distribution of the Mean				
Theoretical	Theoretically from a mathematical equation	$\mu_{\overline{X}}$	$\sigma_{\overline{X}}$	$\sigma_{\overline{X}}^2$
Empirical	Empirically by drawing samples from a population	$\overline{X}_{\overline{X}}$	$s_{\overline{X}}$	$s_{\overline{X}}^2$

The theoretical sampling distribution of the mean for a given sample size is obtained from a mathematical equation. Empirical sampling distributions are typically not employed in actual research. Rather, estimates of μ and $\sigma_{\overline{X}}$ are obtained from the $\overline{X}$ and s of a sample.

Testing Your Knowledge 7–3

On a separate sheet of paper, test your knowledge of the material in this section by answering the following questions.

1. Suppose you have a sample of scores for time on target of a tracking task. In such a task, a person must track a moving target with a cursor on a video display tube. The amount of time the person maintains the cursor on the target during a trial is recorded. The s for these scores is 18.0 seconds.
   a. What is the value of $s_{\overline{X}}$ if the sample size is 4?
   b. What is the value of $s_{\overline{X}}$ if the sample size is 9?
   c. What is the value of $s_{\overline{X}}$ if the sample size is 36?
   e. Must the value of $s_{\overline{X}}$ always decrease as N increases? Explain your answer.
2. Suppose you have three different samples of scores on time on target during a tracking task. The values of s for the three samples are 10, 15, and 20 seconds, respectively. The sample size was 25 ($N = 25$).
   a. Find the value of $s_{\overline{X}}$ for each sample.
   b. What relationship between variability of scores and the value of $s_{\overline{X}}$ is illustrated by these samples?

3. You plan to draw equal-sized samples from two different populations of scores, A_1 and A_2. Population A_1 has a σ of 17.0 and population A_2 has a σ of 30.0. Which population, A_1 or A_2, do you expect will lead to a sample with a larger value of $s_{\overline{X}}$? Explain your answer. ▪

POINT AND INTERVAL ESTIMATION OF THE POPULATION MEAN

Point Estimation

We have indicated that $\overline{X}$ obtained from a sample is an unbiased and consistent estimator of the population mean μ. If we had a mean obtained from a sample of scores and were asked to estimate the mean of the scores in the population from which the sample was drawn, then the best estimate of μ would be the value of $\overline{X}$. Thus, if a researcher obtained Test Anxiety Inventory scores from 100 females and wanted to estimate the value of μ for the population from which these scores were selected, she would use the value of $\overline{X}$ as an estimate of μ. If the obtained value of $\overline{X}$ were 41.6, then this value would be used as the estimate of μ.

This form of estimation of population parameters from sample statistics is called point estimation. **Point estimation** is estimating the value of a parameter as a single point; for example, $\mu = 41.6$, from the value of the statistic, $\overline{X} = 41.6$. From our discussion of sampling error, however, we know that most point estimates will be in error; the true value of μ will not be equal to the value of μ estimated by $\overline{X}$.

Interval Estimation

A point estimate of the population mean almost is assured of being in error; the estimate from the sample will not equal the exact value of the parameter. To gain confidence about the accuracy of this estimate, we may estimate not only a point value for the mean, but we may also construct an interval of scores that is expected to include the value of the population mean. Such intervals are called confidence intervals. A **confidence interval** is a range of score values that is expected to contain the value of μ. For example, rather than estimating the population mean of Test Anxiety Inventory scores as exactly 41.6, a researcher may estimate that an interval from 39.9 to 43.3 contains the value of μ. A level of confidence can be attached to this estimate so that, for example, the scientist can be 95 percent confident that the interval encompasses the population mean. The lower (e.g., 39.9) and upper (e.g., 43.3) scores that determine the interval are called *confidence limits*. Let us see how such intervals are constructed and what it means to say that an experimenter is 95 percent confident that the interval includes the value of μ.

Return to Figure 7–3, the theoretical sampling distribution of the mean. Recall that $\sigma_{\overline{X}}$ is the standard deviation of this sampling distribution and that the distribution is normally distributed. Using these properties, we illustrated in an earlier section of this chapter that the interval from $\mu - 1\sigma_{\overline{X}}$ to $\mu + 1\sigma_{\overline{X}}$ contains 0.6826 of the sample means that could be drawn from this population. Suppose we now asked the question: If you were to draw a single sample mean $\overline{X}$, what is the probability that its value would fall into the interval between $\mu - 1\sigma_{\overline{X}}$ to $\mu + 1\sigma_{\overline{X}}$? The answer is 0.6826, for 0.6826 of the sample means have values between $\mu - 1\sigma_{\overline{X}}$ and $\mu + 1\sigma_{\overline{X}}$. If you were to draw a single sample mean, the probability that its value would be between $\mu - 1\sigma_{\overline{X}}$ to $\mu + \sigma_{\overline{X}}$ is 0.6826. Notice that, to answer the question, we constructed an interval about μ using values of $\sigma_{\overline{X}}$ and the known properties of the normal distribution. But in most instances μ is unknown; indeed, we estimate μ with $\overline{X}$. Suppose we follow the same procedure of constructing an interval around μ, but employ $\overline{X}$ as an estimate of μ. Thus, we obtain an interval of $\overline{X} - 1\sigma_{\overline{X}}$ to $\overline{X} + 1\sigma_{\overline{X}}$. The question we now ask is not whether this interval contains the value of $\overline{X}$, but whether the interval contains μ. We can answer this question with a probability statement also. If the probability that the interval $\mu - 1\sigma_{\overline{X}}$ to $\mu + 1\sigma_{\overline{X}}$ contains a value of $\overline{X}$ is 0.6826, then it is also true that the probability that the interval $\overline{X} - 1\sigma_{\overline{X}}$ to $\overline{X} + 1\sigma_{\overline{X}}$ contains μ is 0.6826.

The interval of $\overline{X} - 1\sigma_{\overline{X}}$ to $\overline{X} + 1\sigma_{\overline{X}}$ is a 68 percent (rounding 0.6826 and then multiplying by 100 to obtain percent) confidence interval. The limits, or extremes, of this interval, $\overline{X} - 1\sigma_{\overline{X}}$ and $\overline{X} + 1\sigma_{\overline{X}}$, are the confidence limits. We can interpret this interval by thinking that if we were to repeatedly draw samples and calculate a sample mean and then construct an interval of plus or minus one $\sigma_{\overline{X}}$ about each mean, 68 percent of the intervals would contain the value of μ. Thus, we could state that any one of the intervals has a probability of 0.68 (or a 68 percent chance) of including μ. Notice that, because μ is a population parameter and thus a specific value, it is either contained or not contained in the interval. Let us consider a numerical example to illustrate this discussion.

Suppose we have a population with $\mu = 50$ and $\sigma = 10$. We draw a sample of size 25 ($N = 25$) from this population and obtain a sample mean, $\overline{X}$, of 51.5. Then, $\sigma_{\overline{X}} = 10/\sqrt{25}$, which equals 2.0. A 68 percent confidence interval for μ is obtained by finding the interval from $\overline{X} - 1\sigma_{\overline{X}}$ to $\overline{X} + 1\sigma_{\overline{X}}$. Substituting values of $\overline{X} = 51.5$ and $\sigma_{\overline{X}} = 2$, the resulting confidence interval is 49.5 to 53.5. We can be 68 percent confident that this interval contains the value of $\mu = 50$. And, in this instance, it does. Suppose, however, that $\overline{X}$ had been 54.0 rather than 51.5. Then the 68 percent confidence interval is 52.0 to 56.0. Again, we can be 68 percent confident that this interval contains μ. But in this instance the interval does not contain $\mu = 50$. In practice, of course, we cannot know for sure if the confidence interval contains μ or not, for we do not know the value of μ. If we did know μ, then we would not need to estimate its value. We can only have a certain level of confidence that the interval actually does contain the value of μ.

Confidence intervals used in actual research are more typically 95 percent or 99 percent confidence intervals rather than 68 percent confidence intervals. We find the limits for these intervals by using the properties of the standard normal distribution with $\mu = 0$ and $\sigma = 1$. From Table A–1, we find that an interval from $z = -1.96$ to $z = +1.96$ will contain .95 of the values of z, and a range of z from -2.58 to $+2.58$ will contain .99 of the values of z. Thus, a 95 percent confidence interval for the mean is obtained by the interval

$$\overline{X} - 1.96\sigma_{\overline{X}} \quad \text{to} \quad \overline{X} + 1.96\sigma_{\overline{X}},$$

and a 99 percent confidence interval by the interval

$$\overline{X} - 2.58\sigma_{\overline{X}} \quad \text{to} \quad \overline{X} + 2.58\sigma_{\overline{X}}.$$

For our example with $\overline{X} = 51.5$ and $\sigma_{\overline{X}} = 2$, a 95 percent confidence interval equals $51.5 - 1.96(2)$ to $51.5 + 1.96(2)$, or 47.6 to 55.4. The 99 percent confidence interval equals $51.5 - 2.58(2)$ to $51.5 + 2.58(2)$, or 46.3 to 56.7.

One aspect of this discussion may be puzzling. We have been estimating μ, a population parameter, because we cannot measure the population to obtain the value of this parameter. Yet, in constructing confidence intervals, we have used the value of σ, another parameter, to find $\sigma_{\overline{X}}$. Why should we know the value of σ when we do not known μ? The answer is that we don't; we must estimate $\sigma_{\overline{X}}$ from $s_{\overline{X}}$. We assumed knowledge of $\sigma_{\overline{X}}$ to simplify the introduction of interval estimation. In practice, $s_{\overline{X}}$, rather than $\sigma_{\overline{X}}$, is used to determine the limits of the confidence interval. When $s_{\overline{X}}$ is used, then the intervals must be made slightly larger than those obtained by using $\sigma_{\overline{X}}$. The concepts of interval estimation are identical, however, whether $\sigma_{\overline{X}}$ or $s_{\overline{X}}$ is used. We discuss the use of $s_{\overline{X}}$ in the construction of confidence intervals in Chapter 8.

 ### Example Problem 7–2
Constructing Confidence Intervals When $\sigma_{\overline{X}}$ Is Known

Problem:
We have a sample of 30 scores from a population with $\sigma = 13.0$. The sample mean is 71.0. Find the 95 percent confidence interval for μ.

Solution:
We must find $\sigma_{\overline{X}}$ and then use Table A–1 to find the value of z that defines an interval containing 95 percent of the area on the standard normal distribution.

$$\sigma_{\overline{X}} = \frac{\sigma}{\sqrt{N}} = \frac{13.0}{\sqrt{30}} = 2.37.$$

From Table A–1, we find that an interval on the standard normal distribution from $z = -1.96$ to $z = +1.96$ contains 95 percent of the area of the distribution. Thus, the 95 percent confidence interval for μ is given by

$$\overline{X} - 1.96\sigma_{\overline{X}} \quad \text{to} \quad \overline{X} + 1.96\sigma_{\overline{X}}.$$

Substituting numerical values for $\overline{X}$ and $\sigma_{\overline{X}}$ provides an interval

$$71.0 - 1.96(2.37) \quad \text{to} \quad 71.0 + 1.96(2.37), \quad \text{or} \quad 66.4 \quad \text{to} \quad 75.6.$$

The 95 percent confidence interval for μ is from 66.4 to 75.6. ▪

Testing Your Knowledge 7–4

On a separate sheet of paper, test your knowledge of the material in this section by answering the following questions.

1. Define: Point estimation, interval estimation, confidence interval, confidence limits.
2. You have drawn a sample of 25 scores from a population with $\sigma = 10.0$. The value of $\overline{X}$ is 73.0.
   a. Provide a point estimate of μ.
   b. Construct a 95 percent confidence interval for μ.
   c. Construct a 99 percent confidence interval for μ.
   Assume for questions 2d, 2e, and 2f that your sample size was 100 ($N = 100$) rather than 25.
   d. Provide a point estimate of μ.
   e. Construct a 95 percent confidence interval for μ.
   f. Construct a 99 percent confidence interval for μ.
   g. The confidence intervals based on $N = 100$ are smaller than those based on $N = 25$. Explain why this difference occurs. ▪

ESTIMATION OF THE POPULATION VARIANCE AND STANDARD DEVIATION

Variance

The population variance σ^2 is obtained by measuring all members of a population and then entering all scores into the formula

$$\sigma^2 = \frac{\sum\limits_{i=1}^{N_{\text{pop}}} (X_i - \mu)^2}{N_{\text{population}}},$$

where X_i represents the individual score of a member of the population, μ is the population mean of the scores, and $N_{\text{population}}$ is the total number of scores in the population. As we have pointed out, it is usually impossible for a researcher to measure all members of a population. Consequently, as was the case for the population mean, μ, the population variance, σ^2, is typically estimated from a sample variance. An unbiased and consistent estimator of σ^2 is provided by

$$s^2 = \frac{\sum_{i=1}^{N}(X_i - \overline{X})^2}{N - 1}.$$

Notice in this formula that the denominator is $N - 1$ rather than N. As we discussed in Chapter 5, the value of S^2 obtained using N in the denominator provides a biased estimate of σ^2. More specifically, the value of S^2 given by

$$S^2 = \frac{\sum_{i=1}^{N}(X_i - \overline{X})^2}{N}$$

is a biased estimator of σ^2; typically it underestimates the value of σ^2.

The value of s^2 given by

$$s^2 = \frac{\sum_{i=1}^{N}(X_i - \overline{X})^2}{N - 1}$$

is an unbiased estimator of σ^2. Consequently, as stated in Chapter 5, unless we indicate differently, this formula is the one utilized whenever s^2 is calculated in this text.

Standard Deviation

The population standard deviation, σ, is obtained by taking the square root of σ^2, or notationally,

$$\sigma = \sqrt{\sigma^2} = \sqrt{\frac{\sum(X_i - \mu)^2}{N_{\text{population}}}}.$$

The sample standard deviation, s, is obtained by taking the square root of the sample variance, s^2, and is used as an estimator of σ. In contrast to s^2 as an estimator of σ^2, however, s is not an unbiased estimator of σ. Rather, s slightly underestimates σ. Because the bias in s is small and becomes smaller as sample size increases, most researchers use s when it is necessary to estimate σ. The slight bias in s is tolerated also because

s^2 proves to be a useful statistic in several inferential statistical tests discussed in later chapters. In these chapters, we will show how s and s^2 are used to estimate σ and σ^2, respectively.

Testing Your Knowledge 7–5

On a separate sheet of paper, test your knowledge of the material in this section by answering the following questions.

1. Is the value of S^2 obtained by

$$S^2 = \frac{\sum (X_i - \overline{X})^2}{N}$$

an unbiased estimator of σ^2? If it is biased, how is it biased?

2. Is the value of s^2 obtained by

$$s^2 = \frac{\sum (X_i - \overline{X})^2}{N - 1}$$

an unbiased estimator of σ^2? If it is biased, how is it biased?

3. Is the value of s obtained by

$$s = \sqrt{\frac{\sum_i (X_i - \overline{X})}{N - 1}}$$

an unbiased estimator of σ? If it is biased, how is it biased? ■

SUMMARY

- Statistical inference is the process of drawing conclusions about unknown population values from sample statistics.
- $\overline{X}$ is an unbiased and consistent estimator of μ.
- To allow accurate estimation, a sample should be representative of the population from which it is drawn. Representativeness is determined by the method of sampling employed.
- The sampling distribution of the mean is the theoretical distribution of sample means for a given size sample.

- The standard error of the mean is the standard deviation of the sampling distribution of the mean.
- $\sigma_{\overline{X}}$ is found by $\sigma/\sqrt{N}$. In most cases it is estimated by $s_{\overline{X}} = s/\sqrt{N}$.
- The sampling distribution of the mean approaches a normal distribution as sample size increases. Thus, $\sigma_{\overline{X}}$ can be used to find confidence intervals for estimates of μ from $\overline{X}$.

KEY TERMS

central limit theorem

confidence interval

confidence limits

consistent estimator

interval estimation

$\mu_{\overline{X}}$

point estimation

sampling distribution of the mean

sampling error

$\sigma_{\overline{X}}$

σ^2

$s_{\overline{X}}$

s^2

simple random sampling

standard error of the mean

statistical inference

stratified random sample

unbiased estimator

variance

$X_{\overline{X}}$

REVIEW QUESTIONS

On a separate sheet of paper, test your knowledge of the material in this chapter by answering the following questions.

1. Match the statistic with the parameter it estimates.

		Statistic	Parameter
a.		s	μ
b.		$\overline{X}$	$\sigma_{\overline{X}}$
c.		s^2	σ
d.		$s_{\overline{X}}$	σ^2

2. You select two samples from a population with mean μ. Sample 1 is of size $N = 10$. Sample 2 is of size $N = 24$. Which sample mean do you expect to be closer to the value of μ? Why?

3. A researcher is taking a poll to predict the outcome of a city election. She knows that the voting population of the city is composed of 34 percent registered Democrats, 29 percent registered Republicans, and 37 percent independents. Which type of sampling, simple or stratified random sampling, will more likely lead to a representative sample of voters? Why?

4. A popular tabloid reported that approximately 24 percent of women agree they should be slapped when it is deserved (*1 in 4 Women Agree*, 1983). They based this estimate on the responses of 746 women who responded to a poll published in an earlier issue of the newspaper. The total readership of the newspaper is about 4.5 million. Do you think this sample is representative of the population of readers of this tabloid? Explain your answer.

5. To estimate the number of cigarettes smoked per day by smokers in a high school population, you randomly sample 16 students from among those who identify themselves as smokers. You find that the sample mean for this group is 9.0 cigarettes per day.

   a. Provide a point estimate of the population mean.

   b. Suppose $\sigma = 3.1$ cigarettes per day. Find the 95 percent confidence interval of the mean.

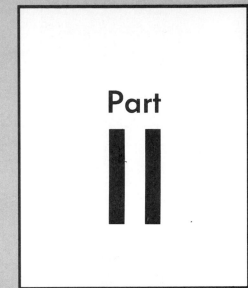

Part
II

Statistical Hypothesis Testing

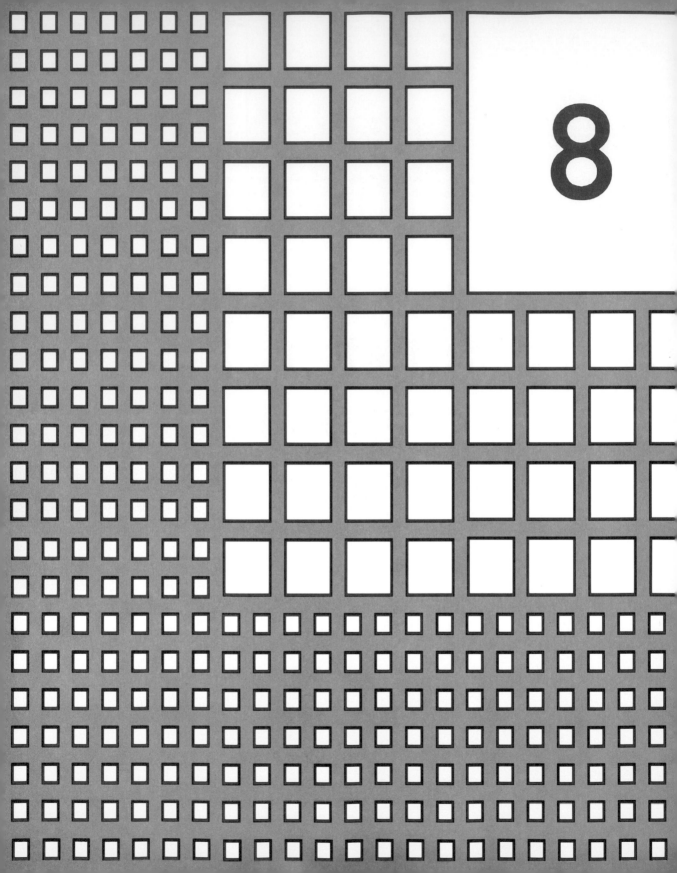

8

Introduction to Statistical Hypothesis Testing with the z Test

OVERVIEW: A PROBLEM AND ITS SOLUTION

We have described the use of statistics for organizing and describing data, and for estimating population parameters. In this chapter, we turn our attention from the use of statistics to organize and describe data to the use of statistics as decision-making tools in behavioral sciences research.

To introduce statistical decision making, we present the following problem. Human factors is that area of behavioral science that attempts to match machines and technology to human capabilities. For example, human factors specialists often are involved in the design of electric power plant control rooms for operators that will eliminate errors in reading instruments or in operating controls. To ensure appropriate design, human factors specialists take measurements of physical characteristics of people so that they can design seats, controls, or display devices to fit the human being. Assume that you are in charge of interior design for a major truck manufacturer. For years the seats in your trucks have been designed for males with a mean popliteal height of 42.1 centimeters (cm) with a σ of 2.6 cm. Popliteal height is the vertical distance from the underside of the thigh to the floor of a seated driver.

Recently, your company has broken into foreign markets and has received complaints that your seats are too high; foreign drivers' feet do not reach the floor of the truck while seated. You wonder if the drivers of these trucks in foreign companies belong to the population for which you have designed the seat, that is, a population with $\mu = 42.1$ cm and $\sigma = 2.6$ cm. Consequently, you obtain a sample of 100 foreign drivers of your truck, sampled randomly and independently from the population of foreign drivers. The mean popliteal height for these drivers is 41.3 cm. Does this mean popliteal height differ from the population mean of 42.1 cm? In statistical terms, this problem resolves to deciding whether the sample mean of 41.3 cm is a commonly found sample mean in the sampling distribution of the mean for samples of size 100 drawn from a population with $\mu = 42.1$ cm and $\sigma = 2.6$ cm, or whether it is a rare ccurrence in this sampling distribution. We provided one method of answering this question in Chapter 7 by finding confidence intervals for a population mean. Thus, we could answer this question by finding the 95 percent confidence interval for the population mean using $\overline{X} = 41.3$ cm and $\sigma = 2.6$ cm. This interval is given by the set of scores from $\overline{X} - 1.96\sigma_{\overline{X}}$ to $\overline{X} + 1.96\sigma_{\overline{X}}$. Substituting numerical values for $\overline{X}$ and $\sigma_{\overline{X}}$, we obtain

$$41.3 - 1.96\left(\frac{2.6}{\sqrt{100}}\right) \quad \text{to} \quad 41.3 + 1.96\left(\frac{2.6}{\sqrt{100}}\right),$$

or 40.79 to 41.81 cm.

The 95 percent confidence interval for μ based on a sample mean is 40.79 to 41.81 cm. We can be 95 percent confident that this interval includes the value of μ for the population from which the sample with mean 41.3 cm was drawn. This interval does not include the value $\mu = 42.1$ cm. Consequently, we conclude that the mean popliteal height of the foreign drivers is not equal to the population mean of $\mu = 42.1$ cm used to design the seats. The seats should be redesigned to fit the population of foreign drivers.

We have answered the question by using confidence intervals for the population mean. The question also could be answered by using statistical hypothesis testing. For the example we have illustrated, statistical hypothesis testing and the use of confidence intervals lead to the same decision with respect to the seat-height question. Statistical hypothesis testing, however, enjoys the advantage of possessing generalizability to a wider variety of decision-making problems than does the use of confidence intervals.

A SECOND SOLUTION TO THE PROBLEM: STATISTICAL HYPOTHESIS TESTING

Parametric and Nonparametric Tests

Two general types of statistical tests frequently are used: parametric and nonparametric tests.

Parametric Tests
Parametric tests test relationships among population parameters such as the population mean, μ, or the population variance, σ^2. Parametric tests often make certain assumptions about the conditions that are regarded as being true for the scores in the sample. As we introduce specific parametric tests we also identify the assumptions of these tests. In this chapter we introduce statistical hypothesis testing employing the parametric one-sample z test. Other parametric tests are introduced in Chapters 9 to 14.

Nonparametric Tests
Nonparametric tests typically make fewer assumptions about the distribution of scores in the population from which the sample is drawn. For this reason, nonparametric tests also are referred to as *distribution-free tests*. Typically, they do not test relationships among population parameters. For many, but not all parametric statistical tests, there are alternative nonparametric tests for analyzing the same data. Nonparametric tests often are used when the assumptions necessary for parametric tests appear to have been violated by the scores. Several nonparametric tests are

presented in Chapter 15. The fundamental concepts of statistical hypothesis testing, though, are much the same for both parametric and nonparametric models.

Statistical Hypotheses

Statistical hypothesis testing—parametric and nonparametric—begins with the formulation of statistical hypotheses. A **hypothesis** is a tentative statement made for the sake of argument. A **statistical hypothesis** is a statement about a characteristic of a population. The statement may or may not be true; it is made simply to establish a testable condition. For example, we could hypothesize that the mean for the population from which we obtained the sample of 100 popliteal height measures is 42.1 cm. In reality, the population mean may or may not be 42.1 cm; we are simply proposing that it is 42.1 cm and that we will test this hypothesis. This statistical hypothesis is a statement about a population parameter. Accordingly, this hypothesis is appropriate for a parametric statistical test. Statistical tests require that two hypotheses be formulated, the null and the alternative hypothesis.

Statistical Null Hypothesis

Statistical hypotheses typically are written in *symbolic* or *notational form* using the letter *H* to indicate that a hypothesis is being offered. In notation the hypothesis that $\mu = 42.1$ cm may be stated as $H: \mu = 42.1$ cm. More specifically, we identify this hypothesis as a **null hypothesis** and designate it by H_0. Hence, the statistically correct expression of the hypothesis that $\mu = 42.1$ cm is $H_0: \mu = 42.1$ cm. The null hypothesis is the statement that tentatively we hold to be true about the population of interest; and it is the hypothesis that is tested by a statistical test.

Statistical Alternative Hypothesis

It is possible, of course, that the null hypothesis is not true and that μ does not equal 42.1 cm. Consequently, there is an alternative hypothesis to $H_0: \mu = 42.1$ cm and it is that μ does not equal 42.1 cm. This **alternative hypothesis** may be identified as H_1 and written as $H_1: \mu \neq 42.1$ cm, where $\neq$ is the symbol for "does not equal."

Properties of Statistical Hypotheses

Every statistical test requires formulation of null and alternative statistical hypotheses. These statistical hypotheses must be expressed such that:

- They are mutually exclusive. That is, both hypotheses cannot be true at the same time. For example, it is logically impossible for $H_0: \mu = 42.1$ cm and $H_1: \mu \neq 42.1$ cm to be simultaneously true for the same population.

- They include all possible values of the parameter being hypothesized. The hypotheses H_0: μ = 42.1 cm and H_1: $\mu \neq$ 42.1 cm meet this requirement; between them they include all possible values of μ for the population of interest.

Because of these characteristics, one of the two hypotheses must represent the true state of affairs in the population — the population mean is either 42.1 cm and H_0: μ = 42.1 cm is true, or it is not, and H_1: $\mu \neq$ 42.1 cm is true.

In summary, then, for our example problem and the statistical test that we are introducing, the statistical hypotheses are:

$$H_0\text{: } \mu = 42.1 \text{ cm} \qquad \text{(null hypothesis)}$$

$$H_1\text{: } \mu \neq 42.1 \text{ cm} \qquad \text{(alternative hypothesis)}.$$

Function of the Statistical Hypotheses

The function of the null hypothesis in a statistical test is to establish a situation under which the theoretical sampling distribution of a statistic may be obtained. In Chapter 7 we defined a sampling distribution of the mean as the frequency distribution of all possible values of $\overline{X}$ if an infinite set of samples of size N were drawn from a population with a mean equal to μ. Thus, for example, assuming the null hypothesis of H_0: μ = 42.1 cm is true, we may obtain the sampling distribution of $\overline{X}$ for samples of size 100. This sampling distribution is shown in Figure 8–1. Notice that

FIGURE 8–1.

Theoretical sampling distribution of the mean for samples of size 100 from a population with μ = 42.1 cm and $\sigma_{\overline{X}}$ = .26 cm.

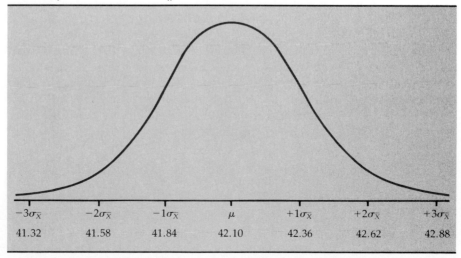

$-3\sigma_{\overline{X}}$	$-2\sigma_{\overline{X}}$	$-1\sigma_{\overline{X}}$	μ	$+1\sigma_{\overline{X}}$	$+2\sigma_{\overline{X}}$	$+3\sigma_{\overline{X}}$
41.32	41.58	41.84	42.10	42.36	42.62	42.88

this sampling distribution is normally distributed with $\mu = 42.1$ cm and a standard error equal to $\sigma_{\overline{X}}$. Further, we also know $\sigma_{\overline{X}}$ because we know $\sigma = 2.6$ cm and the sample size is 100. Thus,

$$\sigma_{\overline{X}} = \frac{\sigma}{\sqrt{N}} = \frac{2.6}{\sqrt{100}} = 0.26 .$$

Examine Figure 8–1 carefully. This figure represents a probability density function for values of $\overline{X}$ with the area under the curve equal to 1.00. Notice that a sample mean of 41.3 cm falls beyond three standard errors of the mean away from μ. Accordingly, under the condition established by H_0: $\mu = 42.1$ cm, a sample mean of 41.3 cm is an infrequent occurrence if samples of size 100 are drawn from a population with $\mu = 42.1$ cm and $\sigma = 2.6$ cm. Hence we might be inclined to reject the null hypothesis H_0: $\mu = 42.1$ cm if we obtained a sample mean of 41.3 cm. Such a mean is a statistically rare event under the null hypothesis. But, before we can decide whether H_0 appears to be true or not, we must do two things:

- We must be able to identify the probability of obtaining a value of $\overline{X}$ as small as 41.3 cm or smaller if H_0: $\mu = 42.1$ cm is true. This step requires utilizing a test statistic.
- We must define what we mean by a statistically rare event. This step requires choosing a significance level.

A Test Statistic: z

To identify the probability of obtaining a value of $\overline{X}$ as small as 41.3 cm or less if H_0: $\mu = 42.1$ cm is true, a test statistic is required. A **test statistic** is a number calculated from the scores of the sample that allows us to test a statistical null hypothesis. For our example, a test statistic will allow us to find the probability of occurrence of a sample mean as small as 41.3 cm or less if H_0: $\mu - 42.1$ cm is true. What test statistic might we use? The sampling distribution of the mean illustrated in Figure 8–1 is normally distributed with $\mu = 42.1$ cm and $\sigma_{\overline{X}} = 0.26$. Consequently, we could transform any value of $\overline{X}$ into a score on the standard normal distribution by employing the relation

$$z = \frac{\overline{X} - \mu}{\sigma_{\overline{X}}} ,$$

where $\overline{X}$ is a sample mean, μ is the hypothesized population mean, and $\sigma_{\overline{X}}$ the standard error of the mean. Accordingly, z is the test statistic to be used here. The value of z locates the sample mean on the standard normal distribution. Notice that this formula is identical in form to that given for z in Chapter 7.

Let us compute the value of z with the $\overline{X}$ of 41.3 cm, the value of μ hypothesized to be 42.1 cm, and $\sigma_{\overline{X}} = 0.26$ cm:

$$z_{obs} = \frac{\overline{X} - \mu}{\sigma_{\overline{X}}}$$

$$z_{obs} = \frac{41.3 - 42.1}{0.26}$$

$$z_{obs} = \frac{-0.8}{0.26}$$

$$z_{obs} = -3.08 \,.$$

We have identified the z statistic as z_{obs} because it is observed from the value of $\overline{X}$ of the sample data. The sampling distribution of the z statistic is provided in Table A–1. From this table, we find that the probability of z being as small as or smaller than -3.08 is $p = 0.001$. Consequently, reverting to our value of $\overline{X} = 41.3$ cm, the probability of obtaining a value of $\overline{X}$ this small or smaller from a sample of size 100 is equal to 0.001 if H_0: $\mu = 42.1$ cm is true. In other words, if H_0 is true and we were to randomly select 1000 samples of $N = 100$ from a population with $\mu = 42.1$ cm and $\sigma = 2.6$, only one of the 1000 sample means would be as small as or smaller than 41.3 cm. Thus, if H_0: $\mu = 42.1$ cm is true, do you think obtaining a sample mean equal to 41.3 cm would be a statistically rare event? We suspect that you would answer "yes." Had we obtained such a sample mean we would certainly reject the hypothesis that it was drawn from a population of individuals with a mean popliteal height of 42.1 cm and we would accept the alternative hypothesis that $\mu \neq 42.1$ cm. Suppose, however, that we had observed a sample mean of 41.7 cm, instead of 41.3 cm. Here the value of z is

$$z_{obs} = \frac{41.7 - 42.1}{0.26}$$

$$z_{obs} = \frac{-0.4}{0.26}$$

$$z_{obs} = -1.54 \,.$$

Consulting Table A–1 we find that the probability of obtaining a value of $z = -1.54$ or smaller is equal to 0.0618. Thus, if H_0 were true and we drew 10,000 samples of $N = 100$, 618 of them would have values of $\overline{X}$ equal to or less than 41.7 cm. Is a sample mean of 41.7 cm a statistically rare event if H_0: $\mu = 42.1$ cm is true? What decision would you make about the null hypothesis in this instance? Would you reject H_0: $\mu =$ 42.1 cm and accept H_1: $\mu \neq 42.1$ cm? Or, would you not reject H_0 and therefore not accept H_1? To answer these questions, we must define what value of z_{obs} we will treat as a statistically rare outcome if H_0 is true. And, the definition of statistical rareness is given by the significance level we adopt for your study.

Testing Your Knowledge 8–1

On a separate sheet of paper, test your knowledge of the material in this section by answering the following questions.

1. Define: alternative hypothesis, null hypothesis, test statistic, hypothesis, H_0, H_1, z_{obs}.
2. Explain the two properties of statistical hypotheses.
3. Write null and alternative statistical hypotheses in notation for each of the following statements.
   a. The population mean for scores on the Wechsler Adult Intelligence Test is 100.
   b. The mean number of murders per year is 8.3 for every 150,000 people.
   c. The mean reaction time of 19-year-old males to a simple stimulus is 423 milliseconds.
4. For each of the following values of μ, $\sigma_{\bar{X}}$, and $\bar{X}$, find the value of z_{obs}. Then, using Table A–1, find the probability associated with z_{obs} equal to or more extreme than the value obtained.

	μ	$\sigma_{\bar{X}}$	$\bar{X}$
a.	50	4.7	40
b.	100	25.0	70
c.	143	0.4	143.9
d.	87	2.9	77

Significance Levels: Statistical Rareness

A statistically rare outcome is defined by the significance level adopted. The **significance level** (also called the **alpha** or α **level**) is the probability value that specifies how improbable an observed value of a test statistic must be under a null hypothesis in order to reject that null hypothesis as true. Traditionally, behavioral scientists have decided that values of a test statistic occurring only 5 or fewer times in 100 occasions if a null hypothesis is true are rare statistically. These values of the test statistic are sufficiently rare occurrences, that it is more reasonable to decide that the alternative hypothesis, H_1, is true if such a value of the test statistic is obtained. Normally, the significance level is stated as a probability value such as $\alpha = 0.05$ or $p \le 0.05$ where the symbol $\le$ implies less than or equal to. Thus, $p \le 0.05$ is read as "p less than or equal to 0.05."

Notice that the significance level is the probability of making a wrong decision if H_0 is true. Because scientists do not want to reject true null hypotheses, significance levels usually are set at $\alpha = .05$ or even less. If it is particularly important to a researcher not to reject a true null hypothesis erroneously, he or she may set $\alpha = 0.01$ or even 0.001. For most of our examples, however, we follow the common usage of $\alpha = 0.05$.

Using the Test Statistic and the Significance Level to Make a Decision about the Statistical Hypotheses

After choosing a test statistic and setting a criterion for statistical rareness, we are in a position to reach a decision about a null hypothesis. Three final steps are involved:

1. Using the significance level to locate a rejection region or regions in the sampling distribution of the test statistic,
2. Calculating the value of the test statistic on the sample data, and
3. Making decisions about the statistical hypotheses by observing whether the observed value of the test statistic does or does not fall into a rejection region.

Locating Rejection Regions
The choice of a value of α, such as $\alpha = .05$ or $\alpha = .01$, allows a researcher to locate a rejection region or regions in the sampling distribution of the test statistic. The **rejection region** represents the values on the sampling distribution of the test statistic (e.g., the z statistic in our example) that have a probability equal to or less than α if the null hypothesis is true. The rejection region defines the observed values of the test statistic (that is, values of z_{obs}) that meet the criterion for rejecting the null hypothesis, H_0, and accepting the alternative hypothesis, H_1. We illustrate locating rejection regions for the z statistic.

The sampling distribution of the z statistic is shown in Figure 8–2. Statistically rare values of z could occur at either tail, or end, of the distribution. For example, z values of either $+3.60$ or -3.60 would be equally improbable values of z if H_0 were true. For our example problem, if either positive or negative values of z this large were found, then it would cast doubt on the truth of H_0: $\mu = 42.1$ cm. Thus, the rejection regions for the z statistic will be in either tail of the sampling distribution. A statistical test that employs rejection regions in both tails of the sampling distribution of the test statistic is identified as a **two-tailed test** or a **nondirectional test**. If a value of z_{obs} falls into either rejection region, then the null hypothesis is rejected and the alternative hypothesis accepted. A value of z_{obs} falling in either rejection region would be quite improbable if H_0 were true,

FIGURE 8–2.
Sampling distribution of the z statistic.

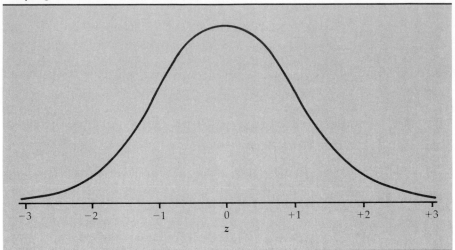

but more likely to occur if H_1 were true. Accordingly, then, a researcher bases the decision to reject or not reject H_0 upon whether or not the observed value of the test statistic falls into a rejection region.

On occasion, a researcher may have reason to place the rejection region in only one tail of the sampling distribution of z. In this instance, a **one-tailed test** is used. The benefit of a one-tailed test is that a smaller value of z_{obs} may fall into the rejection region. But the use of one-tailed rejection regions is controversial and we examine this controversy in Chapter 10. For this chapter and in Chapter 9 we employ two-tailed rejection regions.

Critical Values.   The specific numerical values that define the boundaries of the rejection region are called **critical values.** The critical values for z are found in Table A–1. The first step is to choose a significance level. We use $\alpha = 0.05$ here. Remember that for a two-tailed test, rejection regions are to be located in each tail of the sampling distribution of z. Accordingly, we want the area in each tail of the distribution to equal $\alpha/2$, or in our example, 0.05/2, which equals 0.025. What values of z meet the requirement of locating a boundary such that 0.025 of the area of the sampling distribution of z lies beyond their values in each tail? Consulting Table A–1 we read down Column c until we find the area beyond z equal to 0.025. When we find this area we read the corresponding value of z in Column a. This value of z is 1.96. Thus, the critical values are $z = -1.96$ and $z = +1.96$. For α equal to .05 these are the critical values of z (symbolized as z_{crit}) that locate the rejection regions in the sampling distribution of z.

Decisions about the Statistical Hypotheses

A value of z_{obs} equal to or less than $z_{crit} = -1.96$, or equal to or greater than $z_{crit} = +1.96$, falls into a rejection region. Values of z_{obs} that fall into a rejection region are statistically rare if H_0 is true. They are more common occurrences, however, if H_1 is true. Thus, a value of z_{obs} falling into a rejection region leads the behavioral scientist to reject H_0 and accept H_1. The rejection regions and corresponding decisions regarding H_0 are illustrated in Figure 8–3.

For our example on popliteal height, $z_{obs} = -3.08$. This z_{obs} falls into the lower rejection region; it is less than -1.96. Thus, we reject H_0: $\mu = 42.1$ cm and accept H_1: $\mu \neq 42.1$ cm. We reject the hypothesis that the sample represents a population with a mean of 42.1 cm. The sample was obtained from a population with a mean other than 42.1 cm. Because the sample mean, $\overline{X} = 41.3$ cm, is less than the hypothesized population mean of 42.1 cm, we conclude that the mean popliteal height of the

FIGURE 8–3.

Illustration of rejection regions on the sampling distribution of the z statistic for a two-tailed test and $\alpha = .05$. A value of z_{obs} that falls into either rejection region leads to rejection of H_0 and acceptance of H_1.

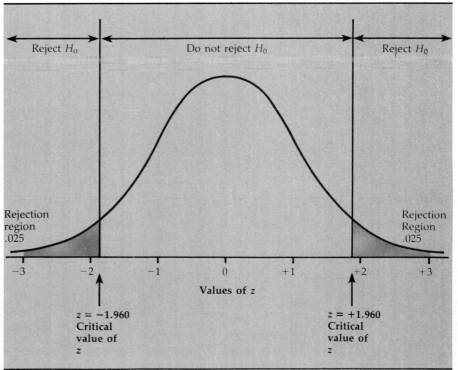

foreign drivers is less than 42.1 cm. The best point estimate we have of this population mean is the sample mean, $\overline{X} = 41.3$ cm.

We may summarize the relationship between the value of z_{obs}, the rejection regions, and decisions about the statistical hypotheses as follows:

- If z_{obs} falls into a rejection region, then H_0 is rejected and H_1 is accepted.
- If z_{obs} does not fall into a rejection region, then H_0 is not rejected (often stated as "failed to reject H_0") and H_1 is not accepted.

Statistically Significant Difference

If the observed test statistic falls into a rejection region when $\alpha = .05$, then we reject the null hypothesis deciding that it is more likely that the observed difference between the sample mean and the hypothesized population mean is due to factors other than chance alone. This difference is then said to be **statistically significant.** The implication of a statistically significant difference between the obtained sample mean and the hypothesized population mean is that the sample mean is considered an estimate of a population mean different from the hypothesized population mean.

Statistically significant results often are reported in scientific articles in the form $z_{obs} = -3.08$, $p \leq .05$. This report tells the reader that the null hypothesis was rejected at the .05 significance level because the probability (p) of z_{obs} when the null hypothesis is true is equal to or less than .05, i.e., $p \leq .05$. The decisions and conclusions reached from a significant difference with the z test are summarized in the left column of Table 8–1.

Statistically Nonsignificant Difference

If the obtained value of the test statistic does not fall into a rejection region, then the null hypothesis is not rejected and the results are regarded as **statistically nonsignificant.** In such an instance, then, a difference between a sample mean and a population mean is not statistically significant and $p > .05$. The observed difference between $\overline{X}$ and the hypothesized μ may be due simply to sampling error. The decisions and conclusions reached from a nonsignificant difference with the z test are summarized in the right column of Table 8–1.

Summary of the Steps of Statistical Hypothesis Testing

All statistical tests require that we:

- formulate two statistical hypotheses, H_0 and H_1,
- obtain the sampling distribution of the test statistic under H_0,
- select a significance level,

TABLE 8–1.

Summary of decisions and conclusions in statistical hypothesis testing using the z test for testing a sample mean against an hypothesized population mean.

If z_{obs} Falls into a Rejection Region for $\alpha = .05$, then:	If z_{obs} Does *Not* Fall into a Rejection Region for $\alpha = .05$, then:
p of z_{obs} is less than or equal to .05, $p \le .05$.	p of z_{obs} is greater than .05, or $p > .05$.
The null hypothesis (H_0) is rejected.	The null hypothesis (H_0) is is not rejected.
The alternative hypothesis (H_1) is accepted. The sample mean estimates a population mean different from the hypothesized population mean.	The alternative hypothesis (H_1) is not accepted.
The difference between the sample mean and the hypothesized population mean is statistically significant at the .05 level.	The difference between the sample mean and the hypothesized population mean is not statistically significant at the .05 level, or a nonsignificant difference was obtained.
It is decided that something in addition to sampling error is responsible for the difference between the sample mean and the hypothesized population mean.	It is decided that sampling error may be the most plausible explanation of the difference between the sample mean and the hypothesized population mean.

- find a critical value or values of the test statistic,
- locate a rejection region or regions in the sampling distribution of the test statistic,
- formulate decision rules regarding the statistical hypotheses,
- calculate the value of the test statistic on the sample data, and
- make decisions about H_0 and H_1 from the observed value of the test statistic, based upon whether the statistic does or does not fall into the rejection region.

 Example Problem 8–1

Does a stop-smoking program have an effect? Using the z statistic

Problem:

Suppose that among a population of adolescent cigarette smokers the mean number of cigarettes smoked per day is 16.4 with a standard deviation of 4.8 cigarettes. A counselor has developed a program of information designed to reduce cigarette smoking among adolescents and asks you to test this program. You randomly select 100 adolescent smokers and enroll them in the program. After the program ends you obtain a measure of the number of cigarettes smoked each day by each subject. You find that the sample mean is 15.1. Is this sample mean different from the population mean of 16.4 cigarettes per day? Use a two-tailed test and a .05 significance level.

Statistic to be used: $z_{obs} = \dfrac{\overline{X} - \mu}{\sigma \overline{X}}$

Assumptions for use:

1. The individuals measured were randomly and independently drawn from a population of adolescent smokers.
2. The number of cigarettes smoked per day in the population sampled is normally distributed.

Statistical hypotheses: H_0: μ = 16.4 cigarettes per day;
H_1: $\mu \neq$ 16.4 cigarettes per day

Significance level: α = .05

Critical value of z: z_{crit} = + or − 1.96

Rejection regions: Values of z_{obs} equal to or less than −1.96 or equal to or greater than +1.96.

Calculation: $z_{obs} = \dfrac{\overline{X} - \mu}{\sigma \overline{X}}$

$z_{obs} = \dfrac{15.1 - 16.4)}{(4.8/\sqrt{100})}$

$z_{obs} = \dfrac{-1.3}{0.48}$

$z_{obs} = -2.71.$

Decision: z_{obs} is less than −1.96. Thus, we reject H_0 and accept H_1.

Conclusion:
The difference between the sample mean of 15.1 cigarettes per day and the population mean of 16.4 cigarettes per day is statistically significant; the sample mean is from a population where the mean number of cigarettes smoked per day is less than 16.4. The sample of adolescent smokers exposed to the program smokes fewer cigarettes per day than the population of adolescent smokers. ■

Example Problem 8–2
Susceptibility to diabetes: Using the z statistic

Problem:

Ethnic and racial groups often differ in their susceptibility to various diseases. It is known, for example, that Mexican Americans are more at risk for noninsulin dependent diabetes mellitus (diabetes that typically develops after age 40) than are non-Hispanic white Americans (Haffner, Stern, Hazuda, Pugh, & Patterson, 1986). To investigate this difference, suppose we obtain a sample of 125 Mexican-American males free of diabetes mellitus. We have them fast for 12 hours and then measure their blood-plasma glucose level. The mean blood-plasma glucose level for the sample is 85.2 milligrams of glucose per deciliter of blood (mg/dl). The population mean of blood-plasma glucose level for non-Hispanic white American males is 84.2 mg/dl with $\sigma = 9.51$ mg/dl. Does the sample mean for the Mexican-American males differ from the population mean for non-Hispanic white American males at the .01 significance level?

Statistic to be used: $z_{obs} = \dfrac{\overline{X} - \mu}{\sigma_{\overline{X}}}$

Assumptions for use:

1. The Mexican Americans measured were randomly and independently drawn from a population of nondiabetic Mexican-American males.
2. The fasting blood-plasma glucose level in the population sampled is normally distributed.

Statistical hypotheses: H_0: $\mu = 84.2$ mg/dl;
$\qquad\qquad\qquad\qquad$ H_1: $\mu \neq 84.2$ mg/dl

Significance level: $\alpha = .01$

Critical value of z: $z_{crit} = +$ or $- 2.58$

Rejection regions: Values of z_{obs} equal to or less than -2.58 or equal to or greater than $+2.58$.

Calculation:

$z_{obs} = (\overline{X} - \mu)/\sigma_{\overline{X}}$
$z_{obs} = (85.2 - 84.2)/(9.51/\sqrt{125})$
$z_{obs} = +1.0/0.85$
$z_{obs} = +1.18.$

Decision: z_{obs} falls into the area between $z_{crit} = -2.58$ and $z_{crit} = +2.58$. Thus, it does not fall into a rejection region; accordingly, we fail to reject H_0 and we do not accept H_1.

Conclusion:

The difference between the sample mean of 85.2 mg/dl and the population mean of 84.2 mg/dl in blood-plasma glucose levels is not statistically significant. The observed difference between the sample mean of 85.2 mg/dl and the population mean of 84.2 mg/dl may be due to sampling error. There is no evidence that the fasting blood-plasma glucose level of Mexican-American males differs from that of the population of non-Hispanic white American males. ■

Testing Your Knowledge 8–2

On a separate sheet of paper, test your knowledge of the material in this section by answering the following questions.

1. Define: significance level, alpha level, α, rejection region, two-tailed test, critical value, z_{crit}, statistically significant difference, statistically non-significant difference.
2. Identify the steps involved in statistical hypothesis testing.
3. For each of the following values of z_{obs}, determine whether the z_{obs} falls into a two-tailed rejection region at the .05 significance level. Then indicate your decision for H_0 and H_1. Remember that you either fail to reject or reject H_0, and you do not accept or accept H_1.

z_{obs}
+3.21
+1.43
−2.65
+2.58
−2.36
−0.63
−3.01

4. Complete the following problem and answer the questions asked. Employ a .05 significance level and a two-tailed test.

Problem: The population mean for an intelligence scale is 100 and $\sigma = 15$. You are the principal of an elementary school in a rural county. For the 117 students in your school, the mean score on this scale is 103.4. Does the mean of the students in your school differ from the population mean?

a. Statistic to be used

b. Assumptions for use

c. Statistical hypotheses

d. Significance level

e. z_{crit}

f. Rejection regions

g. z_{obs}

h. Decision

i. Conclusion

IMPORTANT CONSIDERATIONS IN STATISTICAL HYPOTHESIS TESTING

Why Don't We Accept the Null Hypothesis?

In our discussion of making decisions about the statistical hypotheses, we indicated that if a test statistic does not fall into a rejection region, then we do not reject the null hypothesis. This decision often is stated as "we fail to reject the null hypothesis," or "we cannot reject the null hypothesis." You may wonder why we use this rather awkward phraseology; for, in common terms, if we do not reject something, then we accept it. Why, then, don't we accept the null hypothesis if the test statistic does not fall into a rejection region? To answer this question, let us consider the nature of a null hypothesis and a statistical test.

Return to our example of the height of a truck seat. The seat was designed for a population with a popliteal height of 42.1 cm and $\sigma = 2.6$ cm. Suppose again that you obtained a sample of 100 foreign drivers of your truck and found the mean popliteal height of these drivers was 41.8 cm. The value of z_{obs} for this sample is -1.15 [$z_{obs} = (41.8 - 42.1)/(2.6/\sqrt{100})$]. This z_{obs} does not fall into the rejection region defined by $z_{crit} = +$ or $- 1.96$ for $\alpha = .05$. Thus the value of z_{obs} is statistically nonsignificant, and we fail to reject H_0: $\mu = 42.1$ cm. Does this decision imply that the mean of the population from which the sample was drawn must be exactly 42.1 cm? Clearly, the answer to this question is "no." The observed sample mean of 41.8 cm does not imply that the population mean must be 42.1 cm. On the other hand, the observed sample mean of 41.8 cm does not provide any evidence that the population mean may not be 42.1 cm. That is, an $\overline{X}$ of 41.8 cm does not provide evidence that we should reject H_0:

$\mu = 42.1$ cm, but neither does it provide evidence that we should accept that μ is exactly 42.1 cm. At best, then, it provides evidence only that we should not reject $H_0: \mu = 42.1$ cm.

Suppose, however, the sample mean had been $\overline{X} = 41.3$ cm, so that $z_{obs} = -3.08$. This z_{obs} is statistically significant at the .05 level, and we would reject $H_0: \mu = 42.1$ cm and accept $H_1: \mu \neq 42.1$ cm. It is appropriate to accept H_1 because H_1 states that μ is some value other than 42.1 cm, and the observed mean $\overline{X} = 41.3$ cm indicates that μ is some value other than 42.1 cm. In this case, the sample mean of 41.3 cm would provide the best point estimate of μ for the foreign drivers.

The correct terminology to describe decisions about the statistical hypotheses is

- If the test statistic is statistically significant (i.e., it falls into a rejection region), then: reject H_0 and accept H_1.
- If the test statistic is statistically nonsignificant (i.e., it does *not* fall into a rejection region), then: fail to reject H_0 and do not accept H_1.

Why Is the .05 Significance Level Adopted?

It may appear that scientists are unduly conservative about the criterion used to make decisions about the null hypothesis. You may ask, for example, "What if the outcome had been statistically significant at the .06 level or even the .10 level? After all, the probability of the results being due to chance alone is still small. Why not regard an outcome as 'probably' significant if the null hypothesis could be rejected at the .06 or .07 level? Isn't setting the significance level so that 'it is .05 or nothing at all' an unnecessarily rigid criterion?"

The concern is understandable, but scientists typically adopt a conservative stance with respect to making decisions about data. Thus, although somewhat arbitrary, the .05 significance level is a widely accepted convention for statistical significance. Indeed, any difference between a sample mean and a hypothesized population mean that does not reach the usual .05 level of significance is generally viewed skeptically by researchers and interpreted as a chance difference. It should be noted there is some controversy on this issue (see, for example, Brewer, 1987; Franks & Huck, 1986, 1987; and O'Brien & Israel, 1987). Typically, behavioral scientists adhere to the use of α equal to .05 or less.

Type I and Type II Errors in Statistical Tests

A statistical test allows the experimenter to make one of two decisions about the null hypothesis: (1) to reject H_0, or (2) to fail to reject H_0. Either decision may be correct or incorrect depending on whether the null hypothesis is in fact true or not. A **Type I error** occurs if the null hypothesis

TABLE 8–2.

Errors and correct decisions in statistical decision making.

		State of Nature	
		H_0 *True*	H_1 *True*
Decision	H_0 *True*	Correct decision	Type II error
by the			
Experimenter	H_1 *True*	Type I error	Correct decision

is rejected when it actually is true. On the other hand, failing to reject H_0 when it is false and the alternative hypothesis (H_1) is true results in a **Type II error.** The true state of the statistical hypotheses, the decisions made from the statistical test, and the corresponding correct decisions and errors are presented in Table 8–2.

Type I and Type II errors arise because statistical decision making is probabilistic. The probability of a Type I error, for example, is given by the significance level employed. Hence, if H_0 is true for a statistical test and $\alpha = .05$, there is a 1 in 20 chance of making a Type I error. Uncertainty is inevitable in any decision about H_0 and H_1. From any single statistical test a researcher can never know if the correct decision was made about the statistical hypotheses. A number of factors, including sample size and the variability of scores, affect the probability of the occurrence of a Type I or Type II error. We discuss these factors more fully in Chapter 16.

Statistical and Scientific Significance

The use of the word *significant* to characterize a rare outcome in a statistical hypothesis test is unfortunate. Perhaps the most typical connotation to something significant is that it is important. Yet, it is inappropriate to apply this attribution to a statistically significant difference. In statistical testing, significance has one meaning only: a rare outcome, as Carver (1978) states:

> *Statistical significance simply means statistical rareness. Results are "significant" from a statistical point of view because they occur very rarely in random sampling under the conditions of the null hypothesis. (p. 383)*

A statistical test has only one function and that is to permit the researcher to conclude that the observed difference between the sample mean and the hypothesized population mean is not due to chance by using "formal, objective, communicable, and reproducible procedures rather than by intuition" (Winch and Campbell, 1969, p. 143). If a statistically rare result occurs, then the statistical test provides no indication of the reason for this result. The responsibility for determining the reason rests with the experimenter who must examine carefully the conditions of the study and the nature of the data obtained.

It is important to notice that observed values of the test statistic that do not fall into the rejection region are referred to as *nonsignificant* and not as *insignificant*. The word *insignificant* implies that something is lacking importance or is inconsequential. Yet a statistically nonsignificant difference may be scientifically important. For example, in Example Problem 8–2 it may be important for a scientist to know that there is no evidence for a difference in the mean blood-plasma glucose level of a sample of non-diabetic Mexican-American males from the population mean of non-diabetic non-Hispanic white American males. This result is revealed by a statistically nonsignificant difference between the sample mean and the population mean of blood-plasma glucose levels.

The Importance of the z Test

The use of the z statistic requires knowledge of the population standard deviation, σ. In many instances of actual research, however, σ is unknown. Consequently, the z statistic is used infrequently in practice. Why, then, have we introduced the z statistic in such detail? The answer to this question is that knowledge of principles of statistical hypothesis testing using the z test is immediately transferable to all the statistical tests that follow in this text. Therefore, if you understand the basic concepts of hypothesis testing using the z test, you have established a solid base for understanding statistical hypothesis testing with other statistical tests. In the next chapter we introduce a more widely used statistical test, the t test, which permits the experimenter to use $\sigma_{\overline{X}}$ estimated from sample data. The basic principles of hypothesis testing with this test are identical to those employed with the z test.

Testing Your Knowledge 8–3

On a separate sheet of paper, test your knowledge of the material in this section by answering the following questions.

1. Define: Type I error, Type II error.
2. Explain why the null hypothesis is not accepted if z_{obs} does not fall into a rejection region.

3. H_0 is true, but on the basis of z_{obs}, an experimenter rejects H_0. What type of error is made here?

4. H_1 is true, but on the basis of z_{obs}, an experimenter fails to reject H_0. What type of error is made here?

5. H_0 is true and on the basis of z_{obs} the experimenter fails to reject H_0. Is this a correct decision or an error?

6. H_1 is true and on the basis of z_{obs} the experimenter rejects H_0. Is this a correct decision or an error?

7. What is the difference between a statistically significant result and a scientifically significant result? ■

SUMMARY

- Statistical tests may be either parametric or nonparametric.
- Statistical testing requires formulating a null hypothesis and an alternative hypothesis.
- The null hypothesis is used to find the sampling distribution of the test statistic.
- The z statistic may be used to test a sample mean against a hypothesized population mean when σ is known.
- The significance level is the probability value that specifies how improbable an observed value of a test statistic must be under a null hypothesis in order to reject that null hypothesis as being true.

- The rejection region represents the values on the sampling distribution of the test statistic (e.g., the z statistic in our example) that have a probability equal to or less than α if the null hypothesis is true.
- The difference between a sample mean and a hypothesized population mean is statistically significant if the test statistic falls into a rejection region. The difference is nonsignificant if the test statistic does not fall into a rejection region.
- Statistical decision making is inherently probabilistic. A Type I error occurs if a true H_0 is rejected. A Type II error occurs if a false H_0 is not rejected.

KEY TERMS

α	nonparametric tests	statistically nonsignificant difference
alpha level	null hypothesis	statistically significant difference
alternative hypothesis	one-tailed test	test statistic
assumption	parametric tests	two-tailed test
critical values	rejection region	Type I error
hypothesis	σ	Type II error
H_0	significance level	z_{crit}
H_1	statistical hypothesis	z_{obs}

REVIEW QUESTIONS

On a separate sheet of paper, test your knowledge of the material in this chapter by answering the following questions.

1. Identify the assumptions made when employing the z test.
2. State the requirements that any set of statistical hypotheses must meet.
3. What role does the null hypothesis serve in a statistical test?
4. Explain significance level.
5. What is the critical value of a test statistic?
6. What decision is made regarding H_0 and H_1 if
   a. the obtained value of a test statistic falls into the rejected region?
   b. the obtained value of a test statistic does not fall into the rejection region?
7. What decision do you make about the value of a sample mean if z_{obs} falls into a rejection region?
8. What decision do you make about the value of a sample mean if z_{obs} does not fall into a rejection region?
9. For each of the following values of z_{obs}, determine whether the z_{obs} falls into a two-tailed rejection region at the .01 significance level. Then indicate your decision for H_0 and H_1. Remember that you either fail to reject or reject H_0, and you do not accept or accept H_1.

z_{obs}
+3.71
−2.60
+1.74
−3.05
−1.96
+2.58

10. The population mean for a group intelligence scale is 100 and $\sigma = 16$. A school counselor tests 17 10-year-olds on this scale and obtains $\overline{X} = 94.1$. Conduct a statistical test on these data to determine if the difference between the population mean and the sample mean is likely a result of sampling error or is more likely a real difference. Employ a .05 significance level and a two-tailed test.
11. You are told that based on the outcome of a z test, there is a statistically significant difference between a sample mean and a population mean. Explain what is meant by statistical significance in this case.
12. Explain why a researcher does not accept the statistical null hypothesis if the obtained value of a test statistic does not fall into a rejection region.

13. Answer the following:
    a. Define a Type I error.
    b. What is the probability of making a Type I error if H_0 is true?
    c. What is the probability of making a Type I error if H_0 is false?
14. Answer the following:
    a. Define a Type II error.
    b. Is it possible for an experimenter to make both a Type I and a Type II error in the same statistical test? Explain your answer.
15. Distinguish between statistical significance and scientific significance.

9

The One-Sample *t* Test

In Chapter 8 we indicated when using the z statistic, $z = (\overline{X} - \mu)/\sigma_{\overline{X}}$, it would be unusual to know the value of σ for the population from which the scores were sampled. Thus, $\sigma_{\overline{X}}$ also would be unknown. Typically, σ is estimated by s, the standard deviation of the scores in the sample. Consequently, the value of $\sigma_{\overline{X}}$ also is estimated from $s_{\overline{X}}$. When we estimate $\sigma_{\overline{X}}$ from $s_{\overline{X}}$ we obtain a new statistic, the t, defined as

$$t = \frac{\overline{X} - \mu}{s_{\overline{X}}}$$

or, equivalently, substituting $s/\sqrt{N}$ for $s_{\overline{X}}$,

$$t = \frac{\overline{X} - \mu}{(s/\sqrt{N})}.$$

As with the z test, this t statistic may be used to test the difference between a sample mean and a hypothesized population mean for statistical significance. Because only one sample mean is involved in this test, the statistic is called the **one-sample t** to distinguish it from a t test involving two sample means that we introduce in Chapter 10. The one-sample t is a more widely used test than the z, for it allows σ to be estimated by s.

The t statistic was developed by the British mathematician William Sealy Gosset shortly after the turn of the twentieth century. Gosset, employed as a brewer for Messrs. Guiness, published his work under the pseudonym of "Student." Consequently, the t statistic is often identified as "Student's t."

THE ONE-SAMPLE t TEST: COMPARING A SAMPLE MEAN WITH A HYPOTHESIZED POPULATION MEAN

Theoretical Sampling Distribution of t

The z statistic, because its computation involves the population parameter $\sigma_{\overline{X}}$, has only one sampling distribution, the distribution presented in Table A–1. The t statistic, however, uses s, the sample standard deviation. Therefore, there are many t distributions. In Chapter 5, we defined s as

$$s = \sqrt{\frac{\Sigma(X_i - \overline{X})^2}{(N - 1)}}.$$

Notice that the calculation of *s* involves the sample size, *N*. Therefore, the value of *t* also is sensitive to sample size. Consequently, the theoretical sampling distribution of *t* varies with *N*. As a result, there is a family of theoretical sampling distributions for the *t* statistic. More specifically, the theoretical sampling distributions of *t* depend upon the degrees of freedom of the sample.

Degrees of Freedom

Degrees of freedom (abbreviated *df*) is determined by the number of scores that are free to vary when calculating a statistic. Several examples will be helpful in understanding what is meant by "scores free to vary" when computing a statistic. Suppose we ask you to choose three scores on a test. In response to this request, you may choose any three scores, say 75, 62, and 97. For this request there are no limitations on the scores that you may choose; each score is free to vary. Accordingly, there are *N* or 3 *df* for this set of scores. Consider a second request, however, where you are asked to choose three scores, but the sum of the three scores must be 254. You choose 81 and 78 as your first two scores; they could have any value you desired. These two scores were free to vary. Is the third score also free to vary? It is not. Because the three scores must total 254, the third score must be 95; no other score provides a total of 254. Consequently, if you are told the total of the scores is 254, two scores are free to vary, but the value of the third score is "fixed" by the value of the two scores free to vary and the total that is to be obtained. Accordingly, if we know the total of the three scores, then there are $N - 1 = 3 - 1 = 2$ degrees of freedom for the three scores.

Applying this reasoning to the calculation of common statistics, the sample mean, $\overline{X}$, has *N df*. All scores in a set of scores are free to vary when calculating the mean. To illustrate, suppose we ask you to calculate the sample mean of a set of five scores, four of which are 7, 10, 3, and 6. Given only this information you cannot find the mean. The fifth score may assume any value, and there is no way that you can deduce what the fifth score is from knowledge of the four scores. Thus, all *N* scores (where *N* = 5 for this example) are free to vary when calculating the sample mean.

The degrees of freedom for the sample standard deviation, *s*, however, are *N* − 1. To illustrate why *s* possesses *N* − 1 *df*, suppose you are asked to calculate *s* on a sample of five scores. The sample standard deviation is defined as

$$s = \sqrt{\frac{\Sigma(X_i - \overline{X})^2}{(N - 1)}}$$

or, more briefly as

$$s = \sqrt{\frac{SS}{(N-1)}}.$$

To compute the SS, you must obtain and square each $X_i - \overline{X}$ value. The first step in computation, then, is to obtain $\overline{X}$. Assume that you perform this step and find that the mean of the five scores is 13.4. Now only four of the five scores, or $N - 1$ scores, are free to vary in calculating the sum of squares. Suppose that four of the five scores have values of 13, 15, 13, and 12. Knowing that the mean of the five scores is 13.4, it is now possible for you to determine the value of the fifth score; it must be 14, because no other value of X_i, given that four of the five scores are known, will yield a mean of 13.4.

We can reason to this result also by knowing that $\Sigma(X_i - \overline{X}) = 0$. Suppose we subtract $\overline{X}$ from each of the four known scores:

$$X_i - \overline{X}$$
$$13 - 13.4 = -0.4$$
$$15 - 13.4 = +1.6$$
$$13 - 13.4 = -0.4$$
$$12 - 13.4 = -1.4.$$

The sum of these four $X_i - \overline{X}$ deviations is -0.6. When the fifth score is included in the set, this sum must be zero. Thus, we recognize that the fifth score must result in an $X_5 - \overline{X}$ value of $+0.6$, for $+0.6$ added to -0.6 will equal zero. Thus, if $X_5 - 13.4 = +0.6$, X_5 must equal 14. Accordingly, if $\overline{X}$ is known for the set of five scores, the values of only four of the five scores are free to vary. The value of the fifth score is not free to vary; its value is fixed by the restriction that the value of the mean imposes. Because the sample mean must be known to calculate s, all but one score is free to vary in calculating the sample standard deviation. Generally, when calculating either s or s^2, a set of N scores possesses $N - 1$ df.

We can apply this knowledge of degrees of freedom to the formula for s, $s = \sqrt{SS/(N-1)}$, and write this formula more briefly. Because $N - 1$ represents the degrees of freedom when obtaining an SS, the sample standard deviation can be expressed as the square root of the sum of squared deviations (SS) divided by the degrees of freedom (df), or

$$s = \sqrt{\frac{SS}{df}}.$$

We will find this expression of s very useful in later chapters.

Degrees of Freedom for the One-Sample *t* Test

We now return to the *t* statistic, $t = (\overline{X} - \mu)/s_{\overline{X}}$, and apply our knowledge of *df* to this statistic. The estimated standard error of the mean, $s_{\overline{X}}$, is given by $s/\sqrt{N}$. Because *s* has $N - 1$ *df*, $s_{\overline{X}}$, too, has $N - 1$ *df*. Hence, the degrees of freedom for the sampling distribution of the one-sample *t* statistic are $N - 1$ also. These degrees of freedom determine the shape of the sampling distribution for this *t*.

The Sampling Distribution of the *t* Statistic

There is a different theoretical sampling distribution of *t* for each number of *df*. And because potentially any number of scores can be obtained in a sample, there is virtually an unlimited number of *df* ranging from 1 to infinity for the *t* statistic. Three different sampling distributions of *t*, for 2, 4, and 60 *df* are illustrated in Figure 9–1.

Notice how the shape of the *t* distribution changes with its degrees of freedom and therefore with sample size. Notice also that the *t* distribution is similar to the normal distribution in several respects. Each *t* distribution is symmetrical, unimodal, and has a mean equal to zero. Consider why these properties arise. When a null hypothesis, such as H_0: μ = some hypothesized value of the population mean, is true, the expected value of *t* will be zero, because the average $\overline{X} - \mu$ value in a sampling distribution from such a population will be zero. But, even when H_0 is true, values of $\overline{X} - \mu$ will vary around a mean of zero because of sampling error. Further, we expect that $\overline{X}$ will be larger than μ about as often as it is smaller than μ. Therefore, in the long run, the $\overline{X} - \mu$ values will be positive and negative equally often when the null hypothesis is true. Consequently, the expected *t* values will be symmetrical around a mean of zero.

For an infinite number of degrees of freedom (a theoretical but not actual possibility) the sampling distribution of *t* is the same as the normal. All other *t* distributions differ, however, from a normal distribution. In general, the distribution of *t* is flatter and wider (the possible values are more spread out) than a normal distribution. As you can see in Figure 9–1, the flattest and widest *t* distributions are those based on the smallest sample sizes; for example, compare the top distribution, *df* = 2 (thus *N* = 3), with the bottom distribution, *df* = 60 (thus *N* = 61). In Chapter 6 we discussed ranges within which normally distributed scores were expected to fall. Recall that in a standard normal distribution a range of $\mu \pm 1.96\sigma_{\overline{X}}$ encompasses exactly 95 percent of the values of *z*. Because a *t* distribution is spread out more, however, a larger percentage of *t* values falls in the tails of the distribution than occurs with the value of *z*. Therefore, a larger range of *t* values will always be required to encompass 95 percent of the values of *t*.

Why Are Degrees of Freedom Used Rather than *N*?   If the *df* for the one-sample *t* test are given by $N - 1$, you may wonder why we have not

FIGURE 9–1.

Sampling distributions of the *t* statistic for 2, 4, and 60 *df*.

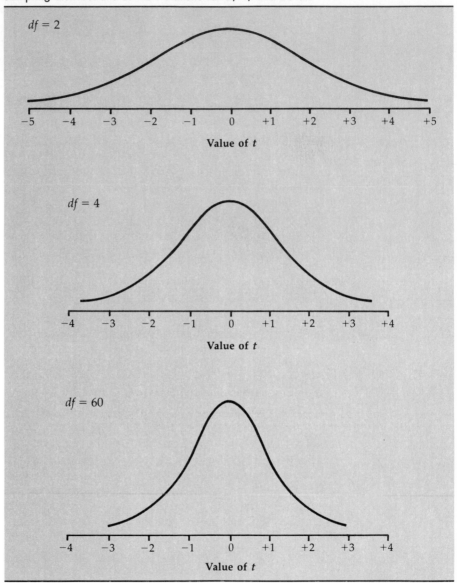

presented the sampling distribution of *t* in terms of *N* rather than degrees of freedom. And, indeed, for the one-sample *t* statistic we have gained no advantage by employing *df* rather than *N*, for the *df* are always one less than *N*. The advantage of employing *df*, however, becomes apparent in

Chapter 10 when we introduce another *t* statistic used for comparing two sample means. For this *t*, the *df* are $N - 2$ rather than $N - 1$. When equated for *df*, however, both *t* tests possess the same sampling distribution.

Testing Your Knowledge 9–1

On a separate sheet of paper, test your knowledge of the material in this section by answering the following questions.

1. Write the formula for the one-sample *t* statistic.
2. Why is the *t* statistic sometimes called Student's *t*?
3. You are given seven scores: 73, 42, 51, 68, 49, 62, and 57. How many *df* does this set of scores possess for calculating
   a. $\overline{X}$?
   b. *s*?
   c. s^2?
4. Assume you plan to compute the one-sample *t* statistic on samples of the following sizes. For each sample, find the *df*.

$$N$$

N
10
16
7
54
100
30

5. Identify three characteristics of the theoretical sampling sample of the *t* statistic.
6. Assume that you have two theoretical sampling distributions of *t*, one with 13 *df* and one with 27 *df*. Which distribution will be wider and flatter?
7. Under what conditions will the sampling distribution of the *t* statistic be identical to the sampling distribution of *z*? ■

STATISTICAL HYPOTHESIS TESTING WITH THE ONE-SAMPLE *t*

Knowing the theoretical sampling distribution of *t* allows us to employ the *t* statistic to determine whether a sample mean differs from a hypothesized population mean by an amount greater than we may expect from sampling error alone. The procedure for statistical hypothesis testing with the t is identical to that described for the z statistic in Chapter 8. The necessary steps include:

- formulating two statistical hypotheses, H_0 and H_1,
- obtaining the sampling distribution of t statistic under H_0,
- setting a significance level,
- finding a critical value or values of the t,
- locating a rejection region or regions in the sampling distribution of the t,
- formulating decision rules regarding the statistical hypotheses,
- calculating the value of t on the sample data, and
- making decisions about H_0 and H_1 from the observed value of t.

Watching Television: An Example Problem

To illustrate the application of these steps, consider the following problem. Suppose a researcher studying a group of 100 third-graders in an experimental after-school care program found that for a weekday the children watched an average of 86.2 minutes of television with an s of 26.5 minutes. Suppose it is also known that the population mean for time spent watching television by third-graders on a weekday is 95.0 minutes. The question asked by the researcher was whether the sample mean of 86.2 minutes differs significantly from the population mean of 95.0 minutes. Because σ is estimated by s, the one-sample t test will be used to answer this question.

Formulating Statistical Hypotheses

The statistical hypotheses for the one-sample t statistic are identical to those of the z statistic. The **null hypothesis,** H_0, is stated as a value of a population mean. The **alternative hypothesis,** H_1, is a statement that the population mean is not that hypothesized in H_0. Accordingly, for our example problem, the statistical hypotheses expressed in notation are:

$$H_0: \mu = 95.0 \text{ minutes},$$

and, $$H_1: \mu \neq 95.0 \text{ minutes}.$$

Obtaining the Sampling Distribution of the t Statistic

The z statistic has only one sampling distribution; thus this step is not of concern to us when using the z. The t statistic, however, possesses a family of sampling distributions, each distribution dependent upon the degrees of freedom for the t calculated on the sample scores. Accordingly, to obtain the sampling distribution of t we must find the df for the t statistic we are calculating. The *df* for *t* are provided by $N - 1$; for our example of a $\overline{X}$ based on 100 scores, the *df* for $t = 100 - 1$, or 99. The sampling distribution for *t* will be based on 99 *df*. After we set a significance level and locate rejection regions we will use this number with a table of the sampling distribution of *t* to find critical values of *t*.

Setting a Significance Level

The significance level is a probability level that establishes how improbable under H_0 an observed value of *t* must be in order to reject H_0 as true. Either the .05 or .01 significance level is typically employed in statistical hypothesis testing. For our example, we employ a .05 level.

Locating the Rejection Regions for *t*

A rejection region is composed of values in the theoretical sampling distribution of a statistic that occur rarely when a null hypothesis is true. For the *t* statistic, similarly to the *z* statistic, these are values in either tail of the sampling distribution of *t*. Let us see why.

As illustrated in Figure 9–1, when H_0 is true, most values of *t* will be clustered around zero in the middle of the distribution. This clustering will occur because most values of $\overline{X}$ will differ only slightly from μ if H_0 is true. Because of sampling error, however, some values of *t* will be at either end of the distribution even when H_0 is true. These values are obtained when the numerator of the statistic (i.e., the difference $\overline{X} - \mu$) is large compared to the denominator (i.e., $s_{\overline{X}}$). But these large values of *t* are rare occurrences if the null hypothesis is true.

On the other hand, if H_1 is true and $\overline{X}$ represents a sample from a population with a mean other than μ, then large values of $\overline{X} - \mu$, and thus of *t*, are expected to occur more frequently. Hence, the rejection region for the *t* is two-tailed. It is composed of large positive and negative values of *t*, which occur with a probability equal to α if the null hypothesis is true but occur much more frequently if H_1 is true. Thus, a rejection region is located in each tail of the theoretical sampling distribution of *t*. The total probability of a rare outcome as defined by the significance level is divided between the tails. Accordingly, when two rejection regions are established — one in each tail of the *t* distribution, and $\alpha = .05$, each rejection region encompasses a probability of $\alpha/2$, or .025. If the value of *t* calculated on the scores of the sample falls into either rejection region, then the null hypothesis is rejected and the alternative hypothesis accepted.

The two rejection regions for the sampling distribution of *t* based upon 8 degrees of freedom are illustrated in Figure 9–2. For 8 *df*, if H_0 is true, then the probability that a *t* value will be equal to or less than -2.306 is .025, and the probability that it will be equal to or larger than

FIGURE 9–2.
Two-tailed rejection regions for the *t* distribution for 8 *df* and $\alpha = .05$.

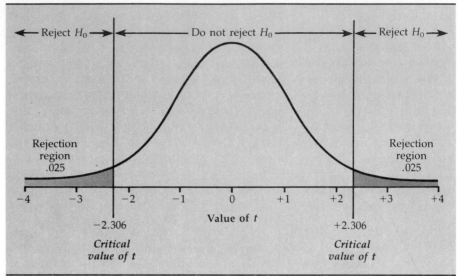

+2.306 is also .025. Any *t* observed from a sample (identified as t_{obs}) equal to or less than −2.306 or equal to or larger than +2.306 lies within a rejection region; such an outcome will occur only 5 percent of the time when the null hypothesis is true. By locating two rejection regions, one in each tail of the theoretical *t* distribution, the experimenter covers both possibilities implied by the alternative hypothesis. The total probability of an outcome in either of the two areas if H_0 is true is .05.

You may be curious about how the values of −2.306 and +2.306 were obtained. We obtained them from a table of critical values of the sampling distribution of *t*. The use of this table is explained in the next section.

Using the Table of Critical *t* Values

The sampling distribution of *t* depends upon the degrees of freedom involved. Consequently, for a particular significance level the critical *t* values needed for locating the rejection regions (identified as t_{crit}) differ depending upon the sample size. Although figures of the sampling distribution of *t*, such as those illustrated in Figure 9–1, are useful to visualize how the shape of the *t* distribution varies with the degrees of freedom, it would be extremely difficult to find exact values of t_{crit} from such figures. Fortunately, however, precise values of t_{crit} for the .05 and .01 significance levels have been calculated and are presented in tables.

To explain the use of a table of critical *t* values, we present in Table 9–1 the two-tailed values of t_{crit} for $\alpha = .05$ and .01. Table 9–1 is part of

Table A–2 in the Appendix. The first column lists degrees of freedom for *t* distributions. The values shown in any row in the .05 or .01 columns are the two-tailed values of t_{crit} for the corresponding degrees of freedom for that significance level. For example, if the significance level is .05, the two-tailed t_{crit} value for 8 degrees of freedom is 2.306. Notice that this value is not preceded by a plus or minus sign. Rather, it is presented as an absolute value of *t*. For purposes of locating rejection regions, however, this value should be treated as both −2.306 and +2.306. Similarly, for α = .01, the two-tailed t_{crit} value for 8 degrees of freedom is 3.355.

Table 9–1 shows that the value of t_{crit} decreases as the degrees of freedom for *t* increase. To understand this relationship, recall that the *t* distribution is more spread out when fewer degrees of freedom are involved; thus, the t_{crit} values will lie farther away from zero with fewer *df*. Moreover, a significance level of .01 imposes a more stringent criterion for defining a rare chance outcome. Therefore, for all degrees of freedom, the t_{crit} value is larger for α = .01 than for α = .05. Any observed $\overline{X} - \mu$ difference will have to be more standard errors away from zero to be regarded as a rare chance occurrence when a .01 significance level is adopted instead of .05.

TABLE 9–1.

Critical Values of the *t* Distribution for α = .05 and α = .01. The values provided are for a two-tailed test.

df	α = .05	α = .01	df	α = .05	α = .01
1	12.706	63.657	18	2.101	2.878
2	4.303	9.925	19	2.093	2.861
3	3.182	5.841	20	2.086	2.845
4	2.776	4.604	21	2.080	2.831
5	2.571	4.032	22	2.074	2.819
6	2.447	3.707	23	2.069	2.807
7	2.365	3.499	24	2.064	2.797
8	2.306	3.355	25	2.060	2.787
9	2.262	3.250	26	2.056	2.779
10	2.228	3.169	27	2.052	2.771
11	2.201	3.106	28	2.048	2.763
12	2.179	3.055	29	2.045	2.756
13	2.160	3.012	30	2.042	2.750
14	2.145	2.977	40	2.021	2.704
15	2.131	2.947	60	2.000	2.660
16	2.120	2.921	120	1.980	2.617
17	2.110	2.898	∞	1.960	2.576

Reprinted with permission from Table IV.1 Percentage Points, Student's *t*-Distribution, *CRC Handbook of Tables for Probability and Statistics* (2nd ed.). Copyright 1968, CRC Press, Inc., Boca Raton, Florida.

Observe that only selected critical values beyond 30 degrees of freedom are included in the table. Thus for many studies employing sample sizes larger than 30, the exact values of t_{crit} are not included. This situation rarely poses a problem for the investigator, however. In such cases we recommend that the t_{crit} value be based upon the number of degrees of freedom in the table that is closest to but smaller than the degrees of freedom associated with the t_{obs}.

For instance, in our example of television watching by third-graders, the sample size is 100; thus the degrees of freedom for t are 99. Table 9–1 shows t_{crit} values for 60 and 120 df but none between. Accordingly, following our recommendation, we use 60 df to determine the t_{crit} (which is 2.000 for $\alpha = .05$) instead of 120 df. This procedure makes the t test slightly more conservative with respect to Type I errors, because the actual significance level used is somewhat smaller than .05. That is, the t_{crit} for 60 df is somewhat larger than the t_{crit} for 99 df. If 120 df were used to find the t_{crit} instead, then the significance level would be slightly greater than .05. If t_{obs} falls into the rejection region for 60 df, then, of course it will also be in the rejection region for 99 df. Should t_{obs} (e.g., t_{obs} = 1.990) fall between the tabled values for the next lower df (e.g., t_{crit} = 2.000 for 60 df) and the next higher df (e.g., t_{crit} = 1.980 for 120 df), then a more accurate value of t_{crit} can be interpolated from the tabled values.

Calculating the Value of *t*

The t statistic for comparing a sample mean to a hypothesized population mean is defined as:

$$t_{obs} = \frac{\overline{X} - \mu}{s_{\overline{X}}}.$$

The calculation of this statistic requires substitution of appropriate values of $\overline{X}$, the hypothesized value of μ, and $s_{\overline{X}}$ into the formula. For our example of 100 scores of third-graders watching television, $\overline{X}$ = 86.2 minutes, s = 26.5 minutes, and N = 100. The hypothesized value of μ is 95.0 minutes. The value of $s_{\overline{X}}$ is obtained from $s/\sqrt{N}$; thus $s_{\overline{X}}$ = $26.5/\sqrt{100}$, which equals 2.65. As a result

$$t_{obs} = \frac{86.2 - 95.0}{2.65}$$

$$t_{obs} = \frac{-8.8}{2.65}$$

$$t_{obs} = -3.321 \text{ with } 99 \ df.$$

Decisions about the Statistical Hypotheses

The decision rules for statistical hypotheses remain the same for all statistical tests. Accordingly, for the one-sample *t* test,

- If t_{obs} falls into a rejection region, then
  reject H_0
  accept H_1.
- If the t_{obs} does not fall into a rejection region, then
  fail to reject H_0
  do not accept H_1.

The two-tailed value of t_{crit} for 99 *df* is 2.000. Accordingly, for a two-tailed test, t_{obs} equal to or less than -2.000 or equal to or larger than $+2.000$ falls into a rejection region. The t_{obs} of -3.321 calculated on the 100 television watching times is more extreme than the tabled critical value of -2.000 and therefore falls into a rejection region for the .05 significance level. The statistical decisions are then to reject H_0: $\mu = 95.0$ minutes, and accept H_1: $\mu \neq 95.0$ minutes. The difference between the sample mean and the population mean is statistically significant at the .05 level. Accordingly, we infer that the sample mean of 86.2 minutes is from a population with a mean less than 95.0 minutes. The mean amount of TV viewing by the third-graders in the experimental after-school program is significantly less than the population mean of 95.0 minutes per day.

If t_{obs} had fallen between the two critical values of -2.000 and $+2.000$ (for example, if $\overline{X}$ had been 90.6 minutes and $t_{obs} = -1.660$), then the opposite statistical decisions would be made: t_{obs} would not lie within a rejection region, and we would fail to reject H_0 and would not accept H_1. The observed difference between the sample mean and hypothesized population mean would be nonsignificant. There is no evidence that the null hypothesis is not true.

The decisions about the statistical hypotheses and the conclusions reached from either a statistically significant or a statistically nonsignificant one-sample *t* test are summarized in Table 9–2.

Assumptions of the One-Sample *t* Test

The one-sample *t* test makes the following assumptions about the scores in the sample.

- The scores in the sample are drawn randomly from a population of scores and each score is independent of each other score.
- The scores in the population sampled are distributed normally.

TABLE 9–2.

Summary of decisions and conclusions in statistical hypothesis testing using the one-sample t test.

If t_{obs} falls into a rejection region for $\alpha = .05$, then:	If t_{obs} does *not* fall into a rejection region for $\alpha = .05$, then:
p of t_{obs} is less than or equal to .05, or $p \leq .05$.	p of t_{obs} is greater than .05, or $p > .05$.
The null hypothesis (H_0) is rejected.	The null hypothesis (H_0) is not rejected.
The alternative hypothesis (H_1) is accepted. The sample mean is from a population with a mean different from the hypothesized population mean.	The alternative hypothesis (H_1) is not accepted.
The difference between the sample mean and the hypothesized population mean is statistically significant at the .05 level.	The difference between the sample mean and the hypothesized population mean is nonsignificant at the .05 level.
It is decided that something in addition to sampling error is responsible for the difference between the sample mean and the hypothesized population mean.	It is decided that sampling error is the most plausible explanation of the difference between the sample mean and the hypothesized population mean.

Example Problem 9–1
Using the one-sample t test

Problem:

Psychologists have hypothesized that in competitive situations, some individuals are motivated to avoid being too successful in order to minimize criticism and ostracism by peers. A self-report inventory measuring this motivation to avoid success has been developed by Good and Good (1973). Suppose it is known that the population mean for female college seniors on this inventory is 8.6 (where the range of scores may be from 0—low motivation to avoid success—to 29—high motivation to avoid success). Suppose an instructor has developed a course dealing with responding to competitive situations. She gives the fear of success inventory to 33 female college seniors who have completed this course and obtains a mean of 8.1 with $s = 1.31$. Does this sample mean differ significantly from a population mean of 8.6 at the .05 level?

Statistic to be used: Because σ is being estimated by s, the one-sample t test is an appropriate statistical test to provide an answer to the question asked. Therefore,

$$t_{obs} = \frac{\overline{X} - \mu}{s_{\overline{X}}}.$$

Assumptions for use:

1. The individuals measured were randomly and independently drawn from a population of female college seniors.
2. Fear of success scores are distributed normally in the population sampled.

Statistical hypotheses: H_0: $\mu = 8.6$
H_1: $\mu \neq 8.6$

Significance level: $\alpha = .05$

df for *t*: $N - 1 = 33 - 1 = 32$

Critical value of *t*: $t_{crit} = 2.042$. (A critical value of t for 32 df is not presented in Table A–2. Thus, we used the t_{crit} for the next lower df tabled, 30 df.)

Rejection regions: Values of t_{obs} equal to or less than -2.042 or equal to or greater than $+2.042$.

Calculation: $t_{obs} = (\overline{X} - \mu)/s_{\overline{X}}$. Substituting numerical values,

$$t_{obs} = \frac{8.1 - 8.6}{(1.31/\sqrt{33})}$$

$$t_{obs} = \frac{-0.5}{0.228} = -2.193$$

Decision: t_{obs} is more extreme than $t_{crit} = -2.042$. Thus, we reject H_0 and accept H_1.

Conclusion:
The difference between the sample mean of 8.1 and the population mean of 8.6 is statistically significant at the .05 level. The sample mean

is from a population with a mean less than 8.6. The mean fear of success in the sample of female college seniors is significantly less than the population mean of female college seniors. ■

Statistics in Use 9–1

Perception of Illusions: Use of the One-Sample *t* Test

Psychologists study illusions in order to better understand how we perceive the world. One little known illusion is the Morinaga misalignment illusion, illustrated below. The figure is an illusion because the points of each angle do not appear to be aligned on the same vertical axis, although they are. The middle point appears to align with an axis different from the axis on which the bottom and top angles align.

Day and Kasperczyk (1984) investigated the question: Does the illusion occur with shapes other than the angles illustrated? The 12 participants in their experiment (thus, $N = 12$) were asked to adjust the center angle so that its point appeared perfectly aligned with the points of the top and bottom. The error in the adjustment was measured in millimeters (mm). If a subject aligned the points of the three angles perfectly, then he or she would have 0 mm error. On the other hand, if a person adjusted the center angle so that it appeared aligned, but was not, then the measured error was recorded. In one experimental condition employing circles in place of the angles, Day and Kasperczyk found a mean error of 1.44 mm with an *s* of 2.07 mm. Does this measured error represent a real error in perception and not simply a chance difference from a 0 mm error? To answer this question, they conducted a one-sample *t* test to compare this sample mean to a hypothesized population mean of 0 mm error. Thus the null hypothesis was H_0: $\mu = 0$ and H_1: $\mu \neq 0$. The *t* statistic is calculated by $t_{obs} = (\overline{X} - \mu) \div (s/\sqrt{N})$. Substituting the sample mean and standard deviation, $t_{obs} = (1.44 - 0.0)/(2.07/\sqrt{12}) = +2.410$. The *df* for this t_{obs} are $N - 1$, or $12 - 1 = 11$; thus the value of t_{crit} for a two-tailed test with 11 *df* and $\alpha = .05$ is 2.201 (see Table A–2). Accordingly, the rejection regions are t_{obs} equal to or less than -2.201 or equal to or larger than $+2.201$. The t_{obs} of $+2.410$ is larger than t_{crit} of $+2.201$; thus, it falls into the rejection region and H_0: $\mu = 0$ is rejected, and H_1: $\mu \neq 0$ is accepted. Accordingly, Day and Kasperczyk concluded that the mean error they found, $\overline{X} = 1.44$ mm, differs significantly from a hypothesized population mean of 0.0 mm error. Rather it represents a population with a mean greater than 0.0 mm error. The Morinaga misalignment illusion can be produced with circles as well as angles. The illusion appears to be a more general perceptual phenomenon that is not dependent upon a specific stimulus, such as an angle. ▇

Testing Your Knowledge 9–2

On a separate sheet of paper, test your knowledge of the material in this section by answering the following questions.

1. Write null and alternative statistical hypotheses in notation for the one-sample *t* test for each of the following statements.
   a. The population mean for time sleeping per night is 493 minutes.
   b. The population mean on an inventory of depression proneness is 36.1.
2. Using Table 9–1, find the values of t_{crit} for the *df* and value of α indicated. Use a two-tailed test.

df	α
6	.05
17	.01
23	.05
32	.05
39	.05
75	.01
103	.05
256	.05

3. Indicate whether each of the following t_{obs} does or does not fall into a rejection region. Then indicate your decision for H_0 and H_1. Remember that you fail to reject or reject H_0 and you do not accept or accept H_1.

Assume $\alpha = .05$ and use a two-tailed test. The *df* for each t_{obs} are given in parentheses.

$$t_{obs}(19) = +3.014$$
$$t_{obs}(19) = -1.989$$
$$t_{obs}(16) = -2.179$$
$$t_{obs}(16) = +2.040$$
$$t_{obs}(30) = -3.961$$
$$t_{obs}(30) = +2.743$$
$$t_{obs}(6) = -2.364$$
$$t_{obs}(6) = +2.447$$
$$t_{obs}(9) = -2.262$$
$$t_{obs}(37) = +2.938$$
$$t_{obs}(42) = -2.410$$

4. Identify the assumptions underlying the use of the one-sample *t* test.
5. Complete the following problem and answer the questions asked. Use a two-tailed test and .05 significance level. Problem: You are interested in how well people can estimate the passage of time without the use of a watch or clock. To investigate this problem, you ask 11 people to tell you when they think a 7-minute interval has passed without using a watch or clock. The mean of the 11 estimates was 5.8 minutes with $s = 0.8$ minutes. Is your sample mean significantly different from a population mean of 7 minutes?
   a. Statistic to be used?
   b. Assumptions for use?
   c. Statistical hypotheses?
   d. Significance level?
   e. Critical value of the test statistic?
   f. Rejection regions?
   g. Calculation?
   h. Decision?
   i. Conclusion? ▪

REPORTING THE RESULTS OF THE ONE-SAMPLE *t* TEST

In a published scientific journal report a brief textual presentation of the data analysis typically is given in the Results section. The presentation is concise and reports both the relevant descriptive and inferential statistics. We present an illustration of how the results of our example problem of 100 television watching time scores might be described in a published scientific report.

The mean daily amount of time spent watching television for the 100 children was 86.2 minutes ($s = 26.5$ minutes). A one-sample t test revealed that the *sample mean differed significantly from a hypothesized population mean of 95.0 minutes, $t(99) = -3.321$, $p \leq .01$.*

This presentation of the results conveys considerable information about a study to the informed reader. Let us see why by examining each of the components of the report of the *t* test separately.

1. $t(99)$: Identifies the name of the test statistic as the *t*. Because the *t* is identified as one-sample *t*, we know that the test is a comparison of a sample mean against a hypothesized population mean. The degrees of freedom for the test statistic are shown in parentheses. Thus we know also that 100 scores were used in the calculation of *t* (because $df = N - 1$; thus $99 = 100 - 1$).
2. $= -3.321$: Gives the value of t_{obs} (not the t_{crit} value found in Table A–2).
3. $p \leq .01$: Tells us that
   a. The *p* and "less than or equal to" sign ($p \leq$) indicates that the probability of t_{obs} if H_0 is true is less than or equal to 0.01. This value is the probability of t_{obs} if H_0 is true; it is not the value of α selected. Unless otherwise indicated in the report, you may assume the significance level employed was 0.05.
   b. $H_0: \mu = 95.0$ minutes was rejected
      $H_1: \mu \neq 95.0$ minutes was accepted.
   c. The difference of the sample mean from the hypothesized population mean is statistically significant at the .01 level.
   d. The sample mean is considered to be from a population with a mean less than the hypothesized population mean of $\mu = 95.0$ minutes.
   e. If $p > .05$ were reported, then the greater than ($>$) sign indicates that the researcher failed to reject H_0 and the sample mean did not differ significantly from the hypothesized population mean at the .05 significance level.

Testing Your Knowledge 9–3

On a separate sheet of paper, test your knowledge of the material in this section by answering the following questions. These exercises present reports of the use of the t test adapted from results of published studies.

1. The mean weight of the male runners was 70.4 kilograms ($s = 7.6$ kg). A one-sample *t* test revealed that the sample mean did not differ significantly from a hypothesized population mean of 75 kg for 25-year-old males, $t(5) = -1.482$, $p > .05$.
   a. What is the value of the sample mean for the runners?
   b. What is the value of the sample standard deviation for the runners?
   c. What *t* test was used in this study?

    d. What are H_0 and H_1 for this t test?

    e. How many scores were obtained in this study?

    f. What is the value of t_{obs} for this study?

    g. What are the df for this t_{obs}?

    h. What is t_{crit} for $\alpha = .05$ and a two-tailed rejection region?

    i. Do you reject or not reject H_0?

    j. Do you accept or not accept H_1?

    k. Do you conclude that the sample mean differs significantly from the hypothesized population mean?

2. The mean hospital stay for males aged 65 and over with nonterminal diseases was 10.4 days ($s = 2.3$ days). A one-sample t test revealed that the sample mean differed significantly from a hypothesized population mean of 8.7 days, $t(24) = +3.696$, $p \leq .05$.

    a. What is the value of the sample mean for the hospitalized patients?

    b. What is the value of the sample standard deviation for the patients?

    c. What t test was employed in this study?

    d. What are H_0 and H_1 for this t test?

    e. How many scores were obtained in this study?

    f. What is the value of t_{obs} for this study?

    g. What are the df for this t_{obs}?

    h. What is t_{crit} for $\alpha = .05$ and a two-tailed rejection region?

    i. Do you reject or not reject H_0?

    j. Do you accept or not accept H_1?

    k. Do you conclude that the sample mean differs significantly from the hypothesized population mean?　▨

USING THE t STATISTIC TO CONSTRUCT CONFIDENCE INTERVALS FOR THE POPULATION MEAN

Confidence intervals for the population mean were defined in Chapter 7 as intervals in which we have a certain degree of confidence that the interval contains the population mean. In that chapter we constructed these intervals using the sample mean, the z statistic, and the value of $\sigma_{\overline{X}}$. Thus, if $\sigma_{\overline{X}}$ is known, a 95 percent confidence interval for the population mean is given by the interval from

$$\overline{X} - 1.96\sigma_{\overline{X}} \quad \text{to} \quad \overline{X} + 1.96\sigma_{\overline{X}},$$

and a 99 percent confidence interval by the interval from

$$\overline{X} - 2.58\sigma_{\overline{X}} \quad \text{to} \quad \overline{X} + 2.58\sigma_{\overline{X}}.$$

We noted, however, that it is unusual to know the value of σ and therefore of $\sigma_{\overline{X}}$. Consequently, we suggested that in practice, $s_{\overline{X}}$, rather than $\sigma_{\overline{X}}$, is used to determine the limits of the confidence interval. When

$s_{\overline{X}}$ is used, the confidence interval is constructed using the *t* statistic rather than the *z* statistic. Employing the *t* and $s_{\overline{X}}$, then, the 95 percent confidence interval for the population mean is given by the interval from

$$\overline{X} - t_{.05}s_{\overline{X}} \quad \text{to} \quad \overline{X} + t_{.05}s_{\overline{X}},$$

where $\overline{X}$ is the observed sample mean, $s_{\overline{X}}$ the estimated standard error of the mean obtained from $s/\sqrt{N}$, and $t_{.05}$ is the value of t_{crit} at the .05 significance level obtained from a table of the critical values of *t* for a two-tailed test (such as Table 9–1 or Table A–2). Similarly, a 99 percent confidence interval for the population mean is given by the interval from

$$\overline{X} - t_{.01}s_{\overline{X}} \quad \text{to} \quad \overline{X} + t_{.01}s_{\overline{X}}.$$

To illustrate, we compute the 95 percent confidence intervals for the 100 third-graders' television watching time scores with a mean of 86.2 minutes and $s = 26.5$ minutes. As we have discussed, because $N = 100$, there are 99 *df* for this sample. The value of t_{crit} for 99 *df* is obtained from Table A–2. Because 99 *df* are not tabled, however, we use the next lower tabled *df*, 60. With 60 *df*, $t_{.05} = 2.000$. The standard error of the mean, $s_{\overline{X}}$, equals $26.5/\sqrt{100}$, or 2.65 minutes. Thus the 95 percent confidence interval for μ is

$$86.2 - (2.000)(2.65) \quad \text{to} \quad 86.2 + (2.000)(2.65),$$

or, carrying out the mathematical operations indicated,

$$80.9 \quad \text{to} \quad 91.5 \text{ minutes}.$$

The interpretation of this confidence interval is identical to the interpretation of a confidence interval constructed using *z* and $\sigma_{\overline{X}}$. That is, we can say that the 95 percent confidence interval of 80.9 to 91.5 minutes has a .95 probability of including the value of μ.

Example Problem 9–2
Constructing confidence intervals using the *t* statistic

Problem:
As principal of a high school you have obtained standardized achievement test scores on graduating seniors. The mean for 127 students taking the test was 960.0 and $s = 141.0$. What is the 95 percent confidence interval for the population mean?

Solution:
To obtain the 95 percent confidence interval we must substitute appropriate numerical values into the formula:

$$\overline{X} - t_{.05}s_{\overline{X}} \quad \text{to} \quad \overline{X} + t_{.05}s_{\overline{X}}.$$

For 126 *df*, $t_{.05} = 1.980$. The required confidence interval is then found by

$$960.0 - (1.980)\left(\frac{141}{\sqrt{127}}\right) \quad \text{to} \quad 960.0 + (1.980)\left(\frac{141}{\sqrt{127}}\right),$$

which equals

$$960.0 - 24.8 \quad \text{to} \quad 960.0 + 24.8, \quad \text{or} \quad 935.2 \quad \text{to} \quad 984.8.$$

Conclusion:
You can be 95 percent confident that the interval from 935.2 to 984.8 includes the value of the population mean for the test scores. ▪

Statistics in Use 9–2

Premarital Cohabitation: Employing Confidence Intervals

Premarital cohabitation among heterosexual couples is a social phenomenon in the United States and other countries. To gain further understanding of this phenomenon, Gwartney-Gibbs (1986) studied premarital cohabitation by utilizing marriage license application data to obtain demographic information on cohabiting and noncohabiting couples. As part of her results, she reported the mean age of marriage for males and females of couples who had either cohabited or had not cohabited prior to marriage. The mean ages were accompanied by 95 percent confidence intervals for the population mean.

As an example, Gwartney-Gibbs presents the following results for cohabiting and noncohabiting females who had not been married previously.

	Cohabiting	Noncohabiting
N	806	877
Mean age at marriage (yrs.)	22.8	21.7
s (yrs.)	4.6	4.4
95 percent confidence interval	22.48 to 23.12	21.41 to 21.99

We can reconstruct these confidence intervals from the information provided above. We illustrate using the statistics for the cohabiting females. Recall that the 95 percent confidence interval is provided by

$$\overline{X} - t_{.05}s_{\overline{X}} \quad \text{to} \quad \overline{X} + t_{.05}s_{\overline{X}}.$$

For $N = 806$, there are 805 *df*. From Table 9–1 the value of *t* at the .05 significance level is 1.960. Notice we used t_{crit} for an infinite degrees of freedom ($t_{crit} = 1.960$), rather than for the next smaller tabled *df*, 120. Eight hundred five is sufficiently large to be treated as an infinite *df*. As a result, the 95 percent confidence interval is found by

$$22.8 - 1.96\left(\frac{4.6}{\sqrt{806}}\right) \quad \text{to} \quad 22.8 + 1.96\left(\frac{4.6}{\sqrt{806}}\right) \text{years},$$

which equals 22.8 − .32 to 22.8 + .32 years, or an interval from 22.48 to 23.12 years. Consequently, Gwartney-Gibbs can be 95 percent confident that the population mean for age of marriage by cohabiting females falls between 22.48 to 23.12 years. For the noncohabiting females, the 95 percent confidence interval is 21.41 to 21.99 years. The two confidence intervals do not overlap; therefore, Gwartney-Gibbs concluded that cohabiting females typically married at least one-half year later in age than noncohabiting females.   ■

Testing Your Knowledge 9–4

On a separate sheet of paper, test your knowledge of the material in this section by answering the following questions.

1. An experimenter observed the amount of time that adolescents spent playing video games in an arcade. The mean time spent playing per day for a sample of 23 males was 97 minutes with a standard deviation of 39 minutes. Construct a 95 percent confidence interval for the population mean for the amount of time spent playing video games by male adolescents.

2. Davidson and Templin (1986) report that for a sample of 119 professional top money-winning golfers their mean driving distance was 258 yards with an *s* of 6.71 yards. Construct a 95 percent confidence interval for the population mean of driving distance.   ■

SUMMARY

- The one-sample *t* test employs the formula

$$t = \frac{\overline{X} - \mu}{s_{\overline{X}}}.$$

- The sampling distribution of the *t* statistic depends upon the *df* of the *t*.
- Statistical hypothesis testing with the *t* follows the steps common to all hypothesis testing:
  - formulating a null and an alternative hypothesis

- obtaining the sampling distribution of the *t*
- setting a significance level
- finding t_{crit}
- locating a rejection region or regions
- formulating decision rules
- calculating t_{obs}
- making decisions about H_0 and H_1.
- The *t* distribution may be used with $s_{\overline{X}}$ to find confidence intervals for the population mean.

KEY TERMS

alternative hypothesis	null hypothesis	$s_{\overline{X}}$
confidence interval	one-sample t	t statistic
degrees of freedom	rejection region	t_{crit}
df	sampling distribution of t	t_{obs}
H_0	statistically nonsignificant difference	
H_1	statistically significant difference	

REVIEW QUESTIONS

On a separate sheet of paper, test your knowledge of the material in this chapter by answering the following questions.

1. Identify the assumptions made when employing the one-sample t test.
2. What decision do you make about the value of a sample mean if t_{obs} falls into a rejection region?
3. What decision do you make about the value of a sample mean if t_{obs} does not fall into a rejection region?
4. Indicate whether each of the following t_{obs} does or does not fall into a rejection region. Assume $\alpha = .01$ and use a two-tailed test. The df for each t_{obs} are given in parentheses.

$$t_{obs}(18) = +3.713$$
$$t_{obs}\ (7) = -2.615$$
$$t_{obs}(35) = +2.794$$
$$t_{obs}(44) = -3.058$$
$$t_{obs}(74) = -1.960$$
$$t_{obs}(15) = -2.368 .$$

5. You are told that based on the outcome of the t test, there is a statistically significant difference between a sample mean and a population mean. Explain what is meant by a statistically significant difference.
6. Mothers with young children often complain that they do not get enough sleep. Suppose you obtained a measure of the typical amount of sleep of 9 mothers of children under one year of age and found the following durations (in hours): 6.4, 7.7, 6.9, 7.3, 7.6, 7.1, 6.5, 8.1, and 7.8.
   a. Does the mean amount of sleep for these mothers differ significantly from a hypothesized population mean for women of

7.8 hours sleep per night? Use a two-tailed test and a .05 significance level.

b. Describe your results in Question 6a following the example illustrated in the Reporting the Results of the One-Sample *t* Test section of this chapter.

c. Could your decision about the statistical hypotheses in 6a represent the occurrence of a Type I error?

d. Could your decision about the statistical hypotheses in 6a represent the occurrence of a Type II error?

e. Compute the 95 percent confidence interval for the population mean of these scores. Is the hypothesized population mean of 7.8 hours per night included in this interval.

7. A medical researcher attempted to learn if a new disease is accompanied by an increase in body temperature. She measured the body temperature of 12 people diagnosed as having the disease and obtained the following temperatures (in °F): 99.3, 99.1, 100.4, 98.4, 98.2, 98.9, 99.7, 100.1, 100.7, 99.0, 98.8, 99.2.

a. Does the mean body temperature of these individuals differ from a hypothesized population mean of 98.6° F? Use a two-tailed test and a .05 significance level.

b. Could your decision regarding the statistical hypothesis represent a Type II error? Explain your answer.

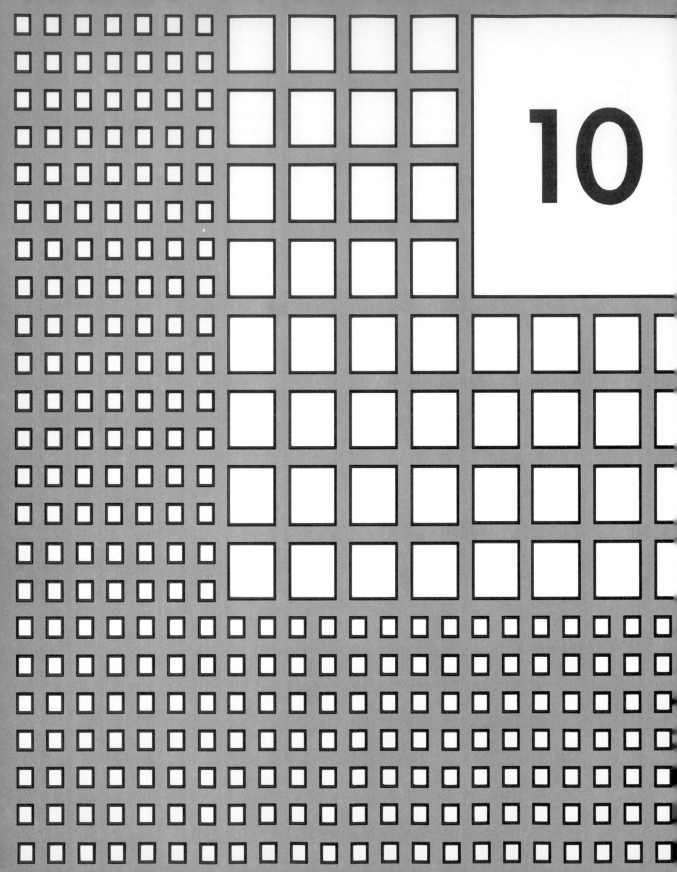

10

Elementary Research Methods and the *t* Test for Two Independent Groups

OVERVIEW: THE NATURE OF A SIMPLE EXPERIMENT

In Chapters 8 and 9 we introduced the use of statistical hypothesis testing to determine if a sample mean differs significantly from a hypothesized population mean. In this chapter, we expand the use of statistical hypothesis testing to compare two sample means to determine if they differ by an amount more than expected by sampling error alone. This form of statistical hypothesis testing is needed to evaluate the results of experimental research. Let us review the characteristics of an experiment.

- A research hypothesis is formulated predicting a relationship of an independent variable and a dependent variable.
- Equivalent groups are formed by randomly assigning individuals to a group. The groups formed thus represent the same population before the independent variable is manipulated.
- Extraneous variables are controlled to prevent confounding.
- The independent variable is manipulated and scores on the dependent variable are recorded.
- Measures of central tendency and variability, frequently the sample mean and standard deviation, are calculated for the scores of each treatment group.
- A statistical test is conducted to determine if the sample means, or other measure of central tendency, differ significantly.
- If the sample means differ significantly, the difference is attributed to the effect of the independent variable.

In this chapter we discuss the design and statistical analysis of the very simplest experiment, one involving only two groups.

TREATMENT OF KAWASAKI SYNDROME: AN EXAMPLE EXPERIMENT

To illustrate the use of statistical hypothesis testing in an experiment, we draw on an example from the area of medical science. Kawasaki syndrome is a serious illness of early childhood that often leads to dangerous cardiovascular problems. The syndrome is characterized by high fever, fissured lips, a bright red tongue, redness of the palms and soles, and a rash. The cause of this syndrome is unknown; treatment typically involves the use of aspirin to reduce the fever. For several reasons, however, Newburger et al. (1986) hypothesized that gamma globulin, a derivative of blood plasma, plus aspirin may be a more effective therapy to reduce the fever than aspirin alone. This statement is a research hypothesis; it predicts a relationship between an independent variable, type of treatment, and a dependent variable, amount of fever. To test this research hypothesis Newburger and her associates conducted an experiment.[1]

The experiment involved creating two equivalent groups of children with Kawasaki syndrome. One group was given a treatment of aspirin every six hours; the other group was given aspirin plus gamma globulin every six hours. The dependent variable measured was body temperature on the second day of treatment. They found the mean body temperature on the second day of treatment to be 38.48°C for the aspirin alone group and 37.60°C for the aspirin plus gamma globulin group.

They analyzed these means using the *t* for independent groups and found the temperature for the aspirin plus gamma globulin group to be significantly lower than the temperature of the aspirin alone group. Consequently, Newburger et al. concluded that aspirin plus gamma globulin more effectively lowers body temperature in Kawasaki syndrome than does aspirin alone.

Conducting an experiment requires a number of steps prior to the statistical analysis of the data. Regardless of the problem investigated, these steps are similar in all experiments and include selection of the participants, assignment of participants to treatment conditions and the creation of equivalent groups, control of extraneous variables, manipulation of the independent variable, and measurement of the dependent variable.

Selection of Participants

Random Sampling

An experiment always is conducted on a sample of participants from a population. To generalize the results of the experiment, the participants in the sample should be representative of the population. To ensure this representativeness, it is recommended that the sample be selected randomly from the population to which inferences are to be made. But, in actual experimentation random sampling rarely is achieved. More typically convenience sampling is employed.

Convenience Sampling

Convenience sampling is obtaining participants from the individuals who are accessible or convenient to the researcher. As an example, Newburger et al. utilized 168 children selected from children with Kawasaki syndrome at six medical centers in the United States. The children were required to meet certain criteria for the presence of Kawasaki syndrome,

---

[1]The methodology and analysis of this experiment has been simplified for this introductory presentation. Newburger et al. employed electrocardiograms and blood analysis as well as body temperature to determine the effectiveness of their treatments.

but they were not selected randomly from among all children in the United States suffering from Kawasaki syndrome.

Convenience sampling clearly would not be adequate if we were trying to accurately estimate the population mean, such as estimating the outcome of an election from a poll. But the purpose of an experiment is not to estimate population means; rather it is to determine if two or more groups differ because of the effect of an independent variable. Provided the groups created are equivalent, convenience sampling typically does not limit the importance of experimentation.

Creation of Equivalent Groups

Equivalent groups means that the participants in the two or more groups are not expected to differ in any systematic or consistent way prior to receiving the treatment conditions. This similarity does not imply that participants in each group will be exactly alike prior to the treatment conditions. Creation of equivalent groups requires using an unbiased procedure to assign individuals to levels of the independent variable. Any differences that may then exist between the groups prior to manipulation of the independent variable will be only chance differences. As we explain later, a *t* test allows us to assess the probability of occurrence of such chance differences.

Random Assignment

The most commonly used method of creating equivalent groups is to randomly assign subjects to treatment conditions. Essentially, **random assignment** means that any individual selected for the experiment has an equal chance of being assigned to any one of the treatment conditions. More specifically, random assignment satisfies two criteria:

1. The probability of assignment to any of the treatment conditions is equal for every individual.
2. The assignment of each individual is independent of the assignment of every other individual; that is, the assignment of one participant to a treatment condition does not affect the assignment of any other individual to that same condition.

Random assignment ensures that the effects of variables — such as motivation, gender, anxiety, intelligence, and age — are distributed without bias among the treatment groups. After random assignment the treatment groups should not differ in any systematic way before the treatments are given.

In practice, researchers may place some limitations upon true random assignment. They may want to obtain an equal number of subjects in each group, or they may want to have each group composed of an equal number of males and females. These limitations still permit the groups to be equivalent. Newburger et al., for example, created two equivalent groups of 84 children each by randomly assigning a child to one of two groups. Several constraints were placed upon the random assignment to ensure that an equal number of boys and girls were in each group and that each group had an equal number of children under the age of one year and over the age of one year.

Administration of the Independent Variable

The **independent variable** is the variable that the researcher is manipulating and administering to individuals in the various groups in order to determine its effects upon behavior. An independent variable must take on at least two different values or levels. A **level of an independent variable** is one particular value of the independent variable. An independent variable often is identified as a *factor*, such as factor A, and the levels noted symbolically as A_1 and A_2. We then indicate the number of subjects in each group by n_{A_1} and n_{A_2}.

Each level of the independent variable is administered to one of the groups that have been formed. In the example experiment, the independent variable (i.e., factor A) is the type of treatment given; and there are two levels: level A_1—aspirin alone and level A_2—aspirin plus gamma globulin. Thus, one group of children (of size $n_{A_1} = 84$) was given the aspirin alone therapy, the other group (of size $n_{A_2} = 84$) was given the aspirin plus gamma globulin therapy. Recall from Chapter 1 that this design is a **one-factor between-subjects design,** for one independent variable is manipulated and the groups formed are composed of different people. Hence the comparison needed to decide if the independent variable has an effect is between subjects.

Control of Extraneous Variables

To ensure that any difference that is created between the groups is due only to the independent variable, extraneous variables must be controlled. **Extraneous variables** are any variables other than the independent variable that can affect the dependent variable. They may arise from subjects' attributes (for example, differences in intelligence, anxiety level, sensitivity to drugs, or motivation), uncontrolled changes in the physical environment in which the experiment is conducted, and variations in the experimental procedure from one participant to another. To be sure that any difference found between treatment groups is due only to the independent variable being manipulated, extraneous variables must not vary in any systematic or consistent way with the independent variable. If the extraneous variable is allowed to vary consistently with the independent variable, then the experiment is confounded. In a **confounded experiment** the effect of the independent variable cannot be separated from the possible effect of the confounded extraneous variable.

In the example experiment, Newburger et al. treated each of the two groups identically except for the administration of the independent variable. For example, the amount of aspirin given the children in each group was held constant at 100 milligrams of aspirin per kilogram of body weight per day. Had the aspirin plus gamma globulin group been given 150 milligrams of aspirin per kilogram of body weight, then the experiment would have been confounded. The aspirin plus gamma globulin group would differ from the aspirin alone group not only in that they received gamma globulin, but in that they also received a larger dose of aspirin.

Avoiding confounding is vital to conducting a meaningful experiment. We illustrate several other possibilities of potential confounding in experiments similar to our example, and control techniques to avoid that confounding.

Whenever someone is given a treatment, he or she may expect that it will have an effect. For example, you have a headache and take a medication for it. Obviously you expect the medication to have an effect. An hour later your headache seems somewhat relieved. Or is it? Perhaps you just think it is relieved because you expected the medication to have an effect. If subjects in the different groups possess different expectancies, the experiment is confounded. We cannot be sure if a difference between the groups is due to the effect of the independent variable or to the subjects' expectations about the effect of the independent variable.

To prevent subjects' expectancies from confounding an experiment, a single blind procedure often is employed. With a **single-blind procedure,** a subject is not told what treatment condition he or she is in and thus should not be able to form an expectancy. In medical or drug research, placebo control groups are also often used to control expectancies. A **placebo control** is a group given a medication or drug with no active ingredients. The purpose of the placebo control is to determine if the mere expectation of taking a medication or drug may have an effect on the dependent variable.

Subjects are not the only individuals who have expectations about the effect of an independent variable; experimenters do also. Certainly the experimenters conducting our example experiment expected the aspirin plus gamma globulin to be a more effective therapy than aspirin alone. How might experimenters' expectancies confound the experiment? Suppose the experimenters (i.e., the doctors) spent more time with the children who received the aspirin plus gamma globulin, telling them that they received an experimental treatment and they will be better soon. Perhaps they also took more care in measuring the body temperature of these children. Would the two groups be equivalent except for the manipulation of the independent variable? Clearly not. The group given the aspirin plus gamma globulin also received more attention and care from the doctors. The amount of attention and care is an extraneous variable varying with the levels of the independent variable, thus confounding the experiment. If the groups differ on the dependent variable, we cannot sort out whether the difference is due to the drug treatment or the confounding variable of attention and amount of care.

To prevent experimenter expectancies from confounding an experiment, a double-blind procedure may be used. With a **double-blind procedure** the experimenter who actually is dealing with the subjects does not know the research hypothesis or the treatment group which the subjects are in. Thus, the experimenter should not have any expectancies about the subjects in a treatment group or about the effect of the independent variable.

Confounding also occurs if the groups created for the experiment are nonequivalent. For example, suppose the children in our experiment were not randomly assigned to groups. Rather, the experimenter judged how ill a child was and then assigned the more severely ill children to the aspirin treatment group. This experiment is confounded; the groups were not equivalent prior to the administration of the independent variable. If the groups differ on body temperature after the treatment is given, we cannot know if the difference is due to the treatment or the severity of the illness of the child.

Measurement of the Dependent Variable

The final step in conducting the experiment is to measure the dependent variable for each participant. The **dependent variable** is the variable that the experimenter expects to be affected by the independent variable. The scores obtained in measuring the dependent variable then are summarized with a measure of central tendency and variability.

The research hypothesis of Newburger et al. predicted that the treatment of aspirin plus gamma globulin would more effectively lower body temperature than would aspirin alone. Their dependent variable was body temperature. As we indicated, they observed mean body temperatures on the second day of treatment of 38.48°C for the aspirin alone group and 37.60°C for the aspirin plus gamma globulin group.

Testing Your Knowledge 10–1

On a separate sheet of paper, test your knowledge of the material in this section by answering the following questions.

1. Define: confounding, random sampling, convenience sampling, random assignment, equivalent groups, independent variable, dependent variable, extraneous variable.
2. Identify the steps in conducting an experiment.

3. What is the purpose of creating equivalent groups?

4. Distinguish between random selection of participants and random assignment of participants to treatment groups.

5. When does confounding occur in an experiment?

6. What difficulties does a confounded experiment pose for reaching conclusions about the effect of an independent variable?

7. An experimenter is investigating the effect of noise on the performance of a tracking task. The task is to keep a pointer on a spot on a rotating turntable (imagine keeping a pencil pointing to a dime on a rotating record turntable). A subject's score is the amount of time that he or she is able to keep the pointer on the spot. The experimenter hypothesized that subjects performing the task when no external noise is present will keep the pointer on the spot for a greater amount of time than subjects who perform the task while listening to a loud noise. Each of the actions by the experimenter described below confounds this experiment by letting an extraneous variable vary along with the independent variable of noise condition. For each action, identify the extraneous variable that confounds the experiment, and then explain why the experiment is confounded.

   a. The experimenter assigns ten 20-year-old males to the no-noise condition and ten 60-year-old males to the noise condition.

   b. The experimenter urges the subjects in the no-noise condition to try very hard, but does not similarly encourage the subjects in the noise condition.

   c. The experimenter assigns males to the no-noise condition and females to the noise condition.

   d. The experimenter assigns physical education majors to the no-noise condition and social science majors to the noise condition.

   e. Subjects in the no-noise condition are run between 9:00 to 10:00 A.M. and subjects in noise condition are run between 4:00 to 5:00 P.M.

DID THE TREATMENT HAVE AN EFFECT? COMPARING THE SAMPLE MEANS: THE NEED FOR STATISTICAL TESTING

The Implications of Sampling Error for an Experiment

The steps of conducting an experiment are quite straightforward, yet they set the stage for the appearance of a dilemma for the experimenter. Any decision about the effect or lack of an effect of an independent variable must be made from comparing the sample means with each other. In principle, if the sample means are equal to each other, then the treatment had no effect. On the other hand, if the sample means are not equal to each other, then it seems reasonable to assume that the treatment had an effect. Unfortunately, however, because of the presence of sampling error this decision is not made as simply as suggested. In Chapter 7, we defined sampling error as the amount a sample mean deviates from the population mean (i.e., $\overline{X} - \mu$). If you were to draw two samples of participants from the same population and measure a behavior, because of sampling error it would be unlikely that the two sample means would be equal to each other or to the population mean. This fact was illustrated by the several empirical sampling distributions of the mean presented in Figure 7–2.

What are the implications of sampling error for reaching conclusions in an experiment? Simply that chance differences between the means of different groups drawn from the same population are anticipated in any experiment, whether or not the independent variable has an effect upon the dependent variable. Thus, our idea of making a decision about the effect of an independent variable merely from an observed difference between sample means is too simplistic. Sample means, even those drawn from the same population, will differ somewhat. Even if the independent variable has no effect whatsoever, the means of the several treatment groups will differ from each other.

We see an example of this problem in the results of Newburger et al. They found the mean body temperature on the second day of treatment to be 38.48°C for the aspirin alone group and 37.60°C for the aspirin plus gamma globulin group. Obviously the two sample means are not identical. But does this lack of identity represent an effect created by the independent variable or might it merely result from sampling error? Before we answer this question, we provide another illustration of sampling error.

Numerical Illustration of Sampling Error

A clear understanding of the nature of sampling error is crucial to grasping the importance of statistical analysis of experimental data. Consequently, we illustrate the problem of reaching a decision about the effect of an independent variable from sample means with another numerical example.

Consider an experiment in which a researcher manipulates two levels (A_1 and A_2) of an independent variable. Suppose, further, that in this instance the independent variable has no effect on the dependent variable. Because the independent variable has no effect, we can simulate this instance by sampling scores from two populations with identical means, $\mu_{A_1} = \mu_{A_2}$. Imagine that we conducted this "experiment" 10 times by drawing 10 sets of two samples of size 5 each ($n_{A_1} = 5$, $n_{A_2} = 5$), one sample from each population, A_1 and A_2, respectively, and then calculated the mean for each sample. Imagine, also, that each population mean is equal to 84, that is, $\mu_{A_1} = 84$ and $\mu_{A_2} = 84$. The 10 outcomes are presented in Table 10–1a. Observe that although the true difference between the population means, $\mu_{A_1} - \mu_{A_2}$, is zero, none of the differences between the sample means, $\overline{X}_{A_1} - \overline{X}_{A_2}$, is exactly zero.

TABLE 10–1.

Results of 10 simulated experiments in which 10 pairs of scores were randomly sampled from two populations. All samples are based upon sample sizes of 5 ($n = 5$).

a. *A Situation Where the Independent Variable Has No Effect; Thus* $\mu_{A_1} = \mu_{A_2} = 84$.

Experiment	Sample Means $\overline{X}_{A_1}$	$\overline{X}_{A_2}$	Difference $\overline{X}_{A_1} - \overline{X}_{A_2}$
1	83.6	83.2	+0.4
2	83.0	85.2	−2.2
3	82.2	86.2	−4.0
4	86.4	82.6	+3.8
5	85.2	84.4	+0.8
6	84.0	81.6	+2.4
7	83.4	84.2	−0.8
8	84.8	85.4	−0.6
9	83.8	84.0	−0.2
10	85.0	84.8	+0.2

b. *A Situation Where* $\mu_{A_1} = 84$ *and* $\mu_{A_2} = 86$. *Thus,* μ_{A_2} *Simulates a Treatment Effect of +2 Added to the Scores of* $\overline{X}_{A_2}$ *in Table 10–1a (Shown in Parentheses). Here* $\mu_{A_1} - \mu_{A_2} = -2.0$.

Experiment	Sample Means $\overline{X}_{A_1}$	$\overline{X}_{A_2}$	Difference $\overline{X}_{A_1} - \overline{X}_{A_2}$
1	83.6	85.2 (83.2 + 2)	−1.6
2	83.0	87.2 (85.2 + 2)	−4.2
3	82.2	88.2 (86.2 + 2)	−6.0
4	86.4	84.6 (82.6 + 2)	+1.8
5	85.2	86.4 (84.4 + 2)	−1.2
6	84.0	83.6 (81.6 + 2)	+0.4
7	83.4	86.2 (84.2 + 2)	−2.8
8	84.8	87.4 (85.4 + 2)	−2.6
9	83.8	86.0 (84.0 + 2)	−2.2
10	85.0	86.8 (84.8 + 2)	−1.8

Consider now a situation where the independent variable does have an effect. Suppose the true effect of the independent variable (or treatment effect) is equivalent to changing the score of each person in population A_2 by +2.0. An illustration of the 10 experiments with a treatment effect present is given in Table 10–1b. The sample means from the A_1 population with $\mu_{A_1} = 84$ are the same as in Table 10–1a. A value of 2 has been added to each score in level A_2, however, to simulate a treatment effect (shown in parentheses). This treatment effect increases the population mean by 2. Thus, μ_{A_2} now equals 86, so that $\mu_{A_1} - \mu_{A_2} = -2$ instead of 0. Observe again, however, that none of the differences between sample means, $\overline{X}_{A_1} - \overline{X}_{A_2}$, is exactly equal to the difference between the population means, $\mu_{A_1} - \mu_{A_2} = -2$. Thus, Tables 10–1a and 10–1b reveal the presence of sampling error in the difference between two sample means.

Consider the task of the experimenter in the context of this example. He or she obtains only two sample means ($\overline{X}_{A_1}$ and $\overline{X}_{A_2}$) in an experiment, one for each treatment condition, and observes the difference between them ($\overline{X}_{A_1} - \overline{X}_{A_2}$). On the basis of this difference the researcher must decide on one of the following alternatives:

- The two sample means were drawn from populations with identical means, $\mu_{A_1} = \mu_{A_2}$. Hence there is no treatment effect present.
- The two sample means were drawn from populations with different means, so that $\mu_{A_1} \neq \mu_{A_2}$. In a controlled experiment this difference is attributed to the effect of the independent variable.

Suppose the experimenter obtains a difference between sample means of -4.0 (i.e., $\overline{X}_{A_1} - \overline{X}_{A_2} = -4.0$). What should he or she decide about the populations from which the samples were drawn? An observed difference of about -4.0 occurs in both Tables 10–1a and 10–1b. Does an observed difference of -4.0 indicate that μ_{A_1} equals μ_{A_2} or that μ_{A_1} does not equal μ_{A_2}? The experimenter cannot be sure. Suppose, on the other hand that the experimenter observes a difference of $+0.4$. Differences of $+0.4$ again occur in both Tables 10–1a and 10–1b. What inference about population means and thus the effect of an independent variable should be made from this observed difference between sample means? The experimenter clearly is faced with a dilemma about the inference to be made on the effect of the independent variable from the observed difference of the sample means.

This dilemma occurs in an actual experiment when an experimenter has an observed difference between two (or more) sample means from groups given different experimental treatments. He or she must decide whether this difference indicates an effect of the independent variable or is likely due to sampling error. Does the difference in body temperature of $0.88°C$ ($38.48° - 37.60°C$) obtained by Newburger et al. indicate an effect of their independent variable or is it more likely due to sampling error?

The absolute size of the difference between the treatment means is of little help in resolving this problem, for as Tables 10–1a and 10–1b demonstrate, there may be overlap in the size of the differences obtained both with and without a treatment effect. How, then, does a behavioral scientist answer the question:

How big a difference between the sample means is big enough to decide that something other than sampling error is at work in the experiment?

The answer to this question is provided by statistical hypothesis testing.

The approach employed in this form of statistical hypothesis testing is to assume that each sample mean is drawn from a different population; $\overline{X}_{A_1}$ is drawn from a population with μ_{A_1}, and $\overline{X}_{A_2}$ is drawn from a population with μ_{A_2}. Then, assuming that if the independent variable has no effect, the two population means will be equal (i.e., that $\mu_{A_1} = \mu_{A_2}$), we can determine the expected extent of sampling error between the means. The observed difference between the sample means is then compared to the differences expected by sampling error alone. If the observed difference is large enough so that it is unlikely to occur from sampling error alone, then we decide that the difference is due not to sampling error, but to the effect of the independent variable.

We have just introduced a very crucial point in understanding statistical testing. To decide whether the means of two or more groups given different levels of an independent variable differ sufficiently to attribute the difference to the independent variable, we must first find the extent of differences expected from sampling error alone. Differences between means expected from sampling error are often referred to as **chance differences.** If the observed difference between the sample means falls among the chance differences, then we treat the observed difference as a chance difference. The independent variable did not affect the dependent variable.

On the other hand, if the observed difference between the means is sufficiently large to be expected rarely by chance, then we decide that the sample means do not differ by chance alone. Rather the difference is attributed to the independent variable. The purpose of the statistical hypothesis test, then, is to estimate the size of expected chance differences.

There are many different inferential statistical tests suitable for use with diverse types of data and research designs. Regardless of the specific test used, however, basic concepts of hypothesis testing are applicable to all statistical tests. We introduce the t test for two independent groups in this chapter. This t test allows us to statistically test the difference between two sample means where each mean is obtained from a different group of individuals.

THE t TEST FOR TWO INDEPENDENT GROUPS

The t test for two independent groups permits us to determine the probability that an observed difference between sample means, that is, $\overline{X}_{A_1} - \overline{X}_{A_2}$, would occur if sampling error alone were responsible for the obtained difference. If the observed difference occurs rarely by chance, then we decide that the sample means do not represent populations with the same means. The observed difference between the sample means is attributed to the independent variable.

As we suggested and illustrated in Table 10–1, however, the simple difference between sample means, $\overline{X}_{A_1} - \overline{X}_{A_2}$, does not provide an adequate basis for making such a decision; it provides no measure of the amount of sampling error to be expected. Rather, this decision must be made on the basis of the t statistic that incorporates a measure of error variation. The t **test for two independent treatment groups** is defined as

$$t = \frac{(\overline{X}_{A_1} - \overline{X}_{A_2}) - (\mu_{A_1} - \mu_{A_2})}{s_{\overline{X}_{A_1} - \overline{X}_{A_2}}}.$$

The numerator of this t reflects how much an observed difference between two sample means (i.e., $\overline{X}_{A_1} - \overline{X}_{A_2}$) differs from the difference between the two population means (i.e., $\mu_{A_1} - \mu_{A_2}$) that the sample means are assumed to represent. In most instances, the population means are hypothesized to be equal; thus the difference between them (i.e., $\mu_{A_1} - \mu_{A_2}$) is zero. The denominator of the t is a measure of error variation called the *standard error of the difference between two sample means.* To understand this measure of error variation, we must develop the concept of a sampling distribution of differences between means.

Sampling Distribution of Differences Between Means

In Table 10–1a we presented the outcomes of 10 hypothetical experiments for each of which two samples of size 5 were drawn randomly from two populations with equal means ($\mu_{A_1} = \mu_{A_2} = 84$). For each experiment, then, a null hypothesis H_0: $\mu_{A_1} = \mu_{A_2}$ was true. Suppose we replicated the hypothetical experiment 100 times and found the resulting $\overline{X}_{A_1} - \overline{X}_{A_2}$ differences. Plotting a frequency distribution of these differences in sample means, i.e., a distribution of $\overline{X}_{A_1} - \overline{X}_{A_2}$ values, results in an **empirical sampling distribution of differences between means.** The sampling distribution of the 100 differences between means is portrayed in Figure 10–1.

The distribution shown in Figure 10–1 is an empirical sampling distribution of differences between means because we observed and calculated the values of 100 $\overline{X}_{A_1} - \overline{X}_{A_2}$ differences. In practice, however, only rarely would a researcher calculate and construct an empirical sampling distribution as we have done in Figure 10–2. Rather, he or she uses the theoretical sampling distribution of the difference between means. We calculated and graphed an empirical distribution in Figure 10–1 to provide a better understanding of a sampling distribution of the differences between means.

A theoretical sampling distribution of the difference between means is presented in Figure 10–2. As discussed in Chapter 7, the theoretical sampling distribution of the mean possesses several important characteristics concerning its shape, mean, and standard error. A theoretical sampling distribution of the difference between means shares these same characteristics.

FIGURE 10–1.

Empirical sampling distribution of the difference between two means $(\overline{X}_{A_1} - \overline{X}_{A_2})$ for 100 samples drawn from two populations with identical means $(\mu_{A_1} = \mu_{A_2})$

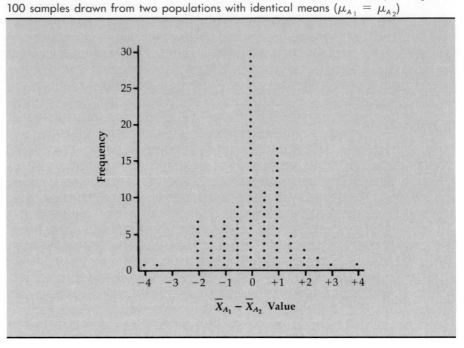

FIGURE 10–2.

Theoretical sampling distribution of the difference between two means

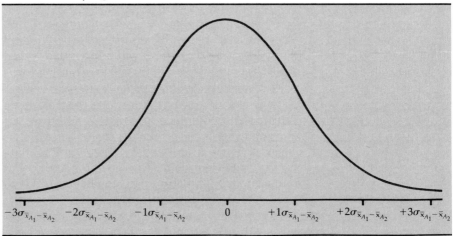

Shape of a Sampling Distribution of Differences Between Means

Observe that the sampling distribution in Figure 10–1 is relatively symmetrical and unimodal. Because of the central limit theorem, as sample size increases, any sampling distribution of the difference between means approaches a normal distribution. Regardless of the shape of the distribution of the underlying population of scores, the theoretical sampling distribution of the difference between means is normally distributed. This characteristic is present in the theoretical distribution illustrated in Figure 10–2.

Mean of a Sampling Distribution of Differences Between Means

The mean of the distribution of an unlimited set of $\overline{X}_{A_1} - \overline{X}_{A_2}$ values, $\overline{X}_{\overline{X}_{A_1} - \overline{X}_{A_2}}$, will be equal to the true difference in population means $\mu_{A_1} - \mu_{A_2}$. Therefore, when $\mu_{A_1} = \mu_{A_2}$, and thus $\mu_{A_1} - \mu_{A_2} = 0$, the mean of the obtained $\overline{X}_{A_1} - \overline{X}_{A_2}$ values will, in the long run, equal zero and the obtained differences in sample means will be clustered around the true difference of zero between the population means. Notice that this characteristic is demonstrated in the distribution shown in Figure 10–1. The mean value of the $\overline{X}_{A_1} - \overline{X}_{A_2}$ difference is +0.07. Even with only 100 sets of samples, the mean of the $\overline{X}_{A_1} - \overline{X}_{A_2}$ differences is quite close to the true population difference of zero.

Standard Error of a Sampling Distribution of Differences Between Means

The standard deviation of a theoretical sampling distribution of $\overline{X}_{A_1} - \overline{X}_{A_2}$ values is called the **standard error of the difference between means,** or more simply the **standard error of the difference.** It is symbolized as $\sigma_{\overline{X}_{A_1} - \overline{X}_{A_2}}$ and defined as:

$$\sigma_{\overline{X}_{A_1} - \overline{X}_{A_2}} = \sqrt{\frac{\sigma^2_{A_1}}{n_{A_1}} + \frac{\sigma^2_{A_2}}{n_{A_2}}}$$

As you see, the standard error of a theoretical sampling distribution of $\overline{X}_{A_1} - \overline{X}_{A_2}$ values is found by combining or pooling the standard errors of each sampling distribution of means. Thus, its value will vary with the standard error of the mean for each distribution. In practice, however, σ or σ^2 is not known and therefore the value of $\sigma_{\overline{X}_{A_1} - \overline{X}_{A_2}}$ cannot be found from this formula. But, recall (see Chapter 7) that a similar difficulty arose for the true standard error of the mean $\sigma_{\overline{X}}$ and was resolved by estimating $\sigma_{\overline{X}}$ by $s_{\overline{X}}$. Similarly, the true standard error of the difference between means ($\sigma_{\overline{X}_{A_1} - \overline{X}_{A_2}}$) can be estimated by using the variances calculated from the sample data, $s^2_{A_1}$ and $s^2_{A_2}$.

Estimating the Value of $\sigma_{\overline{X}_{A_1} - \overline{X}_{A_2}}$ When $n_{A_1} = n_{A_2}$. When the sample sizes for each group are equal, that is, $n_{A_1} = n_{A_2}$, the estimated standard error of the difference for a sampling distribution of $\overline{X}_{A_1} - \overline{X}_{A_2}$ values is given by:

$$s_{\overline{X}_{A_1} - \overline{X}_{A_2}} = \sqrt{\frac{s_{A_1}^2}{n_{A_1}} + \frac{s_{A_2}^2}{n_{A_2}}}$$

where $s_{A_1}^2$ and $s_{A_2}^2$ are the sample variances of groups A_1 and A_2, respectively.

Estimating the Value of $\sigma_{\overline{X}_{A_1} - \overline{X}_{A_2}}$ When $n_{A_1} \neq n_{A_2}$.   If the two samples from which the means are calculated are not equal in size, so that $n_{A_1} \neq n_{A_2}$, then a slightly different formula for $s_{\overline{X}_{A_1} - \overline{X}_{A_2}}$ must be used. In this instance the formula is

$$s_{\overline{X}_{A_1} - \overline{X}_{A_2}} = \sqrt{\left[\frac{(n_{A_1} - 1)s_{A_1}^2 + (n_{A_2} - 1)s_{A_2}^2}{n_{A_1} + n_{A_2} - 2}\right]\left[\frac{1}{n_{A_1}} + \frac{1}{n_{A_2}}\right]}.$$

The Estimated Standard Error of the Difference and the t Statistic.   The estimated standard error of the difference is the denominator of the t statistic. Thus, the value of t reflects how many estimated standard errors away from the mean of the sampling distribution an obtained $\overline{X}_{A_1} - \overline{X}_{A_2}$ difference lies. For example, consider an instance where an observed $\overline{X}_{A_1} - \overline{X}_{A_2} = 3.00$ and $s_{\overline{X}_{A_1} - \overline{X}_{A_2}} = 3.00$. The value of t then equals $3.00 \div 3.00$ or 1.00, indicating that the observed $\overline{X}_{A_1} - \overline{X}_{A_2}$ difference is one standard error away from the mean of the sampling distribution of $\overline{X}_{A_1} - \overline{X}_{A_2}$ values. If $\overline{X}_{A_1} - \overline{X}_{A_2} = 6.00$, then t equals $6.00/3.00$ or 2.00 indicating that the observed $\overline{X}_{A_1} - \overline{X}_{A_2}$ difference is two standard errors away from the mean of the sampling distribution of $\overline{X}_{A_1} - \overline{X}_{A_2}$ values.

Testing Your Knowledge 10–2

On a separate sheet of paper, test your knowledge of the material in this section by answering the following questions.

1. Define: empirical sampling distribution of the difference between means, theoretical sampling distribution of the difference between means.
2. Explain why you cannot look at the difference between the mean scores of two groups given different treatments and decide if the difference between the means is due to the independent variable.
3. Write the formula for the t test for two independent groups.
4. What is the name of the denominator of the t test?

5. Write the formula for the true standard error of the difference in two sample means.
6. Write the formula for the estimated standard error of the difference in two sample means when $n_{A_1} = n_{A_2}$.
7. Write the formula for the estimated standard error of the difference in two sample means when $n_{A_1} \neq n_{A_2}$.
8. Calculate $s_{\bar{X}_{A_1} - \bar{X}_{A_2}}$ for each of the following sets of scores.

a.	Group		b.	Group	
	A_1	A_2		A_1	A_2
	104	99		77	82
	111	107		84	86
	120	105		68	78
	113	110		71	74
	108	115		82	69
					79
					80

c.	Group		d.	Group	
	A_1	A_2		A_1	A_2
	71	85		32	38
	82	80		37	42
	63	73		28	29
	74	76		41	36
	68	70		35	30
	76	67		33	37
					36
					39
					34

STATISTICAL TESTING WITH A *t* TEST FOR INDEPENDENT GROUPS

We have emphasized that experimenters expect to observe some differences between the means of two treatment groups in an experiment whether the independent variable has an effect or not. Some difference between the means will occur because of sampling error alone. The purpose of statistical hypothesis testing, then, is to decide if the observed difference is large enough to be treated as due to something other than sampling error alone. If it is, then we may attribute the difference to the effect of the independent variable, provided, of course, that the experiment is not confounded. We use the *t* test.

In conducting a t test to determine whether there is a significant difference between two means, the steps for statistical hypothesis testing outlined in Chapter 8 are followed:

- Two statistical hypotheses, a null hypothesis, H_0, and an alternative hypothesis, H_1, are formulated. The null hypothesis provides the theoretical sampling distribution of the t statistic.
- A significance level is selected.
- A critical value of t, identified as t_{crit}, is obtained from Table A–2.
- Rejection regions are located in the theoretical sampling distribution of the t statistic.
- The t statistic, identified as t_{obs}, is calculated from the scores collected.
- A decision to reject or not reject H_0 is made on the basis of whether or not t_{obs} falls into a rejection region.

We now consider these steps and then provide an example of the use of the t test for independent groups.

Statistical Hypotheses

Recall that a statistical hypothesis is a statement involving population parameters. The parameters corresponding to a statistical test of two sample means, $\overline{X}_{A_1}$ and $\overline{X}_{A_2}$, are the population means μ_{A_1} and μ_{A_2}. The statistical hypotheses are stated as follows:

$$H_0: \mu_{A_1} = \mu_{A_2} \quad \text{(null hypothesis)}$$
$$H_1: \mu_{A_1} \neq \mu_{A_2} \quad \text{(alternative hypothesis)}.$$

The alternative hypothesis may also be stated equivalently as

$$H_1: \text{not } H_0.$$

These hypotheses are appropriate for any t test for two independent groups. Notice that for any population of scores, one or the other of these hypotheses must be true. It is logically impossible for both to be true at the same time.

Null Hypothesis
Observe that the null hypothesis does not specify numerical values for population parameters, which, of course, are unknown; it only states symbolically that the population means are equal. Essentially, $H_0: \mu_{A_1} = \mu_{A_2}$ corresponds to the situation that exists if the independent variable has no effect on the dependent variable. If the sample means are not affected

by the treatments, then all individuals will be representative of a population with the same μ_A on a measure of the dependent variable. Under the assumption of the null hypothesis an observed difference between sample means is due to sampling error. Thus, the null hypothesis establishes a situation under which the theoretical sampling distribution of the *t* statistic may be obtained.

Recall that a theoretical sampling distribution of a test statistic is a distribution specifying the probability of obtaining values of that statistic if the null hypothesis is true. By knowing the sampling distribution for a test statistic, such as the *t*, a researcher can determine how likely or unlikely any particular value of the test statistic is when sampling error alone is responsible for the difference observed between the sample means. Some values of the test statistic are likely to occur by chance alone. Others—those larger values of *t* reflecting greater differences in group means in comparison to the standard error of the difference—will occur infrequently under the chance conditions expressed in H_0. Thus the decision about whether the null hypothesis or the alternative hypothesis provides a more plausible explanation of the observed difference between the two sample means is made on the basis of comparing the value of *t* obtained on the sample data to the theoretical sampling distribution of *t* under H_0.

Alternative Hypothesis

The alternative hypothesis for the *t* test is written as the negation of the null hypothesis, $H_1: \mu_{A_1} \neq \mu_{A_2}$, or equivalently, H_1: not H_0. This hypothesis represents the situation if the sample means differ because the individuals are not from two populations with identical means. One way in which this difference could happen would be if the independent variable had changed the behavior measured. If the alternative hypothesis is true, we expect the sample means, $\overline{X}_{A_1}$ and $\overline{X}_{A_2}$, to differ by an amount greater than that expected from sampling error alone. Therefore, if H_1 is true, the value of *t* obtained on the sample data should typically be larger than the value of *t* obtained if H_0 is true.

It should be evident, that support for the research hypotheses of the experiment can be obtained only by refuting the null hypothesis of the statistical test. Indeed, the researcher hopes to reject the null hypothesis in favor of accepting the alternative hypothesis. Rejecting the null hypothesis is equivalent to deciding that the observed difference in sample means is not due to sampling error but to the effect of the independent variable.

As an example of this reasoning, Newburger et al.'s research hypothesis predicted that aspirin plus gamma globulin would lower the body temperature of children with Kawasaki syndrome more than would aspirin alone. This hypothesis will be supported only if the mean body temperatures for the two treatment conditions represent populations with different means, the situation stated in the alternative hypothesis. Thus, only if it is decided that H_0 is false, and therefore that H_1 is true, can support for the research hypothesis be established.

Selecting a Significance Level

How improbable under H_0 must t_{obs} be to reject H_0? As we know, behavioral scientists often choose a significance or alpha level of .05. By doing so, they have decided that values of t occurring only 5 or fewer times in 100 occasions if the null hypothesis is true are statistically rare. It is reasonable to decide that the alternative hypothesis, H_1, is true when such a value of t is obtained.

Locating Rejection Regions and Finding Critical Values of t: Two-Tailed Tests

The rejection region represents values of t that have a probability equal to or less than α if the null hypothesis is true. Thus, the rejection region defines values of t_{obs} that meet the criterion for rejecting the null hypothesis, H_0, and accepting the alternative hypothesis, H_1.

Rejection regions for the t test typically are established in either tail of the theoretical sampling distribution as illustrated in Figure 10–3. Most values of t will be clustered around zero in the middle of the distribution

FIGURE 10–3.

Illustration of a two-tailed rejection region for the t distribution for 8 df and $\alpha = .05$

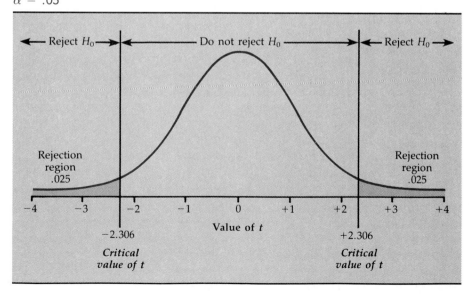

when H_0 is true. This clustering occurs because most values of $\overline{X}_{A_1} - \overline{X}_{A_2}$ will differ only slightly from zero if H_0 is true. But some values of t will fall in either end of the distribution even when H_0 is true. Such values are obtained when the numerator of the t (i.e., the difference between the sample means, $\overline{X}_{A_1} - \overline{X}_{A_2}$) is large compared to the denominator (i.e., the standard error of the difference). These large values of t are rare occurrences, however, if H_0: $\mu_{A_1} = \mu_{A_2}$ is true.

On the other hand, if H_1 is true and $\mu_{A_1} \neq \mu_{A_2}$, then large values of $\overline{X}_{A_1} - \overline{X}_{A_2}$, and thus of t, are expected to occur more frequently. Hence, the rejection regions for the t are located in each tail of the theoretical sampling distribution of t. The total probability of a rare outcome as defined by the significance level is divided between both tails of the t distribution. For instance, where $\alpha = .05$, two rejection regions are established—one in each tail of the t distribution, each with a probability of $\alpha/2 = .05/2 = .025$. If t_{obs} falls into the rejection region in either tail of the t distribution, then the null hypothesis is rejected and the alternative hypothesis accepted.

A t test with rejection regions in either tail of the theoretical sampling distribution is often called a **two-tailed t test.** As with the one-sample t test, the two-tailed critical values given in Table A–2 define the exact location of the rejection regions. To use this table we must know the degrees of freedom associated with the t_{obs}.

Degrees of Freedom for the t for Two Independent Groups

Degrees of freedom represent the number of scores that are free to vary when we estimate a population parameter with a sample statistic. In Chapter 9 we illustrated df by calculating the variance, s^2, from sample scores and demonstrated that s^2 has $N - 1$ df, where N represents the number of scores on which the variance is calculated. For the t statistic, $s_{\overline{X}_{A_1} - \overline{X}_{A_2}}$ is obtained by calculating the variances from each group, $s_{A_1}^2$ and $s_{A_2}^2$. Accordingly, the df for the t statistic are based upon the combined df associated with each variance estimate, $s_{A_1}^2$ and $s_{A_2}^2$. When n_{A_1} and n_{A_2} represent the number of scores in Groups A_1 and A_2, respectively, $s_{A_1}^2$ has $n_{A_1} - 1$ df and $s_{A_2}^2$ has $n_{A_2} - 1$ df. Accordingly, the combined df for the t statistic are $(n_{A_1} - 1)$ plus $(n_{A_2} - 1)$. If N is used to represent the total number of scores in the two groups (i.e., $N = n_{A_1} + n_{A_2}$), then the df for the t for independent groups are $N - 2$.

Locating a Rejection Region: One-Tailed Tests

As we noted, the t test that we have described to this point is sometimes referred to as a *two-tailed* or *nondirectional test*. The null hypothesis is rejected and the alternative hypothesis accepted if t_{obs} falls in a rejection region in either tail of the t distribution. When the research hypothesis is directional and a specific relationship is predicted among the means (e.g.,

$\overline{X}_{A_1} < \overline{X}_{A_2}$), then some researchers employ a directional or one-tailed test. In a **one-tailed test** the rejection region is established in only one tail of the t distribution. Thus, rather than splitting the value of the significance level between two tails, a rejection region encompassing the total value of α is established in the tail of the t distribution corresponding to the direction of the outcome predicted by the research hypothesis. A one-tailed rejection region in the right tail of a t distribution is illustrated in Figure 10–4. Values of t_{crit} for a one-tailed test at the .01 and .05 significance levels also are presented in Table A–2.

When Should a One-Tailed Test Be Used?

The advantage of using a directional t test is that t_{crit} will be smaller because the entire rejection region lies in only one tail of the distribution. Thus, it is easier to reject H_0 in that a smaller difference between sample means will result in a t_{obs} falling into the rejection region. This advantage is accompanied by a limitation, however. The decision to adopt a one-tailed or two-tailed rejection region (and, hence, to conduct a directional or nondirectional t test) must be made before the data are collected and analyzed. If a one-tailed rejection region is adopted, then the experimenter cannot reject the null hypothesis from a difference in means that is in the direction opposite to that hypothesized, because no rejection region for such an outcome has been established.

One wholly unjustifiable strategy is to conduct a one-tailed test if a t_{obs} narrowly misses statistical significance with a two-tailed test. The prob-

FIGURE 10–4.

Illustration of a one-tailed rejection region for the t distribution for 8 df and $\alpha = .05$

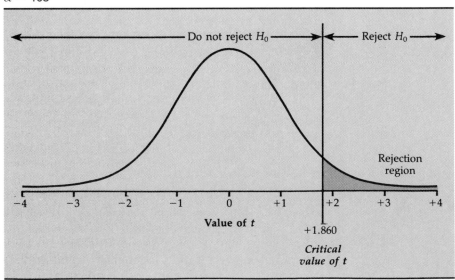

lem with such a procedure is that the significance level for the experiment is then actually greater than the adopted alpha level. If t_{obs} falls into the rejection region in the one-tailed test but not in the two-tailed test, then the probabilities of *t* in the rejection regions for both tests determine the actual significance level. For example, where the significance level adopted for both the two-tailed and one-tailed test is .05, the actual probability of making a Type I error is closer to .075. Thus, conducting both a two-tailed and one-tailed test on the same data is hedging on one's predictions and is statistically dishonest.

There is further statistical controversy about the use of one-tailed tests. The sampling distribution of *t* presented in Table A–2 is developed under H_0: $\mu_{A_1} = \mu_{A_2}$. This distribution is symmetric about zero, and positive and negative differences from zero are expected to occur equally. But for a one-tailed test, H_0 is written as $\mu_{A_1} \leq \mu_{A_2}$ (or $\mu_{A_1} \geq \mu_{A_2}$) and H_1 as $\mu_{A_1} > \mu_{A_2}$ (or $\mu_{A_1} < \mu_{A_2}$). But we cannot develop a sampling distribution for *t* under this null hypothesis. There are an infinite number of ways H_0: $\mu_{A_1} \leq \mu_{A_2}$ could be true. Therefore, the sampling distribution for H_0: $\mu_{A_1} = \mu_{A_2}$ is used to determine critical values of *t* for one-tailed as well as two-tailed tests. For this reason, some researchers recommend against using one-tailed *t* tests (Gaito, 1977). We use only two-tailed rejection regions in our example problems.

Calculating the *t* Statistic

The definitional formula for the *t* test is

$$t = \frac{(\overline{X}_{A_1} - \overline{X}_{A_2}) - (\mu_{A_1} - \mu_{A_2})}{(s_{\overline{X}_{A_1} - \overline{X}_{A_2}})}.$$

The null hypothesis for the *t* test, H_0: $\mu_{A_1} = \mu_{A_2}$, is equivalent to H_0: $\mu_{A_1} - \mu_{A_2} = 0$, however. Thus, the difference of $\mu_{A_1} - \mu_{A_2}$ is hypothesized to be zero. Accordingly, the *t* statistic becomes

$$t = \frac{(\overline{X}_{A_1} - \overline{X}_{A_2}) - 0}{s_{\overline{X}_{A_1} - \overline{X}_{A_2}}},$$

or even more simply

$$t = \frac{\overline{X}_{A_1} - \overline{X}_{A_2}}{s_{\overline{X}_{A_1} - \overline{X}_{A_2}}}.$$

The formula for $s_{\overline{X}_{A_1} - \overline{X}_{A_2}}$ depends upon whether the groups are equal or unequal in sample size.

Equal Number of Scores in Each Treatment Group
When $n_{A_1} = n_{A_2}$, the formula for t becomes

$$t = \frac{\overline{X}_{A_1} - \overline{X}_{A_2}}{\sqrt{(s^2_{A_1}/n_{A_1}) + (s^2_{A_2}/n_{A_2})}}.$$

With this formula only the sample means, standard deviations, and sample sizes are needed for computing the t. We illustrate computation of the t using this formula in Example Problem 10–1.

Unequal Number of Scores in Each Treatment Group
If n_{A_1} does not equal n_{A_2}, then the value of $s_{\overline{X}_{A_1} - \overline{X}_{A_2}}$ is provided by

$$s_{\overline{X}_{A_1} - \overline{X}_{A_2}} = \sqrt{\left[\frac{(n_{A_1} - 1)s^2_{A_1} + (n_{A_2} - 1)s^2_{A_2}}{n_{A_1} + n_{A_2} - 2}\right]\left[\frac{1}{n_{A_1}} + \frac{1}{n_{A_2}}\right]}.$$

Consequently, the formula for the t statistic becomes

$$t = (\overline{X}_{A_1} - \overline{X}_{A_2}) \Bigg/ \sqrt{\left[\frac{(n_{A_1} - 1)s^2_{A_1} + (n_{A_2} - 1)s^2_{A_2}}{n_{A_1} + n_{A_2} - 2}\right]\left[\frac{1}{n_{A_1}} + \frac{1}{n_{A_2}}\right]}.$$

The computation of t employing this formula is illustrated in Example Problem 10–2.

Decisions about the Statistical Hypotheses

Decisions about the statistical hypotheses are made from the value of t_{obs}. If t_{obs} falls into a rejection region, then the null hypothesis is rejected and the alternative hypothesis accepted. The difference between the sample means is *statistically significant*. On the other hand, if t_{obs} does not fall into a rejection region, then the decision is to fail to reject H_0 and not accept H_1. The difference between the sample means is nonsignificant.

Statistically Significant Difference
If the null hypothesis, H_0: $\mu_{A_1} = \mu_{A_2}$, is rejected and the alternative hypothesis, H_1: not H_0, is accepted, then it is inferred that the two sample means involved in t_{obs} are not estimates of identical population means and thus that the observed difference between them is due to something other than sampling error alone. If the experiment has been carefully designed and conducted, then the difference between the sample means is due to the independent variable manipulated. These decision-making procedures and corresponding conclusions are summarized in the left column of Table 10–2.

TABLE 10–2.

Summary of decisions and conclusions in statistical hypothesis testing using the *t* test for two independent groups. A .05 significance level is illustrated.

If t_{obs} Falls into a Rejection Region for $\alpha = .05$, then:	If t_{obs} Does Not Fall into a Rejection Region for $\alpha = .05$, then:
p of t_{obs} is less than or equal to .05, or $p \le .05$.	p of t_{obs} is greater than .05, or $p > .05$.
The null hypothesis (H_0) is rejected.	The null hypothesis (H_0) is not rejected.
The alternative hypothesis (H_1) is accepted. Each sample mean is from a different population.	The alternative hypothesis (H_1) is not accepted.
The difference between the two sample means is statistically significant at the .05 level.	The difference between the two sample means is nonsignificant at the .05 level.
It is decided that something in addition to sampling error is responsible for the difference between the sample means. In a carefully done experiment the difference is attributed to the independent variable.	It is decided that sampling error alone is the most plausible explanation of the difference between the sample means. There is no evidence that the independent variable had an effect.

Statistically Nonsignificant Difference

If we fail to reject H_0 and do not accept H_1, then we have no evidence that the null hypothesis is not true. Despite the observed numerical difference, the two sample means are considered to be from populations with identical means. They differ because of sampling error. Accordingly, the implication for the experiment is that the independent variable had no effect and the observed difference between the sample means is considered to be a chance occurrence. These decisions and conclusions are summarized in the right column of Table 10–2.

Assumptions for Use of the *t* Test for Two Independent Groups

The use of the *t* test for two independent groups rests upon the following assumptions:

1. Each subject of the experiment is randomly and independently drawn from the population.
2. The scores in the population sampled are normally distributed.
3. The variances of scores in the populations are equal.

In practice, these assumptions are often not fully met in an experiment; they are violated. Yet, researchers typically proceed to use the *t* test on the data. This approach raises the question of what assumptions are frequently violated and what the consequences of such violations are.

Typically, the participants in experiments are obtained by convenience sampling. The failure to randomly sample does not alter the outcome of the t test, but it does limit the extent to which the results can be generalized. Although samples may not be randomly drawn, however, the t test for two independent groups requires each score in the experiment to be independent of every other score. That is, it assumes that every individual is involved in only one level of the independent variable and contributes only one score in the experiment. If the person is involved in more than one level of the independent variable and contributes two or more scores for analysis, then the t test for related scores, discussed in Chapter 14, must be used.

Violations of the second (the normal distribution of scores) and the third (the equality of variances, often called the *homogeneity of variances*) assumptions can change the probability of obtaining a particular value of t_{obs}. Consequently, the actual probability of making a Type I error differs from that established by the value of α.

Until relatively recently the t test was thought to be very "robust" against violations of these assumptions. **Robustness** means that violation of the assumptions has little effect on the probability of making a Type I error. Research by Bradley (1980, 1984) has challenged this robustness notion, however. Bradley argues that there is no one set of conditions under which these assumptions may be violated and robustness of the t test assured. But, violations of the normality and equality of variances assumptions are more likely to have minimal effects on the probability of making a Type I error when the following conditions are met:

- The number of participants in each group is the same.
- The shape of the distributions of the scores for each group is about the same and the distributions are neither very peaked nor very flat.
- The significance level is set at .05, rather than .01.

Example Problem 10–1
Calculating the t with an equal number of scores in each group

Problem:
We use the problem faced by Newburger et al. of treatment of Kawasaki syndrome to illustrate calculating t_{obs} for two groups of equal size. Newburger et al. had two treatment groups of 84 children each. On the second day of treatment the temperatures of the groups were 38.48°C for the aspirin alone group and 37.60°C for the aspirin plus gamma globulin group. Suppose the standard deviations for these two groups were 0.96°C for aspirin and 0.92°C for aspirin plus gamma globulin. Is aspirin plus gamma globulin a more effective treatment than aspirin alone?

Solution:

To determine if the observed difference between the two sample means is one that could likely result from sampling error alone or if it is too large to be attributed to only sampling error, a statistical hypothesis test is necessary. Because only two treatment groups are involved, the *t* test for independent groups is an appropriate statistical test. We employ a .05 significance level and a two-tailed test.

Statistic to be used:

$$t = \frac{(\overline{X}_{A_1} - \overline{X}_{A_2})}{\sqrt{[(s_{A_1}^2/n_{A_1}) + (s_{A_2}^2/n_{A_2})]}}.$$

Assumptions:

1. The children were sampled randomly from among children with Kawasaki syndrome and each child is independent of all others.
2. Body temperature is normally distributed.
3. The variances for body temperatures are equal in the populations for the two treatment groups.

Statistical hypotheses: H_0: $\mu_{A_1} = \mu_{A_2}$
H_1: not H_0, or $\mu_{A_1} \neq \mu_{A_2}$.

Significance level $\alpha = .05$

df for *t*: $(n_{A_1} - 1) + (n_{A_2} - 1) = (84 - 1) + (84 - 1) = 166$, or $N - 2 = 168 - 2 = 166$

Critical value of *t*: $t_{crit} = 1.980$. A critical value of *t* for 166 *df* is not presented in Table A–2. Thus we used the t_{crit} for the next lower *df* tabled, 120 *df*.

Rejection regions: Values of $t_{obs} \leq -1.980$ or $\geq +1.980$.

Calculation: Because values of *s* are given, we can calculate t_{obs} directly from the formula above. Substituting numerical values,

$$t_{obs} = \frac{38.48 - 37.60}{\sqrt{[(0.96)^2/84] + [(0.92)^2/84]}}$$

$$t_{obs} = +0.88/\sqrt{0.02105}$$

$$t_{obs} = +0.88/0.145 = +6.069.$$

Decision: t_{obs} falls into the rejection region of equal to or greater than $t_{crit} = +1.980$. Thus, we reject H_0 and accept H_1.

Conclusion:

The two sample means of 38.48°C and 37.60°C differ significantly at the .05 level. The treatment groups were equivalent before the treatment was administered, so the numerical difference between the means is considered to be due to the effect of the independent variable and not sampling error. Aspirin plus gamma globulin more effectively lowers body temperature in Kawasaki syndrome patients than does aspirin alone. ▪

Example Problem 10–2
Calculating the t with an unequal number of scores in each group

Problem:

Suppose that Newburger et al. did not have 84 children in each treatment condition as in Example Problem 10–1, but had 82 children in the aspirin alone group (n_{A_1}) and 68 children in the aspirin plus gamma globulin group (n_{A_2}). Assume that the sample means and standard deviations remained the same: $\overline{X}_{A_1} = 38.48°C$, $s_{A_1} = 0.96°C$ for the aspirin alone group and $\overline{X}_{A_2} = 37.60°C$, $s_{A_2} = 0.92°C$ for the aspirin plus gamma globulin group. Conduct a statistical test to determine if the two sample means differ significantly at the .05 level. Use a two-tailed test.

Statistic to be used:

$$t = \frac{(\overline{X}_{A_1} - \overline{X}_{A_2})}{\sqrt{\left[\frac{(n_{A_1} - 1)s_{A_1}^2 + (n_{A_2} - 1)s_{A_2}^2}{n_{A_1} + n_{A_2} - 2}\right]\left[\frac{1}{n_{A_1}} + \frac{1}{n_{A_2}}\right]}}.$$

Assumptions for use: The assumptions are identical to those of Example Problem 10–1.

Statistical hypotheses: H_0: $\mu_{A_1} = \mu_{A_2}$
$\qquad\qquad\qquad\quad$ H_1: not H_0, or $\mu_{A_1} \neq \mu_{A_2}$.

Significance level: $\alpha = .05$

df for t: $(n_{A_1} - 1) + (n_{A_2} - 1) = (82 - 1) + (68 - 1) = 148$, or $N - 2 = 150 - 2 = 148$

Critical value of t: $t_{crit} = 1.980$. Because t_{crit} for 148 df is not presented in Table A–2 we used t_{crit} for the next lower df tabled, 120 df.

Rejection regions: Values of $t_{obs} \leq -1.980$ or $\geq +1.980$.

Calculation: Because values of s are given, we can calculate t_{obs} directly from the formula above. Substituting numerical values, we obtain

$$t_{obs} = \frac{38.48 - 37.60}{\sqrt{\left[\frac{(81)(0.96)^2 + (67)(0.92)^2}{82 + 68 - 2}\right]\left[\frac{1}{82} + \frac{1}{68}\right]}},$$

$t_{obs} = +0.88/0.1545 = +5.696$.

Decision: t_{obs} falls into the rejection region of equal to or greater than $t_{crit} = +1.980$. Accordingly, we reject H_0 and accept H_1.

Conclusion:

The two sample means of 38.48°C and 37.60°C differ significantly at the .05 level. The observed difference between the sample means is considered to be due to the effect of the independent variable. Aspirin plus gamma globulin more effectively lowers body temperature in Kawasaki syndrome patients than does aspirin alone. ▪

Statistics in Use 10–1

I'll Remember Better if You Look Me in the Eye: Using the t Test for Independent Groups

Social psychologists have demonstrated that nonverbal behaviors, such as eye contact, play a major role in communication between individuals. Thus, Sherwood (1987) was interested in the question of whether direct eye contact between a teacher and a learner might improve recall of material by the learner. To answer this question, in one experiment he formed two groups of 12 subjects each. Participants in each group listened to a six-minute oral presentation by an experimenter and were then given a 10-item test on the material. For a gaze condition given to one group, the experimenter maintained direct eye contact with the participant while giving the oral presentation. For a no-gaze condition given the second group, the experimenter did not maintain eye contact while making the presentation. The mean number of items answered correctly for the gaze group was 6.9 ($s - 1.0$), whereas a mean of 3.3 questions ($s = 1.5$) were answered correctly by the no-gaze group. The t_{obs} (22) was 6.9, a statistically significant value at the .05 level. The subjects in the gaze condition answered more questions correctly than subjects in the no-gaze condition. If you want someone to remember your words, then look them in the eye while you are speaking to them. ▪

Statistics in Use 10–2

Reducing Test Anxiety: Comparing Sample Means with the t

Many students experience test anxiety that severely interferes with their academic performance. One approach to reducing that anxiety, called Test Anxiety Reduction Training (Siegel, 1986) employs classical Pavlovian conditioning. In this approach, a person listens to music that he or she finds relaxing. While listening to the music, the person holds a small object (such as a marble) in his or her hand and attempts to imagine taking a test. The concept behind the training is that individuals should associate relaxation with the object. The object should thus become a stimulus to evoke relaxation in the person. At the time of an exam, then, the person holds the object to become relaxed.

To empirically test this technique, Siegel compared two groups of five highly test-anxious students each. The students were obtained from an introductory psychology course. The treatment group was taught the Test Anxiety Reduction Training technique; the control group was taught nothing about relaxing. After the training, all individuals were given an examination in introductory psychology. The score on this exam then was compared to the person's score on a previous examination in the course and a difference score between the two exams was obtained. Each subject thus had one score, a positive score, such as +2, or a negative score, such as −4. A positive score indicated better performance on the exam after the training period; a negative score indicated poorer performance on this exam. For the treatment group, Siegel found a mean increase of 1.5 items on the second exam (i.e., $\overline{X}_{A_1} = +1.5$) . The control group, on the other hand, revealed a mean decrease of 1.5 items (i.e., $\overline{X}_{A_2} = -1.5$) . The $t_{obs}(8)$ on the scores of the two groups was +5.17, which is statistically significant at the .05 level. The two groups differed significantly in their change on test performance. It appears that the Test Anxiety Reduction Training technique does reduce anxiety and leads to improved test performance. ■

Testing Your Knowledge 10–3

On a separate sheet of paper, test your knowledge of the material in this section by answering the following questions.

1. Define: rejection region, t_{crit}, t_{obs}, two-tailed rejection region, nondirectional test, one-tailed rejection region, directional test.
2. Identify the steps in statistical testing with the t test.
3. Write the statistical hypotheses for the t test for two independent groups.
4. To what situation in an experiment does H_0 correspond?
5. Assume that you have two groups of size n_{A_1} and n_{A_2}, respectively. Complete the following exercise for each set of samples by finding the df for the t test on the two samples and then finding t_{crit} for a two-tailed test for $\alpha = .05$ and $\alpha = .01$. If the exact df are not tabled, then use the next lower tabled value. Then indicate whether the t_{obs} falls into a rejection region. Finally, indicate your decisions with respect to the statistical hypotheses.

	n_{A_1}	n_{A_2}	t_{obs}
a.	10	10	2.341
b.	8	12	1.763
c.	15	15	2.120
d.	16	14	3.479
e.	35	35	2.912
f.	19	16	2.007
g.	65	64	2.002
h.	75	75	2.193

6. Identify the assumptions underlying the use of the *t* test for independent groups.
7. The *t* test is said to be robust. What is meant by this term?
8. Under what conditions is the *t* test likely to be robust?
9. Complete the following problems and answer the questions asked. Use a two-tailed test and a .05 significance level for each problem.

Problem 1: Does time seem to pass more slowly when you are expecting a delay before an event occurs? Suppose that to find an answer for this question you randomly assigned a total of 36 subjects to either a control group or an experimental group ($n_{A_1} = n_{A_2}$). In both groups you told the participants that the experiment would take only a few minutes and that they were going to fill out a questionnaire on anxiety. Subjects in the control group were told that your assistant would arrive with the questionnaires in a few minutes. Individuals in the experimental group were told that the assistant was delayed and that there would be a short delay. For both groups, however, the assistant arrived in exactly five minutes. When your assistant arrived, the participants were asked, without looking at their watches, to write down an estimate of how long they had waited. Suppose you obtained the following mean time estimates and standard deviations (in minutes) for your groups:

	Group	
	Control	*Experimental*
$\overline{X}$	6.9	8.9
s	1.57	1.71

a. State the statistical hypotheses for the *t* test for these scores.
b. What is the value of t_{obs}?
c. What are the *df* for this *t*?
d. What is the value of the two-tailed t_{crit}? at the .05 level?
e. What are the rejection regions for t_{obs}?
f. Does t_{obs} fall into a rejection region?
g. What decisions do you make about the statistical hypotheses? Do you reject or fail to reject H_0? Accept or not accept H_1?
h. Do you conclude that the means are from the same or different populations?
i. Is the difference between the means statistically significant?
j. Did the groups differ in their estimates of the time they spent waiting? If so, what is the direction of the difference?

Problem 2: Suppose you were interested in finding an answer to the same question as in problem 1; does time seem to pass more slowly when you are expecting a delay before an event occurs? Again, you randomly assign individuals to one of two groups. Rather than an equal number of people in each group, however, you assign 13 people to the control group and 17 to the experimental group. In all other respects the experiment is identical to that described in problem 1. Suppose you obtained the following mean estimates and standard deviations (in minutes) for your groups:

	Group	
	Control	Experimental
$\overline{X}$	6.6	7.8
s	1.80	1.92

a. State the statistical hypotheses for the t test for these scores.
b. What is the value of t_{obs}?
c. What are the df for this t?
d. What is the value of the two-tailed t_{crit} at the .05 level?
e. What are the rejection regions for t_{obs}?
f. Does t_{obs} fall into a rejction region?
g. What decisions do you make about the statistical hypotheses? Do you reject or fail to reject H_0? Accept or not accept H_1?
h. Do you conclude that the means are from the same or different populations?
i. Is the difference between the means statistically significant?
j. Did the groups differ in their estimates of the time they spent waiting? If so, what is the direction of the difference? ▪

REPORTING THE RESULTS OF THE t TEST FOR INDEPENDENT GROUPS

The results of the statistical analysis presented in Example Problem 10–1 might be described in a published scientific report as follows:

The mean body temperature for the aspirin alone group was 38.48°C ($s = 0.96$°C) and 37.60°C ($s = 0.92$°C) for the aspirin plus gamma globulin group. The means differed significantly, $t(166) = +6.069$, $p < .001$.

This presentation of the results conveys considerable information about the experiment to the reader. We see how this information is provided by examining each of the components of the report of the t test separately.

1. $t(166)$: Identifies the test statistic as the t. Therefore, we know that a t test was used to analyze the data, and because a t test may be used to compare only two sample means, two levels of an independent variable were employed in the experiment. The

degrees of freedom for the test statistic are shown in parentheses. Thus we know also that scores were analyzed from 168 different participants (because $df = N - 2$).

2. $= +6.069$: Gives the value of t_{obs} (not the t_{crit} value found in Table A–2).

3. $p < .001$: Tells us that

   a. The p and "less than" sign ($p <$) indicate that the probability of t_{obs} if H_0 is true is less than (or equal to) .001. This value is the probability of t_{obs} if H_0 is true; it is not the value of α selected. Unless otherwise indicated in the report, you may assume the significance level employed was 0.05.

   b. H_0: $\mu_{A_1} = \mu_{A_2}$ was rejected. H_1: not H_0 was accepted.

   c. The difference between the sample means is statistically significant (at the .001 level).

   d. Something other than sampling error is responsible for the observed difference in the means.

   e. If $p > .05$ were reported, then the greater than ($>$) sign indicates that the researcher failed to reject H_0 and the two means did not differ significantly at the .05 significance level.

Testing Your Knowledge 10–4

On a separate sheet of paper, test your knowledge of the material in this section by answering the following questions. These exercises present reports of the use of the t test adapted from results of published studies.

1. A t test for independent groups indicated that participants correctly detected a larger percentage of targets while listening to the familiar passage ($\overline{X} = 79.7$, $s = 8.57$) than while listening to the unfamiliar passage ($\overline{X} = 73.0$, $s = 5.85$), $t(60) = 3.60$, $p < .001$.

   a. How many levels of the independent variable were used in this experiment?

   b. How many participants were involved in this experiment?

   c. What is the value of the sample mean for the familiar passage group?

   d. What is the value of the sample standard deviation for the familiar passage group?

   e. What is the value of t_{obs}?

   f. What is the value of t_{crit} at the .05 level (two-tailed)?

   g. Do you reject or not reject H_0?

   h. Do you accept or not accept H_1?

   i. Is the difference between the means statistically significant or nonsignificant?

   j. To what do you attribute the observed difference in the sample means?

2. A t test for independent groups revealed no difference in the number of words recalled after an interval of 5 minutes ($\overline{X} = 22.78$) and an interval of 0.5 minutes ($\overline{X} = 24.33$), $t(28) = -0.80$, $p > .10$.
   a. How many levels of the independent variable were used in this experiment?
   b. How many participants were utilized in this experiment?
   c. What is the value of the sample mean for the five-minute group?
   d. What is the value of the sample mean for the 0.5-minute group?
   e. What is the value of t_{obs}?
   f. What is the value of t_{crit} at the .05 level (two-tailed)?
   g. Do you reject or not reject H_0?
   h. Do you accept or not accept H_1?
   i. Is the difference between the means statistically significant or nonsignificant?
   j. To what do you attribute the observed difference in the sample means? ■

WHAT DOES A t TEST ACTUALLY TEST?

The outcome of a t test provides the basis for drawing conclusions about the effect of an independent variable in an experiment, and therefore for deciding whether a research hypothesis is or is not supported by the data of the experiment. It is important to recognize, however, that a research hypothesis is not tested directly by the t test. The t test for independent groups is simply a procedure for testing the statistical hypothesis, H_0: $\mu_{A_1} = \mu_{A_2}$. Regardless of the independent and dependent variables stated in the research hypothesis, the null and alternative hypotheses for the t are always H_0: $\mu_{A_1} = \mu_{A_2}$ and H_1: not H_0, respectively. On the other hand, a research hypothesis for a two-group experiment is a declarative sentence predicting a relationship between an independent variable and a dependent variable. As an example, the statement, "it is expected that the body temperature of Kawasaki syndrome patients administered aspirin plus gamma globulin will be lower than the body temperature of patients given aspirin only," is an example of a research hypothesis.

A statistically significant t_{obs} with a nondirectional alternative hypothesis (i.e., H_1: $\mu_{A_1} \neq \mu_{A_2}$ does not necessarily provide support for the research hypothesis. Support for the research hypothesis stated above is obtained if $\overline{X}_{A_1}$, the mean body temperature for the aspirin alone group, is significantly higher in value than $\overline{X}_{A_2}$, the mean body temperature for the aspirin plus gamma globulin group. But a value of $\overline{X}_{A_1}$ significantly less than $\overline{X}_{A_2}$ does not agree with this research hypothesis. After obtaining a statistically significant t, we must always examine the direction of the difference between the means to find if it agrees or disagrees with the research hypothesis.

STATISTICAL AND SCIENTIFIC SIGNIFICANCE REVISITED

We have pointed out that use of the word *significant* in statistics is to identify a statistically rare result. A statistically significant difference between the means in an experiment bears no necessary relation to the scientific significance of the experiment. The scientific importance of an experiment is determined before the data are subjected to statistical analysis. In a well-conceived and well-designed experiment both statistically significant and nonsignificant differences may be important scientifically. Indeed, if a particular relationship is predicted between the independent variable and the dependent variable, a failure to find that relationship empirically may have scientific significance. However, in a poorly designed experiment where the independent variable is confounded with an extraneous variable, even a statistically significant difference between two sample means cannot be interpreted meaningfully.

TRUE EXPERIMENTS AND EX POST FACTO STUDIES

True Experiments. The Use of Active Independent Variables

This chapter has developed the *t* test for two independent groups in the context of a true experiment. To conduct a true experiment two equivalent groups are formed by randomly assigning participants to one of two groups. Extraneous variables are controlled, each group is given a different level of the independent variable, and a dependent variable measured. If the sample means of the two groups are found to differ significantly, then we may conclude that the independent variable caused the difference. The key to the conclusion that the independent variable caused the difference is that equivalent groups are created and then an independent variable is actively manipulated. By actively manipulated, we mean that the experimenter can decide which group receives which level of the independent variable. For instance, in our example of the treatment of children with Kawasaki syndrome, the experimenters decided which group of children would receive the aspirin alone and which group would receive the aspirin plus gamma globulin. Independent variables that the researcher has direct control over and can decide which participants will get what level of the independent variable are called **active independent variables.** In order to have a true experiment, the independent variable must be an active independent variable.

Ex Post Facto Studies: The Use of Attribute Independent Variables

Many independent variables of interest to behavioral scientists cannot be manipulated actively, but are attributes or characteristics of individuals. For example, a behavioral scientist may be interested in comparing males to females on a test of verbal ability. Here, gender of the participant, male or female, is the independent variable. But such an independent variable cannot be manipulated actively, for it is a personal attribute. In order to have two levels of gender in a study, a researcher must select individuals who possess the appropriate level of the independent variable, either male or female. **Attribute independent variables** are characteristics or attributes of a participant—such as gender, age, handedness, anxiety, intelligence, amount of schooling, drug use or nonuse, smoking habits, or level of depression. An experimenter can select participants who possess the attribute, but he or she cannot assign, administer, or present the characteristic to a person.

Ex post facto studies (also called **retrospective studies**) employ attribute independent variables. As an example of an ex post facto study, suppose a behavioral scientist is interested in comparing people who are high and low on test anxiety (an attribute independent variable) on their performance on a difficult intellectual task. In this study people would be measured on test anxiety prior to their selection to participate. Those people who represent the highest and lowest 20 percent of the scores on a test anxiety measure then would be selected to form the high and low test anxiety groups, respectively. Subsequently, their performance on the intellectual task would be measured. Notice that the individuals who participate in this study have self-determined which level of test anxiety they are in. Essentially, then, the "manipulation" of the independent variable of test anxiety took place before the individual was selected as a participant in the research.

The term *ex post facto* is of Latin origin and refers to something "done, made, or formulated after the fact" (*Webster's Ninth New Collegiate Dictionary*, 1983, p. 438). Thus, in the sense that by possessing the attribute of interest to the experimenter, the participants in an ex post facto study themselves determine which treatment condition they are in. The experimenter's employment of the attribute variable occurs after the fact, that is, after the attribute variable already has been manipulated in nature. If you were to participate in the test-anxiety study described, the factors determining whether you are high or low in test anxiety would have occurred before you participated in the study.

Statistical Hypothesis Testing in Ex Post Facto Studies

The use of statistical hypothesis testing in ex post facto studies is identical to its use in true experiments. We illustrate using an ex post facto study on perceived locus of control. Locus of control refers to the perception a person has over the control of events that affect his or her life. A person with an external locus of control perceives that he or she has little control over these events, whereas a person with an internal locus of control perceives that he or she has a great deal of control over such events. Several rating scales are available to measure locus of control.

Wiehe (1986) hypothesized that children who have been removed from the custody of their parents might have a more external locus of control than children who live with their biological parents. To test this hypothesis, Wiehe formed two groups from among adolescents in a residential maternity home: 45 pregnant adolescents who had been removed from their biological parents and had become pregnant while in foster care, and 45 pregnant adolescents who had become pregnant while living with their biological parents.

Each adolescent was given a rating scale to measure locus of control and Wiehe reported a mean locus of control score of 15.76 ($s = 4.65$) for the foster parents group and a mean score of 12.27 ($s = 5.74$) for the biological parents group. (For this measure, higher scores indicate greater external locus of control.) To determine if the two means differed significantly, Wiehe conducted a *t* test for two independent groups on the two sample means. We can compute t_{obs} from the information given above by

$$t = \frac{\overline{X}_{A_1} - \overline{X}_{A_2}}{\sqrt{(s_{A_1}^2/n_{A_1}) + (s_{A_2}^2/n_{A_2})}}.$$

Substituting numerical values,

$$t_{obs} = \frac{15.76 - 12.27}{\sqrt{[(4.65)^2/45] + [(5.74)^2/45]}},$$

$$t_{obs} = +3.49/1.101 = +3.170.$$

Thus, t_{obs} for $N - 2$ or $90 - 2 = 88$ *df* is +3.170. For 88 *df* and a .05 significance level, $t_{crit} = 2.000$ (based on the tabled value for 60*df*); thus rejection regions for t_{obs} are values of t_{obs} equal to or less than -2.000 or equal to or greater than +2.000. The t_{obs} of $+3.170$ falls into a rejection region; accordingly, H_0: $\mu_{A_1} = \mu_{A_2}$ is rejected, and H_1: not H_0 is accepted. The two sample means differ significantly and represent samples from different populations. The adolescents in the foster parents group demonstrated greater external locus of control than adolescents in the biological parents group.

Conclusions from an Ex Post Facto Study

Whenever an attribute variable is employed as an independent variable, nothing can ensure that the groups differing on the attribute are equivalent in all respects other than the attribute that is of interest. One can be certain that they are not equivalent. That is, the groups will differ systematically on many characteristics other than the attribute that is being compared. It may be that one of these characteristics is the variable that leads to the differences in behavior and not the attribute on which the participants were grouped. Unfortunately, there are so many related characteristics that a behavioral scientist is unlikely to ever know and be able to control all of them in one study. Therefore, ex post facto studies are confounded, and one cannot establish cause-and-effect relationships between the independent and dependent variables.

In our example ex post facto study, the author was quite cautious to note that one could only state that a relation had been found between type of custody and locus of control. He noted that there are at least several aspects of foster care status that might cause an adolescent to change her locus of control to a more external focus: the actual parental abuse or neglect, intervention by a social services agency and removal of the child from the biological parents, and placing the child into a foster home. It is also possible that locus of control may lead to type of custody status. Adolescents with an external locus of control may engage in the types of behavior that evoke abuse from parents.

Why Are Ex Post Facto Studies Conducted?

You may be wondering why ex post facto studies are conducted if a scientist is unable to determine causal relations between the independent variable and dependent variable from any single study. The answer to this question is that ex post facto studies offer the only way to study many of the independent variables of interest to behavioral scientists. Many independent variables cannot be manipulated actively either for pragmatic or ethical reasons—gender, handedness, drug usage, occupation, body weight, physical attractiveness, ethnic origin, type of schooling, level of anxiety, intelligence—are some examples. Consequently, scientists interested in studying these and similar variables must use ex post facto studies.

Statistics in Use 10–3

Course Grades and Time of Day: Analyzing an Ex Post Facto Study

One college student stereotype is that they like both to stay up late and sleep late. If this is so, then might course grades be related to the time of day that the course is offered? Morning classes may lead to poorer grades than afternoon classes if students are forced to waken for the classes after an abbreviated sleep period. To find if course grades differ between morning and afternoon classes, Skinner (1985) compared the mean grades for 74 morning courses against 67 afternoon courses at a small liberal arts college. This research was an ex post facto study; Skinner had to take courses and students as they exist, he could not randomly assign either students or courses to morning or afternoon times.

The scores analyzed were the mean grade for a class. The mean grade for morning classes was 68.9, whereas the mean grade for afternoon classes was 71.9. The t_{obs} on these scores, 2.33, was statistically significant at the .05 level. The mean grade for morning classes was significantly lower than the mean grade for afternoon classes. ■

Statistics in Use 10–4

Investigating Learning Disabilities: Using the *t* Test for Independent Groups

Learning disabilities tend to run in families; thus, might the parents of normal and learning disabled children differ in personality and motivational variables? To find if such differences exist, Miletic (1986) employed an ex post facto study to compare parents of normal and learning disabled children on a number of interpersonal variables. The independent variable, type of parent, is an attribute independent variable. Miletic selected parents based on possessing the attribute of either having a learning disabled or a normal child.

A number of comparisons were done; we report only several here. Mothers of learning disabled girls ($n = 15$) were more supportive ($\overline{X} = 17.7$, $s = 1.7$ on the Gordon Survey of Interpersonal Values) than mothers of normal children ($\overline{X} = 15.6$, $s = 3.1$, $n = 16$), $t_{obs}(29) = 2.10$, $p < .05$. No differences were found between the mothers of learning disabled and normal girls on conformity ($\overline{X} = 16.1$, $s = 2.0$ for learning disabled, $\overline{X} = 14.0$, $s = 4.5$ for normal), $t_{obs}(29) = 1.28$, $p > .05$, or independence ($\overline{X} = 16.9$, $s = 3.9$ for learning disabled, $\overline{X} = 18.7$, $s = 6.5$ for normal), $t_{obs}(29) = 1.20$, $p > .05$. Thus it appears that parents of normal and learning disabled children may differ on selected personality variables and research comparing the parents may lead to a better understanding of learning disabilities. ■

Testing Your Knowledge 10–5

On a separate sheet of paper, test your knowledge of the material in this section by answering the following questions.

1. Define: active independent variable, equivalent groups, true experiment, attribute independent variable, ex post facto study.
2. Distinguish between a research hypothesis and a statistical hypothesis.
3. Why is statistical hypothesis testing needed in an experiment or an ex post facto study?
4. Does a statistically significant difference necessarily imply a scientifically important result? Explain.
5. Explain why causal conclusions cannot be reached from an ex post facto study.

6. Hughey (1985) compared the grade point average (GPA) of college students cited for residence hall disruptions with students not involved in residence hall disruptions. The mean GPA of 1,794 students involved in disruptions was 1.68 with $s = 0.34$. For 3,606 students not involved in disruptions, the mean GPA was 2.19 with $s = 0.83$.
   a. What type of study is described here? Explain your answer.
   b. Do the GPAs differ significantly? Use a two-tailed test and a .05 significance level? ■

SUMMARY

- An experiment requires:
  - Creating equivalent groups by random assignment.
  - Controlling extraneous variables.
  - Manipulating an active independent variable.
- The t test for independent groups may be used to determine if two sample means are significantly different. The formula for this t is

$$t = \frac{(\overline{X}_{A_1} - \overline{X}_{A_2})}{s_{\overline{X}_{A_1} - \overline{X}_{A_2}}}.$$

- The standard error of the difference be

tween means is the denominator of the t statistic. The formula for $s_{\overline{X}_{A_1} - \overline{X}_{A_2}}$ depends upon whether $n_{A_1} = n_{A_2}$ or $n_{A_1} \neq n_{A_2}$.

- Statistical testing with the t for independent groups follows the steps common to all statistical testing.
- Ex post facto studies utilize attribute independent variables. With attribute independent variables, subjects self-determine the group to which they are assigned.
- The t test may be used to test for differences between sample means in ex post facto studies as well as experiments.

KEY TERMS

active independent variables
attribute independent variables
central limit theorem
chance difference
confounding
convenience sampling
dependent variable
directional test
double blind procedure
empirical sampling distribution
   of the difference between
   means
equivalent groups

ex post facto studies
extraneous variables
independent variable
level of an independent
   variable
nondirectional test
one-tailed rejection region
one-tailed test
placebo control
random assignment
random sampling
rejection region
robustness

single blind procedure
standard error
standard error of the difference between means
$s_{\overline{X}_{A_1} - \overline{X}_{A_2}}$
theoretical sampling distri-
   bution of the difference
   between means
t_{crit}
t_{obs}
true experiment
two-tailed rejection region
two-tailed test

REVIEW QUESTIONS

On a separate sheet of paper, test your knowledge of the material in this chapter by answering the following questions.

1. For each statement, indicate whether the statement applies to a true experiment, to an ex post facto study, or both.
   a. Equivalent groups are formed by randomly assigning individuals to a group.
   b. An active independent variable is manipulated.
   c. An attribute independent variable is varied.
   d. Participants self-determine which level of the independent variable they are in.
   e. Measures of typical performance, frequently the sample means, are obtained for each group.
   f. A research hypothesis is formulated stating the relationship of the independent variable and the dependent variable.
   g. The independent variable is manipulated or varied and scores on the dependent variable are recorded.
   h. Extraneous variables are controlled to prevent confounding.
   i. A *t* test is used to determine if the sample means differ significantly.
   j. If the sample means differ significantly, then the experimenter can state only that the independent variable and the dependent variable are related.
   k. If the sample means differ significantly, then the experimenter can state that the independent variable caused the dependent variable to vary.

2. Noise is an ever present phenomenon in modern society and you are interested in finding if it has any physiological effects. Suppose you randomly assigned 22 individuals to either a control or an experimental group ($n_{A_1} = n_{A_2}$). Subjects in the control group relaxed in a comfortable chair for 30 minutes. At the end of the 30 minutes you measured their systolic blood pressure (i.e., the blood pressure during the contraction of the heart). Subjects in the experimental group also sat in the same chair for 30 minutes. During the 30-minute wait, however, they listened to a recording of traffic noise from a large city during rush hour. After listening to the noise for 30 minutes, the systolic blood pressure of these individuals also was recorded. Suppose you obtained the following blood pressure measures (in millimeters of mercury).

Group

Quiet	Noise
106	141
117	136
124	124
129	139
115	121
131	119
121	147
115	128
128	115
136	134
127	140

a. Find the mean and standard deviation for each group. Then use a *t* test to answer the question: Does noise affect systolic blood pressure? Use a two-tailed test and a .05 significance level.

b. Describe your results in question 2a following the example illustrated in the Reporting the Results of the *t* Test for Independent Groups section of this chapter.

3. Suppose you had obtained the blood pressure scores given below for question 2. Does noise affect systolic blood pressure? Use a .05 significance level and a two-tailed test.

Group

Quiet	Noise
110	116
114	111
106	120
117	119
108	123
116	108
120	122
111	115
115	117
109	101
118	116

4. Do sex differences exist in the need for privacy among college students? To find an answer to this question, Pedersen (1987) gave the Privacy Questionnaire (Pederson, 1979) to male and female college students. One aspect of this questionnaire measures the need for solitude. Scores on this scale may range from 6 (never need solitude) to 30 (usually need solitude). Suppose the following scores were obtained for 13 males and 17 females.

Gender	
Male	*Female*
23	16
16	29
13	11
25	14
17	17
21	19
10	18
19	21
24	9
16	15
11	17
22	20
14	14
	24
	23
	25
	24

Do males and females differ in the rated need for solitude?

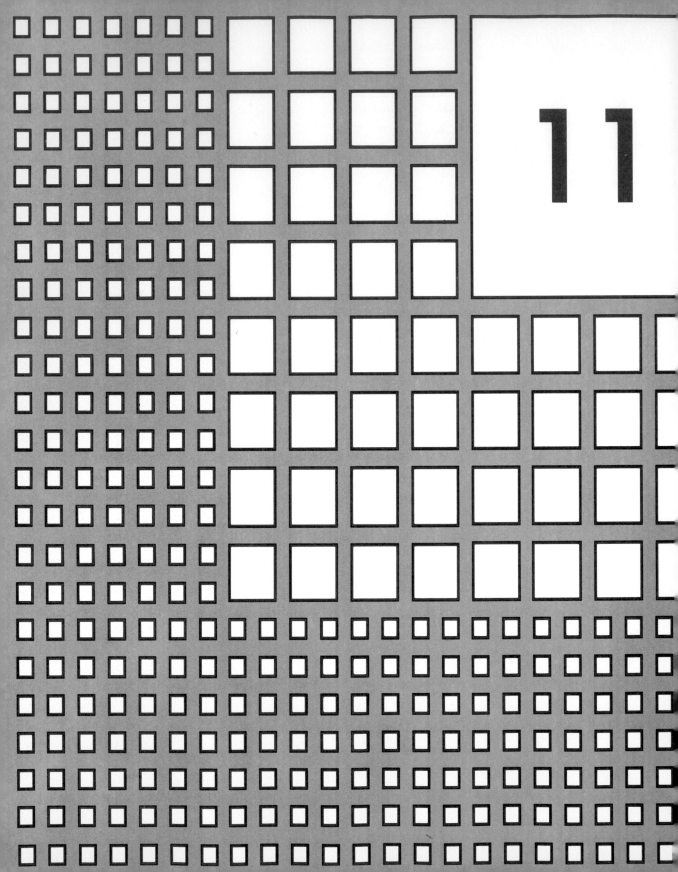

11

One-Factor Between-Subjects Analysis of Variance

The *t* test introduced many of the important concepts of statistical hypothesis testing in behavioral science experimentation. But the *t* test possesses one major limitation — it can be used to compare the means from only two groups at a time. Many behavioral science experiments, however, are multilevel designs. A **one-factor multilevel design** is an experiment with one independent variable and three or more levels of that independent variable. Most frequently, the analysis of variance is employed as a statistical hypothesis test for multilevel designs.

The **analysis of variance** (abbreviated **ANOVA**) is a statistical test used to compare two or more means simultaneously. If used to analyze an experiment involving only two treatment conditions, then the conclusions reached from the analysis of variance are identical to the conclusions reached from a *t* test. But, if three or more treatment conditions are compared — i.e., the independent variable has three or more levels — then an analysis of variance is necessary to analyze the data statistically.

In psychological research, analysis of variance is the most widely used statistical test; indeed, Rucci and Tweney (1980) characterize analysis of variance as "the workhorse statistic of experimental psychology" (p. 166). Analysis of variance is a versatile statistical test. It can be utilized for both between- and within-subjects designs, and for designs in which two or more independent variables are varied. Consequently, knowledge of the analysis of variance is fundamental to understanding much of current behavioral science research. This chapter presents the analysis of variance for the one-factor between-subjects design, the design in which one independent variable is manipulated and each level of the independent variable is administered to a different group of subjects. Its uses in other designs are presented in subsequent chapters.

The name *analysis of variance* provides an insight into the approach of this statistical technique. Essentially, an analysis of variance for a one-factor between-subjects design breaks down the total variation in the scores of an experiment into two sources: (1) a variance that varies with both the systematic effect of an independent variable and sampling error among the means, and (2) a variance that varies only with nonsystematic error variation among individual scores. In the analysis of variance, however, a variance usually is called a **mean square**. Mean square (abbreviated *MS*) is another term for a sample variance, but its use is unique to analysis of variance. Although the terminology may be confusing initially, just keep in mind that a mean square is another name for a variance.

This sorting of the total variation into systematic variance and error variance results in a test statistic called *F* and named after Sir Ronald A. Fisher (1890–1962), the British statistician who developed the concepts of analysis of variance. The *F* statistic is a ratio of two different mean squares (i.e., variances) obtained from the scores of an experiment and may be stated in general terms as

$$F = \frac{MS_A}{MS_{Error}}.$$

The variance estimate in the numerator, **MS_A**, called the **between-groups variance,** is derived from variation in sample means. Recall that treatment means in an experiment may differ from each other for two reasons: (1) the effect of an independent variable, and (2) sampling error. Thus, the numerator of the *F* statistic reflects systematic variation among the means of the treatment groups due to the effect of the independent variable as well as variation due to sampling error. The variance estimate in the denominator of the *F* ratio, **MS_{Error}**, called the **within-groups variance,** measures only variation in scores within treatment conditions. If the independent variable has no effect, then the variation among the treatment group means will be due only to sampling error. Consequently, MS_A and MS_{Error} will be about the same, and the *F* ratio will be about 1.00. But when an independent variable has an effect, the treatments will increase the differences among sample means beyond the differences expected from sampling error alone. In this instance, the between-groups variance of the numerator, MS_A, will be greater than the within-groups variance of the denominator, MS_{Error}, and the value of the *F* ratio will be larger than 1.00. Thus, the *F* ratio will increase in value as a treatment has an effect. Accordingly, the *F* statistic provides the basis for a statistical hypothesis test.

MEMORY FOR DRAWINGS: AN EXAMPLE EXPERIMENT

Our visual world presents us with stimuli of varying complexity and detail. What aspects of a stimulus determine how well we remember the stimulus? One research hypothesis, the elaboration hypothesis, predicts that the more elaborate the memory representation of a stimulus, the better the stimulus should be remembered (Craik & Tulving, 1975). A second research hypothesis, the effort hypothesis, predicts that stimuli that require more effort to process will be better recalled than stimuli requiring less effort to process (Coulter, Coulter, & Glover, 1984). Suppose we create three different types of drawings of common objects — detailed, outline, and incomplete drawings. The elaboration hypothesis predicts that detailed drawings should lead to the most memory elaboration and thus be best recalled, with outline and incomplete outline drawings leading to less memory elaboration and thus progressively poorer recall. The effort

hypothesis leads to an opposite prediction, the incomplete outline drawings require the most effort to process; thus they will be best remembered. The outline and detailed drawings require increasingly less effort;
hence detailed drawings will be the most poorly recalled.

   To determine which of these hypotheses best predicts memory for visual stimuli suppose we manipulated the independent variable of type of
drawing (factor A) over three levels—incomplete (A_1), outline (A_2), and
detailed (A_3) using a one-factor between-subjects design. Three treatment
groups were created by randomly assigning 5 individuals to each group.
The subjects were shown a set of drawings of 30 common items. For one
group the drawings were detailed, for the second group the drawings
were outlines, and for the third group the drawings were incomplete outlines. After viewing each of the 30 drawings for 4 seconds, each subject
was asked to orally recall as many of the drawings as possible. The number of items recalled by each person is presented in Table 11–1. Is the
number of drawings recalled affected by the type of drawing? To answer
this question we use the analysis of variance.

TABLE 11–1.

Hypothetical scores for number of items recalled as a function of
type of drawing. The mean ($\overline{X}_A$) and standard deviation (s_A)
are provided for each condition. $\overline{X}_G$ is the grand mean of the
15 scores.

	Type of Drawing (A)		
	Incomplete Outline	*Outline*	*Detailed*
	(A_1)	(A_2)	(A_3)
	17	14	15
	13	13	10
	16	16	11
	19	12	12
	20	10	12
$\overline{X}_A$	17.0	13.0	12.0	$\overline{X}_G = 14.0$
s_A	2.74	2.24	1.87	

OBTAINING THE *F* RATIO

The F statistic utilizes two variances, MS_A and MS_{Error}. A variance, or in
analysis of variance terminology, an **MS**, is defined as $SS/(n-1)$. The denominator, $n-1$, corresponds to the degrees of freedom (df) involved in
obtaining the variance estimate. Thus, the formula for a sample variance

providing an unbiased estimate of the population variance can be expressed as $MS = SS/df$. Accordingly, to obtain the mean squares necessary for an analysis of variance we must find SS_A and SS_{Error} from the scores and then divide each sum of squares by its df. The process of obtaining the sums of squares begins by partitioning a score. The partitioned scores then are used to obtain sums of squares and finally the sums of squares are divided by the degrees of freedom to obtain the needed mean squares.

Partitioning a Score

The analysis of variance sorts the total variation of the scores in an experiment into between-groups and within-groups variance by assuming a simple model for an individual's score. Although our example uses only three levels of an independent variable, the model introduced here applies to the analysis of variance for any number of levels of a one-factor between-subjects design.

The scores in Table 11–1 are represented symbolically in Table 11–2. The symbols are similar to those used to this point. The independent variable is identified as factor A with three levels, A_1, A_2, and A_3. Generally, a represents the number of levels of factor A. For Tables 11–1 and 11–2, $a = 3$. A score for an individual is represented by X_{ij}, where the subscripted i represents a number identifying the subject within a group and the subscripted j represents the number of the group, A_1, A_2, or A_3. For example, X_{52} is the fifth subject in Group A_2. The sample means for each

TABLE 11–2.

Notational representation of scores from the hypothetical experiment in Table 11–1 with three levels of an independent variable, factor A. The means for each level of factor A are represented by $\overline{X}_A$ and the grand mean by $\overline{X}_G$.

Factor A			
A_1	A_2	A_3	
X_{11}	X_{12}	X_{13}	
X_{21}	X_{22}	X_{23}	
X_{31}	X_{32}	X_{33}	
X_{41}	X_{42}	X_{43}	
X_{51}	X_{52}	X_{53}	
$\overline{X}_{A_1}$	$\overline{X}_{A_2}$	$\overline{X}_{A_3}$	$\overline{X}_G$

level of the independent variable are indicated by $\overline{X}_{A_1}$, $\overline{X}_{A_2}$, and $\overline{X}_{A_3}$, or more generally by $\overline{X}_A$. The grand mean, which is the mean of all the scores in the experiment, is labeled $\overline{X}_G$. The number of scores in a level of the independent variable is represented as n_A, and the total number of scores in the experiment is represented by N. For Table 11–1 therefore, $n_{A_1} = 5$, $n_{A_2} = 5$, $n_{A_3} = 5$, $N = 15$, $\overline{X}_{A_1} = 17.0$, $\overline{X}_{A_2} = 13.0$, $\overline{X}_{A_3} = 12.0$, and $\overline{X}_G = 14.0$.

The analysis of variance develops the F statistic by taking the total variation of a score, that is, the total amount by which a score (i.e., X_{ij}) differs or deviates from the grand mean of the scores (i.e., $\overline{X}_G$), and partitions this total difference or deviation into two components. One component, which becomes the between-groups variance (i.e., MS_A), varies with an effect of the independent variable and error variation. The other component, which becomes the within-groups variance (i.e., MS_{Error}), varies with error variation only. This model for representing a score can be expressed as

$$\begin{array}{c}\text{Total variation} \\ \text{in a score}\end{array} = \begin{array}{c}\text{Variation due} \\ \text{to a treatment} \\ \text{effect}\end{array} + \begin{array}{c}\text{Variation due} \\ \text{to error}\end{array}. \qquad \textbf{Eq. 11–1}$$

This breaking up, or partitioning, of a score can be represented symbolically as

$$X_{ij} - \overline{X}_G \quad = \quad (\overline{X}_A - \overline{X}_G) \quad + \quad (X_{ij} - \overline{X}_A). \qquad \textbf{Eq. 11–2}$$

| Deviation of a score from the grand mean | Deviation of treatment group mean from the grand mean | Deviation of a score from its treatment group mean |

Let us examine each component of equation 11–2.

$X_{ij} - \overline{X}_G$

The deviation of a score from the grand mean represents the total variation of the score from the grand mean. As equation 11–2 indicates, a portion of this variation is due to the effect of the independent variable and a portion of it is due to error variation.

$\overline{X}_A - \overline{X}_G$

The $\overline{X}_A - \overline{X}_G$ term enters into the computation of MS_A. Accordingly, it varies with the effect of an independent variable and with sampling error.

Effect of the Independent Variable.   The deviation of a treatment group mean from the grand mean varies with the effect of the independent variable. Recall that with the t test the effect of the independent variable is found from the difference $\overline{X}_{A_1} - \overline{X}_{A_2}$. This difference cannot be used to assess the effect of the independent variable when three or more sample means are being compared. Thus, analysis of variance uses the difference $\overline{X}_A - \overline{X}_G$ to measure the effect of the independent variable. The grand mean is used to represent the typical performance of a person before any treatment has acted upon his or her score. Any effect of the independent variable is expected to affect all individuals in a treatment condition equally and either adds to or subtracts from the base score of the grand mean. Thus, a treatment effect changes the value of the treatment means. The treatment means will then differ from the grand mean. A numerical illustration helps to clarify this important point.

Table 11–3 presents three possible outcomes of an experiment involving only three scores in each of two treatment groups. In panel a of this table no treatment effect is present. Each treatment mean is equal to the grand mean. Further, each of the two values of $\overline{X}_A - \overline{X}_G$ that may be calculated is equal to 0. A treatment effect of +2 added to the scores of A_2 is present in panel b. Notice here that neither treatment mean is equal to the grand mean. This treatment effect of +2 is represented by a value of −1 for the $\overline{X}_{A_1} - \overline{X}_G$ deviation and a value of +1 for the $\overline{X}_{A_2} - \overline{X}_G$ deviation. Panel c represents a treatment effect of +6 added to the scores of A_2. Now $\overline{X}_{A_2} - \overline{X}_{A_1} = +6$. In the analysis of variance this effect is broken into a −3 for the $\overline{X}_{A_1} - \overline{X}_G$ deviation and a value of +3 for the $\overline{X}_{A_2} - \overline{X}_G$ deviation. Thus, you can see that if a treatment has an effect, it will be reflected

TABLE 11–3.

Demonstration that the term $\overline{X}_A - \overline{X}_G$ responds to the effect of an independent variable in an experiment. Treatment means are represented by $\overline{X}_A$ and the grand mean for each set of scores by $\overline{X}_G$. The difference between each treatment group mean and the grand mean is shown at the bottom of each set of scores.

a. **No treatment effect present: $\overline{X}_{A_2} - \overline{X}_{A_1} = 0.$**
b. **Treatment effect of +2 present: $\overline{X}_{A_2} - \overline{X}_{A_1} = +2.$**
c. **Treatment effect of +6 present: $\overline{X}_{A_2} - \overline{X}_{A_1} = +6.$**

	a		b		c	
	A_1	A_2	A_1	A_2	A_1	A_2
	11	12	11	14	11	18
	12	13	12	15	12	19
	13	11	13	13	13	17
$\overline{X}_A$	12	12	12	14	12	18
$\overline{X}_G$	12		13		15	
	$X_{A_1} - \overline{X}_G = 0$		$X_{A_1} - \overline{X}_G = -1$		$X_{A_1} - \overline{X}_G = -3$	
	$X_{A_2} - \overline{X}_G = 0$		$X_{A_2} - \overline{X}_G = +1$		$X_{A_2} - \overline{X}_G = +3$	

in the value of the $\overline{X}_A - \overline{X}_G$ deviations that can be calculated in an experiment.

Sampling Error.   In addition to any treatment effect, however, the treatment means also differ from each other because of sampling error. Even if the independent variable has no effect, a $\overline{X}_A - \overline{X}_G$ is expected to have a value different from zero simply because of sampling error.

$X_{ij} - \overline{X}_A$

The deviation of an individual score from a treatment mean, $X_{ij} - \overline{X}_A$ enters into the computation of MS_{Error}. It varies only with within-groups error variation in the experiment. In fact, this deviation was introduced in Chapter 5 without subscripting as the numerator of the standard deviation and variance, measures of error variability among scores within a group. The numerical value of this deviation does not vary with an effect of an independent variable. Because any effect of the independent variable is assumed to increase or decrease equally the scores of all individuals receiving a particular treatment, the treatment mean will change by an equal amount, and thus $X_{ij} - \overline{X}_A$ will remain constant regardless of the effect of an independent variable. Notice that for the second person in A_2 of Table 11–3 (i.e., the score represented by X_{22}; $X_{22} = 13$ in panel a), the $X_{ij} - \overline{X}_A$ deviation remains a +1 regardless of the absence or presence of a treatment effect. Thus, the values of $X_{ij} - \overline{X}_A$ reflect only error variation among the scores within a particular treatment condition.

Numerical Illustration of Partitioning a Score

To illustrate the numerical partitioning of a score we use the score of person 4 of group A_1 (i.e., X_{41}) of Table 11–1, which is 19.0. For this score equation 11–2 becomes

$$X_{41} - \overline{X}_G = (\overline{X}_{A_1} - \overline{X}_G) + (X_{41} - \overline{X}_{A_1}).$$

Substituting the appropriate numerical values for X_{41}, X_{A_2}, and $\overline{X}_G$, we obtain

$$19.0 - 14.0 = (17.0 - 14.0) + (19.0 - 17.0), \quad \text{or}$$
$$+5.0 \quad = \quad (+3.0) \quad + \quad (+2.0).$$

We have separated the total deviation of this subject's score from the grand mean into two components or parts. The partitioning shows that the score deviates from the grand mean ($X_{41} - \overline{X}_G = +5.0$) as much as it does because of the treatment condition the person is in (reflected in $\overline{X}_{A_1} - \overline{X}_G = +3.0$) and because of the unsystematic influences of error or chance factors (reflected in $X_{41} - \overline{X}_{A_1} = +2.0$). A similar partitioning could be done for each of the other scores in Table 11–1.

On a separate sheet of paper, test your knowledge of the material in this section by answering the following questions.

1. Define: one-factor multilevel designs, between-groups variance, within-groups variance, factor A, A_1 and A_2, a, n_A, N, $X_{ij} - \overline{X}_G$, $\overline{X}_A - \overline{X}_G$, $X_{ij} - \overline{X}_A$.
2. What is the limitation upon using the t test to analyze the data of an experiment?
3. What is the test statistic employed in analysis of variance?
4. Write the general equation for the F statistic.
5. Into what two sources does a one-factor between-subjects analysis of variance break down the total variation of the scores in an experiment?
6. An experimenter used a one-factor experiment with four levels: A_1, A_2, A_3, and A_4. There were 11 different individuals in each level. What are the values of a, n_A, and N?
7. Write the general equation for partitioning scores obtained in a one-factor between-subjects experiment.
8. Explain why the value of $\overline{X}_A - \overline{X}_G$ varies with the effect of an independent variable in an experiment.
9. Explain why the value of $X_{ij} - \overline{X}_A$ varies with error variation in an experiment.
10. Partition the score of subject 3 in the outline drawing condition (A_2) of Table 11–1 (i.e., $X_{23} = 16$) following equation 11–2.

Obtaining Mean Squares from Partitioned Scores

The benefit of partitioning a score into several components is that it establishes the basis for obtaining MS_A and MS_{Error} necessary for the F statistic. Recall that the sample variance was found from

$$s^2 = \frac{\sum\limits_{i=1}^{n_A} (X_i - \overline{X})^2}{(n - 1)}.$$

Notice that each term in equation 11–2 resembles the numerator of a variance. By using MS in place of s^2, *sum of squares (SS)* to represent $\Sigma(X_i - \overline{X})^2$, and df to represent $n - 1$, we may express the sample variance in more general form as

$$MS = \frac{SS}{df}.$$

This more general formula for the variance suggests that if each deviation represented in equation 11–2 were squared for each subject and then summed over all subjects in an experiment, the result would be a sum of squared deviations, or *SS*, the numerator of a mean square. From equation 11–2, three such *SS* terms can be obtained. The term $X_{ij} - \overline{X}_G$ leads to SS_{Total}, which represents the total deviation of a score from the grand mean. The $X_A - \overline{X}_G$ deviation leads to SS_A, which is a measure of between-group variation due to an effect of the independent variable, factor *A*. Finally, $X_{ij} - \overline{X}_A$ leads to SS_{Error}, which is a measure of within-group, or error variation in the experiment.

Obtaining the Three Sums of Squares

Let us illustrate how equation 11–2 may be used to obtain the sums of squares used in forming the mean squares needed for the *F* statistic. We demonstrate each step of this process numerically in Table 11–4 using the 15 scores shown in Table 11–1. Table 11–4 may appear intimidating to you; but the computations in the table require only the simple mathematical operations of addition, subtraction, and multiplication, and proceed in a step-by-step fashion. The steps also indicate what an analysis of variance does with the scores to obtain the *F* statistic. Follow each step carefully.

> **Step 1.** The scores of all 15 subjects in the experiment are partitioned following equation 11–2.
> **Step 2.** The numerical values of each deviation for each component of each score are obtained.

TABLE 11–4.

Obtaining sums of squares for a one-factor between-subjects analysis of variance. The scores employed are those in Table 11–1.

		Step 1: Partition scores for the 15 individuals				
		$X_{ij} - \overline{X}_G$	=	$(\overline{X}_A - \overline{X}_G)$	+	$(X_{ij} - \overline{X}_A)$
Scores in A_1	X_{11}	$17 - 14$	=	$(17 - 14)$	+	$(17 - 17)$
	X_{21}	$13 - 14$	=	$(17 - 14)$	+	$(13 - 17)$
	X_{31}	$16 - 14$	−	$(17 - 14)$	+	$(16 - 17)$
	X_{41}	$19 - 14$	=	$(17 - 14)$	+	$(19 - 17)$
	X_{51}	$20 - 14$	=	$(17 - 14)$	+	$(20 - 17)$
Scores in A_2	X_{12}	$14 - 14$	=	$(13 - 14)$	+	$(14 - 13)$
	X_{22}	$13 - 14$	=	$(13 - 14)$	+	$(13 - 13)$
	X_{32}	$16 - 14$	=	$(13 - 14)$	+	$(16 - 13)$
	X_{42}	$12 - 14$	=	$(13 - 14)$	+	$(12 - 13)$
	X_{52}	$10 - 14$	=	$(13 - 14)$	+	$(10 - 13)$
Scores in A_3	X_{13}	$15 - 14$	=	$(12 - 14)$	+	$(15 - 12)$
	X_{23}	$10 - 14$	=	$(12 - 14)$	+	$(10 - 12)$
	X_{33}	$11 - 14$	=	$(12 - 14)$	+	$(11 - 12)$
	X_{43}	$12 - 14$	=	$(12 - 14)$	+	$(12 - 12)$
	X_{53}	$12 - 14$	=	$(12 - 14)$	+	$(12 - 12)$

Step 2: Perform the subtractions in Step 1 to obtain deviations

		$X_{ij} - \overline{X}_G$	=	$(\overline{X}_A - \overline{X}_G)$	+	$(X_{ij} - \overline{X}_A)$
Scores in A_1	X_{11}	+3	=	+3	+	-0
	X_{21}	-1	=	+3	+	-4
	X_{31}	+2	=	+3	+	-1
	X_{41}	+5	=	+3	+	+2
	X_{51}	+6	=	+3	+	+3
Scores in A_2	X_{12}	-0	=	-1	+	+1
	X_{22}	-1	=	-1	+	-0
	X_{32}	+2	=	-1	+	+3
	X_{42}	-2	=	-1	+	-1
	X_{52}	-4	=	-1	+	-3
Scores in A_3	X_{13}	+1	=	-2	+	+3
	X_{23}	-4	=	-2	+	-2
	X_{33}	-3	=	-2	+	-1
	X_{43}	-2	=	-2	+	-0
	X_{53}	-2	=	-2	+	-0

Step 3: Square each deviation

		$(X_{ij} - \overline{X}_G)^2$	$(\overline{X}_A - \overline{X}_G)^2$	$(X_{ij} - \overline{X}_A)^2$
Scores in A_1	X_{11}	9	9	0
	X_{21}	1	9	16
	X_{31}	4	9	1
	X_{41}	25	9	4
	X_{51}	36	9	9
Scores in A_2	X_{12}	0	1	1
	X_{22}	1	1	0
	X_{32}	4	1	9
	X_{42}	4	1	1
	X_{52}	16	1	9
Scores in A_3	X_{13}	1	4	9
	X_{23}	16	4	4
	X_{33}	9	4	1
	X_{43}	4	4	0
	X_{53}	4	4	0

Step 4: Sum the squared deviations for each partition over all individuals

$$\sum_{j=1}^{a=3} \sum_{i=1}^{n_A=5} (X_{ij} - \overline{X}_G)^2 = \sum_{j=1}^{a=3} \sum_{i=1}^{n_A=5} (\overline{X}_A - \overline{X}_G)^2 + \sum_{j=1}^{a=3} \sum_{i=1}^{n_A=5} (X_{ij} - \overline{X}_A)^2$$

134.0	=	70.0	+	64.0
SS_{Total}	=	SS_A	+	SS_{Error}

Step 3. Each of the positive and negative deviations obtained in step 2 is squared.

Step 4. The values of the squared deviations are summed over all scores in the experiment. This summing is achieved simply by adding the 15 values in each of the columns. The result, as expected, is three sums of squares: SS_{Total}, SS_A, and SS_{Error}.

As shown in step 4, the SS_{Total} is represented mathematically by

$$\sum_{j=1}^{a} \sum_{i=1}^{n_A} (X_{ij} - \overline{X}_G)^2.$$

The double summation sign

$$\sum_{j=1}^{3} \sum_{i=1}^{5}$$

indicates that the squared deviations $(X_{ij} - \overline{X}_G)^2$ are to be summed over all subjects in each treatment group (from the first subject, $i = 1$, to the last subject, n_A, in a particular group) and over all groups (from the first level of the independent variable, $j = 1$, to the last level, a). In our example there are five scores in each group ($n_A = 5$) and three groups ($a = 3$); thus the summation limits are from $i = 1$ to $n_A = 5$ and from $j = 1$ to $a = 3$. Similarly, to obtain the SS_A value, the squared deviations of the treatment group mean from the grand mean are summed over all subjects in the experiment; accordingly, SS_A is represented by

$$\sum_{j=1}^{3} \sum_{i=1}^{5} (\overline{X}_A - \overline{X}_G)^2.$$

Finally, SS_{Error} is obtained by summing each squared deviation of a subject's score from the mean of his or her treatment group, or

$$\sum_{j=1}^{3} \sum_{i=1}^{5} (X_{ij} - \overline{X}_A)^2.$$

An important relationship that exists among the sum of squares terms is shown at the bottom of Table 11–4. The SS_{Total} is equal to the sum of SS_A and SS_{Error}, or

$$SS_{Total} = SS_A + SS_{Error}. \hspace{3em} \textbf{Eq. 11–3}$$

Equation 11–3 may also be written in more general mathematical notation as

$$\sum_{j=1}^{a} \sum_{i=1}^{n_A} (X_{ij} - \overline{X}_G)^2 = \sum_{j=1}^{a} \sum_{i=1}^{n_A} (\overline{X}_A - \overline{X}_G)^2 + \sum_{j=1}^{a} \sum_{i=1}^{n_A} (X_{ij} - \overline{X}_A)^2. \qquad \textbf{Eq. 11–4}$$

Thus, we see that the total variation in scores of an experiment, SS_{Total}, is the result of systematic variation that occurs between groups receiving different treatments, SS_A (sometimes identified as $SS_{between\text{-}groups}$ or $SS_{Treatments}$), and error variation that occurs within groups, SS_{Error} (sometimes expressed as $SS_{within\text{-}groups}$).

Obtaining SS values for scores is the major computational procedure involved in analysis of variance. In practice, however, it is unlikely that you would perform the necessary calculations following the steps presented in Table 11–4, for these steps are tedious and easily open to error, especially as the number of scores involved becomes large. Instead, simplified raw-score computational formulas leading to identical numerical values commonly are used to obtain the SS values and we illustrate them later in this chapter. Following the steps shown in Table 11–4 should help you to understand the concept of sums of squares as used in analysis of variance. The computational formulas do not lead to this understanding easily.

Determining Degrees of Freedom

The final step in obtaining MS_A and MS_{Error} is to divide each SS by its df. Recall that degrees of freedom refers to the number of values that are free to vary in the computation of a statistic. The df for each of the sum of squares components of equation 11–3 are determined easily by applying the definition of degrees of freedom to each term: SS_{Total}, SS_A, and SS_{Error}.

Total Degrees of Freedom.   To compute the total sum of squares, SS_{Total}, the grand mean, $\overline{X}_G$, must be known. Because the total sum of squares is based upon the deviation of every score in the experiment from the grand mean (i.e., $X_{ij} - \overline{X}_G$), then one less than the total number of scores are free to vary. To illustrate, refer to the scores in Table 11–1. The grand mean $\overline{X}_G$ for the 15 scores is 14.0. To derive the SS_{Total} the grand mean is subtracted from each of the 15 scores. The sum of the 15 $(X_{ij} - \overline{X}_G)$ deviations must equal 0. Thus, any 14 of the 15 scores are free to vary, but the 15th score becomes fixed if $\overline{X}_G$ is known. Accordingly, there are 14 df associated with the SS_{Total}.

More generally, the **total degrees of freedom,** or df_{Total}, is equal to one less than the total number of scores analyzed. In notation

$$df_{Total} = N - 1,$$

where N represents the total number of scores in the experiment.

Degrees of Freedom for SS$_A$.   The SS_A is computed from the deviations of the means of the treatment conditions (e.g., $\overline{X}_{A_1}$, $\overline{X}_{A_2}$, and $\overline{X}_{A_3}$ for our example) from the grand mean $\overline{X}_G$. For a research design with three levels of the independent variable and an equal number of scores in each condition, if the grand mean is known, then only two treatment means are free to vary. For example, where $\overline{X}_G = 14.0$, $\overline{X}_{A_1} = 17.0$, and $\overline{X}_{A_3} = 12.0$, as in Table 11–1, then $\overline{X}_{A_2}$ becomes known; it must equal 13.0. Any other value of $\overline{X}_{A_2}$ would not be consistent with a grand mean $\overline{X}_G$ of 14.0. Accordingly, there are 2 df for SS_A in the example.

In general, the *df* for SS_A, or *df$_A$*, is equal to one less than the number of levels of the independent variable. In notation,

$$df_A = a - 1,$$

where a represents the number of levels of the independent variable A.

Degrees of Freedom for SS$_{Error}$.   The SS_{Error} is based upon subtracting the mean of each treatment condition, $\overline{X}_A$, from the scores of all subjects within that treatment condition for each treatment condition in the experiment. Thus, for each level of the independent variable, after X_A is determined, only $n_A - 1$ scores are free to vary within that level. In Table 11–1, only four of the five scores are free to vary within each treatment condition A_1, A_2, and A_3. Because there are three levels of the independent variable and four scores are free to vary within each of the levels, there are 12 *df* associated with the SS_{Error} (4 *df* for A_1 + 4 *df* for A_2 + 4 *df* for $A_3 = 12$).

More generally, where a represents the number of levels of the independent variable and there are n_A scores within each level of the independent variable, the **df for error**, or *df$_{Error}$* $= a(n_A - 1)$. Because $(a)(n)$ equals the total number of scores (N), the *df$_{Error}$* may also be expressed as the total number of scores (N) minus the number of levels of the independent variable (a), or

$$df_{Error} = N - a.$$

Additivity of Degrees of Freedom.   The degrees of freedom are additive in the same manner as the corresponding sums of squares values. Thus

$$df_{Total} = df_A + df_{Error}. \qquad\qquad \textbf{Eq. 11–5}$$

This relationship holds in our example, for $df_{Total} = 14$, $df_A = 2$, and $df_{Error} = 12$.

Calculating Variance Estimates from SS and df: Mean Squares

The F statistic is a ratio of two mean squares, MS_A and MS_{Error}. The two required MS values are derived from the SS obtained in equation 11–3 and the df value associated with each SS. More specifically, these mean squares are defined as follows:

$$MS_A = \frac{SS_A}{df_A}$$

$$MS_{Error} = \frac{SS_{Error}}{df_{Error}}.$$

Although it is possible to obtain a MS_{Total} by dividing the SS_{Total} by the df_{Total}, this value provides no useful information in an analysis of variance and it typically is not calculated. For the scores in Table 11–1 we have found $SS_A = 70.00$ and $SS_{Error} = 64.00$ (see Table 11–4). Further, $df_A = 2$ and $df_{Error} = 12$. Consequently

$$MS_A = \frac{SS_A}{df_A} = \frac{70.00}{2} = 35.00, \quad \text{and}$$

$$MS_{Error} = \frac{SS_{Error}}{df_{Error}} = \frac{64.00}{12} = 5.33.$$

Computing the F Statistic

At the beginning of this chapter we introduced the F statistic as

$$F = \frac{MS_A}{MS_{Error}}.$$

The numerator variance, MS_A, is a variance that varies with the effect of the independent variable and sampling error, whereas the denominator variance, MS_{Error}, measures only error variation among the scores within the several treatment groups. We have now obtained those two variances, MS_A and MS_{Error}. For the scores of Table 11–1, $MS_A = 35.00$ and $MS_{Error} = 5.33$. Thus

$$F_{obs} = \frac{35.00}{5.33} = 6.57,$$

where F_{obs} is used to indicate the value of F obtained from the scores analyzed.

The numerical values of an analysis of variance are summarized frequently in a table that identifies the sources of variation, the relevant df, SS, and MS values, and the value of F_{obs}. Table 11–5 illustrates how such a summary table is organized. We also have presented the formulas for each of the computations involved using the notation introduced in this chapter. A numerical summary of the analysis of variance performed on the data of Table 11–1 is presented in Table 11–6. We will discuss how to interpret and use this table shortly.

TABLE 11–5.

Notational summary of a one-factor between-subjects analysis of variance.

Source	df [a]	SS	MS	F
Factor A	$a - 1$	$\sum_{j=1}^{a} \sum_{i=1}^{n_A} (\overline{X}_A - \overline{X}_G)^2$	SS_A / df_A	MS_A / MS_{Error}
Error	$N - a$	$\sum_{j=1}^{a} \sum_{i=1}^{n_A} (X_{ij} - \overline{X}_A)^2$	SS_{Error} / df_{Error}	
Total	$N - 1$	$\sum_{j=1}^{a} \sum_{i=1}^{n_A} (X_{ij} - \overline{X}_G)^2$	Not calculated	

[a] a = number of levels of factor A; n_A = number of scores in a treatment condition. N = total number of scores.

TABLE 11–6.

Summary of the analysis of variance on the scores in Table 11–1.

Source	df	SS	MS	F [a]
Type of drawing (A)	2	70.00	35.00	6.57*
Error	12	64.00	5.33	
Total	14	134.00		

*$p < .05$.

[a] Significant values of F are indicated by a probability level footnote on a summary table, i.e., *$p < .05$.

Testing Your Knowledge 11–2

On a separate sheet of paper, test your knowledge of the material in this section by answering the following questions.

1. Write the definitional equation for a sample variance.
2. Write the equation for a sample variance in sum of squares notation.
3. Complete the following equations for a one-factor between-subjects analysis of variance.
   a. $\sum_{j=1}^{a} \sum_{i=1}^{n_A} (X_{ij} - \overline{X}_G)^2 =$
   b. $SS_{Total} =$

c. $df_A =$

d. $df_{Error} =$

e. $MS_A =$

f. $MS_{Error} =$

4. What is the value of SS_{Total} if $SS_A = 50$ and $SS_{Error} = 100$?

5. What is the value of SS_A if $SS_{Total} = 75.3$ and $SS_{Error} = 51.2$?

6. What is the value of df_{Total} if $df_A = 4$ and $df_{Error} = 76$?

7. What is the value of MS_A if $SS_A = 100$ and $df_A = 4$?

8. What is the value of MS_{Error} if $SS_{Error} = 760$ and $df_{Error} = 76$?

9. An experimenter used a one-factor experiment with four levels: A_1, A_2, A_3, and A_4. There were 11 different individuals in each level. What are the values of df_A, df_{Error}, and df_{Total}?

10. Suppose you conducted an experiment with two levels of an independent variable and three participants in each group and obtained the following scores:

Factor A

A_1	A_2
30	34
32	36
28	32

Partition these scores following the approach illustrated in Table 11–4. Obtain the SS_{Total}, SS_A, and SS_{Error} and the corresponding degrees of freedom for each partition. Then complete a numerical summary table for the analysis.

11. Suppose you now conducted an experiment with three levels of an independent variable and three participants in each group and obtained the following scores:

Factor A

A_1	A_2	A_3
30	34	37
32	36	35
28	32	33

Partition these scores following the approach illustrated in Table 11–4. Obtain the SS_{Total}, SS_A, and SS_{Error} and the corresponding degrees of freedom for each partition. Then complete a numerical summary table for the analysis.

12. Tables 1 and 2 below are incomplete summary tables for a one-factor between-subjects analysis of variance. Assume an equal number of subjects in each level of the independent variable. Provide the missing values in each table by using the relationships among SS and df given in

equations 11–3 and 11–5, respectively, and the formulas in Table 11–5. Then answer the following questions for each table.

a. How many levels of the independent variable were used?
b. How many subjects participated in the study?
c. How many subjects were measured in each treatment condition?

Table 1

Source	df	SS	MS	F
Factor A	1	50	_____	_____
Error	26	260	_____	
Total	_____	_____		

Table 2

Source	df	SS	MS	F
Factor A	3	_____	6.0	_____
Error	76	_____	_____	
Total	79	170		

STATISTICAL HYPOTHESIS TESTING WITH THE F RATIO

The purpose of obtaining a test statistic, such as the F ratio, is to decide if the treatment means differ significantly. To understand how this decision is made using the F ratio, it is necessary to review briefly the factors influencing MS_A and MS_{Error}, and the relationship of MS_A and MS_{Error}.

Factors Affecting the Value of MS_A and MS_{Error}

MS_A
The value of MS_A is given by

$$MS_A = \frac{SS_A}{df_A}.$$

Accordingly, the numerical value of MS_A depends upon the value of SS_A, where

$$SS_A = \sum_{j=1}^{a} \sum_{i=1}^{n_A} (\overline{X}_A - \overline{X}_G)^2.$$

If each treatment mean is identical to each other treatment mean and thus equal to the grand mean, then the value of MS_A is equal to zero. For example, the value of MS_A for the scores in panel a of Table 11–3 is 0. MS_A

takes on values different from zero, however, whenever the means of two or more treatment groups are not equal to each other. As the values of $\overline{X}_A$ become more disparate from each other and, consequently, different from the value of $\overline{X}_G$, the numerical value of MS_A becomes larger. As an example, for panel b of Table 11–3, MS_A is 6 and for panel c, MS_A is 54.

As we indicated in our discussion of partitioning a score, two sources of variation affect the value of

$$\sum_{j=1}^{a} \sum_{i=1}^{n_A} (\overline{X}_A - \overline{X}_G)^2$$

in any experiment: the effect of the independent variable, and sampling error.

Hence, MS_A, too, varies with the effect of the independent variable and sampling error. Because MS_A increases with an effect of an independent variable, it is treated as the mean square associated with the systematic variance created by factor A, the independent variable.

MS_{Error}

The MS_{Error} is obtained by

$$\frac{\sum_{j=1}^{a} \sum_{i=1}^{n_A} (X_{ij} - \overline{X}_A)^2}{df_{Error}}.$$

Thus it measures only the within-groups error variation in an experiment. The value of MS_{Error} will not be affected by an independent variable. This result occurs because any systematic changes in scores due to a treatment effect will also be accompanied by a corresponding increase or decrease in the treatment mean. Thus, the difference between an individual's score and the group mean, $(X_{ij} - \overline{X}_A)$, will not change. Hence, MS_{Error} is a measure of only within-groups error variation in the scores of an experiment. The factors affecting each mean square are summarized in Table 11–7.

TABLE 11–7.
Factors affecting MS_A and MS_{Error} in an experiment.

Variance	Affected by
MS_A	Sampling error The effect of the independent variable
MS_{Error}	Within-groups error variation

The Relationship of MS_A and MS_{Error}

Unbiased Estimates.   Both MS_A and MS_{Error} are unbiased estimates of the population variance of scores σ^2. They are unbiased because in deriving each variance estimate, the sum of squares is divided by degrees of freedom rather than by the actual number of scores involved in the computation of the variance. As unbiased estimates, neither mean square value should be systematically smaller nor larger than the population variance when error variation alone is responsible for the variability in scores on which the estimate is based.

Independent Estimates.   Our discussion of the factors affecting MS_A and MS_{Error} indicated that these mean squares are independent estimates of the population variance. **Independent estimates** means that either mean square may change in value without affecting the value of the other. We illustrate how a treatment effect influences MS_A but not MS_{Error} and, therefore, why each variance estimate is independent, in Table 11–8. Table 11–8a presents an analysis of variance summary on scores simulating a situation in which an independent variable has no effect; each sample was randomly selected from a population with $\mu = 14.0$ and $\sigma^2 = 4.56$. Therefore, each sample mean (13.4 and 14.2) is an unbiased estimate of the same population mean ($\mu = 14.0$); the observed difference between the sample means is due only to sampling error. The MS_A and

TABLE 11–8.

a. Analysis of variance on scores without a treatment effect. The scores for each group were randomly selected from a population with $\mu = 14.0$.

Factor A		Source	df	SS	MS	F
A_1	A_2					
13	16	Factor A	1	1.60	1.60	1.07
15	15	Error	8	12.00	1.50	
13	13	Total	9	13.60		
12	14					
14	13					
$\overline{X}_A$ 13.4	14.2					

b. Analysis of variance on scores with a treatment effect of $+2$ for level A_2. The treatment effect added to scores is shown in parentheses.

Factor A			Source	df	SS	MS	F
A_1	A_2						
13	18	(16 + 2)	Factor A	1	19.60	19.60	13.07*
15	17	(15 + 2)	Error	8	12.00	1.50	
13	15	(13 + 2)	Total	9	31.60		
12	16	(14 + 2)	*$p < .05$				
14	15	(13 + 2)					
$\overline{X}_A$ 13.4	16.2						

MS_{Error} values in the summary table (1.60 and 1.50, respectively) are both smaller than the actual population variance they estimate; however, they are unbiased and independent estimates of σ^2. Because both samples were drawn from the same population and no treatment effect was present, both are estimating only error variation in the scores. Thus, we do not expect MS_A and MS_{Error} to differ greatly from each other. As expected, F_{obs}, 1.07, is slightly greater than 1.00.

Table 11–8b shows what happens to MS_A and MS_{Error} when an independent variable does have an effect. Here a treatment effect is simulated by adding +2 to each score in the A_2 column, thus increasing $\overline{X}_{A_2}$ from 14.2 to 16.2. This "treatment effect" is equivalent to drawing the A_2 sample from a population with $\mu = 16.0$. As a result of this treatment effect, SS_A, and correspondingly MS_A, is increased. The SS_{Error}, and thus MS_{Error}, remain unchanged. As a result, F_{obs} in Table 11–8b is larger than the value in Table 11–8a (13.07 versus 1.07).

This example demonstrates that if the independent variable has no effect upon the dependent variable (as in Table 11–8a), then only error variation affects the MS_A and MS_{Error} values. Both mean squares are expected to be approximately equal, and therefore, F_{obs} should be equal to about 1.00. If the independent variable does produce an effect (as in Table 11–8b), then MS_A responds to the systematic variation contributed by the independent variable in addition to the existing sampling error. Consequently, MS_A will be larger than MS_{Error} and F_{obs} will be greater than 1.00.

With this understanding of the factors affecting the value of F, we are ready to use the F in a statistical hypothesis test. Statistical testing with the F follows the now familiar steps:

- Two statistical hypotheses, a null hypothesis, H_0, and an alternative hypothesis, H_1, are formulated. The null hypothesis provides the theoretical sampling distribution of the F statistic.
- A significance level is selected.
- A critical value of F, identified as F_{crit}, is obtained from Table A–3.
- A rejection region is located in the theoretical sampling distribution for F.
- The F ratio, identified as F_{obs}, is calculated from the scores collected.
- A decision to reject or not reject H_0 is made on the basis of whether or not F_{obs} falls into the rejection region.

Statistical Hypotheses

Null Hypothesis
The null hypothesis establishes a condition under which the sampling distribution of the F statistic may be obtained. For an experiment with

three levels of an independent variable, the null hypothesis tested in an analysis of variance is that the populations from which the three samples were obtained are identical and hence have the same means, μ_A. In mathematical notation, this null hypothesis may be written

$$H_0: \mu_{A_1} = \mu_{A_2} = \mu_{A_3}.$$

This null hypothesis represents the situation that exists if the independent variable has no effect. If this null hypothesis is true for an experiment, then any observed difference among the sample means is due to sampling error.

The number of population means identified in the null hypothesis always corresponds to the number of levels of the independent variable. If an experiment involves five levels of an independent variable, then the null hypothesis is written as

$$H_0: \mu_{A_1} = \mu_{A_2} = \mu_{A_3} = \mu_{A_4} = \mu_{A_5}.$$

Alternative Hypothesis
The alternative hypothesis, H_1, is stated typically as the negation of the null hypothesis, or

$$H_1: \text{not } H_0$$

regardless of the number of population means involved in the null hypothesis. The alternative hypothesis states that the population means from which the samples in the experiment are drawn are not equal to each other, a situation that exists if the independent variable does have an effect.

The Sampling Distribution of F

The decision to reject or not reject the null hypothesis depends upon how rare or unlikely a value of F_{obs} would be if H_0 were true. The sampling distribution of a statistic is a probability density function of values taken on by the statistic when H_0 is true. Thus, the probability of obtaining a value of F if H_0 is true is determined from the sampling distribution of the F statistic. There is not just one sampling distribution of F, for the sampling distribution of F depends upon the number of means being compared and the number of scores in each treatment condition. Specifically, the sampling distribution of F varies with the degrees of freedom associated with the numerator mean square (i.e., MS_A) and denominator mean square (i.e., MS_{Error}) of the F ratio.

The sampling distribution for F with 1 df for the numerator (i.e., 1 df for MS_A) and 8 degrees of freedom for the denominator (i.e., 8 df for

FIGURE 11–1.

Theoretical sampling distribution of F for 1 and 8 degrees of freedom.

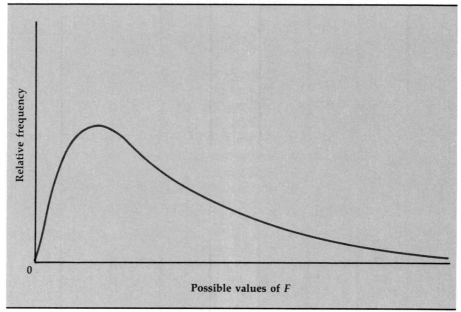

MS_{Error}) is illustrated in Figure 11–1. Because the df for MS_A are found by $a - 1$, and the df for MS_{Error} are found by $a(n - 1)$, we know that this sampling distribution is appropriate for an F calculated on an experiment with two treatment groups (i.e., $a = 2$, so that $2 - 1 = 1$ df for MS_A) and five subjects in each treatment group [i.e., $n_A = 5$ so that $2(5 - 1) = 8$ df for the MS_{Error}].

Unlike the t distribution, the distribution of F is positively skewed. The lowest possible value of F is zero; this value would be obtained if the sample means were equal to each other and the resulting MS_A value were zero. The most probable value is about 1.00, for if H_0 is true, then MS_A should be about the same as MS_{Error}.[1] There is no upper limit to the values that F may assume; F may take on any value between 0 and positive infinity. Because the probability of obtaining a value of F between 0 and positive infinity is 1.00, the area under the distribution is equal to 1.00.

Selecting a Significance Level

The significance level specifies how improbable an obtained value of F must be under a null hypothesis to reject H_0 as being true. In effect, it is our definition of statistical rareness for the test statistic if H_0 is true. The

---

[1]The actual expected value of F under the null hypothesis is given by $df_{Error}/(df_{Error} - 2)$, where $df_{Error} > 2$.

significance level usually adopted in behavioral science research is either $\alpha = .05$ or $\alpha = .01$. We illustrate locating a rejection region for a .05 significance level.

Locating the Rejection Region for F

The rejection region represents values of F that have a probability equal to or less than α if the null hypothesis is true. Thus, the rejection region defines values of F_{obs} that meet the criterion for rejecting the null hypothesis, and accepting the alternative hypothesis. The rejection region for F_{obs} always lies in the tail of the sampling distribution for F. We can see why the rejection region is located here if we recall how the value of F_{obs} varies with the effect of an independent variable.

If an independent variable has no effect and therefore H_0 is true, then it is expected that MS_A and MS_{Error} will be nearly equal; consequently, F_{obs} should be about 1.00. If the independent variable does have an effect and therefore H_0 is not true, then MS_A will be larger than MS_{Error} and F_{obs} will be greater than 1.00. (Review Table 11–8 for an illustration of this relation.) In order to reject the null hypothesis then, the value of F_{obs} must be sufficiently greater than 1.00 that the probability of such a value of F occurring if H_0 were true is equal to or less than the alpha level selected. Therefore, the rejection region for F always lies among the larger values of F in the tail of the distribution.

Critical values of F (identified as F_{crit}) identifying the lower limit of the rejection region for $\alpha = .05$ and .01 are presented in Table A–3 in the Appendix. For purposes of illustration, a section of Table A–3 of F_{crit} for the .05 significance level is presented in Table 11–9. Notice that this table

TABLE 11–9.
Values of F_{crit} for $\alpha = .05$.

Degrees of Freedom for Denominator	Degrees of Freedom for Numerator				
	1	2	3	4	5
1	161.4	199.5	215.7	224.6	230.2
2	18.51	19.00	19.16	19.25	19.30
3	10.13	9.55	9.28	9.12	9.01
4	7.71	6.94	6.59	6.39	6.26
5	6.61	5.79	5.41	5.19	5.05
6	5.99	5.14	4.76	4.53	4.39
7	5.59	4.74	4.35	4.12	3.97
8	**5.32**	4.46	4.07	3.84	3.69
9	5.12	4.26	3.86	3.63	3.48
10	4.96	4.10	3.71	3.48	3.33

Reprinted with permission from Table VI.1 Percentage Points, F-Distribution, *CRC Handbook of Tables for Probability and Statistics* (2nd ed.). Copyright 1968, CRC Press, Inc., Boca Raton, Florida.

is arranged so that the degrees of freedom associated with the numerator (i.e., MS_A) of the F ratio appear in a row across the top of the table. The degrees of freedom for the denominator (i.e., MS_{Error}) appear in the column on the left side of the table.

As an example, to locate the value of F_{crit} for 1, 8 degrees of freedom, we find the column for 1 df and then locate the row for 8 df. This column and row intersect at the value of 5.32 (boldfaced in Table 11–9). This value is F_{crit} and locates the rejection region for an F_{obs} with 1 and 8 df. Any value of F_{obs} with 1, 8 df that is equal to or larger than 5.32 falls into the rejection region. Such values of F_{obs} occur only 5 or fewer times in every 100 experiments if the null hypothesis is true. Figure 11–2 illustrates the location of this rejection region on the theoretical sampling distribution of F for 1, 8 df.

Decisions about the Statistical Hypotheses

The value of F_{obs} provides the basis for making decisions about the statistical hypotheses. If F_{obs} falls into a rejection region, then the null hypothesis is rejected and the alternative hypothesis accepted. There is a **statistically significant** difference among the sample means. On the other hand, if F_{obs} does not fall into a rejection region, then we fail to reject H_0 and do not accept H_1. The differences among the sample means are **statistically nonsignificant.**

FIGURE 11–2.

Location of the rejection region on sampling distribution of F for 1 and 8 degrees of freedom. The F_{crit} from Table A–3 is 5.32.

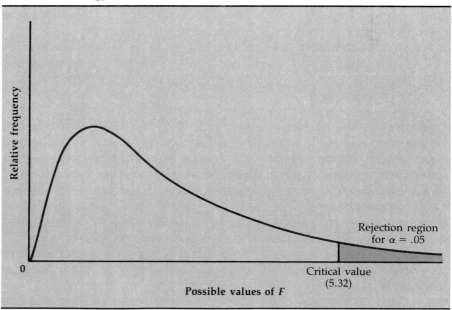

Statistically Significant Difference

The interpretation of a significant difference among the means is more complex in a multilevel design than it is for the simple two-group experiment discussed in Chapter 10. To illustrate, we use our example experiment on the retention of drawings. In this experiment we manipulated three levels of type of drawing to determine if the type of drawing affected recall of the items depicted in the drawings. The mean number of items recalled as a function of type of drawing is portrayed below.

	Type of Drawing (A)		
	Incomplete Outline (A_1)	Outline (A_2)	Detailed (A_3)
$\overline{X}_A$	17.0	13.0	12.0

The analysis of variance on the scores (given in Table 11–1) resulted in $F_{obs}(2, 12) = 6.57$ (see Table 11–6). For 2, 12 df, F_{crit} at the .05 level is 3.89. F_{obs} is larger than F_{crit} and thus falls into the rejection region. Accordingly, we reject the null hypothesis

$$H_0: \mu_{A_1} = \mu_{A_2} = \mu_{A_3}$$

and accept the alternative

$$H_1: \text{not } H_0.$$

We conclude that the three sample means are not all equal to each other. The independent variable did affect the number of items recalled. Notice, however, there are many ways for H_1: not H_0 to be true. The null hypothesis would be true, for example, if μ_{A_1} was greater than either μ_{A_2} or μ_{A_3}, and μ_{A_2} and μ_{A_3} were equal; or if μ_{A_1} was greater than μ_{A_2}, and μ_{A_2} was greater than μ_{A_3}. Which relationship holds for the pattern of means in the example? The analysis of variance alone does not answer this question with certainty, for rejection of H_0 when there are three or more treatment conditions being tested simply lets us conclude that there is at least one statistically significant difference among the means. In our example, a visual inspection of the means suggests that the incomplete outline drawing condition led to the largest number of items recalled and that there was little difference between the outline and detailed drawing conditions.

A visual inspection of the treatment means after finding a statistically significant F_{obs} always will not be sufficient to determine the exact nature of the differences among the sample means. In many instances, the researcher will follow up the analysis of variance with multiple comparison tests. We discuss two such tests in Chapter 12. The decision-making procedures and corresponding conclusions for a statistically significant difference are summarized in the left column of Table 11–10.

TABLE 11–10.

Summary of decisions and conclusions in statistical hypothesis testing using the analysis of variance for a one-factor between-subjects design. A .05 significance level is illustrated.

If F_{obs} Falls into the Rejection Region for $\alpha = .05$, then:	If F_{obs} Does Not Fall into the Rejection Region for $\alpha = .05$, then:
p of F_{obs} is less than or equal to .05, or $p \leq .05$.	p of F_{obs} is greater than .05, or $p > .05$.
The null hypothesis (H_0) is rejected.	The null hypothesis (H_0) is not rejected.
The alternative hypothesis (H_1) is accepted. The sample means are not all from the same populations.	The alternative hypothesis (H_1) is not accepted.
The difference among the sample means is statistically significant at the .05 level.	The difference among the sample means is nonsignificant at the .05 level.
It is decided that something in addition to sampling error is responsible for the differences among the sample means. In a carefully done experiment the difference is attributed to the independent variable. Follow-up tests may be needed.	It is decided that sampling error is the most plausible explanation of the differences among the sample means. There is no evidence that the independent variable had an effect.

Nonsignificant Difference

If we fail to reject H_0 and do not accept H_1, then we have no evidence that the null hypothesis is not true. Despite any observed numerical differences among the means, they are considered to be drawn from populations with identical means. The implication for the experiment is that the independent variable had no effect and the observed difference between the sample means is a chance occurrence readily explained by sampling error alone. These decisions and conclusions are summarized in the right column of Table 11–10.

An example of a statistically nonsignificant difference is provided by the analysis of variance summarized in Table 11–8a. The F_{obs} of 1.07 is smaller than the critical value of 5.32 and thus does not fall into the rejection region (see Figure 11–2). Accordingly, we fail to reject H_0 and do not accept H_1 for this value of F_{obs}. We decide that the treatment means do not differ significantly at the .05 level and that the two sample means presented in Table 11–8a ($\overline{X}_{A_1} = 13.4$ and $\overline{X}_{A_2} = 14.2$) are from the same population. The observed difference between them is most likely due to sampling error.

Assumptions of One-Factor Between-Subjects Analysis of Variance

Similarly to the t test, the between-subjects analysis of variance is based upon three assumptions about the scores obtained in an experiment:

1. Each subject in the experiment is randomly and independently drawn from the population.
2. The scores in the populations sampled are normally distributed.
3. The variances of scores in the populations are equal.

These assumptions are important because the sampling distribution of F, and therefore the values of F_{crit} given in Table A–3 are generated from populations that meet these assumptions. As with the t test, these assumptions may be violated in an experiment. The results of such violations are similar to those discussed for the t test for two independent groups in Chapter 10. In order for the between-subjects analysis of variance to be used, each score in the experiment must be independent of every other score. That is, every individual may be involved in only one level of the independent variable and contribute only one score in the experiment. If a subject is involved in more than one level of the independent variable, and two or more scores are analyzed for a person, then the within-subjects analysis of variance must be used. This analysis of variance is discussed in Chapter 14.

Violations of the second (the normal distribution of scores) and the third (the equality of variances) assumptions can change the probability of obtaining a particular value of F_{obs} and thus affect the probability of making a Type I error. Again we suggest that violations of these assumptions are more likely to have minimal effects on the probability of making a Type I error when the following conditions are met:

- The number of participants in each group is the same.
- The shape of the distributions of the scores for each treatment condition is about the same and the distributions are neither very peaked nor very flat.
- The significance level is set at .05 rather than at .01.

Testing Your Knowledge 11–3

On a separate sheet of paper, test your knowledge of the material in this section by answering the following questions.

1. Define: F_{crit}, F_{obs}, rejection region.
2. What factors affect the value of MS_A in an experiment?

3. Explain why MS_A increases in value with the effect of the independent variable.

4. What factors affect the value of MS_{Error} in an experiment?

5. Explain why the value of MS_{Error} is not affected by an independent variable.

6. What value of F_{obs} is expected if an independent variable has no effect in an experiment?

7. What is expected to happen to the value of F_{obs} if an independent variable has an effect in an experiment?

8. Identify the steps necessary in statistical hypothesis testing with the F test.

9. Write the statistical hypotheses for the F test for two independent groups.

10. Write the statistical hypotheses for the F test for four independent groups.

11. To which inference in an experiment does H_0 of an analysis of variance correspond: the independent variable has an effect on the dependent variable, or the independent variable has no effect?

12. To which inference in an experiment does H_1 of an analysis of variance correspond: the independent variable has an effect on the dependent variable, or the independent variable has no effect?

13. What is the lower limit for the value of F if H_0 is true?

14. What is the upper limit for the value of F if H_0 is true?

15. The following exercise provides values for df_A, df_{Error} and F_{obs} for several hypothetical one-factor between-subjects experiments. For each set of values, obtain the value of F_{crit} for a .05 significance level from Table A–3. Then indicate whether the value of F_{obs} falls into the rejection region. Finally, indicate your decision with respect to H_0 and H_1. If the exact df are not tabled for df_{Error}, then use the next lower tabled value.

	df_A	df_{Error}	F_{obs}
a.	1	10	5.12
b.	2	24	3.29
c.	1	24	4.26
d.	2	90	3.24
e.	2	12	3.94
f.	2	15	3.60
g.	4	45	1.93
h.	3	20	1.46
i.	6	60	98.19
j.	4	95	2.13

16. Identify the assumptions underlying the use of the one-factor between-subjects analysis of variance.

17. Under what conditions will violation of normality of the distribution of scores in the population have the least effect on Type I errors? ■

CALCULATING THE ANALYSIS OF VARIANCE: RAW-SCORE COMPUTATIONAL FORMULAS

The definitional formulas for the sums of squares in an analysis of variance and the computation of SS and MS by partitioning scores as in Table 11–4 provide the basis for a conceptual understanding of the analysis of variance. But, this approach requires computations that are prone to error. Thus, simplified computational procedures have been developed. These procedures give no conceptual insight into the analysis of variance, but they ease considerably the computations involved.

The computational formulas are based upon the raw scores, the total of the scores in a treatment (rather than the treatment mean), and the grand total of the scores in the experiment (rather than the grand mean). Following the notational representation introduced in Table 11–2, an experiment with three levels of an independent variable A and five subjects in each level is represented as

Factor A

A_1	A_2	A_3	
X_{11}	X_{12}	X_{13}	
X_{21}	X_{22}	X_{23}	
X_{31}	X_{32}	X_{33}	
X_{41}	X_{42}	X_{43}	
X_{51}	X_{52}	X_{53}	
T_{A1}	T_{A2}	T_{A3}	G (grand total)

where
X_{ij} = raw score of a subject
T_A = total of scores for a treatment condition
G = grand total of the scores
n_A = number of scores in a treatment condition
a = number of levels of independent variable A
N = total number of scores.

Three numerical terms are computed using these values:

$[1] = \sum\limits_{j=1}^{a} \sum\limits_{i=1}^{n_A} X_{ij}^2$ the sum of all the raw scores squared

$[2] = \sum\limits_{j=1}^{a} T_A^2/n_A$ the sum of each treatment group total squared, divided by the number of scores in a treatment condition

$[3] = G^2/N$ the grand total squared, divided by the total number of scores.

Using these numerical values, an analysis of variance is computed as follows:

Source of Variance	df	SS	MS	F
Factor A	$a - 1$	[2] − [3]	SS_A/df_A	MS_A/MS_{Error}
Error	$N - a$	[1] − [2]	SS_{Error}/df_{Error}	
Total	$N - 1$	[1] − [3]	Not calculated	

To illustrate the computations, we use the example scores given in Table 11–1 for which an analysis of variance is summarized in Table 11–6.

	Factor A	
A_1	A_2	A_3
17	14	15
13	13	10
16	16	11
19	12	12
20	10	12
$T_A = 85$	65	60

$G = 85 + 65 + 60 = 210$

$n_A = 5$, $a = 3$, and $N = 15$.

The values of the necessary numerical computation terms are:

$[1] = 17^2 + \cdots + 20^2 + 14^2 + \cdots + 10^2 + 15^2 + \cdots + 12^2 = 3,074.00$

$[2] - (85^2 + 65^2 + 60^2)/5 = 15,050.00/5 = 3,010.00$

$[3] = 210^2/15 = 44,100/15 = 2,940.00$

Then

$$SS_A = [2] - [3] = 3,010.00 - 2,940.00 = 70.00$$

$$df_A = a - 1 = 3 - 1 = 2$$

$$SS_{Error} = [1] - [2] = 3,074.00 - 3,010.00 = 64.00$$

$$df_{Error} = N - a = 15 - 3 = 12$$

$$SS_{Total} = [1] - [3] = 3,074.00 - 2,940.00 = 134.00$$

$$df_{Total} = N - 1 = 15 - 1 = 14.$$

The summary of the analysis of variance is then

Source	df	SS	MS	F
Factor A	2	70.00	$70.00/2 = 35.00$	$35.00/5.33 = 6.57$
Error	12	64.00	$64.00/12 = 5.33$	
Total	14	134.00	—	

The numerical values obtained by this computational approach are identical to those presented in Table 11–6 obtained from the definitional formulas of an analysis of variance.

Example Problem 11–1
Using the one-factor between-subjects analysis of variance with two levels of an independent variable

Problem:
We introduced the Morinaga misalignment illusion in Statistics in Use 9–1: Perception of Illusions. There we illustrated how Day and Kasperczyk (1984) used the one-sample t to determine if their participants actually saw an illusion in certain stimulus conditions. In other aspects of the experiment, however, Day and Kasperczyk were interested in comparing the illusion magnitude under different stimulus conditions.

To illustrate the use of analysis of variance in experimental research, suppose it is hypothesized that a greater illusion will be seen with stimuli that form angles in comparison with stimuli that are circular in nature. To test this research hypothesis, suppose an experimenter created two equivalent groups of individuals by randomly assigning 20 people to one of two groups. The individuals in group A_1 were shown the stimulus created from angled points and the participants in Group A_2 saw a stimulus made from partial circles as illustrated below.

Figure shown Group A_1 Figure shown Group A_2

The error in the perception of the stimulus was measured for both groups. (See Statistics in Use 9–1 for a description of how perceptual error may be measured.) Suppose the following error scores were obtained (in millimeters).

Type of Figure (A)	
Angular (A₁)	*Circular (A₂)*
2.01	1.62
1.96	1.74
1.84	1.80
2.11	1.61
2.04	1.53
1.76	1.77
1.93	1.65
1.87	1.79
1.91	1.69
1.74	1.59
$\overline{X}_A$ 1.917	1.679
s_A 0.119	0.093

Does the amount of error perceived depend upon the type of stimulus?

Solution:
To determine if the means differ by more than expected from sampling error alone, a statistical test is needed. For this example, we use the one-factor between-subjects analysis of variance. (Although, because only two groups are involved, a t test for independent groups also is an appropriate statistical test.) We adopt a .05 significance level.

Statistic to be used: $F = MS_A/MS_{Error}$

Assumptions for use:

1. The subjects were sampled randomly and independently from a population.
2. The error in perceiving the illusion is normally distributed in the population.
3. The variances for the perceptual error scores are equal in the populations sampled.

Statistical hypotheses: $H_0: \mu_{A_1} = \mu_{A_2}$
$\quad\quad\quad\quad\quad\quad\quad H_1:$ not H_0

Significance level: $\alpha = .05$

df for F:

$$df_A = a - 1 = 2 - 1 = 1$$
$$df_{Error} = N - a = 20 - 2 = 18$$
$$df \text{ for } F: df_{Total} = N - 1 = 20 - 1 = 19$$

Critical value of F: $F_{crit}\ (1, 18) = 4.41$

Rejection region: Values of F_{obs} equal to or greater than 4.41.

Calculation: We calculate the analysis of variance using the raw-score computational formulas. Accordingly

$$[1] = \sum_{j=1}^{a} \sum_{i=1}^{n_A} X_{ij}^2 = 65.1448$$

$$[2] = \frac{\sum_{j=1}^{a} T_A^2}{n_A} = 64.9393$$

$$[3] = G^2/N = 64.6561.$$

And

$$SS_A = [2] - [3] = 64.9393 - 64.6561 = 0.2832$$
$$SS_{Error} = [1] - [2] = 65.1448 - 64.9393 = 0.2055$$
$$SS_{Total} = [1] - [3] = 65.1448 - 64.6561 = 0.4887.$$

The summary of the analysis of variance is then

Source	df	SS	MS	F
Type of figure (A)	1	0.2832	0.2832	24.84
Error	18	0.2055	0.0114	
Total	19	0.4887		

Decision: F_{obs} falls into the rejection region; thus we reject H_0 and accept H_1.

Conclusion:
The means of 1.917 mm and 1.679 mm differ significantly at the .05 level; the mean of 1.917 mm is significantly larger than the mean of 1.679 mm. Because the treatment groups were equivalent groups before the independent variable was administered and extraneous variables were controlled, the difference is presumed to be due to the effect of the independent variable. Individuals see a larger illusion with angular stimuli than with circular stimuli. ▪

Example Problem 11–2
Using the one-factor between-subjects analysis of variance with three levels of an independent variable.

Problem:
Does drinking alcohol make one more open to the effects of social influence? Gustafson (1987b) attempted to answer this question by having subjects estimate the length of a line that ranged in length from 5 to 100 centimeters. The subjects were then given written feedback about the length of the line and asked to give another estimate of the line. Each individual estimated the length of 75 lines. For 60 of the

75 estimates the written feedback indicated to the subject that his or her first estimate was incorrect. The number of times that each person changed his or her second estimate was recorded as a measure of the person's responsiveness to social influence. Three treatment groups were employed. One group of individuals was a control group, given a drink of only orange juice 15 minutes before the line length estimation task. The second group was a placebo group. A placebo is a simulated treatment given to subjects. Subjects in this group were given only orange juice 15 minutes before the line length estimation task, but they were led to believe that the drink contained alcohol. The third group was an alcohol group. These individuals were given 0.8 milliliters of alcohol per kilogram of body weight in an orange juice solution 15 minutes before the task began. The expectation was that the alcohol and placebo groups would be more responsive to social influence and the written feedback and would thus change their second estimates more often than the control group. Suppose the number of estimates changed for each of 13 individuals in a group were as follows:

	Treatment Group (A)		
	Control (A_1)	Placebo (A_2)	Alcohol (A_3)
	18	17	31
	2	19	27
	11	26	16
	3	4	24
	26	18	11
	18	23	17
	9	31	12
	24	35	32
	17	11	16
	21	8	19
	14	29	35
	19	25	26
	33	38	17
$\overline{X}_A$	16.5	21.8	24.1
s_A	8.83	10.29	8.81

Does alcohol make individuals more open to social influence in a line length estimation task?

Solution:
To answer this question, a statistical hypothesis test is needed. For this example, because three treatment groups are involved, we use the one-factor between-subjects analysis of variance. Again, we use a .05 significance level.

Statistic to be used: $F = MS_A/MS_{Error}$

Assumptions for use:

1. The individuals were sampled randomly and independently from a population.
2. The number of changes made in line length estimates is normally distributed in the population.
3. The variances for the number of changes in line length estimates are equal in the populations sampled.

Statistical hypotheses: $H_0: \mu_{A_1} = \mu_{A_2} = \mu_{A_3}$
$H_1:$ not H_0

Significance level: $\alpha = .05$

df:
$$df_A = a - 1 = 3 - 1 = 2$$
$$df: df_{Error} = N - a = 39 - 3 = 36$$
$$df_{Total} = N - 1 = 39 - 1 = 38$$

Critical value of F: $F_{crit}(2, 36) = 3.32$

Rejection region: Values of F_{obs} equal to or greater than 3.32.

Calculation: We calculate the analysis of variance using the raw-score formulas.

$$[1] = \sum_{j=1}^{a} \sum_{i=1}^{n_a} X_{ij}^2 = 20{,}434.000$$

$$[2] = \frac{\sum_{j=1}^{a} T_A^2}{n_A} = 17{,}296.154$$

$$[3] = G^2/N = 16{,}906.256$$

Accordingly

$$SS_A = [2] - [3] = 17{,}296.154 - 16{,}906.256 = 389.898$$
$$SS_{Error} = [1] - [2] = 20{,}434.000 - 17{,}296.154 = 3{,}137.846$$
$$SS_{Total} = [1] - [3] = 20{,}434.000 - 16{,}906.256 = 3{,}527.744.$$

The summary of the analysis of variance is then

Source	df	SS	MS	F
Treatment group (A)	2	389.898	194.949	2.24
Error	36	3,137.846	87.162	
Total	38	3,527.744		

Decision: F_{obs} does not fall into the rejection region; thus we fail to reject H_0 and do not accept H_1.

Conclusion:

The observed difference between the means is nonsignificant; the sample means of 16.5, 21.8, and 24.1 are all samples from the same population. There is no evidence for an effect of the independent variable. Individuals given an alcoholic drink do not change their line length estimates more often than do individuals given a placebo drink or no drink at all. ▪

Statistics in Use 11–1

The Effectiveness of Dbsmecarl Nseawrs: Using the One-Factor Analysis of Variance

After taking multiple-choice examinations students often are given feedback about the correct alternative for a question. One purpose for giving the feedback is for students to learn the correct answer and to be able to answer the question correctly in the future. What form of feedback best enhances this learning? Lhyle and Kulhavy (1987) hypothesized that the effectiveness of feedback depends upon the amount of effort needed to cognitively process the correct answers. To test this hypothesis, they created three equivalent groups with 20 undergraduate students randomly assigned to each group. Each group was given a learning program on the human eye and 20 multiple-choice questions on the material in this program. After completing the multiple-choice items, the groups were given different forms of feedback of the correct answer. The control group, Group A_1, was given no feedback of the correct answer. A repeated answer group, Group A_2, was given the item and the correct answer twice. A scrambled answer group, Group A_3, was given the item and the correct alternative. The words in the alternative were randomly ordered, however, and subjects were told to rearrange them mentally to form the correct answer. It was expected that the scrambled answers would require more cognitive effort to process the feedback than would the repeated answer condition; thus, subjects in this condition should better remember the correct answer.

   After completing the learning program and receiving the feedback on the correct alternatives, the subjects took a criterion test composed of the same 20 multiple-choice alternatives they had just studied. The mean number of items correct on the criterion test were 9.00 ($s = 3.20$) for the control group, A_1, 13.55 ($s = 3.83$) for the repetition group, A_2, and 12.50 ($s = 2.84$) for the scrambled answer group, A_3. The analysis of variance summary for the scores calculated from information presented by Lhyle and Kulhavy is shown below.

Source	df	SS	MS	F
Type of feedback (A)	2	227.08	113.54	10.34
Error	57	625.86	10.98	
Total	59	852.94		

F_{crit} at the .05 level for 2, 57 *df* is 3.23 (using the tabled value for 2, 40 *df*); thus $F_{obs} = 10.34$ falls into the rejection region. The null hypothesis,

$$H_0: \mu_{A_1} = \mu_{A_2} = \mu_{A_3},$$

was rejected and the alternative hypothesis,

$$H_1: \text{not } H_0,$$

was accepted. Accordingly, there is at least one statistically significant difference among the three means. A visual examination of the means indicates that there was no difference between the scrambled and repeated feedback groups (A_2 and A_3), but both of these groups correctly answered more items than the control group (A_1). These results were not in agreement with the research hypotheses, which predicted that the scrambled answer feedback, Group A_3, would show the best performance on the criterion task, followed by the repeated feedback condition, Group A_2, which would show better recall than the control group, Group A_1. Their explanation for these results was that subjects in the scrambled feedback group did not expend the necessary effort to fully unscramble the feedback. To test this hypothesis, Lhyle and Kulhavy conducted a second experiment in which greater effort was required to unscramble the feedback. Here scrambled feedback produced the desired improvement in criterion test performance. ▪

Testing Your Knowledge 11–4

On a separate sheet of paper, test your knowledge of the material in this section by answering the following questions. Complete these problems using the one-factor between-subjects analysis of variance following the format illustrated in the example problems. Use a .05 significance level for each problem.

1. In Testing Your Knowledge 10–3, problem 9 presented an experiment dealing with the effects of an expected delay on the estimation of a time interval. Subjects in the control group were not led to expect a delay in the start of an experiment, whereas subjects in the experimental group were told the experimenter's assistant was delayed. The delay period was 5 minutes for both groups. Suppose you replicated this experiment

with a total of 20 subjects and obtained the following estimates of the 5-minute delay period (in minutes):

	Group	
	Control	Experimental
	6	8
	7	9
	9	11
	7	10
	6	9
	8	8
	5	7
	9	6
	6	10
	8	10
$\overline{X}_A$	7.1	8.8
s_A	1.37	1.55

a. State the statistical hypotheses for the F test for these scores.
b. What is the value of F_{obs}?
c. What are the df for this F?
d. What is the value of F_{crit} at the .05 level?
e. What is the rejection region for F_{obs}?
f. Does F_{obs} fall into the rejection region?
g. What decisions do you make about the statistical hypotheses? Do you reject or fail to reject H_0? Accept or not accept H_1?
h. Do you conclude that the means are from the same or different populations?
i. Is the difference between the means statistically significant?
j. Did the groups differ in their estimates of the time they spent waiting? If so, what is the direction of the difference?

2. Do beards make males feel more masculine? To find an answer to this question, Wood (1986) randomly assigned clean-shaven males to one of three treatment conditions. The dependent variable measured was the subject's self-rating of masculinity. Subjects in Group A_1 wore a theatrical beard while completing the ratings, subjects in Group A_2 wore an outlaw-style bandana around the face while rating themselves, and subjects in Group A_3 formed a control condition where nothing was worn on the face while completing the ratings. Each subject looked at himself in a mirror for one minute and then completed the masculinity ratings. Suppose the following scores were obtained (lower scores indicate greater rated masculinity).

	Treatment Group		
	Beard	*Bandana*	*Control*
	A_1	A_2	A_3
	26	34	40
	24	39	41
	19	38	39
	23	40	36
	18	34	35
	21	35	32
	23	29	31
	29	36	34
$\overline{X}_A$	22.9	35.6	36.0
s_A	3.60	3.50	3.70

a. State the statistical hypotheses for the F test for these scores.
b. What is the value of F_{obs}?
c. What are the df for this F?
d. What is the value of F_{crit} at the .05 level?
e. What is the rejection region for F_{obs}?
f. Does F_{obs} fall into the rejection region?
g. What decisions do you make about the statistical hypotheses? Do you reject or fail to reject H_0? Accept or not accept H_1?
h. Do you conclude that the means are from the same or different populations?
i. Is the difference between the means statistically significant?
j. Did the groups differ in rated masculinity? If so, describe the differences found. ▪

REPORTING THE RESULTS OF THE ANALYSIS OF VARIANCE

In a typical scientific report of the outcome of the analysis of variance on experimental data, descriptive statistics, the value of F_{obs}, the df for F_{obs}, the MS_{Error}, and significance level are reported in only a few sentences. We illustrate using the results from Example Problem 11–1.

The mean perceptual error for the angular stimulus condition was 1.917 mm (s = 0.119 mm), and the mean error for the circular stimulus condition was 1.679 mm (s = 0.093 mm). A one-factor between-subjects analysis of variance indicated a significant effect for the type of stimulus condition, F(1, 18) = 24.84, MS$_{Error}$ = 0.0114, p < .01.

To see the information provided by this presentation of the results we examine each part of the report separately.

1. $F(1, 18)$: Identifies the name of the test statistic as the F. Therefore, we know that an analysis of variance was used to analyze the data. The df for the numerator (i.e., 1) and the denominator (i.e., 18) of F_{obs} are shown in parentheses. From these df you can determine the number of groups involved and the number of participants employed in the experiment. The df for the numerator are equal to $a - 1$. In this report, $df_A = 1$; thus $a = 2$. The df for the denominator, $df_{Error} = N - a$. In our example, $df_{Error} = 18$ and $a = 2$; therefore $18 = N - 2$, and the total number of participants in the experiment equals 20.

2. $= 24.84$: Gives the value of F_{obs} (not the F_{crit} value found in Table A–3).

3. $p < .01$: Indicates that
   a. the probability of F_{obs} if H_0 is true is less than (or equal to) .01,
   b. H_0: $\mu_{A_1} = \mu_{A_2}$ was rejected; H_1: not H_0 was accepted,
   c. the difference between the sample means is statistically significant (at the .01 level),
   d. something other than sampling error is responsible for the observed difference in sample means, and
   e. if $p > .05$ were reported, then the greater than sign would indicate that the researcher failed to reject H_0 and the sample means did not differ significantly at the .05 significance level.

4. $MS_{Error} = 0.0114$: Provides the value of the MS_{Error} for the F_{obs}. This value provides a measure of the error variation in the scores.

On a separate sheet of paper, test your knowledge of the material in this section by answering the following questions. These exercises present sample reports of the use of the one-factor between-subjects analysis of variance. For each report, answer the questions from the information presented in the report.

a. How many levels of the independent variable were used in this experiment?
b. How many participants were utilized in this experiment?
c. What is the value of F_{obs}?
d. What is the value of F_{crit} at the .05 significance level?
e. Do you reject or fail to reject H_0?
f. Do you accept or not accept H_1?
g. Are the results statistically significant or nonsignificant?
h. To what do you attribute the observed differences among the sample means?

1. The mean number of tones detected while listening to a familiar passage was 79.9 compared to a mean of 73.0 when listening to an unfamiliar passage. A one-factor between-subjects analysis of variance revealed that the means differed significantly, $F(1, 60) = 14.15$, $MS_{Error} = 5.74$, $p < .05$.
2. No difference was found in the number of words recalled as a function of retention interval, $F(3, 36) = 1.13$, $MS_{Error} = 14.34$, $p > .05$. ■

STATISTICAL DECISIONS AND THE RESEARCH HYPOTHESIS

Behavioral scientists conduct research to obtain evidence that provides a test of a research hypothesis. Recall that for an experiment a research hypothesis is stated in the form of a declarative sentence predicting a relationship between an independent variable and a dependent variable. In Example Problem 11–1, the research hypothesis was that the extent of the Morinaga misalignment illusion depends upon the nature of the stimulus producing it; angled stimuli produce a greater illusion than do circular stimuli. This research hypothesis is supported if the mean perceptual error of the subjects who saw the angled stimuli (Group A_1) is significantly greater than the mean of those who saw the circular stimuli (Group A_2). But, rejection of H_0 in an analysis of variance does not necessarily imply this relation between the means. The alternative hypothesis, H_1: not H_0, will be accepted if the sample means differ significantly in either direction, that is, if $\overline{X}_{A_1} < \overline{X}_{A_2}$ or if $\overline{X}_{A_1} > \overline{X}_{A_2}$. Acceptance of the alternative hypothesis merely indicates the means differ in one or the other direction. The outcome $\overline{X}_{A_1} > \overline{X}_{A_2}$ is in agreement with the research hypothesis, but the outcome $\overline{X}_{A_1} < \overline{X}_{A_2}$ is not.

Thus, if F_{obs} is statistically significant, then we must examine the group means to determine if the significant difference is in the direction predicted by the research hypothesis. If only two groups are being compared, then a visual inspection of the means after a significant F_{obs} will indicate the direction of the difference between them, and whether the direction is that predicted by the research hypothesis. When three or more sample means are being compared, a visual inspection may not be sufficient and multiple comparison tests may be required. We present these tests in Chapter 12.

THE RELATIONSHIP BETWEEN *t* AND *F*

The *t* test and the one-factor between-subjects analysis of variance lead to the same statistical decisions when analyzing data from two treatment groups. If we reject the null hypothesis at the .05 level with the t test (two-tailed), then we would also reject H_0 with an analysis of variance on the same data. The reason is that $t^2 = F$ or $t = \sqrt{F}$. This relation also holds for the tabled critical values of t and F for the analysis of two sample means when the same significance level is adopted. As an example, for $\alpha = .05$, F_{crit} for 1, 8 df is 5.32. The value of t_{crit} for 8 df and $\alpha = .05$ in a two-tailed test is 2.306, which is the square root of 5.32. Thus, $(2.306)^2 = 5.32$, and $t^2 = F$. Because of this relationship of t and F, either test may be used for comparing two independent sample means; the tests provide identical outcomes and one is not preferred over the other. The advantage of analysis of variance appears only when three or more treatment conditions are compared.

EX POST FACTO DESIGNS AND THE ANALYSIS OF VARIANCE

We have developed the one-factor between-subjects analysis of variance in the context of a true experiment—the independent variable used in all our examples to this point has been an active independent variable and subjects were randomly assigned to treatment conditions. Accordingly, in Example Problem 11–1 we were able to conclude that the type of stimulus presented—angular or circular—affected the error in perception of the Morinaga misalignment illusion. Similarly to the t test, however, analysis of variance also may be used for the statistical analysis of ex post facto studies. Ex post facto studies employ attribute independent variables, consequently a researcher cannot reach causal conclusions about the effect of the attribute independent variable from an ex post facto study.

The analysis of variance is used with ex post facto studies to determine if the means of the various groups formed differ significantly. The use of analysis of variance to analyze the data of an ex post facto study does not in any way change the nature of the study or the limited conclusions from an ex post facto study. Statistical tests are tools to help a scientist decide if two or more sample means differ by more than expected from sampling error alone. If the test results in a decision to reject H_0 and accept H_1, the statistical test cannot explain why the means differ. It is the experimenter's task to discover why the difference occurred. The statistical test cannot answer this question. As Boneau (1961) observes:

> The statistical test cares not whether a Social Desirability scale measures social desirability, or number of trials to extinction is an indicator of habit strength. . . . Given unending piles of numbers from which to draw small samples, the t test and the F test will methodically decide for us whether the means of the piles are different. (p. 261)

Statistics in Use 11–2

Use of the Analysis of Variance with an Ex Post Facto Study

Obesity and its causes are of considerable interest in our society. One hypothesis is that eating disorders may be related to underlying emotional states. Based on this hypothesis, Weinstein and Pickens (1988) compared anxiety and depression levels in normal weight and obese subjects. They formed two groups of subjects, 10 overweight females (mean weight = 182.9 lbs) and 10 normal weight females (mean weight = 126.4 lbs). The independent variable of body weight is an attribute of the subject; the subjects themselves determined which level of the independent variable they were in. Subjects in both groups completed an anxiety inventory and a depression inventory. The mean anxiety scores for the overweight subjects were 17.3 and for the normal weight subjects, 3.5. (Higher scores indicate a higher level of anxiety.) The analysis of variance for these means resulted in $F_{obs}(1, 18) = 6.58$. At the .05 level, $F_{crit} = 4.41$; accordingly, Weinstein and Pickens rejected $H_0: \mu_{A_1} = \mu_{A_2}$ for this analysis. The mean anxiety score of the overweight subjects was significantly higher than the mean for the normal weight subjects.

A similar analysis was done on the means for the depression inventory. For this analysis, $F_{obs}(1, 18) = 20.87$, $p < .05$. The overweight subjects were higher in depression level (mean score = 17.2) than the normal weight subjects (mean score = 0.2).

These results indicate that overweight and normal weight females differ in anxiety and level of depression. Because the study is ex post facto, however, we cannot reach causal conclusions about the relation of body weight and emotional states. But it is evident that body weight and emotional state are related and deserve further research to find the causal relations. ▧

Testing Your Knowledge 11–6

On a separate sheet of paper, test your knowledge of the material in this section by answering the following questions.

1. Does rejection of H_0 and acceptance of H_1 in an analysis of variance necessarily provide support for a research hypothesis? Explain your answer.
2. You have conducted a *t* test on two independent groups and $t_{obs}(18) = 2.931$. If you had analyzed the scores with an analysis of variance what value of F_{obs} would you have found? Indicate the *df* for F_{obs}.
3. You have conducted an analysis of variance on two independent groups and $F_{obs}(1, 22) = 9.00$. If you had analyzed the scores with a *t* test what value of t_{obs} would you have found? Indicate the *df* for t_{obs}.
4. Explain why a statistical test cannot identify the reason for two groups differing. ▧

SUMMARY

- The one-factor between-subjects analysis of variance is used to analyze scores when two or more treatment groups are employed.
- The F statistic is given by

$$F = MS_A / MS_{Error}.$$

- An MS is a variance and is found by SS/df.
- MS_A varies with the effect of the independent variable and sampling error.
- MS_{Error} varies with the within-groups error variation.
- If the independent variable has no effect, then MS_A and MS_{Error} estimate only error variation in the scores and the F should be about equal to 1.00.

- When an independent variable has an effect, MS_A increases in value, but MS_{Error} is not affected. The value of F becomes larger than 1.00.
- Using the F statistic in a statistical test follows the usual steps of formulating statistical hypotheses, setting a significance level, locating a rejection region, calculating F_{obs}, and making decisions concerning the statistical hypotheses.
- A statistically significant F when three or more treatments are used requires examination of the sample means to determine the nature of the relationship among them. Follow-up tests may be necessary to find which means differ significantly.

KEY TERMS

A_1, A_2, and A_3
a
analysis of variance
ANOVA
between-groups variance
degrees of freedom
df_A
df_{Error}
df_{Total}
factor A
F_{crit}

F_{obs}
independent estimates
mean square
MS_A
MS_{Error}
MS_{Total}
N
n_A
one-factor multilevel designs
rejection region
sum of squares

SS_A
SS_{Error}
SS_{Total}
statistically nonsignificant
statistically significant
within-groups variance
$X_{ij} - \overline{X}_G$
$\overline{X}_A - \overline{X}_G$
$X_{ij} - \overline{X}_A$

REVIEW QUESTIONS

On a separate sheet of paper, test your knowledge of the material in this chapter by answering the following questions.

1. Weinstein and de Man (1987) compared 16 U.S. college students against 16 foreign college students on knowledge of world

geography. Suppose the scores below represent the number of countries the students could identify on a world map.

	Type of Student	
	U.S. (A₁)	*Foreign (A₂)*
	6	12
	3	8
	10	16
	4	9
	7	7
	2	18
	12	10
	5	8
	2	12
	4	14
	5	16
	7	9
	3	13
	6	17
	11	7
	7	14
$\overline{X}_A$	5.9	11.9
s_A	3.05	3.70

a. Do U.S. and foreign students differ in their knowledge of geography? Analyze the scores with a one-factor between-subjects analysis of variance. Use a .05 significance level.

b. Describe your results in Question 1a following the example illustrated in the Reporting the Results of the Analysis of Variance section of this chapter.

2. Elementary school teachers must have many talents, among them the ability to teach children the physical skills needed for certain sports and other skilled activities. To determine how well elementary education majors could learn the necessary skills from instructional videotapes, Morrison and Reeve (1986) created three equivalent groups of subjects and varied the instructional videotape shown them. Group A_1 was a control group and saw no videotape. Group A_2 saw a videotape on soccer kicks, and Group A_3 saw a video tape on throwing, catching, and striking skills. After viewing the instructional videotape, or no tape for Group A_1, the subjects were shown a second videotape on throwing, catching, and striking and asked to identify correct and incorrect performances displayed on the tape. Suppose the following scores were obtained for nine subjects in each instructional videotape condition.

Instructional Videotape Condition

	None (A₁)	Soccer (A₂)	Throwing, Catching (A₃)
	50	53	61
	46	48	58
	39	37	49
	52	49	56
	44	46	45
	51	48	66
	41	37	58
	36	41	64
	48	40	57
$\overline{X}_A$	45.2	44.3	57.1
s_A	5.63	5.74	6.68

a. Did the instructional videotape condition affect a subject's skill to correctly identify throwing, catching, and striking performance? Use a .05 significance level.

b. Examine the treatment group means. The overall analysis indicates only that there is at least one statistically significant difference among the means. Which means do you think differ significantly? Which do not?

3. Problem 2 of the Chapter 10 Review Questions dealt with the physiological effects of noise. In the experiment described, participants either sat quietly for 30 minutes or listened to a recording of traffic noise for 30 minutes. At the end of 30 minutes their systolic blood pressures were measured and the following scores obtained (in millimeters of mercury).

Group

	Quiet	Noise
	106	141
	117	136
	124	124
	129	139
	115	121
	131	119
	121	147
	115	128
	128	115
	136	134
	127	140
$\overline{X}_A$	122.6	131.3
s_A	8.76	10.45

a. Does noise affect systolic blood pressure? Use a one-factor between-subjects analysis of variance and a .05 significance level.

b. Compare the value of F_{obs} to the value of t_{obs} for Problem 2 of the Chapter 10 Review Questions. Do you find the expected relationship between t and F?

4. An experimenter used a one-factor experiment with six levels: A_1, A_2, A_3, A_4, A_5, and A_6. There were 7 different individuals in each level. What are the values of a, n_A, and N?

5. An experimenter used a one-factor experiment with six levels: A_1, A_2, A_3, A_4, A_5, and A_6. There were 7 different individuals in each level. What are the values of df_A, df_{Error}, and df_{Total}?

6. Assume that you plan to conduct a one-factor between-subjects experiment with five levels of the independent variable and 12 subjects in each treatment condition.

a. Write out, in notation, the sum of squares partitioning equation for the scores of this experiment. Include the summation limits on the equation.

b. Find the numerical values of the df for each SS identified in Question 6a.

c. Write the statistical null and alternative hypotheses for the analysis of variance for this research design.

d. What is the value of F_{crit} at the .05 significance level for this analysis of variance?

e. Suppose the value of F_{obs} was larger than F_{crit}. What decisions do you make about H_0 and H_1?

7. The following tables are incomplete summary tables for an analysis of variance. Assume an equal number of people in each level of the independent variable. By using the relationships among SS and df, provide the missing values in each table. Then answer the following questions for each table.

a. How many levels of the independent variable were used?

b. How many subjects participated in the study?

c. How many subjects were measured in each treatment condition?

d. Is the value of F_{obs} statistically significant at the .05 level?

Table 1

Source	df	SS	MS	F
Factor A	2	50	——	——
Error	27	270	——	
Total	——	——		

Table 2

Source	df	SS	MS	F
Factor A	——	60	12.0	——
Error	72	——	——	
Total	77	276		

Table 3

Source	df	SS	MS	F
Factor A	——	——	——	3.00
Error	——	320	5.0	
Total	67	365		

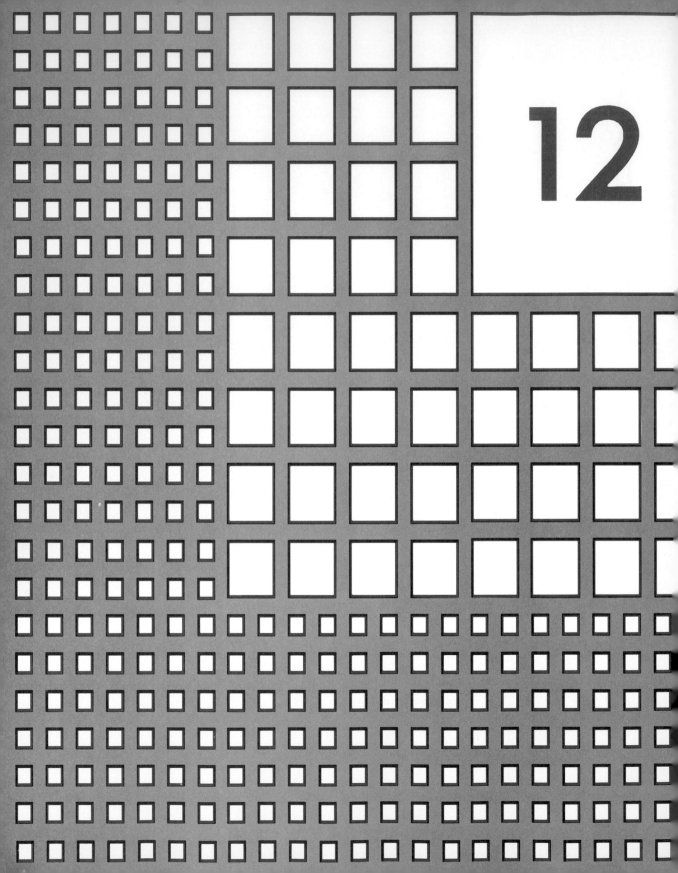

12

Multiple Comparison Procedures for the One-Factor Between-Subjects Analysis of Variance

This chapter introduces multiple comparison tests that often are used in conjunction with the analysis of variance. To illustrate the need for and use of multiple comparison tests, consider the example problem of Chapter 11 dealing with the effect of type of drawing on the number of items recalled in a retention task. Three levels of the independent variable of type of drawing were manipulated in this experiment: incomplete outline (A_1), outline (A_2), and detailed (A_3) drawings. The mean number of items recalled as a function of type of drawing was

Type of Drawing (A)		
Incomplete Outline	Outline	Detailed
(A_1)	(A_2)	(A_3)
17.0	13.0	12.0

An analysis of variance on these scores resulted in a statistically significant $F_{obs}(2, 12) = 6.57$, $p < .05$ (see Table 11–6 for a summary of this analysis). Recall that because three sample means are tested by this analysis, the null hypothesis is

$$H_0: \mu_{A_1} = \mu_{A_2} = \mu_{A_3}.$$

This null hypothesis states that the means of the populations from which the samples were obtained are identical, a situation that holds if the independent variable has no effect on the dependent variable. This null hypothesis was rejected in this experiment and the alternative hypothesis, H_1: not H_0, was accepted. An alternative hypothesis expressed in this form is called an **omnibus alternative hypothesis** because many possible relationships among the population means could hold if "not H_0" were true. (The word *omnibus* means to include many things at once.) To illustrate, Figure 12–1 presents, symbolically and graphically, nine possible relationships that may occur under H_1 for an experiment with three treatment conditions. For example, Figure 12–1b displays an instance where two population means, μ_{A_1} and μ_{A_2} are equal to each other but both are greater than μ_{A_3}. In the context of an experiment, this example represents a situation where there is a nonsignificant difference between two sample means, $\overline{X}_{A_1}$ and $\overline{X}_{A_2}$, but both are significantly larger than $\overline{X}_{A_3}$. As another example, panels g, h, and i present outcomes where each population mean differs from each of the other population means. In an experiment, this situation corresponds to an instance where each sample mean differs significantly from each of the other means. Panel i, for instance, illus-

FIGURE 12–1.

Some of the relationships among three population means that are possible under H_1: not H_0.

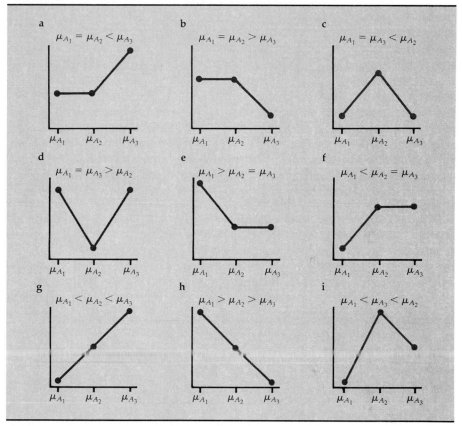

trates a case where $\overline{X}_{A_1}$ is significantly less than $\overline{X}_{A_2}$ and $\overline{X}_{A_3}$, and $\overline{X}_{A_3}$ is significantly less than $\overline{X}_{A_2}$.

The inference for our example experiment of the decision from the overall analysis of variance to accept H_1: not H_0 is that the three sample means are not all from the same population. There is at least one significant difference among them. But as Figure 12–1 illustrates, there are many relationships possible among three population means when H_1: not H_0 is true. Which of these relationships exists among the sample means of our experiment? To answer this question, suppose we construct a figure of the means and compare it to Figure 12–1. Figure 12–2 presents the three sample means as a function of type of drawing. Comparing Figure 12–2 with Figure 12–1, we see that the relationship among the sample means most resembles the relationship illustrated in panel e of Figure 12–1. Panel e represents a situation where μ_{A_1} is greater than μ_{A_2}

FIGURE 12–2.
Mean number of items recalled as a function of type of drawing.

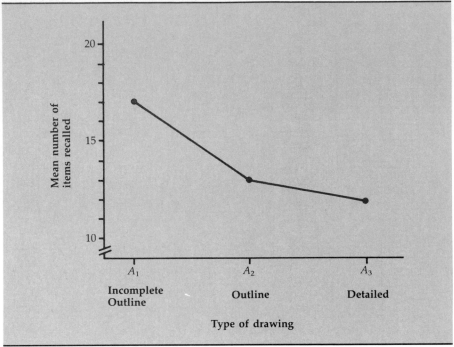

and μ_{A_3}, and μ_{A_2} and μ_{A_3} are equal to each other. For sample means, the relationship expressed in panel e occurs when $\overline{X}_{A_1}$ is significantly larger than both $\overline{X}_{A_2}$ and $\overline{X}_{A_3}$, and $\overline{X}_{A_2}$ and $\overline{X}_{A_3}$ do not differ significantly. But from the overall analysis of variance can we be sure that the relationship seen in Figure 12–2 corresponds to that shown in panel e of Figure 12–1? The answer to this question is "No, we can't be sure," for by rejecting H_0 we know only that at least one significant difference exists among the sample means.

In Chapter 11 we dealt with the problem of deciding which of the means differ significantly by visually inspecting the means. But this approach is not entirely appropriate, for visual inspection does not take into account the amount of sampling error in the experiment. Although it appears that the relationship in Figure 12–2 most resembles Figure 12–1e it is possible that the apparent nonsignificant difference between the means for outline ($\overline{X}_{A_2} = 13.0$) and detailed ($\overline{X}_{A_3} = 12.0$) drawings is statistically significant. If this relationship were the case, then the means in Figure 12–2 would demonstrate the relationship of panel h of Figure 12–1 rather than panel i. Obviously, then, a researcher needs to know which of these relationships holds for the scores he or she has obtained using a procedure that is more objective than visual inspection. Multiple comparison tests provide this procedure.

ISSUES IN THE USE OF MULTIPLE COMPARISON TESTS

Multiple comparison procedures are statistical tests used to find which means differ significantly from one another in a one-factor multilevel design. Such tests are also identified as **individual comparisons, analytic comparisons,** or **specific comparisons.** Many comparison tests have been developed, each only slightly different from another. These varied tests have been developed to address one or more problems that arise when we make multiple comparisons. In this chapter, we introduce the nature of simple comparisons and the problems associated with making such comparisons. Then we develop two tests used for multiple comparisons. Although the discussion deals with only three sample means from the example experiment on the effect of type of drawing on recall, the tests developed are appropriate for comparing any number of means from a one-factor design.

A Simple Comparison

Given the three sample means from the example experiment, we could make three simple two-mean comparisons among them: $\overline{X}_{A_1}$ compared to $\overline{X}_{A_2}$, $\overline{X}_{A_1}$ compared to $\overline{X}_{A_3}$, and $\overline{X}_{A_2}$ compared to $\overline{X}_{A_3}$. Because these comparisons each involve two means, they are called **pairwise comparisons.** By conducting statistical tests on these three pairwise comparisons we could find which pairs of means differ significantly, and thus infer which of the relationships among the population means shown in Figure 12–1 holds for the experiment.

One way of making pairwise comparisons is to use the t test for comparing two independent groups. This method involves conducting three t tests, one for each comparison. From the outcome of these three tests, we could determine which means differ significantly from each other. The issue is not resolved so easily, however. Two problems require further discussion, the Type I error rate and the nature of planned versus post hoc comparisons.

The Problem of Type I Errors

One problem that arises has to do with the probability of a Type I error occurring in the comparisons to be made. Recall that a Type I error occurs when the null hypothesis actually is true, but is rejected in the statistical hypothesis test. Researchers want to keep the probability of making a Type I error low and thus usually set the significance level at .05 or .01.

For the overall analysis of variance in our example (reported in Table 11–6) the probability of a Type I error is equal to the value of α, or .05. But when conducting multiple comparisons, an investigator runs many more statistical tests, the exact number depending upon the number of comparisons to be made. Consider, for example, conducting a t test on each of the three pairwise comparisons in the example experiment. For each t test the probability of a Type I error is equal to α. Hence the probability of making at least one Type I error among all the comparisons becomes greater with an increasing number of comparisons. Very quickly this probability attains a level unacceptable to a researcher. As an example, for three sample means, there are three possible pairwise comparisons. But, only two of them are independent comparisons because each mean is involved in two of the three possible comparisons.[1] If, for each of these two independent comparisons, the probability of a Type I error is equal to $\alpha = .05$, then the probability of making a Type I error over the two comparisons is found by $1 - (1 - \alpha)^k$, where k is the number of independent comparisons. Substituting numerical values for two independent comparisons, the probability of a Type I error equals $1 - (1 - .05)^2$, which equals 0.0975, or nearly 0.10. If one conducts the three possible pairwise comparisons, then the probability of a Type I error will be even larger, about 0.14.

Error Rates

The **error rate** in an experiment (often called the **familywise error rate**) is the probability of making at least one Type I error in the various statistical comparisons conducted. The error rate in an experiment increases very rapidly with a growing number of comparisons. For example, consider employing the t test for five independent comparisons among six means with $\alpha = .05$ for each comparison. If H_0 is true, then the probability of at least one Type I error in the five comparisons is equal to $1 - (1 - .05)^5$, or 0.23. This error rate is obviously too high for most researchers. It is for this reason that alternatives to the t test have been developed to make multiple comparisons.

Planned versus Post Hoc Comparisons

Planned Comparisons

Many research studies are based on well-developed theoretical formulations that lead to specific research hypotheses. These research hypotheses

---

[1]Independent comparisons are those that do not depend upon the outcome of any other comparison. Here is a simple analogy: If you know three means, e.g., 8, 10, and 12, then you can obtain three possible differences between pairs of two means: $8 - 10 = -2$, $8 - 12 = -4$, and $10 - 12 = -2$. Notice, however, that only two of the differences are independent; if you know the numerical value of any two of them, then you know the third.

structure the design of the study and dictate which levels of the independent variable are to be compared. **Planned comparisons** (also called **a priori comparisons**) are pairwise comparisons that the researcher plans to make before he or she has conducted the experiment. These comparisons are planned on the basis of the research hypothesis prior to conducting the experiment. These comparisons are limited in number in relation to the total number of comparisons possible among the means. For example, in our experiment on the effect of type of drawing on retention, two competing theoretical formulations were tested. The elaboration hypothesis predicted the ordering of means from largest to smallest to be detailed ($\overline{X}_{A_3}$), outline ($\overline{X}_{A_2}$), and incomplete outline ($\overline{X}_{A_1}$) drawings, respectively. The effort hypothesis, on the other hand, predicted the largest to smallest ordering to be incomplete outline ($\overline{X}_{A_1}$), outline ($\overline{X}_{A_2}$), and detailed ($\overline{X}_{A_3}$) drawings, respectively. To see which hypothesis better predicts the ordering of the means requires comparing $\overline{X}_{A_1}$ with $\overline{X}_{A_2}$, and $\overline{X}_{A_2}$ with $\overline{X}_{A_3}$. The comparison of $\overline{X}_{A_1}$ with $\overline{X}_{A_3}$ is not required, however.

Post Hoc Comparisons

Post hoc comparisons (also called **a posteriori comparisons** or **incidental comparisons**) are comparisons that are suggested after one has conducted the experiment and seen the means obtained. Often experiments are conducted because the researcher suspects the independent variable will affect behavior, but has little or no theoretical framework or empirical evidence on which to base specific predictions about the ordering of the treatments. For example, we may expect that the type of drawing will affect the amount of recall, but we have no anticipation of the specific relation to be obtained among the sample means. After we obtain the means, however, we decide to compare each mean against the others—a total of three comparisons. Such pairwise comparisons are post hoc, or after-the-fact, because we have decided on the comparisons to be conducted after the data have been obtained.

The willingness of a researcher to risk a Type I error depends upon whether the comparisons to be conducted are planned or post hoc. Fundamentally, the issue relates to the belief that predictions of behavior are more valuable scientifically than after-the-fact, post-hoc attempts to interpret and explain the data. After all, don't we think that someone who can predict behavior accurately must have a better understanding of that behavior than someone who cannot make such predictions? Scientists believe that planned comparisons, made on the basis of predicted relationships among the treatment conditions, are less likely to capitalize on chance differences among means than are unplanned, post hoc comparisons suggested by the obtained data. For this reason, researchers are more willing to risk a Type I error when they are conducting planned comparisons than when they are "data snooping" with post hoc comparisons.

On a separate sheet of paper, test your knowledge of the material in this section by answering the following questions.

1. Define: multiple comparison test, pairwise comparison, Type I error, error rate, planned comparison, post hoc comparison.
2. Explain why multiple comparison procedures are required in a one-factor multilevel experiment after a statistically significant overall analysis of variance.
3. Are multiple comparison procedures required in an experiment that employs only two levels of the independent variable? Explain your answer.
4. What relationship among three sample means corresponds to Figure 12–1a?
5. What relationship among three sample means corresponds to Figure 12–1c?
6. What relationship among three sample means corresponds to Figure 12–1d?
7. What relationship among three sample means corresponds to Figure 12–1h?
8. Suppose you found that $\overline{X}_{A_1}$ is significantly less than either $\overline{X}_{A_2}$ or $\overline{X}_{A_3}$, and that $\overline{X}_{A_2}$ does not differ significantly from $\overline{X}_{A_3}$. Which relationship in Figure 12–1 corresponds to this finding?
9. Identify the pairwise comparisons that can be made in a one-factor experiment with four levels of the independent variable. ■

PLANNED COMPARISONS

The Multiple *F* Test

A number of multiple comparison procedures have been developed for planned comparisons. We present the **multiple *F* test** procedure here. This technique is a frequently used multiple comparison procedure for planned comparisons and has the added benefit of building directly upon the analysis of variance.

The multiple *F* test procedure obtains a **critical difference (*CD*)** that specifies the minimum difference between two treatment means that is statistically significant at the α level chosen. The absolute value of an observed difference in a pairwise comparison is compared with the critical difference. If the absolute value of the obtained difference between the means is equal to or larger than the *CD*, then the sample means differ significantly and are treated as representing different populations.

The *CD* for the multiple *F* test is found by

$$CD = (\sqrt{2F_{crit}})\left(\sqrt{\frac{MS_{Error}}{n_A}}\right),$$

where
F_{crit} is the value of F_{crit} with 1 *df* for the numerator and df_{Error} from the analysis of variance for the denominator at the significance level chosen,
MS_{Error} is the error term from the overall analysis of variance, and
n_A is the number of scores in each treatment condition. The values of n_A for each treatment condition must be equal to use this formula.

Using the Multiple F Test

We illustrate using the multiple *F* test for planned comparisons with our example experiment on the effect of type of drawing on memory for items. Table 12–1 presents the means and standard deviations for each type of drawing condition and a summary of the analysis of variance on these scores.

TABLE 12–1.

a. Hypothetical scores for number of items recalled as a function of type of drawing. The mean ($\overline{X}$) and standard deviation (s) are provided for each condition.

	Type of Drawing (A)		
	Incomplete Outline (A_1)	Outline (A_2)	Detailed (A_3)
	17	14	15
	13	13	10
	16	16	11
	19	12	12
	20	10	12
$\overline{X}_A$	17.0	13.0	12.0
s_A	2.74	2.24	1.87

b. Summary of the analysis of variance on the scores in a.

Source	df	SS	MS	F
Type of drawing (A)	2	70.00	35.00	6.57*
Error	12	64.00	5.33	
Total	14	134.00		

*$p < .05$

The F_{obs}, 6.57, is statistically significant at the .05 level; thus we reject H_0: $\mu_{A_1} = \mu_{A_2} = \mu_{A_3}$ and accept H_1: not H_0. The statistically significant F_{obs} from the overall analysis of variance indicates there is at least one significant difference among the three means being compared. To find specifically which means differ from each other, multiple comparison tests are necessary. Although two different research hypotheses were stated, each hypothesis provided a specific ordering of the treatment conditions in terms of population parameters. The elaboration hypothesis predicted the ordering to be

$$\mu_{A_1} \text{ (incomplete outline)} < \mu_{A_2} \text{ (outline)} < \mu_{A_3} \text{ (detailed)}.$$

On the other hand, the effort hypothesis predicted

$$\mu_{A_1} \text{ (incomplete outline)} > \mu_{A_2} \text{ (outline)} > \mu_{A_3} \text{ (detailed)}.$$

To determine whether one of these two orderings occurred, two pairwise comparisons are necessary:

$\overline{X}_{A_1}$ (incomplete outline) to $\overline{X}_{A_2}$ (outline), found by the difference $\overline{X}_{A_1} - \overline{X}_{A_2}$, and

$\overline{X}_{A_2}$ (outline) to $\overline{X}_{A_3}$ (detailed drawing), found by the difference $\overline{X}_{A_2} - \overline{X}_{A_3}$.

Calculating the CD for the Multiple F Test.   The numerical values needed to find the multiple F CD for our example are obtained as follows:

- F_{crit} is the value of F_{crit} at the desired significance level from Table A–3 for 1 df in the numerator and 12 df in the denominator (12 is the df_{Error} from the analysis of variance in Table 12–1). For a .05 significance level, this value is 4.75.
- MS_{Error} is obtained from the analysis of variance in Table 12–1, and is 5.33 for our example.
- n_A is the number of scores in each mean being compared and equals 5 for our example.

Substituting these numerical values into the formula,

$$CD = (\sqrt{2F_{crit}})\left(\sqrt{\frac{MS_{Error}}{n_A}}\right),$$

$$CD = [\sqrt{2(4.75)}]\left[\sqrt{\frac{5.33}{5}}\right]$$

$$CD = (\sqrt{9.5})(\sqrt{1.066})$$

$$CD = 3.2.$$

Interpreting the CD

The CD for the multiple F test for our example is 3.2. A difference between two treatment means equal to or larger in absolute value (i.e., the value of the difference ignoring the + or − sign) than 3.2 items recalled is a statistically significant difference at the .05 level. A useful method of presenting the obtained differences and indicating whether they are statistically significant is shown in Table 12–2. This table was constructed by listing the three means both horizontally and vertically. The values in the table are the absolute values of the differences between the means. For example, the value of 4.0 is the absolute difference of the means of the incomplete outline (row A_1) and outline drawing (column A_2) conditions (i.e., $17.0 - 13.0 = 4.0$).

TABLE 12–2.

Means and pairwise differences between the means for the three types of drawing treatment conditions. The mean for each group is shown in parentheses. The absolute values of the differences between corresponding means are presented. A_1 = incomplete outline drawing, A_2 = outline drawing, and A_3 = detailed drawing group.

	Type of Drawing (A)		
	A_1 (17.0)	A_2 (13.0)	A_3 (12.0)
A_1 (17.0)	—	4.0*	5.0[a]
Type of Drawing (A) A_2 (13.0)		—	1.0[a]
A_3 (12.0)			—

*$p < .05$, multiple F test, $CD = 3.2$
[a]This comparison was not planned; thus no test was conducted.

The planned comparisons suggested earlier for this experiment are the comparisons of the incomplete outline ($\overline{X}_{A_1}$) with the outline drawing ($\overline{X}_{A_2}$) means and the outline ($\overline{X}_{A_2}$) with detailed drawing ($\overline{X}_{A_3}$) means. From Table 12–2, the absolute values of these comparisons are 4.0 and 1.0, respectively. The comparison of $\overline{X}_{A_1}$ with $\overline{X}_{A_2}$ (i.e., a difference of 4.0 items recalled) exceeds the CD of 3.2, but the comparison of $\overline{X}_{A_2}$ with $\overline{X}_{A_3}$ (i.e., a difference of 1.0 item recalled) does not. Accordingly, we reach the following decisions regarding these comparisons:

Comparison	Decision
$\overline{X}_{A_1}$ vs. $\overline{X}_{A_2}$	reject H_0: $\mu_{A_1} = \mu_{A_2}$ accept H_1: $\mu_{A_1} \neq \mu_{A_2}$
$\overline{X}_{A_2}$ vs. $\overline{X}_{A_3}$	fail to reject H_0: $\mu_{A_2} = \mu_{A_3}$ do not accept H_1: $\mu_{A_2} \neq \mu_{A_3}$

The multiple F test leads to the conclusion that recall for incomplete outline drawings ($\overline{X}_{A_1}$) is greater than recall for outline drawings ($\overline{X}_{A_2}$), but recall for outline drawings ($\overline{X}_{A_2}$) does not differ from detailed drawings ($\overline{X}_{A_3}$). Accordingly, the conclusion is that the population means are ordered

$$\mu_{A_1} > \mu_{A_2} = \mu_{A_3},$$

the relationship illustrated in panel e of Figure 12–1. These results agree partially with the effort hypothesis. The greatest recall occurred with incomplete outline drawings as predicted by this hypothesis, but the difference predicted between the outline and detailed drawings was not found.

Notice that with the use of planned comparisons we did not make all possible pairwise comparisons; we did not compare $\overline{X}_{A_1}$ to $\overline{X}_{A_3}$. Planned comparisons do not involve all possible comparisons but only those that the experimenter is most interested in, and only those for which a specific prediction of the relationships among the means is made before the experiment is conducted. We emphasize that planned comparisons are dictated by well-formulated predictions expressed in the research hypothesis. A statement prior to conducting the experiment that certain comparisons will be performed is not an example of a planned comparison. A planned comparison implies there is a well-developed theoretical or empirical reason for expecting the to-be-compared means to differ. Thus, each planned comparison should provide meaningful information concerning the experiment.[2]

Is It Appropriate to Conduct Planned Comparisons if the Overall Analysis of Variance Is Nonsignificant?

In our example of the effect of type of drawing on object recall we obtained a statistically significant F_{obs} in the overall analysis of variance. What if the F_{obs} had been nonsignificant, would it be appropriate to carry out planned comparisons using the multiple F test? The answer to this question is "Yes"; it is accepted practice to carry out the comparisons planned regardless of whether the overall analysis of variance reaches statistical significance (Wilcox, 1987). You may be tempted to ask why one should then perform an overall analysis of variance on the groups before the planned comparisons are performed. One practical reason is that the multiple F test utilizes the MS_{Error} from the analysis of variance. A second reason is that the overall analysis of variance provides an indication if there is any difference at all among the means while holding the Type I

---

[2]There is controversy about whether planned comparisons should also be orthogonal, that is, independent. We have taken the approach that the comparisons need not be independent, but that they should be planned to provide meaningful information about the results of an experiment. See Keppel (1982) or Kennedy and Bush (1985) for a summary of the issues.

error rate to the significance level selected. The multiple F test does not do this; the Type I error rate for the multiple F test is equal to α for each comparison made.

Least Significant Difference Test

Because the F and the t statistics are identical when comparing only two treatment groups, a value of t_{crit} may be used to calculate the CD. This test, often called the **least significant difference (LSD) test,** is given by

$$CD = (\sqrt{2})\,(t_{crit})\left(\sqrt{\frac{MS_{Error}}{n_A}}\right),$$

where t_{crit} is the value of t_{crit} for a two-tailed t test obtained from Table A–2 with df equal to df_{Error} for the analysis of variance. The least significant difference test gives a CD identical to the multiple F test CD; thus, the choice of test is a matter of personal preference.

REPORTING THE RESULTS OF THE ANALYSIS OF VARIANCE AND MULTIPLE COMPARISON TESTS

The scientific report of the results of our example problem typically would summarize the results in only a few sentences.

> *The mean number of items correctly recalled was 17.0 for the incomplete outline drawings (s = 2.74), 13.0 for the outline drawings (s = 2.24), and 12.0 for the detailed drawings (s = 1.87). A one-factor between-subjects analysis of variance resulted in a significant effect for the type of drawing F(2, 12) = 6.57, MS_Error = 5.33, p < .05. Planned comparisons using the multiple F test (CD = 3.2 with α = .05) indicated significantly more objects recalled for the incomplete outline drawings compared with the outline drawings, but no significant difference in the number of objects recalled for outline drawings compared with the detailed drawings condition.*

Example Problem 12–1
Planned comparisons with the multiple F test

Problem:
Use of addictive drugs, such as heroin, is often thought to be accompanied by impaired intellectual functioning (Cipolli & Galliani, 1987). Evidence to support this supposition is not widely available, however. To

gather evidence, suppose we used an ex post facto study comparing heroin nonusers against short- and long-term heroin users on a test of intellectual functioning. The nonusers were 12 males for whom it could be verified that they were drug nonusers. The drug users were males who were under court order to be evaluated for heroin use. The short-term users were 12 males who had used heroin for 1 to 2 years and the long-term users were 12 males who had used heroin for 4 to 5 years. Suppose we hypothesized that intellectual functioning, ordered from highest to lowest, would be nonuser, short-term user, and long-term user. Assume we obtained the following raw scores on the comprehension subtest of the Wechsler Adult Intelligence Scale—Revised.

	Drug User Group		
	Nonuser (A₁)	Short-Term User (A₂)	Long-Term User (A₃)
	27	21	17
	31	30	24
	25	16	19
	23	20	10
	19	28	19
	33	17	12
	29	26	26
	15	32	21
	24	23	13
	18	28	20
	26	19	17
	29	21	21
$\overline{X}_A$	24.9	23.4	18.2
s_A	5.45	5.26	4.77

Do the intellectual functioning scores reveal the hypothesized ordering of means?

Solution:

The design employed is a one-factor between-subjects design with three levels of the independent variable, drug user group. The research hypothesis provides a specific prediction of the ordering of the sample means and indicates that two pairwise comparisons are needed: $\overline{X}_{A_1}$ (nonusers) versus $\overline{X}_{A_2}$ (short-term users) and $\overline{X}_{A_2}$ (short-term users) versus $\overline{X}_{A_3}$ (long-term users). The first step in data analysis is to conduct a one-factor between-subjects analysis of variance on the scores. The MS_{Error} from this analysis is then used in a multiple F test to conduct the two planned pairwise comparisons.

Calculating the Analysis of Variance

The analysis of variance may be calculated on the scores using the raw-score computational formulas given in Chapter 11. Use of these formulas results in the following summary table.

Source	df	SS	MS	F
Drug user group (A)	2	293.55	146.78	5.49*
Error	33	882.08	26.73	
Total	35	1175.63		

*$p < .05$.

For 2 and 33 df, $F_{crit} = 3.32$ at the .05 level. (Because 33 df for the denominator are not tabled, we used the value of F_{crit} for 30 df in the denominator.) Thus, $F_{obs} = 5.49$ falls into the rejection region; we reject $H_0: \mu_{A_1} = \mu_{A_2} = \mu_{A_3}$, and accept H_1: not H_0. To determine whether the ordering of the means follows the predicted order of

$$\text{nonuser} > \text{short-term user} > \text{long-term user}$$

we conduct the two planned comparisons using the multiple F test.

Multiple F Test

The numerical values needed for this test are obtained as follows:

- F_{crit} is the critical value of F for 1 df in the numerator and df_{Error} from the analysis of variance in the denominator. For 1, 33 df, F_{crit} at the .05 level is 4.17. Because 33 df are not given in Table A–3 we used the next lower tabled df, 30 df for MS_{Error}.
- MS_{Error} is obtained from the analysis of variance, and is 26.73.
- n_A, the number of scores in each of the means to be compared, is 12.

Substituting these numerical values into the formula,

$$CD = (\sqrt{2F_{crit}}) \left(\sqrt{\frac{MS_{Error}}{n_A}} \right),$$

$$CD = [\sqrt{2(4.17)}] \left[\sqrt{\frac{26.73}{12}} \right]$$

$$CD = (\sqrt{8.34})(\sqrt{2.23})$$

$$CD = 4.3.$$

A difference between two means of a planned comparison equal to or larger in absolute value than 4.3 test items is statistically significant at the .05 level with the multiple F test. The table below presents the means and the absolute values of the pairwise differences between the means. In this table A_1 = nonuser group, A_2 = short-term user group, and A_3 = long-term user group.

| | | Drug User Group (A) | | |
		A_1 (24.9)	A_2 (23.4)	A_3 (18.2)
Drug User Group (A)	A_1 (24.9)	—	1.5	not planned
	A_2 (23.4)		—	5.2*
	A_3 (18.2)			—

*$p < .05$, CD = 4.3, multiple F test.

The planned pairwise comparisons, the statistical hypotheses tested, and the decisions reached on the statistical hypotheses for each comparison are:

Comparison	Statistical Hypothesis	Decision
$\overline{X}_{A_1}$ vs. $\overline{X}_{A_2}$	$H_0: \mu_{A_1} = \mu_{A_2}$ $H_1: \mu_{A_1} \neq \mu_{A_2}$	Fail to reject Do not accept
$\overline{X}_{A_2}$ vs. $\overline{X}_{A_3}$	$H_0: \mu_{A_2} = \mu_{A_3}$ $H_1: \mu_{A_2} \neq \mu_{A_3}$	Reject Accept

Conclusions:

The planned comparisons reveal that there was no evidence for a difference in the intellectual functioning of the nonusers and short-term users, but the long-term users had significantly lower comprehension scores than the short-term users. Thus, the inferred relationship among the population means is $\mu_{A_1} = \mu_{A_2} > \mu_{A_3}$. ▪

Statistics in Use 12–1

Studying the Ethics of Research Using Planned Comparisons

Behavioral science research must be conducted ethically. When humans are used in experiments, ethical guidelines require that the subjects give informed consent to their participation in the research. The principle of informed consent requires that the experimenter tell the participant about the general nature of what he or she will be doing in the experiment, what physical or emotional risks or discomfort may be involved, and that the participant has the right to withdraw from the experiment at any time. Often this informed consent must be obtained in writing from the participant.

What effect might obtaining informed consent have upon the emotional status of the participant? Holliman, Soileau, Hubbard, and Stevens (1986) reasoned that the process of obtaining informed consent itself may be anxiety evoking. As part of an experiment to test this hypothesis, they administered different treatments to three groups of participants. A control group was first measured on their level of state anxiety before being given a standard informed consent form to sign. One experimental group was first given a short informed consent form to sign and then measured on state anxiety. A second treatment group was given a more involved long informed consent form to sign followed by the measure of state anxiety. Holliman et al. expected the experimental groups, given the consent form before the anxiety measure, to have higher state anxiety than the control group. Accordingly, they planned to compare each treatment group against the control group. The mean anxiety scores obtained were 37.1 for the control group, 38.1 for the short-consent form group, and 36.0 for the long-consent form group.

A multiple F test (used in the form of a least significant differences t) found no difference between the control and short-consent form group, but did reveal that the individuals in the long-consent form group had significantly less anxiety than the control group. These results do not agree with the research hypothesis that obtaining informed consent from participants in an experiment raises state anxiety. Holliman et al. suggested that perhaps the longer informed consent form permits greater rapport to develop between the subject and the experimenter, thus producing a decrease in state anxiety. ■

Testing Your Knowledge 12–2

On a separate sheet of paper, test your knowledge of the material in this section by answering the following questions.

1. **a.** Write the formula for the *CD* found by the multiple *F* test.
   b. What are the *df* used to obtain F_{crit} for this test?
   c. Where do you obtain MS_{Error} for this test?
   d. What is the value of n_A for this test?
2. You are interested in determining whether seeing a laughing model can increase a person's laughter to cartoons. Specifically, you expect that seeing and hearing a laughing model will lead someone to laugh more than will either no model or a nonlaughing model. To test this hypothesis, you randomly assign eight people to each of one of three treatment

groups: A_1—exposure to no model, A_2—exposure to a nonlaughing model, and A_3—exposure to a laughing model, immediately before the participant reads a book of cartoons. The participant's total laughter to the cartoons is measured (in seconds). Suppose you obtained the following duration of laughter scores.

	Type of Model (A)		
	None (A_1)	Nonlaughing (A_2)	Laughing (A_3)
	23	37	53
	38	28	47
	42	43	36
	31	32	38
	27	22	42
	33	41	45
	44	46	51
	25	39	40
$\overline{X}_A$	32.9	36.0	44.0
s_A	7.85	8.11	6.09

Analyze the scores with the analysis of variance and answer the following questions.

a. Complete a summary table for the analysis with the values for df, SS, MS, and F.

b. What are the statistical hypotheses for this analysis of variance?

c. What is the value of F_{crit} at the .05 significance level?

d. What is the rejection region for F_{obs}?

e. Does F_{obs} fall into this rejection region?

f. What decision do you make about H_0 and H_1 from the value of F_{obs}?

g. What conclusion can you reach at this point about differences among the sample means from your decisions about the statistical hypotheses?

Now perform a multiple F test on the scores and complete the following questions.

h. Why is a test for planned comparisons appropriate for this experiment?

i. What are the df for the value of F_{crit} for this test?

j. What is the value of F_{crit} for this test?

k. What is the value of MS_{Error} for this test?

l. What is the value of n_A for this test?

m. Find the value of the CD for this test?

n. Describe in a sentence or two how this *CD* is used to find significant differences between the treatment means.

o. Find the absolute pairwise differences between the three group means and construct a table similar to Table 12–2.

p. The research hypothesis indicated that the experimenter planned to compare the no model group to the laughing model group, and the nonlaughing model group to the laughing model group. Do these two comparisons using the *CD* of the multiple *F* test and indicate whether or not they are statistically significant by placing an asterisk (*) next to the numerical value of the appropriate differences in the table you completed for Question 2o.

q. What are the statistical hypotheses for the tests conducted in Question 2p and what are your decisions about them?

r. Based upon the comparisons you have made, which relationship among population means illustrated in Figure 12–1 is reflected by the outcome of the experiment?

3. This report describes the outcome of a one-factor between-subjects experiment.

The mean number of items recalled was 16.4 for the 0.05-second retention interval, 9.6 for the 3-second retention interval, and 8.9 for the 12-second retention interval. An analysis of variance revealed a significant effect for retention interval $F(2, 24) = 4.39$, $MS_{Error} = 21.47$, $p < .05$. Planned comparisons using the multiple F test ($CD = 4.5$, $\alpha = .05$) revealed a statistically significant decrease in number of items recalled between the 0.05-second and 3-second retention intervals but no significant difference between the 3-second and 12-second intervals.

a. How many levels of the independent variable were used in this experiment?

b. How many participants were involved in this experiment?

c. What is the value of F_{obs}?

d. What is the value of F_{crit} for the analysis of variance at the .05 level?

e. Do you reject or not reject H_0?

f. Do you accept or not accept H_1?

g. What is the value of F_{crit} used for the multiple *F* test?

h. What is the value of MS_{Error} used for the multiple *F* test?

i. What is the value of n_A used for the multiple *F* test?

j. Using these values of F_{crit}, MS_{Error}, and n_A, calculate the *CD* for the multiple *F* test. Does your value agree with the reported value?

k. Based on the results of the multiple *F* test, which planned pairwise comparisons differ significantly?

POST HOC COMPARISONS

The Control of Type I Error

The Type I error rate for the multiple F test approach is equal to α for each comparison made. Consequently, if an experimenter performs a number of comparisons using this test, the probability of making at least one Type I error becomes rather substantial. The problem usually is not major if the comparisons are planned. Planned comparisons are limited in number and reflect a knowledgeable prediction of the effect of the independent variable.

With post hoc comparisons, however, there is greater concern with the error rate, especially if there are many comparisons to be made. To control the Type I error rate, a large number of post hoc comparison tests have been developed. We present one widely used pairwise post hoc comparison procedure here, the Tukey test.

Tukey Test

The **Tukey test,** often referred to as the **honestly significant difference (HSD) test,** obtains a critical value for pairwise comparisons by

$$CD = q_k\left(\sqrt{\frac{MS_{Error}}{n_A}}\right).$$

Again, MS_{Error} is the error term from the overall analysis of variance on the experiment and n_A is the number of scores in each treatment condition. The value of q_k depends upon: (1) the level of α selected, (2) the number of different treatment means involved in the comparisons, and (3) the df for MS_{Error} in the analysis of variance. Values of q_k are given in Table A–4 for $\alpha = .01$ and $\alpha = .05$ for up to 10 means being compared. The Tukey test holds the probability of a Type I error equal to or less than α for all possible pairwise comparisons.

Calculating the CD for the Tukey Test

We illustrate the calculation of the CD for the Tukey test using the item recall scores of Table 12–1. For this application, assume that a research hypothesis making specific predictions about the differences between the means had not been formulated. Rather, suppose the researchers had predicted type of drawing to affect recall, but the specific direction of the effect was not stated. Post hoc comparisons among means would be appropriate for this instance.

From the analysis of variance summarized in Table 12–1, $MS_{Error} = 5.33$. The number of scores in each treatment group is 5; thus $n_A = 5$.

The value of q_k is obtained from Table A–4. Notice that this table requires knowing: (1) the total number of different means involved in the comparison; in our example it is 3, and (2) the df_{Error} from the analysis of variance, in this case, 12. At the .05 level, for 3 means and 12 df_{Error}, $q_k = 3.77$. Substituting these values into the formula for the CD leads to

$$CD = q_k\left(\sqrt{\frac{MS_{Error}}{n_A}}\right);$$

$$CD = (3.77)\left(\sqrt{\frac{5.33}{5}}\right)$$

$$CD = (3.77)\,(1.03)$$

$$CD = 3.9\,.$$

Any difference between two means equal to or greater than 3.9 items recalled in absolute value is statistically significant using the Tukey test. Notice that in comparison with the CD for the multiple F test on the same scores, the Tukey CD is larger, 3.9 compared with 3.2, respectively. A larger difference between the means being compared is required for statistical significance in post hoc comparisons than for planned comparisons.

Interpreting the Tukey CD

The CD for the Tukey test for our example is 3.9. Therefore, a difference between two treatment means in Table 12–1 equal to or larger in absolute value than 3.9 items recalled is statistically significant at the .05 level. Consulting Table 12–2, we note that two pairwise comparisons are larger than 3.9 in absolute value: $\overline{X}_{A_1}$ versus $\overline{X}_{A_2}$ ($17 - 13 = 4$), and $\overline{X}_{A_1}$ versus $\overline{X}_{A_3}$ ($17 - 12 = 5$). Thus, for the three pairwise comparisons we reach the following decision:

Comparison	Decision
$\overline{X}_{A_1}$ vs. $\overline{X}_{A_2}$	reject H_0: $\mu_{A_1} = \mu_{A_2}$
	accept H_1: $\mu_{A_1} \neq \mu_{A_2}$
$\overline{X}_{A_1}$ vs. $\overline{X}_{A_3}$	reject H_0: $\mu_{A_1} = \mu_{A_3}$
	accept H_1: $\mu_{A_1} \neq \mu_{A_3}$
$\overline{X}_{A_2}$ vs. $\overline{X}_{A_3}$	fail to reject H_0: $\mu_{A_2} = \mu_{A_3}$
	do not accept H_1: $\mu_{A_2} \neq \mu_{A_3}$

The Tukey test leads to the conclusion that recall for incomplete outline drawings ($\overline{X}_{A_1}$) is greater than recall for outline drawings ($\overline{X}_{A_2}$) or detail drawings ($\overline{X}_{A_3}$), but recall for outline drawings ($\overline{X}_{A_2}$) does not differ from that of detailed drawings ($\overline{X}_{A_3}$). Accordingly, the conclusion is that the population means are ordered

$$\mu_{A_1} > \mu_{A_2} = \mu_{A_3}\,.$$

In this example, planned and post hoc comparisons lead to the same conclusions regarding the order of the treatment means. This outcome will not necessarily occur, for the *CD* for planned comparisons always will be smaller than the *CD* for post hoc comparisons. An obtained pairwise difference that is statistically significant in a planned comparison may not be so in a post hoc comparison. We illustrate such an instance in question 4 of the Chapter Review Questions. Normally, however, only one type of a comparison—either planned or post hoc—is appropriate for a set of data, and the problem does not arise in practice.

Is It Appropriate to Conduct Post Hoc Comparisons if the Overall Analysis of Variance Is Nonsignificant?

We stated that a planned comparison could be made using the multiple *F* test regardless of whether or not the overall F_{obs} was statistically significant. Conducting post hoc comparisons, however, requires that the overall F_{obs} be statistically significant. If the overall analysis of variance is not statistically significant, then post hoc comparisons should not be performed. The basis for this recommendation is that a researcher typically wants to hold the Type I error rate to the selected value of α. A statistically nonsignificant overall analysis of variance indicates that there are no significant differences among the means being compared. Because no specific predictions were made about the direction of the difference before the experiment was conducted, any post hoc comparisons after a nonsignificant overall F_{obs} simply capitalize on chance differences.

Example Problem 12–2
Using the Tukey test for post hoc comparisons

Problem:

Animals and insects often form dominance hierarchies; certain members of the species become dominant over other members in a group. The dominant member of the group may then have special priviledges in courtship and mating. But does a female discriminate between dominant and nondominant males when mating? Moore and Breed (1986) used cockroaches to investigate this question. Cockroaches were employed because male cockroaches establish clear dominance hierarchies and the dominance is signified by specific odors of the dominant male. As part of their experiment, Moore and Breed created four different groups of male cockroaches and measured the length of time for a female cockroach to approach the male. A control group (A_1) was composed of one male cockroach that had been raised in isolation and had not developed dominance odors. A second group (the lacking status group, A_2) was composed of two males that had not established a dominance hierarchy. One member of the group was restrained in a small wire mesh cage while the other cockroach was free to move about the test cage. The third group (the dominant male free group, A_3) was composed of two male cockroaches that had established a dominance hierarchy. The non-dominant male was restrained and the dominant male allowed free movement about the cage. The fourth group (the subordinate male free group, A_4) was again composed of two males that had established a dominance hierarchy; in this case the nondominant male was allowed free movement while the dominant male was restrained. In each test a female was introduced into the test cage and the length of time for the female to approach the unrestrained male was measured. Because the female would have to discriminate between the dominant and non-dominant male, Moore and Breed expected the presence of a second male to affect the female's response latency (i.e., the amount of time for the female to approach the male). They did not make specific predictions about the expected relation among the groups, however. Suppose the following response latency scores, in seconds, were obtained using 10 different females in each group.

	Treatment Group (A)			
	Control (A₁)	Lacking Status (A₂)	Dominant Male Free (A₃)	Subordinate Male Free (A₄)
	27	31	61	75
	55	62	43	123
	23	44	36	114
	34	39	74	129
	47	57	52	86
	49	51	31	99
	21	69	79	135
	28	46	63	117
	64	77	72	104
	25	66	54	142
$\overline{X}_A$	37.3	54.2	56.5	112.4
s_A	15.21	14.52	16.31	21.46

Determine which group means differ significantly from each other at the .05 level.

Solution:
The design employed is a one-factor between-subjects design with four levels of the independent variable, type of treatment group. Because the research hypothesis did not make a specific prediction of the relationship among the treatment means, a post hoc test is required for the pairwise comparisons needed to find which group means differ significantly from each other. The first step in data analysis is to conduct a one-factor between-subjects analysis of variance on the scores. If a statistically

significant F_{obs} is found, we will use the Tukey test to find the specific pairwise differences between the treatment means.

Calculating the Analysis of Variance

The analysis of variance may be calculated on the scores using the raw-score computational formulas given in Chapter 11. Use of these formulas results in the following summary analysis of variance table.

Source	df	SS	MS	F
Treatment group (A)	3	32,029.02	10,676.34	36.54*
Error	36	10,518.58	292.18	
Total	39	42,547.60		

*$p < .05$

For 3 and 36 df, $F_{crit} = 2.92$ at the .05 level. Thus F_{obs} of 36.54 falls into the rejection region; we reject H_0: $\mu_{A_1} = \mu_{A_2} = \mu_{A_3} = \mu_{A_4}$, and accept H_1: not H_0. Rejection of H_0 lets us conclude there is at least one statistically significant difference between the sample means. To find specifically which means differ from which other means we will utilize the Tukey test for post hoc comparisons.

Tukey Test

The numerical values needed for this test are obtained as follows:

- q_k is obtained from Table A–4. There are four means involved in the comparisons, and 36 df for MS_{Error} from the analysis of variance summary table. Because 36 df are not given in Table A–4 we use 30 df, the next lower tabled df from the 36 df for MS_{Error}. Thus, $q_k = 3.85$ for a .05 significance level.
- MS_{Error}, obtained from the analysis of variance, is 292.18.
- n_A, the number of scores in each of the means to be compared, is 10.

Substituting these numerical values into the formula,

$$CD = q_k\left(\sqrt{\frac{MS_{Error}}{n_A}}\right),$$

$$CD = 3.85\left(\sqrt{\frac{292.18}{10}}\right)$$

$$CD = 3.85(\sqrt{29.218})$$

$$CD = 20.8.$$

A difference between two means equal to or larger in absolute value than 20.8 seconds is statistically significant at the .05 level with the

Tukey test. The table below presents the means and the absolute values of the pairwise differences between the means. In this table A_1 = control group, A_2 = lacking status group, A_3 = dominant male free group, and A_4 = subordinate male free group.

		Group (A)			
		A_1 (37.3)	A_2 (54.2)	A_3 (56.5)	A_4 (112.4)
Group (A)	A_1 (37.3)	—	16.9	19.2	75.1*
	A_2 (54.2)		—	2.3	58.2*
	A_3 (56.5)			—	55.9*

*$p < .05$, CD = 20.8, Tukey test

The pairwise comparisons, the statistical hypotheses tested, and the decisions reached on the statistical hypotheses for each comparison are

Comparison	Statistical Hypothesis	Decision
$\overline{X}_{A_1}$ vs. $\overline{X}_{A_2}$	H_0: $\mu_{A_1} = \mu_{A_2}$	Fail to reject
	H_1: $\mu_{A_1} \neq \mu_{A_2}$	Do not accept
$\overline{X}_{A_1}$ vs. $\overline{X}_{A_3}$	H_0: $\mu_{A_1} = \mu_{A_3}$	Fail to reject
	H_1: $\mu_{A_1} \neq \mu_{A_3}$	Do not accept
$\overline{X}_{A_1}$ vs. $\overline{X}_{A_4}$	H_0: $\mu_{A_1} = \mu_{A_4}$	Reject
	H_1: $\mu_{A_1} \neq \mu_{A_4}$	Accept
$\overline{X}_{A_2}$ vs. $\overline{X}_{A_3}$	H_0: $\mu_{A_2} = \mu_{A_3}$	Fail to reject
	H_1: $\mu_{A_2} \neq \mu_{A_3}$	Do not accept
$\overline{X}_{A_2}$ vs. $\overline{X}_{A_4}$	H_0: $\mu_{A_2} = \mu_{A_4}$	Reject
	H_1: $\mu_{A_2} \neq \mu_{A_4}$	Accept
$\overline{X}_{A_3}$ vs. $\overline{X}_{A_4}$	H_0: $\mu_{A_3} = \mu_{A_4}$	Reject
	H_1: $\mu_{A_3} \neq \mu_{A_4}$	Accept

Conclusions:

The Tukey test leads to the conclusion that the longest latency occurred in the subordinate male free group; this mean ($\overline{X}_{A_4}$) was significantly longer than each of the three other means. The means for the lacking status group ($\overline{X}_{A_2}$) and the dominant male free group ($\overline{X}_{A_3}$) did not differ significantly from each other or from the control group mean ($\overline{X}_{A_1}$). Accordingly, the inferred relationship among the population means is

$$\mu_{A_1} = \mu_{A_2} = \mu_{A_3} < \mu_{A_4}.$$

Moore and Breed arrived at the same relationship among their groups, leading them to conclude that female cockroaches discriminate dominance cues when approaching a male. They respond less rapidly to a nondominant male when a dominant male is present. ■

Using the Tukey Test for Post Hoc Comparisons

Researchers in short-term memory have found a phenomenon known as release from proactive interference (PI). Release from PI is demonstrated as follows. A subject is asked to remember a consonant-vowel-consonant (CVC) trigram, such as *XEQ*, for a very brief period of time. After seeing the CVC the subject is asked to count backward by threes from a three-digit number. After a short period of counting backward by threes, perhaps 15 seconds, the participant is asked to recall the CVC. On the first such trial the subject usually recalls the trigram quite well. Several more trials then are given using different CVCs. By the fourth or fifth trial, recall of the CVC usually drops to about 40 to 50 percent correct. The drop in recall is explained by interference from the CVCs learned on the earlier trials (i.e., proactive interference). On the next trial the stimulus to be recalled changes — for example, to a consonant-consonant-consonant (CCC) trigram. Recall of this stimulus is higher than recall of the immediately preceding CVC. This increase in recall is assumed to be due to a release from the proactive interference of the preceding CVC items.

To find characteristics of stimuli that affect release from PI, Wickens and Cammarata (1986) created four treatment conditions with 24 subjects per group in a one-factor between-subjects design. For the first three trials all subjects saw word trigrams from the same category, such as fruits (for example, *banana, peach, apple*; or *grapefruit, apricot, lemon*). After seeing the word trigram for 2 seconds the subjects counted backwards by threes for 18 seconds and then attempted to recall the trigram. After three trials of this task, three experimental groups were asked to read aloud 40 words, the fourth group simply rested for an equivalent length of time. For the first experimental group the 40 words were from the *same* category as the word trigrams (e.g., fruits), for the second experimental group from a *similar* category (e.g., vegetables), and for the third experimental group from a *different* category (e.g., occupations). After this task, each subject had one more trial recalling a trigram of fruit words. The percentage of items correct on the fourth trial as a function of treatment condition was

| | | Group | |
Rest	Same	Similar	Different
46	29	35	49

A one-factor between-subjects analysis of variance resulted in a statistically significant difference among the means of the four groups: F_{obs} (3, 92) = 3.22, $p < .05$. Wickens and Cammarata then employed the Tukey test to conduct pairwise post hoc comparisons among the four means. From the Tukey test they arrived at the following ordering of their treatment conditions (p. 268):

different = rest > similar = same. These results indicate that the interpolation of a task between trials 3 and 4 was not sufficient to create release from PI. The material in the interpolated task must be different from that learned on earlier trials for release from PI to occur. ■

Testing Your Knowledge 12–3

On a separate sheet of paper, test your knowledge of the material in this section by answering the following questions.

1. **a.** Write the formula for the CD found by the Tukey test.
   b. What are the df used to obtain q_k for this test?
   c. Where do you obtain MS_{Error} for this test?
   d. What is the value of n_A for this test?
2. One hypothesis offered to explain eating disorders, such as anorexia nervosa and bulimia, is that they represent a means of escaping the anxiety of everyday life (Keck & Fiebert, 1986). To test this hypothesis, suppose you conducted an ex post facto study by forming four groups of individuals—a control group of normal weight, nondieting individuals, a group of normal dieters, a group of individuals diagnosed as anorectic, and a group diagnosed as bulimic. There were nine individuals in each group. Each subject was measured on a scale of anxiety avoidance; scores on the scale may range from 10 to 80, with higher scores representing greater avoidance of anxiety. You are unable to predict a specific relationship among the means of the group. Suppose the following avoidance of anxiety scores were obtained.

	Subject Group (A)			
	Normal (A_1)	Dieters (A_2)	Anorectic (A_3)	Bulimic (A_4)
	31	43	67	74
	40	36	60	56
	26	28	55	63
	17	20	59	69
	27	31	71	50
	29	46	48	71
	19	36	54	68
	35	34	66	63
	39	46	50	51
$\overline{X}_A$	29.2	35.6	58.9	62.8
s_A	8.04	8.63	7.91	8.71

Analyze the scores with an analysis of variance and answer the questions below.

a. Complete a summary table with the values for df, SS, MS, and F.
b. What are the statistical hypotheses for this analysis of variance?

    c. What is the value of F_{crit} for this analysis?

    d. What is the rejection region for F_{obs}?

    e. Does F_{obs} fall into this rejection region?

    f. What decision do you make about H_0 and H_1 from the value of F_{obs}?

    g. What conclusion can you reach at this point about differences between the sample means from your decisions about the statistical hypotheses?

Now perform a Tukey's test to compare the means and complete the following questions.

    h. Why is a test for post hoc comparisons appropriate for this study?

    i. What is the value of q_k at the .05 level for this test?

    j. What is the value of MS_{Error} for this test?

    k. What is the value of n_A for this test?

    l. Find the value of the CD for this test.

    m. Find the absolute pairwise differences between the four group means and construct a table similar to Table 12–2.

    n. Using the CD of the Tukey test, indicate which of the differences in the table of Question 2m are statistically significant by placing an asterisk (*) next to the significant differences.

    o. In several sentences, describe the relationship among the sample means.

    p. What is the inferred relationship among the population means?

SUMMARY

- Multiple comparison procedures are statistical tests used to find which means differ significantly from one another in a one-factor multilevel design. A comparison of two means is a pairwise comparison.
- The error rate in an experiment is the probability of making at least one Type I error in the various statistical comparisons conducted.
- Planned comparisons are planned on the basis of predictions from the research hypothesis prior to conducting the experiment.
- The multiple F test is used for planned comparisons. The Type I error rate for the multiple F test is equal to α for each comparison made.

- Planned comparisons may be performed even if the overall analysis of variance is nonsignificant.
- Post hoc comparisons are comparisons that are suggested after one has conducted the experiment and seen the means obtained.
- The Tukey test is used for all possible pairwise post hoc comparisons for a set of means. The Tukey test holds the probability of a Type I error equal to or less than α for all possible pairwise comparisons.
- The overall analysis of variance should be statistically significant before post hoc comparisons are performed.

KEY TERMS

analytical comparison test
a posteriori comparisons
a priori comparisons
critical difference
CD
error rate
familywise error rate
honestly significant difference
   (HSD) test

incidental comparisons
individual comparison test
least significant difference
   (LSD) test
multiple comparison test
multiple *F* test
omnibus alternative hypothesis

pairwise comparisons
planned comparisons
post hoc comparisons
q_k
specific comparison test
Tukey test
Type 1 error

REVIEW QUESTIONS

On a separate sheet of paper, test your knowledge of the material in this chapter by answering the following questions.

1. For each or these situations, indicate which follow-up test—the multiple *F* or the Tukey—is most appropriate.
   a. One independent variable is varied with six levels. All possible pairwise comparisons will be made.
   b. One independent variable is varied with five levels. Based upon the research hypothesis, the experimenter will compare the following means: $\overline{X}_{A_1}$ to $\overline{X}_{A_3}$, $\overline{X}_{A_1}$ to $\overline{X}_{A_5}$, $\overline{X}_{A_2}$ to X_{A_4}, and $\overline{X}_{A_2}$ to $\overline{X}_{A_3}$.
   c. One independent variable is varied with four levels. The experimenter conducts four pairwise post hoc comparisons.

2. Statistics in Use 11–1 presented an example of a one-factor design employing three levels of an independent variable, type of feedback for a multiple choice test (Lhyle & Kulhavy, 1987). A control group, Group A_1, was given no feedback of the correct answer. A repeated answer group, Group A_2, was given the item and the correct answer twice. A scrambled answer group, Group A_3, was given the item and the correct alternative. The words in the alternative were randomly ordered, however, and subjects were told to rearrange them mentally to form the correct answer. It was expected that the scrambled answers would require more cognitive effort to process than would the repeated answers; thus subjects in this condition should better remember the correct answer. After completing the learning program and receiving the feedback on the correct alternatives, the subjects took a criterion test composed of the same 20 multiple-choice alternatives they had just studied. The experimenters predicted that the scrambled answer feedback, Group A_3,

would show the best performance on the criterion task, followed by the repeated feedback condition, Group A_2, which would show better recall than the control group Group, A_1. The mean number of items correct on the criterion test were 9.00 ($s = 3.20$) for the control group, A_1, 13.55 ($s = 3.83$) for the repetition group, A_2, and 12.50 ($s = 2.84$) for the scrambled answer group, A_3. The analysis of variance summary for the scores is shown below.

Source	df	SS	MS	F
Type of feedback (A)	2	227.08	113.54	10.34*
Error	57	625.86	10.98	
Total	59	852.94		

*$p < .01$

Conduct planned comparisons of $\overline{X}_{A_1}$ versus $\overline{X}_{A_2}$ and $\overline{X}_{A_2}$ versus $\overline{X}_{A_3}$ using the multiple F test. Are the sample means ordered as the experimenters expected?

3. Problem 2 of Testing Your Knowledge 11–4 presented an experiment employing three treatment groups with eight subjects in each group. Subjects in Group A_1 wore a theatrical beard while completing the ratings, subjects in Group A_2 wore an outlaw-style bandana around the face while rating themselves, and subjects in Group A_3 formed a control condition where nothing was worn on the face. It was expected that the groups would differ in masculinity ratings, but a specific ordering of the group means was not predicted. The masculinity ratings were 22.9 for the theatrical beard group (A_1), 35.6 for the bandana group (A_2), and 36.0 for the control group (A_3). The analysis of variance summary for the scores is:

Source	df	SS	MS	F
Group (A)	2	893.250	446.625	34.39*
Error	21	272.750	12.988	
Total	23	1166.000		

*$p < .01$

Use the Tukey test to conduct the three possible pairwise comparisons on the means. What are your conclusions about the observed relationship among the means?

4. Klintman (1984) hypothesized that a person's capability for original thinking is related to his or her ability to see perceptual reversals of an ambiguous figure. An ambiguous figure is a figure that can be seen in one of two ways. To test this hypothesis, he employed an ex post facto design using three groups of subjects classified on their performance on a test of original thinking. Suppose nine subjects

were utilized in each level of original thinking and the following scores were obtained. Each score represents the number of reversals reported by a subject during a two-minute viewing period of an ambiguous figure.

	Low (A_1)	Medium (A_2)	High (A_3)
	5	10	8
	9	11	12
	6	8	11
	4	9	13
	10	10	9
	7	7	8
	6	6	10
	5	9	9
	6	6	7
$\overline{X}_A$	6.4	8.4	9.7
s_A	1.94	1.81	2.00

Level of Original Thinking (A)

a. Suppose no specific predictions were made concerning the ordering of the groups. Use the Tukey test to conduct the three possible pairwise comparisons among the groups. What conclusions about the relationship among the group means do you reach from this test?

b. Suppose now a specific prediction was that the ordering of the groups means would be

$$Low < Medium < High.$$

Use the multiple F test to conduct the following comparisons:

$$\overline{X}_{A_1} \text{ versus } \overline{X}_{A_2}$$
$$\overline{X}_{A_2} \text{ versus } \overline{X}_{A_3}.$$

What conclusions about the relationship among the group means do you reach from this test?

c. Why do you reach different conclusions with the multiple F test compared with the Tukey test?

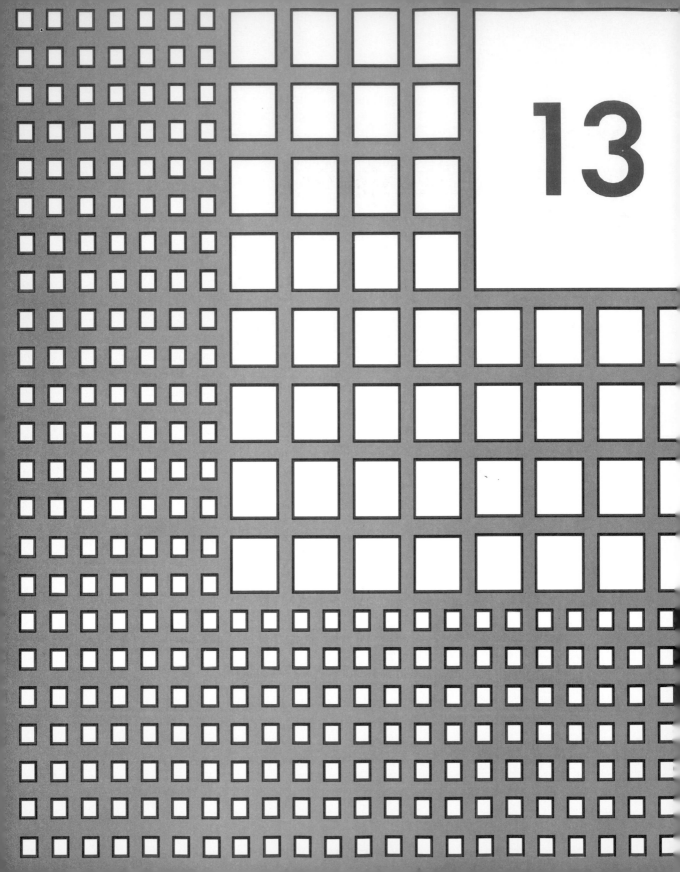

13

Two-Factor Between-Subjects Analysis of Variance

OVERVIEW: FACTORIAL DESIGNS

The one-factor analysis of variance is an important statistical test for data analysis in behavioral science research. But this analysis often is limited in its application because it permits the manipulation of only one independent variable at a time. As you have observed, many behaviors are determined by two or more independent variables. For example, the amount of opinion change (the dependent variable) in a member of an audience listening to a speaker depends upon both the physical attractiveness of the speaker (one independent variable) and the speaker's announced desire to influence or not influence listeners (a second independent variable) (Mills and Aronson, 1965). Or, as another example, memory for a list of noun pairs (the dependent variable) depends upon the imagery ability of the person learning the list (one independent variable), the type of image provided to the learner (a second independent variable), and the length of the retention interval (a third independent variable) (O'Brien and Wolford, 1982). One-factor designs do not permit the manipulation of more than one independent variable at a time; thus, to study the influence of two or more independent variables in combination, factorial designs are used. **Factorial designs** are research designs in which two or more independent variables are simultaneously varied. In the simplest factorial design, two independent variables are varied and each independent variable assumes two levels. Such a design is often called a 2×2 ("two-by-two") design. The first 2 of the 2×2 indicates there are two levels of the first independent variable (often identified as **factor A**) and the second 2 indicates the number of levels of the second independent variable (often identified as **factor B**). A $2 \times 2 \times 2$ design is a three factor design with factors A, B, and C, and each independent variable varies over two levels. Among the many possible factorial designs are a 2×4 design (two levels of factor A, four levels of factor B), a $3 \times 3 \times 2$ design (three levels of factors A and B, two levels of factor C), a $2 \times 2 \times 2 \times 2$ design (four factors, A, B, C, and D, with two levels of each), and so on. Factorial designs may also be totally between-subjects, totally within-subjects, or a combination of the two resulting in a mixed design. In this chapter we discuss only the between-subjects factorial design.

The 2 × 2 Between-Subjects Design

The 2×2 between-subjects design is most convenient for discussing and illustrating the important concepts associated with statistical data analysis of factorial designs. This design is represented in Table 13–1. The table illustrates two independent variables or factors identified simply as A and B, each taking on two levels — factor A with levels A_1 and A_2, and factor B with levels B_1 and B_2. More generally, there are a levels of factor A and b

TABLE 13–1.

Plan of a two-factor between-subjects design with two levels of each independent variable.

		Factor A	
		A_1	A_2
Factor B	B_1	A_1B_1 treatment condition (A_1B_1 cell)	A_2B_1 treatment condition (A_2B_1 cell)
	B_2	A_1B_2 treatment condition (A_1B_2 cell)	A_2B_2 treatment condition (A_2B_2 cell)

levels of factor B. The combination of the two independent variables creates four treatment conditions, often called **cells**, in the table: A_1B_1, A_1B_2, A_2B_1, and A_2B_2. Each cell or **treatment condition** represents a combination formed from one level of each independent variable. An equal number of individuals is typically randomly assigned to each of the treatment conditions. Thus, if 20 people are to be utilized in a 2 × 2 design, five individuals are assigned to each treatment condition or cell. Although there are four treatment conditions in the entire experiment, an individual experiences only one of those conditions.

MUM'S THE WORD: AN EXAMPLE EXPERIMENT

People generally don't like to give other people bad news. This phenomenon is called the MUM effect. Several hypotheses have been proposed to explain this effect. The personal discomfort hypothesis states that the bearer of bad news may feel personal discomfort when delivering the bad news. A second hypothesis, the self-presentational hypothesis, suggests that individuals do not feel discomfort when delivering the bad news; rather the failure to deliver the bad news is a public display following a social norm; after all, who wants to be known as the bearer of bad news? To provide a test of these hypotheses, Bond and Anderson (1987) employed a 2 × 2 between-subjects design. Two independent variables were manipulated: the visibility of the subject to the person to whom the bad news was to be delivered (subject visibility, factor A) and the type of news to be delivered (type of news, factor B). Each independent variable was manipulated over two levels. For subject visibility, the subject was either not visible (level A_1) or visible (level A_2) to the person to whom the news was to be delivered. The type of news was either good (level B_1) or bad (level B_2). The experimental procedure was as follows. A subject was to administer a multiple-choice intelligence test to another individual who, unknown to the subject, was a confederate of the experimenter. The subject and the confederate were in separate rooms joined by a one-way mirror. In the subject not visible condition (level A_1) the subject was told that the confederate could not see him or her through the mirror. For the subject visible condition (level A_2) the subject was told that the confederate could see him or her through the mirror. The type of news was manipulated by the confederate's success on the test. For the good news condition (level B_1) the subject informed the confederate that her performance was in the top 20 percent of the scores on the test. In the bad news condition (level B_2) the subject informed the confederate that her performance was in the bottom 20 percent of the scores on the test. The dependent variable was the latency of feedback of the test score from the subject to the confederate. This latency was the length of time from the completion of the test to the subject's telling the confederate what her score was.

Two different outcomes for the experimenter were predicted from the two hypotheses explaining the MUM effect. If the MUM effect occurs because subjects experience personal discomfort, then it should take longer to deliver the bad news than the good news regardless of whether the subject is or is not visible to the confederate. In other words, the difference between the good (level B_1) and bad (level B_2) news conditions should not depend upon the level of subject visibility, not visible or visible. On the other hand, if the MUM effect is simply a public display, then the latency to deliver the bad news should depend upon whether the subject is or is not visible to the confederate. That is, an interaction of the independent variables should occur. When good news is delivered there should be no difference in the latencies of the not visible and visible conditions. When bad news is delivered, however, the latency of the visible condition should be significantly longer than the latency of the not visible condition. Correspondingly, for the not visible condition, there should be no difference between the latencies of the good and bad news conditions. For the visible condition, however, the latency of the bad news condition should be significantly longer than the good news condition.

Suppose five male subjects were randomly assigned to each of the treatment cells and the latency scores (in seconds) presented in Table 13–2 were obtained. Which prediction, if either, do the results agree with, those of the personal discomfort hypothesis, or those of the public display hypothesis?

INFORMATION OBTAINED FROM A FACTORIAL DESIGN

A factorial design provides information about the main effects of each independent variable and the interaction of the two independent variables. As with the data of a one-factor design, the first step in data analysis

TABLE 13–2.

Hypothetical response latencies (in seconds) as a function of subject visibility and type of news for 20 subjects in the example 2 × 2 between-subjects design experiment.

		Subject Visibility (Factor A)	
		Not Visible (A₁)	*Visible (A₂)*
Type of News (Factor B)	*Good (B₁)*	97.0	70.0
		90.0	87.0
		80.0	81.0
		107.0	95.0
		80.0	90.0
	Bad (B₂)	68.0	114.0
		87.0	96.0
		92.0	127.0
		80.0	110.0
		84.0	115.0

begins with computing measures of central tendency, the sample means. The scores in Table 13–2 are represented notationally in Table 13–3. A score for a subject is represented by X_{ijk}, where the subscripts provide the following information:

i A number identifying the subject within a treatment condition,
j The level of the A variable that the subject receives, and
k The level of the B variable that the subject receives.

TABLE 13–3.

Notational representation of scores in a 2 × 2 between-subjects design with two levels of each independent variable and five subjects per cell.

		Factor A	
		A₁	*A₂*
Factor B	*B₁*	X_{111}	X_{121}
		X_{211}	X_{221}
		X_{311}	X_{321}
		X_{411}	X_{421}
		X_{511}	X_{521}
	B₂	X_{112}	X_{122}
		X_{212}	X_{222}
		X_{312}	X_{322}
		X_{412}	X_{422}
		X_{512}	X_{522}

For example, X_{311} is the third subject in the A_1B_1 treatment condition, X_{421} is the fourth subject in the A_2B_1 treatment condition, X_{212} is the second subject in the A_1B_2 treatment condition, and X_{522} is the fifth subject in the A_2B_2 treatment condition.

Table 13–4 illustrates the nine different sample means that may be calculated from these scores in a 2 × 2 factorial design: four cell means, four main effect means, and one grand mean.

Cell Means

The **cell means,** symbolized by $\overline{X}_{A_1B_1}$, $\overline{X}_{A_1B_2}$, $\overline{X}_{A_2B_1}$, and $\overline{X}_{A_2B_2}$, or in general, by $\overline{X}_{AB}$, are the means of the n_{AB} scores for a treatment combination (see Table 13–4a). Thus, a cell mean indicates the typical performance of subjects in a treatment condition. The numerical cell means for the scores of Table 13–2 are presented in Table 13–5. Notice that each cell mean is based upon 5 scores (e.g., $n_{AB} = 5$ for this experiment).

TABLE 13–4.
Obtaining cell and main effect means in a 2 × 2 between-subjects design.

(a) Cell Means That May Be Calculated

		Factor A	
		A_1	A_2
Factor B	B_1	$\overline{X}_{A_1B_1}$	$\overline{X}_{A_2B_1}$
	B_2	$\overline{X}_{A_1B_2}$	$\overline{X}_{A_2B_2}$

(c) Main Effect Means for Factor B

	Factor A		
	A_1	A_2	
B_1			$\overline{X}_{B_1}$
B_2			$\overline{X}_{B_2}$

Ignore classification of scores by factor A to obtain main effect means for factor B.

(b) Main Effect Means for Factor A

		Factor A	
		A_1	A_2
Factor B	B_1		
	B_2		
		$\overline{X}_{A_1}$	$\overline{X}_{A_2}$

Ignore classification of scores by factor B to obtain main effect means for factor A

TABLE 13–5.
Cell and main effect means for the data of Table 13–2. Standard deviations of cell means are given in parentheses.

| | | Subject Visibility (Factor A) | | Main Effect Means |
		Not Visible (A_1)	Visible (A_2)	for Type of News ($\overline{X}_B$)
Type of News (Factor B)	Good (B_1)	90.8 (11.56)	84.6 (9.61)	87.7
	Bad (B_2)	82.2 (9.07)	112.4 (11.15)	97.3
Main Effect Means for Subject Visibility ($\overline{X}_A$)		86.5	98.5	Grand Mean 92.5

Measures of Variability

The standard deviations for the scores in each cell of Table 13–2 also are presented in Table 13–5. In a factorial design the s typically is calculated only for the cell means and not for the main effect means.

Main Effect Means

Main effect means indicate the typical performance of all individuals given one level of an independent variable while ignoring the classification by the other independent variable. Thus, there are two sets of main effect means, those for factor A and those for factor B.

Factor A

The **main effect means for factor A,** which reflect the overall effect of independent variable A, are symbolized by $\overline{X}_{A_1}$ and $\overline{X}_{A_2}$. These means, sometimes called **column means,** are obtained by essentially treating the design as a one-factor design manipulating only factor A and ignoring factor B. That is, the main effect means for factor A are found for all subjects given either treatment A_1 or A_2 while disregarding the level of factor B they received. Collapsing the data over levels of factor B to obtain main effect means for factor A is shown in Table 13–4b. Following the approach illustrated in Table 13–4b, the main effect means for factor A, subject visibility in Table 13–2, are based upon the 10 scores of subjects either not visible or visible to the confederate. Type of news (factor B) is ignored when determining the main effect means of factor A. The numerical values of $\overline{X}_{A_1}$ and $\overline{X}_{A_2}$ are presented in Table 13–5. The **main effect for independent** variable A is then the difference $\overline{X}_{A_1} - \overline{X}_{A_2}$. If factor A has an effect upon the dependent variable, then this effect will be reflected in the value of $\overline{X}_{A_1} - \overline{X}_{A_2}$.

Factor B

A similar logic applies to obtaining the main effect for independent variable B. The design is now treated as a one-factor design manipulating only factor B. The **main effect means for factor B** (sometimes called *row means*), symbolized as $\overline{X}_{B_1}$ and $\overline{X}_{B_2}$, are obtained by collapsing over factor A as shown in Table 13–4c. To obtain the main effect means for factor B, type of news, the categorization by subject visibility (factor A) is ignored. The numerical values of $\overline{X}_{B_1}$ and $\overline{X}_{B_2}$ are also presented in Table 13–5. The main effect for independent variable B is then the difference $\overline{X}_{B_1} - \overline{X}_{B_2}$. If factor B has an effect upon the dependent variable, then this effect will be reflected in the value of $\overline{X}_{B_1} - \overline{X}_{B_2}$.

Grand Mean

The grand mean $(\overline{X}_G)$ is found by obtaining the mean of all the scores in the table. For the data in Table 13–2, the grand mean is the mean of all 20 scores. Because the grand mean represents average performance over all treatment conditions, it is not typically presented as a descriptive statistic. But it is needed in this chapter for developing an analysis of variance for this design.

Interaction of the Independent Variables

An **interaction** occurs in a factorial design when the effect of one independent variable (e.g., factor A) depends upon the level of the other independent variable (e.g., B_1 or B_2) with which it is combined. For example, if an interaction occurs in a 2×2 design, then the effect of factor A, the difference in behavior between treatments A_1 and A_2, depends upon the level of factor B. Similarly, the effect of factor B, the difference in behavior between treatments B_1 and B_2, depends upon the level of factor A. Thus, an **interaction of independent variables** is their joint effect upon the dependent variable, which cannot be predicted by knowing the main effect of each independent variable separately. The public display hypothesis predicted an interaction for our example experiment. This hypothesis predicted no difference in the response latency between the nonvisible (A_1) and visible (A_2) conditions for good news (level B_1 of factor B). For bad news (level B_2 of factor B), however, the hypothesis predicted significantly longer latencies for the visible (A_2) condition compared to the nonvisible (A_1) condition. The occurrence of an interaction must be analyzed by comparing differences among the cell means rather than among the main effect means. We introduce a technique for doing these comparisons later in this chapter.

On a separate sheet of paper, test your knowledge of the material in this section by answering the following questions.

1. Define: factorial design, factor, level of an independent variable, treatment condition, cell, cell mean, main effect mean, grand mean, column mean, row mean, main effect for factor A, main effect for factor B, $\overline{X}_{AB}$, $\overline{X}_A$, $\overline{X}_B$, $\overline{X}_G$, interaction.
2. For each of the following factorial designs, identify how many independent variables are involved and indicate the number of levels for each factor. Then, assuming that the design is a between-subjects design, indicate how many individuals would be needed if 10 subjects were to be tested in each treatment combination. Type of design: 3×3, 3×2, 2×3, 6×2, 4×4, $2 \times 2 \times 2$, $2 \times 4 \times 3$, $3 \times 3 \times 2$.
3. Find cell means, main effect means, and the grand mean for the scores below.

Table 1				Table 2		
		Factor A			**Factor A**	
		A_1	A_2		A_1	A_2
		10	17		23	41
		13	23		13	22
	B_1	8	17	B_1	28	27
		17	21		11	32
		12	19		19	26
		20	24		20	24
Factor B					18	39
		19	27	**Factor B**		
		13	21		29	28
	B_2	10	16		33	31
		20	19	B_2	18	26
		22	30		29	34
		17	24		36	39
					47	44
					27	35

ANALYSIS OF VARIANCE OF A TWO-FACTOR BETWEEN-SUBJECTS DESIGN

Overview

The analysis of variance of a factorial design involves hypothesis testing to determine if the main effect means differ significantly from each other for each independent variable, and to determine if the interaction of the independent variables is statistically significant. Again, this analysis of variance partitions the total variation of scores into unique sources of variation that are independent of each other. The one-factor between-subjects analysis of variance (discussed in Chapter 11) partitions the total variation into two independent sources: that due to the effect of the independent variable (i.e., factor A), and that due to error variation among individual scores. In a two-factor between-subjects design, however, two independent variables are manipulated; thus the total variation of scores is partitioned into four sources:

1. The effect of the particular treatment level of factor A;
2. The effect of the particular treatment level of factor B;
3. The interaction of factors A and B; and
4. Error variation.

The two-factor between-subjects analysis of variance model thus partitions a score into a set of four components and uses these components to generate four mean squares: MS_A, which varies with the effect of factor A, MS_B, which varies with the effect of factor B, $MS_{A \times B}$, which varies with the effect of the interaction of factors A and B, and MS_{Error}, which varies with the error variation of the scores. Following this step, three separate F ratios are generated:

Source of Variation	F Ratio
Factor A	MS_A/MS_{Error}
Factor B	MS_B/MS_{Error}
Interaction of $A \times B$	$MS_{A \times B}/MS_{Error}$

Each of the three F ratios is then used in a statistical hypothesis test to determine if the source of variation that the F ratio corresponds to is statistically significant.

Partitioning a Score

To understand each of the three F ratios, we must see how the two-factor between-subjects analysis of variance sorts the total variation in an experiment into components varying with factor A, factor B, the $A \times B$ interaction, and error variation. The model for representing a score in a two-factor between-subjects design can be expressed as

$$\begin{array}{l} \text{Total variation} \\ \text{in a subject's} \\ \text{score} \end{array} = \begin{array}{l} \text{Variation due} \\ \text{to the effect} \\ \text{of factor } A \end{array} + \begin{array}{l} \text{Variation due} \\ \text{to the effect} \\ \text{of factor } B \end{array} + \begin{array}{l} \text{Variation due to} \\ \text{interaction of} \\ \text{factors } A \text{ and } B \end{array} + \begin{array}{l} \text{Variation due} \\ \text{to error} \end{array}$$

Eq. 13–1

This partitioning of a score can be represented symbolically as

$$(X_{ijk} - \overline{X}_G) = (\overline{X}_A - \overline{X}_G) + (\overline{X}_B - \overline{X}_G) + (\overline{X}_{AB} - \overline{X}_A - \overline{X}_B + \overline{X}_G) + (X_{ijk} - \overline{X}_{AB}).$$

| Deviation of subject's score from the grand mean | Deviation of factor A main effect mean from the grand mean | Deviation of factor B main effect mean from the grand mean | Deviation of a cell mean from the grand mean after main effects of factors A and B have been removed, i.e., interaction | Deviation of subject's score from his or her treatment group mean |

Eq. 13–2

Let us examine each component of equation 13–2.

$X_{ijk} - \overline{X}_G$

The deviation of a score from the grand mean represents the total deviation of the subject's score from the grand mean of the experiment. As equation 13–2 indicates, a portion of this deviation is due to the effect of each independent variable and the interaction of the independent variables, and a portion of it is due to error variation.

$\overline{X}_A - \overline{X}_G$

This component of the equation varies with the effect of factor A and with sampling error among the main effect means of factor A. Its use is identical to its use in the one-factor between-subjects design to measure the effect of the independent variable in that design. The **grand mean** is used to represent the typical performance of a person before any treatment has acted upon his or her score. Any effect of factor A is expected to affect all individuals who receive a given level of this factor equally and either adds to or subtracts from the base score of the grand mean. Thus, an effect of factor A changes the value of the main effect means for factor A. These main effect means will then differ from the grand mean. Hence, the difference $\overline{X}_A - \overline{X}_G$ reflects any effect of factor A (the treatment effect for factor A in equation 13–1). In addition to any treatment effect, the main effect means for factor A will also differ from each other because of sampling error. Therefore, the value of any $\overline{X}_A - \overline{X}_G$ difference reflects both a treatment effect of factor A and sampling error affecting the values of $\overline{X}_A$.

$\overline{X}_B - \overline{X}_G$

This component of the equation varies with the effect of factor B and sampling error among the main effect means of factor B. As with factor A, any effect of factor B is expected to affect all individuals who receive a given level of this factor equally and either adds to or subtracts from the base score of the grand mean. Consequently, an effect of factor B changes the value of the main effect means for factor B, which will then differ from the grand mean. Therefore, the difference $\overline{X}_B - \overline{X}_G$ reflects any effect of factor B (the treatment effect for factor B in equation 13–1). In addition, the main effect means for factor B will also differ from each other because of sampling error. Hence, the difference $\overline{X}_B - \overline{X}_G$ reflects both a treatment effect of factor B and sampling error affecting the values of $\overline{X}_B$.

$\overline{X}_{AB} - \overline{X}_A - \overline{X}_B + \overline{X}_G$

The interaction of factors A and B is the remaining deviation of the cell means from the grand mean after the main effect of each independent variable has been removed. Symbolically, this statement may be represented as

$$A \times B \quad = \quad (\overline{X}_{AB} - \overline{X}_G) \quad - \quad (\overline{X}_A - \overline{X}_G) \quad - \quad (\overline{X}_B - \overline{X}_G).$$

Interaction of A and B	Deviation of cell mean from grand mean	Main effect of factor A	Main effect of factor B

The variation remaining in the cell means after the main effect of each independent variable has been removed must then be due to the joint effect of the independent variables.

Carrying out the subtractions indicated in the equation results in the simplified expression of the interaction as

$$\overline{X}_{AB} - \overline{X}_A - \overline{X}_B + \overline{X}_G.$$

The interaction is expressed in this form in equation 13–2.

$X_{ijk} - \overline{X}_{AB}$

The difference of a score from its cell mean reflects only error variation in the experiment. This error is what is left over in the score after the main effects of both factors and their interaction have been taken into account. As in a one-factor analysis of variance, the error reflects the uniqueness of a person's score in a group of individuals all of whom receive the same treatment.

Numerical Illustration of Partitioning a Score

To illustrate the numerical partitioning of a score, we use the score for the fourth subject in the not visible/bad news treatment group (i.e., X_{412}) of Table 13–2, which is 80. For this score, equation 13–2 becomes

$$X_{412} - \overline{X}_G = (\overline{X}_{A_1} - \overline{X}_G) + (\overline{X}_{B_2} - \overline{X}_G) + (\overline{X}_{A_1 B_2} - \overline{X}_{A_1} - \overline{X}_{B_2} + \overline{X}_G)$$
$$+ (X_{412} - \overline{X}_{A_1 B_2}).$$

Substituting numerical values for the score and appropriate means, we obtain

$$80.0 - 92.5 = (86.5 - 92.5) + (97.3 - 92.5)$$
$$+ (82.2 - 86.5 - 97.3 + 92.5) + (80.0 - 82.2)$$

and, carrying out the arithmetic functions indicated,

$$-12.5 = (-6.0) + (+4.8) + (-9.1) + (-2.2) \,.$$

Notice that we have separated the total deviation of this score from the grand mean into four components or parts. The partitioning shows that a score deviates from the grand mean as much as it does because of the systematic effect of the level of factor A received (reflected in $\overline{X}_{A_1} - \overline{X}_G = -6.0$), the systematic effect of the level of factor B received (reflected in $\overline{X}_{B_2} - \overline{X}_G = +4.8$), the interaction of factors A and B (reflected in $\overline{X}_{A_1 B_2} - \overline{X}_{A_1} - \overline{X}_{B_2} + \overline{X}_G = -9.1$), and because of the unsystematic influences of within-groups error variation (reflected in $X_{412} - \overline{X}_{A_1 B_2} = -2.2$). A similar partitioning could be done for each of the other scores in Table 13–2.

Testing Your Knowledge 13–2

On a separate sheet of paper, test your knowledge of the material in this section by answering the following questions.

1. Identify the sources of variation in scores from a two-factor between-subjects design.
2. Write the equation to partition a score for the two-factor between-subjects analysis of variance.
3. Explain why the value of $\overline{X}_A - \overline{X}_G$ varies with the effect of factor A in a factorial experiment.
4. Explain why the value of $\overline{X}_B - \overline{X}_G$ varies with the effect of factor B in a factorial experiment.
5. Explain why the value of $\overline{X}_{AB} - \overline{X}_A - \overline{X}_B + \overline{X}_G$ varies with the effect of the interaction of factors A and B in a factorial experiment.
6. Explain why the value of $X_{ijk} - \overline{X}_{AB}$ varies only with error variation in a factorial experiment.
7. Partition the score of subject 4 in the visible/good news condition $(X_{421} = 95.0)$ in Table 13–2.

Obtaining Mean Squares from Partitioned Scores

Obtaining Sums of Squares
Using the approach presented in Chapter 11, sums of squares (SS) are obtained by partitioning each score in the form of equation 13–2. This partitioning is shown in step 1 of Table 13–6. The remaining steps in the table obtain sums of squares from these partitioned scores.

Step 1. The scores of all 20 subjects in the experiment are partitioned following equation 13–2.
Step 2. The numerical values of each deviation for each component of each score are obtained.
Step 3. Each of the positive and negative deviations obtained in step 2 is squared.

Step 4. The values of the squared deviations are summed over all subjects in the experiment. This summing is achieved by adding the 20 values in each of the columns. The result is five sums of squares:

$$SS_{Total} = 4567.00,$$
$$SS_A = 720.00,$$
$$SS_B = 460.80,$$
$$SS_{A \times B} = 1656.20, \quad \text{and}$$
$$SS_{Error} = 1730.00.$$

The steps illustrated in Table 13–6, and the sums of squares resulting from those steps, may be expressed in mathematical notation as

$$\sum_{k=1}^{b} \sum_{j=1}^{a} \sum_{i=1}^{n_{AB}} (X_{ijk} - \overline{X}_G)^2 = \sum_{k=1}^{b} \sum_{j=1}^{a} \sum_{i=1}^{n_{AB}} (\overline{X}_A - \overline{X}_G)^2 + \sum_{k=1}^{b} \sum_{j=1}^{a} \sum_{i=1}^{n_{AB}} (\overline{X}_B - \overline{X}_G)^2$$

$$+ \sum_{k=1}^{b} \sum_{j=1}^{a} \sum_{i=1}^{n_{AB}} (\overline{X}_{AB} - \overline{X}_A - \overline{X}_B + \overline{X}_G)^2 + \sum_{k=1}^{b} \sum_{j=1}^{a} \sum_{i=1}^{n_{AB}} (X_{ijk} - \overline{X}_{AB})^2. \quad \textbf{Eq. 13–3}$$

TABLE 13–6.
Obtaining sums of squares for a two-factor analysis of variance.

Step 1. Partition Scores for the 20 Participants.				
$X_{ijk} - \overline{X}_G$	$= (\overline{X}_A - \overline{X}_G)$	$+ (\overline{X}_B - \overline{X}_G)$	$+ (\overline{X}_{AB} - \overline{X}_A - \overline{X}_B + \overline{X}_G)$	$+ (X_{ijk} - \overline{X}_{AB})$

Scores in $A_1 B_1$

$97.0 - 92.5$	$= (86.5 - 92.5)$	$+ (87.7 - 92.5)$	$+ (90.8 - 86.5 - 87.7 + 92.5)$	$+ (97.0 - 90.8)$
$90.0 - 92.5$	$= (86.5 - 92.5)$	$+ (87.7 - 92.5)$	$+ (90.8 - 86.5 - 87.7 + 92.5)$	$+ (90.0 - 90.8)$
$80.0 - 92.5$	$= (86.5 - 92.5)$	$+ (87.7 - 92.5)$	$+ (90.8 - 86.5 - 87.7 + 92.5)$	$+ (80.0 - 90.8)$
$107.0 - 92.5$	$= (86.5 - 92.5)$	$+ (87.7 - 92.5)$	$+ (90.8 - 86.5 - 87.7 + 92.5)$	$+ (107.0 - 90.8)$
$80.0 - 92.5$	$= (86.5 - 92.5)$	$+ (87.7 - 92.5)$	$+ (90.8 - 86.5 - 87.7 + 92.5)$	$+ (80.0 - 90.8)$

Scores in $A_2 B_1$

$70.0 - 92.5$	$= (98.5 - 92.5)$	$+ (87.7 - 92.5)$	$+ (84.6 - 98.5 - 87.7 + 92.5)$	$+ (70.0 - 84.6)$
$87.0 - 92.5$	$= (98.5 - 92.5)$	$+ (87.7 - 92.5)$	$+ (84.6 - 98.5 - 87.7 + 92.5)$	$+ (87.0 - 84.6)$
$81.0 - 92.5$	$= (98.5 - 92.5)$	$+ (87.7 - 92.5)$	$+ (84.6 - 98.5 - 87.7 + 92.5)$	$+ (81.0 - 84.6)$
$95.0 - 92.5$	$= (98.5 - 92.5)$	$+ (87.7 - 92.5)$	$+ (84.6 - 98.5 - 87.7 + 92.5)$	$+ (95.0 - 84.6)$
$90.0 - 92.5$	$= (98.5 - 92.5)$	$+ (87.7 - 92.5)$	$+ (84.6 - 98.5 - 87.7 + 92.5)$	$+ (90.0 - 84.6)$

Scores in $A_1 B_2$

$68.0 - 92.5$	$= (86.5 - 92.5)$	$+ (97.3 - 92.5)$	$+ (82.2 - 86.5 - 97.3 + 92.5)$	$+ (68.0 - 82.2)$
$87.0 - 92.5$	$= (86.5 - 92.5)$	$+ (97.3 - 92.5)$	$+ (82.2 - 86.5 - 97.3 + 92.5)$	$+ (87.0 - 82.2)$
$92.0 - 92.5$	$= (86.5 - 92.5)$	$+ (97.3 - 92.5)$	$+ (82.2 - 86.5 - 97.3 + 92.5)$	$+ (92.0 - 82.2)$
$80.0 - 92.5$	$= (86.5 - 92.5)$	$+ (97.3 - 92.5)$	$+ (82.2 - 86.5 - 97.3 + 92.5)$	$+ (80.0 - 82.2)$
$84.0 - 92.5$	$= (86.5 - 92.5)$	$+ (97.3 - 92.5)$	$+ (82.2 - 86.5 - 97.3 + 92.5)$	$+ (84.0 - 82.2)$

Scores in $A_2 B_2$

$114.0 - 92.5$	$= (98.5 - 92.5)$	$+ (97.3 - 92.5)$	$+ (112.4 - 98.5 - 97.3 + 92.5)$	$+ (114.0 - 112.4)$
$96.0 - 92.5$	$= (98.5 - 92.5)$	$+ (97.3 - 92.5)$	$+ (112.4 - 98.5 - 97.3 + 92.5)$	$+ (96.0 - 112.4)$
$127.0 - 92.5$	$= (98.5 - 92.5)$	$+ (97.3 - 92.5)$	$+ (112.4 - 98.5 - 97.3 + 92.5)$	$+ (127.0 - 112.4)$
$110.0 - 92.5$	$= (98.5 - 92.5)$	$+ (97.3 - 92.5)$	$+ (112.4 - 98.5 - 97.3 + 92.5)$	$+ (110.0 - 112.4)$
$115.0 - 92.5$	$= (98.5 - 92.5)$	$+ (97.3 - 92.5)$	$+ (112.4 - 98.5 - 97.3 + 92.5)$	$+ (115.0 - 112.4)$

Step 2. Perform the Subtractions in Step 1 to Obtain Deviations.

Scores in A_1B_1	+4.5	=	−6.0	+	−4.8	+	+9.1	+	+6.2
	−2.5	=	−6.0	+	−4.8	+	+9.1	+	−0.8
	−12.5	=	−6.0	+	−4.8	+	+9.1	+	−10.8
	+14.5	=	−6.0	+	−4.8	+	+9.1	+	+16.2
	−12.5	=	−6.0	+	−4.8	+	+9.1	+	−10.8
Scores in A_2B_1	−22.5	=	+6.0	+	−4.8	+	−9.1	+	−14.6
	−5.5	=	+6.0	+	−4.8	+	−9.1	+	+2.4
	−11.5	=	+6.0	+	−4.8	+	−9.1	+	−3.6
	+2.5	=	+6.0	+	−4.8	+	−9.1	+	+10.4
	−2.5	=	+6.0	+	−4.8	+	−9.1	+	+5.4
Scores in A_1B_2	−24.5	=	−6.0	+	+4.8	+	9.1	|	−14.2
	−5.5	=	−6.0	+	+4.8	+	−9.1	+	+4.8
	−0.5	=	−6.0	+	+4.8	+	−9.1	+	+9.8
	−12.5	=	−6.0	+	+4.8	+	−9.1	+	−2.2
	−8.5	=	−6.0	+	+4.8	+	−9.1	+	+1.8
Scores in A_2B_2	+21.5	=	+6.0	+	+4.8	+	+9.1	+	+1.6
	+3.5	=	+6.0	+	+4.8	+	+9.1	+	−16.4
	+34.5	=	+6.0	+	+4.8	+	+9.1	+	+14.6
	+17.5	=	+6.0	+	+4.8	+	+9.1	+	−2.4
	+22.5	=	+6.0	+	+4.8	+	+9.1	+	+2.6

Step 3. Square Each Deviation.

	$(X_{ijk} - \overline{X}_G)^2$	$(\overline{X}_A - \overline{X}_G)^2$ +	$(\overline{X}_B - \overline{X}_G)^2$ +	$(\overline{X}_{AB} - \overline{X}_A - \overline{X}_B + \overline{X}_G)^2$ +	$(X_{ijk} - \overline{X}_{AB})^2$
Scores in A_1B_1	20.25	36.00 +	23.04 +	82.81 +	38.44
	6.25	36.00 +	23.04 +	82.81 +	0.64
	156.25	36.00 +	23.04 +	82.81 +	116.64
	210.25	36.00 +	23.04 +	82.81 +	262.44
	156.25	36.00 +	23.04 +	82.81 +	116.64
Scores in A_2B_1	506.25	36.00 |	23.04 |	82.81 +	213.16
	30.25	36.00 +	23.04 +	82.81 +	5.76
	132.25	36.00 +	23.04 +	82.81 +	12.96
	6.25	36.00 +	23.04 +	82.81 +	108.16
	6.25	36.00 +	23.04 +	82.81 +	29.16
Scores in A_1B_2	600.25	36.00 +	23.04 +	82.81 +	201.64
	30.25	36.00 +	23.04 +	82.81 +	23.04
	0.25	36.00 +	23.04 +	82.81 +	96.04
	156.25	36.00 +	23.04 +	82.81 +	4.84
	72.25	36.00 +	23.04 +	82.81 +	3.24
Scores in A_2B_2	462.25	36.00 +	23.04 +	82.81 +	2.56
	12.25	36.00 +	23.04 +	82.81 +	268.96
	1190.25	36.00 +	23.04 +	82.81 +	213.16
	306.25	36.00 +	23.04 +	82.81 +	5.76
	506.25	36.00 +	23.04 +	82.81 +	6.76

Step 4. Sum the Squared Deviations for Each Partition Over All Individuals.

$$\sum_{k=1}^{b=2}\sum_{j=1}^{a=2}\sum_{i=1}^{n_{AB}=5}(X_{ijk}-\overline{X}_G)^2 = \sum_{k=1}^{b=2}\sum_{j=1}^{a=2}\sum_{i=1}^{n_{AB}=5}(\overline{X}_A-\overline{X}_G)^2 + \sum_{k=1}^{b=2}\sum_{j=1}^{a=2}\sum_{i=1}^{n_{AB}=5}(\overline{X}_B-\overline{X}_G)^2 + \sum_{k=1}^{b=2}\sum_{j=1}^{a=2}\sum_{i=1}^{n_{AB}=5}(\overline{X}_{AB}-\overline{X}_A-\overline{X}_B+\overline{X}_G)^2 + \sum_{k=1}^{b=2}\sum_{j=1}^{a=2}\sum_{i=1}^{n_{AB}=5}(X_{ijk}-\overline{X}_{AB})^2$$

4567.00	=	720.00	+	460.80	+	1656.20	+	1730.00
SS_{Total}	=	SS_A	+	SS_B	+	$SS_{A\times B}$	+	SS_{Error}

365

The summing notation $\sum_{k=1}^{b} \sum_{j=1}^{a} \sum_{i=1}^{n_{AB}}$ indicates that each term is first summed over all n_{AB} subjects within a treatment condition (from the first person, $i = 1$, to the last person, n_{AB}, in a particular group), then summed over all a levels of factor A (from the first level of the independent variable, $j = 1$, to the last level, a), and finally over all b levels of factor B (from the first level of the independent variable, $k = 1$, to the last level, b). In our example, because there are five scores in each treatment condition ($n_{AB} = 5$) and two levels of each independent variable ($a = 2$, $b = 2$), the summation limits are from $i = 1$ to $n_{AB} = 5$, from $j = 1$ to $a = 2$, and from $k = 1$ to $b = 2$.

Using the sums of squares notation introduced in Chapter 11, equation 13–3 may be written more simply as

Eq. 13–4 $$SS_{Total} = SS_A + SS_B + SS_{A \times B} + SS_{Error}.$$ **Eq. 13–4**

These sums of squares indicate that the total variation of the scores in the experiment (SS_{Total}) is the result of systematic variation that occurs from factor A (SS_A), factor B (SS_B), the interaction of factors A and B ($SS_{A \times B}$), and the error variation that occurs within groups (SS_{Error}). Thus, the analysis of variance for a two-factor between-subjects design enables a researcher to partition the total variation in scores into four unique and independent sources of variation.

Obtaining SS values for scores is the major computational procedure involved in analysis of variance. In practice it is unlikely that you would perform the necessary calculations following the steps presented in Table 13–6, as these steps are tedious and open to error. Rather, you would use simplified computational formulas that are presented later in this chapter. The steps shown in Table 13–6, however, permit you to understand the conceptual basis for the factorial analysis of variance. The computational formulas do not lead easily to this understanding.

Determining Degrees of Freedom

Mean squares (MS) are obtained by dividing the sums of squares (SS) by the appropriate degrees of freedom (df). Recall that degrees of freedom are defined as the number of scores that are free to vary in the computation of a statistic. Using this definition it is simple to calculate the df for each term of equation 13–3.

Total Degrees of Freedom.   To compute the SS_{Total}, the grand mean, $\overline{X}_G$, must be known. Because the total sum of squares is based upon the deviation of every score in the experiment from the grand mean (i.e., $X_{ijk} - \overline{X}_G$), then one less than the total number of scores are free to vary when calculating SS_{Total}. In notation

$$df_{Total} = N - 1,$$

where N represents the total number of scores in the experiment. With $N = 20$, $df_{Total} = 2 - 1 = 19$.

Degrees of Freedom for SS_A.   The SS_A is computed from the deviations of the main effect means of factor A (i.e., $\overline{X}_{A_1}$ and $\overline{X}_{A_2}$ for our example) from the grand mean, $\overline{X}_G$. For a factorial design with two levels of factor A, if the grand mean is known, then only one main effect mean for factor A is free to vary. Thus, the df for SS_A are equal to one less than the number of levels of factor A. In notation,

$$df_A = a - 1,$$

where a represents the number of levels of independent variable A. For our example $a = 2$, thus $df_A = 2 - 1 = 1$.

Degrees of Freedom for SS_B.   The SS_B is computed from the deviations of the main effect means of factor B (i.e., $\overline{X}_{B_1}$ and $\overline{X}_{B_2}$ in our example) from the grand mean, $\overline{X}_G$. For a factorial design with two levels of factor B, if the grand mean is known, then only one main effect mean for factor B is free to vary. Thus, the df for SS_B are equal to one less than the number of levels of factor B. In notation,

$$df_B = b - 1,$$

where b represents the number of levels of independent variable B. For our example $b = 2$, thus $df_B = 2 - 1 = 1$.

Degrees of Freedom for $SS_{A \times B}$.   The $SS_{A \times B}$ is computed by subtracting the appropriate main effect means from each cell mean. For a 2×2 design, if each main effect mean is known, then only one cell mean is free to vary. Given one cell mean and knowing the main effect means for factors A and B, you can find the other three cell means. More generally,

$$df_{A \times B} = (a - 1)(b - 1).$$

In the 2×2 design that we are discussing, $a = 2$, and $b = 2$, thus $df_{A \times B} = (2 - 1)(2 - 1) = 1$.

Degrees of Freedom for SS_{Error}.   The SS_{Error} is found by subtracting each cell mean, $\overline{X}_{AB}$, from all the scores within that treatment condition, for all the treatment conditions in the experiment. Thus, for each treatment combination, after $\overline{X}_{AB}$ is determined, only $n_{AB} - 1$ scores are free to vary within that cell. For example, in Table 13–2 only four of the five scores are free to vary within each treatment condition if $\overline{X}_{AB}$ is known. Because there are two levels of each independent variable and four scores are free to vary within treatment combination, there are 16 df associated with the SS_{Error} [(4 df for each treatment combination) $\times$ (4 treatment cells)]. Generally, where a represents the number of levels of factor A, b the levels of factor B and n_{AB} the number of scores within each treatment combination,

$$df_{Error} = ab(n_{AB} - 1).$$

Additivity of Degrees of Freedom.   The degrees of freedom for a factorial analysis are additive in the same manner as they are for the one-factor analysis of variance. Thus

$$df_{Total} = df_A + df_B + df_{A \times B} + df_{Error}.$$

This relationship holds in our example, for $df_{Total} = 19$, $df_A = 1$, $df_B = 1$, $df_{A \times B} = 1$, and $df_{Error} = 16$.

Calculating Variance Estimates from SS and df: Mean Squares

Recall that the F statistic is a ratio of two mean squares. Dividing each SS in equation 13–4 by its corresponding df produces the four mean squares needed for the two-factor between-subjects analysis of variance:

$$MS_A = SS_A/df_A$$
$$MS_B = SS_B/df_B$$
$$MS_{A \times B} = SS_{A \times B}/df_{A \times B}, \quad \text{and}$$
$$MS_{Error} = SS_{Error}/df_{Error}.$$

We typically do not obtain MS_{Total} because it is not used in this analysis of variance.

For the scores in Table 13–2 we have found $SS_A = 720.00$, $SS_B = 460.80$, $SS_{A \times B} = 1656.20$, and $SS_{Error} = 1730.00$. Further, $df_A = 1$, $df_B = 1$, $df_{A \times B} = 1$, and $df_{Error} = 16$. Consequently

$$MS_A = 720.00/1 = 720.00$$
$$MS_B = 460.80/1 = 460.80$$
$$MS_{A \times B} = 1656.20/1 = 1656.20, \quad \text{and}$$
$$MS_{Error} = 1730.00/16 = 108.12.$$

Computation of F Statistics

An F statistic is formed by the ratio of two mean squares, one MS a variance estimate varying with the effect of an independent variable as well as with sampling error, and the other MS varying only with error variation in the experiment. In the two-factor between-subjects analysis of variance, MS_A varies with factor A, MS_B varies with factor B, $MS_{A \times B}$ varies with the interaction of factors A and B, and MS_{Error} varies only with error variation within the treatment conditions. Thus, three F ratios are formed, one for each of the systematic sources of variation in the experiment:

Source of Variation	F Ratio
Factor A	MS_A/MS_{Error}
Factor B	MS_B/MS_{Error}
Interaction of $A \times B$	$MS_{A \times B}/MS_{Error}$

For the scores of Table 13–2, $MS_A = 720.00$, $MS_B = 460.80$, $MS_{A \times B} = 1656.20$, and $MS_{Error} = 108.12$. Thus, we obtain the following F ratios:

Source of Variation	F Ratio
Factor A	$720.00/108.12 = 6.66$
Factor B	$460.80/108.12 = 4.26$
Interaction of $A \times B$	$1656.20/108.12 = 15.32$

We discuss how to use and interpret each ratio shortly.

Table 13–7 provides a notational summary of the sources of variance in a two-factor between-subjects analysis of variance, along with the formulas for df, SS, MS, and the F ratios. A numerical summary of the analysis of variance on the data of Table 13–2 is presented in Table 13–8.

TABLE 13–7.

Notational summary of a two-factor between-subjects analysis of variance.

Source	df [a]	SS	MS	F
Factor A	$a - 1$	$\sum_{k=1}^{b} \sum_{j=1}^{a} \sum_{i=1}^{n_{AB}} (\overline{X}_A - \overline{X}_G)^2$	SS_A/df_A	MS_A/MS_{Error}
Factor B	$b - 1$	$\sum_{k=1}^{b} \sum_{j=1}^{a} \sum_{i=1}^{n_{AB}} (\overline{X}_B - \overline{X}_G)^2$	SS_B/df_B	MS_B/MS_{Error}
Interaction of A and B	$(a - 1) \times (b - 1)$	$\sum_{k=1}^{b} \sum_{j=1}^{a} \sum_{i=1}^{n_{AB}} (\overline{X}_{AB} - \overline{X}_A - \overline{X}_B + \overline{X}_G)^2$	$SS_{A \times B}/df_{A \times B}$	$MS_{A \times B}/MS_{Error}$
Error	$ab(n_{AB} - 1)$	$\sum_{k=1}^{b} \sum_{j=1}^{a} \sum_{i=1}^{n_{AB}} (X_{ijk} - \overline{X}_{AB})^2$	SS_{Error}/df_{Error}	
Total	$N - 1$	$\sum_{k=1}^{b} \sum_{j=1}^{a} \sum_{i=1}^{n_{AB}} (X_{ijk} - \overline{X}_G)^2$	Not calculated	

[a] a = number of levels of factor A, b = number of levels of factor B, n_{AB} = number of scores in each treatment condition, N = total number of scores.

TABLE 13–8.

Summary of the analysis of variance on the scores of Table 13–2.

Source	df	SS	MS	F
Subject visibility (A)	1	720.00	720.00	6.66
Type of news (B)	1	460.80	460.80	4.26
A × B	1	1656.20	1656.20	15.32
Error	16	1730.00	108.12	
Total	19	4567.00		

Testing Your Knowledge 13–3

On a separate sheet of paper, test your knowledge of the material in this section by answering the following questions.

1. Complete the following equations for a two-factor between-subjects analysis of variance.
   a. $\sum_{k=1}^{b} \sum_{j=1}^{a} \sum_{i=1}^{n_{AB}} (X_{ijk} - \overline{X}_G)^2 =$
   b. $SS_{Total} =$
   c. $SS_A =$
   d. $SS_B =$
   e. $SS_{A \times B} =$
   f. $SS_{Error} =$
   g. $df_A =$
   h. $df_B =$
   i. $df_{A \times B} =$
   j. $df_{Error} =$
   k. $df_{Total} =$
   l. $MS_A =$
   m. $MS_B =$
   n. $MS_{A \times B} =$
   o. $MS_{Error} =$

2. If $SS_A = 40$, $SS_B = 70$, $SS_{A \times B} = 30$, and $SS_{Error} = 100$, what is the value of SS_{Total}?

3. If $SS_{Total} = 224.6$, $SS_B = 14.7$, $SS_{A \times B} = 64.3$, and $SS_{Error} = 101.9$, what is the value of SS_A?

4. If $SS_{Total} = 302.4$, $SS_A = 75.1$, $SS_B = 19.7$, and $SS_{Error} = 153.2$, what is the value of $SS_{A \times B}$?

5. If $SS_{Total} = 98.9$, $SS_A = 14.2$, $SS_B = 7.9$, and $SS_{A \times B} = 17.6$, what is the value of SS_{Error}?

6. Find df_A, df_B, $df_{A \times B}$, df_{Error}, and df_{Total} for a 2 × 3 between-subjects analysis of variance with 6 scores in each cell.

7. Find df_A, df_B, $df_{A \times B}$, df_{Error}, and df_{Total} for a 3 × 2 between-subjects design with 13 subjects in each treatment condition.

8. If $df_A = 3$, $df_B = 1$, $df_{A \times B} = 3$, and $df_{Error} = 72$, what is the value of df_{Total}?

9. Find the numerical values of mean squares for the following SS and df:
$SS_A = 14$, $SS_B = 26$, $SS_{A \times B} = 44$, $SS_{Error} = 480$, $df_A = 1$, $df_B = 2$, $df_{A \times B} = 2$, $df_{Error} = 60$.

10. Suppose you conducted a 2×2 factorial experiment with three participants in each cell and obtained the following scores:

		Factor A	
		A_1	A_2
	B_1	30	34
		32	36
		28	32
Factor B			
	B_2	28	38
		30	34
		26	36

a. Partition these scores following the approach illustrated in Table 13–6. Obtain the SS_{Total}, SS_A, SS_B, $SS_{A \times B}$, and SS_{Error} and the corresponding degrees of freedom for each partition. Then complete a numerical summary table with values of MS and F.

b. Why is SS_B equal to 0?

11. The following tables are incomplete summary tables for a factorial between-subjects analysis of variance. Assume an equal number of scores in each cell. By using the relationships among SS and df given in equations 13–3 and 13–4 you can provide the missing values in each table. Then answer these questions for each table.

a. How many levels of factor A were employed?
b. How many levels of factor B were employed?
c. How many subjects were measured in each cell?
d. How many subjects participated in the study?

Table 1

Source	df	SS	MS	F
Factor A	2	_____	16.0	_____
Factor B	1	24.0	_____	3.00
A × B	_____	_____	12.0	_____
Error	_____	_____	_____	
Total	65	560.0		

Table 2

Source	df	SS	MS	F
Factor A	2	_____	_____	4.50
Factor B	4	24.0	_____	1.50
A × B	_____	160.0	_____	5.00
Error	_____	_____	4.0	
Total	224	_____		

STATISTICAL HYPOTHESIS TESTING WITH THE TWO-FACTOR BETWEEN-SUBJECTS ANALYSIS OF VARIANCE

To understand statistical hypothesis testing using the F statistics obtained from a factorial analysis of variance, we must know what factors in an experiment affect MS_A, MS_B, $MS_{A \times B}$, and MS_{Error}.

Factors Affecting the Value of Mean Squares in a Factorial Analysis of Variance

Each MS in a factorial analysis is affected by a different source of variation in the experiment. If neither of the independent variables has an effect on the dependent variable and there is no interaction of the independent variables, then each MS estimates only error variation. Under these circumstances, all four mean squares should be approximately equal in value and reflect only the effects of sampling error. But, if either or both of the independent variables have a main effect, or if they interact, then the effect is reflected in the value of the corresponding MS. For example, if factor A produces a main effect, then MS_A will increase in value relative to MS_{Error}, but MS_B, $MS_{A \times B}$, and MS_{Error} will not be affected by the main effect of factor A. A similar situation holds if factor B has a main effect. If factor B produces a main effect, then MS_B will increase in value relative to MS_{Error}, but MS_A, $MS_{A \times B}$, and MS_{Error} will not be affected by this main effect. Similarly, if the independent variables interact, $MS_{A \times B}$ will increase in value but MS_A, MS_B, and MS_{Error} will not be affected. The MS_{Error} is not affected by either main effects or interaction of the independent variables. It reflects only error variance in the experiment. Each MS in a factorial design is thus an independent estimate of the population variance of the scores.

The four mean squares and the sources of variation affecting them may be summarized:

Mean Square	Responsive to
MS_A	Systematic variance due to factor A
	Sampling error
MS_B	Systematic variance due to factor B
	Sampling error
$MS_{A \times B}$	Systematic variance due to the interaction of factors A and B
	Sampling error
MS_{Error}	Error variance

We may relate this understanding of the factors affecting each MS to the three F ratios obtained in Table 13–7. Notice that each F ratio employs

MS_{Error} as the denominator and the appropriate MS for the independent variable or the interaction as the numerator. If the independent variable affecting the MS in the numerator of a particular F ratio does not have an effect, then that F ratio should be equal to about 1.00, for both the numerator and denominator MS will measure only error variation in the experiment. But, if the independent variable does have an effect, then the value of the MS for that variable becomes larger and the particular value of F for that factor becomes greater than 1.0. This reasoning is identical to that expressed in Chapter 11 for the one-factor analysis of variance.

Statistical Decision Making with Factorial Analysis of Variance

The purpose of conducting a two-factor analysis of variance on the data of an experiment is to allow the researcher to decide if the main effect means for either independent variable differ because of sampling error or because of something other than sampling error, the effect of the independent variable. In addition, this analysis allows a decision of whether the variation in cell means results only from the main effects of each independent variable, or if there is some variation in the cell means that can be explained only by an interaction of the independent variables. Thus, a factorial analysis of variance allows us to decide if either or both independent variables have a main effect, or if the two independent variables interact.

These decisions are made by comparing the appropriate value of F_{obs} from the data of the experiment to the sampling distribution of F obtained under a null hypothesis. The steps used are identical to those discussed in Chapter 11. For each of the three F_{obs}:

- Two statistical hypotheses, a null hypothesis, H_0, and an alternative hypothesis, H_1, are formulated. The null hypothesis provides the theoretical sampling distribution of the F statistic.
- A significance level is selected.
- A critical value of F, identified as F_{crit}, is obtained from Table A–3.
- A rejection region is located in the theoretical sampling distribution for the F statistic based upon the value of F_{crit}.
- F_{obs} is calculated from the scores in the experiment.
- A decision to reject or not reject H_0 is made on the basis of whether or not F_{obs} falls into the rejection region.

Statistical Hypotheses

There are three different F ratios for a two-factor between-subjects analysis of variance, thus three different null hypotheses are tested, one for each of the F ratios. In mathematical notation, the null (H_0) and alternative hypotheses (H_1) for each F ratio in a 2×2 factorial analysis of variance are

F Ratio for	Statistical Hypotheses
Factor *A*	H_0: $\mu_{A_1} = \mu_{A_2}$
	H_1: not H_0
Factor *B*	H_0: $\mu_{B_1} = \mu_{B_2}$
	H_1: not H_0
A × *B*	H_0: all $(\mu_{AB} - \mu_A - \mu_B + \mu_G) = 0$
	H_1: not H_0

Main Effects.   The null and alternative hypotheses for the main effects of factors *A* and *B* are identical in form to the statistical hypotheses for the one-factor analysis of variance. For the main effect of an independent variable the factorial analysis of variance is treating the data as if they were obtained from a one-factor design, a point emphasized in Table 13–4. The number of population means identified in the null hypothesis for either factor *A* or *B* always must correspond to the number of levels of that factor in the experiment. For example, if an experiment involves three levels of factor *A*, then the null hypothesis for factor *A* is written as

$$H_0\text{: } \mu_{A_1} = \mu_{A_2} = \mu_{A_3}.$$

The null hypothesis for each factor represents the situation that exists if the independent variable has no effect. If the null hypothesis is true, then any observed difference between the corresponding main effect means is treated as due to sampling error.

The alternative hypothesis, H_1, is again stated as the negation of the null hypothesis

$$H_1\text{: not } H_0$$

regardless of the number of population means involved in the null hypothesis. This hypothesis states that the population means are not equal to each other, a situation that exists if the independent variable does have an effect.

Interaction.   The null hypothesis for the interaction states that in the population, if no interaction occurs, then the deviation of a cell mean, μ_{AB}, from the grand mean, μ_G, will be equal to zero after the main effects of each independent variable [i.e., $(\mu_A - \mu_G)$ and $(\mu_B - \mu_G)$] have been subtracted from it. In other words, this null hypothesis states that with no interaction of the independent variables the value of each cell mean may be exactly predicted from the main effects of the independent variables. The alternative hypothesis states this is not the case and that the variation in cell means is not predictable from the main effects alone.

Decision Making from the F Ratio

Statistical decision making from each F_{obs} in a factorial analysis of variance is identical to the process followed in a one-factor analysis of variance. A value of α defining the size of the rejection region is chosen prior to conducting the analysis. The sampling distribution of F under H_0 then is determined for each of the three F ratios and a rejection region located in each sampling distribution. This step requires looking up three values of F_{crit} with the appropriate numerator and denominator df in Table A–3. Then, for each F_{obs}, if F_{obs} is equal to or larger than its corresponding F_{crit} value, the null hypothesis for that F is rejected and the alternative hypothesis accepted. If F_{obs} is less than its F_{crit} value, then the decision is to fail to reject the null hypothesis and to not accept the alternative hypothesis for that source of variance. The two sets of decisions for each F_{obs} in a two-factor analysis of variance are summarized in Table 13–9.

To illustrate this decision-making process, we turn to the analysis of variance on the example data of Table 13–2, summarized in Table 13–8. Notice that in this table each F_{obs} has 1 df for its numerator and 16 df for its denominator. Hence, each F_{obs} has the same value of F_{crit} and thus the same rejection region. This result is not necessarily the case in all factorial analyses of variance. Depending upon the number of levels of each independent variable, it is possible for F_{obs} to have a different df for the numerator, and thus a different rejection region.

For $\alpha = .05$, F_{crit} with 1, 16 df is 4.49 (obtained from Table A–3). Hence, for each of the three values of F in Table 13–8 the rejection region consists

TABLE 13–9.

Summary of statistical decision making in a two-factor analysis of variance.

F Ratio for	Value of F_{obs}	Statistical Decision
Factor A	Less than F_{crit}	Fail to reject H_0 Do not accept H_1
	Equal to or greater than F_{crit}	Reject H_0 Accept H_1
Factor B	Less than F_{crit}	Fail to reject H_0 Do not accept H_1
	Equal to or greater than F_{crit}	Reject H_0 Accept H_1
$A \times B$	Less than F_{crit}	Fail to reject H_0 Do not accept H_1
	Equal to or greater than F_{crit}	Reject H_0 Accept H_1

of values of F_{obs} equal to or larger than 4.49. Accordingly, we make the following decisions from this analysis of variance.

F Ratio for	F_{obs}	Falls into Rejection Region	Statistical Decision
Factor A	6.66	Yes	Reject H_0 Accept H_1
Factor B	4.26	No	Fail to reject H_0 Do not accept H_1
$A \times B$	15.32	Yes	Reject H_0 Accept H_1

Assumptions of Factorial Between-Subjects Analysis of Variance

The factorial between-subjects analysis of variance is based upon the same three assumptions about the scores obtained in an experiment as is the one-factor between-subjects analysis.

1. Each subject in the experiment is randomly and independently drawn from a population.
2. The scores in the populations sampled are normally distributed.
3. The variances of scores in the populations sampled are equal.

Violations of the normality and variance assumptions are more likely to have minimal effects on the probability of making a Type I error when the following conditions are met:

- The number of subjects in each treatment condition is the same.
- The shape of the distributions of the scores for each treatment condition is about the same and the distributions are neither very peaked nor very flat.
- The value of α is set at .05 rather than .01.

Testing Your Knowledge 13–4

On a separate sheet of paper, test your knowledge of the material in this section by answering the following questions.

1. Identify the factors affecting each MS in a between-subjects factorial analysis of variance.
2. Explain why MS_A increases in value if factor A has an effect in a factorial experiment.
3. Explain why MS_B increases in value if factor B has an effect in a factorial experiment.
4. Explain why $MS_{A \times B}$ increases in value if factors A and B interact in a factorial experiment.

5. Explain why the value of MS_{Error} is not affected by either factors A or B or their interaction in a factorial experiment.
6. What is expected to happen to the value of F_{obs} for factor A if factor A has an effect in an experiment?
7. What is expected to happen to the value of F_{obs} for $A \times B$ if the independent variables interact in an experiment?
8. Identify the steps in statistical testing with a factorial analysis of variance.
9. Write the statistical hypotheses for a 2×4 between-subjects analysis of variance.
10. Write the statistical hypotheses for a 3×2 between-subjects analysis of variance.
11. The following exercise provides incomplete analysis of variance summary tables for several two-factor between-subjects designs. For each table, obtain the value of F_{crit} for a .05 significance level from Table A–3 and indicate whether each value of F_{obs} falls into the rejection region. Then indicate your decision with respect to H_0 and H_1. If the exact df are not tabled for df_{Error}, then use the next lower tabled value.

Table 1

Source	df	F_{obs}
Factor A	1	4.63
Factor B	3	2.11
$A \times B$	3	3.97
Error	56	
Total	63	

Table 2

Source	df	F_{obs}
Factor A	3	1.42
Factor B	2	3.51
$A \times B$	6	2.37
Error	144	
Total	155	

12. Identify the assumptions underlying the use of the factorial between-subjects analysis of variance. ▪

INTERPRETING A 2 × 2 FACTORIAL ANALYSIS OF VARIANCE

Computing a factorial analysis of variance and making decisions with respect to the statistical hypotheses becomes routine with sufficient practice. The interpretation of the outcome of the analysis with respect to the data obtained, however, is never routine. It always requires a careful examination of the various treatment means obtained in the experiment. To do this examination, often it is useful to present the sample means in graphic as well as in table form. In addition, interpreting a statistically significant interaction requires preparing a table of the simple effects for each independent variable.

Graphic Presentation of Cell Means

In the published results of designs employing factorial analysis of variance, the cell means frequently are presented graphically in a figure rather than in a table such as Table 13–5. Compared to a table, a graphic presentation often provides a much clearer portrayal of any interaction that may have occurred. For this reason, we present a brief discussion of plotting and interpreting a figure of cell means from a 2×2 factorial experiment.

The cell means from Table 13–5 are plotted in Figure 13–1. Each cell mean is identified in this figure, but this identification is not done with

FIGURE 13–1.

Latency of response in the example experiment as a function of the type of news (good versus bad) and subject visibility (not visible versus visible).

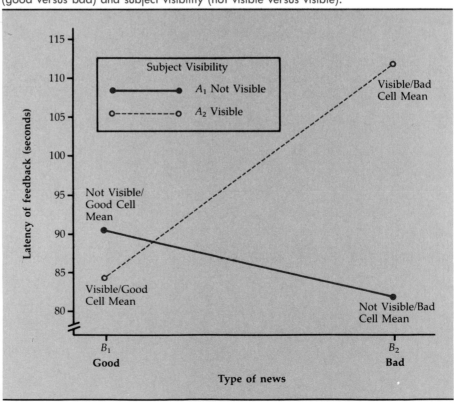

figures in published articles; the cell means are represented by a symbol such as the filled or open circles used in our figure. When plotting such a figure, one of the independent variables is plotted on the abscissa (i.e., horizontal axis), the second independent variable is represented as a function on the figure, and the measure of the dependent variable is plotted on the ordinate (i.e., vertical axis). Which of the two independent variables should be plotted on the abscissa? The rule generally followed is that the independent variable that is more quantitative in nature or with a more continuous underlying dimension is plotted on the abscissa. In the example experiment this variable is factor B, the type of news, as the good-bad dimension of news is a continuum. That is, the type of news may vary over the good-bad dimension in a continuous manner; some news may be very good, whereas other news may be very bad. Thus, the type of news variable was chosen to be placed on the abscissa. The second independent variable, subject visibility, varies in a less continuous manner: there is not a continuous gradation from not visible to visible. Thus, this independent variable is represented by the two functions within the figure. The filled circles connected by the solid line represent the subject not visible condition (A_1) and the open circles connected by the dashed line indicate the subject visible condition (A_2).

Tabular Presentation of Sample Means and Simple Effects

An interaction of two independent variables occurs when the effect of one independent variable depends upon the level of the other independent variable with which it is combined. Consequently, a statistically significant interaction may be interpreted by comparing differences among the cell means. These differences between the cell means reveal the simple effects of the independent variables. The **simple effect of an independent variable** in a factorial design is the effect of that independent variable at only one level of the other independent variable. Table 13–10 illustrates the four simple effect comparisons as well as the two main effect comparisons in a 2 × 2 design.

Although Table 13–10 may appear complex, the information in it is grasped easily. The various simple effects for each independent variable are presented in the rectangular boxes between cells. In a 2 × 2 design there are only two simple effect comparisons for each independent variable.

Simple Effects of Factor A
The simple effect of factor A at level B_1 of factor B is given by $\overline{X}_{A_1B_1} - \overline{X}_{A_2B_1}$. This simple effect reveals the influence of factor A at level B_1 of factor B. Similarly, the simple effect of factor A at level B_2 of factor B, $\overline{X}_{A_1B_2} - \overline{X}_{A_2B_2}$, reveals the effect of factor A at level B_2. In finding the numerical values of the simple effects, it is important to maintain a consistency of direction in the comparisons. Notice that we always

TABLE 13–10.
Simple and main effects in a 2 × 2 between-subjects analysis of variance.

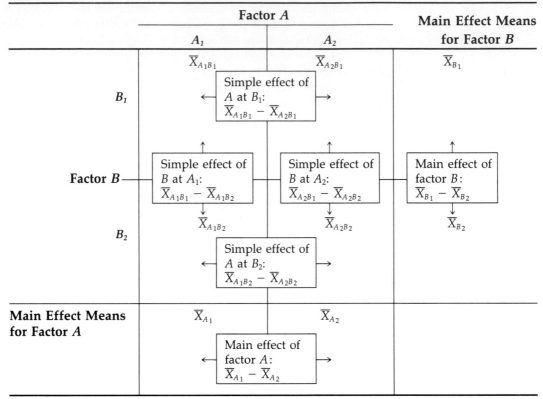

subtract the A_2 cell mean from the A_1 cell mean. You should retain the sign (+ or −) of the effect.

Simple Effects of Factor B

There are also two possible simple effects for factor B; the simple effect of factor B at level A_1 of factor A, $\overline{X}_{A_1B_1} - \overline{X}_{A_1B_2}$, and the simple effect of factor B at level A_2 of factor A, $\overline{X}_{A_2B_1} - \overline{X}_{A_2B_2}$. Each of these simple effect comparisons reveals the effect of factor B at only one level of factor A.

Interpretation of Simple Effects When a Statistically Significant Interaction Occurs

If a statistically significant interaction of the independent variables occurs in an analysis of variance, then the two simple effects for a factor are not equal to each other or to the main effect for that factor. Thus, if there is an interaction, the simple effect of factor A at level B_1, $\overline{X}_{A_1B_1} - \overline{X}_{A_2B_1}$, is not equal to the simple effect of factor A at level B_2, $\overline{X}_{A_1B_2} - \overline{X}_{A_2B_2}$. In addition, neither of these simple effects of factor A is equal to the main effect of factor A, $\overline{X}_{A_1} - \overline{X}_{A_2}$. This description also applies to the simple effects of factor B. If a statistically significant interaction occurs, then the simple effect of factor B at level A_1, $\overline{X}_{A_1B_1} - \overline{X}_{A_1B_2}$, is not equal to the simple effect of B at level A_2, $\overline{X}_{A_2B_1} - \overline{X}_{A_2B_2}$. And, neither of these simple effects equals the main effect of factor B, $\overline{X}_{B_1} - \overline{X}_{B_2}$.

Interpretation of Simple Effects When No Statistically Significant Interaction Occurs

If no statistically significant interaction of the independent variables occurs, then the simple effects and the main effect for a factor are the same. This relationship will be the case for each of the independent variables. The simple effects of factor A are equal to each other and to the main effect of factor A, and the simple effects of factor B are equal to each other and to the main effect of factor B. The lack of an interaction does not mean that the simple effects of factor A equal the simple effects of factor B. This equality occurs only if there also is no main effect for either independent variable. Table 13–11 summarizes these relationships among simple and main effects.

TABLE 13–11.

Interaction and the interpretation of simple effects in a factorial analysis of variance.

If the F ratio for interaction is statistically significant, then:

- The simple effect of factor A at B_1 ($\overline{X}_{A_1B_1} - \overline{X}_{A_2B_1}$) is not equal to the simple effect of factor A at B_2 ($\overline{X}_{A_1B_2} - \overline{X}_{A_2B_2}$). The observed difference between the two simple effects for factor A is due to the interaction of the independent variables and not simply to sampling error.
- The simple effect of factor B at A_1 ($\overline{X}_{A_1B_1} - \overline{X}_{A_1B_2}$) is not equal to the simple effect of factor B at A_2 ($\overline{X}_{A_2B_1} - \overline{X}_{A_2B_2}$). The observed difference between the two simple effects for factor B is due to the interaction of the independent variables and not simply to sampling error.
- The simple effects of factor A are not equal to the main effect of factor A.
- The simple effects of factor B are not equal to the main effect of factor B.

If the F ratio for interaction is statistically nonsignificant, then:

- The simple effect of factor A at B_1 ($\overline{X}_{A_1B_1} - \overline{X}_{A_2B_1}$) does not differ significantly from the simple effect of factor A at B_2 ($\overline{X}_{A_1B_2} - \overline{X}_{A_2B_2}$). The observed difference between the two simple effects for factor A is due to sampling error.
- The simple effect of factor B at A_1 ($\overline{X}_{A_1B_1} - \overline{X}_{A_1B_2}$) does not differ significantly from the simple effect of factor B at A_2 ($\overline{X}_{A_2B_1} - \overline{X}_{A_2B_2}$). The observed difference between the two simple effects for factor B is due to sampling error.
- The simple effects of factor A do not differ from the main effect of factor A.
- The simple effects of factor B do not differ from the main effect of factor B.

A Numerical Example of Simple and Main Effects.   The numerical values of the simple and main effect differences from the means of Table 13–5 are presented in Table 13–12. The main effect and simple effect differences between means are shown in the rectangular boxes. For example, the simple effect of subject visibility for good news (the simple effect of factor A at B_1) is $\overline{X}_{A_1B_1} - \overline{X}_{A_2B_1}$, which equals $90.8 - 84.6$, or $+6.2$ seconds. Likewise, the simple effect of type of news under a subject not visible condition (the simple effect of B at A_1) is $\overline{X}_{A_1B_1} - \overline{X}_{A_1B_2}$, which equals $90.8 - 82.2$, or $+8.6$ seconds.

A table such as 13–12 rarely is presented in published research, but it is helpful in understanding the outcome of an analysis of variance and its relation to the data of an experiment. Notice that Tables 13–5 and 13–12 and Figure 13–1 present the same information, but each in a different form. Both the tabular and graphic approaches will be useful as we discuss the interpretation of the analysis of variance with respect to the main effects and interaction of the example experiment.

Interpretation of Main Effects When an Interaction Occurs

When a statistically significant interaction occurs, the main effects for the independent variables may not lend themselves to meaningful interpretation. This condition happens because the main effect of an independent variable is the mean of the simple effects for that variable. For example, the main effect for subject visibility (-12.0 seconds) in Table 13–12 is the

TABLE 13–12.

Main effect and simple effect differences for subject visibility and type of news in the example experiment.

	Subject Visibility (A)		Main Effect Means for Type of News (B)
	Not Visible (A₁)	*Visible (A₂)*	
Good (B₁)	90.8 ← +6.2 →	84.6	87.7
Type of News (B)	+8.6	−27.8	−9.6
Bad (B₂)	82.2 ← −30.2 →	112.4	97.3
Main Effect Means for Subject Visibility (A)	86.5 ← −12.0 →	98.5	

mean of the simple effects for subject visibility for good and bad news (i.e., [(+6.2) + (−30.2)]/2 = −12.0 seconds). A similar relationship holds for main effects for type of news, −9.6 seconds. It is the mean of the simple effects for type of news for the subject not visible condition, +8.6 seconds, and the subject visible condition, −27.8 seconds. Thus, when an interaction occurs, so that the simple effects of a factor are not equal to each other, the main effect of the independent variable may not accurately represent the effect of that variable. Such main effects are **artifacts of the interaction** and cannot be meaningfully interpreted. An **artifactual main effect,** then, is a main effect that cannot be meaningfully interpreted for it occurs only because of the specific pattern of interaction obtained. It is an artificial result of the pattern of simple effects for that variable. Consequently, we may formulate an important note of caution about interpreting main effects in a factorial design:

- If F_{obs} for interaction is statistically significant, then main effects for either factor A or factor B may be artifactual and not lend themselves to meaningful interpretation.
- If F_{obs} for interaction is statistically nonsignificant, then main effects for either factor A or factor B may be interpreted meaningfully.

A statistically significant interaction in an analysis of variance does not ensure that the main effects will be artifactual, but it is a warning signal to examine carefully any significant main effects to find whether they lend themselves to a meaningful interpretation.

Interpreting the Analysis of Variance on the Example Experiment

Understanding the results of a factorial experiment requires that we look carefully at each main effect and the interaction and interpret them with respect to the decisions made in the analysis of variance. Whenever a statistically significant interaction is obtained, as in our example experiment, we begin our interpretation with understanding the interaction obtained.

Interpreting the Interaction of Independent Variables A and B

The value of F_{obs} for interaction = 15.32 in Table 13–8 is greater than the F_{crit} value of 4.49 and thus falls into the rejection region. Consequently, the null hypothesis for the interaction of factors A and B, H_0: all $(\mu_{AB} - \mu_A - \mu_B + \mu_G) = 0$, is rejected and the alternative, H_1: not H_0, is accepted. We can understand the specific nature of the interaction that occurred by examining Table 13–12 and Figure 13–1. In Table 13–12 the simple effects for factor A, subject visibility, differ for good and bad news. That is, the simple effect of factor A at B_1 (i.e., +6.2 seconds) does not equal the simple effect of factor A at B_2 (i.e., −30.2 seconds). In addition, neither of these simple effects equals the main effect for subject visibility (i.e., −12.0 seconds). Similarly, the simple effects for factor B, type of news, depend upon the subject visibility level. For the subject not visible condition, the difference between good and bad news is +8.6 seconds; whereas for the subject visible condition the difference between good and bad news is −27.8 seconds. Notice, also, that neither of the simple effects for type of news is equal to the main effect for type of news (i.e., −9.6 seconds).

Figure 13–1 also portrays these differences in the simple effects for each of the two independent variables. An interaction is defined as an instance where the effect of one independent variable depends upon the level of the other independent variable with which it is combined. This "it depends" nature of an interaction becomes clear from this figure. If you were asked "What is the effect of subject visibility on response latency?" your answer would have to be, "It depends upon the type of news delivered. For good news there is only a small difference between the subject visible and subject not visible conditions, but for bad news the subject visible condition results in a considerably longer response latency than the subject not visible condition." Likewise, if you were asked, "What is the effect of type of news on response latency?" your answer would take the form, "It depends upon the subject visibility condition. For the subject not visible condition there is only a small difference in the latency of delivery of good and bad news. For the subject visible condition, however, there is a much larger difference between good and bad news with a considerably longer latency for the bad news condition."

The lines connecting data points in Figure 13–1 are nonparallel, a distinguishing characteristic of a figure of a statistically significant interaction. Because an interaction implies that the simple effects of an independent variable are not equal to its main effect, the plot of an interaction must necessarily yield nonparallel lines. But the lines need not cross as they do in Figure 13–1; they will do so only when the simple effects for an independent variable have opposite signs as they do in this example.

In practice, it is rare to find any two lines in a figure to be exactly parallel geometrically. Because of sampling error, the lines will not be precisely parallel, even when there is no statistically significant interaction. Thus, visual inspection alone is insufficient to determine whether or not the lines are to be treated as statistically parallel. An interaction is present in data only if a statistically significant value of F_{obs} is found for the interaction term in an analysis of variance.

Interpreting the Main Effect for Independent Variable A: Subject Visibility

The value of F_{obs} (1, 16) = 6.66 for factor A in Table 13–8 is greater than F_{crit}(1, 16) = 4.49. Thus, this F_{obs} falls into the rejection region. Accordingly, the null hypothesis, H_0: $\mu_{A_1} = \mu_{A_2}$, for factor A, subject visibility, is rejected and the alternative hypothesis, H_1: not H_0, is accepted. This decision implies that the main effect means for subject visibility (86.5 and 98.5 seconds, for subject not visible and subject visible, respectively) each arise from populations with different means, μ_{A_1} and μ_{A_2}, respectively. The main effect difference between the column means, -12.0 seconds (shown in Table 13–12), is considered due to the effect of the independent variable, subject visibility. Because only two means are involved in the comparison, a visual inspection is sufficient to indicate that the direction of the difference is for longer latency in the subject visible condition. Because of the significant interaction, this main effect is artifactual, however. The subject visible condition leads to a longer latency only when bad news is delivered. For good news, latency under subject not visible conditions and subject visible conditions differs only slightly and the subject visible condition even has a slightly shorter latency than the subject not visible condition. Thus, it is misleading to conclude there is an interpretable main effect for subject visibility in this experiment.

Interpreting the Main Effect for Independent Variable B: Type of News

The value of F_{obs} for factor B, the type of news, is 4.26. This value of F_{obs} is less than F_{crit} of 4.49 and hence the null hypothesis for factor B, H_0: $\mu_{B_1} = \mu_{B_2}$ is not rejected and the alternative hypothesis is not accepted. The implication of this decision is that the main effect means for type of news (87.7 and 97.3 seconds for good and bad news, respectively) do not differ significantly. From this nonsignificant main effect difference alone we would conclude that type of news does not affect the response latency of a subject, the 9.6 second difference between the good and bad news conditions due to sampling error. But does this conclusion accurately describe the effect of type of news? An examination of either Figure 13–1 or Table 13–12 indicates clearly that it does not; the effect of the type of news depends upon the visibility of the subject. When the subject is not visible to the confederate there is little difference in the response latency between good and bad news. However, when the subject is visible to the confederate, the bad news is delivered more slowly than the good news. As we can see, the statistically significant interaction has made it inappropriate to attempt to interpret the nonsignificant main effect for type of news.

Patterns of Interaction

The pattern of interaction among the cell means obtained in the example experiment is only one of many that may result in a statistically significant interaction. Obtaining a statistically significant interaction in the analysis of variance ensures only that the simple effect and main effect differences for an independent variable will not be equal. It alone does not provide any further information about the numerous possible ways in which this result may occur. The exact nature of the interaction can be determined only by carefully analyzing the relationships among the cell means. As part of this analysis, it may be necessary to conduct follow-up statistical tests on the values of the simple effects. These tests are discussed in a later section of this chapter.

Testing Your Knowledge 13–5

On a separate sheet of paper, test your knowledge of the material in this section by answering the following questions.

1. Define: artifactual main effect.
2. Each of the examples below represents the cell means obtained in an experiment. A summarized analysis of variance is included for each set of means. In the summarized analysis, a statistically significant F_{obs} is indicated by $p < .05$. A nonsignificant F_{obs} is indicated by $p > .05$. Assume that factor A is teaching method with two levels, inductive teaching (A_1) and deductive teaching (A_2). Factor B is type of material to be learned, quantitative (B_1) or qualitative (B_2). The dependent variable is test score. Interpret each set of means by determining the simple and main effects for each factor and relating the obtained effects to the summarized analysis of variance. Then answer the following questions for each example:
   a. Do the main effect means of factor A differ significantly from each other?
   b. Do the main effect means of factor B differ significantly from each other?
   c. Is there a statistically significant interaction of factors A and B?
   d. What is the effect of teaching method (factor A) on test scores?
   e. What is the effect of type of material (factor B) on test scores?
   f. Is it possible to meaningfully interpret the main effects in this example?

Table 1

		Factor A		ANOVA Summary
		A_1	A_2	Factor A $p < .05$
	B_1	91	85	Factor B $p > .05$
Factor B				$A \times B$ $p > .05$
	B_2	92	87	

Table 2

		Factor A		ANOVA Summary
		A_1	A_2	Factor A $p > .05$
	B_1	88	90	Factor B $p < .05$
Factor B				$A \times B$ $p > .05$
	B_2	81	80	

Table 3

		Factor A		ANOVA Summary
		A_1	A_2	Factor A $p < .05$
	B_1	85	94	Factor B $p < .05$
Factor B				$A \times B$ $p > .05$
	B_2	78	86	

Table 4

		Factor A		ANOVA Summary
		A_1	A_2	Factor A $p > .05$
	B_1	88	75	Factor B $p > .05$
Factor B				$A \times B$ $p < .05$
	B_2	76	90	

Figure 1

ANOVA Summary

Factor A $p < .05$
Factor B $p > .05$
$A \times B$ $p < .03$

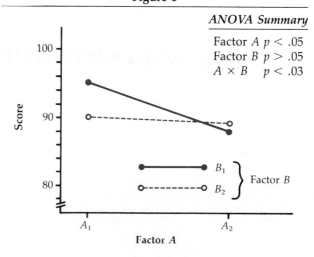

Figure 2

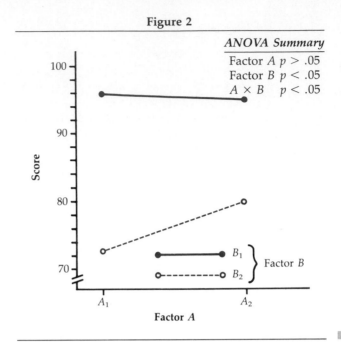

ANOVA Summary

Factor A $p > .05$
Factor B $p < .05$
$A \times B$ $p < .05$

CALCULATING A FACTORIAL ANALYSIS OF VARIANCE: RAW-SCORE COMPUTATIONAL FORMULAS

This section provides the computational format for a factorial between-subjects analysis of variance with an equal number of subjects in each cell. The notational representation for computation of an analysis of variance of a two-factor between-subjects design with two levels of each factor and five scores per cell is

		Factor A				
		A_1		A_2		
	B_1	X_{111} X_{211} X_{311} X_{411} X_{511}	$T_{A_1B_1}$	X_{121} X_{221} X_{321} X_{421} X_{521}	$T_{A_2B_1}$	T_{B_1}
Factor B						
	B_2	X_{112} X_{212} X_{312} X_{412} X_{512}	$T_{A_1B_2}$	X_{122} X_{222} X_{322} X_{422} X_{522}	$T_{A_2B_2}$	T_{B_2}
						G
		T_{A_1}		T_{A_2}		

where

X_{ijk} = raw score of a subject
T_A = total of scores for a level of factor A
T_B = total of scores for a level of factor B
T_{AB} = total of scores in a cell
G = grand total of scores
n_{AB} = number of scores in a cell
a = number of levels of factor A
b = number of levels of factor B
N = total number of scores.

Five numerical terms needed to obtain SS are then computed using these values:

$$[1] = \sum_{k=1}^{b} \sum_{j=1}^{a} \sum_{i=1}^{n_{AB}} X_{ijk}^2 \qquad \text{the sum of all the raw scores squared}$$

$$[2] = \sum_{k=1}^{b} \sum_{j=1}^{a} T_{AB}^2 / n_{AB} \qquad \text{the sum of each cell total squared, divided by the number of scores in a cell}$$

$$[3] = \sum_{j=1}^{a} T_A^2 / bn_{AB} \qquad \text{the sum of each main effect level total for factor } A \text{ squared, divided by the number of scores entering into each total}$$

$$[4] = \sum_{k=1}^{b} T_B^2 / an_{AB} \qquad \text{the sum of each main effect level total for factor } B \text{ squared, divided by the number of scores entering into each total}$$

$$[5] = G^2 / N \qquad \text{the grand total squared, divided by the total number of scores.}$$

Using these numerical values, an analysis of variance is computed as follows:

Source of Variance	df	SS	MS	F
Factor A	$a - 1$	$[3] - [5]$	SS_A / df_A	MS_A / MS_{Error}
Factor B	$b - 1$	$[4] - [5]$	SS_B / df_B	MS_B / MS_{Error}
$A \times B$	$(a - 1) \times (b - 1)$	$[2] - [3] - [4] + [5]$	$SS_{A \times B} / df_{A \times B}$	$MS_{A \times B} / MS_{Error}$
Error	$ab(n_{AB} - 1)$	$[1] - [2]$	SS_{Error} / df_{Error}	
Total	$N - 1$	$[1] - [5]$	Not calculated	

To illustrate the computations, we use the scores from the example problem given in Table 13–2 for which an analysis of variance is summarized in Table 13–8.

		Factor A			
		A_1		A_2	
Factor B	B_1	97 90 80 107 80	$T_{A_1B_1} = 454$	70 87 81 95 90	$T_{A_2B_1} = 423$ $T_{B_1} = 877$
	B_2	68 87 92 80 84	$T_{A_1B_2} = 411$	114 96 127 110 115	$T_{A_2B_2} = 562$ $T_{B_2} = 973$
		$T_{A_1} = 865$		$T_{A_2} = 985$	$G = 1850$

and $n_{AB} = 5$, $a = 2$, $b = 2$, and $N = 20$.

The values of the necessary numerical computational terms are:

$$[1] = 97^2 + \cdots + 80^2 + 70^2 + \cdots + 90^2 + 68^2 + \cdots + 84^2 + 114^2$$
$$+ \cdots + 115^2 = 175{,}692.00$$

$$[2] = (454^2 + 423^2 + 411^2 + 562^2)/5 = 869{,}810.00/5 = 173{,}962.00$$

$$[3] = (865^2 + 985^2)/[(2)\,(5)] = 1{,}718{,}450.00/10 = 171{,}845.00$$

$$[4] = (877^2 + 973^2)/[(2)\,(5)] = 1{,}715{,}858.00/10 = 171{,}585.80$$

$$[5] = 1850^2/20 = 3{,}422{,}500.00/20 = 171{,}125.00$$

Then

$$SS_A = [3] - [5] = 171{,}845.00 - 171{,}125.00 = 720.00$$

$$df_A = a - 1 = 2 - 1 = 1$$

$$SS_B = [4] - [5] = 171{,}585.80 - 171{,}125.00 = 460.80$$

$$df_B = b - 1 = 2 - 1 = 1$$

$$SS_{A \times B} = [2] - [3] - [4] + [5] = 173{,}962.00 - 171{,}845.00 - 171{,}585.80$$
$$+ 171{,}125.00 = 1{,}656.20$$

$$df_{A \times B} = (a - 1)(b - 1) = (2 - 1)(2 - 1) = 1$$

$$SS_{Error} = [1] - [2] = 175{,}692.00 - 173{,}962.00 = 1{,}730.00$$

$$df_{Error} = ab(n_{AB} - 1) = (2)(2)(5 - 1) = 16$$

$$SS_{Total} = [1] - [5] = 175{,}692.00 - 171{,}125.00 = 4{,}567.00$$

$$df_{Total} = N - 1 = 20 - 1 = 19$$

The summary of the analysis of variance is then

Source	df	SS	MS	F
Factor A	1	720.00	$720.00/1 = 720.00$	$720.00/108.12 = 6.66^*$
Factor B	1	460.80	$460.80/1 = 460.80$	$460.80/108.12 = 4.26$
$A \times B$	1	1,656.20	$1{,}656.20/1 = 1{,}656.20$	$1{,}656.20/108.12 = 15.32^*$
Error	16	1,730.00	$1{,}730.00/16 = 108.12$	
Total	19	4,567.00		

$^*p < .05$

The numerical values obtained by this computational approach are identical to those presented in Table 13–8 obtained from the definitional formulas of an analysis of variance.

Example Problem 13–1
Using the two-factor between-subjects analysis of variance

Problem:

Vision and hearing are thought of as two independent sensory modalities, yet there may be a common dimension of experience across these modalities. Visual stimuli sometimes are described as loud and sounds as bright. Thus, Lindner and Hynan (1987) attempted to determine if listening to a certain type of music would affect the perception of an abstract painting. They varied two independent variables in a 2×2 between-subjects design: the type of music listened to, avant-garde or minimalistic; and gender of the participant, male or female. While listening to the music, each individual viewed eight abstract paintings. After this procedure, each person rated the paintings on several 7-point rating scales. One rating scale was composed of the adjective pairs *constrained* (1)—*free* (7), *rigid* (1)—*flexible* (7), and *constricted* (1)—*expanded* (7). Suppose scores were obtained by summing over the three sets of adjective pairs so that a rating could range from 3 to 21. Assume the following scores were obtained from 24 participants.

		Type of Music (A)	
		Avant-garde (A₁)	*Minimalistic (A₂)*
	Male (B₁)	4	16
		5	14
		7	17
		6	19
		10	16
		4	20
Gender (B)			
	Female (B₂)	12	5
		15	9
		18	7
		13	6
		16	10
		16	5

Is there an effect of type of music on the ratings of pictures, do males and females differ in the ratings given, and is there an interaction of type of music with gender of the participants?

Solution:
To determine if each set of main effect means differ by more than would be expected from sampling error alone, and to determine if the pattern of cell means reveals an interaction, a two-factor between-subjects analysis of variance is necessary. We adopt a .05 significance level.

Assumptions for use:

1. The individuals were sampled randomly and independently from a population.
2. The error in ratings is normally distributed in the population.
3. The variances for the rating scores are equal in the populations sampled.

Statistical hypotheses:

Factor A H_0: $\mu_{A_1} = \mu_{A_2}$
  H_1: not H_0

Factor B H_0: $\mu_{B_1} = \mu_{B_2}$
  H_1: not H_0

A × B H_0: all $(\mu_{AB} - \mu_A - \mu_B + \mu_G) = 0$
  H_1: not H_0

Significance level: $\alpha = .05$

df:

$df_A = a - 1 = 2 - 1 = 1$

$df_B = b - 1 = 2 - 1 = 1$

$df_{A \times B} = (a - 1)(b - 1) = (2 - 1)(2 - 1) = 1$

$df_{Error} = ab(n_{AB} - 1) = (2)(2)(6 - 1) = 20$

$df_{Total} = N - 1 = 24 - 1 = 23$

Critical value of F: $F_{crit}(1, 20) = 4.35$

Rejection region: Values of F_{obs} equal to or greater than 4.35.

Calculation: We calculate the analysis of variance using raw-score computational formulas. The necessary cell and main effect totals are given in the table below.

		Type of Music (A)			
		Avant-garde (A₁)	*Minimalistic (A₂)*		
	Male (B₁)	$T_{A_1B_1} = 36$	$T_{A_2B_1} = 102$	$T_{B_1} = 138$	
Gender (B)					
	Female (B₂)	$T_{A_1B_2} = 90$	$T_{A_2B_2} = 42$	$T_{B_2} = 132$	
		$T_{A_1} = 126$	$T_{A_2} = 144$	$G = 270$	

The numerical values necessary to obtain SS are then

$$[1] = \sum_{k=1}^{b} \sum_{j=1}^{a} \sum_{i=1}^{n_{AB}} X_{ijk}^2 = 3690.00$$

$$[2] = \sum_{k=1}^{b} \sum_{j=1}^{a} T_{AB}^2 / n_{AB} = 21564.00/6 = 3594.00$$

$$[3] = \sum_{j=1}^{a} T_A^2 / bn_{AB} = 36612.00/[(2)(6)] = 3051.00$$

$$[4] = \sum_{k=1}^{b} T_B^2 / an_{AB} = 36468.00/[(2)(6)] = 3039.00$$

$$[5] = G^2/N = 72900.00/24 = 3037.50$$

Then

$$SS_A = [3] - [5] = 3051.00 - 3037.50 = 13.50$$

$$SS_B = [4] - [5] = 3039.00 - 3037.50 = 1.50$$

$$SS_{A \times B} = [2] - [3] - [4] + [5] = 3594.00 - 3051.00 - 3039.00$$
$$+ 3037.50 = 541.50$$

$$SS_{Error} = [1] - [2] = 3690.00 - 3594.00 = 96.00$$

$$SS_{Total} = [1] - [5] = 3690.00 - 3037.50 = 652.50$$

The summary of the analysis of variance is

Source	df	SS	MS	F
Music (A)	1	13.50	13.50	2.81*
Gender (B)	1	1.50	1.50	0.31*
A × B	1	541.50	541.50	112.81*
Error	20	96.00	4.80	
Total	23	652.50		

*$p < .01$.

Decision: Three decisions must be made for the statistical hypotheses of this analysis, one for each F_{obs}.

- Type of music (Factor A): $F_{obs} = 2.81$. This F_{obs} does not fall into the rejection region; we fail to reject H_0 and we do not accept H_1.
- Gender (Factor B): $F_{obs} = 0.31$. This F_{obs} does not fall into the rejection region; we fail to reject H_0 and we do not accept H_1.
- Type of music by gender (A × B): $F_{obs} = 112.81$. This F_{obs} falls into the rejection region; we reject H_0 and we accept H_1.

Conclusions:

To interpret the statistically significant interaction, it is useful to construct a table of simple and main effects similar to Table 13–11.

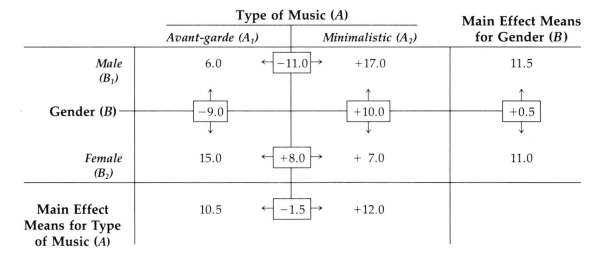

This table shows how the effect of type of music depends upon the gender of the participant. Males hearing avant-garde music typically rate pictures as 6.0 (constrained, rigid, and constricted), but males hearing minimalistic music rate pictures as 17.0 (free, flexible, and expanded). This rating pattern is reversed for females. When listening to avant-garde music, females rate the pictures as 15.0, whereas when listening to minimalistic music they typically give a 7.0 rating. The simple effects for type of music (−11.0 for males, +8.0 for females) are not equal to each other, nor are they equal to the nonsignificant main effect of −1.5 for music. Similarly, the difference between males and females depends upon the type of music. Females rate avant-garde music as more free, flexible, and expanded than do males. However, males rate the minimalistic music higher in this dimension than do the females. Thus, the simple effects for gender (−9.0 for avant-garde music, +10.0 for minimalistic music) are not equal to each other or to the nonsignificant main effect of +0.5 for gender. The main effect means do not provide interpretable information about the outcome of this experiment. From analysis of the main effect means alone, we would conclude that there is no effect for type of music and that males and females do not differ on their ratings. Our interpretation of the interaction, however, indicates that type of music does have an effect, but the direction of the effect depends upon the gender of the subject. Males and females differ also in their ratings, but the difference depends upon the type of music.

Statistics in Use 13–1

Do Token Rewards Increase Intelligence Test Scores? Using the Two-Factor Analysis of Variance

Factorial designs are used widely in behavioral science; accordingly, the factorial analysis of variance is employed in many discipline areas. Our first example is drawn from the area of school psychology. School children frequently are given individual intelligence tests and it is assumed that when taking these tests children are motivated highly and will perform to the best of their abilities. To ensure the highest level of motivation, examiners are trained to provide praise for a child's efforts on the test. But does this praise necessarily lead to the highest level of performance for a child? What if a child was given a token for a correct answer and then allowed to trade tokens for a toy after completing the test? Would the token rewards improve performance over the standard testing conditions? Employing a 2 × 2 between-subjects design, Bradley-Johnson, Graham, and Johnson (1986) varied administration of the *Wechsler Intelligence Scale for Children — Revised* (WISC–R) (factor A) over two conditions — standard administration (identified as the control condition, A_1) and tokens given for correct answers (identified as the token reward condition, A_2). Two different grade levels of children (factor B) were employed — 20 first- and second-graders (B_1) and 20 fourth- and fifth-graders (B_2). Ten students from each grade level were tested under each administration condition. The mean WISC–R verbal score for each condition is shown in the figure below.

Mean WISC–R scores as a function of type of administration conditions and grade level. (Adapted with permission of publisher and authors from Table 1 of "Token reinforcement on WISC-R performance for white, low-socioeconomic, upper and lower elementary-school-age students." Sharon Bradley-Johnson, Dixie Payne Graham, and C. Merle Johnson, *Journal of School Psychology*, 1986, 24, 73–79.)

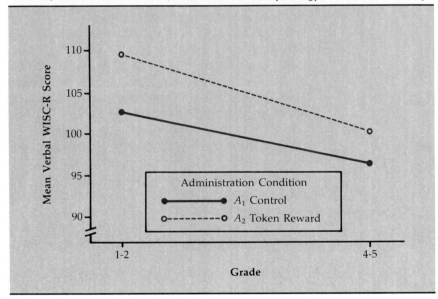

A summary table of a 2 × 2 between-subjects analysis of variance on the intelligence test scores is given below.

Source	df	SS	MS	F
Administration (*A*)	1	313.60	313.60	5.66*
Grade level (*B*)	1	577.60	577.60	10.42*
A × *B*	1	25.60	25.60	0.46*
Error	36	1995.27	55.42	
Total	39	2912.07		

*$p < .05$

The analysis of variance revealed that the main effects of both independent variables were statistically significant, but the interaction was nonsignificant. Notice from the figure of the results that the use of tokens led to higher verbal intelligence scores for both grade levels. Notice also that first- and second-graders obtained higher scores than fourth- and fifth-graders in both administration conditions. Because there is no statistically significant interaction, the effect of the token did not depend upon the grade level of the child. The two lines in the figure thus are considered parallel.

These results indicate that standard testing conditions do not lead necessarily to maximal performance on an intelligence test. Bradley-Johnson et al.
suggest that additional research is necessary to understand conditions that
improve performance on these tests. ■

Statistics in Use 13–2

Rules and Strategies in Filmmaking: Using the Two-Factor Analysis of Variance

A second example of the use of the factorial between-subjects analysis of
variance is drawn from a study investigating techniques of cinematography.
Writers on filmmaking have proposed rules and strategies to be followed to
convey the intended message of the film. Rules provide guidelines for struc-
turing shots so that the scene will be coherent to the viewer. As an example,
one rule indicates that directional continuity should be maintained in filming
scenes; if not, the viewer's perceptual expectations will not be met and the
scene will be perceptually incoherent.

Strategies are guidelines for making shots convey the intended meaning.
An example of a strategy is that of camera angle. Low-angle shots of an individual are intended to convey the impression of strength and superiority
of the person. High-angle shots of the individual convey an impression of
weakness and insignificance. To determine if these rules and strategies function as proposed, Kraft (1987) manipulated rules and strategies in a 2 × 2
between-subjects design. Two levels of the directional continuity rule (factor
A) were employed, the rule followed (A_1) and the rule violated (A_2). The
second independent variable was the strategy of camera angle (factor B),
again with two levels, high camera angle (B_1) and low camera angle (B_2).
Each group of 15 participants viewed four stories constructed under one of
the four treatment combinations (e.g., A_1B_1—directional continuity rule
followed/high camera angle). After viewing the stories, participants reconstructed the order of scenes in the stories and the number of errors made
were recorded (the measure of the dependent variable). If filmmaking theo-
rists are correct, reconstruction should be affected by the directional continuity rule, but not by the camera angle strategy.

The mean number of reconstruction errors obtained are shown below.

	Directional Continuity (A)		Main Effect Means for Factor B
	Followed (A_1)	*Violated (A_2)*	
High (B_1)	0.4	3.1	1.8
Camera Angle (B)			
Low (B_2)	0.2	2.7	1.4
Main Effect Means for Factor A	0.3	2.9	

The analysis of variance summary table for these data is

Source	df	SS	MS	F
Rule (A)	1	101.398	101.398	45.47*
Strategy (B)	1	1.668	1.668	0.75*
A × B	1	0.069	0.069	0.03*
Error	56	124.880	2.230	
Total	59	228.015		

*$p < .05$

The results were in accord with the predictions; the statistically significant main effect for factor A indicated that the two main effect means, 0.3 errors for rule followed and 2.9 errors for rule violated, are significantly different from each other. The main effect means for camera angle do not differ significantly; however, the observed difference is due to sampling error. The lack of a statistically significant interaction indicates that the effect of the continuity rule does not depend upon the camera angle. ◼

Statistics in Use 13–3

Employment Policy and Salary: Using the Two-Factor Analysis of Variance

A third example of the use of a between-subjects factorial analysis of variance is from the area of industrial psychology. Does a company's statement of a fair employment policy (i.e., a policy on the hiring of women and minorities) affect the behavior of managers and administrators responsible for hiring employees? To investigate this problem, Rosen and Mericle (1979) varied two independent variables in a 2 × 2 between-subjects design. The first independent variable (factor A) was the strength of a company's fair employment policy statement, strong (A_1) or weak (A_2). The second independent variable (factor B) was the gender of an applicant, male (B_1) or female (B_2). As part of the experiment, participants assigned to one of the treatment conditions were asked to make a salary offer to a hypothetical applicant. The mean salary offers made are a function of the treatment conditions shown on the next page.

A 2 × 2 between-subjects analysis of variance revealed a statistically significant interaction, $F(1, 37) = 6.25$, $p < .05$, but no significant main effects for either factor. Examine the figure to identify the nature of the interaction. Notice that a strong fair employment policy statement actually worked against females with respect to salary offered. Females were offered a lower salary under a strong policy than under a weak policy. This relationship did not hold for males; they were offered approximately equal salaries in both employment policy conditions. ◼

Mean salary offer to males and females as a function of strength of fair employment policy. (Adapted with permission of publisher and authors from Table 1 of "Influence of strong versus weak fair employment policies and applicant's sex on selection decisions and salary recommendations in a management simulation." Benson Rosen and Mary F. Mericle, *Journal of Applied Psychology*, 1979, *64*, 435–439.)

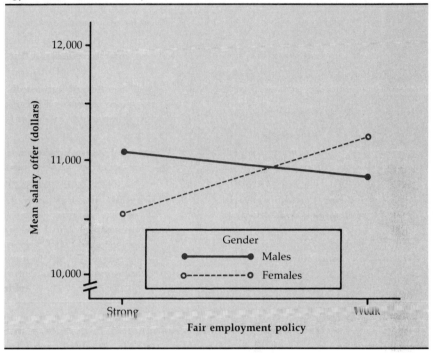

Testing Your Knowledge 13–6

On a separate sheet of paper, test your knowledge of the material in this section by answering the following questions. Complete these problems using a two-factor between-subjects analysis of variance using the format illustrated in the example problem. Use a .05 significance level for each problem.

1. A researcher hypothesized that the effect of type of instructions upon a person's performance would depend upon that individual's perceived locus of control. To evaluate this hypothesis, she obtained 12 females who scored low on a locus of control scale (thus indicating an internal locus of control) and 12 females who scored high on the scale (thus indicating an external locus of control). Half the females in each group were then randomly assigned to one of two instructional conditions—skill or chance instructions. In the skill instructions condition participants were

told that their performance on an anagram solution task depended upon their verbal ability and was under their control. The chance instructions indicated that performance on this task does not depend upon verbal ability and is beyond a person's control. The participants then solved a series of anagrams and the amount of time devoted to the task was recorded. Suppose the following amounts of time (in seconds) that each participant worked on solving the anagrams were obtained:

		Locus of Control (A)	
		Internal (A_1)	External (A_2)
Instructions (B)	Skill (B_1)	175	115
		202	106
		193	87
		186	93
		150	99
		212	157
	Chance (B_2)	125	218
		100	202
		77	196
		101	244
		131	237
		152	180

a. Analyze the scores to determine: (1) if there is a main effect for either independent variable, and (2) if there is an interaction of the independent variables.

b. Are you able to meaningfully interpret any statistically significant main effects or are they artifactual?

c. Describe the pattern of any interaction that occurred.

2. In many jurisdictions, potential jurors are shown a film to acquaint them with the legal process and the nature of the jury system. Suppose a lawyer was interested in finding out whether the film alters a juror's behavior. Further, the lawyer wanted to know if any effect of the film may depend upon the type of crime the juror is to evaluate. To answer these questions, the lawyer conducted a 2×2 between-subjects factorial experiment with 9 subjects serving as mock jurors in each cell. Factor A was the type of instruction given to jurors: A_1—normal oral instructions by a court officer, and A_2—filmed instructions. Factor B was the type of crime the subject was asked to evaluate; this variable was manipulated by having the subjects read a description of an auto theft case (level B_1) or of a rape case (level B_2). Each subject was then asked to assign a prison term to the defendant described in the case. The prison terms assigned (in years) were

	Type of Instruction (A)	
	Normal (A₁)	Filmed (A₂)

Type of Crime (B)

	Normal (A_1)	Filmed (A_2)
Theft (B_1)	15	13
	10	16
	10	9
	14	11
	17	14
	9	8
	8	10
	12	10
	10	12
Rape (B_2)	25	30
	20	33
	23	26
	20	25
	19	30
	17	35
	18	30
	22	28
	20	32

a. Analyze the scores to determine: (1) if there is a main effect for either independent variable, and (2) if there is an interaction of the independent variables.

b. Are you able to meaningfully interpret any statistically significant main effects or are they artifactual?

c. Describe the pattern of any interaction that occurred. ▪

REPORTING THE RESULTS OF A FACTORIAL ANALYSIS OF VARIANCE

A journal summary of a factorial experiment typically would report descriptive statistics and the outcome of the analysis of variance in only a few sentences. We illustrate using the results of Example Problem 13–1 on the relation of type of music and gender to judgments of pictures.

As predicted, there was a significant interaction of type of music with subject gender, $F(1, 20) = 112.81$, $MS_{Error} = 4.80$, $p < .01$. Males listening to avant-garde music rated pictures as constrained, rigid, and constricted ($\overline{X} = 6.0, s = 2.3$), whereas males listening to minimalistic music rated the pictures as free, flexible, and expanded ($\overline{X} = 17.0, s = 2.2$). Females demonstrated a reverse pattern, rating pictures viewed while listening to *avant-garde music as free, flexible, and expanded ($\overline{X}$ = 15.0, s = 2.2) and pictures viewed with minimalistic music as constrained, rigid, and constricted ($\overline{X}$ = 7.0, s = 2.1). The main effect for type of music was non-significant, $F(1, 20)$ = 2.81, MS_{Error} = 4.80, p > .05, as was the main effect for subject gender, $F(1, 20)$ < 1.00, MS_{Error} = 4.80, p > .05.*

As with the one-factor analysis of variance, this presentation of the results conveys considerable information about the experiment to the informed reader.

1. $F(1, 20)$: Identifies the name of the test statistic as the F. Therefore, we know that an analysis of variance was used to analyze the data. The *df* for each F_{obs} reported are shown in parentheses. The *df* indicates the *df* for the numerator (i.e., 1) and the denominator (i.e., 20) of the F_{obs}, respectively. Three values of F_{obs} are reported, one for each independent variable and one for the interaction of the independent variables. Also, the order in which the F ratios are reported is not necessarily factor A, factor B, and $A \times B$. Often an experimenter has more interest in the interaction and thus will present this F_{obs} value first in the description of the results.

2. = 112.81: Gives the value of F_{obs} (not the F_{crit} value found in Table A–3). If F_{obs} is less than 1.00, it may be reported as $F < 1.00$ as was done for the gender variable in this example. In some instances you may find that an author reports only two of the three F ratios obtained in the analysis of variance. In this circumstance, you may assume that the unreported value of F_{obs} was nonsignificant.

3. $p < .01$: Tells us that
   a. H_0 was rejected and H_1 was accepted;
   b. the difference in sample means is statistically significant at the .01 level; and
   c. it is inferred that something other than sampling error was responsible for the obtained difference in sample means.

4. MS_{Error} = 4.80: Provides the value of the MS_{Error} for the F_{obs}. This value is a measure of the error variation in the scores.

Testing Your Knowledge 13–7

On a separate sheet of paper, test your knowledge of the material in this section by answering the following questions.

The following exercises present sample reports of factorial between-subjects analyses of variance. For each exercise, answer the following questions from information provided in the report.

     a. How many levels of factor A were used in this experiment?
     b. How many levels of factor B were used in this experiment?
     c. How many participants were employed in the experiment?
     d. What is the value of F_{crit} at the .05 significance level for each F_{obs} reported?
     e. Is the value of F_{obs} for factor A statistically significant?
     f. Is the value of F_{obs} for factor B statistically significant?
     g. Is the value of F_{obs} for $A \times B$ statistically significant?

1. The main effect of drug level (factor A) was statistically significant, $F(2, 36) = 9.43$, $p < .05$, $MS_{Error} = 17.81$. There was also a main effect for retention interval (factor B), $F(1, 36) = 5.60$, $p < .05$, $MS_{Error} = 17.81$. There was no interaction of the variables, however, $F(2, 36) = 2.46$, $p > .05$, $MS_{Error} = 17.81$.

2. There was a significant gender of athlete (factor A) by type of sport (factor B) interaction on self-esteem ratings, $F(3, 88) = 3.28$, $p < .05$, $MS_{Error} = 42.16$. In addition, males gave higher rated self-esteem than females, $F(1, 88) = 4.82$, $p < .05$, $MS_{Error} = 42.16$, but there were no main effect differences among sport types, $F(3, 88) = 1.65$, $p > .05$, $MS_{Error} = 42.16$. ▪

FOLLOW-UP TESTS FOR THE 2 × 2 BETWEEN-SUBJECTS ANALYSIS OF VARIANCE

After obtaining the statistically significant value of F for the interaction of type of strategy with type of word in Table 13–8, we interpreted the interaction effect among the cell means (Figure 13–1 and Table 13–12) by simple visual inspection. But, visual inspection of the cell means and simple effects is not always a satisfactory basis for determining the pattern of interaction. As we discussed in Chapter 12 with a one-factor analysis of variance, if a null hypothesis involving more than two population means (i.e., there are three or more levels of one independent variable) is rejected, then follow-up or multiple-comparison tests are needed to find exactly which means differ. A similar problem arises in a factorial analysis of variance for interpreting both statistically significant main effects when three or more means are involved and for interpreting a statistically significant interaction.

Follow-Up Tests for Statistically Significant Main Effects

If a statistically significant main effect in an analysis of variance involves three or more means (i.e., the independent variable has three or more levels, for example, a 3 × 3 design), then a follow-up test is required to find which pairs of means differ from each other. On the other hand, if only two means are involved in a main effect (i.e., the independent variable has only two levels, e.g., a 2 × 2 design), then a statistically significant main effect may be interpreted by visual inspection of the means. When a follow-up test is required, the multiple F test may be used for *planned* comparisons and the Tukey test for *post hoc* comparisons. The MS_{Error} employed in each test is the MS_{Error} from the factorial analysis of variance. The value of n is the number of scores that entered into the main effect means being compared. Interpretation of these multiple comparisons is identical to the interpretation for the one-factor analysis of variance discussed in Chapter 12.

Follow-Up Tests for a Statistically Significant Interaction

The approach to interpreting an interaction is to analyze the simple effects of each independent variable. Return to Table 13–10 for a moment. Notice that in a 2 × 2 analysis of variance there are two simple effect comparisons for each independent variable. Each simple effect comparison is a pairwise comparison—the two cell means are compared with each other. To determine if the two cell means differ significantly from each other, a familiar procedure is followed; a critical difference (CD) for the pairwise comparison is determined. If the obtained value of the difference between the two cell means being compared is equal to or exceeds the CD, then the difference between the cell means is statistically significant. The choice of which statistical test to employ depends upon whether the comparison is planned or post hoc.

Planned Comparisons of Simple Effects

For planned comparisons of simple effects, the multiple F test may be used. The critical difference for this test is provided by

$$CD = (\sqrt{2F_{crit}})\left(\sqrt{\frac{MS_{Error}}{n_{AB}}}\right),$$

where F_{crit} is the tabled critical value of F at the α level selected with 1 and MS_{Error} df for the numerator and denominator, respectively. MS_{Error} is the value of MS_{Error} calculated in the factorial analysis of variance, and n_{AB} is the number of scores in each cell. For our example problem on subject visibility and type of news with the analysis of variance summarized in Table 13–8, F_{crit} for 1, 16 df at the .05 significance level equals 4.49, $MS_{Error} = 108.12$, and $n_{AB} = 5$. Thus,

$$CD = [\sqrt{(2)(4.49)}]\left[\sqrt{\frac{(108.12)}{5}}\right] = 13.9.$$

Any simple effect comparison in Table 13.12 equal to or greater than 13.9 in absolute value is statistically significant at the .05 level. Thus, the simple effect of subject visibility for bad news (-30.2 seconds) and the simple effect of type of news for a visible subject (-27.8 seconds) are significant at the .05 level with the multiple F test. Accordingly, this test leads to the following description of the outcome of this experiment.

> *There was a statistically significant interaction of subject visibility with type of news. For good news there was no significant difference between visible and not visible subjects. For bad news, however, the response latency of visible subjects was significantly longer than the latency of the not visible subjects. Not visible subjects delivered good and bad news with equal latencies. Visible subjects, however, took longer to deliver bad news compared to good news.*

Post Hoc Comparisons of Simple Effects

The Tukey test is frequently used for post hoc comparisons of simple effects. The CD for the Tukey test is given by

$$CD = q_k \left(\sqrt{\frac{MS_{Error}}{n_{AB}}} \right).$$

The value of q_k depends upon the number of simple effect comparisons to be made and df error. We may find the value of q_k by using the following conversion:

Type of Design	Use q_k from Table A–4 Found in the Column for _____ Groups
2 × 2	3
2 × 3	5
3 × 2	5
3 × 3	7
3 × 4	8
4 × 3	8
4 × 4	10

The MS_{Error} is the value of MS_{Error} calculated in the factorial analysis of variance, and n_{AB} is the number of scores in each cell.

For our example experiment, a 2 × 2 design, with 16 df for MS_{Error}, and $\alpha = .05$, the value of q_k (3, 16) is 3.65. Hence, the numerical value of the Tukey CD is:

$$CD = 3.65 \left(\sqrt{\frac{108.12}{5}} \right) = 17.0.$$

Any simple effect difference between cell means equal to or greater than 17.0 seconds in absolute value is statistically significant at the .05 level. From Table 13–12, we see that the simple effect of subject visibility for bad news (−30.2 seconds) and the simple effect of type of news for visible subjects (−27.8 seconds) are significant at the .05 level with the Tukey procedure. Although the Tukey CD is larger than the multiple F CD, both tests lead to the same interpretation of results for the example problem.

SUMMARY

- Factorial designs are research designs in which two or more independent variables are varied simultaneously.
- Each cell or treatment condition of a factorial design represents a combination formed from one level of each independent variable.
- Main effect means indicate the typical performance of all individuals given one level of an independent variable while ignoring the classification by the other independent variable.
- An interaction occurs in a factorial design when the effect of one independent variable depends upon the level of the other independent variable with which it is combined.
- Three F ratios are generated in the two-factor between-subjects analysis of variance, as shown below.

- The steps in statistical testing with these F ratios are identical to those discussed in Chapter 11.
- The simple effect of an independent variable in a factorial design is the effect of that independent variable at only one level of the other independent variable.
- If a statistically significant interaction of the independent variables occurs, then the two simple effects for a factor are not equal to each other or to the main effect for that factor.
- An artifactual main effect is a main effect that cannot be meaningfully interpreted; it occurs only because of the specific pattern of interaction obtained.
- Follow-up tests are needed to statistically analyze the simple effects if a significant interaction is obtained. The multiple F test is used for planned comparisons and the Tukey test for post hoc comparisons.

Source of Variation	F Ratio
Factor A	MS_A/MS_{Error}
Factor B	MS_B/MS_{Error}
Interaction of $A \times B$	$MS_{A \times B}/MS_{Error}$

KEY TERMS

$A \times B$ interaction
artifactual main effect
cells
cell means
column means
df_A
df_B
$df_{A \times B}$
df_{Error}
df_{Total}
factor
factor A
factor B
factorial design
grand mean

interaction
level of an independent variable
main effect means
main effect for factor A
main effect for factor B
MS_A
MS_B
$MS_{A \times B}$
MS_{Error}
MS_{Total}
n_{AB}
row means
simple effects
SS_A
SS_B

$SS_{A \times B}$
SS_{Error}
SS_{Total}
treatment condition
$\overline{X}_{AB}$
$\overline{X}_A$
$\overline{X}_B$
$\overline{X}_G$
X_{ijk}
$X_{ijk} - \overline{X}_G$
$\overline{X}_A - \overline{X}_G$
$\overline{X}_B - \overline{X}_G$
$\overline{X}_{AB} - \overline{X}_A - \overline{X}_B + \overline{X}_G$
$X_{ijk} - \overline{X}_{AB}$

REVIEW QUESTIONS

On a separate sheet of paper, test your knowledge of the material in this chapter by answering the following questions.

1. How does level of physiological arousal change when we are engaged in social exchange with others? In an attempt to partially answer this question, Wellens (1987) employed a 2 × 2 between-subjects design in which subjects were interviewed by an experimenter. One independent variable (factor A) was eye-contact of the experimenter with the subject during the interview. Two levels were manipulated: no eye-contact (A_1) and eye-contact (A_2) made. The second independent variable (factor B) was a manipulation of affect with two levels: positive (B_1) and negative (B_2). In the positive affect condition subjects were given a written "first impression" of them by the interviewer that was favorable. For the negative affect condition they were given a written first impression of them by the interviewer that was very unfavorable. The dependent variable was the subject's heart rate in beats per minute while the interview was being conducted. Suppose you replicated this experiment with eight subjects per cell and obtained the following heart rates.

	Eye-Contact (A)	
	No Eye-Contact (A₁)	Eye-Contact (A₂)

Affect (B)		No Eye-Contact (A_1)	Eye-Contact (A_2)
	Positive (B_1)	75	61
		77	68
		68	71
		72	59
		83	74
		78	66
		70	67
		65	57
	Negative (B_2)	79	84
		82	79
		75	88
		77	90
		84	75
		72	75
		78	77
		69	85

a. Does eye-contact affect heart rate? If so, describe the nature of the effect.

b. Does the effect of eye-contact depend upon the level of affect? If so, use a multiple F test to make the pairwise comparisons possible among the cell means. Describe the relationship between eye-contact and affect level that you found.

c. Are you able to meaningfully interpret any main effects or are they artifactual?

d. Describe the results of this experiment following the example illustrated in the Reporting the Results of a Factorial Analysis of Variance section of this chapter.

2. What effect does headline size and position in an advertisement have upon the consumer? Bellizzi and Hite (1987) hypothesized that headline size may convey an impression of the magnitude of a sale. To test this hypothesis they employed a 2 × 2 between-subjects design. Subjects in the experiment were shown an advertisement and asked to judge the magnitude of the sale by estimating the percentage off the regular price they would expect in the sale. One independent variable (factor A) was the size of the word *sale* in the ad. The small size (A_1) was 0.5 inch and the large size (A_2) was 2.0 inches. The second independent variable (factor B) was the placement of the word *sale* on the ad. One placement (B_1) was horizontal, the second (B_2) was diagonal across the page. Suppose you conducted a similar experiment with 12 subjects per cell and obtained the following estimates of the percentage reduction in prices.

| | Word Size | |
| | Small (A₁) | Large (A₂) |

Word Placement (B)		Small (A_1)	Large (A_2)
		7	15
		9	10
		13	17
		5	12
		6	10
		8	16
	Horizontal (B_1)	9	11
		11	14
		10	15
		10	15
		5	9
		16	20
		10	15
		6	17
		8	20
		8	11
		14	11
		5	10
	Diagonal (B_2)	5	14
		5	13
		11	15
		9	17
		7	16
		7	13

a. Does word size affect the perceived magnitude of the sale? If so, describe the nature of the effect.

b. Does word placement affect the perceived magnitude of the sale? If so, describe the nature of the effect.

c. Does the effect of word size depend upon the level of word placement? Does the effect of word placement depend upon the word size?

d. Are you able to meaningfully interpret any main effects or are they artifactual?

3. One aspect of teaching children to read is to have them learn to process information from the material read. A strategy proposed to enhance this processing is to ask the reader to answer questions after reading each page of a story. To test if this strategy does indeed increase reading comprehension, Seretny and Dean (1986) divided a sample of second graders into three reading level ability groups (factor A): below average (A_1), average (A_2), and above average (A_3). Half the subjects in each group were given reading instruction (factor B) in which the children read orally and the teacher did not ask questions each time a page was completed (level B_1). The other half of the subjects (the questions group, level B_2) were given reading instruction in which they too read orally but the teacher asked questions each time the child finished a page. After eight weeks of instruction the children were tested on reading comprehension. Suppose the following scores were obtained for nine children in each cell (larger scores indicate higher levels of reading comprehension.

| | | Reading Ability (A) | | |
		Below Average (A_1)	Average (A_2)	Above Average (A_3)
		10	16	21
		14	17	24
		16	23	23
		12	19	20
	Control (B_1)	14	20	23
		13	15	25
		15	19	21
		11	18	26
		13	21	22
Type of Instruction (B)				
		15	18	21
		18	24	19
		22	19	20
		18	22	23
	Questions (B_2)	21	21	24
		17	20	24
		18	20	22
		16	22	25
		16	23	20

a. Does type of instruction affect reading comprehension scores? If so, describe the nature of the effect.

b. Does effect of type of instruction depend upon the level of reading ability? If so, use a Tukey test to make the nine pairwise comparisons possible among the cell means. Then describe the relationship between type of instruction and reading level ability that you found.

c. Are you able to meaningfully interpret any main effects or are they artifactual?

4. The following tables are incomplete summary tables for between-subjects factorial analyses of variance. Assume an equal number of subjects in each cell. By using the relationships that exist among df, SS, and MS in an analysis of variance, you can provide the missing values in each table. Answer the following questions for each table.

a. How many levels of factor A were employed?
b. How many levels of factor B were employed?
c. How many subjects were used in each cell?
d. What was the total number of subjects employed in the experiment?
e. Which values of F_{obs} are statistically significant at the .05 level?
f. What decision do you make for each null and alternative hypotheses for this analysis?

Table 1

Source	df	SS	MS	F
Type of task (A)	3	_____	5.00	_____
Noise level (B)	_____	16.00	_____	_____
$A \times B$	6	36.00	_____	_____
Error	60	_____	2.00	
Total	_____	_____		

Table 2

Source	df	SS	MS	F
Training length (A)	_____	40.00	10.00	_____
Skill level (B)	3	_____	40.00	_____
$A \times B$	_____	960.00	80.00	_____
Error	160	3200.00	_____	
Total	179	_____		

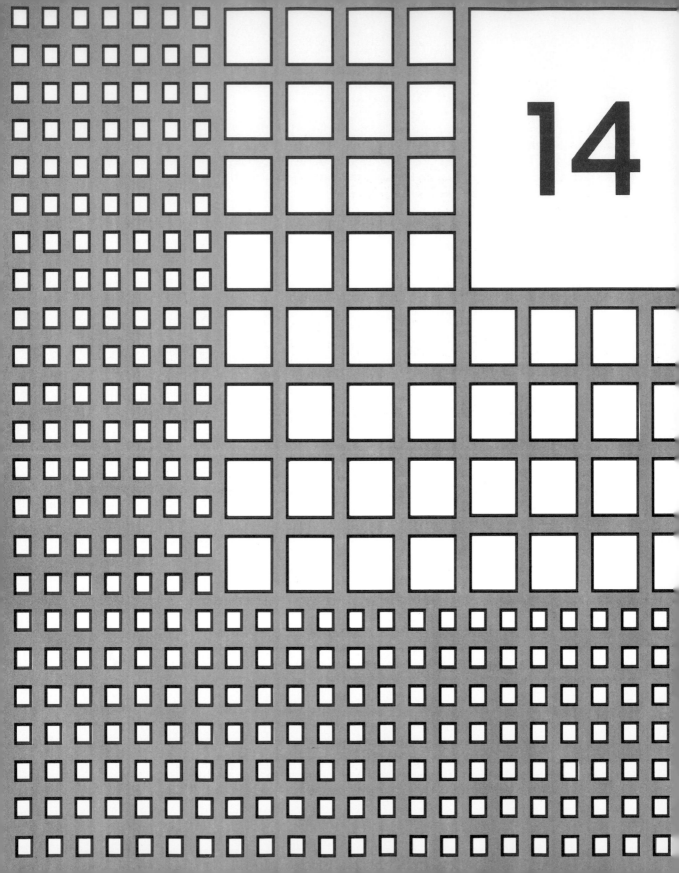

14

One-Factor Within-Subjects Designs

To this point our concern has been with the analysis of between-subjects designs in which each treatment condition is administered to a different group of participants. In this chapter we introduce a second major type of research design, the within-subjects design. In a **within-subjects design** a single group of participants is exposed to all levels of each independent variable. For a one-factor within-subjects design only one independent variable is manipulated and each subject is exposed to and measured under each level of this variable. Because individuals are measured repeatedly in a within-subjects design, this design also is referred to as a **repeated measures design.** It is sometimes called a **treatments-by-subjects design,** a reminder that each person is tested under all levels of the independent variable.

Table 14–1 represents notationally a one-factor within-subjects design with four levels of an independent variable and five subjects. The notation is similar to that used to this point. The independent variable is identified as factor A with levels, A_1, A_2, A_3, and A_4. The number of levels of factor A is represented by a; for Table 14–1, $a = 4$. A score for an individual is represented by X_{ij}, where the subscripted i represents a number identifying the subject (e.g., X_{1j}, X_{2j}, ..., X_{5j}) and the subscripted j represents a number identifying the level of the independent variable. The sample means for each level of the independent variable are indicated by $\overline{X}_{A_1}$, $\overline{X}_{A_2}$, $\overline{X}_{A_3}$, and $\overline{X}_{A_4}$, or more generally by $\overline{X}_A$. The grand mean, which is the mean of all the scores in the experiment, is labeled $\overline{X}_G$. The number of scores in a level of the independent variable is represented by n_S, and the total number of scores in the experiment is represented by N. Notice

TABLE 14–1.

Notational representation of scores from a one-factor within-subjects design with four levels of the independent variable and five subjects.

	Independent Variable A				
Subject	A_1	A_2	A_3	A_4	*Means for Subject*
S_1	X_{11}	X_{12}	X_{13}	X_{14}	$\overline{X}_{S_1}$
S_2	X_{21}	X_{22}	X_{23}	X_{24}	$\overline{X}_{S_2}$
S_3	X_{31}	X_{32}	X_{33}	X_{34}	$\overline{X}_{S_3}$
S_4	X_{41}	X_{42}	X_{43}	X_{44}	$\overline{X}_{S_4}$
S_5	X_{51}	X_{52}	X_{53}	X_{54}	$\overline{X}_{S_5}$
Means for Factor A	$\overline{X}_{A_1}$	$\overline{X}_{A_2}$	$\overline{X}_{A_3}$	$\overline{X}_{A_4}$	$\overline{X}_G$

that n_s, the number of scores in a level of the independent variable, is also the number of subjects in a within-subjects design. For Table 14–1 therefore, $n_s = 5$ and $N = 20$. The mean for a person over the four levels of factor A is represented by X_s. This mean represents the typical performance of a subject over all levels of the independent variable.

SUBJECTIVE CONTOURS: AN EXAMPLE ONE-FACTOR WITHIN-SUBJECTS EXPERIMENT

Observe Figure 14–1a. Although there are only partially filled dots present, it appears that there are edges forming a triangle between the dots. These edges are called **subjective contours** for they exist only in the eye of the beholder; no actual change in the physical energy of reflected light occurs at the perceived edge. Is it possible to use such subjective contours to induce an illusion in perception? Suppose we decide to investigate this question by employing a variety of forms of the Ponzo illusion, as did Meyer (1986). Figure 14–1b illustrates the standard Ponzo illusion. This figure is an illusion because the two horizontal lines are physically equal

FIGURE 14–1.
(a) Subjective contours forming a triangle. (b) The standard form of the Ponzo illusion.

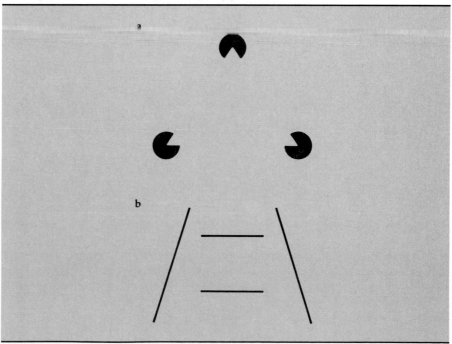

in length although they certainly do not appear to be equal. The top line appears longer than the bottom line.

Consider now the four versions of the Ponzo illusion shown in Figure 14–2. Figure 14–2a presents the standard version. A subjective contours version is illustrated in Figure 14–2b. The version in Figure 14–2c provides orientation information, but the solid dots do not introduce a subjective contour. Finally, Figure 14–2d presents a control condition in which no illusion should occur. Suppose we ask a person to adjust the length of the bottom horizontal line so that it appears equal in length to the top horizontal line; and suppose further that the length of the top line is 14.0 centimeters (cm). If no illusion appears, then the bottom line also should be adjusted to 14.0 cm. If, however, an illusion appears, then the top line should appear to be longer than it really is (i.e., it should appear to be longer than 14.0 cm) and the bottom line should be adjusted to match its perceived length.

We now conduct a within-subjects experiment with four levels of the independent variable, type of illusion (factor A) and five subjects. Each of the subjects views each of the four stimuli shown in Figure 14–2 and ad-

FIGURE 14–2.

Four versions of the Ponzo illusion: (a) standard, (b) subjective contours, (c) solid dots, (d) control — no illusion.

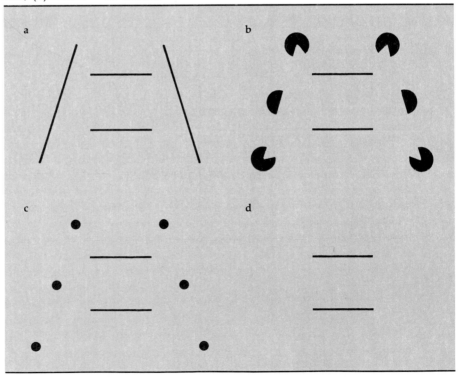

TABLE 14–2.

Perceived equal line lengths (in cm) from five subjects viewing four versions of the Ponzo illusion.

Subject	Type of Illusion (A)				Subject Means
	Standard (A_1)	Subjective Contours (A_2)	Solid Dots (A_3)	Control (A_4)	
1	16.6	15.8	14.7	14.4	15.38
2	16.9	15.6	15.1	13.8	15.35
3	17.1	16.1	14.8	13.9	15.48
4	17.2	16.3	15.2	14.1	15.70
5	16.8	15.7	15.3	14.3	15.53
$\overline{X}_A$	16.92	15.90	15.02	14.10	
s_A	0.239	0.292	0.259	0.255	$X_G = 15.49$

justs the bottom horizontal line to look equal in length to the top horizontal line. The adjusted length, in centimeters, of the bottom horizontal line is the dependent variable. Suppose the scores obtained are those presented in Table 14–2. Is the magnitude of the perceived illusion affected by the type of illusion condition?

As with between-subjects designs, the analysis for the data in Table 14–2 begins with the computation of descriptive statistics. Thus, treatment means and standard deviations are shown at the bottom of each column in the table. If the independent variable does affect the perception of the illusion, then the treatment means should differ from each other. But as we know, any differences observed between treatment means always must be viewed against a background of error variation. How much might the means differ by sampling error alone? A visual inspection of the means does not permit us to assess whether the systematic variation due to the independent variable is relatively greater than the error variation. As before, we resolve this decision-making problem by using a statistical test, the one-factor within-subjects analysis of variance.

ONE-FACTOR WITHIN-SUBJECTS ANALYSIS OF VARIANCE

Overview

The one-factor within-subjects analysis of variance partitions the total variation of scores in an experiment into three sources:

- The effect of the independent variable (**factor** A),
- The effect of individual differences among subjects (**factor** S), and
- The interaction of the treatments with the subjects ($A \times S$).

These three partitions are used to generate three mean squares:

- MS_A, which varies with the effect of the independent variable and error variation,
- MS_S, which varies with differences among subjects, and
- $MS_{A \times S}$, which varies with the interaction of treatments with subjects and provides a measure of the error variation in the experiment.

The F ratio employed in the statistical hypothesis test is

$$F = \frac{MS_A}{MS_{A \times S}}.$$

To understand how sources of variance from a within-subjects design are partitioned, it is useful to think of the within-subjects design as a two-factor design with the independent variable as one factor (A) and the individuals being tested as the second factor (factor S, where S represents the subject). Because each subject is tested under each level of the independent variable, a one-factor within-subjects design can be regarded as an $A \times S$ factorial design with a levels of factor A and n_S levels of factor S. Accordingly, there is a total of AS conditions, or cells, and each condition represents one level of the independent variable combined with a particular subject. In our example, there are four levels of factor A and five subjects; therefore, the experiment can be viewed as employing a 4 (levels of illusion condition) $\times$ 5 (number of subjects) factorial design producing a total of 20 different treatment-by-subject ($A \times S$) conditions. But, only one score is obtained for each of the AS cells.

Consequently, we can think of the one-factor within-subjects analysis of variance as a two-factor analysis of variance with "main effect" means derived for factors A and S. Notice in Table 14–2 that means are given for each row of scores as well as for each column. The four column means are the treatment means needed for evaluating the effect of the independent variable. Each of the five row means is derived by averaging the scores obtained from a single subject in all treatment conditions. These row means reflect individual differences in performance among the subjects in the experiment. Although the subject means are relevant to the analysis of variance, these values typically are not reported as descriptive statistics for experiments using a within-subjects design.

Thinking of a one-factor within-subjects analysis of variance as a two-factor analysis does not change the nature of the experiment; only one independent variable is manipulated and its effect analyzed. Conceptualizing the analysis this way, however, should help you to understand the introduction of the $A \times S$ interaction as the error term in the one-factor within-subjects analysis of variance.

Partitioning a Score

The model for representing a subject's score in a one-factor within-subjects design can be expressed as

$$
\begin{array}{l}
\text{Total variation} \\
\text{in a score}
\end{array}
=
\begin{array}{l}
\text{Variation due} \\
\text{to the effect} \\
\text{factor } A
\end{array}
+
\begin{array}{l}
\text{Variation due} \\
\text{to factor } S
\end{array}
+
\begin{array}{l}
\text{Variation due to} \\
\text{interaction of} \\
\text{factors } A \text{ and } S
\end{array}
$$

Eq. 14–1

This partitioning of a score can be represented symbolically as

$$
X_{ij} - \overline{X}_G = (\overline{X}_A - \overline{X}_G) + (\overline{X}_S - \overline{X}_G) + (X_{ij} - \overline{X}_A - \overline{X}_S + \overline{X}_G).
$$

| Deviation of a score from the grand mean | Deviation of treatment mean from the grand mean | Deviation of subject's mean from the grand mean | Deviation of subject's score from the grand mean after the effects of factor A and factor S have been removed |

Eq. 14–2

Let us examine each component of equation 14–2.

$X_{ij} - \overline{X}_G$

This deviation represents the total deviation of the person's score from the grand mean of the experiment. As equation 14–2 indicates, part of this deviation is due to the effect of the independent variable, part is due to individual differences, and part is due to the treatments-by-subjects interaction.

$\overline{X}_A - \overline{X}_G$

This component of the equation varies with the effect of factor A. Its use is identical to the one-factor between-subjects design to measure the effect of an independent variable. The grand mean is used to represent the typical performance of a subject before any treatment has acted upon his or her score. An effect of factor A is expected to affect all subjects equally and thus change the value of the treatment means. The treatment means will then differ from the grand mean. Hence, the difference $\overline{X}_A - \overline{X}_G$ varies with an effect of factor A (the treatment effect for factor A in equation 14–1).

$\overline{X}_S - \overline{X}_G$

This deviation varies with individual differences among the subjects in the experiment, factor S.

$$X_{ij} - \overline{X}_A - \overline{X}_S + \overline{X}_G$$

The interaction of the treatment with the subjects is the remaining deviation of a score from the grand mean after the effect of the treatment (factor A) and the influence of individual differences (factor S) are removed from this score. This statement may be represented symbolically as

$$A \times S \quad = \quad [(X_{ij} - X_G) \quad - \quad (\overline{X}_A - \overline{X}_G) \quad - \quad (\overline{X}_S - \overline{X}_G)].$$

Treatments-by-subjects interaction	Deviation of subject's score from grand mean	Deviation of treatment mean from grand mean	Deviation of subject's mean from grand mean

This equation indicates that the treatments-by-subjects interaction represents the variation remaining in a score after the effect of the independent variable and individual differences have been removed. Any remaining variation cannot be attributed to the effect of the treatments alone (factor A) or to individual differences among subjects (factor S). The remaining variation in this score thus reflects chance variation from treatment-to-treatment and any treatment-by-subject interaction that may occur.

Carrying out the subtractions indicated in the equation permits us to write the interaction component more simply as

$$A \times S = (X_{ij} - \overline{X}_A - \overline{X}_S + \overline{X}_G).$$

The interaction is expressed in this form in equation 14–2.

Numerical Illustration of Partitioning a Score

To illustrate the use of equation 14–2, we partition the score of the third subject in the subjective contours condition (i.e., $X_{32} = 16.1$) of Table 14–2 by substituting appropriate values into equation 14–2. The specific levels of factors A and S for this score are identified in notation as

$$X_{32} - \overline{X}_G = (\overline{X}_{A_2} - \overline{X}_G) + (\overline{X}_{S_3} - \overline{X}_G) + (X_{32} - \overline{X}_{A_2} - \overline{X}_{S_3} + \overline{X}_G).$$

Substituting numerical values for the score and appropriate means, we obtain

$$16.1 - 15.49 = (15.90 - 15.49) + (15.48 - 15.49)$$
$$+ (16.1 - 15.90 - 15.48 + 15.49),$$

or, carrying out the arithmetic functions indicated,

$$+0.61 = (+0.41) + (-0.01) + (+0.21).$$

This partitioning shows that a subject's score in a one-factor within-subjects design differs from the grand mean because of the systematic effect of the level of factor A received (reflected in $\overline{X}_{A_2} - \overline{X}_G = +0.41$), the effect of individual differences (factor S, reflected in $X_{S_3} - \overline{X}_G = -0.01$), and the interaction of factors A and S (reflected in $X_{32} - \overline{X}_{A_2} - \overline{X}_{S_3} + \overline{X}_G = +0.21$). Although we do not do so in this chapter, we can similarly partition each of the other scores in Table 14–2.

Obtaining Mean Squares from Partitioned Scores

Obtaining Sums of Squares

Sums of squares are obtained by partitioning each score in the experiment in the form of equation 14–2. Each component of each partitioned score is then squared and the values of the squared deviations are summed over all subjects and all levels of factor A. These steps may be expressed in mathematical notation as

$$\sum_{j=1}^{a} \sum_{i=1}^{n_S} (X_{ij} - \overline{X}_G)^2 = \sum_{j=1}^{a} \sum_{i=1}^{n_S} (\overline{X}_A - \overline{X}_G)^2 + \sum_{j=1}^{a} \sum_{i=1}^{n_S} (\overline{X}_S - \overline{X}_G)^2$$
$$+ \sum_{j=1}^{a} \sum_{i=1}^{n_S} (X_{ij} - \overline{X}_A - \overline{X}_S + \overline{X}_G)^2. \qquad \textbf{Eq. 14–3}$$

The summing notation $\sum_{j=1}^{a} \sum_{i=1}^{n_S}$ indicates that each term is first summed over all the n_S scores for a treatment condition (from the first score, $i = 1$, to the last score, n_1), then summed over all a levels of factor A (from the first level of the independent variable, $j = 1$, to the last level, a). Because there are five scores in each treatment condition ($n_S = 5$) and four levels of factor A in our example, the summation limits are from $i = 1$ to $n_S = 5$ and from $j = 1$ to $a = 4$.

Using sums of squares notation, equation 14–3 may be written more simply as

$$SS_{Total} = SS_A + SS_S + SS_{A \times S}. \qquad \textbf{Eq. 14–4}$$

These sums of squares indicate that the total variation of the scores in the experiment (SS_{Total}) is the result of systematic variation that occurs from factor A (SS_A), factor S (SS_S), and the interaction of factors A and S ($SS_{A \times S}$). For the scores in Table 14–2, this process leads to the numerical values:

$$SS_{Total} = 22.926$$
$$SS_A = 21.830$$
$$SS_S = 0.314$$
$$SS_{A \times S} = 0.782 .$$

Again, obtaining SS values for scores is the major computational procedure involved in analysis of variance. Equation 14–3 helps to provide an understanding of the conceptual basis for the one-factor within-subjects analysis of variance, but the steps required by this equation are tedious and open to error. Thus, simplified computational formulas leading to the numerical values above are presented later in this chapter.

Determining Degrees of Freedom

To obtain the mean squares needed for the F ratio, each SS is divided by its corresponding degrees of freedom. The general approach to finding degrees of freedom is again to find the number of scores free to vary in each SS. We apply this procedure to each SS of equation 14–3.

Total Degrees of Freedom.   To compute SS_{Total}, the grand mean, $\overline{X}_G$, must be known. Because the total sum of squares is based upon the deviation of every score in the experiment from the grand mean (i.e., $X_{ij} - \overline{X}_G$), then one less than the total number of scores are free to vary when calculating SS_{Total}. In notation,

$$df_{Total} = N - 1,$$

where N represents the total number of scores in the experiment. For our example experiment, $N = 20$; thus $df_{Total} = 20 - 1 = 19$.

Degrees of Freedom for SS_A.   The SS_A is computed from the deviations of the treatment means of factor A (e.g., $\overline{X}_{A_1}$, $\overline{X}_{A_2}$, $\overline{X}_{A_3}$, and $\overline{X}_{A_4}$) from the grand mean, X_G. Thus, the df for SS_A are equal to one less than the number of levels of factor A. In notation,

$$df_A = a - 1,$$

where a represents the number of levels of the independent variable A. For the four levels of factor A in our example, $a = 4$; hence $df_A = 4 - 1 = 3$.

Degrees of Freedom for SS_S.   The SS_S is computed from the deviation of each subject's mean ($\overline{X}_S$) from the grand mean, $\overline{X}_G$. If the grand mean is known, then one less than the number of subject means (or $n_S - 1$) is free to vary. Thus, with n_S subjects in the experiment,

$$df_S = n_S - 1.$$

There are five subjects in our example experiment; accordingly, $n_S = 5$ and $df_S = 5 - 1 = 4$.

Degrees of Freedom for $SS_{A \times S}$.   The $SS_{A \times S}$ is computed by subtracting the treatment mean and the subject's mean from each score in a particular treatment. If both the treatment means $(\overline{X}_A)$ and the subject's means $(\overline{X}_S)$ are known, then $(a - 1)(n_S - 1)$ scores will be left to vary. Hence

$$df_{A \times S} = (a - 1)(n_S - 1).$$

In our example, $a = 4$ and $n_S = 5$, therefore

$$df_{A \times S} = (4 - 1)(5 - 1) = 12.$$

Additivity of Degrees of Freedom

The degrees of freedom are additive, so that

$$df_{Total} = df_A + df_S + df_{A \times S}.$$

This relationship holds for our example, for

$$df_{Total} = 19, \quad df_A = 3, \quad df_S = 4, \quad \text{and} \quad df_{A \times S} = 12.$$

Calculating Variance Estimates from SS and df: Mean Squares

Three mean squares are obtained from the SS in equation 14–4 by dividing each SS by its corresponding df:

$$MS_A = \frac{SS_A}{df_A}$$

$$MS_S = \frac{SS_S}{df_S}, \quad \text{and}$$

$$MS_{A \times S} = \frac{SS_{A \times S}}{df_{A \times S}}.$$

MS_{Total} is not obtained because it is not used in the analysis of variance. For the scores in Table 14–1,

$$SS_A = 21.830,$$
$$SS_S = 0.314, \quad \text{and}$$
$$SS_{A \times S} = 0.782.$$

The degrees of freedom for these sums of squares are

$$df_A = 3,$$
$$df_S = 4, \quad \text{and}$$
$$df_{A \times S} = 12.$$

Therefore,

$$MS_A = \frac{21.830}{3} = 7.277$$

$$MS_S = \frac{0.314}{4} = 0.078$$

$$MS_{A\times S} = \frac{0.782}{12} = 0.065 .$$

Computation of the F Statistic

The F ratio for the one-factor within-subjects analysis of variance is given by

$$F = \frac{MS_A}{MS_{A\times S}} .$$

For the scores of Table 14–1, $MS_A = 7.277$ and $MS_{A\times S} = 0.065$. Thus,

$$F_{obs} = \frac{7.277}{0.065} = 111.95 .$$

This F ratio is the only F to be computed in this analysis; no F may be found for factor S. Table 14–3 summarizes the sources of variance in a one-factor within-subjects analysis of variance, and the formulas for df, SS, MS, and the F ratio. A numerical summary of the analysis of variance on the scores of Table 14–2 is presented in Table 14–4.

TABLE 14–3.

Notational summary of a one-factor within-subjects analysis of variance.

Source	df [a]	SS	MS	F
Factor A	$a - 1$	$\sum_{j=1}^{a} \sum_{i=1}^{n_S} (\overline{X}_A - \overline{X}_G)^2$	SS_A/df_A	$MS_A/MS_{A\times S}$
Factor S	$n_S - 1$	$\sum_{j=1}^{a} \sum_{i=1}^{n_S} (\overline{X}_S - \overline{X}_G)^2$	SS_S/df_S	
$A \times S$	$(a - 1) \times (n_S - 1)$	$\sum_{j=1}^{a} \sum_{i=1}^{n_S} (X_{ij} - \overline{X}_A - \overline{X}_S + \overline{X}_G)^2$	$SS_{A\times S}/df_{A\times S}$	
Total	$N - 1$	$\sum_{j=1}^{a} \sum_{i=1}^{n_S} (X_{ij} - \overline{X}_G)^2$	Not calculated	

[a] a = number of levels of factor A, n_S = number of scores in a treatment condition, or equivalently, the number of subjects, N = total number of scores.

TABLE 14–4.

Analysis of variance summary table for hypothetical scores of Table 14–2.

Source	df	SS	MS	F
Type of illusion (A)	3	21.830	7.277	111.95*
Subjects (S)	4	0.314	0.078	
A × S	12	0.782	0.065	
Total	19	22.926		

*$p < .05$

Testing Your Knowledge 14–1

On a separate sheet of paper, test your knowledge of the material in this section by answering the following questions.

1. Define: within-subjects design, repeated measures design, treatments-by-subjects design, factor A, factor S, $A \times S$ interaction, n_S, $\overline{X}_S$, $X_{ij} - \overline{X}_G$, $\overline{X}_A - \overline{X}_G$, $\overline{X}_S - \overline{X}_G$, $X_{ij} - \overline{X}_A - \overline{X}_S + \overline{X}_G$, SS_A, SS_S, $SS_{A \times S}$, SS_{Total}, df_A, df_S, $df_{A \times S}$, df_{Total}, MS_A, MS_S, $MS_{A \times S}$, MS_{Total}.

2. Identify the sources of variation in scores from a one-factor within-subjects design.

3. Write the equation to partition a score for the one-factor within-subjects analysis of variance.

4. Explain why the value of $\overline{X}_A - \overline{X}_G$ varies with the effect of factor A in a one-factor within subjects analysis of variance.

5. Explain why the value of $\overline{X}_S - \overline{X}_G$ varies with the effect of factor S in a one-factor within-subjects analysis of variance.

6. Explain why the value of $X_{ij} - \overline{X}_A - \overline{X}_S + \overline{X}_G$ varies with the interaction of factors A and S in a one-factor within-subjects analysis of variance.

7. Complete the following equations for a one-factor within-subjects analysis of variance:
   a. $\sum_{j=1}^{a} \sum_{i=1}^{n_S} (X_{ij} - \overline{X}_G)^2 =$
   b. $SS_{Total} =$
   c. $df_A =$
   d. $df_S =$
   e. $df_{A \times S} =$
   f. $MS_A =$
   g. $MS_S =$
   h. $MS_{A \times S} =$

8. What is the value of SS_{Total}, if $SS_A = 73.7$, $SS_S = 29.4$, and $SS_{A \times S} = 96.8$?

9. What is the value of SS_A, if $SS_{Total} = 426.9$, $SS_S = 92.4$, and $SS_{A\times S} = 301.2$?

10. What is the value of SS_S, if $SS_{Total} = 95.7$, $SS_A = 15.8$, and $SS_{A\times S} = 56.6$?

11. What is the value of $SS_{A\times S}$, if $SS_{Total} = 173.0$, $SS_A = 41.1$, and $SS_S = 36.4$?

12. Find the degrees of freedom for a one-factor within-subjects analysis of variance with 5 levels of factor A and 13 participants.

13. What is the value of df_{Total}, if $df_A = 2$ and $df_S = 19$?

14. Find the numerical values of mean squares for the following SS and df.

$$SS_A = 22, \ SS_S = 18, \ SS_{A\times S} = 36, \ df_A = 2, \ df_S = 9, \ df_{A\times S} = 18.$$

15. The following tables are incomplete summary tables for a one-factor within-subjects analysis of variance. By using the relationships among SS and df, you can provide the missing values in each table. Then answer these questions for each table:

   a. How many levels of factor A were employed?

   b. How many scores were obtained in each treatment condition?

   c. How many subjects participated in the study?

Table 1

Source	df	SS	MS	F
Factor A	4	48.0	———	———
Factor S	9	27.0	———	
$A \times S$	———	72.0	———	
Total	———	———		

Table 2

Source	df	SS	MS	F
Factor A	———	6.0	———	———
Factor S	12	36.0	3.0	
$A \times S$	24	———	———	
Total	———	78.0		

STATISTICAL HYPOTHESIS TESTING WITH THE ONE-FACTOR WITHIN-SUBJECTS ANALYSIS OF VARIANCE

The purpose of computing an F statistic is to test a statistical hypothesis that allows an inference to be made about whether the treatment means differ by more than would be expected from sampling error alone. To understand how this decision is made using the F_{obs} from a one-factor within-subjects analysis of variance, we must know what affects MS_A, MS_S, and $MS_{A\times S}$ in an experiment.

Factors Affecting the Value of Mean Squares

Each mean square in a within-subjects analysis of variance varies with a different source of variation in an experiment.

$MS_{A \times S}$

The $MS_{A \times S}$ represents the amount of variation left in a subject's score for a particular treatment after the effects of the independent variable and individual differences have been removed. Consequently, its value varies with the extent of the treatments-by-subjects interaction in the experiment. This treatments-by-subjects interaction can be seen in Figure 14–3, which graphically depicts the hypothetical data in Table 14–2. The four types of illusion figures are represented on the abscissa. The functions within the figure depict the four scores obtained from the five individuals. The perceived equal line length is longest for all individuals at the standard illusion condition. Thus, there is an apparent effect of type of illusion on perceived line length. Because the five functions are not parallel, however, a treatments-by-subjects interaction is present too. The difference in perceived line length between the illusion conditions is not the same for all subjects. For example, for subject 1, the difference in A_1 and A_2 scores is $16.6 - 15.8 = 0.8$ cm, but for subject 2 the difference is $16.9 - 15.6 = 1.3$ cm. Thus, the effect of type of illusion on perceived line length depends upon the subjects. The $MS_{A \times S}$ provides a measure of the extent of the treatments-by-subjects interaction in a within-subjects experiment. But, because only one score is obtained from each subject in each treatment condition, the treatments-by-subjects interaction cannot be separated from any error that may be affecting the score. Accordingly, $MS_{A \times S}$ is considered to be a measure of the error variation in a one-factor within-subjects design; it is used as the error term for the F ratio for this design.

MS_A

As with a one-factor between-subjects analysis of variance, the mean square for the independent variable (MS_A) varies with an effect of the independent variable. However, MS_A also varies with the treatments-by-subjects interaction. A treatments-by-subject interaction not only affects the value of $MS_{A \times S}$, it also affects the value of the treatment means and consequently MS_A. Thus, MS_A increases in value if there is an effect of the treatment (factor A) or if there is an interaction of the treatments with the subjects ($A \times S$).

MS_S

The value of MS_S depends upon the deviation of each person's mean from the grand mean. Thus, its value reflects the extent of individual differences in the experiment.

FIGURE 14–3.
Perceived equal line lengths (in cm) for each subject as a function of type of illusion.

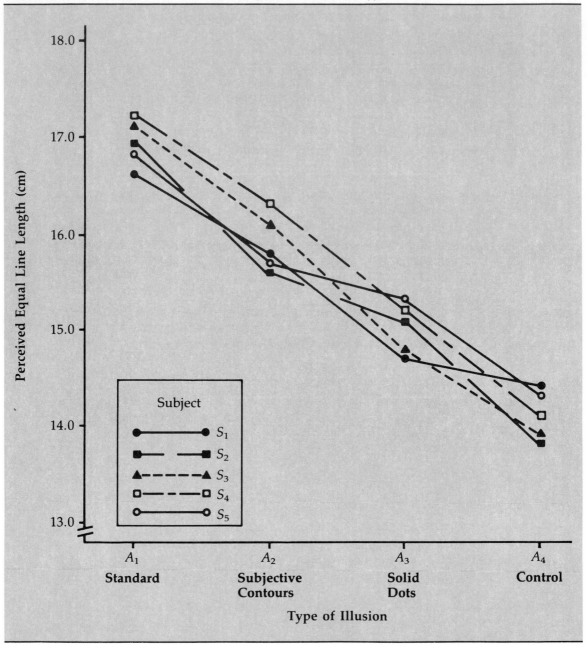

The three mean squares and the sources of variation affecting them may then be summarized as:

Mean Square	Varies with
MS_A	Systematic variance due to factor A Variance due to treatments-by-subjects interaction
MS_S	Variance due to individual differences
$MS_{A \times S}$	Variance due to treatments-by-subjects interaction

The F ratio in a one-factor within-subjects analysis of variance is found by

$$F = \frac{MS_A}{MS_{A \times S}}.$$

The numerator of this ratio, MS_A, varies with the systematic effect of the independent variable and the treatments-by-subjects interaction. If variation in the treatment means is due only to treatments-by-subjects interaction, then the value of F_{obs} should be approximately 1.00. If factor A has an effect, and the treatment means differ because of this effect as well as because of treatments-by-subjects interaction, then MS_A should have a value larger than $MS_{A \times S}$ and the F_{obs} should be greater than 1.00. No F ratio may be constructed involving MS_S for individual differences. Although MS_S varies with the extent of the differences among the subjects in the experiment, there is no MS calculated in this analysis of variance that provides an estimate of the chance variation expected among individuals. Therefore, the value of MS_S, although calculated in this analysis of variance, is not used in statistical decision making.

Statistical Decision Making

The purpose of conducting an analysis of variance on the data of an experiment is to allow the researcher to decide if the variation in sample means is more than expected from sampling error alone. Such variation occurs, of course, if the independent variable has an effect. This decision is made by comparing the value of F_{obs} from the experiment to the sampling distribution of F obtained under a null hypothesis. Again, the steps followed are identical to those presented in Chapter 11. A null hypothesis, H_0, and alternative hypothesis, H_1, are formulated; a significance level is selected and the value of F_{crit} obtained; a rejection region is located in the theoretical sampling distribution of the F statistic; F_{obs} is calculated on the data of the experiment; and, a decision to reject or not reject H_0, and therefore to accept or not accept H_1, is made on the basis of whether or not F_{obs} falls into the rejection region.

Statistical Hypotheses

Null Hypothesis.   In notation, the null hypothesis for a design with four levels of factor A is expressed as

$$H_0: \mu_{A_1} = \mu_{A_2} = \mu_{A_3} = \mu_{A_4}.$$

This null hypothesis represents the situation that exists if the independent variable has no effect. If the null hypothesis is true, then any observed difference among treatment means is due simply to error variation. The number of population means identified in the null hypothesis always corresponds to the number of the number of levels of the independent variable in the experiment.

Alternative Hypothesis.   The alternative hypothesis is again stated as the negation of the null hypothesis:

$$H_1: \text{not } H_0,$$

regardless of the number of population means involved in the null hypothesis. The alternative hypothesis represents a situation that exists if the independent variable does have an effect.

Decision Making from the F Ratio

The statistical decision-making process in a one-factor within-subjects design is identical to that followed in the one-factor between-subjects analysis of variance. A value of α defining the size of the rejection region for F_{obs} is selected prior to conducting the analysis. The sampling distribution of F under H_0 is then determined by finding the value of F_{crit} with the appropriate numerator and denominator df in Table A–3. If F_{obs} is equal to or larger than F_{crit}, then F_{obs} falls into the rejection region. The null hypothesis is rejected and the alternative hypothesis accepted. There is at least one significant difference among the treatment means. However, if F_{obs} is less than F_{crit}, then F_{obs} does not fall into the rejection region. The decision then is to fail to reject the null hypotheses and to not accept the alternative hypothesis. The treatment means do not differ significantly. The observed differences among the means are most likely due to error variation. We then conclude that the independent variable did not have an effect. The two possible sets of decisions and the conclusions that follow are summarized in Table 14–5.

To illustrate this decision-making process from F_{obs}, we use the analysis summarized in Table 14–4 on the example scores of Table 14–2. F_{obs} has

TABLE 14–5.

Summary of decisions and conclusions in statistical hypothesis testing using the analysis of variance for a one-factor within-subjects design. A .05 significance level is illustrated.

If F_{obs} Falls into the Rejection Region for $\alpha = .05$, Then:	If F_{obs} Does Not Fall into the Rejection Region for $\alpha = .05$, Then:
p of F_{obs} is less than or equal to .05, or $p < .05$.	p of F_{obs} is greater than .05, or $p > .05$.
The null hypothesis (H_0) is rejected.	The null hypothesis (H_0) is not rejected.
The alternative hypothesis (H_1) is accepted. The sample means are not all estimates of the same population mean.	The alternative hypothesis (H_1) is not accepted.
At least one difference between treatment means is statistically significant at the .05 level.	The difference among the treatment means is nonsignificant at the .05 level.
It is decided that something in addition to sampling error is responsible for the differences among the means. In a carefully done experiment the difference is attributed to the independent variable.	It is decided that sampling error is the most likely explanation of the differences among the means. The independent variable did not affect the dependent variable.

3 (numerator) and 12 (denominator) df. Thus, for $\alpha = .05$, $F_{crit} = 3.49$ (obtained from Table A–3). The value of F_{obs}, 111.95, is larger than F_{crit} and thus falls into the rejection region. Accordingly, we reject

$$H_0: \mu_{A_1} = \mu_{A_2} = \mu_{A_3} = \mu_{A_4},$$

and accept

$$H_1: \text{not } H_0.$$

This decision indicates that there is at least one statistically significant difference among the four means of Table 14–2, but it does not indicate exactly which means differ from each other. To locate the specific difference or differences among the means, a follow-up test is conducted.

Follow-Up Tests for Within-Subjects Analysis of Variance

The problems and issues of follow-up tests for the within-subjects analysis of variance are the same as those discussed in Chapter 12 for the between-subjects analysis of variance.

Planned Comparisons.   For planned comparisons, the multiple F test with a critical difference given by

$$CD = (\sqrt{2F_{crit}})\left(\sqrt{\frac{MS_{A\times S}}{n_S}}\right)$$

may be used. $MS_{A\times S}$ is the error term from the one-factor within-subjects analysis of variance conducted on the scores and n_S is the number of scores in each treatment condition. The value of F_{crit} is the tabled critical value of F from Table A–3 for 1 df for the numerator and $df_{A\times S}$ for the denominator.

Post Hoc Comparisons.   For post hoc comparisons, the Tukey test with a critical difference of

$$CD = q_k\left(\sqrt{\frac{MS_{A\times S}}{n_S}}\right)$$

may be used. We illustrate the use of the Tukey test to make pairwise comparisons among the four means for our example experiment. This test is the approach of choice for this experiment, for the research hypothesis did not make a specific statement of the outcome expected among the treatment conditions. For this test, $MS_{A\times S}$ is 0.065 (obtained from Table 14–5), $n_S = 5$, and q_k at the .05 level for 4 groups and 12 df for $MS_{A\times S}$ is 4.20 (obtained from Table A–4). Substituting the numerical values, we obtain

$$CD = (4.20)\left(\sqrt{\frac{0.065}{5}}\right) = 0.48\,.$$

For each pairwise comparison a difference between the treatment means larger in absolute value than 0.48 cm is a statistically significant difference at the .05 level. The absolute values of the four pairwise comparisons possible among the treatment means are shown in Table 14–6. Each obtained difference is larger than the CD of 0.48; thus each comparison is statistically significant at the .05 level. Accordingly, it is concluded that the population means are ordered

$$\mu_{A_1} > \mu_{A_2} > \mu_{A_3} > \mu_{A_4}\,.$$

The standard illusion creates the greatest illusion of the four conditions, the subjective contours create a significantly lesser amount of illusion, the solid dots significantly less illusion yet, and the control condition the least illusion.

TABLE 14–6.

Mean perceived equal line lengths and absolute differences between means (in cm) for the four types of illusions in the example experiment. The mean for each type of illusion is shown in parentheses.

		Type of Illusion			
		Standard (16.92)	Subjective Contours (15.90)	Solid Dots (15.02)	Control (14.10)
Type of Illusion	Standard (16.92)	—	1.02*	1.90*	2.82*
	Subjective Contours (15.90)		—	0.88*	1.80*
	Solid Dots (15.02)			—	0.92*
	Control (14.10)				—

*$p < .05.$, Tukey test $CD = 0.48$ cm

Assumptions of a Within-Subjects Analysis of Variance

Four assumptions are presumed to be met by the data when a one-factor within-subjects analysis of variance is employed:

1. Each subject is tested under each level of the independent variable.
2. The scores are normally distributed in the populations.
3. The variances of scores are equal in the populations sampled.
4. The contribution of the individual differences of a person remains the same for his or her scores over all treatment conditions.

The first assumption is necessary for the within-subjects analysis of variance to be the appropriate statistical test for the data; thus, it cannot be violated. The second and third assumptions are identical to assumptions for a between-subjects analysis of variance. They are sometimes violated in experiments, but the analysis of variance maintains some robustness toward such violations. The fourth assumption states that the person's behavior, independent of the treatment effect, remains stable over all levels of the independent variable. It is likely that this assumption is violated in many cases of behavioral research. The effect of such a violation is to increase the probability of making a Type I error above the value established by the significance level.

Most of the work concerning the robustness of the analysis of variance against violations of assumptions has been with between-subjects analysis of variance. Generalizing from this work to the within-subjects analysis of variance, it is likely that violations of the assumptions have the least effect on the probability of making a Type I error when:

- The shape of the distributions of the scores for each treatment condition is about the same and the distributions are neither very peaked nor very flat.
- The significance level is set at .05 rather than .01.

If any of these assumptions are violated seriously, then the nonparametric Wilcoxon signed-ranks test or the Friedman analysis of variance may be used in place of the within-subjects analysis of variance. The Wilcoxon test is presented in Chapter 15.

Testing Your Knowledge 14–2

On a separate sheet of paper, test your knowledge of the material in this section by answering the following questions.

1. Identify the factors affecting each MS in a one-factor within-subjects analysis of variance.
2. Explain why MS_A will increase in value if factor A has an effect in a one-factor within-subjects experiment.
3. Write the statistical hypotheses for a one-factor within-subjects analysis of variance with five levels of the independent variable.
4. Identify the assumptions underlying the use of the one-factor within-subjects analysis of variance.

CALCULATING THE ONE-FACTOR WITHIN-SUBJECTS ANALYSIS OF VARIANCE: RAW-SCORE COMPUTATIONAL FORMULAS

This section provides the computational format for a one-factor within-subjects analysis of variance. The computational formulas are based upon the raw scores, the total of the scores in a treatment condition, the total of the scores for a subject, and the grand total of the scores in the experiment. An experiment with four levels of an independent variable A and five subjects in each level is represented as:

	Factor A				
Subject	A_1	A_2	A_3	A_4	
S_1	X_{11}	X_{12}	X_{13}	X_{14}	T_{S_1}
S_2	X_{21}	X_{22}	X_{23}	X_{24}	T_{S_2}
S_3	X_{31}	X_{32}	X_{33}	X_{34}	T_{S_3}
S_4	X_{41}	X_{42}	X_{43}	X_{44}	T_{S_4}
S_5	X_{51}	X_{52}	X_{53}	X_{54}	T_{S_5}
	T_{A_1}	T_{A_2}	T_{A_3}	T_{A_4}	G

where

X_{ij} = raw score of a subject
T_A = total of scores for a treatment condition
T_S = total of scores for a subject
G = grand total of scores
n_S = number of subjects
a = number of levels of independent variable A
N = total number of scores.

Four numerical terms needed to obtain SS are then computed using these values:

$$[1] = \sum_{j=1}^{a} \sum_{i=1}^{n_S} X_{ij}^2 \quad \text{the sum of all the raw scores squared}$$

$$[2] = \sum_{j=1}^{a} T_A^2/n_S \quad \text{the sum of each treatment condition total squared, divided by the number of scores in a treatment condition}$$

$$[3] = \sum_{i=1}^{n_S} T_S^2/a \quad \text{the sum of each subject's scores squared, divided by the number of scores entering into that total}$$

$$[4] = G^2/N \quad \text{the grand total squared, divided by the total number of scores.}$$

Using these numerical values, an analysis of variance is computed as follows:

Source	df	SS	MS	F
Factor A	$a - 1$	$[2] - [4]$	SS_A/df_A	$MS_A/MS_{A \times S}$
Subjects (S)	$n_S - 1$	$[3] - [4]$	SS_S/df_S	
$A \times S$	$(a - 1) \times (n_S - 1)$	$[1] - [2] - [3] + [4]$	$SS_{A \times S}/df_{A \times S}$	
Total	$N - 1$	$[1] - [4]$	Not calculated	

To illustrate the computations, we use the example scores given in Table 14–2 for which an analysis of variance is summarized in Table 14–4.

Type of Illusion (A)

Subject	Standard (A_1)	Subjective Contours (A_2)	Solid Dots (A_3)	Control (A_4)	Subject Totals
1	16.6	15.8	14.7	14.4	$T_{S_1} = 61.50$
2	16.9	15.6	15.1	13.8	$T_{S_2} = 61.40$
3	17.1	16.1	14.8	13.9	$T_{S_3} = 61.90$
4	17.2	16.3	15.2	14.1	$T_{S_4} = 62.80$
5	16.8	15.7	15.3	14.3	$T_{S_5} = 62.10$
T_A =	84.60	79.50	75.10	70.50	$G = 309.70$

[1] $= 16.6^2 + \cdots + 16.8^2 + 15.8^2 + \cdots + 15.7^2 + 14.7^2$
$+ \cdots + 15.3^2 + 14.4^2 + \cdots + 14.3^2 = 4818.630$

[2] $= (84.60^2 + 79.50^2 + 75.10^2 + 70.50^2)/5 = 4817.534$

[3] $= (61.50^2 + 61.40^2 + 61.90^2 + 62.80^2 + 62.10^2)/4 = 4796.018$

[4] $= 309.70^2/20 = 4795.704$

Then:

$$SS_A = [2] - [4] = 4817.534 - 4795.704 = 21.830$$

$$df_A = a - 1 = 4 - 1 = 3$$

$$SS_S = [3] - [4] = 4796.018 - 4795.704 = 0.314$$

$$df_S = n_S - 1 = 5 - 1 = 4$$

$$SS_{A \times S} = [1] - [2] - [3] + [4] = 4818.630 - 4817.534 - 4796.018$$
$$+ 4795.704 = 0.782$$

$$df_{A \times S} = (a - 1)(n_S - 1) = (4 - 1)(5 - 1) = 12$$

$$SS_{Total} = [1] - [4] = 4818.630 - 4795.704 = 22.926$$

$$df_{Total} = N - 1 = 20 - 1 = 19$$

The summary of the analysis of variance is:

Source	df	SS df	MS	F
Factor A	3	21.830	$21.830/3 = 7.277$	$7.277/0.065 = 111.95^*$
Subjects	4	0.314	$0.314/4 = 0.078$	
$A \times S$	12	0.782	$0.782/12 = 0.065$	
Total	19	22.926		

$^*p < .05$

Example Problem 14–1
Using the one-factor within-subjects analysis of variance

Problem:

The yawn of a student during a class often is interpreted by an instructor as a sign of boredom. But is yawning actually such a sign? To explore this question, Provine and Hamernik (1986) designed an experiment to determine if uninteresting material does actually increase the frequency of yawning. In their experiment, individuals saw, in two different sessions, 30-minutes of rock music videos (A_1 — the interesting stimulus) and 30-minutes of a color-bar test pattern without sound (A_2 — the uninteresting stimulus). The number of times that person yawned during the two sessions was observed and recorded. Suppose we replicated this experiment using 11 subjects and observed the following number of yawns for each session:

Subject	Type of Video (A)	
	Interesting (A₁)	*Uninteresting (A₂)*
1	5	7
2	2	1
3	4	7
4	3	8
5	0	2
6	4	5
7	7	6
8	6	9
9	3	3
10	1	4
11	8	9
$\overline{X}_A$	3.9	5.5
s_A	2.47	2.77

Does the type of task affect the amount of yawning that occurs?

Solution:

To determine if the means of the two video conditions differ significantly, a statistical test is needed. Because the individuals were tested under both video conditions, a within-subjects design was employed. Thus a one-factor within-subjects analysis of variance is an appropriate statistical test for these data. We adopt a .05 significance level.

Statistic to be used: $F = MS_A/MS_{A \times S}$

Assumptions for use:

1. Each subject is tested under each level of the independent variable.
2. The scores are normally distributed in the populations sampled.
3. The variances of scores are equal in the populations sampled.
4. The contribution of the individual differences of a subject remains the same for his or her scores over all treatment conditions.

Statistical hypotheses: $H_0: \mu_{A_1} = \mu_{A_2}$
$H_1:$ not H_0

Significance level: $\alpha = .05$

df for F:

$$df_A = a - 1 = 2 - 1 = 1$$

df for F: $df_S = n_S - 1 = 11 - 1 = 10$

df for F: $df_{A \times S} = (a - 1)(n_S - 1) = (2 - 1)(11 - 1) = 10$

df for F: $df_{Total} = N - 1 = 22 - 1 = 21$

Critical value of F: F_{crit} (1, 10) = 4.96

Rejection region: Values of F_{obs} equal to or greater than 4.96.

Calculation: We calculate the analysis of variance using the raw-score formulas. The necessary treatment and subject totals are

$$T_{A_1} = 43, \quad T_{A_2} = 61;$$
$$T_{S_1} = 12, \quad T_{S_2} = 3, \quad T_{S_3} = 11, \quad T_{S_4} = 11,$$
$$T_{S_5} = 2, \quad T_{S_6} = 9, \quad T_{S_7} = 13, \quad T_{S_8} = 15,$$
$$T_{S_9} = 6, \quad T_{S_{10}} = 5, \quad T_{S_{11}} = 17;$$
$$G = 104.$$

The numerical values necessary to obtain SS are

$$[1] = \sum_{j=1}^{a} \sum_{i=1}^{n_S} X_{ij}^2 = 644.000$$

$$[2] = \sum_{j=1}^{a} T_A^2/n_S = 5{,}570/11 = 506.364$$

$$[3] = \sum_{i=1}^{n_S} T_S^2/a = 1{,}224/2 = 612.000$$

$$[4] = G^2/N = 10{,}816/22 = 491.636$$

Accordingly,

$$SS_A = [2] - [4] = 506.364 - 491.636 = 14.728,$$
$$SS_S = [3] - [4] = 612.000 - 491.636 = 120.364,$$
$$SS_{A \times S} = [1] - [2] - [3] + [4] = 644.000 - 506.364 - 612.000$$
$$+ 491.636 = 17.272,$$
$$SS_{Total} = [1] - [4] = 644.000 - 491.636 = 152.364.$$

The summary of the analysis of variance is then

Source	df	SS	MS	F
Type of video (A)	1	14.728	14.728	8.53*
Subjects (S)	10	120.364	12.036	
$A \times S$	10	17.272	1.727	
Total	21	152.364		

*$p < .05$

Decision: F_{obs} falls into the rejection region; thus we reject H_0 and accept H_1.

Conclusions:

The two treatment means of 3.9 and 5.5 yawns do not represent the same population mean; the observed difference between the two means is statistically significant. When viewing the interesting video, individuals yawned less often than when watching the uninteresting video. Notice that because only two means are involved, no follow-up tests are necessary after the null hypothesis is rejected in the analysis of variance. ▪

Example Problem 14–2
Analyzing a one-factor within-subjects design with four levels of an independent variable

Problem:

Many tasks require that an operator maintain a level of vigilance over a prolonged period of time. For example, an air traffic controller monitoring a radar screen must be vigilant to maintain the proper distance between planes being controlled. Thus, psychologists have studied the factors affecting vigilance over time. As an example, Pfendler and Widdel (1986) had subjects monitor a simulated display of the dials in the control room of a ship for a 2 1/2-hour period. As time progressed, subjects took longer to detect changes in the readings of the controls. Suppose a similar study was conducted requiring subjects to monitor a set of dials for a 4-hour period. The subject's task was to indicate whenever a dial changed its displayed value. The dependent variable measured was the amount of time it took the subject to detect the change. It was expected that for the first hour there would be no decrement in performance, but there would be significant decrements in performance between each of the succeeding hours. The mean detection times (in seconds) for each of the four 1-hour periods for 13 subjects were:

Subject	Time Period (in Hours) (A)			
	1 (A_1)	2 (A_2)	3 (A_3)	4 (A_4)
1	6.2	6.7	7.4	7.8
2	5.9	4.8	6.1	6.9
3	8.4	8.7	9.9	10.3
4	7.6	7.8	8.7	8.9
5	4.1	4.7	5.4	6.6
6	5.4	5.3	5.9	7.1
7	6.6	6.7	7.2	7.5
8	6.1	5.8	6.4	6.7
9	4.9	5.1	5.2	6.8
10	8.2	8.6	9.3	10.4
11	5.7	5.7	6.5	7.2
12	5.9	6.4	6.9	7.6
13	6.9	6.6	7.1	7.5
$\overline{X}_A$	6.3	6.4	7.1	7.8
s_A	1.24	1.34	1.45	1.28

Did the expected decrement in detection time occur?

Solution:

The design employed was a one-factor within-subjects design with four levels of the independent variable, time period. Because the experimenter predicted a specific outcome of the experiment, planned pairwise comparisons are appropriate and the multiple F test may be used. The first step in data analysis is to perform a one-factor within-subjects analysis of variance to obtain the necessary mean square for the multiple F test. We will use a .05 significance level.

Statistic to be used: $CD = (\sqrt{2F_{crit}})(\sqrt{MS_{A \times S}/n_A})$

Assumptions for use:

1. Each subject is tested under each level of the independent variable.
2. The scores are normally distributed in the populations sampled.
3. The variances of scores are equal in the populations sampled.
4. The contribution of the individual differences of a subject remains the same for his or her scores over all treatment conditions.

Statistical hypotheses: Three sets of statistical hypotheses will be tested with the multiple F.

Comparison	Statistical Hypotheses
$\overline{X}_{A_1}$ vs. $\overline{X}_{A_2}$	H_0: $\mu_{A_1} = \mu_{A_2}$
	H_0: $\mu_{A_1} \neq \mu_{A_2}$
$\overline{X}_{A_2}$ vs. $\overline{X}_{A_3}$	H_0: $\mu_{A_2} = \mu_{A_3}$
	H_1: $\mu_{A_2} \neq \mu_{A_3}$
$\overline{X}_{A_3}$ vs. $\overline{X}_{A_4}$	H_0: $\mu_{A_3} = \mu_{A_4}$
	H_1: $\mu_{A_3} \neq \mu_{A_4}$

Significance level: $\alpha = .05$

Calculation of the analysis of variance.

We calculate the analysis of variance using the raw-score formulas. The necessary treatment and subject totals are:

$$T_{A_1} = 81.9, \quad T_{A_2} = 82.9, \quad T_{A_3} = 92.0, \quad T_{A_4} = 101.3;$$
$$T_{S_1} = 28.1, \quad T_{S_2} = 23.7, \quad T_{S_3} = 37.3, \quad T_{S_4} = 33.0,$$
$$T_{S_5} = 20.8, \quad T_{S_6} = 23.7, \quad T_{S_7} = 28.0, \quad T_{S_8} = 25.0,$$
$$T_{S_9} = 22.0, \quad T_{S_{10}} = 36.5, \quad T_{S_{11}} = 25.1,$$
$$T_{S_{12}} = 26.8, \quad T_{S_{13}} = 28.1;$$
$$G = 358.1.$$

The numerical values necessary to obtain SS are

$$[1] = \sum_{j=1}^{a} \sum_{i=1}^{n_S} X_{ij}^2 = 2{,}569.9700$$

$$[2] = \sum_{j=1}^{a} T_A^2 / n_S = 32{,}305.71/13 = 2{,}485.0546$$

$$[3] = \sum_{i=1}^{n_S} T_S^2 / a = 10{,}189.03/4 = 2{,}547.2575$$

$$[4] = G^2/N = 128{,}235.61/52 = 2{,}466.0694$$

Accordingly,

$$SS_A = [2] - \lfloor 4 \rfloor = 2{,}485.0546 - 2{,}466.0694 = 18.9852$$

$$SS_S = [3] - [4] = 2{,}547.2575 - 2{,}466.0694 = 81.1881$$

$$SS_{A \times S} = [1] - [2] - [3] + [4] = 2{,}569.9700 - 2{,}485.0546$$
$$- 2{,}547.2575 + 2{,}466.0694 = 3.7273$$

$$SS_{Total} = [1] - [4] = 2{,}569.9700 - 2{,}466.0694 = 103.9006$$

df for *F*:

$$df_A = a - 1 = 4 - 1 = 3$$
$$df_S = n_S - 1 = 13 - 1 = 12$$
$$df_{A \times S} = (a - 1)(n_S - 1) = (4 - 1)(13 - 1) = 36$$
$$df_{Total} = N - 1 = 52 - 1 = 51$$

The summary of the analysis of variance is then:

Source	df	SS	MS	F
Time period (A)	3	18.9852	6.3284	61.14*
Subjects (S)	12	81.1881	6.7657	
A × S	36	3.7273	0.1035	
Total	51	103.9006		

*$p < .05$

Performing the multiple F test. The CD of the multiple F test is found by

$$CD = (\sqrt{2F_{crit}}) \left(\sqrt{\frac{MS_{A \times S}}{n_S}} \right).$$

For this problem, F_{crit} at the .05 level for 1 *df* for the numerator and 36 *df* for the denominator is 4.17. Because 1, 36 *df* is not included in Table A–3, we used the critical value for 1, 30 *df*. $MS_{A \times S} = 0.1035$ and $n_S = 13$. Substituting these numerical values,

$$CD = [\sqrt{(2)(4.17)}] \left[\sqrt{\left(\frac{0.1035}{13} \right)} \right] = 0.26.$$

Any planned comparison difference equal to or larger in absolute value than 0.26 seconds is statistically significant at the .05 level.

Comparisons and decisions:

Comparison	Numerical Value	Decision on Statistical Hypotheses
$\overline{X}_{A_1}$ vs. $\overline{X}_{A_2}$	$6.3 - 6.4 = -0.1$	Fail to reject H_0: $\mu_{A_1} = \mu_{A2}$ Do not accept H_1: $\mu_{A_1} \neq \mu_{A2}$
$\overline{X}_{A_2}$ vs. $\overline{X}_{A_3}$	$6.4 - 7.1 = -0.7$	Reject H_0: $\mu_{A2} = \mu_{A3}$ Accept H_1: $\mu_{A2} \neq \mu_{A3}$
$\overline{X}_{A_3}$ vs. $\overline{X}_{A_4}$	$7.1 - 7.8 = -0.7$	Reject H_0: $\mu_{A3} = \mu_{A4}$ Accept H_1: $\mu_{A3} \neq \mu_{A4}$

Conclusions:

The planned comparisons reveal that there is no decrement in the detection times between the first and second hours of the task. A statistically significant decrement occurs between hours 2 and 3, and a further statistically significant decrement occurs between hours 3 and 4. Accordingly, detection times are ordered as follows:

$$\text{Time period in hours}$$
$$\overline{X}_{A_1} = \overline{X}_{A_2} < \overline{X}_{A_3} < \overline{X}_{A_4}. \quad \blacksquare$$

Statistics in Use 14–1

Strength and Time of Day: Using a One-Factor Within-Subjects Design

Does physical strength vary with time of day? No doubt many people feel more tired later in the day, but does this subjective feeling correspond to actual decreases in physical strength? To investigate this problem, Ishee and Titlow (1986) employed a one-factor within-subjects design and measured a subjects' hand-grip strength at different times of the day: 9:00 A.M., 12 Noon, and 3:00 P.M. Eighteen subjects were used and each subject was tested for hand-grip strength at each of the three times. To avoid confounding by repeated tests on the same day, the test for each time was conducted on a separate day. In addition, three different orders of the time sequence were used (e.g., 9:00 A.M., 12:00 Noon, 3:00 P.M.; 12:00 Noon, 3:00 P.M., 9:00 A.M.; 3:00 P.M., 9:00 A.M., 12:00 Noon) with six subjects in each sequence.

Mean hand-grip strength, in kilograms was 44.3 for 9:00 A.M. ($s = 16.2$), 44.2 for 12:00 Noon, ($s = 14.0$), and 42.7 for 3:00 P.M. ($s = 15.0$). A one-factor analysis of variance indicated that the obtained differences were nonsignificant, $F(2, 34) = 0.78$, $p > .05$. Although we may feel more tired in the afternoon, there is no change in hand-grip strength over the three times employed in this experiment. ■

REPORTING THE RESULTS OF THE ANALYSIS OF VARIANCE

A brief description of the results of the analysis of our example experiment on type of illusion and perceived line length (see Tables 14–2 and 14–4) might be written for the Results section of an article as follows:

> *The mean perceived equal line lengths for the standard, subjective contours, solid dots, and control illusion conditions were 16.92 (s = 0.239), 15.90 (s = 0.292), 15.02 (s = 0.259), and 14.10 (s = 0.255) cm, respectively. A within-subjects analysis of variance indicated that the means differ significantly, $F(3, 12) = 111.95$, $MS_{A \times S} = 0.065$, $p < .01$. A Tukey test on the four pairwise comparisons revealed that each illusion condition differed significantly from each other illusion condition, $p < .05$ (CD = 0.48 cm). The ordering of the extent of the illusion among the treatment conditions was standard illusion > subjective dots illusion > solid dots illusion > control condition.*

This journal presentation of results conveys a great deal of information. Because much of the information is similar to that of a between-subjects analysis of variance, however, we review this presentation of results briefly.

1. **Sample means:** The obtained values of the sample means and standard deviations are presented in the first sentence. Because only four means were obtained, they are presented in the form of a sentence rather than in a table or a figure.
2. **$F(3, 12)$:** Identifies the name of the test statistic as the F. The numbers shown in parentheses indicate the *df* for the numerator (i.e., 3) and the denominator (i.e., 12) of F_{obs}, respectively.
3. **= 111.95:** Gives the value of F_{obs}. If F_{obs} is less than 1.00, it may simply be reported as $F > 1.00$.
4. **$p < .05$:** Tells us that
   a. H_0 was rejected and H_1 was accepted.
   b. the difference in treatment means is statistically significant at the .01 level.
   c. it is inferred that something other than sampling error alone was responsible for the observed difference in treatment means.
5. **$MS_{A \times S} = 0.065$:** Provides the value of the $MS_{A \times S}$ for F_{obs}. Because this MS is the error term for the F ratio, it may also be identified as MS_{Error}.
6. **Tukey test:** Identifies the name of the follow-up test used for pairwise comparisons.
7. **$CD = 0.48$ cm:** Gives the critical difference for the Tukey test.

Testing Your Knowledge 14–3

On a separate sheet of paper, test your knowledge of the material in this section by answering the following questions. Complete the following problem using a one-factor within-subjects analysis of variance using the format illustrated in the example problem. Use a .05 significance level.

1. Emling and Yankell (1985) evaluated a mouthrinse containing sodium benzoate for its ability to remove and loosen tooth plaque. In one study participants were measured under three treatment conditions—a baseline control condition (A_1), after using an experimental mouthrinse (A_2), and after using a nonactive placebo mouthrinse (A_3). For each treatment condition the amount of plaque on the teeth was rated on a 0 (no plaque) to 5 (plaque covering two thirds or more of the crown) scale. Suppose the following ratings were obtained for 14 participants.

Person	Treatment Condition (A)		
	Control (A_1)	Experimental (A_2)	Placebo (A_3)
1	6	5	6
2	5	5	5
3	4	3	5
4	6	4	5
5	3	4	4
6	3	1	2
7	6	3	5
8	4	4	6
9	4	5	4
10	6	5	6
11	5	2	6
12	2	2	3
13	5	4	3
14	4	1	3
$\overline{X}_A$	4.5	3.4	4.5
s_A	1.29	1.45	1.34

Did the experimental mouthrinse reduce plaque compared to the control or placebo conditions? If a follow-up test is needed, use the Tukey test to make the possible pairwise comparisons.
   a. Statistic to be used
   b. Assumptions for use
   c. Statistical hypotheses
   d. Significance level
   e. F_{crit}
   f. Rejection region
   g. Calculation

   h. Decision
   i. Conclusion
2. The following exercises present sample reports of the use of the one-factor within-subjects analysis of variance. For each report, answer these questions from the information presented in the report.
   a. How many levels of the independent variable were used in this experiment?
   b. How many participants were employed in this experiment?
   c. What is the value of F_{obs}?
   d. What is the value of F_{crit}?
   e. Do you reject or fail to reject H_0?
   f. Do you accept or not accept H_1?
   g. Do the treatment means differ significantly?

Report 1
The mean reaction time for the simple stimulus condition was 396 ms, whereas the mean for the complex stimulus condition was 472 ms. A one-factor within-subjects analysis of variance revealed a significant difference between the means, $F(1, 18) = 4.76$, $MS_{A \times S} = 12.80$, $p < .05$.

Report 2
The mean number of faces correctly recognized was 13.9 on trial 1, 14.4 on trial 2, and 14.1 on trial 3. A one-factor within-subjects analysis of variance indicated no difference in the number of correct recognitions on the trials, $F(2, 22) = 2.81$, $MS_{A \times S} = 25.38$, $p > .05$. ▪

THE *t* TEST FOR RELATED MEASURES

The one-factor within-subjects analysis of variance may be employed to analyze an experiment with any number of levels of an independent variable. When only two levels of an independent variable are manipulated in a within-subjects design, however, the *t* test for related measures may be used in place of the analysis of variance. Because the *t* and *F* statistics are related by $t = \sqrt{F}$ when only two levels of an independent variable are manipulated, identical conclusions are reached from either test. The *t* test for related measures is defined as:

$$t_{rel} = \frac{(\overline{X}_{A_1} - \overline{X}_{A_2}) - (\mu_{A_1} - \mu_{A_2})}{s_D},$$

where s_D is the standard error of the mean difference between each X_{A_1} and X_{A_2} score. Because the same subjects are measured under each treatment condition, the two sets of scores are correlated to some extent. Therefore, this *t* test employs a computational formula different from that of the *t* test for independent groups presented in Chapter 10. Other than differences in deriving the *t* value, however, the *t* test for related measures is interpreted identically to the *t* test for independent groups.

When the null hypothesis $H_0: \mu_{A_1} = \mu_{A_2}$ is tested, the computational formula for t_{rel} becomes

$$t_{rel} = \frac{\overline{X}_{A_1} - \overline{X}_{A_2}}{\sqrt{\dfrac{[\Sigma D^2 - (\Sigma D)^2/N]}{[N(N-1)]}}}.$$

The value of D is the difference between the two scores of a subject, or $X_{i_1} - X_{i_2}$, and N represents the number of pairs of scores, or equivalently, the number of subjects. The denominator of this t test is simply the standard error of the mean difference between the $\overline{X}_{A_1}$ and $\overline{X}_{A_2}$ scores, i.e., s_D. The df are equal to $N - 1$, which represents the number of pairs of scores that are free to vary.

Statistical Hypothesis Testing with a *t* Test for Related Measures

To illustrate the use of t_{rel}, consider the following problem. When scouting college baseball pitchers for professional teams it is common practice for the scout to measure the velocity of fastball pitches with a speed gun. Often the speed gun is used in clear view of the pitcher (Weinstein, Prather, and de Man, 1987). Does sight of the speed gun affect the pitcher's velocity? To answer this question, suppose you measured the velocity of pitches of eight college pitchers both with the speed gun in open view of the pitcher (condition A_1) and with the gun hidden from view (condition A_2). You measured 25 fastball pitches in each condition and found the mean velocity given in Table 14–7 for each pitcher in each condition. Do the mean velocities differ in the two conditions?

TABLE 14–7.

Mean velocities (in mph) of eight right-handed college pitchers with a speed gun in open view and a speed gun hidden from view.

Subject	Speed Gun Condition (*A*)	
	Open View (A₁)	*Hidden (A₂)*
1	72.4	77.9
2	67.1	69.4
3	77.8	77.1
4	73.2	76.5
5	62.5	64.6
6	68.7	75.3
7	71.4	69.8
8	81.7	84.2
$\overline{X}_A$	71.85	74.35
s_A	6.03	6.13

TABLE 14–8.

Computation of the t test for related measures on the scores of Table 14–7.

(a)	(b)	(c)	(d)	(e)
	Speed Gun Condition (A)			
	Open View	**Hidden**		
Subject	**(A_1)**	**(A_2)**	**D**	**D^2**
1	72.4	77.9	−5.5	30.25
2	67.1	69.4	−2.3	5.29
3	77.8	77.1	+0.7	0.49
4	73.2	76.5	−3.3	10.89
5	62.5	64.6	−2.1	4.41
6	68.7	75.3	−6.6	43.56
7	71.4	69.8	+1.6	2.56
8	81.7	84.2	−2.5	6.25
$\overline{X}_A$	71.85	74.35	Σ −20.0	103.70
s_A	6.03	6.13		

$$t_{rel} = \frac{\overline{X}_{A_1} - \overline{X}_{A_2}}{\sqrt{[\Sigma D^2 - (\Sigma D)^2/N]/[N(N-1)]}}.$$

$$t_{obs} = \frac{71.85 - 74.35}{\sqrt{[103.70 - (-20.00)^2/8]/[(8)(7)]}}$$

$$t_{obs} = \frac{71.85 - 74.35}{\sqrt{[103.70 - (400/8)]/56}}$$

$$t_{obs} = \frac{-2.5}{\sqrt{(103.70 - 50)/56}}$$

$$t_{obs} = \frac{-2.5}{\sqrt{(53.7/56)}}$$

$$t_{obs} = \frac{-2.5}{\sqrt{0.959}}$$

$$t_{obs} = \frac{-2.5}{0.979}$$

$$t_{obs} = -2.554.$$

The calculation of the value of t_{rel} is illustrated in Table 14–8. The steps in this calculation are as follows:

1. Find $\overline{X}_{A_1}$ and $\overline{X}_{A_2}$. For our example, these values are 71.85 and 74.35 mph, respectively.
2. Find the value of $D = X_{i_1} - X_{i_2}$ for each subject as shown in column d of Table 14–8. Maintain the algebraic sign of the difference for each subject.

3. Square each value of D as shown in column e of the table.
4. Find ΣD (the sum of column d, -20.0 for the example) and ΣD^2 (the sum of column e, 103.70).
5. Determine N. For our example, $N = 8$.
6. Substitute the numerical values into the equation for t_{rel}.

The t_{obs} for the scores of Table 14–7 is -2.554. The remaining steps in the use of this t_{obs} are identical to those for the t test for independent groups. A value of α is selected and the value of t_{crit} obtained from Table A–2. If the value of t_{obs} is equal to or greater than t_{crit}, then the null hypothesis H_0: $\mu_{A_1} = \mu_{A_2}$ is rejected and the alternative hypothesis H_1: not H_0 is accepted.

For the t obtained on the scores of Table 14–7, the df are $N - 1 = 8 - 1 = 7$. Thus, for a .05 significance level, t_{crit} for a two-tailed rejection region is 2.365. The rejection region is thus composed of values of t_{obs} less than or equal to -2.365 or equal to or greater than $+2.365$. The t_{obs} of -2.554 is less than -2.365; hence it falls into the rejection region; H_0 is rejected and H_1 accepted. The difference between the sample means is statistically significant at the .05 level. The college pitchers in this study threw more slowly when a speed gun was in open view compared to when the speed gun was hidden from view.

SUMMARY

- In a within-subjects design a single group of participants is exposed to all levels of each independent variable.
- Three mean squares are generated in a one-factor within-subjects analysis of variance: MS_A, which varies with the effect of the independent variable and error variation; MS_S, which varies with differences among subjects; and $MS_{A \times S}$, which varies with the interaction of treatments with subjects and provides a measure of the error variation in the experiment.
- The F ratio employed in the one-factor within-subjects analysis of variance is

$$F = \frac{MS_A}{MS_{A \times S}}.$$

- The steps in statistical testing with this F ratio are identical to those discussed in Chapter 11.
- The multiple F test may be used for planned comparisons in a within-subjects design. For post hoc comparisons, the Tukey test may be employed.
- The t test for related measures may be used when there are only two levels of an independent variable in a one-factor within-subjects design.

KEY TERMS

$A \times S$ interaction	$MS_{A \times S}$	treatments-by-subjects design
df_A	MS_{Total}	t_{rel}
df_S	n_S	within-subjects design
$df_{A \times S}$	repeated measures design	$\overline{X}_S$
df_{Total}	SS_A	$X_{ij} - \overline{X}_G$
factor A	SS_S	$\overline{X}_A - \overline{X}_G$
factor S	$SS_{A \times S}$	$\overline{X}_S - \overline{X}_G$
MS_A	SS_{Total}	$X_{ij} - \overline{X}_A - \overline{X}_S + \overline{X}_G$
MS_S		

REVIEW QUESTIONS

On a separate sheet of paper, test your knowledge of the material in this chapter by answering the following questions.

1. Suppose you are interested in whether the type of mood reflected by a word, happy, neutral, or sad, affects how well the word is re- membered from a list. You construct a list composed of six happy words (e.g., joyful, bright), six neutral words (e.g., derive, convey) and six sad words (e.g., gloomy, lonely). Each of eight subjects then learns the list to learn a criterion of two complete correct recitations. One week later each subject attempts to recall the list. The number of items correctly recalled as a function of the type of word was

	Type of Word		
Subject	*Happy (A_1)*	*Neutral (A_2)*	*Sad (A_3)*
1	5	4	3
2	6	3	4
3	4	5	2
4	5	3	1
5	3	1	2
6	6	3	4
7	2	2	3
8	5	3	1
$\overline{X}_A$	4.5	3.0	2.5
s_A	1.41	1.20	1.20

a. Does the type of word affect recall? If a follow-up test is neces- sary, use the Tukey test to make the possible pairwise compari- sons. Employ a .05 significance level.

b. Describe your results in Question 1a following the example illustrated in the Reporting the Results of the Analysis of Variance section of this chapter.

2. Evidence exists that pressure on the carotid arteries at the neck reduces blood flow to the brain and eye. Langan and Watkins (1987) found also that in a sample of 94 men wearing a shirt and tie, the shirt and tie were providing pressure on the neck. To find if tight neckwear affects visual functioning, Langan and Watkins measured critical flicker frequency (CFF) of men wearing a loose collar and then wearing a tight collar and tie. The CFF is a test of the ability to perceive when a rapidly blinking light changes from a solid light to a blinking light. The higher the frequency of the on-off blinks of the light at which this perceptual change occurs, the more sensitive the retinal functioning. Suppose you conducted a similar study with 12 men. Each man participated in two conditions, wearing a loose collar and wearing a tight collar and necktie. The critical flicker frequencies (in Hertz, or cycles per second) for each subject were

	Type of Neckwear (A)	
Subject	Loose (A_1)	Tight (A_2)
1	17	16
2	19	17
3	23	20
4	22	21
5	22	22
6	20	18
7	18	20
8	21	17
9	23	19
10	19	21
11	20	16
12	17	18
$\overline{X}_A$	20.1	18.8
s_A	2.15	2.05

Did the type of neckwear affect the CFF scores? Use a .05 significance level.

a. Analyze the scores and answer the question using a one-factor within-subjects analysis of variance.

b. Analyze the scores and answer the question using a t test for related measures.

c. Compare F_{obs} to t_{obs}. Does $F_{obs} = t_{obs}^2$?

d. Do you reach the same or different answers to this question from the analysis of variance and the t test?

3. Assume that you plan to conduct a one-factor within-subjects experiment with five levels of the independent variable and 12 subjects.
   a. Write out, in notation, the sum of squares partitioning equation for the scores of this experiment. Include the summation limits on the equation.
   b. Write the statistical hypothesis tested by the analysis of variance on the scores you would obtain.
   c. Find the df for the analysis of variance of this design.
   d. What is the value of F_{crit} at the .05 significance level for the analysis of variance of this design?
   e. Suppose the value of F_{obs} was larger than F_{crit}. What decision would you make about H_0 and H_1?
   f. Suppose that you reject H_0 and accept H_1 for this experiment. What inference would you make about the treatment means from these decisions?

4. The following tables are incomplete summary tables for an analysis of variance. By using the relationships among SS and df in an analysis of variance, you can provide the missing values in each table. Then answer the following questions for each table:
   a. How many levels of factor A were employed?
   b. How many scores were obtained in each treatment condition?
   c. How many subjects participated in the study?
   d. Is the value of F_{obs} statistically significant at the .05 level?

Table 1

Source	df	SS	MS	F
Factor A	————	————	11.0	————
Factor S	23	138.0	6.0	
A × S	46	253.0	————	
Total	71	————		

Table 2

Source	df	SS	MS	F
Factor A	————	60.0	————	————
Factor S	19	133.0	7.0	
A × S	95	————	————	
Total	————	573.0		

15

Nonparametric Statistical Tests

Overview

Analysis of Frequency Data: The Chi Square Test
    The Walker Problem: An Example of Frequency Scores
    Contingency Tables
    The Chi Square Test
    Statistical Hypothesis Testing with the χ^2 Statistic
    Assumptions for the Use of the Chi Square Test

Mann-Whitney U Test
    Perception of Ambiguous Figures: An Example Problem
    Statistical Hypothesis Testing with the Mann-Whitney U
    Assumptions of the Mann-Whitney U Test
    Computational Formulas for U

The Wilcoxon Signed-Ranks Test
    Vocal Expression of Emotion: An Example Experiment
    Statistical Testing with the Wilcoxon Signed-Ranks Test

Using Nonparametric Tests

OVERVIEW

We have developed concepts of statistical hypothesis testing emphasizing the t test and the analysis of variance. Both tests are **parametric tests**—they use sample statistics (e.g., $\overline{X}$ and s^2) to estimate the values of population parameters (μ or σ^2, respectively). Further, both tests make certain assumptions about the scores being analyzed, including

- The scores in the populations sampled are normally distributed.
- The variances of scores in the populations are equal.

In practice the data collected may violate these assumptions. Yet, because parametric tests are thought to be robust, researchers may use the t test or analysis of variance on the data even if the assumptions are not met.

In some instances, however, it is not reasonable to presume that these assumptions are met sufficiently to allow appropriate use of a parametric test on the data. For example, in measuring the reaction time of an individual, a large majority of the measured reaction times are likely to be short (e.g., perhaps about 500 milliseconds or less). No reaction time can be less than 0 seconds; but there is no upper limit on the maximum time that may be measured. A few individuals may have long reaction times compared to other people. Thus, a frequency distribution of reaction-time measures is likely to be positively skewed and look like a capital L—most reaction times are quite short, a few may be much longer. Such a distribution clearly is not an approximately normal distribution.

An assumption, too, in the use of the t test or analysis of variance is that it makes sense to compute an arithmetic mean (i.e., $\overline{X}$) on the scores obtained. This requirement implies that the scores should achieve either an interval or ratio scale of measurement. But often behaviors cannot be measured at these levels. An experimenter simply may count the number of people displaying a certain behavior, thus obtaining frequencies of occurrence of the behavior, a nominal scale measure. Or, the scores obtained may form an ordinal scale, such as rank-ordering individuals on a certain personality trait. Because both the t test and analysis of variance require $\overline{X}$ to be calculated, neither test is appropriate for use if the scores represent nominal or ordinal scales of measurement.

In instances where the assumptions of parametric tests are not met, or where the scores obtained are either at the nominal or ordinal scale of measure, nonparametric statistical tests often are used for statistical hypothesis testing. **Nonparametric** or **distribution-free tests** make fewer assumptions about the shapes of population distributions and usually do not test relations among population parameters.

TABLE 15–1.

Parametric and nonparametric tests for one-factor designs as a function of type of design and scale of measurement.

	Scale of Measure of Data	Type of Design			
		Between-Subjects		Within-Subjects	
		2 Levels	*3 or More Levels*	*2 Levels*	*3 or More Levels*
Parametric Tests	Ratio or interval	*t* for independent groups Between-subjects ANOVA	Between-subjects ANOVA	*t* for related groups Within-subjects ANOVA	Within-subjects ANOVA
Nonparametric Tests	Ordinal	Mann-Whitney *U*	Kruskal-Wallis ANOVA by ranks	Wilcoxon signed-ranks	Friedman ANOVA by ranks
	Nominal	Chi square	Chi square		

Table 15–1 presents the parametric tests and corresponding nonparametric tests for one-factor designs. We discuss the chi square, Mann-Whitney *U*, and the Wilcoxon signed-ranks tests in this chapter. A nonparametric test of correlation, the Spearman rank-order correlation coefficient, is presented in Chapter 17. Table 15–1 is limited to nonparametric tests for one-factor designs. In general, there is no nonparametric equivalent to the factorial analysis of variance.

ANALYSIS OF FREQUENCY DATA: THE CHI SQUARE TEST

Many research studies often lead to the collection of scores that merely indicate whether a behavior occurred or not. For example, when observing animals in the wild, a scientist may record only whether an animal does or does not emit a certain behavior. These scores achieve nominal scale of measurement; the scores simply fall into mutually exclusive categories. A tally of the frequency of occurrence of responses in the various categories may be obtained, but the individual scores themselves convey no numerical information about the animal's response. Statistical tests, such as the analysis of variance or *t* test, which assume that a score conveys some numerical information about behavior, are inappropriate for analyzing frequency data. Rather, a nonparametric test, the chi square test, provides an appropriate test for these scores when a between-subjects design is used. The **chi square test** (pronounced "ky square") is a widely used statistical test for scores that represent only the frequency of occurrence of a response.

The Walker Problem: An Example of Frequency Scores

The work of McCloskey and his associates on intuitive physics is an example of a study utilizing a chi square analysis of frequency measures. McCloskey, Washburn, and Felch (1983) were interested in studying people's knowledge of falling objects. In some of their studies they presented individuals with a *walker problem.* In this problem, a subject is shown a side view of a man walking at a constant speed. The walker is holding his arm straight out from the shoulder and is holding a small metal ball in his hand. As he is walking, the man drops the ball. The task of a subject is to indicate on the picture where he or she believes the ball will fall. The correct answer is that the ball, because it is moving at the same forward speed as the walker, will fall in a forward arc and land even with the walker. The majority of people, however, indicate that the ball will fall straight down or in a backward arc.

In one study, McCloskey et al. used this task to compare students who had training in physics (physics-trained) against students who did not have training in physics (physics-untrained) to see if there was any difference in their response to the problem. The independent variable, then, is the type of student, which takes on two levels — physics trained and physics untrained. Suppose the results of a similar study employing 40 physics-trained and 40 physics-untrained students were those shown in Table 15–2. A student's response was classified as either correct or incorrect. This measure represents nominal measurement; a response is assigned to one of two mutually exclusive categories; it is either correct or incorrect, but it cannot be both. Thus, the values in Table 15–2 designated by O (for *observed frequency*) represent the frequency of correct and incorrect answers given by the subjects with each person contributing only one response to the table.

TABLE 15–2.

Hypothetical data for responses of physics-trained and physics-untrained students on the walker problem. The values given for O are the obtained frequencies and the values given for E are the expected frequencies obtained from the marginal frequencies.

		Type of Student		
		Physics Trained	*Physics Untrained*	*(Marginal)*
Response	*Correct*	O = 26 E = 17	O = 8 E = 17	34
	Incorrect	O = 14 E = 23	O = 32 E = 23	46
	(Marginal)	40	40	(Total) 80

Contingency Tables

A table, such as Table 15–2, is called a **rows (*r*) by columns (*c*) contingency table** or a **two-way frequency table.** The columns (symbolized by *c*) of the table represent the categories into which subjects may be placed. The categories may represent levels of an independent variable as in our example problem. The rows (symbolized by *r*) provide the response categories. Table 15–2 is thus a 2 rows (*r* = two categories of the dependent variable — correct and incorrect response) by 2 columns (*c* = two levels of the independent variable) contingency table. It is called a contingency table because we are trying to find if the person's response is contingent upon the type of training experienced. The **marginal frequencies** shown in the table are the row totals (i.e., the *row marginals*) and the column totals (i.e., the *column marginals*) of the obtained frequencies.

Expected Frequencies

Consider the scores in Table 15–2. Correct responses were given by 34 participants and incorrect responses by 46 participants. If correctness of response is not related to the type of student, then it would be reasonable to expect that of the 34 correct responses, about one-half of them (i.e., 17) would be given by physics-trained students and about one-half of them by physics-untrained students. These values are called **expected frequencies,** the frequencies of response expected if correctness of response is not related to type of student. A similar expectation holds for the incorrect responses if there is no relation between type of student and correctness of response. About 23 incorrect responses should be given by each type of student group. These expected frequencies under chance conditions, where type of student and correctness of response are unrelated, are given in Table 15–2 by the value of *E* (for *expected frequency*) in each cell of the table. Expected frequencies, then, are obtained under a hypothesis of no relation of the dependent variable to the independent variable.

The Chi Square Test

The chi square test uses the expected frequencies obtained under a hypothesis of no relation between the independent variable and the dependent variable to develop a test statistic. If there is no relation among the variables in the population sampled, then the observed frequencies typically should be about the same as the expected frequencies. Large deviations of the observed frequencies from the expected frequencies should occur only rarely by chance if the column and row variables are not associated. But if the column and row variables are related in the population sampled, then the observed frequencies should differ from the expected frequencies by larger amounts. For example, if the frequency of correct and incorrect responses is related to the type of student, then it is likely that the physics-trained students will produce more correct responses than the 17 expected by chance and that the physics-untrained students will produce more incorrect answers than the 23 expected.

The χ^2 Statistic

The chi square test measures the difference of the obtained frequencies from the expected frequencies with the test statistic:

$$\chi^2 = \sum_{k=1}^{c} \sum_{j=1}^{r} \frac{(O_{jk} - E_{jk})^2}{E_{jk}},$$

where χ (pronounced "ky") is a letter from the Greek alphabet. In this formula O_{jk} is the observed frequency in the jk cell, where j represents the row number and k the column number; E_{jk} is the expected frequency of the jk cell; r is the number of categories of the row variable (correctness of response in this example); and c is the number of levels of the columns variable (type of student in this example).

Statistical Hypothesis Testing with the χ^2 Statistic

Using the χ^2 statistic to determine whether the correctness of response is related to type of student in our example requires statistical hypothesis testing. To do so we follow the now familiar steps of statistical hypothesis testing:

- Two statistical hypotheses, a null hypothesis, H_0, and an alternative hypothesis, H_1, are formulated. The null hypothesis provides the theoretical sampling distribution of the χ^2 statistic.
- A significance level is selected.
- A critical value of χ^2, identified as χ^2_{crit}, is obtained from Table A–6.
- Using the value of χ^2_{crit} a rejection region is located in the theoretical sampling distribution of the χ^2 statistic.
- χ^2 is calculated from the scores in the study.
- A decision to reject or not reject H_0 is made on the basis of whether or not χ^2_{obs} falls into the rejection region.

Statistical Hypotheses

Null Hypothesis.   The null hypothesis under which the sampling distribution of χ^2 is developed and under which expected frequencies for each cell are found is:

H_0: There is no relationship between the row variable and the column variable in the population.

For our example study, H_0 may be stated specifically as:

H_0: The correctness of the response is not related to the type of student.

Alternative Hypothesis.   The alternative hypothesis is:

H_1: The row and column variables are related in the population.

For our example study, H_1 may be stated specifically as:

H_1: The correctness of the response is related to the type of student.

Choosing a Significance Level
The task of choosing a significance level is identical to the problem faced in earlier chapters. In line with common practice, we choose $\alpha = .05$.

The Sampling Distribution of χ^2
If the null hypothesis is true and correctness of the response is not related to the type of student, then the calculated value of χ^2 (indicated by χ^2_{obs}) should be relatively small; the expected and observed frequencies for a cell of the contingency table should be much alike. On the other hand, if the row variable is related to the column variable, then the value of χ^2_{obs} should grow larger; the expected and observed frequencies will differ from each other. Consequently, relatively large values of χ^2_{obs} should be rare if the null hypothesis is true, but common if the alternative hypothesis is true. Thus, critical values of χ^2 will be large values of χ^2 that occur 5 or less times out of 100 if H_0 is true.

Degrees of Freedom of χ^2
The specific sampling distribution of χ^2 depends upon the degrees of freedom of the statistic. The df for χ^2 are given by $(r - 1)(c - 1)$, where r represents the number of rows and c represents the number of columns in the contingency table. For our example, $r = 2$ and $c = 2$; thus $df = (2 - 1)(2 - 1)$, which equals 1.

Locating a Rejection Region
Values of χ^2_{crit} for $\alpha = .05$ and $\alpha = .01$ from the sampling distribution of χ^2 at various df are given in Appendix Table A–6. Values of χ^2_{obs} equal to or greater than the tabled critical value are statistically significant at the value of α selected. The critical value of χ^2 for 1 df and $\alpha = .05$ from Table A–6 is 3.84. A value of χ^2 for 1 df equal to or larger than 3.84 will occur with a probability less than or equal to .05 if the null hypothesis is true. Thus, if χ^2_{obs} is equal to or greater than 3.84, it falls into the rejection region and will lead to rejection of H_0 and acceptance of H_1.

Calculating χ^2

Calculating χ^2_{obs} requires knowing both the observed and expected frequencies of response. The expected frequencies for each cell of a contingency table may be obtained from the marginal frequencies by

$$\text{Expected frequency of a cell} = \frac{(\text{Row marginal for cell})(\text{Column marginal for cell})}{\text{Total number of responses}}$$

For example, the expected frequency for the physics-trained/correct response cell (row 1, column 1) is found by

$$E_{11} = \frac{(\text{Row 1 marginal})(\text{Column 1 marginal})}{\text{Total}}, \quad \text{or}$$

$$E_{11} = \frac{(34)(40)}{80} = 17.$$

Notice that this expected frequency is the E shown in Table 15–2.

After expected frequencies for each cell are obtained, χ^2_{obs} is found by subtracting the expected frequency (E) from the observed frequency (O) for each cell. Each $O - E$ difference is then squared and divided by the expected frequency of the cell. The resulting $(O - E)^2/E$ values are summed over all cells in the contingency table. For example, the numerical value of χ^2_{obs} for the frequencies shown in Table 15–2 is calculated as follows:

$$\chi^2_{obs} = \frac{(26 - 17)^2}{17} + \frac{(14 - 23)^2}{23} + \frac{(8 - 17)^2}{17} + \frac{(32 - 23)^2}{23},$$

$$\chi^2_{obs} = \frac{81}{17} + \frac{81}{23} + \frac{81}{17} + \frac{81}{23},$$

$$\chi^2_{obs} = 16.57.$$

Decisions about the Statistical Hypotheses

The χ^2_{obs} of 16.57 is larger than χ^2_{crit} of 3.84 and thus falls into the rejection region. Accordingly, the null hypothesis is rejected and the alternative hypothesis is accepted at the .05 level. There is a statistically significant relationship between the row and column variables.

Conclusions

The rejection of the null hypothesis indicates that the type of student and correctness of response are related. The nature of the relationship may be seen by examining Table 15–2: A greater than chance frequency of a correct response is associated with a physics-trained student and a greater than chance frequency of an incorrect response is associated with a physics-untrained student.

Assumptions for the Use of the Chi Square Test

A chi square test may be used on a contingency table of any size (e.g., 2×3, 3×4, 4×4, etc.). Several assumptions apply to its use, however.

- Each person may contribute only one response to the contingency table.
- The number of responses obtained should be large enough so that no expected frequency is less than 10 in a 2×2 contingency table or less than 5 in a contingency table larger than 2×2. If this condition is not met, then either more responses should be collected or an alternative test such as the Fisher exact test should be used.

Further details of the use of chi square and alternative tests for frequency data may be found in Marascuilo and McSweeney (1977) or Siegel (1956).

Testing Your Knowledge 15–1

On a separate sheet of paper, test your knowledge of the material in this section by answering the following questions.

1. Define: two-way frequency table, rows-by-columns contingency table, observed frequencies, c, r, marginal frequencies, expected frequencies, parametric test, nonparametric test, chi square test.
2. Under what circumstances would it be inappropriate to use a parametric test to analyze data from an experiment?
3. For each of the following one-factor designs and scale of measurement of the scores, identify the appropriate statistical test.
   a. Within-subjects, two levels, ratio measurement.
   b. Between-subjects, two levels, nominal measurement.
   c. Between-subjects, two levels, ratio measurement.
   d. Between-subjects, two levels, ordinal measurement.
   e. Within-subjects, two levels, ordinal measurement.
4. What form of data is suitable for analysis by the chi square test?
5. What is represented by the columns of a rows-by-columns contingency table?
6. What is represented by the rows of a rows-by-columns contingency table?
7. Write the formula for the χ^2 statistic.
8. Write the formula for obtaining the expected frequency of a cell in a contingency table.

9. Write the formula for the degrees of freedom of the χ^2 statistic.
10. Given below are values of χ^2_{obs} for various degrees of freedom (given in parentheses). For each value of χ^2_{obs} and df, find the value of χ^2_{crit} at the .05 level. Then indicate whether χ^2_{obs} falls into the rejection region and the decisions you make concerning H_0 and H_1.

$\chi^2_{obs}(2) = 7.26$ $\chi^2_{obs}(4) = 8.33$

$\chi^2_{obs}(8) = 15.51$ $\chi^2_{obs}(20) = 26.94$

11. Identify the assumptions of the chi square test. ■

Example Problem 15–1
Using the chi square test

Problem:

Being a firstborn often appears to confer certain advantages to a child. Several studies have indicated that firstborn children typically do better on academic-type measures than do later born children. Eisenman (1987) was interested in whether birth order may also relate to an individual's creativity. For his study he employed 100 firstborn and 100 later born adult males. One measure of creativity employed was for the participants to give as many uses as they could think of for a brick. The participants' responses on this test were placed in one of two categories: either above or below the median of a college population on number of uses and originality of those uses. The following frequencies of responses as a function of birth order were reported:

		Birth Order	
		Firstborn	Later Born
	Above Median	67	45
Creativity Test Score			
	Below Median	33	55

Is there a relationship between birth order and creativity in males? Use a .05 significance level.

Solution:

The independent variable in this study is birth order, an attribute independent variable with two levels, firstborn and later born. The dependent variable, test score, was measured at the nominal level of measurement. An individual's score was categorized as either above or below the median number of uses and originality of those uses for a college population. Because each person contributes only one score or count to the frequency, the chi square test is an appropriate statistical test for these data.

Statistic to be used: χ^2
Assumptions for use:

1. Each person contributes only one response to the contingency table.
2. No expected frequency will be less than 10.

Statistical hypotheses:
H_0: There is no relationship between birth order and creativity in the male population sampled.
H_1: Birth order and creativity are related in the male population sampled.

Significance level: $\alpha = .05$
df for χ^2: $(r - 1)(c - 1) = (2 - 1)(2 - 1) = 1$

Critical value: $\chi^2_{crit}(1) = 3.84$

Rejection region: Values of χ^2_{obs} equal to or greater than 3.84.

Calculation: The formula for χ^2_{obs} requires finding expected frequencies; to do so we must find the marginal frequencies. The observed frequencies (indicated by O), the expected frequencies (indicated by E) and the marginal frequencies are provided in the contingency table below.

		Birth Order	
	Firstborn	*Later Born*	*(Row Marginals)*
Above Median	$O = 67$	$O = 45$	112
	$E = 56$	$E = 56$	
Creativity Test			
Below Median	$O = 33$	$O = 55$	88
	$E = 44$	$E = 44$	
(Column marginals)	100	E 100	(Total) 200

The column marginals are obtained by summing the observed frequencies in each column. Row marginals are obtained analogously by summing the observed frequencies in each row. Given the marginal frequencies, expected frequencies are found using

$$\begin{array}{c} \text{Expected} \\ \text{frequency} \\ \text{of a cell} \end{array} = \frac{\text{(Row marginal for cell) (column marginal for cell)}}{\text{Total number of responses}}.$$

The expected frequencies for each cell of the table are then:

$$\text{Firstborn-above median cell: } E_{11} = \frac{(112)(100)}{200} = 56,$$

$$\text{Later born-above median cell: } E_{12} = \frac{(112)(100)}{200} = 56,$$

$$\text{Firstborn-below median cell: } E_{21} = \frac{(88)(100)}{200} = 44,$$

$$\text{Later born-below median cell: } E_{22} = \frac{(88)(100)}{200} = 44.$$

The value of χ^2_{obs} is found by

$$\chi^2_{obs} = \sum_{k=1}^{c} \sum_{j=1}^{r} \frac{(O_{jk} - E_{jk})^2}{E_{jk}}.$$

Substituting numerical values,

$$\chi^2_{obs} = \frac{(67 - 56)^2}{56} + \frac{(33 - 44)^2}{44} + \frac{(45 - 56)^2}{56} + \frac{(55 - 44)^2}{44},$$

$$\chi^2_{obs} = 2.16 + 2.75 + 2.16 + 2.75,$$

$$\chi^2_{obs} = 9.82.$$

Decision: The $\chi^2_{obs} = 9.82$ is greater than $\chi^2_{crit} = 3.84$; it thus falls into the rejection region. Consequently, we reject H_0 and accept H_1.

Conclusions:
Birth order and creativity are related in the male population sampled. Firstborn males' creativity scores more frequently are above the median on creativity and later born males' creativity scores more frequently are below the median. ▪

Statistics in Use 15–1

Using the χ^2 Test for Goodness of Fit
Have you ever described someone as a lunatic? If so, you are following the belief that behavior is affected by phases of the moon. Indeed, often it is popularly expressed that unusual or abnormal behavior is more likely to occur during the full moon phase. Does empirical evidence support this belief, however? Little, Bowers, and Little (1987) tabulated all the reports of unusual behavior to a correction center mental health unit over a six-year

period. The 364 incidents reported were then categorized according to the lunar phase in which they occurred. The distribution was as follows:

Lunar Phase

Full Moon	New Moon	First Quarter	Third Quarter
83	95	88	98

Do the incidents vary with the phase of the moon? The chi square test may be used to answer this question.

The table above categorizes behavior only one way — by lunar phase. To run a chi square test, we need to find expected frequencies. Because we do not have row and column marginals to obtain expected frequencies from, we use the following reasoning to obtain the expected frequencies. If behavior is unrelated to phase of the moon, then the frequency of occurrence of reported behaviors should be equal in each phase, any observed differences reflecting only sampling error. If, however, behavior is related to phase of the moon, then the reported incidents should not be equal among the phases. Under the null hypothesis that behavior is not related to phases of the moon, about one-fourth of the 364 incidents should occur in each lunar phase. Hence, expected frequencies of incidents may be obtained by dividing the total frequency, 364, by 4, the number of categories of lunar phase. Thus E for each phase is $364/4 = 91$. Using these expected frequencies, χ^2_{obs} is obtained using the formula given earlier:

$$\chi^2_{obs} = \frac{(83 - 91)^2}{91} + \frac{(95 - 91)^2}{91} + \frac{(88 - 91)^2}{91} + \frac{(98 - 91)^2}{91}, \quad \text{or}$$

$$\chi^2_{obs} = 1.52 .$$

The degrees of freedom for this χ^2_{obs} are $c - 1$, where c represents the number of categories used. For our example $c = 4$; thus $df = 4 - 1 = 3$. For $\alpha = .05$, $\chi^2_{crit}(3) = 7.81$. Thus $\chi^2_{obs} = 1.52$ is nonsignificant and we fail to reject the null hypothesis. There is no evidence that the frequency of incidents reported is related to phases of the moon in the population sampled.

The chi square test as illustrated in this example is known as the **chi square goodness-of-fit** test. In a goodness-of-fit test only the dimension of categorization of response is used. Expected frequencies are obtained from a theoretical hypothesis, such as the hypothesis that the frequencies of all categories should be equal. The assumptions for this use of the chi square are similar to those stated earlier; each person must contribute only one observation to the categories and the expected frequencies should not be less than 10 if there are only two categories or not less than 5 if there are three or more categories. ■

Testing Your Knowledge 15–2

On a separate sheet of paper, test your knowledge of the material in this section by answering the following questions.

1. Complete the following problem using the chi square test following the format illustrated in the example problem. Use a .05 significance level.

   Have you ever run a red traffic light while driving? Perhaps not, but no doubt you have seen others do so. How frequently do drivers fail to stop for traffic lights, and does the frequency of occurrence of such behaviors depend upon the time of day or day of the week? One researcher investigated this problem by observing the number of vehicles passing a red traffic light at a major intersection in a large city. He observed traffic during 45 one-hour periods. The observations were divided equally among Tuesday, Wednesday, and Thursday, and between two one-hour periods on each of these days, from 10:00 A.M. to 11:00 A.M. and from 2:00 P.M. to 3:00 P.M. Suppose the investigator reported the following frequency of vehicles running the red light during these two times on each of the days of the week observed.

		Day of Week		
		Tuesday	*Wednesday*	*Thursday*
	10:00 to 11:00 A.M.	38	46	58
Time				
	2:00 to 3:00 P.M.	46	54	63

Is there a relationship between day of the week and time of day with respect to cars running red lights? ▦

MANN-WHITNEY *U* TEST

Perception of Ambiguous Figures: An Example Problem

The **Mann-Whitney *U* test** is a nonparametric test for a between-subjects design using two levels of an independent variable and the scores realize at least an ordinal scale. To develop and illustrate the Mann-Whitney *U* test, we borrow from the research of Reisberg (1983) on the perception of ambiguous figures. Ambiguous figures are perceptual stimuli that involve two or more possible perceptual organizations. For example, Figure 15–1 illustrates the Schroeder staircase. This well-known figure has two possible perceptual organizations: In one, a set of stairs appears normal; in the other, the stairs seem upside down. The stairs will reverse perceptually if you view them for a while. If attention and memory are required to reverse the perception from one organization to the other, then an

FIGURE 15–1.

The Schroeder staircase, an ambiguous figure.

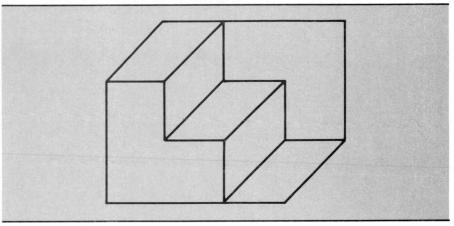

additional task that occupies attention and memory should prolong the amount of time needed to reverse the perception. To test this hypothesis, Reisberg formed two groups of participants. Both groups viewed the Schroeder staircase and were to report to the experimenter when they had seen both organizations of the stimulus. The independent variable was the type of interfering task. Participants in the control group simply viewed the figure and reported the reversal. Individuals in the experimental group were required to count backward by threes from a three-digit number while they viewed the stimulus. It was hypothesized that counting backward required both attention and memory. If the perceptual task also required attention and memory, then counting backward should interfere with its performance and delay the reports of a reversal. The experimenter timed how long it took the participant to make the report of a reversal. If a subject did not report a reversal at the end of 2 minutes, the test was stopped and the subject assigned an "infinite" (∞) latency.

Table 15–3 presents hypothetical data for a similar experiment employing nine subjects in each of the two treatment conditions. The scores are presented in order of increasing latency in each treatment condition. The scores recorded from subjects as tested would not be so ordered. These scores do not appear to approximate a normal distribution, even if a considerably larger number of scores were to be obtained. Most of the latencies, particularly of the control subjects (i.e., no counting task), are short. For both conditions, however, several of the latencies are long, resulting in distributions appearing more L-shaped than normally distributed. In addition, for the counting backward group, because one person did not report a reversal within 2 minutes, there is an infinite latency that cannot be assigned a numerical value. Therefore, neither the t test nor the analysis of variance can be used to analyze these data. Rather, we will analyze the scores with the Mann-Whitney U test.

TABLE 15–3.

Hypothetical perceptual reversal latencies (in seconds) as a function of type of task.

Task	
No Counting (A_1)	*Counting Backward (A_2)*
2	4
5	10
6	11
8	12
9	14
13	17
15	85
21	98
42	∞^a

Note. For ease of discussion, the scores are presented in order of increasing latency in each treatment condition.

[a]This score represents an "infinite" reversal latency; this person did not see the reversal within the 2-minute time limit.

Statistical Hypothesis Testing with the Mann-Whitney *U*

Ranking Scores
The Mann-Whitney *U* test requires ranking the scores in order to develop a test statistic and a sampling distribution of that statistic. This ranking is done even though the scores actually recorded in the experiment may represent an interval or ratio scale of measurement; the scores are converted to ordinal measurement by ranking them. The first step in ranking scores for the Mann-Whitney *U* is to combine the scores of both groups (for a total of *N* scores) and then place the scores in order of increasing magnitude from smallest to largest. This procedure is shown in step 1 of Table 15–4 for the data of Table 15–3. In performing the ranking, the group identity of the scores should be maintained (see step 2 of Table 15–4). Then the ranks from 1 to *N* are assigned to the scores, giving the smallest score the rank of 1 and the largest score the rank of *N*. This ranking is done in step 3 of Table 15–4.

The *U* Statistic
The **U statistic** is the number of times that the rank of a score in one group precedes the rank of a score in the other group. This calculation is illustrated in steps 4 and 5 of Table 15–4. For example, the score of 2 (given in step 1) from the A_1 group (identified in step 2) precedes all the A_2 scores in rank (given in step 3). Thus this score precedes nine of the A_2 scores in rank. Scores of 5, 6, 8, and 9 from the A_1 group each precede eight of the scores in the A_2 group in rank. Step 4 of Table 15–4 presents

the number of times that an A_1 score precedes an A_2 in rank. Examine the numerical values in this step carefully and understand how they were obtained. The total number of times that an A_1 score precedes an A_2 score in rank is 56, the total of the values in step 4 (i.e., $9 + 8 + \cdots + 3 + 3 = 56$). Thus, the value of U for the A_1 group, or U_{A_1}, is 56.

There is also a value of U for the A_2 group. This value represents the number of times that the rank of an A_2 score precedes the rank of an A_1 score. Step 5 of Table 15–4 indicates the number of times that an A_2 score precedes an A_1 score in rank. The sum of the values in this step provides U_{A_2}; in this case $U_{A_2} = 25$.

Characteristics of the U Statistic

If a treatment has no effect, then we expect that when the scores are combined and ordered as they are in Table 15–4, scores from each group will be approximately equally distributed over the rankings. We do not expect the scores from one group to be represented exclusively among the lower ranks and the scores of the other condition to be exclusively among the higher ranks. Consequently, the value of U_{A_1} should be about equal to U_{A_2}. For example, if the treatment had no effect in our example, then U_{A_1} and U_{A_2} would each equal about 40. If the treatment has an exceptionally strong effect, however, and all the A_1 scores have lower ranks than the A_2 scores, then the value of U_{A_1} would be 81 and the value of U_{A_2} equal to 0. Such values of U would, of course, be unlikely by chance alone. Thus, if an experimenter obtains a U equal to 0, he or she would likely reject a hypothesis of chance occurrence for this outcome.

The values of U_{A_1} and U_{A_2} are perfectly inversely related. As U_{A_1} increases, U_{A_2} must decrease by an equal amount. Hence, only one value of U, most typically the smaller value, need be calculated. One can easily determine if the smaller value has been calculated by using the relation

$$U_{A_2} = n_{A_1} n_{A_2} - U_{A_1},$$

TABLE 15–4.
Illustration of rank ordering scores of Table 15–3.

Step 1. Latency scores ordered from smallest to largest	2	4	5	6	8	9	10	11	12	13	14	15	17	21	42	85	98	∞
Step 2. Group identity[a]	1	2	1	1	1	1	2	2	2	1	2	1	2	1	1	2	2	2
Step 3. Rank	1	2	3	4	5	6	7	8	9	10	11	12	13	14	15	16	17	18
Step 4. Number of times an A_1 score precedes A_2 scores	9		8	8	8	8				5		4		3	3			
Step 5. Number of times an A_2 score precedes A_1 scores		8					4	4	4		3		2					

[a]1 indicates the score is from group A_1—no counting, 2 indicates the score is from group A_2—counting backward.

where n_{A_1} is the number of scores in group A_1 and n_{A_2} is the number of scores in group A_2. In our example we can find U_{A_2} from U_{A_1} by

$$U_{A_2} = (9)(9) - 56 = 81 - 56 = 25,$$

and 25 is the smaller of the two values of U for the data of Table 15–3.

We may use the U statistic in a statistical hypothesis test by following the familiar steps of statistical hypothesis testing.

Statistical Hypotheses

Null Hypothesis.   The null hypothesis under which the sampling distribution of U is developed is

H_0: The population distribution of A_1 scores is identical to the population distribution of A_2 scores.

If this statistical null hypothesis is true, then the value of U_{A_1} should be about the same as U_{A_2}.

Alternative Hypothesis.   The alternative hypothesis for the U test is

H_1: The population distribution of A_1 scores is not identical to the population distribution of A_2 scores.

If this alternative hypothesis is true, then U_{A_1} and U_{A_2} should differ considerably from each other.

Sampling Distributions and Critical Values of U

The sampling distribution of U varies with n_{A_1} and n_{A_2}. To simplify the use of the U statistic, tables of its sampling distribution and critical values of U at the .01 and .05 levels have been developed for various sizes of n_{A_1} and n_{A_2}. Because the maximum value of U is determined by n_{A_1} and n_{A_2}, the tables of the sampling distribution of U present only the smaller of the two possible values of U that may be obtained in an experiment. The sampling distribution for the smaller value of U for groups ranging in size from 1 to 20 for $\alpha = .01$ and $\alpha = .05$ is presented in Appendix Table A–7. Values of the smaller U_{obs} less than or equal to U_{crit} are statistically significant for the value of α selected. Notice, here, in contrast to the t, F, and χ^2 statistics, the rejection region for U_{obs} consists of values of the smaller U_{obs} that are less than or equal to U_{crit}. For the example data, $n_{A_1} = 9$ and $n_{A_2} = 9$; the critical value of U is 17 at the .05 significance level.

Decisions about the Statistical Hypotheses

If the smaller U_{obs} is less than or equal to U_{crit}, then we reject H_0 and accept H_1. If the smaller U_{obs} is greater than U_{crit}, then we fail to reject H_0

and do not accept H_1. For our example of the reversal latency scores of Table 15–3, $U_{A_1} = 56$ and $U_{A_2} = 25$. U_{A_2} is the smaller of the two values and it is this value that we use for the statistical hypothesis test. $U_{A_2} = 25$ is larger than the value of $U_{crit} = 17$. Accordingly, the value of U_{A_2} does not fall into the rejection region and is thus nonsignificant. Consequently, we fail to reject the null hypothesis and we do not accept H_1.

Conclusions

The failure to reject H_0 leads to the conclusion that there is no evidence to indicate that the population distribution of the A_1 scores differs from the population distribution of A_2 scores. In the context of our example experiment, we conclude that counting backward did not change the latency of a reversal in comparison to the control condition.

Assumptions of the Mann-Whitney U Test

As the null hypothesis for the Mann-Whitney U indicates, the U provides a test of equality of the population distributions from which the samples were selected. It does not test the equality of a parameter such as μ as does the t test. If a significant value of U is obtained, then we can conclude only that the distribution of A_1 scores is either higher or lower than the distribution of A_2 scores.

The U requires that the scores be rank ordered. Thus, it assumes the scores attain at least an ordinal scale. In many instances, as in our example problem, obtained scores will reflect either interval or ratio scales of measurement and these measures will be converted to ranks for application of the Mann-Whitney U. The only other requirement is that the underlying dimension of the dependent variable is continuous in nature even though the actual measurements may be only ordinal in nature.

Computational Formulas for U

The approach taken in Table 15–4 to obtain U_{A_1} and U_{A_2} is cumbersome, but it indicates conceptually what U_{A_1} and U_{A_2} represent. For research purposes, however, simplified computational formulas have been developed.

U_{A_1}

The value of U_{A_1} may be found from the formula

$$U_{A_1} = n_{A_1}n_{A_2} + \frac{n_{A_1}(n_{A_1} + 1)}{2} - \sum R_{A_1},$$

where n_{A_1} is the number of scores in group A_1, n_{A_2} is the number of scores in the A_2 group, and $\sum R_{A_1}$ is the sum of the ranks assigned to scores in group A_1. The ΣR_{A_1} is obtained by adding the ranks assigned to the A_1 scores in step 3 of Table 15–4. For our example, $\Sigma R_{A_1} = 70$. Substituting values into the equation for U_{A_1} provides:

$$U_{A_1} = (9)(9) + \frac{9(9 + 1)}{2} - 70 = 56.$$

U_{A_2}
The value of U_{A_2} may be obtained from the formula

$$U_{A_2} = n_{A_1} n_{A_2} + \frac{n_{A_2}(n_{A_2} + 1)}{2} - \Sigma R_{A_2},$$

where ΣR_{A_2} is the sum of the ranks assigned to scores in A_2. For our example, $\Sigma R_{A_2} = 101$. When values are substituted into the formula

$$U_{A_2} = (9)(9) + \frac{9(9 + 1)}{2} - 101 = 25.$$

Table 15–5 summarizes the U test employing these computational formulas. This table also includes the procedure to be followed if ranks are tied. Example Problem 15–2 illustrates the steps in this table.

TABLE 15–5.
Employing the Mann-Whitney U test with computational formulas.

Step 1. Rank order the combined scores of both groups from the smallest score (rank = 1) to the largest score (rank = N). Maintain the group designation (A_1 or A_2) of each score. Assign each of the tied scores the mean of the ranks they would have been assigned if they were not tied.

Step 2. Find ΣR_{A_1} and ΣR_{A_2}.

Step 3. Compute U_{A_1}:

$$U_{A_1} = n_{A_1} n_{A_2} + \frac{n_{A_1}(n_{A_1} + 1)}{2} - \Sigma R_{A_1}.$$

Step 4. Compute U_{A_2}:

$$U_{A_2} = n_{A_1} n_{A_2} + \frac{n_{A_2}(n_{A_2} + 1)}{2} - \Sigma R_{A_2} \quad \text{or}$$

$$U_{A_2} = n_{A_1} n_{A_2} - U_{A_1}.$$

Step 5. Choose the smaller of the two obtained values of U.

Testing Your Knowledge 15–3

On a separate sheet of paper, test your knowledge of the material in this section by answering the following questions.

1. Rank-order the following scores from 1 to N. Maintain the group identity of the related scores. Then find U_{A_1}, the number of times an A_1 score precedes an A_2 score, and U_{A_2}, the number of times an A_2 score precedes an A_1 score.

Group	
A_1	A_2
15	7
23	26
10	14
19	16

    a. Which value of U is the smaller value?
    b. Is the smaller U statistically significant at the .05 level?
2. Find U_{A_1} and U_{A_2} for the scores of question 1 using the computational formulas for U.
    a. Do the values of U_{A_1} and U_{A_2} obtained with the computational formulas agree with those obtained by counting precedence in Question 1?
3. Write the statistical hypotheses for the Mann-Whitney U test.
4. If H_0 is true, then what should be the relation of U_{A_1} to U_{A_2}?
5. If H_1 is true, then what should be the relation of U_{A_1} to U_{A_2}?
6. Given below are the smaller values of U_{obs} for various group sizes. For each value of U_{obs} and group size, find the value of U_{crit} at the .01 level. Then indicate whether U_{obs} falls into the rejection region and the decisions you make concerning H_0 and H_1.

	U_{obs}	n_{A_1}	n_{A_2}
a.	3	6	4
b.	12	10	10
c.	28	16	9
d.	21	7	19
e.	4	13	19
f.	126	18	19

7. Identify the characteristics of the Mann-Whitney U test.

Example Problem 15–2
Using the Mann-Whitney U test

Problem:

Many colleges and universities are discovering that the major drug use problem of students is alcohol abuse. Suppose a college counselor developed an alcohol education program for students. At the beginning of an academic year the counselor randomly selected eight freshmen males and presented the educational program to them. Six weeks after presenting the program she gave the students a questionnaire on their alcohol consumption behaviors. At the same time, she randomly chose 10 other freshmen males who had not been given the alcohol education program and also gave them the questionnaire. The estimated daily alcohol consumption of the two groups in ounces of pure alcohol was as follows:

Group	
Educational Program A₁	*No Educational Program A₂*
0.31	0.41
0.53	0.63
0.58	1.14
0.14	0.21
0.16	0.89
0.52	0.55
0.53	0.89
0.02	0.91
	0.08
	0.59

Because the scores obtained represent estimates of a behavior, the counselor believed that they do not meet the requirements of interval scale of measurement. Consequently, she treated them as presenting ordered information only. Did the educational program affect the alcohol consumption of those students exposed to it? Use a .05 significance level.

Solution:

The research design used is a between-subjects design with two levels of the independent variable. The dependent variable, estimated alcohol consumption, is considered to achieve only ordinal measurement. Accordingly, the Mann-Whitney U test is an appropriate statistical test for these data.

Statistic to be used: Smaller U_{obs}

Assumptions for use:

1. The independent variable is manipulated as a between-subjects variable.
2. The dependent variable is measured at least at the ordinal scale of measurement.

Statistical hypotheses:

H_0: The population distribution of A_1 scores is identical to the population distribution of A_2 scores.

H_1: The population distribution of A_1 scores is not identical to the population distribution of A_2 scores.

Significance level: $\alpha = .05$

Critical value of U: For $n_{A_1} = 8$, $n_{A_2} = 10$, and $\alpha = .05$, $U_{crit} = 17$.

Rejection region: Values of the smaller U_{obs} equal to or less than 17.

Calculation: To calculate U, the steps of Table 15–5 are followed.

Step 1.

Ordered scores:	.02	.08	.14	.16	.21	.31	.41	.52	.53	.53	.55	.58	.59	.63	.89	.89	.91	1.14
Group identity:	1	2	1	1	2	1	2	1	1	1	2	1	2	2	2	2	2	2
Rank:	1	2	3	4	5	6	7	8	9.5	9.5	11	12	13	14	15.5	15.5	17	18

Notice that two sets of estimates are tied, 0.53 and 0.89. For 0.53 the scores occupy the ranks of 9 and 10; hence each score was assigned the mean (i.e., 9.5) of the two ranks. Similarly, the two scores of 0.89 occupy the ranks of 15 and 16; thus each score was assigned the mean (i.e., 15.5) of the two ranks.

Step 2.

$$\sum R_{A_1} = 1 + 3 + 4 + 6 + 8 + 9.5 + 9.5 + 12 = 53.$$

$$\sum R_{A_2} = 2 + 5 + 7 + 11 + 13 + 14 + 15.5 + 15.5 + 17 + 18 = 118.$$

Step 3.

$$U_{A_1} = (8)(10) + \frac{8(8 + 1)}{2} - 53 = 63.$$

Step 4.

$$U_{A_2} = (8)(10) + \frac{10(10 + 1)}{2} - 118 = 17, \quad \text{or}$$

$$U_{A_2} = (8)(10) - 63 = 17.$$

Step 5.

$$U_{A_2} = 17 \text{ is the smaller } U_{obs}.$$

Decision: The smaller U_{obs}, $U_{A_2} = 17$, is equal to $U_{crit} = 17$. Thus, it falls into the rejection region. The null hypothesis is rejected and the alernative hypothesis is accepted.

Conclusions:
The alcohol education program changed the amount of alcohol consumed as measured by students' estimates of daily alcohol consumption. Students who had taken the educational program estimated they drank less alcohol than students who had not taken the program. ▪

Statistics in Use 15–2

What is the Effect of a Stott? Analyzing Data with the Mann-Whitney U Test

When approached by a predator, Thomson's gazelles often leap straight up with all four feet simultaneously off the ground. This behavior, known as stotting, appears to be costly to the animal, for it delays the onset of the animal's flight from the predator. In an effort to learn more about the nature and function of stotting, Caro (1986) studied gazelles in Serengeti National Park, Tanzania. One behavior measured was the estimated distance the gazelle traveled when fleeing from a predator, such as a cheetah. Caro also timed the length of flight so that he was able to obtain a speed measure by dividing the distance traveled by the length of time taken to travel the distance. Because flight distance was estimated rather than actually measured, Caro treated this measure as ordinal. Correspondingly, flight speed also was treated as an ordinal measurement.

One question of interest was whether flight speed differed if the flight was or was not preceded by a stott. To answer this question, Caro compared the flight speed for flights with and without initial stotts. One such comparison on neonate gazelles (less than 2 weeks old) involved 16 neonates that did not stott before fleeing and 15 neonates that did. A Mann-Whitney U test comparing the two distributions of flight speed revealed the smaller $U_{obs} = 119.5$. From Table A–7, U_{crit} for group sizes of 16 and 15 is 70 for $\alpha = .05$. Thus the rejection region consists of values of U_{obs} equal to or less than 70. Clearly, the $U_{obs} = 119.5$ does not fall into the rejection region. Caro failed to reject the null hypothesis. There is no evidence that the distribution of flight speeds either preceded or not preceded by a stott differ in this population. A similar result occurred when comparing flight speeds of fawns (2 weeks to 4 months in age) preceded or not by a stott. Similar comparisons could not be completed for older gazelles because almost all flights were preceded by a stott. Accordingly, Caro concluded that, at least for neonates and fawn gazelles, flight speed was not affected by the occurrence of a stott before the flight.

Testing Your Knowledge 15–4

On a separate sheet of paper, test your knowledge of the material in this section by answering the following questions.

1. Complete the following problem using the Mann-Whitney U test using the format illustrated in the example problem. Use a .05 significance level.

   The use of music to induce relaxation in dental patients is becoming more widespread. Suppose a dentist tested the effectiveness of music in relaxing patients by randomly assigning patients to one of two groups. Thirteen patients in the music group listened to music while dental procedures were performed; 12 patients in the no music group did not listen to music while similar dental procedures were performed. Midway through the appointment each patient was asked to estimate his or her anxiety on a scale of 1 (not at all anxious) to 100 (extremely anxious). The anxiety estimates obtained were

Group	
No Music	Music
52	44
75	21
66	66
33	54
17	37
78	84
94	30
89	29
27	54
49	49
53	33
78	10
	78

Do the groups differ in their anxiety estimates?

THE WILCOXON SIGNED-RANKS TEST

Vocal Expression of Emotion: An Example Experiment

The **Wilcoxon signed-ranks test** is a parametric test for within-subjects designs with two levels of an independent variable. Thus it is a nonparametric analog of the *t* test for related groups. This test assumes only that the underlying dimension of behavior measured is continuous and that scores may be placed in rank order. To illustrate the Wilcoxon signed-ranks test, we introduce an experiment modeled after research reported by Cosmides (1983) on the problem of how emotion is expressed in voice patterns. Specifically, Cosmides wanted to know whether vocal expression of emotion is similar from person to person as is the facial expression of emotion. To investigate this problem, she measured certain sound characteristics of a person's speech as he or she read a part from a script. One of her dependent variables, the frequency span of sounds in a person's utterance, required using nonparametric statistical analyses.

Given this brief introduction to the problem, suppose we employ a one-factor within-subjects design with two levels of an independent variable, the type of script a person is to read—a script reflecting a happy scene (A_1) and a script reflecting a sad scene (A_2). In each condition the participant's task is to simply read the script silently and, on signal from the experimenter, say aloud the words "I'll do it." The frequency span of the vocal expression of "I'll do it" is the dependent variable for each individual and is measured in cycles per second (cps, or Hertz). That is, a score is the range of the highest vocal frequency minus the lowest vocal frequency in a person's expression of the three words.

Suppose the frequency spans for 10 people tested under both script conditions are those presented in Table 15–6. The means, standard deviations, and variances for these scores also are shown here. Notice that not only do the mean frequency ranges appear to differ, but there also is a large difference in the variability of the two conditions. Recall that the *t* test requires the sample variances to be estimates of the same population variance. In the example, however, it appears that the two variances (704.37 and 10,281.96 for the happy and sad scripts, respectively) are unequal. Thus, one of the assumptions of the *t* test is violated by these data. The Wilcoxon signed-ranks test does not make assumptions about the variances and thus it is a more appropriate test for these scores.

Statistical Hypothesis Testing with the Wilcoxon Signed-Ranks Test

The *T* Statistic
The Wilcoxon test employs ranked scores to obtain a test statistic for which a sampling distribution is known. The test statistic utilized is called

TABLE 15–6.

Hypothetical scores for vocal-frequency span (in Hertz) as a function of type of script read.

Subject	Type of Script	
	Happy (A_1)	*Sad (A_2)*
1	305	214
2	275	385
3	360	519
4	299	307
5	317	483
6	326	454
7	284	501
8	347	463
9	331	382
10	314	297
$\overline{X}_A$	315.8	400.5
s_A	26.54	101.40
s_A^2	704.37	10281.96

the T, and it is the smaller sum of the ranks from the two treatment conditions.

Statistical Hypotheses

Null Hypothesis.   The statistical null hypothesis tested with the T is

H_0: The population distributions of the related A_1 and A_2 scores are identical.

Alternative Hypothesis.   The statistical alternative hypothesis is

H_1: The population distributions of the related A_1 and A_2 scores are not identical.

Sampling Distribution and Critical Values of *T*

Values of T_{crit} for $\alpha = .05$ and $\alpha = .01$ are presented in Appendix Table A–8 for samples up to size 50. This table is entered with the value of N, the number of paired scores, or equivalently, the number of participants. Values of T_{obs} equal to or less than T_{crit} fall into the rejection region and are statistically significant for the value of α selected. In our example with $N = 10$ and $\alpha = .05$, $T_{crit} = 8$. The rejection region is thus defined by values of T_{obs} equal to or less than 8.

Calculating *T*

The computations involved in obtaining the T statistic are shown in Table 15–7 using the example vocal-frequency span scores. The approach

TABLE 15–7.
Computation of the Wilcoxon T on the scores of Table 15–86.

Subject	Type of Script Happy (A_1)	Sad (A_2)	a d_i	b $|d_i|$	c Ranked d_i	d Signed Rank
1	305	214	+ 91	91	4	+ 4
2	275	385	−110	110	5	− 5
3	360	519	−159	159	8	− 8
4	299	307	− 8	8	1	− 1
5	317	483	−166	166	9	− 9
6	326	454	−128	128	7	− 7
7	284	501	−217	217	10	−10
8	347	463	−116	116	6	− 6
9	331	382	− 51	51	3	− 3
10	314	297	+ 17	17	2	+ 2

Step 1. Find the difference ($d_i = X_{i_1} - X_{i_2}$) between the participant's two scores as shown in column a. Maintain the sign (+ or −) of the difference.

Step 2. Find the absolute value of each difference (the value without regard to sign) as shown in column b.

Step 3. Rank the absolute differences from smallest (rank = 1) to largest (rank = N) as shown in column c. Differences of 0 are not ranked and the value of n used to obtain T_{crit} is reduced by the number of 0 differences occurring. Tied values of d_i are assigned the mean of the ranks that would have been assigned had no tie occurred.

Step 4. Give each rank the sign of the difference found in step 1 as shown in column d.

Step 5. Sum the ranks of like sign (i.e., the sum of the positive-signed ranks and the sum of the negative-signed ranks). For example, the sum of the positive-signed ranks in column d equals 6 [i.e., $(+4) + (+2)$] and the sum of the negative-signed ranks equals −49 [i.e., $(−5) + (−8) + (−1) + (−9) + (−7) + (−10) + (−6) + (−3)$].

Step 6. Find the absolute value of each sum of the ranks. Then choose the smaller of the two sums of the ranks. In this case it is 6, the sum of the positive ranks. This sum is the value of T_{obs}.

is to find the absolute value of the difference between each set of paired scores (steps 1 and 2, columns a and b). The values of the absolute differences are then ranked (step 3, column c). Next the ranked differences are assigned the sign of the difference (column d) and the sum of the positive ranks and the sum of the negative ranks obtained (steps 4 and 5). The value of T_{obs} is the smaller sum of the ranks in absolute value (step 6). In our example, the smaller sum of the ranks in absolute value is 6, the sum of the positive ranks. Thus, $T_{obs} = 6$.

Decisions about the Statistical Hypotheses

The value of T_{crit} for 10 paired scores is 8. Thus the rejection region is composed of scores of T_{obs} equal to or less than 8. T_{obs} is 6; hence, it falls into the rejection region, and we reject H_0 and accept H_1.

Conclusions
The rejection of H_0 and acceptance of H_1 leads to the conclusion that the two distributions of scores differ; the type of script produced differences in the vocal-frequency span. The vocal-frequency span for a sad script is greater than for a happy script.

Testing Your Knowledge 15–5

On a separate sheet of paper, test your knowledge of the material in this section by answering the following questions.

1. For what type of research design is the Wilcoxon test appropriate?
2. What is the test statistic used by the Wilcoxon signed-ranks test?
3. Write the statistical hypotheses for the Wilcoxon signed-ranks test.
4. Given below are the smaller absolute values of the sum of the signed ranks for experiments of different group sizes. For each smaller rank and value of N, identify the value of T_{obs}. Then find T_{crit} for the .05 significance level and indicate whether T_{obs} falls into the rejection region. Lastly, identify the decisions you make concerning H_0 and H_1.

	Smaller Rank	N
a.	2	8
b.	9	10
c.	17	13
d.	40	19
e.	98	25

Example Problem 15–3
Using the Wilcoxon signed-ranks test

Problem:
It has been suggested that music tempo affects the speed of behaviors, with fast tempo music increasing the speed with which a behavior may occur (Roballey et al., 1985). To investigate this hypothesis, a researcher conducts the following study. Eleven cafeteria patrons were observed unobtrusively on two different days under two different background music conditions, slow (A_1) and fast (A_2) tempo. The same individuals were observed on both days. The number of bites per minute taken by each person under each music condition was recorded. Suppose the following median bites per minute were observed for each person under the two music tempo conditions.

	Music Tempo	
Subject	Slow (A_1)	Fast (A_2)
1	3	4
2	4	6
3	2	3
4	3	3
5	3	8
6	4	2
7	1	4
8	5	4
9	3	6
10	5	9
11	2	8

The experimenter considered the scores to achieve an ordinal scale of measurement. Does music tempo affect biting rate? Use a .05 significance level.

Solution:
The research design is a one-factor within-subjects design with two levels of the independent variable, music tempo. The dependent variable is measured at least at the ordinal scale of measurement; thus the Wilcoxon signed-ranks test is an appropriate statistical test for these data.
Statistic to be used: T

Assumptions for use:

1. The independent variable is manipulated as a within-subjects variable.
2. The dependent variable is measured at least at the ordinal scale of measurement.

Statistical hypotheses:

H_0: The population distributions of the related A_1 and A_2 scores are identical.

H_1: The population distributions of the related A_1 and A_2 scores are not identical.

Significance level: $\alpha = .05$
Critical value of T: For $N = 11$ and $\alpha = .05$, $T_{crit} = 11$. In the calculation of T, however, subject 4 shows a zero change between the music conditions. This subject is dropped from the analysis. Accordingly, N becomes 10 and T_{crit} for $N = 10$ is 8.

Rejection region: Values of T_{obs} equal to or less than 8.

Calculation: To calculate T, the steps of Table 15–7 are followed.

Step 1. The value of $d_i = X_{i_1} - X_{i_2}$ is found for each subject (column *a* of the table below).

	Music Tempo		a	b	c	d
Subject	Slow (A₁)	Fast (A₂)	d_i	$|d_i|$	Ranked d_i	Signed d_i
1	3	4	−1	1	2	−2
2	4	6	−2	2	4.5	−4.5
3	2	3	−1	1	2	−2
4	3	3	−0	0	—	—
5	3	8	−5	5	9	−9
6	4	2	+2	2	4.5	+4.5
7	1	4	−3	3	6.5	−6.5
8	5	4	+1	1	2	+2
9	3	6	−3	3	6.5	−6.5
10	5	9	−4	4	8	−8
11	2	8	−6	6	10	−10

Step 2. Absolute values of d_i are obtained (column *b* of the table above.)
Step 3. The absolute values of d_i are ranked from 1 to 10; $d_i = 0$ is not included in the ranking (column *c*). Notice the ranking of the several sets of tied d_i values.
Step 4. The sign of each d_i is attached to the rank of d_i (column *d*).
Step 5. Like-signed ranks are summed.
The absolute value of the sum of the positive-signed ranks = 6.5.
The absolute value of the sum of the negative-signed ranks = 48.5.
Step 6. The absolute value of the sum of the positive-signed ranks is the smaller sum of the ranks; hence it provides $T_{obs} = 6.5$.

Decisions: $T_{obs} = 6.5$ is less than $T_{crit} = 8$. Accordingly, it falls into the rejection region and H_0 is rejected and H_1 accepted.

Conclusions:
The distributions of the number of bites taken per minute differ under the two music tempos. Examining the scores indicates that more bites are taken per minute under a fast tempo than under a slow tempo. ■

Statistics in Use 15–3

Agonistic Behavior in Preschoolers: Data Analysis Using the Wilcoxon Signed-Ranks Test

Agonistic behavior is defensive or aggressive interaction between individuals. Anyone who has observed children knows that such behavior often occurs in their social interactions. Addison (1986) was interested in the occurrence of such behavior in preschool children and the sex of the recipient of the behavior. He observed preschool children and recorded several types of agonistic behavior, including threats to other children and displacement. Displacements were instances where one child caused another child to move away from a location. For each child observed, the behaviors were categorized according to the sex of the recipient, same sex or opposite sex of the initiator. Addison analyzed the number of occurrences of each type of behavior using the Wilcoxon signedranks test. For nine children who displayed displacement behavior, the smaller sum of the ranks was 3, which is statistically significant at the .05 level. The percentage of same-sex displacements was significantly greater than the percentage of opposite-sex displacements. The difference between same-sex and opposite-sex threats was nonsignificant, however. For 14 children displaying threat behaviors, the smaller sum of the ranks was 22.5, larger than the T_{crit} of 21 at the .05 level.

The results indicate that certain forms of agonistic behavior in preschoolers most frequently occur between members of the same sex. Addison suggests that this finding may be related to the development of dominance relationships among children. He suggests also that the results may reflect the reinforcement of sex-appropriate interactions among children by adults. ▪

Testing Your Knowledge 15–6

On a separate sheet of paper, test your knowledge of the material in this section by answering the following questions.

1. Complete the following problem using the Wilcoxon signed-ranks test and the format illustrated in the example problem. Use a .05 significance level.

    Sport psychologists have recently become interested in the relationship of anxiety to performance in sports competition. For example, Maynard and Howe (1987) measured anxiety of rugby players before games 1 and 2 of a playoff series. Suppose you attempted a similar study and obtained the anxiety scores on the next page. The range of possible scores is from 12 — very low reported anxiety — to 84 — very high reported anxiety. It is likely that the population distribution of anxiety of scores is negatively skewed (most players reporting very high anxiety, a few reporting very low anxiety levels); thus you plan to use a nonparametric statistical analysis for these scores. Does anxiety level change from game 1 to game 2?

Player	Game 1 (A_1)	Game 2 (A_2)
1	68	72
2	56	65
3	78	77
4	49	54
5	66	64
6	43	53
7	77	70
8	68	78
9	28	29
10	69	75
11	75	78
12	80	72
13	75	75
14	65	76
15	71	70

USING NONPARAMETRIC TESTS

As we have seen, nonparametric tests usually do not make assumptions about the population distribution of scores for a sample. Further, they typically require only that we be able to rank-order the scores obtained. Parametric tests, such as the t or analysis of variance, require stronger assumptions about the nature of scores in an experiment, assumptions that sometimes may be questionable for the scores collected in a study. Nevertheless, nonparametric statistical tests are much less widely used in behavioral science research than are parametric statistical tests. Why?

There are several answers to this question. In general, nonparametric tests are less likely to detect an effect of an independent variable than are parametric tests if the population distributions are indeed normal. That is, they are more likely to lead to Type II errors in this case. Nonparametric tests also typically provide different information than do parametric tests. For example, the t test leads to conclusions about the equality or inequality of the population means, but conclusions with the U test concern the equality or inequality of the population distributions.

For more complex designs, such as the factorial designs discussed in Chapter 13, there are no nonparametric tests that provide as much information as the parametric factorial analysis of variance. Accordingly, many behavioral scientists routinely analyze their data with parametric tests.

There also are no hard and fast rules about when a nonparametric test should be employed. The example we used to introduce the U test, the perception of reversals in the Schroeder staircase, provides an unusually clear-cut instance when a nonparametric statistical test is necessary. One of the scores in this experiment was an infinite value. With such a value, a mean or standard deviation of scores cannot be computed. Obviously, then, a parametric test cannot be used on these data.

Other instances often are not so clear cut. For example, how much must the underlying distribution of a population of scores differ from a normal distribution before the use of a parametric test is inappropriate? When are the variances of two or more populations considered to be unequal? Behavioral scientists are not in agreement on the answers to these questions; consequently, they often do not agree upon whether a parametric or nonparametric test should be used to analyze a set of scores.

SUMMARY

- The chi square test is used for scores that represent only the frequency of occurrence of a response.
- The chi square test statistic is obtained by:

$$\chi^2_{obs} = \sum_{k=1}^{c} \sum_{j=1}^{r} \frac{(O_{jk} - E_{jk})^2}{E_{jk}}.$$

- The Mann-Whitney U test is a nonparametric test for a between-subjects design using two levels of an independent variable and scores at least at an ordinal scale.
- The U statistic is the number of times that the rank of a score in one group precedes the rank of a score in the other group.
- The value of U_{A_1} is found from:

$$U_{A_1} = n_{A_1} n_{A_2} + \frac{n_{A_1}(n_{A_1} + 1)}{2} - \sum R_{A_1},$$

- and the value of U_{A_2} from:

$$U_{A_2} = n_{A_1} n_{A_2} + \frac{n_{A_2}(n_{A_2} + 1)}{2} - \sum R_{A_2}.$$

- The smaller obtained value of U is used as the test statistic.
- The Wilcoxon signed-ranks test is a parametric test for within-subjects designs with two levels of an independent variable.
- The test statistic utilized by the Wilcoxon signed-ranks test is the T; the smaller sum of the ranks from the two treatment conditions.

KEY TERMS

chi square test	Mann-Whitney U test	T
contingency table	marginal frequencies	T_{crit}
χ^2	nonparametric test	T_{obs}
χ^2_{crit}	observed frequencies	U
χ^2_{obs}	parametric test	U_{crit}
distribution-free test	rows-by-columns contingency table	U_{obs}
expected frequencies	$\sum R_A$	Wilcoxon signed-ranks test
goodness-of-fit test	two-way frequency table	

REVIEW QUESTIONS

On a separate sheet of paper, test your knowledge of the material in this chapter by answering the following questions.

1. Many individuals in psychotherapy terminate the therapy before its scheduled completion. These individuals (known as psychotherapy dropouts) appear to comprise a substantial minority of those individuals in psychotherapy (Stahler & Eisenman, 1987). Suppose that in an attempt to gain more knowledge of this problem you obtain the records of several community mental health centers and categorize dropouts and nondropouts by gender and severity of problem they exhibit.

   a. You obtained the following frequencies of dropouts and non-dropouts for males and females:

	Gender	
	Male	*Female*
Non-dropout	99	130
Dropout	75	78

   Is the dropout frequency related to gender at the .05 significance level? If so, what is the relationship?

   b. The subjects were then categorized by severity of the problem: mild, moderate, and severe. The following frequencies were obtained:

	Severity of Problem		
	Mild	*Moderate*	*Severe*
Non-dropout	51	66	112
Dropout	64	54	35

   Is the dropout rate related to severity of the problem at the .05 significance level? If so, what is the relationship?

2. Example Problem 14–1 introduced a study testing whether yawning is a sign of boredom. Employing a one-factor within-subjects design, subjects saw a 30-minute rock music video (A_1—the interesting stimulus) and 30-minutes of a color-bar test pattern without sound (A_2—the uninteresting stimulus). The number of times that a subject yawned during the two sessions was observed and recorded.

Suppose we replicated this experiment using 11 subjects and observed the following number of yawns for each session:

Subject	Type of Video (A)	
	Interesting (A₁)	Uninteresting (A₂)
1	5	7
2	2	1
3	4	7
4	3	8
5	0	2
6	4	5
7	7	6
8	6	23
9	3	3
10	1	4
11	8	9

Does the type of task affect the amount of yawning that occurs? Use the Wilcoxon signed-ranks test and a .05 significance level.

a. Why might the Wilcoxon signed-ranks test be more appropriate for these data than the *t* for related groups? (Hint, examine the scores.)

b. What conclusions do you reach from the Wilcoxon test?

3. Chapter 10, Review Question 2, presented a study to determine the effect of noise on blood pressure. In that study, two groups of subjects were formed. Subjects in the control group relaxed in a comfortable chair for 30 minutes and at the end of the 30 minutes their systolic blood pressure was measured. Subjects in the experimental group also sat in the same chair for 30 minutes. During the 30-minute wait, however, they listened to a recording of traffic noise from a large city during rush hour. After listening to the noise for 30 minutes, the systolic blood pressure of these individuals was recorded. Suppose the following blood pressure measurements (in millimeters of mercury) were obtained:

Group	
Quiet	Noise
106	141
117	136
124	124
129	139
115	121
147	119
121	147
115	128
128	115
136	134
127	140

Do the distributions differ? Use the U test and a .05 significance level. If they differ, describe the difference.

4. To find if sex differences exist in trait anxiety, a researcher gave an anxiety inventory to 9 females and 13 males. The scores on the inventory may range from 20 (low anxiety) to 80 (high anxiety). Suppose the following scores were obtained:

Gender	
Female	Male
36	54
25	70
47	34
39	53
55	41
41	56
29	32
59	44
38	40
	61
	50
	30
	37

Does the distribution of female anxiety scores differ from that of the males? Use the Mann-Whitney U test and a .05 significance level. Describe your conclusions.

5. In Chapter 14 we presented a problem dealing with pitching speed of college baseball pitchers. In that study, the velocity of pitches of eight college pitchers was measured both with a speed gun in open view of the pitcher (condition A_1) and with the gun hidden from view (condition A_2). The following speeds were obtained:

	Speed Gun Condition (A)	
	Open View	Hidden
Subject	(A_1)	(A_2)
1	72.4	77.9
2	67.1	69.4
3	77.8	77.1
4	73.2	76.5
5	62.5	64.6
6	68.7	75.3
7	71.4	69.8
8	81.7	84.2

Analyze the scores with the Wilcoxon signed ranks test. Do the distributions differ at the .05 level?

16

Errors, Power, and Strength of Effect

For each statistical test we have discussed, the end result of the test is a decision by the researcher about the statistical hypotheses of the test. The two decision choices are:

- If the test statistic falls into the rejection region, then reject H_0 and accept H_1.
- If the test statistic does not fall into the rejection region, then fail to reject H_0 and do not accept H_1.

We pointed out in Chapter 8 that these decisions may be either correct or incorrect with respect to the true state of affairs in nature. A **Type I error** occurs if the null hypothesis is rejected when it is actually true. A **Type II error** occurs if we fail to reject H_0 when the alternative hypothesis (H_1) is true. Table 16–1 portrays the errors and correct decisions that may be made from a statistical test.

Type I and Type II errors occur because statistical decision making is probabilistic. If H_0 is true, the probability of a Type I error is given by α, the value of the significance level. If α is the probability of falsely rejecting H_0 when it is actually true, then the probability of making a correct decision and not rejecting H_0 when it is true is provided by $1 - \alpha$. The probability of a Type II error is given by β (the lower-case Greek letter **beta**). The value of β depends upon a number of factors and we discuss those factors in a following section. Finally, the probability of correctly accepting H_1 when H_1 is true is provided by $1 - \beta$. This value, $\mathbf{1 - \beta}$, often is identified as the power of a statistical test. Therefore, the **power of a statistical test,** or **power,** is the probability of rejecting H_0 when H_0 is false, and H_1 is true. Power plays an important role in statistical hypothesis test-

TABLE 16–1.
Errors and correct decisions in statistical decision making and the probability associated with each outcome.

		State of Nature	
		H_0 *True*	H_1 *True*
Decision by the Experimenter	H_0 *True*	Correct decision $p = 1 - \alpha$	Type II error $p = \beta$
	H_1 *True*	Type I error $p = \alpha$	Correct decision $p = 1 - \beta$

ing and we discuss it in later sections of this chapter. Each of these probabilities also is identified in Table 16–1.

TYPE I ERRORS

The purpose of conducting a statistical test is, of course, to determine whether differences on the dependent variable among treatment conditions are likely to be due to chance or to nonchance factors. Only if the null hypothesis is rejected does the experimenter have a basis for concluding that the independent variable affects behavior. Moreover, if a treatment effect is present, then the experimenter wants to detect it. After all, determining the effect of the independent variable is the reason for conducting an experiment. But a researcher does not want to conclude that a treatment has an effect when it really does not. Indeed, scientists typically view this latter possibility with some concern and want to keep the probability of this occurrence low in the research. Deciding that the alternative hypothesis is true when actually it is not corresponds to the conclusion that the treatment has an effect when, in reality, it does not. Thus, the scientist does not want to make a Type I error.

A Type I error can occur only when H_0 is true; hence the probability of making a Type I error depends directly upon the significance level selected. Recall that the significance level is the probability of obtaining a value of the test statistic that leads to rejection of the null hypothesis when the null hypothesis actually is true. The value of α therefore defines the probability of making a Type I error. When the alpha level is selected for a statistical test, the risk of making a Type I error is established. With a .05 significance level, for example, the probability of wrongly rejecting a true null hypothesis is .05. Similarly, if the alpha level is established at .01, then there is only a 1 in 100 chance of making a Type I error by incorrectly rejecting the null hypothesis when it is true. The possibility of making a Type I error is particularly loathesome to most scientists; who wants to go on record saying that an independent variable has an effect when, in reality, it does not? Consequently, the value of α typically is selected to be a small value such as $\alpha = .05$ or $\alpha = .01$.

TYPE II ERRORS

The probability of a Type II error depends upon four factors: (1) the significance level selected; (2) the magnitude of the effect induced by the independent variable; (3) the amount of variability in the measure of the dependent variable; and (4) the sample size.

Significance Levels and Type II Errors

The probability of making a Type II error depends upon the significance level selected. The effect of changing the value of α is reflected in the location of the rejection region for the test statistic. As the value of α is decreased (say from .05 to .01), the critical value of the test statistic locating the rejection region is increased for t and F and most other parametric tests. Thus, as α decreases, it becomes less likely that small but real differences between population means (i.e., small but real treatment effects) will produce values of a test statistic that fall into the rejection region. Consequently, as α decreases the experimenter is less likely to accept a true alternative hypothesis and is thus more likely to make a Type II error.

This relationship is illustrated in Figure 16–1 using the theoretical sampling distribution of F for 1 and 8 degrees of freedom (given by the distribution plotted in solid lines). This sampling distribution is obtained by assuming H_0: $\mu_{A_1} = \mu_{A_2}$ is true. The distribution represented by the dashed lines is one possible sampling distribution of F that may occur when H_1 is true.[1] If this H_1 is true, then the probability of a Type II error is provided by the shaded area under the distribution. This area represents the probability of obtaining values of F that do not fall into the rejection region. The probability of making a correct decision of rejecting H_0 and accepting H_1, or the power of the test, is shown by the unshaded area of the distribution beyond the value of F_{crit}. By decreasing α from .05 (panel a) to .01 (panel b), the value of F_{crit} increases. Therefore, if H_1 is true, fewer values of F_{obs} will fall into the rejection region. Accordingly, as α decreases from .05 to .01, β increases and power decreases correspondingly.

As Figure 16–1 illustrates, there is an inverse relationship between the probability of Type I and Type II errors. If the researcher decreases α to reduce the probability of making a Type I error, then β increases; it is more likely that a Type II error will occur if H_1 is true. On the other hand, if the experimenter increases α to reduce the probability of making a Type II error, the probability of making a Type I error, if H_0 is true, increases.

Size of the Effect of the Independent Variable

The probability of making a Type II error also varies with the size, or magnitude, of the effect of the independent variable. To illustrate, we use the analysis of variance. In an analysis of variance, the effect of an independent variable increases the differences among the sample means beyond the differences expected from sampling error alone. These differ-

---

[1]There are many possible ways for H_1 to be true; hence there are many possible sampling distributions for F when H_1 is true. For each of these distributions we expect the values of F to be larger than those obtained if H_0 is true. The figure illustrates one arbitrarily selected sampling distribution for H_1.

FIGURE 16–1.

Probability of Type I and II errors as a function of the significance level. Significance levels of $\alpha = .05$ and $\alpha = .01$ are illustrated.

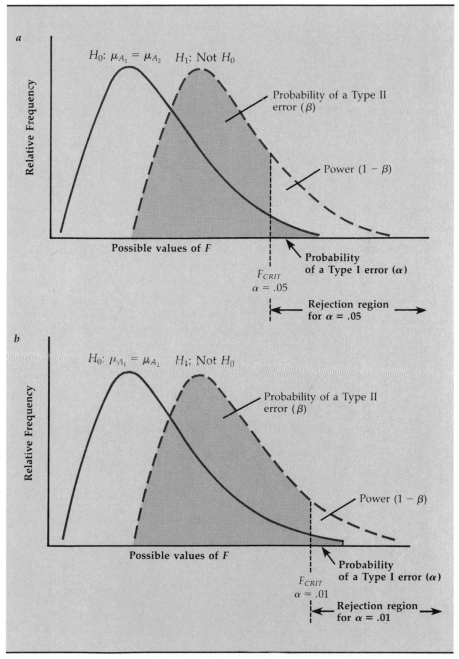

ences increase the value of MS_A, thus increasing the value of F_{obs}. For each possible treatment effect, then, there is a different but always unknown sampling distribution of F. This relation is illustrated in Figure 16–2 for the theoretical sampling distribution of F under H_0: $\mu_{A_1} = \mu_{A_2}$, and under two hypothetical instances of H_1, a smaller (panel a) and a larger (panel b) treatment effect. Similarly to Figure 16–1, the probability of a Type II error (β) is illustrated by the shaded area of the sampling distribution under H_1. The power is shown by the nonshaded area of this distribution falling beyond the value of F_{crit}. By comparing panels a and b, we note that as the treatment effect increases, β decreases (i.e., it becomes less probable that a Type II error will be made). Hence, power, $1 - \beta$, correspondingly increases. The treatment effect illustrated in panel b will more likely lead to a correct rejection of the null hypothesis and a correct acceptance of the alternative hypothesis than will the treatment effect shown in panel a.

Amount of Variability in the Dependent Variable

The probability of a Type II error also depends upon the amount of variability in the scores within treatment conditions. We demonstrate this relationship using the F statistic. The analysis of variance compares a variance varying with the effect of the independent variable (MS_A) with the error variation among scores within the treatment conditions (i.e., MS_{Error}). If F_{obs} indicates that the systematic variation is sufficiently greater than the error variation (i.e., F_{obs} falls into the rejection region), then H_0 is rejected and H_1 accepted. If a treatment has an effect, the decision about whether an observed difference between sample means is a chance occurrence or not depends not only upon the size of the treatment effect, but also upon the amount of error variation in the experiment.

Numerical Example of the Effect of Error Variation

An example of this relationship is shown in Table 16–2. Part a of the table illustrates two sets of two samples of $n_A = 5$ each. For each set, the two samples were selected from two populations whose means differed by a value of 2.0. Thus each set of scores simulates an experiment where a treatment effect is present and consequently H_1 is true. The observed difference between the sample means for both sets 1 and 2 is 3.4. Consequently, in the analysis of variance of each set (presented in part b of Table 16–1), MS_A is the same for each set ($MS_A = 28.90$). Notice, however, in set 1 the error variance is greater than in set 2. The cause of this larger error variance can been seen by comparing the standard deviations associated with set 1 ($s_{A_1} = 3.51$ and $s_{A_2} = 1.87$) to those associated with set 2 ($s_{A_1} = 1.41$ and $s_{A_2} = 1.14$). The scores in set 2 show less error variation than the scores in set 1. This difference in error variation is also reflected in the analysis of variance, where the MS_{Error} for set 1, 7.90, is nearly five

FIGURE 16–2.

Probability of Type I and II errors as a function of effect size of the independent variable. A smaller and a larger treatment effect are illustrated.

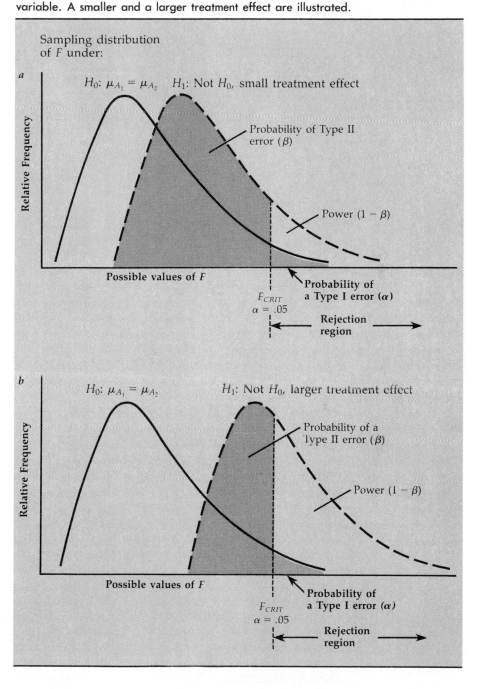

TABLE 16–2.

a. Two sets of two randomly drawn samples of size 5 each. Sample A_1 was drawn from a population with a mean $= \mu_{A_1}$. Sample A_2 was drawn from a population with a mean $= \mu_{A_1} + 2$.

	Set 1		Set 2	
	A_1	A_2	A_1	A_2
	10	17	14	18
	14	14	14	17
	14	18	12	19
	11	17	14	17
	19	19	16	16
$\overline{X}_A$	13.6	17.0	14.0	17.4
s_A	3.51	1.87	1.41	1.14

b. Analysis of variance summary tables for the two sets of scores shown in part a.

Set 1

Source	df	SS	MS	F
Factor A	1	28.90	28.90	3.66
Error	8	63.20	7.90	
Total	9	92.10		

Set 2

Source	df	SS	MS	F
Factor A	1	28.90	28.90	17.52*
Error	8	13.20	1.65	
Total	9	42.10		

*$p < .05$.

times greater than the MS_{Error} for set 2, 1.65. For $\alpha = .05$, F_{obs} for set 1, $F_{obs}(1, 8) = 3.66$, is statistically nonsignificant, whereas, F_{obs} for set 2, $F_{obs}(1, 8) = 17.52$ is statistically significant. For set 1, H_0 is not rejected, but in set 2, H_0 is rejected and H_1 accepted. The important point to notice here is that given the same observed numerical difference between the sample means $(\overline{X}_{A_2} - \overline{X}_{A_1} = 3.4)$, two different conclusions regarding the statistical hypotheses are reached. Because a treatment effect is present in the population, the decision for set 1 reflects a Type I error. The decision for set 2, however, is correct. The reason for these two differing decisions rests in the amount of error variation among the scores in each of the two sets of samples. The relevance of this example is clear. To decrease the probability of a Type II error, and to increase the power of a test, a scientist should reduce the error variation in his or her experiment to the smallest amount possible.

Reducing Error Variation

Error variation in an experiment may be diminished by: (1) controlling extraneous variables, and (2) reducing errors of measurement associated with measuring the dependent variable.

Controlling Extraneous Variables.   In Chapter 10 **extraneous variables** are defined as variables other than the independent variable in an experiment that can affect the dependent variable. They may arise from subjects' attributes such as differences in intelligence, anxiety level, sensitivity to drugs, or motivation; uncontrolled changes in the physical environment in which the experiment is being conducted; and variations in the experimental procedure from one participant to another. In Chapter 10 our concern was in preventing confounding by not allowing extraneous variables to vary along with the levels of the independent variable.

Extraneous variables also may have another effect; they may increase the error variation in an experiment if allowed to vary within a treatment condition. To illustrate, consider an experiment described in problem 7 of Testing Your Knowledge 10–1. An experimenter is investigating the effect of noise on the performance of a tracking task. The task is to keep a pointer on a spot on a rotating turntable. A subject's score is the amount of time that he or she is able to keep the pointer on the spot. Suppose that females generally are better at this task than males and will typically have longer time on target scores than males. Here gender is an extraneous variable, for the time on target score is related to gender. Consider the scores (in seconds) that might arise from a group of female subjects:

Subject	Time on Target Score
Janet	25
Kim	29
Joanna	26
Rita	23

The standard deviation for these scores is 2.5.

Consider now the scores that might arise when gender is allowed to vary within a group. Remember that males usually do not do as well on this task as females.

Subject	Time on Target Score
Janet	25
Kim	29
Leon	19
Mike	17

The s for these scores is 5.5. By assigning both males and females to the group we have increased the error variation among the scores.

The lesson is clear: Extraneous variables allowed to vary within a treatment group increase the within-groups error variation. Thus experimenters control extraneous variables not only to prevent confounding, but also to minimize error variation to increase the power of their tests.

Reducing Errors of Measurement.   Errors of measurement are due to problems that arise in measuring the dependent variable and can occur in numerous ways. It often is difficult to measure the behavior of all participants in an experiment with equal precision or accuracy. For example, recording the latency or duration of a behavior with a hand-operated stopwatch often leads to variability in scores because observers who operate the stopwatch have different reaction times to different events. Experimenters also can make perceptual errors in reading dials, meters, or instruments used in the experiment. Sometimes the criteria for identifying a response may be ambiguous or open to interpretation. In such cases, an experimenter may not be consistent in scoring the behavior from one participant to another.

Some errors of measurement may arise from within the participants themselves. Individuals may guess at answers in certain tasks, or their attention to the task they are performing may lapse momentarily. In perceptual tasks where stimuli often are presented for less than a second, even an eyeblink may lead to an erroneous response. And, if individuals are filling out a rating scale or performing some other paper-and-pencil task, they may not fully understand the instructions, or they may accidentally mark an incorrect answer. Such errors of measurement, because they usually do not occur in a systematic fashion, are often called **random errors.**

Errors of measurement often can be minimized. For example, to measure an individual's response time, instrumentation can be used that automatically starts a timer with the onset of a stimulus and stops it at the moment the individual responds either orally or manually. Where individuals' responses may be ambiguous or unclear, several raters or judges can be used to independently score such responses. Subjects should always be instructed fully on tasks they are to perform, and practice given if needed. And experimenters must be careful when recording scores.

Sample Size

Sample size also affects the probability of a Type II error. To illustrate, we return to using $\overline{X}$ to estimate μ (see Chapter 7). Recall that we can find the error associated with $\overline{X}$ as an estimate of μ from the standard error of the mean, $s_{\overline{X}}$. Recall also, that $s_{\overline{X}}$ is obtained from the value of the standard deviation, s, by

$$s_{\overline{X}} = \frac{s}{\sqrt{n_A}},$$

where n_A is the size of the sample used to obtain $\overline{X}$ and s. For a given value of s, the value of $s_{\overline{X}}$ decreases as the size of n_A increases. Suppose, for example, that we obtain a sample of $n_A = 4$ and $s = 12$. Then, $s_{\overline{X}} = 12/\sqrt{4} = 6$. If the value of $s = 12$ had been obtained from a sample of $n_A = 9$, then $s_{\overline{X}} = 12/\sqrt{9} = 4$. Had our sample size been 16 with $s = 12$, then $s_{\overline{X}} = 12/\sqrt{16} = 3$. This example demonstrates that as the size of the sample increases, the standard error of the mean decreases.

A similar relationship holds for $s_{\overline{X}_{A_1}-\overline{X}_{A_2}}$, the standard error of the difference between two means, used as the denominator of the t test for independent groups. If the two samples are of equal size, then

$$s_{\overline{X}_{A_1}-\overline{X}_{A_2}} = \sqrt{\left(\frac{s^2_{A_1}}{n_{A_1}} + \frac{s^2_{A_2}}{n_{A_2}}\right)}.$$

To illustrate the relationship of $s_{\overline{X}_{A_1}-\overline{X}_{A_2}}$ to sample size, suppose $s^2_{A_1} = 30$ and $s^2_{A_2} = 36$. Consider also that these values of s^2 arose from one of three sample sizes: $n_{A_1} = n_{A_2} = 3$, $n_{A_1} = n_{A_2} = 6$, or $n_{A_1} = n_{A_2} = 9$. Then

for $n_{A_1} = n_{A_2} = 3$,

$$s_{\overline{X}_{A_1}-\overline{X}_{A_2}} = \sqrt{\left(\frac{30}{3} + \frac{36}{3}\right)} = \sqrt{22} = 4.7,$$

for $n_{A_1} = n_{A_2} = 6$,

$$s_{\overline{X}_{A_1}-\overline{X}_{A_2}} = \sqrt{\left(\frac{30}{6} + \frac{36}{6}\right)} = \sqrt{11} = 3.3, \quad \text{and}$$

for $n_{A_1} = n_{A_2} = 9$,

$$s_{\overline{X}_{A_1}-\overline{X}_{A_2}} = \sqrt{\left(\frac{30}{9} + \frac{36}{9}\right)} = \sqrt{7.3} = 2.7.$$

Here we see that as the sample size increases, the standard error of the difference decreases. Thus for a given difference between two sample means, $\overline{X}_{A_1} - \overline{X}_{A_2}$, the value of t_{obs},

$$t_{obs} = \frac{\overline{X}_{A_1} - \overline{X}_{A_2}}{s_{\overline{X}_{A_1}-\overline{X}_{A_2}}},$$

will increase as sample size becomes larger. And, as t_{obs} increases, it becomes more likely that t_{obs} will fall into a rejection region and H_0 will be rejected and H_1 accepted.

A general principle arises here and it is that any treatment effect, no matter how small, may be detected if sample size is large enough. Using the t test as an illustration, as sample size increases, the denominator of the t, $s_{\overline{X}_{A_1} - \overline{X}_{A_2}}$, decreases in size. Regardless of the value of $\overline{X}_{A_1} - \overline{X}_{A_2}$, as sample size increases, $s_{\overline{X}_{A_1} - \overline{X}_{A_2}}$ will eventually become small enough so that t_{obs} is statistically significant. Although we will not demonstrate it here with an example, a similar relationship holds for analysis of variance. As sample size increases, MS_{Error} becomes smaller because the df_{Error}, which are divided into SS_{Error} to obtain MS_{Error}, increase.

In principle, then, any treatment effect, no matter how small, can be detected if a large enough sample is used. Thus, a researcher can minimize the probability of making a Type II error by maximizing sample size. But reality must intrude here, for increasing the size of a sample often is costly and time consuming. And, if it takes a sample of 1000 people in each group to detect the effect of an independent variable, then certainly we expect this independent variable to have a minimal effect on behavior. To make an informed decision about the sample size needed to detect a treatment of a given magnitude and to avoid making a Type II error, the experimenter must consider the power of a statistical test.

Testing Your Knowledge 16–1

On a separate sheet of paper, test your knowledge of the material in this section by answering the following questions.

1. Define: Type I error, Type II error, errors of measurement, random errors, extraneous variables, α, β, power.
2. For each of the following statements, indicate if you have made a correct decision, or if not, what type of error you made.
   a. H_0 is true and you fail to reject H_0.
   b. H_0 is true and you reject H_0.
   c. H_1 is true and you fail to reject H_0.
   d. H_1 is true and you reject H_0.
3. You have selected $\alpha = .10$ for an experiment. If H_0 is true, what is the probability of a Type I error?
4. You have selected $\alpha = .10$ for an experiment. If H_0 is true, what is the probability of correctly failing to reject H_0?
5. Explain why scientists typically select α equal to a small value such as .05 or .01.

6. Identify four factors that affect the probability of making a Type II error in a statistical test.

7. An experimenter reduces α from .05 to .01. Does this action increase or decrease β? Does this action increase or decrease the power of the statistical test?

8. Which condition, large effect size or small effect size, leads to
   a. a larger probability of a Type II error in a statistical test?
   b. a smaller value of β in a statistical test?
   c. a larger value of power in a statistical test?

9. Problem 4 of Chapter 10 Review Questions described a study to determine if sex differences exist in the need for privacy among college students. Two groups were formed, males and females, and a score obtained on the Privacy Questionnaire (Pederson, 1979). What extraneous variables, if uncontrolled, would you expect to increase error variation in this study? (Hint, year in college may be one. Why?)

10. Two sets of two samples each are obtained. For set 1, $s_{A_1} = 6.3$ and $s_{A_2} = 7.6$. For set 2, $s_{A_1} = 11.7$ and $s_{A_2} = 10.3$.
    a. Which set of scores has greater error variation?
    b. If H_1 is true, which set of scores will more likely lead to a Type II error in a statistical test?
    c. Which set of scores will lead to a more powerful statistical test?

11. Suppose you are attempting to measure anxiety level with a paper-and-pencil rating scale. What steps could you take to reduce any errors of measurement on this scale?

12. Two samples of unequal size were drawn from the same population. The $s_{\bar{x}}$ for sample 1 was 3.7, whereas, for sample 2, $s_{\bar{x}} = 6.8$. Which sample more likely had the larger n?

13. Which of the following two sample sizes would be expected to lead to a smaller value of $s_{\bar{X}_{A_1} - \bar{X}_{A_2}}$ in a t test: $n_{A_1} = n_{A_2} = 12$, or $n_{A_1} = n_{A_2} = 20$? Why?

14. Which of the following two sample sizes would be expected to lead to a smaller value of MS_{Error} in an F test: $n_{A_1} = n_{A_2} = 29$, or $n_{A_1} = n_{A_2} = 17$? Why? ▪

POWER

What Power Should We Seek?

The power of a statistical test is the probability of rejecting H_0 when H_0 is false, or equivalently, the probability of accepting H_1 when H_1 is true. Because power equals $1 - \beta$, the factors that affect β affect power also: (1) the significance level adopted; (2) the magnitude of the effect induced by the independent variable; (3) the amount of variability in the measure of the dependent variable; and (4) the sample size. A decrease in α (e.g., $\alpha = .01$ rather than .05), a weak effect of an independent variable, a great deal of error variation, or a small sample size decreases the power of a test. Conversely, increasing α (e.g., $\alpha = .05$ rather than .01), increasing the effect of the independent variable, reducing error variation, or increasing sample size increases the power of a test.

The goal in research is to assure reasonable power to detect the effect of an independent variable while maintaining a low probability of a Type I error. Scientists usually establish the upper limit for the probability of a Type I error as .05. On the other hand, values of β, the probability of a Type II error, acceptable in an experiment are not at all well defined. Cohen (1977) suggests that researchers should make the decision concerning the acceptable size of β by comparing the relative importance of a Type II to a Type I error. For example, if we select $\alpha = .05$ and are willing to accept $\beta = .30$, then $\beta/\alpha = .30/.05 = 6$ to 1. We are six times more willing to tolerate a Type II error than a Type I error. Cohen proposes that in many cases it may be reasonable to realize a β of about .20, thus suggesting that we be four times more willing to tolerate a Type II than a Type I error. Consequently, if $\beta = .20$, then power $= 1 - .20 = .80$. Hence, Cohen suggests that a power of .80 might be a reasonable goal for many instances of research. We accept and use this value of power, recognizing, however, that .80 is only a suggested value and should be ignored if an experimenter finds reason to use an alternative value.

Assume for a moment that we plan to conduct a statistical test and we wish to have power $= .80$. How do we assure that our test will have such power? As we have observed, power of a statistical test depends upon the value of α, size of the treatment effect, error variance, and sample size. The values of α and sample size are directly under the experimenter's control. Error variance can be minimized by controlling extraneous variables. But, what of treatment effect size? An experimenter cannot be sure if an independent variable has an effect and if it does have an effect, what is the extent of the effect. In fact, if the experimenter did know the effect of the independent variable, then there would be no need to conduct the experiment in the first place. We seem at an impasse for finding the power of our statistical test for we do not know the size of the treatment effect. Fortunately, however, there is a way out of this difficulty.

One resolution to this problem is to state the power that we wish to have to be able to detect a specified treatment-effect size. That is, we decide on a certain minimum treatment effect that we wish to detect with a certain power. By specifying the treatment effect and power, then the sample size can be selected to provide the power desired. The only question remaining is how should we specify treatment-effect size?

Treatment-Effect Size for an Independent Variable with Two Levels

A specification of **treatment-effect size,** or **effect size,** must be applicable to any experiment. Consequently, the measure must be free of the particular units of measurement in any experiment. For an experiment involving two levels of an independent variable, and thus statistically analyzable by the t test, Cohen (1977) suggests a measure called d:

$$d = \frac{|\mu_{A_1} - \mu_{A_2}|}{\sigma},$$

where μ_{A_1} and μ_{A_2} represent the population means estimated by the two sample means of the experiment, and σ represents the standard deviation of each population (i.e., $\sigma_{A_1} = \sigma_{A_2} = \sigma$). Notice that an effect of an independent variable corresponds to changing the value of a population mean. Notice, also, that d describes effect size in terms of how many standard deviations the population means differ. For example, suppose $\mu_{A_1} = 20$, $\mu_{A_2} = 25$, and $\sigma = 5$. Then

$$d = \frac{|20 - 25|}{5} = 1.0.$$

The effect size is 1.0; the two population means differ by one standard deviation. As a second example, suppose $\mu_{A_1} = 80$, $\mu_{A_2} = 87$, and $\sigma = 7$. Then

$$d = \frac{|80 - 87|}{7} = 1.0.$$

The effect size in this case is also 1.0. Thus, two experiments in which an effect size of 1.0 (i.e., $d = 1.0$) occurred would, at least in one sense, be equivalent in the effect of the independent variable; the independent variable changed a population mean by one standard deviation.

To help researchers select an effect size that they wish to detect in an experiment, Cohen proposes that $d = 0.2$ be considered a small effect size, $d = 0.5$ be considered a medium effect size, and $d = 0.8$ be considered a large effect size.[2] A visual representation of these effect sizes, as well as an effect size of $d = 0$, is presented in Figure 16–3. This figure illustrates the difference in population means for two normal distributions with $\sigma_{A_1} = \sigma_{A_2} = \sigma$ for each effect size in terms of a standard deviation. To use d as a measure of effect size we do not have to know μ_{A_1}, μ_{A_2}, or σ. We need to decide what effect size we would like to detect in an experiment or judge what effect size the independent variable may have.

[2]These effect sizes are simply suggestions. Sechrest and Yeaton (1982) discuss other suggested effect sizes.

FIGURE 16–3.

Illustration of effect size of $d = 0$, $d = 0.2$, $d = 0.5$, and $d = 0.8$ for two normal distributions.

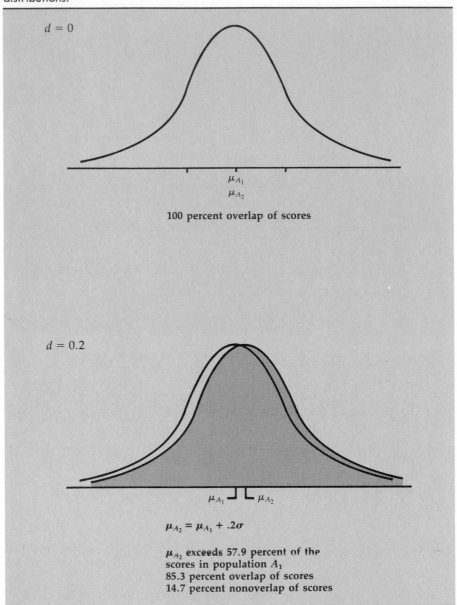

$d = 0$

μ_{A_1}
μ_{A_2}

100 percent overlap of scores

$d = 0.2$

μ_{A_1} μ_{A_2}

$\mu_{A_2} = \mu_{A_1} + .2\sigma$

μ_{A_2} exceeds 57.9 percent of the scores in population A_1
85.3 percent overlap of scores
14.7 percent nonoverlap of scores

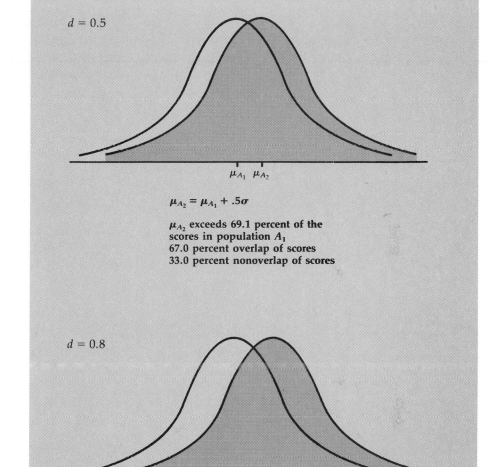

$d = 0.5$

μ_{A_1} μ_{A_2}

$\mu_{A_2} = \mu_{A_1} + .5\sigma$

**μ_{A_2} exceeds 69.1 percent of the
scores in population A_1
67.0 percent overlap of scores
33.0 percent nonoverlap of scores**

$d = 0.8$

μ_{A_1} μ_{A_2}

$\mu_{A_2} = \mu_{A_1} + .8\sigma$

**μ_{A_2} exceeds 78.8 percent of the
scores in population A_1
52.6 percent overlap of scores
47.4 percent nonoverlap of scores**

Achieving the Desired Power Value in an Experiment

We now have all the pieces necessary to design an experiment with two levels of an independent variable to achieve a certain power in the statistical test: α, n_A, and the effect size we wish to detect. The relationship between power, n_A, and effect size is presented in Table A–5 for $\alpha = .05$. A portion of Table A–5 is reproduced in Table 16–3 for n_A up to 25. Tables A–5 and 16–3 present approximate power values for a t test as a function of sample size (n_A) and effect size in terms of d for $\alpha = .05$. The table may be used several ways:

- To find the power of a t test at the .05 significance level for a given value of n_A and d, or
- To find the n_A needed to achieve a certain power for a given value of d at the .05 significance level.

TABLE 16–3.

Approximate power of the t test for $\mu_{A_1} = \mu_{A_2}$ at $\alpha = .05$ for a two-tailed test. n_A is the size of each group and d is the effect size.

	d		
n_A	0.20	0.50	0.80
6	0.06	0.14	0.28
7	0.07	0.16	0.32
8	0.07	0.17	0.36
9	0.07	0.18	0.40
10	0.07	0.20	0.44
11	0.08	0.21	0.47
12	0.08	0.23	0.50
13	0.08	0.25	0.52
14	0.08	0.27	0.57
15	0.08	0.28	0.59
16	0.09	0.29	0.61
17	0.09	0.30	0.64
18	0.09	0.32	0.67
19	0.09	0.34	0.69
20	0.10	0.35	0.72
21	0.10	0.37	0.74
22	0.10	0.38	0.75
23	0.11	0.40	0.77
24	**0.11**	0.41	0.78
25	0.11	0.43	0.81

The example below illustrates both uses of these tables.

Using a Power Table: Finding Power Given n_A and d

Suppose you are designing an experiment to test the effect of an advertising message on a consumer's attitude toward a new toothpaste. You expect the effect size to be small; thus you expect a d of about 0.20. You have two treatment conditions: no message and message; and 24 people in each group. What is the power of your test at $\alpha = .05$?

To find the power of the test you enter Table 16–3 in the column headed by $d = 0.20$ and the row labeled $n_A = 24$. The number given where this column and row intersect is the power of your test. This value is 0.11 (boldfaced in Table 16–3); thus the power of your test, the probability of rejecting a false H_0, is approximately 0.11. In other words, the probability of detecting the effect of the message is 0.11, a very low value. It is likely that you would consider this value to be unacceptably low for your experiment.

Using a Power Table: Finding n_A Given Power and d

Suppose you wished to increase the power of your test to the 0.80 level suggested by Cohen. Given that you expect a small effect size, the only factor that you can change to increase power is n_A, the sample size. To determine n_{A_1} for $\alpha = .05$, $d = 0.2$, and power = 0.80, enter Table A–5 in the column headed by $d = 0.20$. The values in the column are values of power. Read down the column until you encounter power = 0.80 or the value nearest to 0.80. In our example the value nearest to 0.80 is a power of 0.81. Reading across the row with power = 0.81 to the column labeled n_A provides the n_A necessary to obtain this power; $n_A = 400$. Thus you must have 400 subjects in each of your groups, or a total of 800 subjects to obtain power of about 0.80.

Anyone practiced in research recognizes that a sample size of 400 individuals per group is an exceedingly large sample. Will it be worthwhile for you to conduct this experiment? We cannot answer the question of the value of the experiment to you. If, for instance, the experiment were being sponsored by a toothpaste company, and if an advertising message that had even a small effect could have large financial consequences for the company, then you may decide to proceed with the experiment utilizing 800 participants.

On the other hand, suppose you are planning the experiment to determine what factors affect the effectiveness of an advertising message but have no specific product that you are trying to sell. Now you may decide that you do not have the resources to conduct the experiment with sufficient participants to assure a power of 0.80. One resolution would be to alter the manipulation of your independent variable so that effect size may be increased. Suppose you could increase the anticipated effect size of your independent variable to 0.50. What sample size would now be needed to have power of 0.80 at $\alpha = .05$? Entering Table A–5 in the column headed by $d = 0.50$, read down the column until you find power = 0.80. You find that the n_A required for this power is 65. Thus, with a medium effect size the n_A necessary to obtain power equal to about 0.80 at $\alpha = .05$ is 65 individuals per group, or a total of 130 for the experiment.

Power and Analysis of Variance

The approach to power analysis for the analysis of variance is analogous to that for the t test. Indeed, for the instance where two levels of an independent variable are manipulated and $t_{obs} = \sqrt{F_{obs}}$, the power of the F test is identical to that of the t. Thus, the power of analysis of variance for this instance may be obtained by using Table A–5. Where three or more levels of an independent variable are manipulated, d, because it involves only two population means (μ_{A_1} and μ_{A_2}) cannot be used as a measure of effect size. A different measure of effect size, f, which involves all the population means, then is employed.

Power tables for the analysis of variance for values of f are extensive, however, for power depends upon α, n_A, f, and the number of levels of the independent variable. Thus, we do not present power tables for the F statistic in this text.[3] You may gain some idea of the power of the analysis of variance, however, by choosing the most important pairwise comparison in the analysis and finding the power of this comparison using Table A–5. Although the approach does not provide the power of the overall analysis of variance, it does provide an idea of the power of the most important comparison to be made.

Statistics in Use 16–1

Power in Published Research Studies

Power analysis is a useful tool for designing an experiment so that the effect of an independent variable can be detected when it is present. When reading behavioral sciences research, however, you will notice that researchers rarely report whether or not they conducted a power analysis in order to determine the size of the sample used. The issue is of no concern when the test statistic was statistically significant and the effect of the independent

---

[3]The interested reader may consult Cohen (1977, pages 289–354) for these tables.

variable detected. In this instance, the statistical test was sufficiently powerful to detect the treatment effect. But, when no effect of the independent variable is detected a power analysis becomes important to deciding whether the independent variable has no effect, or if the statistical test was not sufficiently powerful to detect an effect. To illustrate, we do a power analysis on a study where no difference was found between levels of the independent variable.

Several studies have found differences in perceptual sensitivities between males and females. An unanswered question, however, is whether males and females differ in their ability to estimate line length? To answer this question, Verrillo (1982) compared 26 males to 26 females on a line length estimation task. A t test comparing the mean line length estimated by males and females was nonsignificant. How sure can we be that there are no sex differences in line length estimation? To answer this question, we may do a power analysis of the statistical test used in this study. If we set $\alpha = .05$, then we find the following power levels from Table A–5 for $n_A = 26$ and three possible levels of a sex difference: small, medium, and large:

Effect Size	Small ($d = .20$)	Medium ($d = .50$)	Large ($d = .80$)
Power	.11	.42	.83

From this analysis, only for a large effect size does the power of this test reach the .80 level suggested by Cohen (1977). We can be quite sure that a difference between males and females on line length estimation with an effect size of $d = 0.80$ (i.e., males and females differ by $.8\sigma$) does not exist. We can be less sure, however, that smaller differences do not exist. If a difference between males and females equal to d of 0.20 does exist, this study had about a one-in-ten chance of detecting the difference. ■

Testing Your Knowledge 16–2

On a separate sheet of paper, test your knowledge of the material in this section by answering the following questions.

1. What factors affect the power of a statistical test?
2. Write the equation for the measure of effect size, d.
3. If $d = 0.7$, then two populations that are normal and possess equal standard deviations differ by how many standard deviations?

4. Identify the values of d suggested by Cohen to reflect a small, medium, and large effect size.

5. Find the approximate power of the t test for independent groups at the .05 significance level for the following values of n_A for each group and d.

	n_A	d
a.	10	0.80
b.	45	0.80
c.	11	0.50
d.	80	0.50
e.	14	0.20
f.	29	0.20

6. Find the n_A required for each group of a t test for independent groups to achieve the power indicated for the effect size, d, at the .05 significance level.

	Power	d
a.	0.60	0.80
b.	0.75	0.50
c.	0.50	0.50
d.	0.60	0.20
e.	0.99	0.80
f.	0.99	0.50
g.	0.75	0.20

7. An experimenter reports a nonsignificant t_{obs} for independent groups, $t(18) = 1.23$, $p > .05$.
   a. What is the power of this test for an effect size of $d = .50$?
   b. Suppose the experimenter argued that the independent variable does not affect behavior. How would you respond to this conclusion? Your answer should be in terms of power to detect certain effect sizes. ◼

MEASURING THE STRENGTH OF A TREATMENT EFFECT

Our discussion has involved estimating a potential effect size (i.e., d) for an experiment and then using this estimated effect size to: (1) determine the power of the t test (or the F when only two treatment conditions are being compared) for a given n_A, α, and d; or (2) to find the value of n_A necessary to achieve a certain power at a given value of α and d. We turn now to measuring the effect size after the experiment has been completed.

Eta Squared

A number of statistical measures have been developed for quantifying the strength of effect of an independent variable after an experiment has been completed. These statistics often are referred to as **strength of association measures, magnitude of effect measures,** or **utility indices.** The statistic we discuss is called **eta squared** and represented by η^2, where η is the lower-case Greek letter for *eta.* Eta squared may be calculated from either the t test or the analysis of variance.

Calculation of Eta Squared for the t Test
From the t test, η^2 is obtained from the t_{obs} value and degrees of freedom for t by

$$\eta^2 = \frac{t^2_{obs}}{t^2_{obs} + df}.$$

Example of Calculating η^2 for the t Test for Independent Groups.   In Example Problem 10–1 of Chapter 10 we calculated the t test for two independent groups using two groups of children suffering from Kawasaki syndrome and who had been given different treatments — either aspirin alone or aspirin plus gamma globulin. The t test was done on the mean body temperatures of the two groups. This t_{obs} for the difference in body temperature was 6.069 with 166 df. The t_{obs} is statistically significant at the .05 level. Eta squared for this t_{obs} then equals:

$$\eta^2 = \frac{t^2_{obs}}{t^2_{obs} + df},$$

$$\eta^2 = \frac{(6.069)^2}{(6.069)^2 + 166},$$

$$\eta^2 = \frac{36.833}{202.833} = 0.182.$$

Calculation of Eta Squared for the Analysis of Variance

For the analysis of variance η^2 may be obtained from several alternative formulas. If sums of squares values are known, η^2 is given by

$$\eta^2 = \frac{SS_A}{SS_A + SS_{Error}}.$$

For a one-factor between-subjects analysis of variance, SS_A plus SS_{Error} equals SS_{Total}; thus η^2 may be expressed in this case as

$$\eta^2 = \frac{SS_A}{SS_{Total}}.$$

Where only the F_{obs} and the df are known for a one-factor between-subjects analysis of variance, η^2 can be obtained by

$$\eta^2 = \frac{df_A(F_{obs})}{df_A(F_{obs}) + df_{Error}}.$$

Example of Calculating η^2 for the One-Factor Between-Subjects Analysis of Variance.   Example Problem 11–1 employed the analysis of variance to determine if the extent of the Morinaga misalignment illusion depends upon the type of stimulus presented—either angled points or partial circles. An analysis of variance summary table on the example scores from this problem is presented in Table 16–4. Eta squared may be calculated either from the SS values or the F_{obs} and df values of this table.

TABLE 16–4.

Analysis of variance summary for the effect of type of stimulus on the amount of illusion perceived in the Morinaga misalignment illusion. See Example Problem 11–1 for details of the experiment.

Source	df	SS	MS	F
Type of stimulus	1	0.2832	0.2832	24.84*
Error	18	0.2055	0.0114	
Total	19	0.4887		

*$p < .05$

η^2 *from SS values*

$$\eta^2 = \frac{SS_A}{SS_A + SS_{Error}}.$$

$$\eta^2 = \frac{0.2832}{0.2832 + 0.2055}$$

$$\eta^2 = 0.58.$$

η^2 *from F_{obs} and df values*

$$\eta^2 = \frac{df_A(F_{obs})}{df_A(F_{obs}) + df_{Error}},$$

$$\eta^2 = \frac{1(24.84)}{1(24.84) + 18},$$

$$\eta^2 = 0.58.$$

Interpreting η^2

Eta squared provides two complimentary types of information: (1) η^2 may be converted to a value of d, the effect size in the experiment; and (2) η^2 indicates the proportion of the total variation in the dependent variable that is systematic variation and can be accounted for by the independent variable.

η^2 as a Value of d for a Test of Two Independent Means

In our discussion of power we used d to estimate effect size where

$$d = \frac{|\mu_{A_1} - \mu_{A_2}|}{\sigma}.$$

The value of η^2 for a t test or an analysis of variance employing two levels of an independent variable may be converted to d by using Table 16–5. To use this table to convert η^2 to d, enter the η^2 column, find the value of η^2 obtained in your experiment, and read the equivalent d. For example, suppose you obtained a value of $\eta^2 = 0.06$. The value of d for this η^2 is 0.505; approximately a medium effect size. As another example, an η^2 of 0.14 is equivalent to an effect size of $d = 0.807$, a large effect size. For

TABLE 16–5.

Eta squared to d equivalencies for selected values of η^2 and d.

η^2	d	η^2	d
.00	.000	.15	.840
.01	.201	.16	.873
.02	.286	.17	.905
.03	.352	.18	.937
.04	.408	.19	.969
.05	.459	.20	1.000
.06	.505	.25	1.155
.07	.549	.30	1.309
.08	.590	.40	1.633
.09	.629	.50	2.000
.10	.667	.60	2.449
.11	.703	.70	3.055
.12	.739	.80	4.000
.13	.773	.90	6.000
.14	.807		

Values of η^2 were calculated using the relation $d = (2\sqrt{\eta^2})/(\sqrt{1 - \eta^2})$ by the author.

values of η^2 larger than 0.20 we present values only for $\eta^2 = 0.25$, 0.30, and then to a value of 0.90 in 0.10 increments.

η^2 as a Proportion of Variation Accounted For

Eta squared also provides an index of the total amount of variation in the dependent variable that is in common with the independent variable. Consider the total amount of observed variation in the dependent variable to be 1.00. Then η^2 indicates what proportion of that variation can be variance accounted for by the independent variable. In a true experiment in which an active independent variable is manipulated, the value of η^2 reveals what proportion of the total variation of the dependent variable is due to the effect of the independent variable. In an ex post facto study employing an attribute independent variable, η^2 reveals what proportion of the total variation the attribute independent variable and the dependent variable have in common.

Interpreting η^2 as the proportion of variation in the dependent variable accounted for by the independent variable, or in common with the independent variable, is not conceptualized easily, however. Suppose you manipulate an independent variable, find a statistically significant t_{obs} and obtain $\eta^2 = 0.06$. Is 6 percent a small, medium, or large amount of the total variance in the dependent variable to account for? In comparison to a maximum 100 percent to be accounted for, 6 percent appears small. What percentage of the variance in the dependent variable can one realistically expect to account for by an independent variable?

Accounting for 100 percent of the variance in an experiment is an impossible goal. In all instances, some of the variance in a dependent measure is due to errors of measurement and to uncontrolled extraneous variables. Because errors of measurement typically do not occur in any systematic fashion in an experiment, it is unlikely that they can be eliminated entirely. Further, all extraneous variables cannot be controlled in any experiment, and we can be sure that individuals will always differ from each other on any dependent variable measured. Consequently, there will always be error variance in an experiment, and an investigator will have to settle for accounting for less than 100 percent of the total variance.

Interpreting η^2 in terms of Cohen's suggestions for small, medium, and large d values helps us understand η^2. From Table 16–5 a small d of .2 is about equivalent to $\eta^2 = 0.01$, a medium d of 0.5 is equivalent to $\eta^2 = 0.06$, and a large d of 0.8 is about equivalent to $\eta^2 = 0.14$. In these terms, $\eta^2 = 0.01$, an effect accounting for about 1 percent of the variance, represents a small effect size, $\eta^2 = 0.06$, an effect accounting for about 6 percent of the variance, a medium effect size, and $\eta^2 = 0.15$, an effect accounting for about 15 percent of the variance, a large effect size.

These suggested interpretations of η^2 find support in published behavioral science research. For example, Haase, Waechter, and Solomon (1982) calculated η^2 on 11,044 tests of statistical significance reported in issues of the *Journal of Counseling Psychology* published between 1970 to 1979. They found a median η^2 value of 0.083, equivalent to a d of about 0.60, somewhat larger than a medium effect size. The interquartile range for the η^2 values was 0.043 to 0.268. Linton and Gallo (1975) report a similar study they conducted "on most of the published studies in American Psychological Association journals for the year 1964" (p. 330). They found strength of association values of less than 0.05 for over 50 percent of the published studies. This result gives some idea of the typical strength of association found in current behavioral science research, and provides a basis for evaluating the magnitude of an effect from a value of η^2.

Example Problem 16–1
Calculating η^2 in an experiment

Problem:
Does a counselor's response to a client affect the client's perception of the expertness of the counselor? To find an answer to this question,

McCarthy and Betz (1978) formed two equivalent groups of female college undergraduates. One group ($n_{A_1} = 54$) listened to an audio tape of a simulated counseling session in which a counselor responded to a client in a self-disclosing fashion (i.e., the counselor revealed a similar personal experience). The second group ($n_{A_2} = 53$) heard a simulated counseling session in which a counselor responded to a client in a self-involving manner (i.e., the counselor indicated a positive feeling or reaction to the client). At the end of the counseling session, the participants in each group rated the expertness of the counselor on a scale that could range from 12 (very inexpert) to 84 (very expert). The mean expertness ratings and standard deviations obtained were:

Type of Counselor Response to Client

	Self-Disclosing	*Self-Involving*
$\overline{X}_A$	63.1	68.5
s_A	14.6	11.1

The value of t_{obs} for the scores was $t_{obs}(105) = -2.172$. This t_{obs} is statistically significant at the .05 level for a two-tailed test. Thus, McCarthy and Betz rejected H_0: $\mu_{A_1} = \mu_{A_2}$ and accepted H_1: not H_0. Accordingly, they concluded that their independent variable of type of counselor response affected the expertness ratings of the counselor — self-involving responses of a counselor lead to greater perceived expertness scores than do self-disclosing responses.

An analysis of variance on the expertness scores is summarized below. Because the t and F tests are identical when only two levels of an independent variable are manipulated, the analysis of variance leads to the same conclusions as does the t test. We present the analysis of variance here only so that we can calculate η^2 from both the t and the F tests on the same data.

Source	df	SS	MS	F
Counselor response	1	790.21	790.21	4.69*
Error	105	17700.95	168.58	
Total	106	18491.16		

*$p < .05$

Find the value of η^2 for this experiment using the formulas for the t test and for the analysis of variance.

Solution:

Computation of η^2 using t_{obs}.

$$\eta^2 = \frac{t_{obs}^2}{t_{obs}^2 + df}$$

$$\eta^2 = \frac{(2.172)^2}{(2.172)^2 + 105} = 0.04 .$$

Solution:

Computation of η^2 using SS from the analysis of variance.

$$\eta^2 = \frac{SS_A}{SS_A + SS_{Error}}$$

$$\eta^2 = \frac{790.21}{790.21 + 17700.95} = 0.04 .$$

Solution:

Computation of η^2 using df and F_{obs} from the analysis of variance.

$$\eta^2 = \frac{df_A(F_{obs})}{df_A(F_{obs}) + df_{Error}}$$

$$\eta^2 = \frac{1(4.69)}{1(4.69) + 105} = 0.04 .$$

Conclusion:

Based on the value of $\eta^2 = 0.04$, 4 percent of the total variation of the dependent variable may be accounted for by the effect of the independent variable in this experiment. Because McCarthy and Betz's study was a true experiment, it is appropriate to state that the independent variable is responsible for 4 percent of the variance in the dependent variable. The d equivalent for $\eta^2 = 0.04$ is 0.408, the two sample means differ by about 0.4 of a within-groups standard deviation, somewhat less than a medium effect size. ▪

Statistics in Use 16–2

Cognitive Gender Differences: Measuring Strength of Effect

Men and women think differently. Of course! We all know this simple fact, but how differently? Hyde (1981) reviewed a large number of empirical studies on gender differences in various cognitive skills and abilities. For those studies that reported a difference between males and females on verbal ability, she found a typical effect size of $d = 0.24$ with females demonstrating greater verbal ability. This value of d indicates that male and female verbal ability scores typically differ by about one fourth of a standard deviation. An equivalent η^2 is about 0.015. The difference between males and females on verbal skills may be considered a small effect size. What of quantitative ability? For this ability, Hyde found a typical effect size of $d = 0.43$, with males showing the greater ability; the difference between males and females being about 0.4σ. The equivalent η^2 is about 0.044. The difference between males and females on quantitative ability is somewhat less than a medium effect size. ▪

Testing Your Knowledge 16–3

On a separate sheet of paper, test your knowledge of the material in this section by answering the following questions.

1. Find the value of η^2 for each of the following values of t. The df for each t are presented in parentheses. Each t is statistically significant at the .05 level with a two-tailed test.
   a. $t(8) = 2.413$
   b. $t(14) = 2.284$
   c. $t(20) = 2.174$
   d. $t(29) = 2.939$
   e. $t(60) = 2.306$

2. Find the value of η^2 for each of the following values of SS_A and SS_{Error} from an analysis of variance.

	SS_A	SS_{Error}
a.	13.94	46.21
b.	1,009.26	10,929.87
c.	693.70	11,416.08
d.	274.53	8,624.13
e.	117.37	927.61

3. Find the value of η^2 for each of the following values of F. The df for each F are presented in parentheses. Each F is statistically significant at the .05 level.
   a. $F(1, 14) = 4.93$
   b. $F(1, 26) = 4.78$
   c. $F(2, 18) = 4.04$
   d. $F(3, 28) = 3.35$
   e. $F(4, 55) = 5.24$

4. Assume the following values of η^2 were obtained from a t test for two independent groups. Find the value of d equivalent to η^2.

	η^2
a.	.11
b.	.04
c.	.06
d.	.17
e.	.50

SUMMARY

- A Type I error occurs if the null hypothesis is rejected when it is actually true.
- A Type II error occurs if we fail to reject H_0 when the alternative hypothesis (H_1) is true.
- The probability of a Type I error is given by α.
- The probability of a Type II error is given by β.
- The power of a statistical test is the probability of rejecting H_0 when H_0 is false, and H_1 is true; this probability is $1 - \beta$.
- Factors affecting power include the significance level adopted, the magnitude of the effect induced by the independent variable, the amount of variability in the measure of the dependent variable, and sample size.

- A measure of effect size is given by

$$d = \frac{|\mu_{A_1} - \mu_{A_2}|}{\sigma}$$

- $d = 0.2$ is a small effect size, $d = 0.5$ is a medium effect size, and $d = 0.8$ is a large effect size.
- Eta squared (η^2) is a measure of the strength of association and may be calculated from either the t test or the analysis of variance.
- Eta squared provides two complimentary types of information: (1) η^2 may be converted to a value of d, the effect size in the experiment; and (2) η^2 indicates the proportion of the total variation in the dependent variable that is systematic variation and can be accounted for by the independent variable.

KEY TERMS

alpha	eta squared	strength of association
α	η^2	treatment-effect size
beta	extraneous variables	Type I error
β	magnitude of effect measures	Type II error
d	$1 - \beta$	utility indices
effect size	power	variance accounted for
errors of measurement	random errors	

REVIEW QUESTIONS

On a separate sheet of paper, test your knowledge of the material in this chapter by answering the following questions.

1. An experimenter reported that in an experiment, a t test for independent groups indicated that participants correctly detected a larger percentage of targets while listening to the familiar passage than while listening to the unfamiliar passage, $t(60) = 3.62$, $p < .05$.
   a. What is the value of η^2 for this experiment?
   b. Convert the value of η^2 into a value of d.
   c. How would you describe the effect size for this experiment: small, medium, or large?

2. A researcher provided the following report of the outcome of an experiment.

   A t test for independent groups revealed no difference in the number of words recalled after an interval of 5 minutes ($\overline{X} = 22.78$) and an interval of 0.5 minutes ($\overline{X} = 24.33$), $t(28) = 0.80$, $p > .10$.

   What is the power of this test with $\alpha = .05$ for
   a. a small effect size ($d = 0.20$)?
   b. a medium effect size ($d = 0.50$)?
   c. a large effect size ($d = 0.80$)?

3. An experimenter found a statistically significant difference at the .05 level between two groups. She concluded that the manipulated independent variable affected behavior. A second researcher argued that this was an incorrect conclusion because the power of her test to detect a medium effect size was only 0.40. Is the second researcher's argument correct or incorrect? Explain your answer.

4. You are interested in finding whether a drug has an effect upon behavior. You plan to have two treatment groups, one group a placebo control, the other a drug treatment group. You will analyze the scores with a one-factor between-subjects analysis of variance. Based upon this information, answer the following questions. Use $\alpha = .05$ for each question.
   a. You expect the drug to have an effect size of approximately $d = 0.50$. You would like to achieve a power of about 0.80. How many subjects will you need for each treatment condition?
   b. You expect the drug to have an effect size of approximately $d = 0.80$. You will have 20 subjects in each group. What will be the power of your test?

c. You have available 25 subjects for each group and you want to realize a power of 0.80. What must the effect size of the drug be to reach this power?

d. The effect size of the drug is $d = 0.20$. You have 15 subjects in each group. What is the probability that a Type II error will occur in your statistical test?

e. The effect size of the drug is $d = 0.00$. You have 54 subjects in each group. What is the probability that a Type I error will occur in your statistical test?

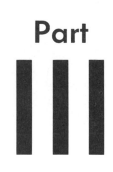

Part

III

Correlation
and
Regression

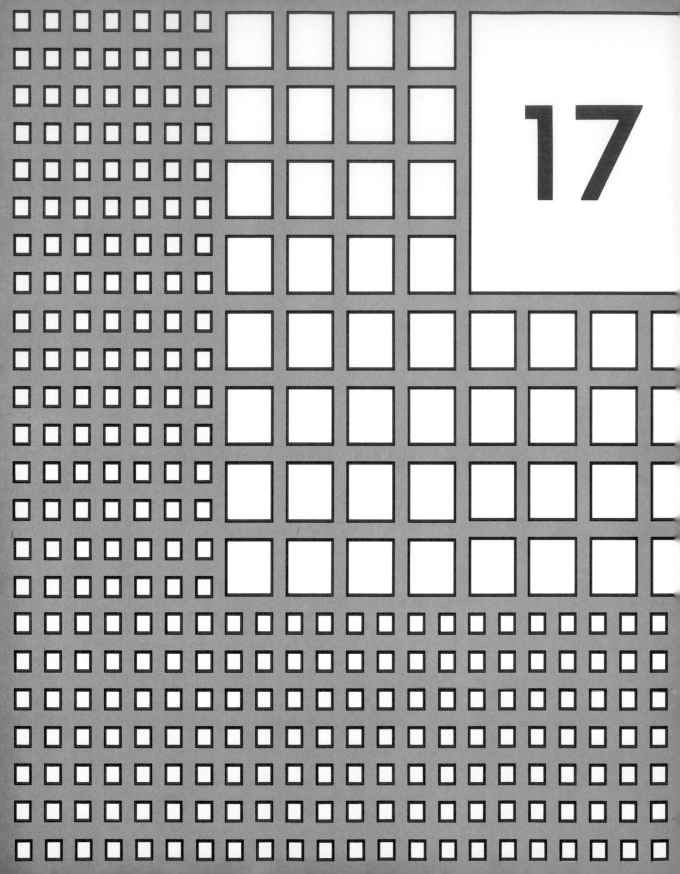

17

Correlation

OVERVIEW: CORRELATIONAL STUDIES

In many research studies, two different scores will be obtained from the individuals in a group. The scientist's interest is to find if the scores are related to each other. As an example, in Chapter 1 we discussed a study that obtained both loneliness and depression scores on a group of college undergraduates (Ouellet & Joshi, 1986). Each student thus provided two scores: a loneliness score and a depression score. A statistical analysis of these scores indicated that these characteristics are related; lonely people also tend to be depressed. In this chapter we introduce concepts of correlation needed to understand such research and a statistic called the **correlation coefficient.** Using the correlated scores to predict one score from another is introduced in Chapter 18.

Two variables that are related, or that vary together, such as loneliness and depression, are said to be *correlated.* Accordingly, **correlational studies** are attempts to find the extent to which two or more variables are related. Typically, in a correlational study, no variables are manipulated as in an experiment—the investigator measures naturally occurring events, behaviors, or personality characteristics and then attempts to determine if the measured scores covary.

The simplest instance of a correlational study involves obtaining a pair of observations or measures on two different variables from a number of individuals. The paired measures then are statistically analyzed to determine if any relationship exists between them. As examples, behavioral scientists have explored such areas as the relationship between anxiety level and self-esteem, attendance at classes in college and course grades, avocational interests and career success, scholastic aptitude and academic performance, and body weight and self-esteem.

PERSONALITY AND BELIEF IN EXTRAORDINARY PHENOMENA: AN EXAMPLE CORRELATIONAL STUDY

Are certain personality characteristics related to possessing a belief in extraordinary phenomena such as reincarnation, witchcraft, astrology, and extrasensory perception? To answer this question, Windholz and Diamant (1974) had 297 college students complete a *Scale of Belief in Extraordinary Phenomena* (SOBEP) questionnaire and the *reflectivity* scale of the Thorndike Dimensions of Temperament personality inventory (Thorndike, 1966). Reflective individuals are characterized by an interest in ideas and knowledge for its own sake rather than for immediate application. Thus, for each person two scores were obtained, one a score on belief in extraordinary phenomena and the other a score on reflectivity.

TABLE 17–1.

Hypothetical scores for 10 people on the reflectivity scale of the *Thorndike Dimensions of Temperament* (Thorndike, 1966) and on the *Scale of Belief in Extraordinary Phenomena.*

Person	Reflectivity Score (X_i)	SOBEP (Y_i)
1	9	3
2	10	2
3	16	4
4	5	1
5	9	4
6	7	1
7	5	3
8	11	5
9	1	2
10	17	5

Windholz and Diamant then examined the paired scores to see if belief in extraordinary phenomena is correlated with reflectivity.

Suppose the reflectivity scores (designated variable X) and the SOBEP scores (designated variable Y) obtained for ten individuals are those presented in Table 17–1. In this example, higher scores indicate greater reflectivity or a greater belief in extraordinary phenomena. The Scores in Table 17–1 represent a **bivariate distribution of scores.** The prefix *bi* means two; thus these scores are bivariate in that two scores are obtained from each person. The designation of reflectivity scores as X and SOBEP scores as Y is entirely arbitrary. We could reverse the designations and call the reflectivity scores Y and the SOBEP scores X if desired.

Are these scores related? Perhaps higher SOBEP scores are associated with higher reflectivity scores and lower SOBEP scores related to lower scores on reflectivity? Or perhaps the relationship is the inverse: Higher SOBEP scores are associated with lower reflectivity scores and lower scores on the SOBEP related to higher scores on reflectivity. It is also possible that the scores do not covary. We will answer this question first with a visual examination of a scatterplot of the scores. Then we will calculate a Pearson product-moment correlation coefficient on the scores.

SCATTERPLOTS

One way to gain a visual impression of the relationship is to construct a scatterplot of the scores as we have done in Figure 17–1. In a **scatterplot** (sometimes called a **scattergram**), one of the two measures (typically the

FIGURE 17–1.

Scatterplot of *reflectivity* scores and *Scale of Belief in Extraordinary Phenomena* (SOBEP) scores for 10 participants. The numbers next to the plotted scores identify the individuals.

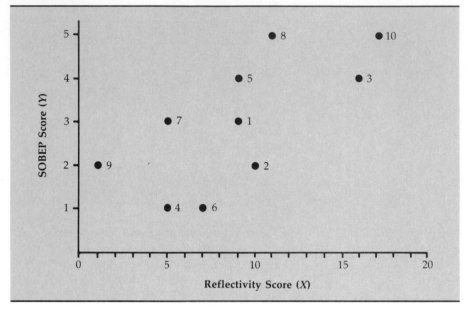

variable labeled X) is represented on the horizontal axis (the abscissa) and the other measure (the Y variable) is plotted on the vertical axis (the ordinate). The score of an individual on each of the two measures then is depicted by one point on the scatterplot. For example, in Figure 17–1, the scores for person 1 are plotted at the point within the figure that intersects a value of 9 on the reflectivity score and 3 on the SOBEP scale. To illustrate how the scatterplot was constructed, we have identified each individual by placing the number of the person from Table 17–1 next to the point that represents his or her scores on both measures. Typically only the scores are plotted with a dot; participants are not identified by name or number on a scatterplot. The scatterplot in Figure 7–1 is a bivariate distribution, for it illustrates the joint distribution of two paired variables, X and Y.

Positive Relationships

The scatterplot indicates that there is a relationship between SOBEP and reflectivity scores. Generally, higher SOBEP scores appear to be associated with higher reflectivity scores and lower SOBEP scores appear to be related to lower reflectivity scores. Accordingly, the relationship among the scores is positive. In a **positive relationship** (also identified as a **direct relationship**), as the value of one variable increases, so does the value of the other variable. Thus, in Figure 17–1, as the reflectivity scores increase, the SOBEP scores tend also to increase. Because both variables are measured, and not manipulated, it is equally appropriate to state that as the SOBEP scores increase, the reflectivity scores tend to increase also. In Figure 17–1 the positive relationship is not perfect. Person 6, for example, has a higher reflectivity score than person 4, but both have a SOBEP score of 1. Similarly, individuals 1 and 5 have reflectivity scores of 9, but SOBEP scores of 3 and 4, respectively.

A perfect positive relationship between SOBEP and reflectivity scores is illustrated in Figure 17–2. In this instance the plot of the scores results in a straight line. Relationships between two variables that can be described by a straight line are called **linear relationships**. In a perfect positive relationship, such as that illustrated in Figure 17–2, knowing the value of one score permits us to know or predict perfectly the score on the second variable. For example, a person who obtained a reflectivity score of 9 scored 3 on the SOBEP measurement. Or, a person who scored 4 on the SOBEP obtained a 12 on reflectivity. There is no error in predicting one score from the other in a perfect relationship. Perfect positive

FIGURE 17–2.

A perfect positive relationship between reflectivity scores and Scale of Belief in Extraordinary Phenomena (SOBEP) scores.

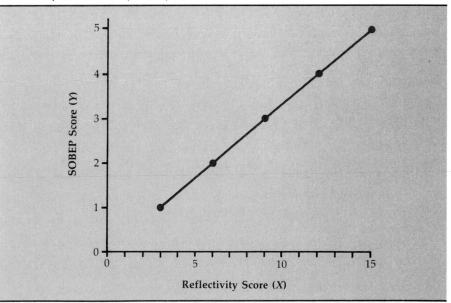

relationships seldom, if ever, occur between scores obtained in actual research, however.

Negative Relationships

Suppose the relationship obtained between the reflectivity and SOBEP scores was that shown in Figure 17–3. This figure illustrates a negative relationship between the two variables. In a **negative relationship,** as the value of one variable increases, the value on the second variable decreases. From Figure 17–3 you can see that low scores on reflectivity tend to be associated with high SOBEP scores and high reflectivity scores are associated with low SOBEP scores. Negative relationships are sometimes identified as **inverse relationships,** for the variables are oppositely related—low values on X to high values on Y, and high values on X to low values on Y.

The negative relationship illustrated in Figure 17–3 is not a perfect relationship between reflectivity and SOBEP scores. For example, two individuals have SOBEP scores of 3, but one has a reflectivity score of 7, the other a reflectivity score of 11. Similarly, two individuals have reflectivity scores of 9, but SOBEP scores of 4 and 2, respectively.

FIGURE 17–3.

A negative relationship between reflectivity scores and Scale of Belief in Extraordinary Phenomena (SOBEP) scores for ten individuals.

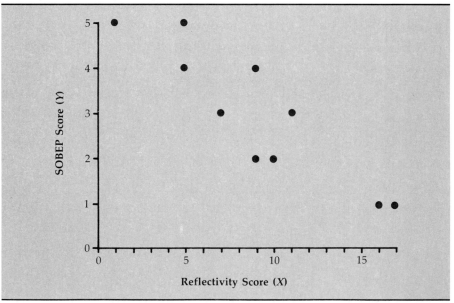

FIGURE 17–4.

A perfect negative relationship between reflectivity scores and Scale of Belief in Extraordinary Phenomena (SOBEP) scores.

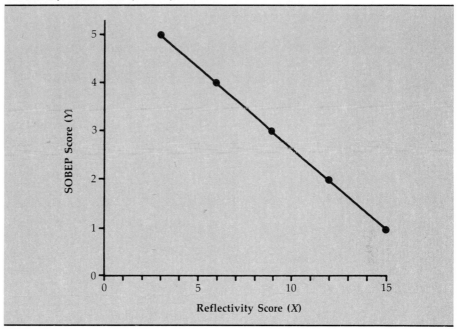

A perfect negative relationship between SOBEP and reflectivity scores is illustrated in Figure 17–4. In this instance the plot of the scores again creates a straight line. As with the perfect positive relationship, if two variables are perfectly negatively (or inversely) related, knowledge of one score permits us to predict perfectly the other score. For example, from the scores illustrated in Figure 17–4, if we know that a person obtained a 5 on the SOBEP, we also know that his or her reflectivity score was a 3. Similarly, if we know a person obtained a reflectivity score of 12, then his or her SOBEP score was 2. As with perfect positive relationships, perfect negative relationships rarely occur with actual scores.

Which Is More Useful, a Positive or a Negative Relationship?

Be careful not to attribute more meaning to the direction of the relationship than it represents. A positive relationship between variables is not better in any way than a negative relationship. The positive or negative sign merely indicates the direction, not the strength, of a relationship. For predicting one score from knowledge of another, positive and negative relationships are equally useful.

Testing Your Knowledge 17–1

On a separate sheet of paper, test your knowledge of the material in this section by answering the following questions.

1. Define: correlational approach, covary, scatterplot, bivariate distribution of scores, positive relationship, direct relationship, linear relationship, negative relationship, inverse relationship.
2. Plot a scatterplot of the following scores on a sheet of graph paper.

Person	Loneliness	Depression
1	21	32
2	36	45
3	44	50
4	38	49
5	52	60
6	45	56
7	29	34
8	29	37
9	66	75
10	70	82

   a. Does the relationship between the scores appear to be positive or negative, or is there no relationship between the scores?
   b. Is the relationship between the scores perfect or less than perfect?
   c. If you knew only the loneliness score of a person, would you be able to accurately predict the depression score for that person?
3. Plot a scatterplot of the following scores on a sheet of graph paper.

Person	Loneliness	Depression
1	21	81
2	36	56
3	44	50
4	38	56
5	52	49
6	45	37
7	29	75
8	29	60
9	66	34
10	70	32

   a. Does the relationship between the scores appear to be positive or negative, or is there no relationship between the scores?
   b. Is the relationship between the scores perfect or less than perfect?

    c. If you knew only the depression score of a person, would you be able to accurately predict the loneliness score for that person?

4. Plot a scatterplot of the following scores on a sheet of graph paper.

Person	Body Weight	Self-Esteem
1	100	39
2	111	47
3	117	54
4	124	23
5	136	35
6	139	30
7	143	48
8	151	20
9	155	28
10	164	46

    a. Does the relationship between the scores appear to be positive or negative, or is there no relationship between the scores?

    b. Is the relationship between the scores perfect or less than perfect?

    c. If you knew only the body weight of a person, would you be able to accurately predict the self-esteem score for that person? ◼

THE PEARSON PRODUCT-MOMENT CORRELATION COEFFICIENT

An inspection of a scatterplot can give an impression of whether two variables are related and the direction of their relationship. But it alone is not sufficient to determine whether there is an association between two variables. The relationship depicted in the scatterplot needs to be described quantitatively. Descriptive statistics that express the degree of relation between two variables are called *correlation coefficients*. A commonly employed correlation coefficient for scores at the interval or ratio level of measurement is the **Pearson product-moment correlation coefficient**, symbolized as r_{xy}. The Pearson correlation coefficient is defined as

$$r_{XY} = \frac{\sum_{i=1}^{N}(X_i - \overline{X})(Y_i - \overline{Y})}{\sqrt{\left[\sum_{i=1}^{N}(X_i - \overline{X})^2\right]\left[\sum_{i=1}^{N}(Y_i - \overline{Y})^2\right]}}.$$

In this formula, X_i is the score of a person on the X variable, $\overline{X}$ is the mean of all N scores on the X variable, Y_i is the score of a person on the Y variable, and $\overline{Y}$ is the mean of all N scores on the Y variable.

This formula may also be written as

$$r_{XY} = \frac{CP_{XY}}{\sqrt{(SS_X)(SS_Y)}},$$

where CP_{XY} represents $\sum_{i=1}^{N}(X_i - \overline{X})(Y_i - \overline{Y})$, the cross products of X and Y, SS_X is the sum of squares for the X scores [i.e., $\sum_{i=1}^{N}(X_i - \overline{X})^2$], and SS_Y is the sum of squares of the Y scores [i.e., $\sum_{i=1}^{N}(Y_i - \overline{Y})^2$]. We illustrate the derivation of these equivalent formulas in the next section.

Obtaining a Measure of Covariation: Cross Products

To see how these formulas provide a measure of covariation of two variables, return to the scores of Table 17–1. The scatterplot of these scores indicated that the scores tended to be positively related—low scores on the SOBEP are related to low reflectivity scores and high scores on the SOBEP are related to high reflectivity scores. Consider how we might develop a statistic that indicates whether two variables covary. As an index of whether a score (e.g., X_i) is high or low on a variable, we could subtract the mean of the scores on the variable (i.e., $\overline{X}$) from the particular score. For example, the mean of the reflectivity scores in Table 17–1 is 9. Person 3 obtained a reflectivity score of 16, well above the mean. We could index this performance by finding $X_3 - \overline{X}$, or $16 - 9 = +7$. Person 3 thus obtained a reflectivity score 7 points above the mean of the reflectivity scores. Similarly, person 9 obtained a reflectivity score of 1, well below the mean. This person's reflectivity score could also be expressed as $X_9 - \overline{X}$; in this case, $1 - 9 = -8$, or 8 points below the mean reflectivity score. Thus, converting a score into a deviation from the mean of the scores indicates both whether the score is above or below the mean and how far below or above it is.

Of course, the Y scores could be indexed similarly with respect to their mean, $\overline{Y}$. For example, the mean of the SOBEP scores is 3. Person 3 obtained a SOBEP score of 4. Converting this score to a deviation from the mean, we obtain $Y_3 - \overline{Y} = 4 - 3 = +1$. On the other hand, person 9 obtained a SOBEP score of 2. Expressed as a deviation from the mean, this score is $Y_9 - \overline{Y} = 2 - 3 = -1$, or 1 point below the mean SOBEP score.

From the conversions of scores to deviations from the mean, we see that person 3 was above the mean on both the reflectivity and SOBEP scores, whereas person 9 was below the mean on both scores. Suppose now that we obtain such deviation scores for all the individuals measured. We have done so in columns c and e, respectively, of Table 17–2.

A measure of how much the scores covary over all the scores can now be found. We obtain this measure by multiplying each person's deviation

TABLE 17–2.
Calculation of the cross products of X and Y. Scores in column b are the reflectivity scores of Table 17–1 and scores in column d are the SOBEP scores of Table 17–1.

	Reflectivity (X)		SOBEP (Y)		
(a)	(b)	(c)	(d)	(e)	(f)
Person	X_i	$X_i - \overline{X}$	Y_i	$Y_i - \overline{Y}$	$(X_i - \overline{X})(Y_i - \overline{Y})$
1	9	0	3	0	0
2	10	+1	2	−1	−1
3	16	+7	4	+1	+7
4	5	−4	1	−2	+8
5	9	0	4	+1	0
6	7	−2	1	−2	+4
7	5	−4	3	0	0
8	11	+2	5	+2	+4
9	1	−8	2	−1	+8
10	17	+8	5	+2	+16
	$\overline{X}$ 9		$\overline{Y}$ 3		Sum +46

from the mean on the X variable by his or her deviation from the mean on the Y variable and then summing the product of each multiplication over all the individuals measured. We illustrate the multiplication for each person's scores in column f of Table 17–2. For example, for person 4, $(X_i - \overline{X})(Y_i - \overline{Y}) = (-4)(-2) = +8$. The sum of the products in this column is +46.

The $\sum_{i=1}^{N}(X_i - \overline{X})(Y_i - \overline{Y})$ is called the **cross products of X and Y** and is symbolized as CP_{XY}. This term forms the numerator of the formula for r_{XY}. The cross products of X and Y will take on a large positive value if X and Y are positively linearly related, a large negative value if X and Y are negatively linearly related, and a value closer to zero if X and Y are not linearly related. Table 17–2 illustrates the large positive value of CP_{XY} when X and Y are positively related. The value of the CP_{XY} for a negative relationship of X and Y is illustrated in Table 17–3a. These are the scores used to illustrate the negative relationship in Figure 17–3. The CP_{XY} is −59 for these scores.

The CP_{XY} for no relationship of X and Y are presented in Table 17–3b. Figure 17–5 portrays a scatterplot of these scores. Notice from this scatterplot that the X and Y scores do not covary—high scores on X are not consistently related to either high or low scores on Y. Similarly, low scores on X are not consistently related to either high or low scores on Y. The $CP_{XY} = -4$ calculated in Table 17–3 corresponds to this lack of relationship.

We have seen that the CP_{XY} will reflect the amount and direction of a relationship between two sets of scores. If the scores are positively related, the cross products will take on a positive value; the more strongly the X and Y scores covary, the larger the CP_{XY} becomes. For negatively related scores, the CP_{XY} will be negative and will become larger as the negative relationship becomes stronger. When the X and Y values are not related, however, the CP_{XY} will be closer to zero. Clearly, then, the CP_{XY} indicates both the direction and strength of relationship of two sets of scores.

TABLE 17–3.

a. Illustration of the cross products of X and Y for a negative relationship between reflectivity and SOBEP scores.

	Reflectivity (X)		SOBEP (Y)		
Person	X_i	$X_i - \overline{X}$	Y_i	$Y_i - \overline{Y}$	$(X_i - \overline{X})(Y_i - \overline{Y})$
1	9	0	4	+1	0
2	10	+1	2	−1	−1
3	16	+7	1	−2	−14
4	5	−4	5	+2	−8
5	9	0	2	−1	0
6	7	−2	3	0	0
7	5	−4	4	+1	−4
8	11	+2	3	0	0
9	1	−8	5	+2	−16
10	17	+8	1	−2	−16
	$\overline{X}$ 9.0		$\overline{Y}$ 3.0		**Sum** −59

b. Illustration of the cross products of X and Y for no relationship between reflectivity and SOBEP scores.

	Reflectivity (X)		SOBEP (Y)		
Person	X_i	$X_i - \overline{X}$	Y_i	$Y_i - \overline{Y}$	$(X_i - \overline{X})(Y_i - \overline{Y})$
1	9	0	1	−2	0
2	10	+1	3	0	0
3	16	+7	5	+2	+14
4	5	−4	4	+1	−4
5	9	0	4	+1	0
6	7	−2	2	−1	+2
7	5	−4	5	+2	−8
8	11	+2	3	0	0
9	1	−8	2	−1	+8
10	17	+8	1	−2	−16
	$\overline{X}$ 9.0		$\overline{Y}$ 3.0		**Sum** −4

FIGURE 17–5.

No relationship between reflectivity scores and Scale of Belief in Extraordinary Phenomena (SOBEP) scores for ten individuals. The scores are from Table 17–3b.

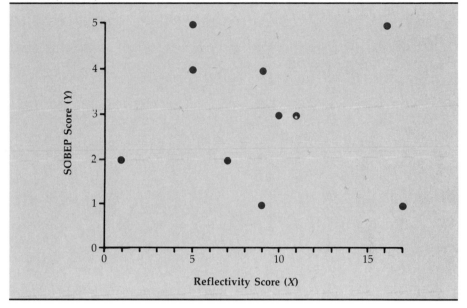

r_{XY}: Comparing the CP_{XY} with a Measure of the Total Variation in Scores

We encounter one difficulty with interpreting the CP_{XY}. The value of the CP_{XY} depends upon the units of measurement of X and Y. To illustrate, suppose the possible SOBEP scores of Table 17–1 were not on a 1 to 5 scale, but a 10 to 50 scale. Table 17–4 presents this possibility. This table was constructed simply by multiplying each SOBEP score of Table 17–1 by 10. The CP_{XY} for Table 17–4 is +460, considerably larger than the CP_{XY} of Table 17–2, $CP_{XY} = +46$. Yet the relationship between X and Y is identical in the two tables. Thus, how do we know if a value of CP_{XY} is to be considered large or small? Clearly, to be useful as a measure of the covariation of X and Y, CP_{XY} must be put into a form that will take on a common range of values regardless of the unit in which the scores are measured and of the number of individuals measured.

One way to make the cross products take on a common range of values is to compare the CP_{XY} to a measure of the total variation in each set of scores. One measure of variation that we have commonly used is the sum of squares (SS). For scores identified as the X variable, $SS_X = \sum_{i=1}^{N}(X_i - \overline{X})^2$ and for the scores identified as the Y variable, $SS_Y = \sum_{i=1}^{N}(Y_i - \overline{Y})^2$. To put the SS into the same units as the cross products, we

TABLE 17–4.

Calculation of CP_{XY} on scores of Table 17–1. The SOBEP scores now range from 10 to 50 rather than 1 to 5 as in Table 17–1.

Person	Reflectivity (X)		SOBEP (Y)		
	X_i	$X_i - \overline{X}$	Y_i	$Y_i - \overline{Y}$	$(X_i - \overline{X})(Y_i - \overline{Y})$
1	9	0	30	0	0
2	10	+1	20	−10	−10
3	16	+7	40	+10	+70
4	5	−4	10	−20	+80
5	9	0	40	+10	0
6	7	−2	10	−20	+40
7	5	−4	30	0	0
8	11	+2	50	+20	+40
9	1	−8	20	−10	+80
10	17	+8	50	+20	+160
	$\overline{X}$ 9.0		$\overline{Y}$ 30.0		**Sum** +460

take the square root of each SS. Then, by multiplying $\sqrt{SS_X}$ by $\sqrt{SS_Y}$, we obtain a measure of the total variation in the two sets of scores, $\sqrt{(SS_X)(SS_Y)}$. We then form a ratio of the CP_{XY} to this measure of the total variation. This ratio is the Pearson product-moment correlation coefficient, r_{XY}. Accordingly, we see that the two formulas for r_{XY},

$$r_{XY} = \frac{\sum_{i=1}^{N}(X_i - \overline{X})(Y_i - \overline{Y})}{\sqrt{\left[\sum_{i=1}^{N}(X_i - \overline{X})^2\right]\left[\sum_{i=1}^{N}(Y_i - \overline{Y})^2\right]}}$$

and

$$r_{XY} = \frac{CP_{XY}}{\sqrt{(SS_X)(SS_Y)}},$$

use identical numerical values to obtain r_{XY}.

Notice that because the terms in the denominator of the formula for r_{XY} involve squared deviations, the denominator always takes on positive values. Thus, the sign of the correlation coefficient, either positive (+) or negative (−), is determined by the sign of the numerator. The computation of r_{XY} on the 10 scores in Table 17–1 using the definitional formula is illustrated in Table 17–5. This table illustrates obtaining SS_X (column d), SS_Y (Column g), and CP_{XY} (Column h) and then substituting them into the formula for r_{XY} to obtain a numerical value of $r_{XY\,obs} = +0.70$ for the scores of Table 17–1.

The definitional formula of r_{XY} permits us to see how r_{XY} measures the covariation between two sets of scores. Because it involves finding deviations of scores from their mean, however, it is easy to make numerical errors with this formula. Accordingly, simplified computational formulas have been developed. We introduce one such formula in a later section.

TABLE 17–5.

Calculation of Pearson r on reflectivity and SOBEP scores of Table 17–1 using the definitional formula of r_{XY}.

Step 1. Finding $SS_X = \sum_{i=1}^{N}(X_i - \overline{X})^2$, $SS_Y = \sum_{i=1}^{N}(Y_i - \overline{Y})^2$, $CP_{XY} = \sum_{i=1}^{N}(X_i - \overline{X})(Y_i - \overline{Y})$:

| | Reflectivity (X) | | | SOBEP (Y) | | | |
| (a) | (b) | (c) | (d) | (e) | (f) | (g) | (h) |
Person	X_i	$X_i - \overline{X}$	$(X_i - \overline{X})^2$	Y_i	$Y_i - \overline{Y}$	$(Y_i - \overline{Y})^2$	$(X_i - \overline{X})(Y_i - \overline{Y})$
1	9	0	0	3	0	0	0
2	10	+1	1	2	−1	1	−1
3	16	+7	49	4	+1	1	+7
4	5	−4	16	1	−2	4	+8
5	9	0	0	4	+1	1	0
6	7	−2	4	1	−2	4	+4
7	5	−4	16	3	0	0	0
8	11	+2	4	5	+2	4	+4
9	1	−8	64	2	−1	1	+8
10	17	+8	64	5	+2	4	+16
	$\overline{X}$ 9.0		SS_X 218	$\overline{Y}$ 3.0		SS_Y 20	CP_{XY} +46

Step 2. Calculating r_{XY}:

$$\sum_{i=1}^{N}(X_i - \overline{X})^2 = SS_X = 218$$

$$\sum_{i=1}^{N}(Y_i - \overline{Y})^2 = SS_Y = 20$$

$$\sum_{i=1}^{N}(X_i - \overline{X})(Y_i - \overline{Y}) = CP_{XY} = +46, \text{ and}$$

$$r_{XY} = \sum_{i=1}^{N}(X_i - \overline{X})(Y_i - \overline{Y}) \Big/ \sqrt{\left[\sum_{i=1}^{N}(X_i - \overline{X})^2\right]\left[\sum_{i=1}^{N}(Y_i - \overline{Y})^2\right]}, \text{ or}$$

$$r_{XY} = CP_{XY}/\sqrt{(SS_X)(SS_Y)}.$$

Substituting numerical values,

$$r_{XY} = +46/\sqrt{(218)(20)}$$

$$r_{XY} = +46/\sqrt{4360}$$

$$r_{XY} = +46/66.03$$

$$r_{XY} = +0.70.$$

Interpreting the Pearson *r*

The Pearson *r* is a statistic that reveals both the direction and the degree of linear relationship between two variables. The direction of the relationship is indicated by the positive or negative sign of the correlation coefficient. The degree to which the points on the scatterplot lie on a straight line is given by the absolute value of *r*, a value that may vary from .00 to 1.00. Combining the sign (+ or −) with the numerical values of *r* allows *r* to vary from −1.00 through 0.00 to +1.00.

Direction of Relationship

The correlation coefficient gains its sign from the sign of the CP_{XY}. A positive CP_{XY}, and thus a positive correlation coefficient, means that there is a direct relationship between the two variables; as the scores on one variable increase, the scores on the other variable do also. The scores in Table 17–1 illustrate a positive relationship, $r_{XY\,obs} = +0.70$.

A negative CP_{XY}, and thus a negative r_{XY}, indicates an inverse relationship between the variables; as scores increase on one variable they tend to decrease on the other variable. A negative relation is illustrated by the scores in Table 17–3*a*. Here, $r_{XY\,obs} = -0.89$.

Degree of Relationship

The numerical value of the correlation coefficient indicates how well the relationship between the two variables is described by a straight line. An *r* of 1.00 means that the relationship is perfectly linear; all points in the scatterplot lie in a straight line. Figure 17–2 portrayed a scatterplot showing a perfect positive correlation, $r_{XY\,obs} = +1.00$, for reflectivity and SOBEP scores. A perfect negative correlation, $r_{XY\,obs} = -1.00$, for the scores is illustrated in Figure 17–4. When *r* achieves a value of 1.00, for every value of one score there is one, and only one, corresponding value of the other score.

We can easily demonstrate that r_{XY} cannot take on a value greater than +1.00 or less than −1.00 by computing r_{XY} for two perfectly related sets of scores. Table 17–6*a* presents the hypothetical reflectivity and SOBEP scores that were used to plot Figure 17–2 and illustrates the computation of r_{XY} on these scores. Notice that CP_{XY} is equal to $\sqrt{(SS_X)(SS_Y)}$ for these scores; thus $r_{XY\,obs} = +1.00$. Table 17–6*b* presents similar scores used to plot Figure 17–4. These scores, however, are perfectly negatively related. Here CP_{XY} is negative in value, but its absolute value ($|-60| = 60$) is equal to $\sqrt{(SS_X)(SS_Y)}$. Accordingly, $r_{XY\,obs} = -1.00$ in this instance. Whenever two sets of scores are perfectly linearly related, the absolute value of CP_{XY} (i.e., $|CP_{XY}|$) will be equal to $\sqrt{(SS_X)(SS_Y)}$; thus the numerical limit for r_{XY} is 1.00.

At the other extreme, if the variables are unrelated, then the value of the correlation coefficient approaches zero. When r_{XY} is about zero, a value of one score is not systematically associated with a value of the other score. Such an instance is shown in Figure 17–5, which presents a scatterplot of the reflectivity and SOBEP scores of Table 17–3*b*.

Values of the correlation coefficient between 0.00 and 1.00 indicate that there is some, but not a perfect, relationship among the variables. Figure 17–6 presents several scatterplots exhibiting different values of r_{XY}. It is often difficult to visualize what an $r_{XY\,obs} = +0.73$ might look like if the scores were placed on a scatterplot. This ability is gained only by comparing values of r_{XY} to a scatterplot of the scores that produced the correlation. Therefore, we suggest that you examine carefully the scatterplots presented in Figure 17–6 and relate the value of r_{XY} to the scores in each figure.

We emphasize that the Pearson r is a measure of the linear or straight-line relationship between two variables. If the relationship between two variables cannot be represented by a straight line (i.e., it is curvilinear), as illustrated in Figure 17–6*f*, then r should not be used.

FIGURE 17–6.

Scatterplots illustrating various correlations between scores on variable X and variable Y for 10 scores. The value of the Pearson correlation coefficient between the sets of scores is given by r_{XY}.

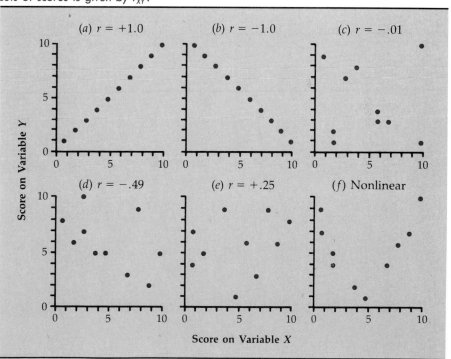

TABLE 17–6.

a. Calculation of Pearson r on perfectly positively related reflectivity and SOBEP scores portrayed in Figure 17–2.

Step 1. Finding $SS_X = \sum_{i=1}^{N} (X_i - \overline{X})^2$, $SS_Y = \sum_{i=1}^{N} (Y_i - \overline{Y})^2$, $CP_{XY} = \sum_{i=1}^{N} (X_i - \overline{X})(Y_i - \overline{Y})$:

		Reflectivity (X)			SOBEP (Y)			
(a)	(b)	(c)	(d)	(e)	(f)	(g)		(h)
Person	X_i	$X_i - \overline{X}$	$(X_i - \overline{X})^2$	Y_i	$Y_i - \overline{Y}$	$(Y_i - \overline{Y})^2$		$(X_i - \overline{X})(Y_i - \overline{Y})$
1	9	0	0	3	0	0		0
2	6	−3	9	2	−1	1		+3
3	15	+6	36	5	+2	4		+12
4	12	+3	9	4	+1	1		+3
5	3	−6	36	1	−2	4		+12
6	6	−3	9	2	−1	1		+3
7	15	+6	36	5	+2	4		+12
8	3	−6	36	1	−2	4		+12
9	9	0	0	3	0	0		0
10	12	+3	9	4	+1	1		+ 3
	$\overline{X}$ 9.0		SS_X 180	$\overline{Y}$ 3.0		SS_Y 20		CP_{XY} +60

Step 2. Calculating r_{XY}:

$SS_X = 180$ Substituting numerical values,

$SS_Y = 20$ $r_{XY} = +60/\sqrt{(180)(20)}$

$CP_{XY} = +60$, and $r_{XY} = +60/\sqrt{3600}$

$r_{XY} = CP_{XY}/\sqrt{(SS_X)(SS_Y)}$. $r_{XY} = +60/60 = +1.00$.

Testing Your Knowledge 17–2

On a separate sheet of paper, test your knowledge of the material in this section by answering the following questions.

1. Define: cross product, CP_{XY}, SS_X, SS_Y.
2. Write the formula for the cross products of two sets of scores.
3. Explain why the cross products provide a measure of the covariation of two sets of scores.
4. We indicated that the value of CP_{XY} will depend upon the units of measurement of the X and Y scores obtained. The value of CP_{XY} also will depend upon the number of sets of scores obtained. Explain this relation.
5. Write the formula for r_{XY} using the definitional formula.
6. Write the formula for r_{XY} using the cross-products and sum of squares notation.

b. Calculation of Pearson r on perfectly negatively related reflectivity and SOBEP scores portrayed in Figure 17–4.

Step 1. Finding $SS_X = \sum_{i=1}^{N}(X_i - \overline{X})^2$, $SS_Y = \sum_{i=1}^{N}(Y_i - \overline{Y})^2$, $CP_{XY} = \sum_{i=1}^{N}(X_i - \overline{X})(Y_i - \overline{Y})$:

		Reflectivity (X)			SOBEP (Y)		
(a)	(b)	(c)	(d)	(e)	(f)	(g)	(h)
Person	X_i	$X_i - \overline{X}$	$(X_i - \overline{X})^2$	Y_i	$Y_i - \overline{Y}$	$(Y_i - \overline{Y})^2$	$(X_i - \overline{X})(Y_i - \overline{Y})$
1	9	0	0	3	0	0	0
2	6	−3	9	4	+1	1	−3
3	15	+6	36	1	−2	4	−12
4	12	+3	9	2	−1	1	−3
5	3	−6	36	5	+2	4	−12
6	6	−3	9	4	+1	1	−3
7	15	+6	36	1	−2	4	−12
8	3	−6	36	5	+2	4	−12
9	9	0	0	3	0	0	0
10	12	+3	9	2	−1	1	− 3
$\overline{X}$ 9.0			SS_X 180	$\overline{Y}$ 3.0		SS_Y 20	CP_{XY} +60

Step 2. Calculating r_{XY}:

$SS_X = 180$

$SS_Y = 20$

$CP_{XY} = -60$, and

$r_{XY} = CP_{XY}/\sqrt{(SS_X)(SS_Y)}$.

Substituting numerical values,

$r_{XY} = -60/\sqrt{(180)(20)}$

$r_{XY} = -60\sqrt{3600}$

$r_{XY} = -60/60 = -1.00$.

7. Given the following scores:

Person	Loneliness	Depression
1	21	32
2	36	45
3	44	50
4	38	49
5	52	60
6	45	56
7	29	34
8	29	37
9	66	75
10	70	82

a. What is the value of CP_{XY} for this set of scores?

b. Does this value of CP_{XY} indicate that the scores are positively, negatively, or not related?

c. Find SS_X and SS_Y for these scores.

d. What is the value of $r_{XY\,obs}$ for these scores?

f. The scores for this question were drawn from Testing Your Knowledge 17–1, Question 2. Compare r_{XY} to the scatterplot of the scores constructed for that question. Use this comparison to visualize the relationship a value of r_{XY} describes.

8. Given the following scores:

Person	Loneliness	Depression
1	21	81
2	36	56
3	44	50
4	38	56
5	52	49
6	45	37
7	29	75
8	29	60
9	66	34
10	70	32

a. What is the value of CP_{XY} for this set of scores?

b. Does this value of CP_{XY} indicate that the scores are positively, negatively, or not related?

c. Find SS_X and SS_Y for these scores.

d. What is the value of $r_{XY\,obs}$ for these scores?

f. The scores for this question were drawn from Testing Your Knowledge 17–1, Question 3. Compare r_{XY} to the scatterplot of the scores constructed for that question. Use this comparison to visualize the relationship a value of r_{XY} describes.

9. Given the following scores:

Person	Body Weight	Self-Esteem
1	100	39
2	111	47
3	117	54
4	124	23
5	136	35
6	139	30
7	143	48
8	151	20
9	155	28
10	164	46

a. What is the value of CP_{XY} for this set of scores?

b. Does this value of CP_{XY} indicate that the scores are positively, negatively, or not related?

c. Find SS_X and SS_Y for these scores.
d. What is the value of $r_{XY obs}$ for these scores?
f. The scores for this question were drawn from Testing Your Knowledge 17–1, Question 4. Compare r_{XY} to the scatterplot of the scores constructed for that question. Use this comparison to visualize the relationship a value of r_{XY} describes. ■

ALTERNATIVE FORMULAS FOR THE PEARSON CORRELATION

The formula that we used to introduce and define the Pearson correlation,

$$r_{XY} = \frac{\sum_{i=1}^{N}(X_i - \overline{X})(Y_i - \overline{Y})}{\sqrt{\left[\sum_{i=1}^{N}(X_i - \overline{X})^2\right]\left[\sum_{i=1}^{N}(Y_i - \overline{Y})^2\right]}},$$

may be expressed in several alternative ways,

Finding r_{XY} from Standard Scores

The formula for r_{XY} may be rewritten separating the denominator into its two separate sums of squares as follows:

$$r_{XY} = \frac{\sum_{i=1}^{N}(X_i - \overline{X})(Y_i - \overline{Y})}{\sqrt{\sum_{i=1}^{N}(X_i - \overline{X})^2}\sqrt{\sum_{i=1}^{N}(Y_i - \overline{Y})^2}},$$

or

$$r_{XY} = \frac{\sum_{i=1}^{N}(X_i - \overline{X})(Y_i - \overline{Y})}{\sqrt{(SS_X)}\sqrt{(SS_Y)}}.$$

Notice that $(X_i - \overline{X})/\sqrt{(SS_X)}$ appears similar to a standard score, $z = (X_i - \overline{X})/S$, introduced in Chapter 6. All that is needed to make this expression a standard score is to divide the SS_X by N, the number of scores entering into SS_X, to obtain S_X, the standard deviation of the X scores. A similar argument follows for $(Y_i - \overline{Y})/\sqrt{(S_Y)}$. Accordingly, r_{XY} also may be found from standard scores by

$$r_{XY} = \frac{\sum_{i=1}^{N}(z_X z_Y)}{N},$$

where

$$z_X = \frac{(X_i - \overline{X})}{S_X},$$

$$z_Y = \frac{(Y_i - \overline{Y})}{S_Y},$$

and N is the number of paired scores. The standard deviation for the X scores, S_X, is found by

$$S_X = \sqrt{\frac{\sum_{i=1}^{N}(X_i - \overline{X})^2}{N}}$$

and S_Y, the standard deviation for the Y scores, by

$$S_Y = \sqrt{\frac{\sum_{i=1}^{N}(Y_i - \overline{Y})^2}{N}}.$$

Table 17–7 illustrates the use of this formula for finding r_{XY} on the scores of Table 17–1. The first step is to obtain S_X and S_Y needed to find the z scores. The values of $\sum(X_i - \overline{X})^2 = 218$ and $\sum(Y_i - \overline{Y})^2 = 20$ in this step were obtained from Table 17–5. From these calculations we find that to convert X_i scores into standard scores, $z_X = (X_i - 9)/4.669$. Similarly, for the Y_i scores, $z_Y = (Y_i - 3)/1.414$.

The second step is to convert each raw score into a standard score using the z conversions found in step 1. Column b of Table 17–7 presents the X_i. Column c presents the $X_i - \overline{X}$ deviations for each person and column d the z score equivalent of the $X_i - \overline{X}$ deviation. Similarly, column e presents the Y_i. Column f presents the $Y_i - \overline{Y}$ deviations for each person and column g the z score equivalent of the $Y_i - \overline{Y}$ deviation. The z_X and z_Y scores of each person are multiplied in column h and the sum of this column, +6.964, provides the value of $\sum(z_X z_Y)$ needed for the numerator of the formula for r_{XY}.

TABLE 17–7.

Calculation of r_{XY} using a standard score formula. The reflectivity (X_i) and SOBEP (Y_i) scores employed are those presented in Table 17–1.

Step 1. Obtaining S_X and S_Y:

$$S_X = \sqrt{\frac{\sum\limits_{i=1}^{N}(X_i - \overline{X})^2}{10}}$$

$$S_Y = \sqrt{\frac{\sum\limits_{i=1}^{N}(Y_i - \overline{Y})^2}{10}}$$

From Table 17–5,

From Table 17–5,

$$\sum_{i=1}^{N}(X_i - \overline{X})^2 = 218$$

$$\sum_{i=1}^{N}(Y_i - \overline{Y})^2 = 20$$

$$S_X = \sqrt{\frac{218}{10}}$$

$$S_Y = \sqrt{\frac{20}{10}}$$

$$S_X = \sqrt{21.8}$$

$$S_Y = \sqrt{2}$$

$$S_X = 4.669$$

$$S_Y = 1.414$$

Step 2. Finding z_X, z_Y, and $\Sigma z_X z_Y$:

	Reflectivity (X)			SOBEP (Y)			
(a)	(b)	(c)	(d)	(e)	(f)	(g)	(h)
Person	X_i	$X_i - \overline{X}$	z_X	Y_i	$Y_i - \overline{Y}$	z_Y	$z_X z_Y$
1	9	0	0.000	3	0	0.000	0.000
2	10	+1	+0.214	2	−1	−0.707	−0.151
3	16	+7	+1.499	4	+1	+0.707	+1.060
4	5	−4	−0.857	1	−2	−1.414	+1.212
5	9	0	0.000	4	+1	−0.707	0.000
6	7	−2	−0.428	1	−2	−1.414	+0.605
7	5	−4	−0.857	3	0	0.000	0.000
8	11	+2	+0.428	5	+2	+1.414	+0.605
9	1	−8	−1.713	2	−1	0.707	+1.211
10	17	+8	+1.713	5	+2	+1.414	+2.422
$\overline{X}$	9.0			$\overline{Y}$ 3.0		**Sum**	+6.964

Step 3.

To convert X scores to standard scores (see column d): $z_X = \dfrac{X_i - 9}{4.669}$.

To convert Y scores to standard scores (see column g): $z_Y = \dfrac{Y_i - 3}{1.414}$.

Step 4. Calculating r_{XY}:

$$\sum_{i=1}^{N} z_X z_Y = +6.964 \quad \text{(see column } h):$$

$N = 10$ pairs of scores, and $\quad r_{XY} = \dfrac{\sum\limits_{i=1}^{N}(z_X z_Y)}{N}$.

Substituting numerical values, $\quad r_{XY\,obs} = \dfrac{+6.964}{10} = +0.696 = +0.70$.

549

Step 3 of the table illustrates substituting the obtained value of $\Sigma(z_X z_Y)$ and N into the formula. The $r_{XY\,obs} = +0.70$. We recommend this method for use when you have obtained data expressed in standard scores. If the obtained scores are not standard scores, then we recommend that you use the raw-score computational formula that follows.

Raw-Score Computational Formula for r_{XY}

The value of r_{XY} using a raw-score computational formula is given by

$$ r_{XY} = \frac{N \sum\limits_{i=1}^{N} X_i Y_i - \left(\sum\limits_{i=1}^{N} X_i \right)\left(\sum\limits_{i=1}^{N} Y_i \right)}{\sqrt{\left[N \sum\limits_{i=1}^{N} X_i^2 - \left(\sum\limits_{i=1}^{N} X_i \right)^2 \right]\left[N \sum\limits_{i=1}^{N} Y_i^2 - \left(\sum\limits_{i=1}^{N} Y_i \right)^2 \right]}} . $$

Table 17–8 illustrates the use of this formula for the computation of r_{XY} on the scores presented in Table 17–1. Columns b and c of this table present the X_i and Y_i scores, respectively. The sums of these columns, $\Sigma X_i = 90$, $\Sigma Y_i = 30$, provide the ΣX_i and ΣY_i needed in both the numerator and denominator of the formula. Column d obtains each X_i^2 and the sum of this column, 1028, provides the value of ΣX_i^2 needed in the denominator of the formula. Column e obtains each Y_i^2 and the sum of this column, 110, is the value of ΣY_i^2. Column f obtains the value of $X_i Y_i$ and the sum of this column, 316, provides the value of $\Sigma X_i Y_i$ needed for the numerator of the equation.

Step 2 of Table 17–8 illustrates substituting the obtained values of ΣX_i, ΣY_i, $\Sigma X_i Y_i$, ΣX_i^2 and ΣY_i^2 into the equation. The $r_{XY\,obs} = +0.70$. Notice that regardless of the formula used—definitional, z score, or raw score—the $r_{XY\,obs} = +0.70$ for the scores of Table 17–1.

TESTING THE STATISTICAL SIGNIFICANCE OF THE PEARSON r

The Population Correlation, ρ

The Pearson r is a descriptive statistic that describes the linear relationship between the X_i and Y_i scores of a sample. As with any sample of scores, the sample is drawn from a larger population of scores. Thus, we may wish to test if a correlation exists among the X_i and Y_i scores in the population. In a population, a linear correlation between X_i and Y_i scores is represented by the parameter ρ (the Greek letter *rho*, pronounced "row"). In our example problem of finding the correlation between reflectivity and belief in extraordinary phenomena scores, the $r_{XY\,obs} = +0.70$ provides an estimated of ρ_{XY}. Of course we realize that because of sampling error,

TABLE 17–8.

Raw-score computations for the Pearson r. The reflectivity (X_i) and SOBEP (Y_i) scores employed are those presented in Table 17–1.

Step 1. Finding $\sum\limits_{i=1}^{N} X_i, \sum\limits_{i=1}^{N} Y_i, \sum\limits_{i=1}^{N} X_i^2, \sum\limits_{i=1}^{N} Y_i^2, \sum\limits_{i=1}^{N} X_i Y_i$:

(a)	(b)	(c)	(d)	(e)	(f)
Person	X_i	Y_i	X^2	Y^2	$X_i Y_i$
1	9	3	81	9	27
2	10	2	100	4	20
3	16	4	256	16	64
4	5	1	25	1	5
5	9	4	81	16	36
6	7	1	49	1	7
7	5	3	25	9	15
8	11	5	121	25	55
9	1	2	1	4	2
10	17	5	289	25	85
Sums	90	30	1,028	110	316

Step 2. Calculating r_{XY}:

$$\sum_{i=1}^{N} X_i = 90 \qquad\qquad \sum_{i=1}^{N} Y_i = 30$$

$$\left(\sum_{i=1}^{N} X_i\right)^2 = 90^2 = 8{,}100 \qquad \left(\sum_{i=1}^{N} Y_i\right)^2 = 30^2 = 900$$

$$\sum_{i=1}^{N} X_i^2 = 1{,}028 \qquad\qquad \sum_{i=1}^{N} Y_i^2 = 110$$

$$\sum_{i=1}^{N} X_i Y_i = 316, \qquad N = 10 \text{ pairs of scores, and}$$

$$r_{XY} = \frac{N\sum\limits_{i=1}^{N} X_i Y_i - \left(\sum\limits_{i=1}^{N} X_i\right)\left(\sum\limits_{i=1}^{N} Y_i\right)}{\sqrt{\left[N\sum\limits_{i=1}^{N} X_i^2 - \left(\sum\limits_{i=1}^{N} X_i\right)^2\right]\left[N\sum\limits_{i=1}^{N} Y_i^2 - \left(\sum\limits_{i=1}^{N} Y_i\right)^2\right]}}$$

Substituting numerical values, we obtain

$$r_{XY} = \frac{(10)(316) - (90)(30)}{\sqrt{[(10)(1{,}028) - 8{,}100][(10)(110) - 900]}}$$

$$r_{XY} = \frac{(3{,}160 - 2{,}700)}{\sqrt{(2{,}180)(200)}}$$

$$r_{XY} = \frac{+460}{\sqrt{436{,}000}}$$

$$r_{XY\,obs} = \frac{+460}{660.30} = +0.697 = +0.70.$$

r_{XY} will not be equal to ρ_{XY}. As with any statistic, r_{XY}, because it is measured on a sample, will vary from sample to sample, even though the samples are from the same population. Accordingly, we may wish to test a statistical hypothesis that $r_{XY\,obs}$ represents a sample from a population with a specific ρ_{XY}. While it is possible to test hypotheses concerning any value of ρ_{XY}, the most commonly tested hypothesis is that ρ_{XY} equals zero in the population sampled.

Testing for a Nonzero Correlation in the Population

The statistical test to determine if r_{XY} is a chance difference from a zero correlation in the population is straightforward. The common steps of statistical hypothesis testing are followed:

- formulate two statistical hypotheses, H_0 and H_1,
- obtain the sampling distribution of the r_{XY} under H_0,
- set a significance level,
- find a critical value of r_{XY},
- locate a rejection region or regions in the sampling distribution of r_{XY},
- formulate decision rules regarding the statistical hypotheses,
- calculate the value of $r_{XY\,obs}$ on the sample data, and
- make decisions about H_0 and H_1 from the value of $r_{XY\,obs}$.

Statistical Hypotheses
Null Hypothesis.   The null hypothesis is

$$H_0\colon \rho_{XY} = 0.$$

This hypothesis states that the population correlation between the X and Y variables is zero.

Alternative Hypothesis.   The alternative hypothesis is

$$H_1\colon \rho_{XY} \neq 0.$$

Sampling Distribution of r_{XY} and Critical Values
Because r_{XY} may take on values only between 0.00 to 1.00, its sampling distribution under $H_0\colon \rho_{XY} = 0$ may be determined readily. As is the case with most other statistical tests, however, the sampling distribution of r_{XY} depends upon its degrees of freedom. The df for r_{XY} are equal to $N - 2$, where N is the number of pairs of scores from which the correlation coefficient is calculated. Critical values of r, identified as r_{crit}, from sampling distributions of r_{XY} with df ranging from 1 to 100 are presented in Appendix Table A–9 for $\alpha = .05$ and $\alpha = .01$.

Locating a Rejection Region

If H_1 is true, then we expect to obtain values of r_{XY} greater than zero. Accordingly, the rejection region for $r_{XY obs}$ is a value of r equal to or greater than r_{crit}. An $r_{XY obs}$ equal to or larger in absolute value (that is, ignoring the $+$ or $-$ sign of the obtained r) than r_{crit} falls into the rejection region. Such an $r_{XY obs}$ is statistically rare if H_0 is true.

Decision Rules

The decision rules for the statistical hypotheses follow the common pattern:

- If $r_{XY obs}$ falls into the rejection region, then we reject H_0: $\rho_{XY} = 0$ and accept H_1: $\rho_{XY} \neq 0$.
- If $r_{XY obs}$ does not fall into the rejection region, then we fail to reject H_0 and we do not accept H_1.

We illustrate this process in the example problems that follow. Table 17–9 summarizes the decisions and conclusions reached from a statistical test on r_{XY}.

Assumptions of the Statistical Test for Significance of r_{XY}

The test for significance of r_{XY} that we have described assumes that the X and Y scores form a **bivariate normal distribution** in the population. A bivariate normal distribution possesses the following characteristics:

- The distribution of the X scores, the reflectivity scores in our example, is normally distributed in the population sampled.

TABLE 17–9.

Summary of decisions and conclusions in statistical hypothesis testing with the Pearson correlation.

If $r_{XY obs}$ Falls Into the Rejection Region for $\alpha = .05$, Then:	If $r_{XY obs}$ Does *Not* Fall Into the Rejection Region for $\alpha = .05$, Then:
p of the $r_{XY obs}$ is less than or equal to .05, or $p \leq .05$.	p of the $r_{XY obs}$ is greater than .05, or $p > .05$.
The null hypothesis H_0: $\rho_{XY} = 0$ is rejected.	The null hypothesis (H_0) is not rejected.
The alternative hypothesis H_1: $\rho_{XY} \neq 0$ is accepted. The $r_{XY obs}$ estimates a population ρ_{XY} different from zero.	The alternative hypothesis H_1: $\rho_{XY} \neq 0$ is not accepted.
The $r_{XY obs}$ is statistically significant at the .05 level.	The $r_{XY obs}$ is not statistically significant at the .05 level.

- The distribution of the Y scores, the SOBEP scores in our example, is normally distributed in the population sampled.
- For each X score, the distribution of Y scores in the population is normal. Using our example, this assumption means that for each reflectivity score in the population, there is a normal distribution of SOBEP scores.
- For each Y score, the distribution of X scores in the population is normal. This assumption is similar to the previous assumption, except now for each SOBEP score in the population, there is a normal distribution of reflectivity scores.

For many paired measures of behavior we may assume that they form a bivariate normal distribution in the population and thus test for a non-zero correlation of the scores in the population.

Example Problem 17–1
Testing the statistical significance of r_{XY}

Problem:
The Pearson correlation for the reflectivity and SOBEP scores of Table 17–1 was found to be $r_{XY\,obs} = +0.70$. Does this sample value indicate the presence of a nonzero correlation between reflectivity and SOBEP scores in the population from which the individuals were sampled?

Solution:
The problem requires that we test the statistical hypothesis that the population correlation, ρ_{XY}, for reflectivity and SOBEP scores is zero.

Statistic to be used: $r_{XY\,obs} = +0.70$.

Assumptions for use: Reflectivity and SOBEP scores possess a bivariate normal distribution in the population from which the scores were sampled.

Statistical hypotheses: H_0: $\rho_{XY} = 0$
$\qquad\qquad\qquad\qquad\quad$ H_1: $\rho_{XY} \neq 0$

Significance level: $\alpha = .05$

Degrees of freedom of r_{XY}: $df = N - 2 = 10 - 2 = 8$

Critical value of r_{XY}: $r_{crit} = 0.632$

Rejection regions: Values of $r_{XY\,obs}$ equal to or less than -0.632 or equal to or greater than $+0.632$.

Calculation: From Table 17–8, $r_{XY\,obs} = +0.70$.

Decision: The $r_{XY\,obs}$ is greater then $r_{crit} = +0.632$. Accordingly, it falls into the rejection region. Therefore, we

$$\text{reject } H_0\text{: } \rho_{XY} = 0,$$
$$\text{accept } H_1\text{: } \rho_{XY} \neq 0.$$

Conclusion:
Reflectivity and SOBEP scores are correlated in the population; the $r_{XY\,obs} = +0.70$ is not simply a chance difference from a true population correlation of zero. The best estimate we have of the population correlation is provided by $r_{XY\,obs} = +0.70$. Reflective individuals also tend to believe in extraordinary phenomena. ▪

Example Problem 17–2
Testing the statistical significance of r_{XY}

Problem:
A study of Ross, Clifford, and Eisenman (1987) investigated the relationship between the communication of sexual preferences and marital satisfaction in married couples. Each member of a couple completed a questionnaire on sexual preferences. The questionnaire was completed twice by each person, once responding to reflect his or her own preferences, and once responding as he or she thought the spouse would respond. An *understanding* score then was derived for each member of the couple. The wife's understanding score was the number of responses that matched when comparing the questionnaire as she thought her husband may have completed it to the husband's questionnaire stating his preferences. Similarly, a husband's understanding score was obtained by matching the number of responses on the questionnaire as he thought his wife might complete it to the wife's questionnaire indicating her preferences. The understanding scores could range from 0 (no understanding of the spouse's preferences) to 100 (perfect understanding of the spouse's preferences). Thus, each couple had two understanding scores, the wife's understanding of the husband's preferences (X_i) and the husband's understanding of the wife's preferences (Y_i). For example, the scores of three couples may have appeared as

Couple	Understanding	
	Wife's (X_i)	Husband's (Y_i)
1	63	68
2	74	60
3	67	65

As part of the study, Ross et al. then calculated a Perason correlation on the paired scores of 61 couples. The $r_{XY\,obs} = +0.21$. Does this correlation reflect a nonzero correlation of the scores in the population from which the sample was drawn?

Solution:

The problem requires that we test a statistical hypothesis that the population correlation, ρ_{XY}, for wife's and husband's understanding scores is zero.

Statistic to be used: $r_{XY\,obs} = +0.21$.

Assumptions for use: The understanding scores possess a bivariate normal distribution in the population from which the scores were sampled.

Statistical hypotheses: H_0: $\rho_{XY} = 0$
$\qquad\qquad\qquad\qquad\quad\; H_1$: $\rho_{XY} \neq 0$

Significance level: $\alpha = .05$

Degrees of freedom of r_{XY}: $df = N - 2 = 61 - 2 = 59$

Critical value of r_{XY}: The critical value of r_{XY} for 59 df is not presented in Table A–9. Following our custom, we then use the critical value for the next lower tabled df, i.e., 50. This value is $r_{crit} = 0.273$.

Rejection regions: Values of $r_{XY\,obs}$ equal to or less than -0.273 or equal to or greater than $+0.273$.

Decision: The value of $r_{XY\,obs} = +0.21$ does not fall into the rejection region. The decisions with respect to H_0 and H_1 are:

$$\text{fail to reject } H_0\text{: } \rho_{XY} = 0,$$
$$\text{do not accept } H_1\text{: } \rho_{XY} \neq 0.$$

Conclusion:

Within couples, husbands' and wives' understanding of each others' sexual preferences are not correlated in the population. There is no evidence that ρ is not zero.   ∎

Statistics in Use 17–1

Talkativeness and Leadership Ratings: Analyzing Scores with the Pearson r

Speech is a unique human capability and there is no doubt that we often use a person's speech to make attributions about that person. To define some of the relationships between talkativeness and aptitudes, Ruback and Dabbs (1986) measured a person's talkativeness in a group. Small groups of subjects were formed and asked to talk about a topic. The amount that each person talked was recorded and scored in the form of a vocalization score. The vocalization score was the percentage of time during the discussion period that a person actually emitted speech sounds. Two other measures also were obtained from the participants in the study, the Scholastic Aptitude Test (SAT) verbal aptitude score and a leadership rating of each person in the group made by the other members of the group. Thus, for each of the 59 people in the study, three scores were obtained—a vocalization score, the person's SAT verbal aptitude score, and a rated leadership score.

To determine if the scores were related, Ruback and Dabbs calculated two separate correlations—the correlation between the vocalization score (i.e., X) and the SAT verbal score (i.e., Y), and the correlation between the vocalization score (i.e., X) and rated leadership (i.e., Y). For 59 pairs of scores there are 57 degrees of freedom; thus r_{crit} at the .05 level is 0.273 (the critical value for 50 df). The $r_{XY\,obs}$ for the vocalization and SAT score was +0.14, a statistically nonsignificant value. The $r_{XY\,obs}$ for vocalization and rated leadership was +0.69, a statistically significant value at the .05 level. Accordingly Ruback and Dabbs concluded that the SAT verbal aptitude score is not related to talkativeness. People who are high on verbal aptitude, at least as measured by the SAT, do not talk any more or less in a group than people of lower verbal aptitude. On the other hand, rated leadership in a group is related to the amount of talking a person does; the more talking, the greater the rated leadership. ■

Testing Your Knowledge 17–3

On a separate sheet of paper, test your knowledge of the material in this section by answering the following questions.

1. Define: ρ_{XY}, bivariate normal distribution.
2. Identify the statistical hypotheses needed to test if $r_{XY\,obs}$ differs significantly from zero.
3. For each of the following values of N, where N represents the number of pairs of scores from which r_{XY} is calculated, determine the df and then find the r_{crit} for $\alpha = .05$ and $\alpha = .01$ from Table A–9.

$$\frac{N}{}$$

8
15
20
32
43
75

4. For each of the following $r_{XY\,obs}$ and N, identify the statistical null and alternative hypotheses, then find r_{crit} at the .05 significance level. Indicate

whether the $r_{XY\,obs}$ falls into the rejection region and then indicate your decisions with respect to the statistical hypotheses.

	$r_{XY\,obs}$	N
a.	+0.580	12
b.	−0.346	12
c.	−0.682	20
d.	+0.204	24
e.	+0.249	80
f.	−0.731	9

5. College professors often contend that class attendance and course grades are highly correlated. Suppose a professor maintained attendance records and found the following number of absences from class and examination averages for 12 students:

Student	Absences	Exam Average
1	22	72
2	6	88
3	1	99
4	8	78
5	6	66
6	11	77
7	10	52
8	6	78
9	10	76
10	0	96
11	5	91
12	10	86

a. Find the value of $r_{XY\,obs}$ for these scores using the computational formula given in Table 17–8.

b. Test to determine if $r_{XY\,obs}$ differs significantly from a population correlation of zero.

c. What do you conclude about the relationship of absences and exam averages for this test? ■

CHARACTERISTICS OF r_{XY}

Restriction of Range and the Value of r_{XY}

The value of r_{XY} is sensitive to the range of values that either the X or Y variable may take on. As the range of values for one or both of the variables becomes smaller, the value of r_{XY} also becomes smaller. To illustrate this relationship, consider the example presented in Statistics in Use 17–1. In this study individuals were measured on their talkativeness and rated leadership in a group discussion. Suppose that talkativeness scores could range from 0 to 100 percent of the time talking and leadership scores could range from 7 (low leadership skills) to 49 (high leadership skills). Assume that in one study of 20 people the scores illustrated in Figure 17–7 were obtained. In this figure, the range of scores on the talkativeness variable was from 7 percent to 82 percent and from 11 to 43 on the rated leadership variable. The scatterplot of Figure 17–7 indicates that the scores appear to be positively linearly related. The $r_{XY\,obs}$ for the scores is +0.51. For 18 df, $r_{crit} = 0.444$ at $\alpha = .05$; there is a statistically significant positive relationship between the talkativeness and rated leadership scores.

Suppose now that we want to examine the relationship of talkativeness and leadership on only the ten highest individuals on the talkativeness variable. These scores are indicated by the dashed envelope on Figure 17–7. The range of scores for the top ten individuals is from 40 to 82 for talkativeness and from 19 to 43 for rated leadership. In comparison to the range of talkativeness and leadership scores for the full 20 individuals, the range of both the talkativeness and leadership scores for the top 10 individuals has become restricted or truncated (i.e., shortened). What effect does this **restriction of range** of scores have on the value of r_{XY}? The answer to this question is discerned easily by examining

FIGURE 17–7.

Scatterplot of hypothetical scores for 20 individuals relating talkativeness and rated leadership scores. The dashed line encloses the 10 highest scores on talkativeness.

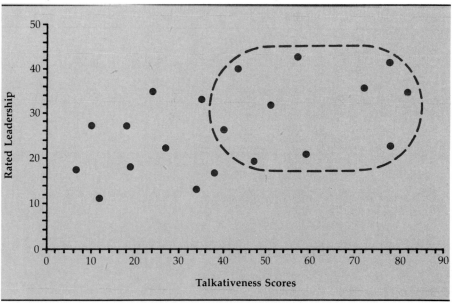

Figure 17–7. The linear relationship of the truncated set of scores is considerably less than the relationship for the full set of scores. This visual observation is confirmed by the value of $r_{XY\,obs}$ for these scores, $r_{XY\,obs} = +0.22$. For 8 df, r_{crit} at .05 is 0.632. Thus, there is no longer a statistically significant relationship existing between the restricted scores.

The implication of this example is clear. Correlation coefficients calculated on scores that have a restricted range may lead us to believe that there is no relationship between two variables, when, had a larger range of scores been employed, a statistically significant relationship would have been found. Accordingly, before calculating a correlation coefficient, we suggest that you examine carefully the sample of individuals measured and the scores obtained to determine if the scores represent a restricted range.

r^2 as a Measure of the Strength of Association of Two Variables

In Chapter 16 we introduced the concept of the strength of association between an independent variable and a dependent variable. Eta square (η^2) was discussed as a measure of the strength of the effect of the independent variable on the dependent variable. In correlation studies, the **coefficient of determination,** r_{XY}^2 (the squared value of the correlation coefficient), provides an analogous measure of the strength of association between the correlated variables.

The interpretation of r_{XY}^2 is similar to that of η^2. That is, r^2 indicates the proportion of variance in one measure that is related to the variance in the other measure. To illustrate, for the 10 hypothetical SOBEP and reflectivity trait scores of Table 17–1, $r_{XY\,obs} = +0.70$; thus r_{XY}^2 is equal to $(+0.70)^2$ or 0.49. This value means that these pairs of scores have 49 percent of their variance in common. In other words, 49 percent of the variance in scores for one variable is associated with the variance in the other measure.

Relationship Between r and r^2

It is evident that the strength of association between two variables is related to the size of the correlation coefficient. Obviously, the closer the value of r_{XY} is to 1.00, the greater is the linear relationship between the two variables. However, the coefficient of determination, r_{XY}^2, is not directly related to r_{XY}. Larger correlation coefficients account for a proportionally larger amount of the common variance than do smaller correlations. As shown in Table 17–10, which illustrates the relationship between r_{XY} and r_{XY}^2, a correlation coefficient of $r_{XY\,obs} = 0.50$, a value midway between 0.00 and 1.00, accounts for only 25 percent of the common variance. Indeed, less than 50 percent of the variance is shared by the two measures for values of r_{XY} between 0.00 and 0.70. The remaining 50 percent of the possible common variance is accounted for by correlation coefficients whose values range from 0.70 to 1.00.

TABLE 17–10.

Relationship of r_{XY}^2 to values of r_{XY}.

r_{XY}	r_{XY}^2
.00	.00
.10	.01
.20	.04
.30	.09
.40	.16
.50	.25
.60	.36
.70	.49
.80	.64
.90	.81
1.00	1.00

Virtually any value of r_{XY} that differs from zero will be statistically significant if the sample size (and therefore *df*) is sufficiently large. After all, with larger samples it should be easier to detect any nonzero relationship that exists between two variables in a population. But a statistically significant relationship obtained with large samples is not necessarily an important one. A value of $r_{XY\,obs}$ as small as 0.062 is statistically significant at the .05 level with 1000 *df*. With a correlation coefficient this small, however, less than 4/10 of 1 percent of the variance in one measure is related to the other ($r_{XY}^2 = 0.062^2 = 0.0038$). Such small but statistically significant correlations are not uncommon in research. In many settings, such as the military or in college aptitude testing, test batteries are administered to thousands of individuals. Many correlations between the variables measured are subsequently analyzed, some of which represent weak but statistically significant relationships.

To illustrate the use of the coefficient of determination, SOBEP and several different personality trait scores were correlated on samples of 72 to 122 individuals in the Windholz and Diamant (1974) study. Six of the 21 correlation coefficients reported were statistically significant at the .05 level, with significant Pearson *r* values ranging from +0.21 (for SOBEP and neuroticism scores) to +0.36 (for SOBEP and hypomania scores). Accordingly, coefficients of determination for the statistically significant correlation coefficients range from 0.04 to 0.13. The smallest significant correlation ($r_{XY} = +0.21$), therefore, accounts for about 4 percent of the variance; meaning that 96 percent of the variance in neuroticism scores is not related to belief in extraordinary phenomena scores. Because r_{XY}^2 indicates the variance common to the two measures being correlated many researchers regard the coefficient of determination as more informative and meaningful than the correlation coefficient.

CORRELATION AND CAUSALITY

Many variables are highly correlated, but the mere existence of a correlational relationship between two variables does not imply a causal relationship between them. If two variables X and Y are correlated, then at least three possibilities exist with respect to the causal relations among the variables:

- X causally affects Y,
- Y causally affects X, or
- neither X nor Y causally affect each other, but both are causally affected by a third variable, Z.

To illustrate the problem, suppose two variables such as the reflectivity personality trait (variable X) and belief in extraordinary phenomena (variable Y) are positively correlated; people who are more reflective have a stronger belief in extraordinary phenomena. Which variable, if either, causally affects the other? Does X cause Y? Or does Y cause X? Perhaps neither of these applies and a third variable, Z, the type of education one experiences causes both. Individuals who are both highly reflective and believe in extraordinary phenomena may have received an education (i.e., variable Z) in which they were taught to contemplate abstract ideas but were not taught physical laws or encouraged to seek empirical evidence for their beliefs. On the other hand, perhaps people who score low on both reflectivity and belief in extraordinary phenomena had an education wherein they were taught to seek data to support their beliefs and learned the physical laws of nature that are violated by purported extraordinary phenomena. These three possible causal relationships are illustrated in Table 17–11.

The **third variable problem** often leads to the misreporting of correlational studies in the popular media. For example, recent newspaper articles have reported studies showing a negative correlation between moderate levels of alcohol consumption and the probability of having a heart attack. One such report was headlined, "Drinking beer can cut your chances of a heart attack in half." This statement implies that drinking beer produces a healthier heart. But, can you conclude this causal relationship from a study that correlated the amount of beer drunk (i.e., X) and heart-attack rates (i.e., Y)? Perhaps a third variable, a person's underlying health (i.e., variable Z), produces the observed correlation between beer consumption and heart-attack rate. Individuals who are not very healthy may avoid drinking beer and also possess a higher probability of having a heart attack, whereas healthy individuals possess a lower probability of heart attack and also drink moderate amounts of beer.

TABLE 17–11.

Possible causal relationships from an observed correlation of two variables, reflectivity (*X*) and belief in extraordinary phenomena (*Y*).

A. The Observed Correlation.

Positive Correlation Obtained
Between Variables X and Y

↙   ↘

Individuals High in | *Individuals Low in*
Reflectivity (X) Are Also | *Reflectivity (X) Are Also*
High in Belief in Extra- | *Low in Belief in Extra-*
ordinary Phenomena (Y) | *ordinary Phenomena (Y)*

B. Possible Causal Relationships That May Explain the Observed Relationship.

- Possibility 1

$$X \quad causes \quad Y$$

Reflectivity (*X*) causes a person to believe or not believe in extraordinary phenomena (*Y*).

- Possibility 2

$$Y \quad causes \quad X$$

Belief in extraordinary phenomena (*Y*) causes a person to be more or less reflective (*X*).

- Possibility 3

$$Z \quad causes \ both \ X \ and \ Y$$

The type of education one experiences (variable *Z*) causes both the reflectivity level (*X*) and the amount of belief in extraordinary phenomena (*Y*).

Another study reported a negative correlation between the reported amount of sleep per night and energy levels during the day; people who sleep less also report higher daytime energy levels. Should you conclude from this relationship that if you lack energy during the day then you should sleep less during the night? A correlational relationship does not allow you to jump to such a causal conclusion. Probably a third variable is present that accounts for the observed relationship, perhaps some physiological condition that affects both daytime energy level and the amount of sleep needed.

A rather curious positive correlation between the use of cellophane tape and diet-margarine has also been reported in a study conducted by an advertising research firm ("You Are," 1976). People who use more cellophane tape also use more diet-margarine. It is unlikely that you will fall into the causality trap with this relationship; it is doubtful you would believe that eating diet-margarine causes one to use more cellophane tape or vice versa. Obviously, a third variable underlies this reported relationship. We let you speculate about what it may be.

Testing Your Knowledge 17–4

On a separate sheet of paper, test your knowledge of the material in this section by answering the following questions.

1. What effect may restricting the range of scores on either the X or Y variable have on the value of r_{XY}?
2. Calculate the coefficient of determination for the following values of r_{XY}.

r_{XY}
$+0.12$
-0.74
-0.59
-0.36
$+0.23$
$+0.19$

3. Explain the third variable problem in determining causality from correlation.
4. You observe a correlation between variables X and Y. Identify the three possible causal relationships that may explain the correlation.
5. Various researchers have reported the following statistically significant correlations. Attempt to identify a third variable that may be responsible for the observed correlation.
   a. A negative correlation between income and blood pressure.
   b. A positive correlation between coffee drinking and cigarette smoking.
   c. A positive correlation between hip size and grade point average in female college students.
   d. A positive correlation between exposure to violence on television and aggressive behavior in children.

THE SPEARMAN RANK-ORDER CORRELATION COEFFICIENT

The Pearson r is appropriate when scores on the variables to be correlated realize interval or ratio measurement. Sometimes, however, measures may represent rank ordering on both variables. Either the scores will be recorded as ranks initially, or the original measures may be converted to ranks. As an example of the latter instance, recall that rating scale scores have no clear identity with respect to scale of measurement. Rating scale measures lie within a gray area; they do not possess true interval scale properties, yet they seem to provide more information than ordinal scales. Thus, some researchers may consider transforming rating scores to ranks. Ranked scores are ordinal measures.

A statistic commonly used to describe the relationship between two sets of ranked scores from a sample is the **Spearman rank-order correlation coefficient,** symbolized by r_s, and found by the formula

$$r_s = 1 - \frac{6 \sum\limits_{i=1}^{N} D^2}{N(N^2 - 1)},$$

where D is the difference in a pair of ranked scores for an individual and N equals the number of pairs of ranks in the study. As with the Pearson r, values of r_s may be positive or negative and range from -1.00 through 0.00 to $+1.00$.

Ranking Behaviors of Animals: An Example of the Use of r_s

We have all observed that animals within a species behave differently from each other. To study differences in animal behaviors, Feaver, Mendl, and Bateson (1986) developed a method of measuring behaviors such as playing, chasing, fleeing, crouching, and so forth. Suppose an investigator using this technique wants to find if playing and chasing behaviors are related in cats. Ten cats are observed for a period of time in a standard environment and ranked separately on playing and chasing behaviors. The most playful cat receives a rank of 1, the least playful a rank of 10. Similarly, the cat that chases most is ranked 1 and the cat that chases least is ranked 10.

Ranks of the 10 cats on playing and chasing behaviors are presented in columns a and b, respectively, in Table 17–12. Cats 1 and 10 were judged to be equal in chasing behavior. Therefore, both cats were assigned the same rank, 6.5, which is the average of the two ranks in question.

The procedures involved in calculating r_s are illustrated in Table 17–12. The first step is to find the difference, D, in each pair of ranks by subtracting one rank from the other. This step is shown in column c, where the chasing rank is subtracted from the playing rank for each cat. Then, each of the differences is squared as shown in column d. The sum of this column, 80.5, provides the value of $\sum_{i=1}^{N} D^2$. The $\sum_{i=1}^{N} D^2$ and N value are substituted into the formula and r_s is calculated: $r_{s\,obs} = +0.512$. Rounded to two decimal places, the Spearman rank-order correlation between playing and chasing behavior in the cats is $+0.51$.

TABLE 17–12.

Calculation of the Spearman rank-order correlation coefficient on playing and chasing behavior of 10 cats.

	(a)	(b)	(c)	(d)
	Behavior			
Cat	Playing	Chasing	D	D²
1	2	6.5	−4.5	20.25
2	6	8	−2	4
3	8	4	+4	16
4	4	1	+3	9
5	7	5	+2	4
6	5	9	−4	16
7	10	10	0	0
8	3	2	+1	1
9	1	3	−2	4
10	9	6.5	+2.5	6.25
			Sum	80.5

The formula for r_s is $r_s = 1 - \dfrac{6 \sum\limits_{i=1}^{N} D^2}{N(N^2 - 1)}$

Substituting the value of $\sum\limits_{i=1}^{N} D^2 = 80.5$,

$r_{s\,obs} = 1 - \dfrac{6(80.5)}{10(10^2 - 1)}$,

$r_{s\,obs} = 1 - \dfrac{483}{10(99)}$,

$r_{s\,obs} = 1 - \dfrac{483}{990}$,

$r_{s\,obs} = 1 - 0.488$,

$r_{s\,obs} = +0.512 = +0.51$.

Statistical Significance of the Spearman Rank-Order Correlation

The test for the statistical significance of r_s is similar to that for the Pearson r. The null hypothesis is that the rank-order correlation in the population, symbolized by ρ_s, is zero, or H_0: $\rho_s = 0$. The alternative hypothesis is that the population correlation is not zero, or H_1: $\rho_s \neq 0$. Minimum values of r_s needed for statistical significance at the .05 and .01 levels are presented in the Appendix, Table A–10. Notice that the critical values are based upon N—the number of pairs of ranks—rather than degrees of freedom. If $r_{s\,obs}$ is equal to or larger than the critical value, then the decision is to reject H_0 and accept H_1.

For our example, the critical value of r_s for $N = 10$ and $\alpha = .05$ is 0.648. Because $r_{s\,obs} = +0.51$ is smaller than the critical value, the null hypothesis is not rejected at the .05 level. Therefore, the relationship between the ranks on playing and chasing is not statistically significant, $p > .05$. The results of this study indicate that playing and chasing behaviors were not related in the sample observed.

Using r_s

One should not routinely convert scores to ranks merely because the Spearman r_s may be easier to compute than the Pearson r. Ordinal measures provide less information than interval or ratio measures. Moreover, the Spearman correlation is not a measure of the degree of linear relationship between two variables. Instead, as Hays (1973) suggests, the Spearman correlation coefficient shows "the tendency of two rank orders to be similar" (p. 787). Consequently, although r_s^2 provides a measure of the strength of association of the two variables, the meaning of the squared correlation is not clear. Because differences in ranks do not correspond to equal differences in the behavior measured, r_s cannot be interpreted strictly as the proportion of variance accounted for by the two variables. Finally, perhaps the most important point is that the Spearman r_s is less sensitive to detecting a statistically significant relationship than is the Pearson r if the latter is suitable for analyzing two sets of scores.

SUMMARY

- Correlational studies are attempts to find the extent to which two or more variables are related.
- In a scatterplot, one of the two scores is represented on the horizontal axis (the abscissa) and the other measure is plotted on the vertical axis (the ordinate). The score of an individual on each of the two measures is then depicted by one point on the scatterplot.
- In a positive relationship, as the value of one variable increases, the value of the other variable also increases.
- In a negative relationship, as the value of one variable increases, the value of the second variable decreases.

- The Pearson correlation coefficient is defined as

$$r_{XY} = \frac{\sum\limits_{i=1}^{N} (X_i - \overline{X})(Y_i - \overline{Y})}{\sqrt{\left[\sum\limits_{i=1}^{N} (X_i - \overline{X})^2\right]\left[\sum\limits_{i=1}^{N} (Y_i - \overline{Y})^2\right]}}$$

- The $\sum_{i=1}^{N} (X_i - \overline{X})(Y_i - \overline{Y})$ is the cross products of X and Y and is symbolized as CP_{XY}. Thus the correlation coefficient may also be expressed as

$$r_{XY} = \frac{CP_{XY}}{\sqrt{(SS_X)(SS_Y)}}.$$

- The direction of a relationship is indicated by the positive or negative sign of the correlation coefficient.
- The degree to which the points on the scatterplot lie on a straight line is given by the absolute value of r, a value that may vary from 0.00 to 1.00.
- r_{XY} may obtained using standard score by

$$r_{XY} = \frac{\sum_{i=1}^{N} (z_X z_Y)}{N}.$$

- The value of r_{XY} using a raw-score computational formula is given by

$$r_{XY} = \frac{N\sum_{i=1}^{N} X_i Y_i - \left(\sum_{i=1}^{N} X_i\right)\left(\sum_{i=1}^{N} Y_i\right)}{\sqrt{\left[N\sum_{i=1}^{N} X_i^2 - \left(\sum_{i=1}^{N} X_i\right)^2\right]\left[N\sum_{i=1}^{N} Y_i^2 - \left(\sum_{i=1}^{N} Y_i\right)^2\right]}}$$

- A linear correlation between X_i and Y_i scores is represented in a population by ρ.
- The coefficient of determination, r_{XY}^2 indicates the proportion of variance in one measure that is related to the variance in the other measure.
- If two variables X and Y are correlated, then at least three possibilities exist with respect to the causal relations among the variables:
  - X causally affects Y,
  - Y causally affects X, or
  - neither X nor Y causally affect each other, but both are causally affected by a third variable, Z.
- The Spearman rank-order correlation coefficient is found by

$$r_s = 1 - \frac{6\sum_{i=1}^{N} D^2}{N(N^2 - 1)}.$$

KEY TERMS

bivariate distribution of scores	inverse relationship	r_{XY}
bivariate normal distribution	linear relationship	r_{xy}^2
coefficient of determination	negative relationship	r_s
correlation coefficient	Pearson product-moment	scatterplot
correlational studies	correlation coefficient	Spearman rank-order correlation coefficient
covary	positive relationship	
cross products	restriction of range	SS_X
CP_{XY}	ρ_s	SS_Y
direct relationship	ρ_{XY}	third variable problem

REVIEW QUESTIONS

On a separate sheet of paper, test your knowledge of the material in this chapter by answering the following questions.

1. Crews, Shirreffs, Thomas, Krahenbuhl, and Helfrich (1986) were interested in variables associated with successful performance of

professional women golfers. One measure that appeared to be related to lower golfing scores was the percentage of body fat. For
their sample they found r_{XY} between percentage of body fat (X_i) and
average score (Y_i) to be +0.64. Suppose you replicated this study
with 12 different professional female golfers and obtained the following values of percentage of body fat and average golf scores
(in strokes).

Golfer	Body Fat (X)	Score (Y)
1	20.1	70
2	28.9	77
3	25.4	75
4	19.6	67
5	36.3	79
6	22.9	73
7	26.5	74
8	30.7	72
9	29.8	83
10	33.2	75
11	24.1	68
12	27.3	75

a. Plot a scatterplot of the percentage of body fat (on the abscissa)
and average golf score (on the ordinate).
b. Does the relationship between the scores appear to be positive or
negative or is there no relationship apparent?
c. Calculate the value of r_{XY} and test to find if the obtained value
differs significantly from a correlation of zero in the population at
the .05 significance level.
d. What conclusions do you reach about the relationship of percentage of body fat to scores in the sample?
e. Calculate r_{XY}^2. What proportion of the variation in percentage
body fat and average score is common to the two measures?
f. Identify a potential third variable that may explain the correlation
found between percentage body fat and average golf score.
2. Our everyday experience indicates to us that often we react to
others based upon their physical appearance. For males, at least,
tallness often seems to evoke positive reactions from others. As the
old adage says, "Tall, dark, and handsome." Following this line of
thinking, Villimez, Eisenberg, and Carroll (1986) were interested in
finding if any relationships exist between physical size and academic
performance for primary school children. They obtained a number of
measures of children's size and related them to test scores and
report card grades. Holding age constant to control for height differences related to age, they found an r_{XY} of −0.12 between height and

report card grades for 53 third-grade girls and a correlation of +0.32 for 42 third-grade boys.

  a. Test each correlation coefficient to determine if it differs significantly at the .05 level from a correlation of zero in the population sampled.

  b. Calculate the coefficient of determination for each value of r_{XY}.

  c. What conclusions do you reach concerning the relationship between height and report card grades in primary school children?

3. Students often are interested in predicting their final examination grade from the grade received on a midterm examination. To make such predictions, grades on the midterm and final exam must be correlated. Suppose that for an elementary statistics class the following grades were obtained for 10 students on a midterm and final examination.

Student	Examination	
	Midterm (X)	Final (Y)
1	87	84
2	89	91
3	97	96
4	80	87
5	73	66
6	85	90
7	81	79
8	74	80
9	80	89
10	89	86

  a. Plot a scatterplot of the midterm exam (on the abscissa) and final exam (on the ordinate).

  b. Does the relationship between the scores appear to be positive or negative or is there no relationship apparent?

  c. Calculate the value of r_{XY} and test to find if the obtained value differs significantly from a correlation of zero in the population at the .05 significance level.

  d. What conclusions do you reach about the relationship of midterm exam grades and final exam grades in the sample?

4. Krantz (1987) found that physical attractiveness and popularity are positively correlated for kindergarten girls, but not for kindergarten boys. Suppose you conducted a similar study and had an observer rank kindergarten children on physical attractiveness and popularity. Twelve girls and 14 boys were ranked. Suppose you found the following rankings.

Girls

Physical Attractiveness (X)	Popularity (Y)
3	1
6	7
2	3
9	10
12	11
1	3
7	8
8	7
4	5
10	9
5	6
11	12

Boys

Physical Attractiveness (X)	Popularity (Y)
5	9
11	1
3	10
9	4
4	6
8	12
12	5
1	13
14	8
10	14
6	2
13	11
2	7
7	3

a. Calculate r_s on the scores of the girls. Test to find if $r_{s\,obs}$ differs significantly from a correlation of zero in the population at the .05 significance level.

b. What conclusions do you reach about the relationship of physical attractiveness and popularity rankings for the girls?

c. Calculate r_s on the scores of the boys. Test to find if $r_{s\,obs}$ differs significantly from a correlation of zero in the population at the .05 significance level.

d. What conclusions do you reach about the relationship of physical attractiveness an popularity rankings for the boys?

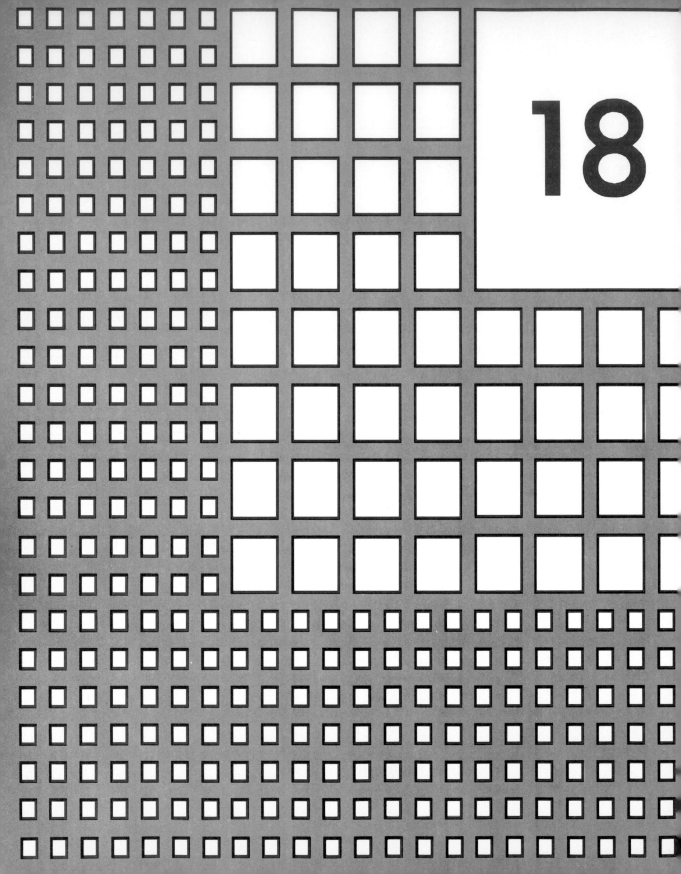

18

Regression

OVERVIEW: THE NEED FOR PREDICTION

When discussing correlation we indicated that if two variables were correlated perfectly, then knowing the value of one score permits a perfect prediction of the score on the second variable. Generally, whenever two variables are significantly correlated, we may use the score on one variable to predict the score on the second. There are many reasons why we want to predict one variable from another. Suppose, for example, you want to know what your first examination score in a course might indicate about your final grade. Here you want to predict your final course grade from the first examination grade. College admission officers want to predict grade point averages from entrance examinations such as the Scholastic Aptitude Test. And, personnel managers want to predict employee performance from aptitude test scores. Later in the chapter we provide examples of predicting depression proneness from body satisfaction ratings, and task performance from personality traits.

This chapter deals with predicting one variable from another when the two variables are linearly related. The approach we take is to fit a straight line to a scatterplot of the two variables and use this straight line to predict one score from the other. This straight line is called a **regression line.** Later we will explain why this line is given this somewhat curious name. The task before us now, however, is to discover how we construct such a line. We begin with several simple examples, then introduce an example of predicting belief in extraordinary phenomena from the personality trait of reflectivity.

LINEAR RELATIONS

Definition of a Linear Relation

We introduced linear relationships in Chapter 17 by indicating that a linear relationship between two variables is a straight line relationship between the variables. Figure 18–1 illustrates two variables, X and Y, that are perfectly positively linearly related. This figure permits us to more completely define a linear relation. In a **linear relation,** each time that one variable changes by one unit, there is a constant change in the second variable. This defining characteristic of a linear relationship is easily seen in Figure 18–1. Each time that X increases by one unit, Y increases by 0.5 unit. For example, as X increases from 3 to 4 (one unit on the X measurement) Y increases from 1.5 to 2.0 (0.5 unit on the Y measurement). Similarly, as X increases from 6 to 7 (again, one unit on the X measurement) Y increases from 3.0 to 3.5 (again, 0.5 unit on the Y measurement). In this

FIGURE 18–1.

A perfect positive linear relationship between variable X and variable Y.

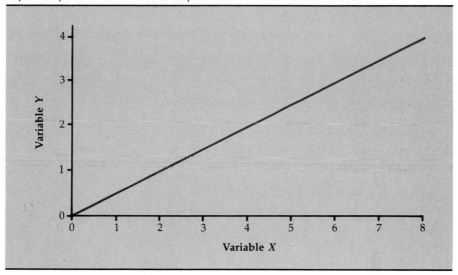

illustration, then, a change in X of one unit of its measurement results in a constant change of 0.5 units on the Y measurement.

The requirement of a linear relationship that a change of one unit in the X variable always be accompanied by a constant amount of change in the Y variable applies whether the relationship is positive or negative. Figure 18–2 illustrates a perfect negative linear relationship between X and Y. Each time X changes by one unit, Y also changes by a constant amount. For example, as X changes one unit from 2 to 3, Y changes from 9.4 to 8.6, a change of -0.8 on the Y measurement. Similarly, a change of X from 8 to 9 results in a change of Y from 4.6 to 3.8, again a change of -0.8 on the Y measurement. From Figure 18–2, we see that every change in X of one unit is accompanied by a corresponding and constant change of Y of -0.8 units.

The **general equation of a straight line,** such as the lines shown in Figures 18–1 and 18–2, is given by

$$Y = bX + a \, ,$$

where b is the **slope of the line** and a is a constant called the **Y-intercept.** We discuss the slope and Y-intercept next.

Slope of a Linear Relationship

In Figures 18–1 and 18–2, every change in X by one unit of its measure is accompanied by a corresponding and constant change in the Y variable.

FIGURE 18–2.
A perfect negative linear relationship between variable *X* and variable *Y*.

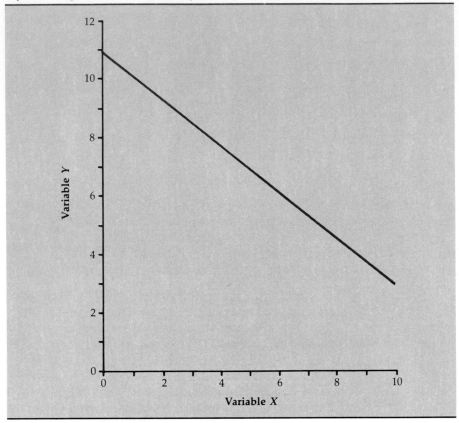

The relationship of the change in the *Y* variable to a one-unit change in the *X* variable is the slope of the straight line relating the two variables. More specifically, the **slope of a linear relationship between two variables, *X* and *Y*,** symbolized by *b*, is defined as

$$b = \frac{Y_2 - Y_1}{X_2 - X_1},$$

where X_1 and X_2 are two values of *X*, and Y_1 and Y_2 are values of *Y* corresponding to X_1 and X_2, respectively.

To illustrate the slope, consider Figure 18–3. This figure presents the same relationship between *X* and *Y* as Figure 18–1, but we have illustrated the computation of the slope on it. The two values of *X* that we have chosen to use to find the slope are $X_1 = 4$ and $X_2 = 5$. The values of

Y that correspond to these X values are $Y_1 = 2$ and $Y_2 = 2.5$, respectively. Thus,

$$b = \frac{Y_2 - Y_1}{X_2 - X_1},$$

$$b = \frac{2.5 - 2}{5 - 4},$$

$$b = \frac{0.5}{1.0} = +0.5.$$

The slope of this straight line is $+0.5$, for every increase of one unit in X, Y increases by one-half unit. The slope of a straight line is constant over its length. Thus, regardless of the values of X that we use in the equation for b, the value of b will always be $+0.5$ for this example. For instance, suppose we choose $X_1 = 6$ and $X_2 = 8$. For these values of X, the corresponding Y values are $Y_1 = 3$ and $Y_2 = 4$. Hence

$$b = \frac{4 - 3}{8 - 6} = \frac{1}{2} = +0.5.$$

Knowing the slope of the line in Figure 18–3, we can now write an equation relating the value of Y to X for this line. This equation is

$$Y = +0.5X.$$

FIGURE 18–3.

Illustration of finding the slope from a linear relationship.

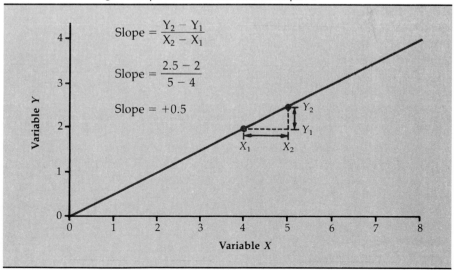

For each value of X, this equation provides the corresponding value of Y. For example, we can solve $Y = +0.5X$ for different values of X as follows:

X_i	Y_i
2	1.0
3	1.5
4	2.0
5	2.5
6	3.0
7	3.5
8	4.0
9	4.5
10	5.0

Compare these values of Y with the values of Y plotted on Figure 18–3 for each of the X values employed. Notice that $Y = +0.5X$ provides an equation describing the linear relationship plotted in Figure 18–3.

The equation $Y = bX$ provides part of the general equation for a straight line. Indeed, this simple equation describes any linear relationship between X and Y provided that $Y = 0$ when $X = 0$. But, what if Y does not equal zero when $X = 0$?

The Y-Intercept of a Linear Relationship

Look at the relationship between variables X and Y presented in Figure 18–4. The slope of this line is also $+0.5$, for every change of one unit in X, Y changes by $+0.5$ units. This line cannot be described by the simple equation $Y = +0.5X$, however. We can demonstrate this lack of relationship by substituting $X = 0$ into this equation. If we do so, we find that Y should equal zero when $X = 0$. But, looking at Figure 18–4, we see that $Y = 3$ when $X = 0$. Let us substitute another value for X, say $X = 10$, into the equation $Y = +0.5X$. Doing so we find that Y should be 5 when $X = 10$. From Figure 18–4, however, we see that $Y = 8$ when $X = 10$. By comparing Y found from the equation $Y = +0.5X$ with the value of Y plotted in Figure 18–4, we see that the equation provides a value of Y that is 3 units less than the value of Y plotted on the figure. Suppose then that we use the equation $Y = +0.5X$ and add 3 to each value of Y obtained from it. Then we write the equation as

$$Y = +0.5X + 3.$$

Using this equation we find that we have described the relationship between X and Y plotted in Figure 18–4. To demonstrate, solving $Y = +0.5X + 3$ for different values of X, we obtain

FIGURE 18–4.

Illustration of a linear relationship between X and Y with a slope of 0.5 and a Y-intercept of +3.

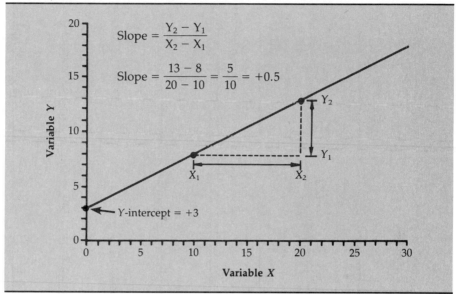

X_i	Y_i
0	3.0
2	4.0
4	5.0
10	8.0
13	9.5
19	12.5
24	15.0
26	16.0
30	18.0

Compare these values of Y with the values of Y plotted on Figure 18–4 for each of the X values employed. Notice that $Y = 0.5X + 3$ provides an equation describing the linear relationship shown in Figure 18–4.

This example provides a specific example of the general equation for a linear relationship between X and Y. To express this general equation for a straight line, we substitute the letter b for the slope of +0.5 and the letter a for the constant of 3 in the equation $Y = +0.5X + 3$. We then obtain $Y = bX + a$, the general equation of a straight line with slope b, and Y-intercept a. The **Y-intercept** is so named because it is the value of Y when $X = 0$. When $X = 0$, the line intercepts, or intersects, the Y-axis. The value of Y at this point is thus called the Y-intercept. In Figure 18–4 we see that the Y intercept is +3, but in Figure 18–3 the Y-intercept is 0.

FIGURE 18–5.
Various linear relationships between X and Y.

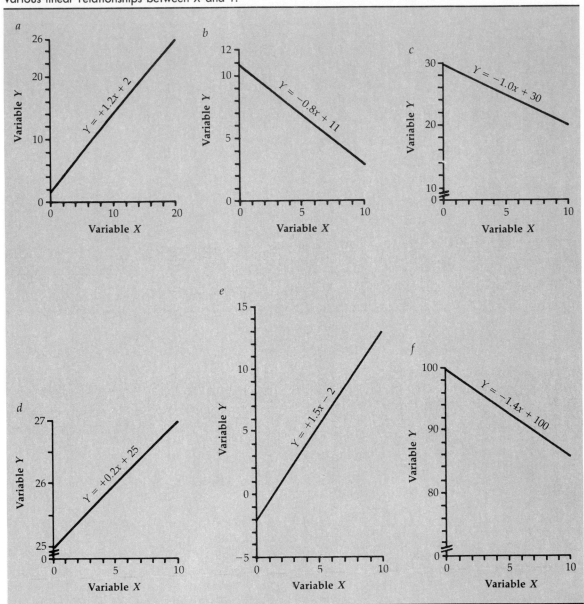

Example Linear Relations and Their Equations

To provide an opportunity to gain familiarity with various linear relationships and the equations describing them, Figure 18–5 provides examples of both positive and negative linear relationships between X and Y. For each relationship illustrated, we have provided the equation with the slope and Y-intercept. You should be sure that you can obtain the value of b and a for each relationship presented. Notice that panel b presents the linear relationship used in Figure 18–2 to illustrate a negative relationship between X and Y. The equation for this relationship is $Y = -0.8X + 11$. Here we see that the slope is -0.8. This value indicates that for every increase of one unit in X, Y decreases by 0.8 units. The value of the slope indicates the relationship is negative. Observe also in this figure that when X is zero, the line intercepts the Y axis at a value of $+11$; thus the Y-intercept for this relationship is $+11$. Examine each relationship carefully and substitute values for X into each equation to ensure that you understand the relation of each equation to its corresponding figure.

Testing Your Knowledge 18–1

On a separate sheet of paper, test your knowledge of the material in this section by answering the following questions.

1. Define: linear relation, slope of a linear relation, Y-intercept, a, b.
2. Write the general equation for a straight line.
3. Write the equation for the slope of a straight line.
4. For each of the figures below, find the slope and Y-intercept. Then write the equation for each linear relationship shown.

a.

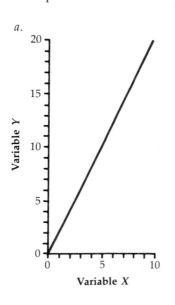

b.

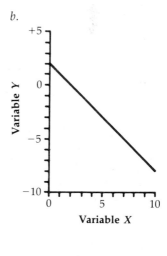

c.

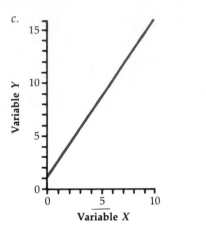

d.

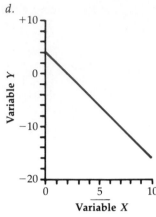

FINDING A LINEAR REGRESSION LINE

Predicting Belief in Extraordinary Phenomena from Reflectivity: An Example Problem

The previous examples have involved variables identified simply as X and Y. To introduce how we find the equation that describes the linear relationship of two sets of scores, we return to the problem introduced in Chapter 17—the relationship between scores on the *reflective* dimension of the *Thorndike Dimensions of Temperament* personality inventory and scores on the *Scale of Belief in Extraordinary Phenomena* (SOBEP). Suppose, for a moment, the scores in Table 18–1 were obtained.

TABLE 18–1.

Hypothetical scores for 10 people on the reflectivity scale of the *Thorndike Dimensions of Temperament* (Thorndike, 1966) and on the *Scale of Belief in Extraordinary Phenomena* (SOBEP, Windholz and Diamant, 1974).

Person	Reflectivity Score (X_i)	SOBEP (Y_i)
1	9	2.9
2	10	3.1
3	16	4.3
4	5	2.1
5	9	2.9
6	7	2.5
7	5	2.1
8	11	3.3
9	1	1.3
10	17	4.5

These scores are perfectly positively related, $r_{XY\,obs} = +1.00$. You can determine this value by applying one of the formulas for r_{XY} from Chapter 17 to these scores. Consequently, we expect a scatterplot of the scores to reveal that the scores fall on a straight line, and indeed, as Figure 18–6 illustrates, they do. We can find the equation for the linear relationship between reflectivity and SOBEP scores by finding the slope and Y-intercept of the line. We have found both these values on the figure: $b = +0.2$ and $a = 1.1$. Thus, the equation relating the SOBEP scores (Y) to the reflectivity scores (X) is

$$Y = bX + a, \quad \text{or}$$
$$\text{SOBEP score} - (+0.2)(\text{Reflectivity score}) + 1.1.$$

Because the correlation of the scores is $+1.00$, we can use this equation to perfectly predict each person's SOBEP score knowing only his or her reflectivity score. The predicted SOBEP scores are given in Table 18–2. For example, person 1 has a reflectivity score of 9. Applying the equation,

$$\text{Predicted SOBEP score} = (+0.2)(\text{Reflectivity score}) + 1.1,$$

FIGURE 18–6.
Scatterplot of the reflectivity and SOBEP scores given in Table 18–1.

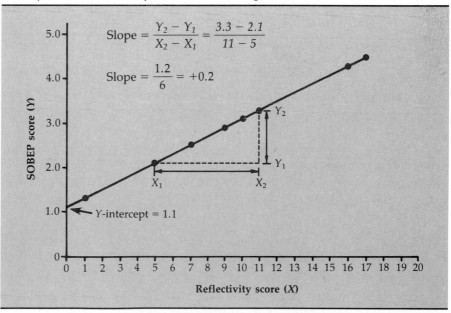

TABLE 18–2.
SOBEP scores predicted from reflectivity scores using the
equation: SOBEP scores = (+0.2) (Reflectivity score) + 1.1.

(a)	(b)	(c)	(d)
Person	Reflectivity Score (X_i)	Predicted SOBEP (Y_i')	Actual SOBEP (Y_i)
1	9	2.9	2.9
2	10	3.1	3.1
3	16	4.3	4.3
4	5	2.1	2.1
5	9	2.9	2.9
6	7	2.5	2.5
7	5	2.1	2.1
8	11	3.3	3.3
9	1	1.3	1.3
10	17	4.5	4.5

we find

$$\text{Predicted SOBEP score} = (+0.2)(9) + 1.1,$$

or
$$\text{Predicted SOBEP score} = 1.8 + 1.1 = 2.9.$$

The predicted SOBEP score from the reflectivity score of 9 is 2.9. The predicted SOBEP scores from the other reflectivity scores are presented in column *c* of Table 18–2. We identify these predicted scores with the letter *Y'* (read as "Y prime" or "Y predicted") to indicate they have been predicted from the *X* score of reflectivity using the equation

$$Y' = bX + a.$$

The actual SOBEP score obtained by each person (symbolized by *Y*) is presented in column *d*. Notice that the predicted and actual SOBEP scores are identical. This identity occurs because *X* and *Y* are correlated perfectly. Because $r_{XY} = +1.00$, *Y'* and *Y* are identical and there is no error in predicting SOBEP scores from reflectivity scores.

Predicting Belief in Extraordinary Phenomena from Reflectivity: A More Realistic Example Problem

From an applied perspective, the scores in Table 18–1 are unusual. Rarely, if ever, would two sets of scores be perfectly correlated as they are in Table 18–1. More realistically, the scores will exhibit a less-than-perfect

TABLE 18–3.

A second set of scores for 10 people on the reflectivity scale of the *Thorndike Dimensions of Temperament* and on the *Scale of Belief in Extraordinary Phenomena*.

Person	Reflectivity Score (X_i)	SOBEP (Y_i)
1	9	3
2	10	2
3	16	4
4	5	1
5	9	4
6	7	1
7	5	3
8	11	5
9	1	2
10	17	5

correlation, such as the scores presented in Table 18–3. These scores were used in Chapter 17 to develop the Pearson correlation coefficient. The $r_{XY\ obs}$ for these scores is +0.70, which is statistically significant at the .05 level.

The scores of Table 18–3 are presented in a scatterplot in Figure 18–7. These scores are positively related; in general, higher SOBEP scores are

FIGURE 18–7.

Scatterplot of the reflectivity and SOBEP scores given in Table 18–3.

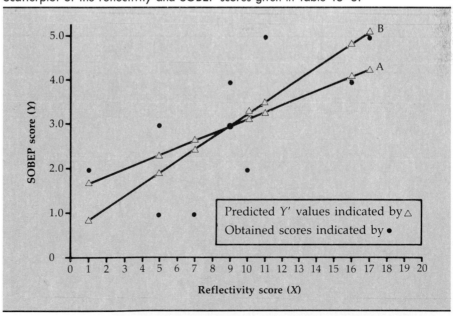

associated with higher scores on reflectivity, and lower SOBEP scores are related to lower reflectivity scores. Although the relationship between the SOBEP and reflectivity scores in Figure 18–7 is not perfect, it does appear to be linear. But what would be the best straight line to describe these scores? Obviously, a number of straight lines could be drawn on the scatter plot. For example, we have drawn two different straight lines on Figure 18–7. The lines were drawn arbitrarily, except we made each line pass through the $\overline{X}, \overline{Y}$ coordinate (i.e., through the point $\overline{X} = 9, \overline{Y} = 3$). Does line A appear to "fit" or describe the scores better or worse than line B? To answer this question, we must have a criterion to decide whether or not a particular straight line fits a set of correlated scores.

The Least Squares Criterion

Each line, A and B, in Figure 18–7 permits us to predict a value of Y (that is, to obtain a Y') for each value of X. For example, for a reflectivity score of 17, line A predicts a Y' of about 4.3, and for a reflectivity score of 1, a Y' equal to about 1.7. On the other hand, line B predicts Y' equal to about 5.15 for an X of 17 and Y' equal to about 0.9 for a reflectivity score of 1. Each line thus leads to error in the Y' scores in comparison with the Y score actually obtained. If we use Y_i to indicate the obtained Y score for a person (e.g., $Y_9 = 2$ from Table 18–3) and Y_i' the predicted Y score for that person (e.g., $Y_9' = 1.7$ from line A in Figure 18–7), then the difference $Y_i - Y_i'$ is a measure of the error in prediction of the Y score from the X score. Table 18–4 illustrates the errors in prediction of each Y score from the X scores using either line A or line B of Figure 18–7.

TABLE 18–4.

Illustration of error of prediction of Y scores from the X scores of Figure 18–7 using either line A or line B.

	Obtained Scores		Predicted from Line A		Predicted from Line B	
			Scores	*Error*	*Scores*	*Error*
Person	X_i	Y_i	Y_i'	$Y_i - Y_i'$	Y_i'	$Y_i - Y_i'$
1	9	3	3.0	0.0	3.0	0.0
2	10	2	3.2	−1.2	3.3	−1.3
3	16	4	4.1	−0.1	4.9	−0.9
4	5	1	2.4	−1.4	1.9	−0.9
5	9	4	3.0	+1.0	3.0	+1.0
6	7	1	2.7	−1.7	2.5	−1.5
7	5	3	2.3	+0.7	1.8	+1.2
8	11	5	3.3	+1.7	3.5	+1.5
9	1	2	1.7	+0.3	0.9	+1.1
10	17	5	4.3	+0.7	5.2	−0.2
			Sums	0.0		0.0

TABLE 18–5.

Obtaining $\sum_{i=1}^{N} (Y_i - Y_i')^2$ for lines A and B of Figure 18–7. The values of $Y_i - Y_i'$ for each person for lines A and B were obtained in Table 18–4.

Person	Predicted from Line A		Predicted from Line B	
	$Y_i - Y_i'$	$(Y_i - Y_i')^2$	$Y_i - Y_i'$	$(Y_i - Y_i')^2$
1	0.0	0.00	0.0	0.00
2	−1.2	1.44	−1.3	1.69
3	−0.1	0.01	−0.9	0.81
4	−1.4	1.96	−0.9	0.81
5	+1.0	1.00	+1.0	1.00
6	−1.7	2.89	−1.5	2.25
7	+0.7	0.49	+1.2	1.44
8	+1.7	2.89	+1.5	2.25
9	+0.3	0.09	+1.1	1.21
10	+0.7	0.49	−0.2	0.04
Sums	0.0	11.26	0.0	11.50

Each line leads to errors in prediction. But does one line lead to smaller errors in prediction than the other? We might try to answer this question by adding up the error in each of the two error columns of Table 18–4. But if we do sum columns, as we have done in Table 18–4, we find that the sum of the errors, $\Sigma(Y_i - Y_i')$, is zero for each line. Clearly, $\Sigma(Y_i - Y_i')$ cannot be used as a criterion to determine the fit of a straight line to the points in a scatterplot; it will always be equal to zero. We faced a similar problem in Chapter 5 when attempting to find a measure of the variation of scores about the mean of a distribution. In that instance we found that $\Sigma(X_i - \overline{X})$ also was always equal to zero. We resolved the problem by squaring each $X_i - \overline{X}$ before the deviations were summed. Then we used $\Sigma(X_i - \overline{X})^2$ to develop a measure of error variation in the scores.

The current problem may be resolved similarly by squaring each $Y_i - Y_i'$ deviation before a sum is found. Then we will use $\Sigma(Y_i - Y_i')^2$ to determine which line best fits the scatterplot. Table 18–5 illustrates obtaining $\Sigma(Y_i - Y_i')^2$ for each line, A and B. The $\Sigma(Y_i - Y_i')^2$ for line A is 11.26, whereas for line B it is 11.50. Based on $\Sigma(Y_i - Y_i')^2$ as a measure of error in prediction, line A produces less error than line B.

When scientists want to find a straight line that best describes a scatterplot of correlated scores, such as those in Figure 18–7, they often use a line that minimizes the value of $\Sigma(Y_i - Y_i')^2$. This line is called a **least squares regression line,** for it minimizes the value of the sum of the squared deviations of every predicted Y score from the obtained Y score. That is, it minimizes $\Sigma(Y_i - Y_i')^2$. Figure 18–8 illustrates a least squares regression line fitted to the scatterplot of the scores in Table 18–3. The equation for this line is $Y' = +0.21X + 1.11$. The $Y_i - Y_i'$ deviations for each

FIGURE 18–8.
The least squares regression line for the reflectivity and SOBEP scores of Table 18–3.

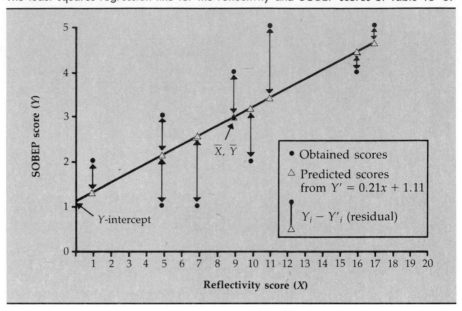

predicted Y score are illustrated on the figure. This line possesses the characteristic that the sum of the $(Y_i - Y_i')^2$ is a minimum; no other straight line fitted to the scores of Table 18–3 will produce a smaller value of $\Sigma(Y_i - Y_i')^2$. We now explain how to find the slope and Y-intercept for this line.

The Slope and Y-Intercept of a Least Squares Regression Line for Predicting Y from X

To find a least squares regression line we must determine the slope and Y-intercept of a straight line that minimizes the value of $\Sigma(Y_i - Y_i')^2$. The mathematics necessary to derive the equations for the slope and Y-intercept of such a line is beyond the scope of this book; hence we present only the end products of this mathematical process.

Formulas for the Slope of a Least Squares Regression Line

Deviational and Cross-Products Formula.   The slope of the least squares regression line for two linearly related variables is given by

$$b = \frac{\sum_{i=1}^{N}(X_i - \overline{X})(Y_i - \overline{Y})}{\sum_{i=1}^{N}(X_i - \overline{X})(X_i - \overline{X})}.$$

Recall that the numerator of this equation, $\sum_{i=1}^{N}(X_i - \overline{X})(Y_i - \overline{Y})$ is called the cross products of X and Y, and is symbolized as CP_{XY} (see Chapter 17). The denominator of the equation

$$\sum_{i=1}^{N}(X_i - \overline{X})(X_i - \overline{X}),$$

is the sum of squares for X, or SS_X. Thus, we may write the equation for b as

$$b = \frac{CP_{XY}}{SS_X}.$$

Raw-Score Computational Formula.   A formula that is more easily accomplished computationally from raw scores is

$$b = \frac{N\left(\sum_{i=1}^{N} X_i Y_i\right) - \left(\sum_{i=1}^{N} X_i\right)\left(\sum_{i=1}^{N} Y_i\right)}{N\sum_{i=1}^{N} X_i^2 - \left(\sum_{i=1}^{N} X_i\right)^2},$$

where N is the number of paired scores.

Correlation Formula.   The value of b may also be obtained from the Pearson correlation, r_{XY}, by using the equation

$$b = r_{XY}\left(\frac{s_Y}{s_X}\right).$$

In this equation r_{XY} is the Pearson correlation between the two sets of scores, s_Y is the standard deviation for the Y scores and s_X is the standard deviation for the X scores. We illustrate use of this equation in Example Problem 18–1.

Which Formula Should You Use to Find b?

Table 18–6 presents each of these formulas for finding the slope. Each formula provides the same value of b when applied to a set of scores. Which formula should you then choose to calculate b from a set of scores? In general, the computations needed for the raw-score computational formula are easier to perform and are less likely to lead to an error than are those needed for the deviational or cross-products formulas.

TABLE 18–6.

Formulas for the slope of a least squares regression line.

Deviational Formula

$$b = \frac{\sum_{i=1}^{N}(X_i - \overline{X})(Y_i - \overline{Y})}{\sum_{i=1}^{N}(X_i - \overline{X})(X_i - \overline{X})}$$

Cross-Products and Sum of Squares Formula

$$b = \frac{CP_{XY}}{SS_X}$$

Raw-Score Computational Formula

$$b = \frac{N\left(\sum_{i=1}^{N} X_i Y_i\right) - \left(\sum_{i=1}^{N} X_i\right)\left(\sum_{i=1}^{N} Y_i\right)}{N\sum_{i=1}^{N} X_i^2 - \left(\sum_{i=1}^{N} X_i\right)^2}$$

N is the number of paired scores

Correlation Formula

$$b = r_{XY}\left(\frac{s_Y}{s_X}\right).$$

Consequently, the raw-score formula is the formula that you would most likely use to obtain b from a set of scores and we illustrate its use below. If, however, you have already found the value of r_{XY} on the scores, then the formula using the Pearson correlation would be most expeditious, for it requires only that you find s_X and s_Y in addition to the value of r_{XY}.

Finding b Using the Raw-Score Formula

We illustrate the use of the raw-score formula to find the slope of the least squares regression line shown in Figure 18–8 fitted to the reflectivity and SOBEP scores of Table 18–3. The value of b using this formula is given by

$$b = \frac{N\left(\sum_{i=1}^{N} X_i Y_i\right) - \left(\sum_{i=1}^{N} X_i\right)\left(\sum_{i=1}^{N} Y_i\right)}{N\sum_{i=1}^{N} X_i^2 - \left(\sum_{i=1}^{N} X_i\right)^2}.$$

The computations required by this formula are illustrated in Table 18–7 for the reflectivity and SOBEP scores of Table 18–3. Columns b and c of this table present the X_i and Y_i scores, respectively. The sums of these columns provide the $\sum_{i=1}^{N} X_i$ and $\sum_{i=1}^{N} Y_i$ needed in both the numerator and

TABLE 18–7.

Calculating b using the raw-score formula. The reflectivity scores (X_i) and SOBEP scores (Y_i) are those from Table 18–3.

Step 1. Finding $\sum\limits_{i=1}^{N} X_i, \sum\limits_{i=1}^{N} Y_i, \sum\limits_{i=1}^{N} X_i^2, \sum\limits_{i=1}^{N} X_i Y_i$:

(a)	(b)	(c)	(d)	(e)
Person	X_i	Y_i	X_i^2	$X_i Y_i$
1	9	3	81	27
2	10	2	100	20
3	16	4	256	64
4	5	1	25	5
5	9	4	81	36
6	7	1	49	7
7	5	3	25	15
8	11	5	121	55
9	1	2	1	2
10	17	5	289	85
Sums	90	30	1028	316

Step 2. Calculating b:

$$\sum_{i=1}^{N} X_i = 90 \,,$$

$$\left(\sum_{i=1}^{N} X_i\right)^2 = 90^2 = 8100 \,,$$

$$\sum_{i=1}^{N} Y_i = 30 \,,$$

$$\sum_{i=1}^{N} X_i^2 = 1028 \,,$$

$$\sum_{i=1}^{N} X_i Y_i = 316 \,,$$

$N = 10$ pairs of scores, and $\quad b = \dfrac{N\left(\sum\limits_{i=1}^{N} X_i Y_i\right) - \left(\sum\limits_{i=1}^{N} X_i\right)\left(\sum\limits_{i=1}^{N} Y_i\right)}{N\sum\limits_{i=1}^{N} X_i^2 - \left(\sum\limits_{i=1}^{N} X_i\right)^2} \,.$

Substituting numerical values,

$$b = \frac{10(31)6 - 90(30)}{10(1028) - 8100}$$

$$b = \frac{3160 - 2700}{2180}$$

$$b = \frac{460}{2180} = +0.21 \,.$$

denominator of the equation. Thus $\sum_{i=1}^{N} X_i = 90$ and $\sum_{i=1}^{N} Y_i = 30$. Column d obtains each X_i^2 and the sum of this column, 1028, provides the value of $\sum_{i=1}^{N} X_i^2$ needed in the denominator of the equation. Column e gives the value of each $X_i Y_i$ and the sum of this column, 316, provides the $\sum_{i=1}^{N} X_i Y_i$ needed for the numerator of the equation.

Step 2 of Table 18–7 illustrates substituting the obtained values of $\sum_{i=1}^{N} X_i$, $\sum_{i=1}^{N} Y_i$, $\sum_{i=1}^{N} X_i Y_i$, and $\sum_{i=1}^{N} X_i^2$ into the equation. The value of b for the scores of Table 18–3 is +0.21.

Y-Intercept of a Least Squares Regression Line

The Y-intercept of a least squares regression line is calculated from the value of b by the formula

$$a = \overline{Y} - b\overline{X},$$

where $\overline{Y}$ is the mean of the Y scores, $\overline{X}$ is the mean of the X scores, and b is the slope of the least squares regression line obtained by using one of the formulas given in the previous section.

To illustrate the use of this formula for the scores of Table 18–3, $\overline{Y} = 3$, $\overline{X} = 9$, and $b = +0.21$. Thus

$$a = 3 - (0.21)(9) = 3 - 1.89 = 1.11.$$

The least squares regression line for these scores intersects the Y-axis at a value of $Y = 1.11$.

The Equation for the Least Squares Regression Line

When the values of b and a are substituted into the equation for a straight line,

$$Y' = bX + a,$$

we find

$$Y' = 0.21X + 1.11.$$

Hence, the least squares regression line for the scores of Table 18–3 is described by the equation $Y' = 0.21X + 1.11$. The line described by this equation is the line illustrated in Figure 18–8.

Fitting a Least Squares Regression Line to Obtained Scores

We now illustrate how the least squares regression line given by the equation $Y' = 0.21X + 1.11$ may be fitted to the scores plotted in Figure 18–8. A linear regression line is a straight line; thus if we know any two points on the line we have sufficient information to plot the line on the figure.

One point on the line is the Y-intercept, the value of Y' when $X = 0$. For our example, the Y-intercept is 1.11. Thus one point on the line has the coordinates $X = 0$, $Y = 1.11$.

A second point may be obtained by substituting a different value of X and solving for Y'. Although we may substitute any value for X, we use the value of $\overline{X}$, where $\overline{X} = 9$ for our example. Substituting $\overline{X} = 9$ into the equation, we obtain

$$Y' = 0.21(9) + 1.11 = 3.$$

Consequently, when $X = 9$, $Y' = 3$. The predicted value of Y, $Y' = 3$, is the value of $\overline{Y}$. For any least squares regression line, when the value of X is equal to the mean of the X scores, the predicted value of Y, Y', will be equal to the mean of the obtained Y scores. Therefore, a second point on the regression line will always be a point with coordinates of $\overline{X}, \overline{Y}$. For the scores in Figure 18–8, $\overline{X} = 9$, $\overline{Y} = 3$. Notice that the regression line on Figure 18–8 passes through these coordinates.

By examining Figure 18–8 you can see why the line described by

$$Y' = 0.21X + 1.11$$

is called the regression line of Y on X. One meaning of the word *regression* is to move toward or approach a mean. Notice that for extreme values of Y (e.g., SOBEP scores of 1 or 5) the Y' values are closer to the value of $\overline{Y} = 3$ than the Y values that they predict. Thus, the Y' values for Y values in the tails of the distribution tend to move or regress toward the mean of Y. For this reason, the line is called a regression line.

Testing Your Knowledge 18–2

On a separate sheet of paper, test your knowledge of the material in this section by answering the following questions.

1. Define: Y', $Y_i - Y_i'$, least squares regression line.
2. Write the general equation for predicting a value of Y from X.
3. Why can $\Sigma(Y_i - Y_i')$ not be used as a measure of error for predicting Y_i from a value of X?
4. Why may $\Sigma(Y_i - Y_i')^2$ be used as a measure of error for predicting Y_i from a value of X?
5. Write the four formulas that may be used to find the slope of a least squares regression line.
6. Write the formula that may be used to find the Y-intercept of a least squares regression line.
7. The slope and Y-intercept for the regression of Test 2 on Test 1 grades are $b = +0.8$, $a = 9$.

    a. Write the equation for the regression line of Test 2 on Test 1 for the scores.

    b. Find values of predicted Test 2 scores (i.e., Y') for the following Test 1 scores (i.e., X): 60, 65, 80, 85, 90.

    c. Plot the regression line on a sheet of graph paper. The value of $\overline{X} = 76$.

8. The slope and Y-intercept for the regression of Task 2 on Task 1 scores are $b = -1.4$, $a = 23$.

    a. Write the equation for the regression line of Task 2 on Task 1 for the scores.

    b. Find values of predicted Task 2 scores (i.e., Y') for the following Task 1 scores (i.e., X): 5, 8, 10, 14, 17.

    c. Plot the regression line on a sheet of graph paper. The value of $\overline{X} = 11$. ▪

Example Problem 18–1
Finding a Regression Line from the Correlation Coefficient

Problem:

Behavioral scientists have done considerable research into the factors affecting eating disorders such as anorexia and bulimia. One avenue of research has been to investigate the relationship of body image to other attributes such as sex role, perceived attractiveness, or self-esteem. Using a correlational approach, Mintz and Betz (1986) measured body satisfaction and depression proneness in a large group of college students. Each variable was measured using a self-report rating scale. Body satisfaction scores could range from 1 (indicating strong positive feelings towards one's body) to 7 (indicating strong negative feelings towards one's body). Depression proneness scores also ranged from 1 (indicating strong resistance to depression) to 7 (indicating proneness to depression). For a subgroup of slightly underweight females, Mintz and Betz found a statistically significant correlation of body satisfaction ratings (variable X) with depression proneness ratings (variable Y) of $r_{XY\,obs} = +0.44$ ($p \leq .05$). Suppose we replicated this study for a group of 15 slightly underweight females and obtained the body satisfaction and proneness to depression ratings given on the next page.

    The mean of the body satisfaction scores is $\overline{X} = 3.7$ and the standard deviation is 1.8. For depression proneness, $\overline{Y} = 3.8$ and $s_Y = 1.9$. The $r_{XY\,obs}$ of these scores is $+0.58$, $p \leq .05$. Construct the regression line of depression proneness on body satisfaction and find predicted depression proneness scores as a function of body satisfaction.

Solution:

The problem requires us to find values for the slope and Y-intercept of the regression line. Because r_{XY} is given, we may obtain the slope using the correlational formula shown in Table 18–6.

Person	Body Satisfaction (X_i)	Depression Proneness (Y_i)
1	2	1
2	4	6
3	6	3
4	1	2
5	3	4
6	5	7
7	6	4
8	3	1
9	7	6
10	1	2
11	4	4
12	2	5
13	3	2
14	5	5
15	4	5

Finding the slope: The slope, b, of the regression line may be found from r_{XY} by

$$b = r_{XY}\left(\frac{s_Y}{s_X}\right).$$

Substituting values of r_{XY}, s_X, and s_Y, we obtain

$$b = +0.58\left(\frac{1.9}{1.8}\right) = +0.61.$$

Finding the Y-Intercept: The Y-intercept is found from

$$a = \overline{Y} - b\overline{X},$$

or

$$a = 3.8 - (+0.61)(3.7) = 1.54.$$

Obtaining the Regression Equation: The regression equation of depression proneness (Y) on body satisfaction (X) is given by

$$Y' = 0.61X + 1.54.$$

Obtaining Predicted Depression Proneness Scores (Y'): Depression proneness scores (Y') predicted from body satisfaction scores (X) are obtained by solving the regression equation for each value of X. For example, for a body satisfaction rating score of 1, the regression equation becomes

$$Y' = 0.61(1) + 1.54 = 2.15.$$

The depression proneness rating predicted from a body satisfaction rating of 1 is 2.15, or rounding to one decimal place, 2.2.

Plotting the Regression Line: The regression line determined by the equation

$$Y' = 0.61X + 1.54$$

is plotted below. The predictor variable, body satisfaction (X) is plotted on the abscissa and the predicted variable, depression proneness score (Y'), is placed on the ordinate. The regression line is located on the graph by identifying the Y-intercept (1.54) and the coordinates of $\overline{X}, \overline{Y}$ (3.7 and 3.8, respectively) and drawing a straight line connecting these two points. The predicted depression proneness scores for each value of X are located on this line and we have identified their position by the dots along the line. ▨

The least squares regression line for the body image and depression proneness ratings. Predicted values of depression proneness for each body image rating are located on the regression line and are indicated by the dots.

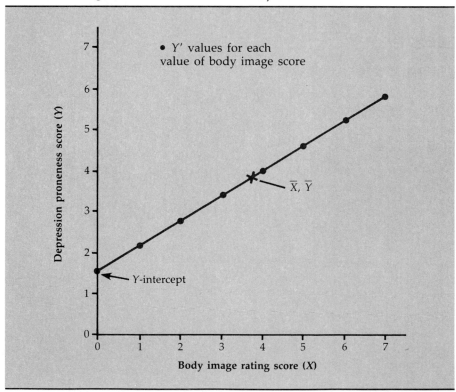

Statistics in Use 18–1

Preference for Sexual Relations and Number of Children: Using a Regression Analysis

One well-established finding in the study of marital relations is that the frequency of sexual intercourse declines as the length of the marriage increases. Indeed, Doddridge, Schumm, and Bergen (1987) cite a press clipping titled "Marriage council says tying the knot can ruin sex life" (p. 395). To investigate this phenomenon more fully, Doddridge et al. asked each partner of 30 married couples to indicate their preferred frequency of sexual intercourse on a weekly basis. They then related this measure (the Y variable) to a variety of other measures, such as the number of children in the marriage and the length of the marriage, among others. They found a significant negative correlation between number of children (variable X) and preferred frequency of intercourse, $r_{XY\,obs}$ for husbands equal to -0.37 and $r_{XY\,obs}$ for wives equal to -0.39.

A linear regression analysis of these scores yielded the equation for preferred frequency of sexual intercourse (Y') as a function of number of children (X) as

$$Y' = -0.50X + 3.5$$

for husbands, and

$$Y' = -0.39X + 2.7$$

for wives. Using these equations we find that for husbands, with no children, the preferred frequency is 3.5 instances per week. With two children, however, the preferred frequency drops to 2.5 instances per week. Similar values for wives are 2.7 instances per week with no children and 1.9 instances per week with two children.

Doddridge et al. caution against wide generalization of these specific values because their sample of couples was not randomly selected from a population. Nevertheless, their research illustrates how linear regression analysis can be used to describe functional relationships between variables. We must be cautious, however, not to ascribe causality to the relationships described. The regression equation simply describes the relationship between preferred frequency of sexual intercourse and number of children in the marriage. The limitations in reaching causal relationships that exist in correlational studies apply equally to linear regression analysis using two measured variables. ■

Testing Your Knowledge 18–3

On a separate sheet of paper, test your knowledge of the material in this section by answering the following questions.

1. Behavioral scientists are interested in the relation between personality attributes and performance of specific tasks. In one study, Gormly and Gormly (1986) correlated ratings of social introversion to performance on a block design test measuring spatial abilities. They found a statistically significant positive correlation—more socially introverted individuals created required block designs more quickly. Suppose you replicated this study rating individuals on a 9-point social introversion scale where 1 indicates highly socially introverted and 9 indicates not at all socially introverted. The amount of time the individual took to create a particular design with nine colored blocks was then recorded. The scores obtained for 12 individuals were:

Person	Introversion (X_i)	Block Design (Y_i)
1	6	217
2	3	230
3	9	315
4	1	224
5	4	271
6	2	198
7	3	256
8	5	263
9	8	321
10	7	289
11	8	265
12	6	291

The Pearson correlation for these scores is statistically significant at the .05 level. Using the raw-score formula for *b*, construct the regression line of block design on introversion scores.
   a. What is the slope of the regression line?
   b. What is the *Y*-intercept of the regression line?
   c. Write the equation for the regression line?
   d. Plot a scatterplot of the introversion and block design scores. Place the regression line on this plot also.
   e. What is the predicted block design score (Y') for each introversion score?
2. Bird watchers will notice that many species often spend a great deal of time scanning the environment. Elgar, McKay, and Woon (1986) observed house sparrows to determine the relationship between amount of scanning and feeding rate. They found a statistically significant negative

correlation between the two variables. Suppose you replicated this study observing 15 house sparrows in your yard. You recorded the number of scans of the environment each bird made per minute and the number of pecks at food each bird made per minute and found the mean scan rate ($\overline{X}$) was 26.2 scans per minute with $s_X = 8.7$. The mean pecks per minute ($\overline{Y}$) was 13.3 ($s_Y = 4.5$). The $r_{XY\,obs}$ between the two variables was -0.84. Using the correlational formula for b, construct the regression line of pecking rate (Y) on scans per minute (X).

a. What is the slope of the regression line?
b. What is the Y-intercept of the regression line?
c. Write the equation for the regression line?
d. What is the predicted pecking rate for a scan rate of 41 scans per minute? For 18 scans per minute?   ■

ERROR IN PREDICTION

Residuals: A Measure of the Error in Prediction

It is clear from Figure 18–8 and from Example Problem 18–1 that using X to predict Y leads to some error in prediction, unless, of course, X and Y are perfectly correlated. Earlier in this chapter, we used $Y_i - Y_i'$ to indicate this error for an individual score. This term, $Y_i - Y_i'$, often is identified as the **residual** in predicting a score. The residual is used as the basis for a measure of the accuracy of prediction called the **standard error of estimate.** To develop this measure of prediction accuracy, we return to the reflectivity and SOBEP scores of Table 18–3. The equation for the regression of these SOBEP scores (Y) on the reflectivity scores (X) is

$$Y' = 0.21X + 1.11\,.$$

Table 18–8 presents the reflectivity and SOBEP scores of Table 18–3 in columns b and c, respectively. Predicted SOBEP scores (i.e., Y') obtained from the regression equation are shown in column d. For example, Y' for person 6 with a reflectivity score of 7 is

$$Y_6' = (0.21)(7) + 1.11 = 2.58\,.$$

To avoid rounding error in later calculations we carried the predicted values to two decimal places rather than only one. You should calculate the remaining Y' values in column d to ensure that you are able to work with the regression equation for this set of scores.

The residual, or error in prediction, $Y - Y_i'$ is shown in column e. The sum of these residuals is equal to zero, so we cannot use the simple sum of these residuals as a measure of error in our prediction. Therefore, to

TABLE 18–8.

Calculating the residual for the predicted Y scores of Table 18–3. The regression equation for the scores is $Y_i' = 0.21X_i + 1.11$. The residual, or error in prediction, is presented in column e and the squared value of the residual is presented in column f.

(a)	(b)	(c)	(d)	(e)	(f)
Person	X_i	Y_i	Y_i'	$Y_i - Y_i'$	$(Y_i - Y_i')^2$
1	9	3	3.00	0.00	0.0000
2	10	2	3.21	−1.21	1.4641
3	16	4	4.47	−0.47	0.2209
4	5	1	2.16	−1.16	1.3456
5	9	4	3.00	+1.00	1.0000
6	7	1	2.58	−1.58	2.4964
7	5	3	2.16	+0.84	0.7056
8	11	5	3.42	+1.58	2.4964
9	1	2	1.32	+0.68	0.4624
10	17	5	4.68	+0.32	0.1024
			Sums	0.00	10.2938

develop a measure of error in prediction, we follow our usual approach and square each $Y_i - Y_i'$ value (see column f). Summing the squared values of $Y_i - Y_i'$ in column f we obtain a sum of squares called the $SS_{Residual}$, the sum of squared residuals. The $SS_{Residual}$ is equal to $\sum_{i=1}^{N}(Y_i - Y_i')^2$, or 10.2938 for our example.

The Standard Error of Estimate

In Chapter 5 we developed a measure of error variation for a set of scores, the standard deviation, s_X, by dividing the SS_X by its degrees of freedom and then taking the square root of the obtained quotient. We can obtain a similar measure of error variation in the prediction of Y from X, the standard error of estimate, by finding the square root of the quotient of the $SS_{Residual}$ divided by its degrees of freedom. The df for $SS_{Residual}$ are $N - 2$ where N is the number of paired scores. Accordingly, the **standard error of estimate,** symbolized as $s_{Y.X}$ to indicate that Y is predicted from X, is found by

$$s_{Y.X} = \sqrt{\frac{SS_{Residual}}{N - 2}},$$

or, equivalently

$$s_{Y.X} = \sqrt{\frac{\sum_{i=1}^{N}(Y_i - Y_i')^2}{N - 2}}.$$

In our example of the reflectivity and SOBEP scores, N is 10; thus the standard error of estimate of predicting SOBEP scores from reflectivity scores is

$$s_{Y.X} = \sqrt{\frac{10.2938}{10 - 2}},$$

$$s_{Y.X} = \sqrt{1.2867}$$

$$s_{Y.X} = 1.13.$$

What Information Does the Standard Error of Estimate Provide?

To understand what information the standard error of estimate provides, we return briefly to a consideration of the standard deviation, s. The standard deviation for a set of scores provides a measure of error variation for those scores. With a single set of scores, if we know no information about the scores other than the mean, then the best prediction we can make for any score is the mean. Of course, this prediction will likely be in error; and on the average, the error will be the value of the standard deviation. For example, suppose you are told that the mean SOBEP score for our example is 3. If you are asked to predict an individual score knowing nothing other than $\overline{Y} = 3$, your best prediction is 3. For the scores in Table 18–3, except for persons 1 and 7, this prediction is in error, however. The average error is the value of the standard deviation, $s_Y = 1.49$, for this set of scores.

Consider the information provided by the standard error of estimate. Suppose you are told there is a linear relation between the SOBEP scores and the reflectivity scores and the relationship is given by

$$Y' = 0.21X + 1.11.$$

Further, suppose you are told that person 8 has a reflectivity score of 11. Using this score and applying the regression equation, you predict this person's Y score to be 3.4. Although this prediction, too, is in error—the person's actual score was 5—the prediction of 3.4 is closer to the actual score than is the prediction of 3 made using only $\overline{Y}$ as a predictor. The standard error of estimate indicates the typical amount of error in predictions from the linear regression line. Notice in our example that $s_{Y.X} = 1.13$ is smaller than $s_Y = 1.49$. Accordingly, if we predict Y from X the error in our prediction will typically be less than if we simply used $\overline{Y}$ as a predictor for all the Y values. When r_{XY} is $+1.00$ or -1.00, as is the case for the scores in Table 18–2, then $s_{Y.X} = 0$ and there will be no error in prediction. On the other hand, if the correlation between two sets of scores approaches zero, then knowing X will not aid in predicting Y, and $s_{Y.X}$ will become as large as s_Y.

Raw-Score Formula for Calculating $s_{Y.X}$

The formula for $s_{Y.X}$,

$$s_{Y.X} = \sqrt{\frac{\sum\limits_{i=1}^{N}(Y_i - Y_i')^2}{N - 2}},$$

illustrates that it is a measure of error variation of the predicted scores compared with the actual scores. Because this formula requires finding $Y_i - Y_i'$ deviations, however, it is both time consuming to use and open to computational error. Thus, a computational formula has been developed that can be applied to the raw scores without obtaining $Y_i - Y_i'$ differences. This formula is

$$s_{Y.X} = \sqrt{\left[\frac{1}{N(N-2)}\right]\left[N\sum_{i=1}^{N}Y_i^2 - \left(\sum_{i=1}^{N}Y_i\right)^2 - \frac{\left[N\left(\sum\limits_{i=1}^{N}XY\right) - \left(\sum\limits_{i=1}^{N}X_i\right)\left(\sum\limits_{i=1}^{N}Y_i\right)\right]^2}{N\sum\limits_{i=1}^{N}X_i^2 - \left(\sum\limits_{i=1}^{N}X_i\right)^2}\right]}$$

where N is the number of pairs of scores.

This equation is not as difficult to solve as it may first appear. The computations using this equation to find $s_{Y.X}$ for the reflectivity and SOBEP scores of Table 18–3 are illustrated in Table 18–9. In step 1 of the table we find $\sum_{i=1}^{N}X_i$ (column b), $\sum_{i=1}^{N}Y_i$ (column c), $\sum_{i=1}^{N}X_i^2$ (column d), $\sum_{i=1}^{N}Y_i^2$ (column e), and $\sum_{i=1}^{N}XY$ (column f). Step 2 illustrates the substitution of these values into the raw-score formula. The obtained value of $s_{Y.X}$ is 1.13, which is the same as the value of $s_{Y.X} = 1.13$ found using the deviational formula.

 ## Example Problem 18–2
Finding a regression line and the standard error of estimate

Problem:
In Example Problem 18–1 we introduced the research of Mintz and Betz (1986) on the relationship of body satisfaction and depression proneness. They also obtained self-ratings of social self-esteem from their subjects. The self-esteem rating scales gave scores ranging from 20 (indicating low self-esteem) to 100 (indicating high self-esteem). Body satisfaction scores could range from 1 (indicating strong positive feelings towards one's body) to 7 (indicating strong negative feelings towards one's body). For slightly underweight females, Mintz and Betz obtained a correlation between body satisfaction (X) and social self-esteem (Y) of $r_{XY\,obs} = -0.60$.

TABLE 18–9.

Calculating $s_{Y.X}$ using the raw-score formula. The reflectivity scores (X_i) and SOBEP scores (Y_i) are those from Table 18–3.

Step 1. Finding $\sum\limits_{i=1}^{N} X_i$, $\sum\limits_{i=1}^{N} Y_i$, $\sum\limits_{i=1}^{N} X_i^2$, $\sum\limits_{i=1}^{N} Y_i^2$, and $\sum\limits_{i=1}^{N} X_i Y_i$:

(a) Person	(b) X_i	(c) Y_i	(d) X_i^2	(e) Y_i^2	(f) $X_i Y_i$
1	9	3	81	9	27
2	10	2	100	4	20
3	16	4	256	16	64
4	5	1	25	1	5
5	9	4	81	16	36
6	7	1	49	1	7
7	5	3	25	9	15
8	11	5	121	25	55
9	1	2	1	4	2
10	17	5	289	25	85
Sums	90	30	1028	110	316

Step 2. Calculating $s_{Y.X}$:

$$\sum_{i=1}^{N} X_i = 90 \qquad\qquad \sum_{i=1}^{N} Y_i = 30$$

$$\left(\sum_{i=1}^{N} X_i\right)^2 = 90^2 = 8100 \qquad\qquad \left(\sum_{i=1}^{N} Y_i\right)^2 = 30^2 = 900$$

$$\sum_{i=1}^{N} X_i^2 = 1028 \qquad\qquad \sum_{i=1}^{N} Y_i^2 = 110$$

$$\sum_{i=1}^{N} X_i Y_i = 316$$

$N = 10$ pairs of scores, and

$$s_{Y.X} = \sqrt{\left[\frac{1}{N(N-2)}\right]\left[N\sum_{i=1}^{N} Y_i^2 - \left(\sum_{i=1}^{N} Y_i\right)^2 - \frac{\left[N\left(\sum_{i=1}^{N} XY\right) - \left(\sum_{i=1}^{N} X_i\right)\left(\sum_{i=1}^{N} Y_i\right)\right]^2}{N\sum_{i=1}^{N} X_i^2 - \left(\sum_{i=1}^{N} X_i\right)^2}\right]},$$

$$s_{Y.X} = \sqrt{\left[\frac{1}{10(8)}\right]\left[10(110) - 900 - \frac{[10(316) - (90)(30)]^2}{10(1028) - 8100}\right]},$$

$$s_{Y.X} = \sqrt{\left(\frac{1}{80}\right)(1100 - 900 - 97.064)},$$

$$s_{Y.X} = 1.134 = 1.13.$$

Suppose in a replication of this study we obtained the body satisfaction and social self-esteem scores below:

Person	Body Satisfaction (X_i)	Self-Esteem (Y_i)
1	2	76
2	4	48
3	6	27
4	1	70
5	3	41
6	5	38
7	6	37
8	3	61
9	7	33
10	1	91
11	4	36
12	2	55
13	3	49
14	5	51
15	4	52

We want to find the following: (a) the least squares regression line of social self-esteem scores on body satisfaction scores, (b) the predicted self-esteem scores from the regression line, (c) the value of $s_{Y.X}$ from the residuals $Y_i - Y_i'$, and (d) the value of $s_{Y.X}$ using the computational formula.

Solution:
The table opposite provides the values necessary to find the information requested. In this table, the following values are given:

Column
a   The body satisfaction scores (X) and the $\sum_{i=1}^{N} X_i$,
b   the self-esteem scores (Y) and the $\sum_{i=1}^{N} Y_i$,
c   the body satisfaction scores squared (X^2) and the $\sum_{i=1}^{N} X_i^2$,
d   the self-esteem scores squared (Y^2) and the $\sum_{i=1}^{N} Y_i^2$,
e   the cross products of the body satisfaction and self-esteem scores and $\sum_{i=1}^{N} XY$,
f   the values of Y', predicted from the regression line found,
g   the residual for each self-esteem score.

	(a)	(b)	(c)	(d)	(e)	(f)	(g)
	Body Satisfaction	Self-Esteem					
Person	X_i	Y_i	X_i^2	Y_i^2	$X_i Y_i$	Y_i'	$Y_i - Y_i'$
1	2	76	4	5776	152	64.859	+11.141
2	4	48	16	2304	192	48.837	−0.837
3	6	27	36	729	162	32.815	−5.815
4	1	70	1	4900	70	72.870	−2.870
5	3	41	9	1681	123	56.848	−15.848
6	5	38	25	1444	190	40.826	−2.826
7	6	37	36	1369	222	32.815	+4.185
8	3	61	9	3721	183	56.848	+4.152
9	7	33	49	1089	231	24.804	+8.196
10	1	91	1	8281	91	72.870	+18.130
11	4	36	16	1296	144	48.837	−12.837
12	2	55	4	3025	110	64.859	−9.859
13	3	49	9	2401	147	56.848	−7.848
14	5	51	25	2601	255	40.826	+10.174
15	4	52	16	2704	208	48.837	+3.163
Sums	56	765	256	43321	2480		
Mean	3.73	51.00					
s	1.83	17.54					

a. Finding the regression line:

Calculating b:

$$\sum_{i=1}^{N} X_i = 56,$$

$$\left(\sum_{i=1}^{N} X_i\right)^2 = 56^2 = 3136$$

$$\sum_{i=1}^{N} X_i^2 = 256,$$

$$\sum_{i=1}^{N} Y_i = 765,$$

$$\sum_{i=1}^{N} X_i Y_i = 2480,$$

$N = 15$ pairs of scores, and

$$b = \frac{N\left(\sum_{i=1}^{N} X_i Y_i\right) - \left(\sum_{i=1}^{N} X_i\right)\left(\sum_{i=1}^{N} Y_i\right)}{N\sum_{i=1}^{N} X_i^2 - \left(\sum_{i=1}^{N} X_i\right)^2}$$

Substituting numerical values,

$$b = \frac{15(2480) - 56(765)}{15(256) - 3136} = -\frac{5640}{704} = -8.011.$$

Calculating a: $\overline{X} = 3.73$ and $\overline{Y} = 51.00$. Substituting these values into $a = \overline{Y} - b\overline{X}$, we obtain

$$a = 51.00 - (-8.011)(3.73),$$

or
$$a = 80.881.$$

Regression line: The regression line is given by

$$Y_i' = -8.011X + 80.881.$$

b. **Predicted self-esteem scores:** Predicted self-esteem scores from the regression equation are given in column f of the table. To avoid rounding error in finding $s_{Y.X}$ from the residuals, we have carried the Y' values to three decimal places.

c. $s_{Y.X}$ **from the residuals:** The residual values are presented in column g of the table. The value of $s_{Y.X}$ is obtained from these residuals by

$$s_{Y.X} = \sqrt{\frac{\sum_{i=1}^{N}(Y_i - Y_i')^2}{N - 2}}.$$

To obtain $\sum_{i=1}^{N}(Y_i - Y_i')^2$ each residual in Column g is squared and then the 15 squared values are summed. The

$$\sum_{i=1}^{N}(Y_i - Y_i')^2 = 1293.7380.$$

Substituting numercial values,

$$s_{Y.X} = \sqrt{\frac{1293.7380}{13}} - \sqrt{99.5183} - 9.98.$$

d. $s_{Y.X}$ **from the raw-score formula:** The value of $s_{Y.X}$ is obtained from the raw scores by

$$s_{Y.X} = \sqrt{\left[\frac{1}{N(N - 2)}\right]\left[N\sum_{i=1}^{N}Y_i^2 - \left(\sum_{i=1}^{N}Y_i\right)^2 - \frac{\left[N\left(\sum_{i=1}^{N}XY\right) - \left(\sum_{i=1}^{N}X_i\right)\left(\sum_{i=1}^{N}Y_i\right)\right]^2}{N\sum_{i=1}^{N}X_i^2 - \left(\sum_{i=1}^{N}X_i\right)^2}\right]}$$

Substituting numerical values,

$$s_{Y.X} = \sqrt{\left[\frac{1}{(15)(13)}\right]\left[15(43{,}321) - (765)^2 - \frac{[(15)(2{,}480) - (56)(765)]^2}{(15)(256) - (56)^2}\right]},$$

$$s_{Y.X} = \sqrt{\left(\frac{1}{195}\right)\left[64{,}590 - \frac{(37{,}200 - 42{,}840)^2}{3{,}840 - 3{,}136}\right]},$$

$$s_{Y.X} = 9.98\,.$$

The value of $s_{Y.X}$ from this formula is the same as the value obtained in step 3 using the definitional formula and residual values.

Conclusions:
The regression equation

$$Y' = -8.011X + 80.881$$

allows the prediction of self-esteem scores from body satisfaction scores with considerable reduction in the error of prediction. The value of $s_{Y.X}$, 9.98, the average amount of error associated with a predicted self-esteem score from the regression equation is smaller than s_Y, 17.54, the average amount of error that is associated with using $\overline{Y}$ (i.e., 51.0) as the predicted value of self-esteem for all individuals. Consequently, knowledge of body satisfaction scores considerably improves our ability to predict self-esteem scores. ∎

Testing Your Knowledge 18–4

On a separate sheet of paper, test your knowledge of the material in this section by answering the following questions.

1. Define: residual, $SS_{Residual}$, standard error of estimate, $s_{Y.X}$.
2. Give the definitional formula for the standard error of estimate.
3. In problem 1 of Testing Your Knowledge 18–3 we gave an example of predicting block design scores (Y') from introversion scores (X). The regression equation that you found was

$$Y' = 11.507X + 202.215\,.$$

The introversion scores (X), obtained block design scores (Y), and predicted block design scores (Y') from this equation are given on the next page.
a. Use the Y' given to find the residual for each person.
b. Find the $SS_{Residual}$.
c. Find $s_{Y.X}$ using the $SS_{Residual}$ obtained in b.

Person	Introversion (X_i)	Block Design (Y_i)	Predicted (Y'_i)
1	6	217	271.3
2	3	230	236.7
3	9	315	305.8
4	1	224	213.7
5	4	271	248.2
6	2	198	225.2
7	3	256	236.7
8	5	263	259.8
9	8	321	294.3
10	7	289	282.8
11	8	265	294.3
12	6	291	271.3

   d. Compare $s_{Y \cdot X}$ to the s_Y, 38.82, for these scores. Does the use of the regression equation to predict block design scores from introversion scores reduce the error of prediction in comparison to using the mean block design score (i.e., 261.7 seconds) as the predicted value for all block design scores?

4. Exercise 2 of Testing Your Knowledge 18–3 presented a study on the relationship of the number of scans per minute (X) and number of pecks per minute (Y) for 15 house sparrows. Suppose the scores obtained were

Bird	Scans (X_i)	Pecks (Y_i)
1	27	13
2	35	10
3	19	12
4	16	19
5	41	10
6	22	13
7	13	22
8	31	11
9	26	10
10	29	12
11	34	8
12	18	21
13	39	9
14	26	12
15	17	18

   a. Use the raw-score formula to find $s_{Y \cdot X}$ for this set of scores.

   b. Compare $s_{Y \cdot X}$ to s_Y for the scores. Does knowledge of X and the regression equation of Y on X permit you to more accurately predict the number of pecks per minute for each bird? ■

Using a Linear Regression Line

The purpose of constructing a linear regression line is to predict one set of scores from another. Two conditions must exist between the sets of scores for this to be achieved successfully. First, the Pearson correlation between the two sets of scores must be statistically significant. When the scores are not correlated, the best prediction one can make of a Y score is to use the mean of the Y scores. If the X and Y scores are not correlated, then if you are given an X score and asked to predict a Y score, the best prediction of Y is simply $\overline{Y}$. The knowledge of X does not give you any information about the value of Y.

A second requirement is that the relationship between the scores must be linear. The formula developed in this chapter for the least squares regression line is for a straight line. Accordingly, if the X and Y scores are not linearly related, then it is inappropriate to fit a least squares regression line to them. For example, if X and Y are related in a U-shaped or an inverted U-shaped (i.e., ⋀) fashion, then constructing a least squares regression line for the scores will not lead to accurate predictions, for the scores are not linearly related.

We must be cautious also to not predict beyond the range of scores encompassed in the sample from which the prediction equation was developed. The relationship may be nonlinear for values outside the range in the sample.

This chapter has provided a brief introduction to regression and prediction. In practice, regression equations become more complex than those we have introduced. Often equations are developed using several predictor variables. An employer may want to predict potential employee performance as a function of an aptitude test score and months of previous work experience. Or, a college admissions officer may want to predict college grade point average from a standardized test score and high school grade point average. These more complex problems are beyond the scope of this introductory chapter.

SUMMARY

- In a linear relation, each time one variable changes by one unit, there is a constant change in the second variable.
- The general equation of a straight line is given by

$$Y = bX + a.$$

- The slope, b, is defined as

$$b = \frac{Y_2 - Y_1}{X_2 - X_1}.$$

- The Y-intercept, a, is the value of Y when $X = 0$.

- A least squares regression line minimizes the value of the sum of the squared deviations of every Y' score from the obtained Y score.
- The residual, $Y_i - Y_i'$, is the error for predicting an individual score from a regression equation.

- The standard error of estimate is found by

$$s_{Y.X} = \sqrt{\frac{SS_{Residual}}{N - 2}}, \quad \text{or}$$

$$s_{Y.X} = \sqrt{\frac{\sum_{i=1}^{N} (Y_i - Y_i')^2}{N - 2}}.$$

KEY TERMS

a

b

least squares regression line

linear relation

regression line

residual

slope of a linear relation

standard error of estimate

s_X

s_Y

$s_{Y.X}$

$SS_{Residual}$

Y-intercept

Y'

$Y_i - Y_i'$

REVIEW QUESTIONS

On a separate sheet of paper, test your knowledge of the material in this chapter by answering the following questions.

1. Jamie has just received her midterm grade in her statistics class. Her instructor said that for a previous semester the following midterm and final examination grades were obtained by 10 students in the course.

Student	Examination	
	Midterm (X)	Final (Y)
1	87	84
2	89	91
3	97	96
4	80	87
5	73	66
6	85	90
7	81	79
8	74	80
9	80	89
10	89	86

    a. Find the slope of the least squares regression line for predicting final exam grades from midterm grades using the raw-score computational formula.

    b. The $r_{XY\,obs}$ for these scores is $+0.781$, $s_X = 7.37$, and $s_Y = 8.34$. Find b using the formula for r_{XY}.

    c. Find the equation of the least squares regression line for predicting Y from X for these scores.

    d. Jamie received a 77 on her midterm examination. Based on the regression line found in 1c, what is her predicted final examination score?

    e. What is the value of $s_{Y.X}$ for this regression line?

2. An investigator observed 12 students on the amount of time playing video games per week (variable X) and correlated this time with their semester grade point averages (variable Y). For a range of 0 to 15 hours per week of video game playing, the $r_{XY\,obs}$ was -0.632 ($p \le .05$). The $s_X = 4.10$ hours and $s_Y = 0.75$. The Y-intercept of the regression line was 3.23.

    a. Find the least squares regression line for predicting grade point average from video playing time.

    b. Brian plays video games about three hours per week. What is his predicted grade point average?

    c. The mean video game playing time in the sample observed was 5.1 hours per week. What is the mean grade point average for the sample?

3. One research study has found a linear relationship between amount of smoking by a pregnant woman and the amount of weight loss of the neonate. For each cigarette smoked per day during pregnancy by the mother, the baby's birth weight is reduced by 4.3 ounces ("Birth Weight," 1986). Assume that if the pregnant mother does not smoke, the average weight of the neonate is 128 ounces.

    a. Write the equation for the linear relationship expressed above. (Hint, both the slope and the Y-intercept are given.)

    b. Plot the linear regression line on a sheet of graph paper. Place the number of cigarettes smoked (X) on the abscissa.

    c. What is the predicted birth weight of a baby whose mother smoked the following number of cigarettes per day during pregnancy? 0, 1, 5, 8, 10, 13, 20.

4. In Chapter 17 (Chapter Review Question 1), we gave the following values of percentage of body fat and average golf scores (in strokes) for 12 professional female golfers.

Golfer	Body Fat (X_i)	Score (Y_i)
1	20.1	70
2	28.9	77
3	25.4	75
4	19.6	67
5	36.3	79
6	22.9	73
7	26.5	74
8	30.7	72
9	29.8	83
10	33.2	75
11	24.1	68
12	27.3	75

a. Find the equation for the regression of golf score (Y) on percent body fat (X) for these scores.

b. What is the predicted golf score for each player as a function of percentage of body fat?

c. Plot a scatterplot of the percentage of body fat (on the abscissa) and average golf score (on the ordinate). Place the regression line on this plot also.

d. Compare each predicted score with the obtained score. Do the predicted scores demonstrate regression to the mean? Explain your answer.

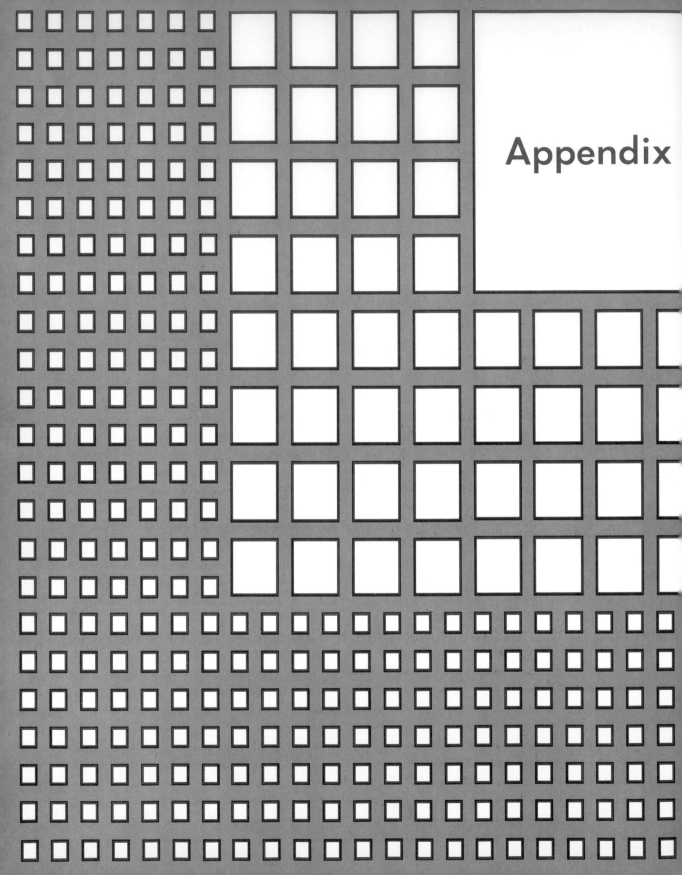

Appendix

Table A–1. Proportions of area under the standard normal distribution.

Table A–2. Critical values of the t distribution for $\alpha = .05$ and $\alpha = .01$.

Tables A–3a and b. Critical values of the F distribution for $\alpha = .05$ and $\alpha = .01$.

Tables A–4a and b. Values of the studentized range statistic q_k, for $\alpha = .05$ and $\alpha = .01$.

Table A–5. Approximate power of the t test for $\mu_{A_1} = \mu_{A_2}$ at $\alpha = .05$ for a two-tailed test.

Table A–6. Critical values of the chi square distribution for $\alpha = .05$ and $\alpha = .01$.

Tables A–7a and b. Critical values of U in the Mann-Whitney U test for $\alpha = .05$ and $\alpha = .01$.

Table A–8. Critical values of T in the Wilcoxon test for $\alpha = .05$ and $\alpha = .01$.

Table A–9. Critical values of r for $\alpha = .05$ and $\alpha = .01$.

Table A–10. Critical values of r_s for $\alpha = .05$ and $\alpha = .01$.

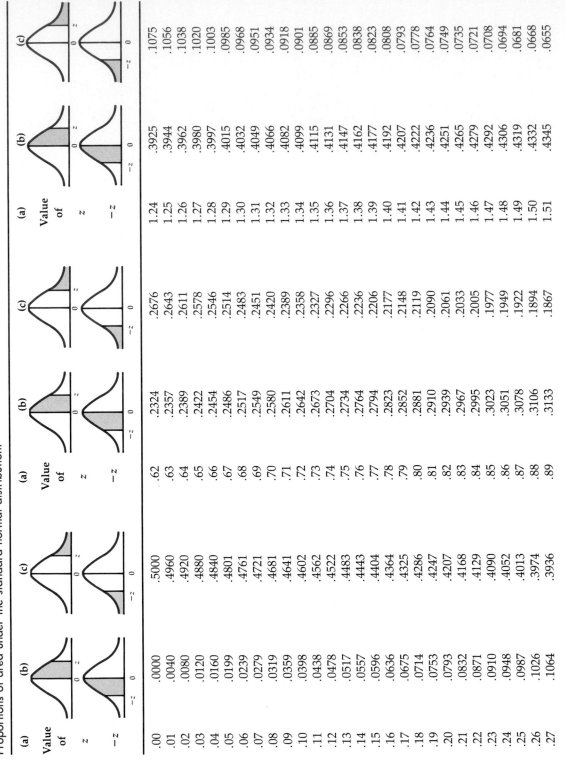

TABLE A–1.
Proportions of area under the standard normal distribution.

(a) Value of z / −z	(b)	(c)	(a) Value of z / −z	(b)	(c)	(a) Value of z / −z	(b)	(c)
.00	.0000	.5000	.62	.2324	.2676	1.24	.3925	.1075
.01	.0040	.4960	.63	.2357	.2643	1.25	.3944	.1056
.02	.0080	.4920	.64	.2389	.2611	1.26	.3962	.1038
.03	.0120	.4880	.65	.2422	.2578	1.27	.3980	.1020
.04	.0160	.4840	.66	.2454	.2546	1.28	.3997	.1003
.05	.0199	.4801	.67	.2486	.2514	1.29	.4015	.0985
.06	.0239	.4761	.68	.2517	.2483	1.30	.4032	.0968
.07	.0279	.4721	.69	.2549	.2451	1.31	.4049	.0951
.08	.0319	.4681	.70	.2580	.2420	1.32	.4066	.0934
.09	.0359	.4641	.71	.2611	.2389	1.33	.4082	.0918
.10	.0398	.4602	.72	.2642	.2358	1.34	.4099	.0901
.11	.0438	.4562	.73	.2673	.2327	1.35	.4115	.0885
.12	.0478	.4522	.74	.2704	.2296	1.36	.4131	.0869
.13	.0517	.4483	.75	.2734	.2266	1.37	.4147	.0853
.14	.0557	.4443	.76	.2764	.2236	1.38	.4162	.0838
.15	.0596	.4404	.77	.2794	.2206	1.39	.4177	.0823
.16	.0636	.4364	.78	.2823	.2177	1.40	.4192	.0808
.17	.0675	.4325	.79	.2852	.2148	1.41	.4207	.0793
.18	.0714	.4286	.80	.2881	.2119	1.42	.4222	.0778
.19	.0753	.4247	.81	.2910	.2090	1.43	.4236	.0764
.20	.0793	.4207	.82	.2939	.2061	1.44	.4251	.0749
.21	.0832	.4168	.83	.2967	.2033	1.45	.4265	.0735
.22	.0871	.4129	.84	.2995	.2005	1.46	.4279	.0721
.23	.0910	.4090	.85	.3023	.1977	1.47	.4292	.0708
.24	.0948	.4052	.86	.3051	.1949	1.48	.4306	.0694
.25	.0987	.4013	.87	.3078	.1922	1.49	.4319	.0681
.26	.1026	.3974	.88	.3106	.1894	1.50	.4332	.0668
.27	.1064	.3936	.89	.3133	.1867	1.51	.4345	.0655

.28	.1103	.3897	.90	.3159	.1841	1.52	.4357	.0643
.29	.1141	.3859	.91	.3186	.1814	1.53	.4370	.0630
.30	.1179	.3821	.92	.3212	.1788	1.54	.4382	.0618
.31	.1217	.3783	.93	.3238	.1762	1.55	.4394	.0606
.32	.1255	.3745	.94	.3264	.1736	1.56	.4406	.0594
.33	.1293	.3707	.95	.3289	.1711	1.57	.4418	.0582
.34	.1331	.3669	.96	.3315	.1685	1.58	.4429	.0571
.35	.1368	.3632	.97	.3340	.1660	1.59	.4441	.0559
.36	.1406	.3594	.98	.3365	.1635	1.60	.4452	.0548
.37	.1443	.3557	.99	.3389	.1611	1.61	.4463	.0537
.38	.1480	.3520	1.00	.3413	.1587	1.62	.4474	.0526
.39	.1517	.3483	1.01	.3438	.1562	1.63	.4484	.0516
.40	.1554	.3446	1.02	.3461	.1539	1.64	.4495	.0505
.41	.1591	.3409	1.03	.3485	.1515	1.65	.4505	.0495
.42	.1628	.3372	1.04	.3508	.1492	1.66	.4515	.0485
.43	.1664	.3336	1.05	.3531	.1469	1.67	.4525	.0475
.44	.1700	.3300	1.06	.3554	.1446	1.68	.4535	.0465
.45	.1736	.3264	1.07	.3577	.1423	1.69	.4545	.0455
.46	.1772	.3228	1.08	.3599	.1401	1.70	.4554	.0446
.47	.1808	.3192	1.09	.3621	.1379	1.71	.4564	.0436
.48	.1844	.3156	1.10	.3643	.1357	1.72	.4573	.0427
.49	.1879	.3121	1.11	.3665	.1335	1.73	.4582	.0418
.50	.1915	.3085	1.12	.3686	.1314	1.74	.4591	.0409
.51	.1950	.3050	1.13	.3708	.1292	1.75	.4599	.0401
.52	.1985	.3015	1.14	.3729	.1271	1.76	.4608	.0392
.53	.2019	.2981	1.15	.3749	.1251	1.77	.4616	.0384
.54	.2054	.2946	1.16	.3770	.1230	1.78	.4625	.0375
.55	.2088	.2912	1.17	.3790	.1210	1.79	.4633	.0367
.56	.2123	.2877	1.18	.3810	.1190	1.80	.4641	.0359
.57	.2157	.2843	1.19	.3830	.1170	1.81	.4649	.0351
.58	.2190	.2810	1.20	.3849	.1151	1.82	.4656	.0344
.59	.2224	.2776	1.21	.3869	.1131	1.83	.4664	.0336
.60	.2257	.2743	1.22	.3888	.1112	1.84	.4671	.0329
.61	.2291	.2709	1.23	.3907	.1093	1.85	.4678	.0322

TABLE A–1. Continued

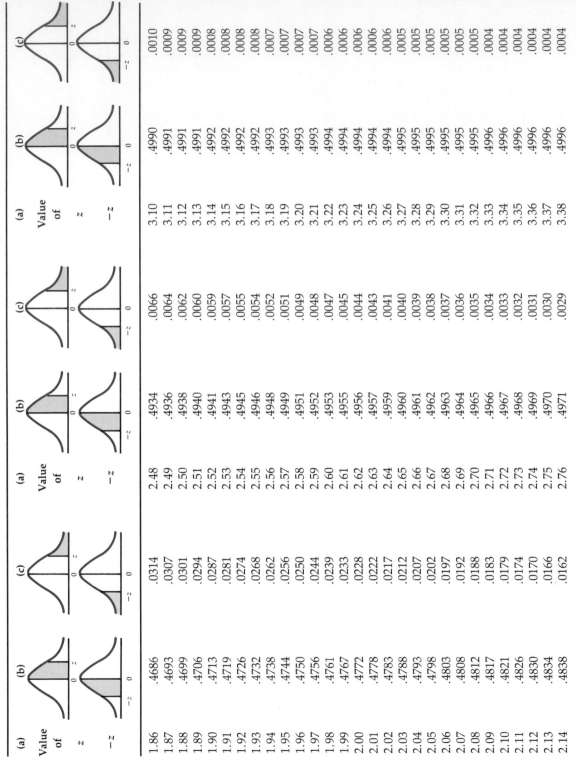

(a) Value of z / $-z$	(b)	(c)	(a) Value of z / $-z$	(b)	(c)	(a) Value of z / $-z$	(b)	(c)
1.86	.4686	.0314	2.48	.4934	.0066	3.10	.4990	.0010
1.87	.4693	.0307	2.49	.4936	.0064	3.11	.4991	.0009
1.88	.4699	.0301	2.50	.4938	.0062	3.12	.4991	.0009
1.89	.4706	.0294	2.51	.4940	.0060	3.13	.4991	.0009
1.90	.4713	.0287	2.52	.4941	.0059	3.14	.4992	.0008
1.91	.4719	.0281	2.53	.4943	.0057	3.15	.4992	.0008
1.92	.4726	.0274	2.54	.4945	.0055	3.16	.4992	.0008
1.93	.4732	.0268	2.55	.4946	.0054	3.17	.4992	.0008
1.94	.4738	.0262	2.56	.4948	.0052	3.18	.4993	.0007
1.95	.4744	.0256	2.57	.4949	.0051	3.19	.4993	.0007
1.96	.4750	.0250	2.58	.4951	.0049	3.20	.4993	.0007
1.97	.4756	.0244	2.59	.4952	.0048	3.21	.4993	.0007
1.98	.4761	.0239	2.60	.4953	.0047	3.22	.4994	.0006
1.99	.4767	.0233	2.61	.4955	.0045	3.23	.4994	.0006
2.00	.4772	.0228	2.62	.4956	.0044	3.24	.4994	.0006
2.01	.4778	.0222	2.63	.4957	.0043	3.25	.4994	.0006
2.02	.4783	.0217	2.64	.4959	.0041	3.26	.4994	.0006
2.03	.4788	.0212	2.65	.4960	.0040	3.27	.4995	.0005
2.04	.4793	.0207	2.66	.4961	.0039	3.28	.4995	.0005
2.05	.4798	.0202	2.67	.4962	.0038	3.29	.4995	.0005
2.06	.4803	.0197	2.68	.4963	.0037	3.30	.4995	.0005
2.07	.4808	.0192	2.69	.4964	.0036	3.31	.4995	.0005
2.08	.4812	.0188	2.70	.4965	.0035	3.32	.4995	.0005
2.09	.4817	.0183	2.71	.4966	.0034	3.33	.4996	.0004
2.10	.4821	.0179	2.72	.4967	.0033	3.34	.4996	.0004
2.11	.4826	.0174	2.73	.4968	.0032	3.35	.4996	.0004
2.12	.4830	.0170	2.74	.4969	.0031	3.36	.4996	.0004
2.13	.4834	.0166	2.75	.4970	.0030	3.37	.4996	.0004
2.14	.4838	.0162	2.76	.4971	.0029	3.38	.4996	.0004

z			z			z		
2.15	.4842	.0158	2.77	.4972	.0028	3.39	.4997	.0003
2.16	.4846	.0154	2.78	.4973	.0027	3.40	.4997	.0003
2.17	.4850	.0150	2.79	.4974	.0026	3.41	.4997	.0003
2.18	.4854	.0146	2.80	.4974	.0026	3.42	.4997	.0003
2.19	.4857	.0143	2.81	.4975	.0025	3.43	.4997	.0003
2.20	.4861	.0139	2.82	.4976	.0024	3.44	.4997	.0003
2.21	.4864	.0136	2.83	.4977	.0023	3.45	.4997	.0003
2.22	.4868	.0132	2.84	.4977	.0023	3.46	.4997	.0003
2.23	.4871	.0129	2.85	.4978	.0022	3.47	.4997	.0003
2.24	.4875	.0125	2.86	.4979	.0021	3.48	.4997	.0002
2.25	.4878	.0122	2.87	.4979	.0021	3.49	.4998	.0002
2.26	.4881	.0119	2.88	.4980	.0020	3.50	.4998	.0002
2.27	.4884	.0116	2.89	.4981	.0019	3.51	.4998	.0002
2.28	.4887	.0113	2.90	.4981	.0019	3.52	.4998	.0002
2.29	.4890	.0110	2.91	.4982	.0018	3.53	.4998	.0002
2.30	.4893	.0107	2.92	.4982	.0018	3.54	.4998	.0002
2.31	.4896	.0104	2.93	.4983	.0017	3.55	.4998	.0002
2.32	.4898	.0102	2.94	.4984	.0016	3.56	.4998	.0002
2.33	.4901	.0099	2.95	.4984	.0016	3.57	.4998	.0002
2.34	.4904	.0096	2.96	.4985	.0015	3.58	.4998	.0002
2.35	.4906	.0094	2.97	.4985	.0015	3.59	.4998	.0002
2.36	.4909	.0091	2.98	.4986	.0014	3.60	.4998	.0002
2.37	.4911	.0089	2.99	.4986	.0014	3.61	.4998	.0002
2.38	.4913	.0087	3.00	.4987	.0013	3.62	.4999	.0001
2.39	.4916	.0084	3.01	.4987	.0013	3.63	.4999	.0001
2.40	.4918	.0082	3.02	.4987	.0013	3.64	.4999	.0001
2.41	.4920	.0080	3.03	.4988	.0012	3.65	.4999	.0001
2.42	.4922	.0078	3.04	.4988	.0012	3.66	.4999	.0001
2.43	.4925	.0075	3.05	.4989	.0011	3.67	.4999	.0001
2.44	.4927	.0073	3.06	.4989	.0011	3.68	.4999	.0001
2.45	.4929	.0071	3.07	.4989	.0011	3.69	.4999	.0001
2.46	.4931	.0069	3.08	.4990	.0010	3.70	.4999	.0001
2.47	.4932	.0068	3.09	.4990	.0010			

Excerpted and adapted from Table II.1 The Normal Probability Function and Related Functions. *CRC Handbook of Tables for Probability and Statistics* (2nd ed.). Copyright 1968, CRC Press, Inc., Boca Raton, Florida. Used by permission.

TABLE A–2.

Critical values of the t distribution for $\alpha = .05$ and $\alpha = .01$. A value of $t_{obs}(df)$ equal to or greater than the tabled value is statistically significant at the α level selected.

	Two-Tailed Test	
df	$\alpha = .05$	$\alpha = .01$
1	12.706	63.657
2	4.303	9.925
3	3.182	5.841
4	2.776	4.604
5	2.571	4.032
6	2.447	3.707
7	2.365	3.499
8	2.306	3.355
9	2.262	3.250
10	2.228	3.169
11	2.201	3.106
12	2.179	3.055
13	2.160	3.012
14	2.145	2.977
15	2.131	2.947
16	2.120	2.921
17	2.110	2.898
18	2.101	2.878
19	2.093	2.861
20	2.086	2.845
21	2.080	2.831
22	2.074	2.819
23	2.069	2.807
24	2.064	2.797
25	2.060	2.787
26	2.056	2.779
27	2.052	2.771
28	2.048	2.763
29	2.045	2.756
30	2.042	2.750
40	2.021	2.704
60	2.000	2.660
120	1.980	2.617
∞	1.960	2.576

	One-Tailed Test	
df	$\alpha = .05$	$\alpha = .01$
1	6.314	31.821
2	2.920	6.965
3	2.353	4.541
4	2.132	3.747
5	2.015	3.365
6	1.943	3.143
7	1.895	2.998
8	1.860	2.896
9	1.833	2.821
10	1.812	2.764
11	1.796	2.718
12	1.782	2.681
13	1.771	2.650
14	1.761	2.624
15	1.753	2.602
16	1.746	2.583
17	1.740	2.567
18	1.734	2.552
19	1.729	2.539
20	1.725	2.528
21	1.721	2.518
22	1.717	2.508
23	1.714	2.500
24	1.711	2.492
25	1.708	2.485
26	1.706	2.479
27	1.703	2.473
28	1.701	2.467
29	1.699	2.462
30	1.697	2.457
40	1.684	2.423
60	1.671	2.390
120	1.658	2.358
∞	1.645	2.326

Reprinted with permission from Table IV.1 Percentage Points, Student's
t-Distribution, *CRC Handbook of Tables for Probability and Statistics* (2nd ed.).
Copyright 1968, CRC Press, Inc., Boca Raton, Florida.

TABLE A–3a.

Critical values of the F distribution for $\alpha = .05$. A value of $F_{obs}(df_{numerator}, df_{denominator})$ equal to or greater than the tabled value is statistically significant at the .05 significance level.

Degrees of Freedom for the Denominator	Degrees of Freedom for the Numerator																		
	1	2	3	4	5	6	7	8	9	10	12	15	20	24	30	40	60	120	∞
1	161.4	199.5	215.7	224.6	230.2	234.0	236.8	238.9	240.5	241.9	243.9	245.9	248.0	249.1	250.1	251.1	252.2	253.3	254.3
2	18.51	19.00	19.16	19.25	19.30	19.33	19.35	19.37	19.38	19.40	19.41	19.43	19.45	19.45	19.46	19.47	19.48	19.49	19.50
3	10.13	9.55	9.28	9.12	9.01	8.94	8.89	8.85	8.81	8.79	8.74	8.70	8.66	8.64	8.62	8.59	8.57	8.55	8.53
4	7.71	6.94	6.59	6.39	6.26	6.16	6.09	6.04	6.00	5.96	5.91	5.86	5.80	5.77	5.75	5.72	5.69	5.66	5.63
5	6.61	5.79	5.41	5.19	5.05	4.95	4.88	4.82	4.77	4.74	4.68	4.62	4.56	4.53	4.50	4.46	4.43	4.40	4.36
6	5.99	5.14	4.76	4.53	4.39	4.28	4.21	4.15	4.10	4.06	4.00	3.94	3.87	3.84	3.81	3.77	3.74	3.70	3.67
7	5.59	4.74	4.35	4.12	3.97	3.87	3.79	3.73	3.68	3.64	3.57	3.51	3.44	3.41	3.38	3.34	3.30	3.27	3.23
8	5.32	4.46	4.07	3.84	3.69	3.58	3.50	3.44	3.39	3.35	3.28	3.22	3.15	3.12	3.08	3.04	3.01	2.97	2.93
9	5.12	4.26	3.86	3.63	3.48	3.37	3.29	3.23	3.18	3.14	3.07	3.01	2.94	2.90	2.86	2.83	2.79	2.75	2.71
10	4.96	4.10	3.71	3.48	3.33	3.22	3.14	3.07	3.02	2.98	2.91	2.85	2.77	2.74	2.70	2.66	2.62	2.58	2.54
11	4.84	3.98	3.59	3.36	3.20	3.09	3.01	2.95	2.90	2.85	2.79	2.72	2.65	2.61	2.57	2.53	2.49	2.45	2.40
12	4.75	3.89	3.49	3.26	3.11	3.00	2.91	2.85	2.80	2.75	2.69	2.62	2.54	2.51	2.47	2.43	2.38	2.34	2.30
13	4.67	3.81	3.41	3.18	3.03	2.92	2.83	2.77	2.71	2.67	2.60	2.53	2.46	2.42	2.38	2.34	2.30	2.25	2.21
14	4.60	3.74	3.34	3.11	2.96	2.85	2.76	2.70	2.65	2.60	2.53	2.46	2.39	2.35	2.31	2.27	2.22	2.18	2.13
15	4.54	3.68	3.29	3.06	2.90	2.79	2.71	2.64	2.59	2.54	2.48	2.40	2.33	2.29	2.25	2.20	2.16	2.11	2.07
16	4.49	3.63	3.24	3.01	2.85	2.74	2.66	2.59	2.54	2.49	2.42	2.35	2.28	2.24	2.19	2.15	2.11	2.06	2.01
17	4.45	3.59	3.20	2.96	2.81	2.70	2.61	2.55	2.49	2.45	2.38	2.31	2.23	2.19	2.15	2.10	2.06	2.01	1.96
18	4.41	3.55	3.16	2.93	2.77	2.66	2.58	2.51	2.46	2.41	2.34	2.27	2.19	2.15	2.11	2.06	2.02	1.97	1.92
19	4.38	3.52	3.13	2.90	2.74	2.63	2.54	2.48	2.42	2.38	2.31	2.23	2.16	2.11	2.07	2.03	1.98	1.93	1.88
20	4.35	3.49	3.10	2.87	2.71	2.60	2.51	2.45	2.39	2.35	2.28	2.20	2.12	2.08	2.04	1.99	1.95	1.90	1.84
21	4.32	3.47	3.07	2.84	2.68	2.57	2.49	2.42	2.37	2.32	2.25	2.18	2.10	2.05	2.01	1.96	1.92	1.87	1.81
22	4.30	3.44	3.05	2.82	2.66	2.55	2.46	2.40	2.34	2.30	2.23	2.15	2.07	2.03	1.98	1.94	1.89	1.84	1.78
23	4.28	3.42	3.03	2.80	2.64	2.53	2.44	2.37	2.32	2.27	2.20	2.13	2.05	2.01	1.96	1.91	1.86	1.81	1.76
24	4.26	3.40	3.01	2.78	2.62	2.51	2.42	2.36	2.30	2.25	2.18	2.11	2.03	1.98	1.94	1.89	1.84	1.79	1.73
25	4.24	3.39	2.99	2.76	2.60	2.49	2.40	2.34	2.28	2.24	2.16	2.09	2.01	1.96	1.92	1.87	1.82	1.77	1.71
26	4.23	3.37	2.98	2.74	2.59	2.47	2.39	2.32	2.27	2.22	2.15	2.07	1.99	1.95	1.90	1.85	1.80	1.75	1.69
27	4.21	3.35	2.96	2.73	2.57	2.46	2.37	2.31	2.25	2.20	2.13	2.06	1.97	1.93	1.88	1.84	1.79	1.73	1.67
28	4.20	3.34	2.95	2.71	2.56	2.45	2.36	2.29	2.24	2.19	2.12	2.04	1.96	1.91	1.87	1.82	1.77	1.71	1.65
29	4.18	3.33	2.93	2.70	2.55	2.43	2.35	2.28	2.22	2.18	2.10	2.03	1.94	1.90	1.85	1.81	1.75	1.70	1.64
30	4.17	3.32	2.92	2.69	2.53	2.42	2.33	2.27	2.21	2.16	2.09	2.01	1.93	1.89	1.84	1.79	1.74	1.68	1.62
40	4.08	3.23	2.84	2.61	2.45	2.34	2.25	2.18	2.12	2.08	2.00	1.92	1.84	1.79	1.74	1.69	1.64	1.58	1.51
60	4.00	3.15	2.76	2.53	2.37	2.25	2.17	2.10	2.04	1.99	1.92	1.84	1.75	1.70	1.65	1.59	1.53	1.47	1.39
120	3.92	3.07	2.68	2.45	2.29	2.17	2.09	2.02	1.96	1.91	1.83	1.75	1.66	1.61	1.55	1.50	1.43	1.35	1.25
∞	3.84	3.00	2.60	2.37	2.21	2.10	2.01	1.94	1.88	1.83	1.75	1.67	1.57	1.52	1.46	1.39	1.32	1.22	1.00

Reprinted with permission from Table VI.1, Percentage Points, *F*-Distribution, *CRC Handbook of Tables for Probability and Statistics* (2nd ed.). Copyright 1968, CRC Press, Inc., Boca Raton, Florida.

TABLE A–3b.

Critical values of the F distribution for $\alpha = .01$. A value of $F_{abs}(df_{numerator}, df_{denominator})$ equal to or greater than the tabled value is statistically significant at the .01 significance level.

	Degrees of Freedom for the Numerator																		
	1	2	3	4	5	6	7	8	9	10	12	15	20	24	30	40	60	120	∞
1	4052	4999.5	5403	5625	5764	5859	5928	5982	6022	6056	6106	6157	6209	6235	6261	6287	6313	6339	6366
2	98.50	99.00	99.17	99.25	99.30	99.33	99.36	99.37	99.39	99.40	99.42	99.43	99.45	99.46	99.47	99.47	99.48	99.49	99.50
3	34.12	30.82	29.46	28.71	28.24	27.91	27.67	27.49	27.35	27.23	27.05	26.87	26.69	26.60	26.50	26.41	26.32	26.22	26.13
4	21.20	18.00	16.69	15.98	15.52	15.21	14.98	14.80	14.66	14.55	14.37	14.20	14.02	13.93	13.84	13.75	13.65	13.56	13.46
5	16.26	13.27	12.06	11.39	10.97	10.67	10.46	10.29	10.16	10.05	9.89	9.72	9.55	9.47	9.38	9.29	9.20	9.11	9.02
6	13.75	10.92	9.78	9.15	8.75	8.47	8.26	8.10	7.98	7.87	7.72	7.56	7.40	7.31	7.23	7.14	7.06	6.97	6.88
7	12.25	9.55	8.45	7.85	7.46	7.19	6.99	6.84	6.72	6.62	6.47	6.31	6.16	6.07	5.99	5.91	5.82	5.74	5.65
8	11.26	8.65	7.59	7.01	6.63	6.37	6.18	6.03	5.91	5.81	5.67	5.52	5.36	5.28	5.20	5.12	5.03	4.95	4.86
9	10.56	8.02	6.99	6.42	6.06	5.80	5.61	5.47	5.35	5.26	5.11	4.96	4.81	4.73	4.65	4.57	4.48	4.40	4.31
10	10.04	7.56	6.55	5.99	5.64	5.39	5.20	5.06	4.94	4.85	4.71	4.56	4.41	4.33	4.25	4.17	4.08	4.00	3.91
11	9.65	7.21	6.22	5.67	5.32	5.07	4.89	4.74	4.63	4.54	4.40	4.25	4.10	4.02	3.94	3.86	3.78	3.69	3.60
12	9.33	6.93	5.95	5.41	5.06	4.82	4.64	4.50	4.39	4.30	4.16	4.01	3.86	3.78	3.70	3.62	3.54	3.45	3.36
13	9.07	6.70	5.74	5.21	4.86	4.62	4.44	4.30	4.19	4.10	3.96	3.82	3.66	3.59	3.51	3.43	3.34	3.25	3.17
14	8.86	6.51	5.56	5.04	4.69	4.46	4.28	4.14	4.03	3.94	3.80	3.66	3.51	3.43	3.35	3.27	3.18	3.09	3.00
15	8.68	6.36	5.42	4.89	4.56	4.32	4.14	4.00	3.89	3.80	3.67	3.52	3.37	3.29	3.21	3.13	3.05	2.96	2.87
16	8.53	6.23	5.29	4.77	4.44	4.20	4.03	3.89	3.78	3.69	3.55	3.41	3.26	3.18	3.10	3.02	2.93	2.84	2.75
17	8.40	6.11	5.18	4.67	4.34	4.10	3.93	3.79	3.68	3.59	3.46	3.31	3.16	3.08	3.00	2.92	2.83	2.75	2.65
18	8.29	6.01	5.09	4.58	4.25	4.01	3.84	3.71	3.60	3.51	3.37	3.23	3.08	3.00	2.92	2.84	2.75	2.66	2.57
19	8.18	5.93	5.01	4.50	4.17	3.94	3.77	3.63	3.52	3.43	3.30	3.15	3.00	2.92	2.84	2.76	2.67	2.58	2.49
20	8.10	5.85	4.94	4.43	4.10	3.87	3.70	3.56	3.46	3.37	3.23	3.09	2.94	2.86	2.78	2.69	2.61	2.52	2.42
21	8.02	5.78	4.87	4.37	4.04	3.81	3.64	3.51	3.40	3.31	3.17	3.03	2.88	2.80	2.72	2.64	2.55	2.46	2.36
22	7.95	5.72	4.82	4.31	3.99	3.76	3.59	3.45	3.35	3.26	3.12	2.98	2.83	2.75	2.67	2.58	2.50	2.40	2.31
23	7.88	5.66	4.76	4.26	3.94	3.71	3.54	3.41	3.30	3.21	3.07	2.93	2.78	2.70	2.62	2.54	2.45	2.35	2.26
24	7.82	5.61	4.72	4.22	3.90	3.67	3.50	3.36	3.26	3.17	3.03	2.89	2.74	2.66	2.58	2.49	2.40	2.31	2.21
25	7.77	5.57	4.68	4.18	3.85	3.63	3.46	3.32	3.22	3.13	2.99	2.85	2.70	2.62	2.54	2.45	2.36	2.27	2.17
26	7.72	5.53	4.64	4.14	3.82	3.59	3.42	3.29	3.18	3.09	2.96	2.81	2.66	2.58	2.50	2.42	2.33	2.23	2.13
27	7.68	5.49	4.60	4.11	3.78	3.56	3.39	3.26	3.15	3.06	2.93	2.78	2.63	2.55	2.47	2.38	2.29	2.20	2.10
28	7.64	5.45	4.57	4.07	3.75	3.53	3.36	3.23	3.12	3.03	2.90	2.75	2.60	2.52	2.44	2.35	2.26	2.17	2.06
29	7.60	5.42	4.54	4.04	3.73	3.50	3.33	3.20	3.09	3.00	2.87	2.73	2.57	2.49	2.41	2.33	2.23	2.14	2.03
30	7.56	5.39	4.51	4.02	3.70	3.47	3.30	3.17	3.07	2.98	2.84	2.70	2.55	2.47	2.39	2.30	2.21	2.11	2.01
40	7.31	5.18	4.31	3.83	3.51	3.29	3.12	2.99	2.89	2.80	2.66	2.52	2.37	2.29	2.20	2.11	2.02	1.92	1.80
60	7.08	4.98	4.13	3.65	3.34	3.12	2.95	2.82	2.72	2.63	2.50	2.35	2.20	2.12	2.03	1.94	1.84	1.73	1.60
120	6.85	4.79	3.95	3.48	3.17	2.96	2.79	2.66	2.56	2.47	2.34	2.19	2.03	1.95	1.86	1.76	1.66	1.53	1.38
∞	6.63	4.61	3.78	3.32	3.02	2.80	2.64	2.51	2.41	2.32	2.18	2.04	1.88	1.79	1.70	1.59	1.47	1.32	1.00

Degrees of Freedom for the Denominator

Reprinted with permission from Table VI.1, Percentage Points, F-Distribution, CRC *Handbook of Tables for Probability and Statistics* (2nd ed.). Copyright 1968, CRC Press, Inc., Boca Raton, Florida.

TABLE A–4a.

Values of the studentized range statistic, q_k, for $\alpha = .05$.

		Number of Means Being Compared								
		2	3	4	5	6	7	8	9	10
	1	17.97	26.98	32.82	37.08	40.41	43.12	45.40	47.36	49.07
	2	6.08	8.33	9.80	10.88	11.74	12.44	13.03	13.54	13.99
	3	4.50	5.91	6.82	7.50	8.04	8.48	8.85	9.18	9.46
	4	3.93	5.04	5.76	6.29	6.71	7.05	7.35	7.60	7.83
	5	3.64	4.60	5.22	5.67	6.03	6.33	6.58	6.80	6.99
	6	3.46	4.34	4.90	5.30	5.63	5.90	6.12	6.32	6.49
	7	3.34	4.16	4.68	5.06	5.36	5.61	5.82	6.00	6.16
Degrees	8	3.26	4.04	4.53	4.89	5.17	5.40	5.60	5.77	5.92
of	9	3.20	3.95	4.41	4.76	5.02	5.24	5.43	5.59	5.74
Freedom	10	3.15	3.88	4.33	4.65	4.91	5.12	5.30	5.46	5.60
for	11	3.11	3.82	4.26	4.57	4.82	5.03	5.20	5.35	5.49
MS_{Error}	12	3.08	3.77	4.20	4.51	4.75	4.95	5.12	5.27	5.39
	13	3.06	3.73	4.15	4.45	4.69	4.88	5.05	5.19	5.32
	14	3.03	3.70	4.11	4.41	4.64	4.83	4.99	5.13	5.25
	15	3.01	3.67	4.08	4.37	4.59	4.78	4.94	5.08	5.20
	16	3.00	3.65	4.05	4.33	4.56	4.74	4.90	5.03	5.15
	17	2.98	3.63	4.02	4.30	4.52	4.70	4.86	4.99	5.11
	18	2.97	3.61	4.00	4.28	4.49	4.67	4.82	4.96	5.07
	19	2.96	3.59	3.98	4.25	4.47	4.65	4.79	4.92	5.04
	20	2.95	3.58	3.96	4.23	4.45	4.62	4.77	4.90	5.01
	24	2.92	3.53	3.90	4.17	4.37	4.54	4.68	4.81	4.92
	30	2.89	3.49	3.85	4.10	4.30	4.46	4.60	4.72	4.82
	40	2.86	3.44	3.79	4.04	4.23	4.39	4.52	4.63	4.73
	60	2.83	3.40	3.74	3.98	4.16	4.31	4.44	4.55	4.65
	120	2.80	3.36	3.68	3.92	4.10	4.24	4.36	4.47	4.56
	∞	2.77	3.31	3.63	3.86	4.03	4.17	4.29	4.39	4.47

TABLE A—4b.

Values of the studentized range statistic, q_k, for $\alpha = .01$.

		Number of Means Being Compared								
		2	**3**	**4**	**5**	**6**	**7**	**8**	**9**	**10**
	1	90.03	135.0	164.3	185.6	202.2	215.8	227.2	237.0	245.6
	2	14.04	19.02	22.29	24.72	26.63	28.20	29.53	30.68	31.69
	3	8.26	10.62	12.17	13.33	14.24	15.00	15.64	16.20	16.69
	4	6.51	8.12	9.17	9.96	10.58	11.10	11.55	11.93	12.27
	5	5.70	6.98	7.80	8.42	8.91	9.32	9.67	9.97	10.24
	6	5.24	6.33	7.03	7.56	7.97	8.32	8.61	8.87	9.10
	7	4.95	5.92	6.54	7.01	7.37	7.68	7.94	8.17	8.37
Degrees	8	4.75	5.64	6.20	6.62	6.96	7.24	7.47	7.68	7.86
of	9	4.60	5.43	5.96	6.35	6.66	6.91	7.13	7.33	7.49
Freedom	10	4.48	5.27	5.77	6.14	6.43	6.67	6.87	7.05	7.21
for	11	4.39	5.15	5.62	5.97	6.25	6.48	6.67	6.84	6.99
MS_{Error}	12	4.32	5.05	5.50	5.84	6.10	6.32	6.51	6.67	6.81
	13	4.26	4.96	5.40	5.73	5.98	6.19	6.37	6.53	6.67
	14	4.21	4.89	5.32	5.63	5.88	6.08	6.26	6.41	6.54
	15	4.17	4.84	5.25	5.56	5.80	5.99	6.16	6.31	6.44
	16	4.13	4.79	5.19	5.49	5.72	5.92	6.08	6.22	6.35
	17	4.10	4.74	5.14	5.43	5.66	5.85	6.01	6.15	6.27
	18	4.07	4.70	5.09	5.38	5.60	5.79	5.94	6.08	6.20
	19	4.05	4.67	5.05	5.33	5.55	5.73	5.89	6.02	6.14
	20	4.02	4.64	5.02	5.29	5.51	5.69	5.84	5.97	6.09
	24	3.96	4.55	4.91	5.17	5.37	5.54	5.69	5.81	5.92
	30	3.89	4.45	4.80	5.05	5.24	5.40	5.54	5.65	5.76
	40	3.82	4.37	4.70	4.93	5.11	5.26	5.39	5.50	5.60
	60	3.76	4.28	4.59	4.82	4.99	5.13	5.25	5.36	5.45
	120	3.70	4.20	4.50	4.71	4.87	5.01	5.12	5.21	5.30
	∞	3.64	4.12	4.40	4.60	4.76	4.88	4.99	5.08	5.16

Reprinted with permission from Table VIII.3, Percentage Points, Studentized Range, *CRC Handbook of Tables for Probability and Statistics* (2nd ed.). Copyright 1968, CRC Press, Inc., Boca Raton, Florida.

TABLE A–5.

Approximate power of the t test for $\mu_{A_1} = \mu_{A_2}$ at $\alpha = .05$ for a two-tailed test. n_A is the size of each group and d is the effect size.

		d				d	
n_A	0.20	0.50	0.80	n_A	0.20	0.50	0.80
6	0.06	0.14	0.28	30	0.12	0.49	0.87
7	0.07	0.16	0.32	35	0.13	0.52	0.92
8	0.07	0.17	0.36	40	0.15	0.60	0.95
9	0.07	0.18	0.40	45	0.16	0.66	0.97
10	0.07	0.20	0.44	50	0.17	0.71	0.98
11	0.08	0.21	0.47	55	0.18	0.75	0.99
12	0.08	0.23	0.50	60	0.19	0.78	0.99
13	0.08	0.25	0.52	65	0.20	0.81	0.99
14	0.08	0.27	0.57	70	0.21	0.84	*
15	0.08	0.28	0.59	75	0.23	0.85	
16	0.09	0.29	0.61	80	0.24	0.88	
17	0.09	0.30	0.64	85	0.26	0.90	
18	0.09	0.32	0.67	90	0.27	0.92	
19	0.09	0.34	0.69	95	0.28	0.93	
20	0.10	0.35	0.72	100	0.29	0.94	
21	0.10	0.37	0.74	150	0.41	0.99	
22	0.10	0.38	0.75	200	0.52	*	
23	0.11	0.40	0.77	250	0.60		
24	0.11	0.41	0.78	300	0.69		
25	0.11	0.43	0.81	350	0.75		
26	0.11	0.44	0.83	400	0.81		
27	0.11	0.45	0.84	450	0.85		
28	0.12	0.46	0.85	500	0.88		
29	0.12	0.48	0.86				

*power values below this point are greater than 0.995.

Values calculated by the author using the approximation method given in Cohen (1970).

TABLE A–6.

Critical values of the chi square distribution for $\alpha = .05$ and $\alpha = .01$. A value of $\chi^2_{obs}(df)$ equal to or greater than the tabled value is statistically significant at the α level selected.

df	$\alpha = .05$	$\alpha = .01$
1	3.84	6.63
2	5.99	9.21
3	7.81	11.3
4	9.49	13.3
5	11.1	15.1
6	12.6	16.8
7	14.1	18.5
8	15.5	20.1
9	16.9	21.7
10	18.3	23.2
11	19.7	24.7
12	21.0	26.2
13	22.4	27.7
14	23.7	29.1
15	25.0	30.6
16	26.3	32.0
17	27.6	33.4
18	28.9	34.8
19	30.1	36.2
20	31.4	37.6
21	32.7	38.9
22	33.9	40.3
23	35.2	41.6
24	36.4	43.0
25	37.7	44.3
26	38.9	45.6
27	40.1	47.0
28	41.3	48.3
29	42.6	49.6
30	43.8	50.9

Reprinted with permission from Table V.1, Percentage Points, Chi-Square Distribution. *CRC Handbook of Tables for Probability and Statistics*, (2nd ed.). Copyright 1968, CRC Press, Inc., Boca Raton, Florida.

TABLE A–7a.

Critical values of U in the Mann-Whitney U test for $\alpha = .05$ (two-tailed test). If the group sizes are unequal, n_1 is the smaller group. A value of U_{obs} equal to or less than the tabled value is statistically significant at the .05 significance level.

										n_2										
n_1	1	2	3	4	5	6	7	8	9	10	11	12	13	14	15	16	17	18	19	20
1																				
2								0	0	0	0	1	1	1	1	1	2	2	2	2
3					0	1	1	2	2	3	3	4	4	5	5	6	6	7	7	8
4				0	1	2	3	4	4	5	6	7	8	9	10	11	11	12	13	13
5			0	1	2	3	5	6	7	8	9	11	12	13	14	15	17	18	19	20
6			1	2	3	5	6	8	10	11	13	14	16	17	19	21	22	24	25	27
7			1	3	5	6	8	10	12	14	16	18	20	22	24	26	28	30	32	34
8		0	2	4	6	8	10	13	15	17	19	22	24	26	29	31	34	36	38	41
9		0	2	4	7	10	12	15	17	20	23	26	28	31	34	37	39	42	45	48
10		0	3	5	8	11	14	17	20	23	26	29	33	36	39	42	45	48	52	55
11		0	3	6	9	13	16	19	23	26	30	33	37	40	44	47	51	55	58	62
12		1	4	7	11	14	18	22	26	29	33	37	41	45	49	53	57	61	65	69
13		1	4	8	12	16	20	24	28	33	37	41	45	50	54	59	63	67	72	76
14		1	5	9	13	17	22	26	31	36	40	45	50	55	59	64	67	74	78	83
15		1	5	10	14	19	24	29	34	39	44	49	54	59	64	70	75	80	85	90
16		1	6	11	15	21	26	31	37	42	47	53	59	64	70	75	81	86	92	98
17		2	6	11	17	22	28	34	39	45	51	57	63	67	75	81	87	93	99	105
18		2	7	12	18	24	30	36	42	48	55	61	67	74	80	86	93	99	106	112
19		2	7	13	19	25	32	38	45	52	58	65	72	78	85	92	99	106	113	119
20		2	8	13	20	27	34	41	48	55	62	69	76	83	90	98	105	112	119	127

TABLE A—7b.

Critical values of U in the Mann-Whitney U test for $\alpha = .01$ (two-tailed test). If the group sizes are unequal, n_1 is the smaller group. A value of U_{obs} equal to or less than the tabled value is statistically significant at the .01 significance level.

		n_2																		
		1	2	3	4	5	6	7	8	9	10	11	12	13	14	15	16	17	18	19	20
	1																				
	2																			0	0
	3									0	0	0	1	1	1	2	2	2	2	3	3
	4					0	0	1	1	2	2	3	3	4	5	5	6	6	7	8
	5				0	1	1	2	3	4	5	6	7	7	8	9	10	11	12	13
	6			0	1	2	3	4	5	6	7	9	10	11	12	13	15	16	17	18
	7			0	1	3	4	6	7	9	10	12	13	15	16	18	19	21	22	24
	8		1	2	4	6	7	9	11	13	15	17	18	20	22	24	26	28	30
	9		0	1	3	5	7	9	11	13	16	18	20	22	24	27	29	31	33	36
n_1	10		0	2	4	6	9	11	13	16	18	21	24	26	29	31	34	37	39	42
	11		0	2	5	7	10	13	16	18	21	24	27	30	33	36	39	42	45	48
	12		1	3	6	9	12	15	18	21	24	27	31	34	37	41	44	47	51	54
	13		1	3	7	10	13	17	20	24	27	31	34	38	42	45	49	53	56	60
	14		1	4	7	11	15	18	22	26	30	34	38	42	46	50	54	58	63	67
	15		2	5	8	12	16	20	24	29	33	37	42	46	51	55	60	64	69	73
	16		2	5	9	13	18	22	27	31	36	41	45	50	55	60	65	70	74	79
	17		2	6	10	15	19	24	29	34	39	44	49	54	60	65	70	75	81	86
	18		2	6	11	16	21	26	31	37	42	47	53	58	64	70	75	81	87	92
	19	0	3	7	12	17	22	28	33	39	45	51	56	63	69	74	81	87	93	99
	20	0	3	8	13	18	24	30	36	42	48	54	60	67	73	79	86	92	99	105

TABLE A–8.

Critical values of T in the Wilcoxon test for $\alpha = .05$ and $\alpha = .01$ (two-tailed test). A value of T_{obs} equal to or less than the tabled value is statistically significant at the α level selected. Dashes indicate that statistical significance cannot be attained at this level for this group size.

N	$\alpha = .05$	$\alpha = .01$	N	$\alpha = .05$	$\alpha = .01$
6	1	—	29	127	100
7	2	—	30	137	109
8	4	0	31	148	118
9	6	2	32	159	128
10	8	3	33	171	138
11	11	5	34	183	149
12	14	7	35	195	160
13	17	10	36	208	171
14	21	13	37	222	183
15	25	16	38	235	195
16	30	19	39	250	208
17	35	23	40	264	221
18	40	28	41	279	234
19	46	32	42	295	248
20	52	37	43	311	262
21	59	43	44	327	277
22	66	49	45	344	292
23	73	55	46	361	307
24	81	61	47	379	323
25	90	68	48	397	339
26	98	76	49	415	356
27	107	84	50	434	373
28	117	92			

Excerpted and adapted from Table X.2, Critical Values of T in the Wilcoxon Matched-Pairs Signed-Ranks Test. *CRC Handbook of Tables for Probability and Statistics* (2nd ed.). Copyright 1968, CRC Press, Inc., Boca Raton, Florida. Used by permission.

TABLE A–9.

Critical values of r for $\alpha = .05$ and $\alpha = .01$ (two-tailed test). A value of r_{obs} equal to or greater than the tabled value is statistically significant at the α level selected.

df^a	$\alpha = .05$	$\alpha = .01$
1	.99692	.999877
2	.9500	.99000
3	.878	.9587
4	.811	.9172
5	.754	.875
6	.707	.834
7	.666	.798
8	.632	.765
9	.602	.735
10	.576	.708
11	.553	.684
12	.532	.661
13	.514	.641
14	.497	.623
15	.482	.606
16	.468	.590
17	.456	.575
18	.444	.561
19	.433	.549
20	.423	.537
25	.381	.487
30	.349	.449
35	.325	.418
40	.304	.393
45	.288	.372
50	.273	.354
60	.250	.325
70	.232	.302
80	.217	.283
90	.205	.267
100	.195	.254

$^a df$ are equal to $N - 2$ where N is the number of paired observations.

TABLE A–10.

Critical values of r_s for $\alpha = .05$ and $\alpha = .01$ (two-tailed test). N is the number of pairs of ranks. A value of $r_{s\,obs}$ equal to or greater than the tabled value is statistically significant at the α level selected.

N	$\alpha = .05$	$\alpha = .01$
5	—	—
6	0.886	—
7	0.786	0.929
8	0.738	0.881
9	0.700	0.833
10	0.648	0.794
11	0.618	0.818
12	0.591	0.780
13	0.566	0.745
14	0.545	0.716
15	0.525	0.689
16	0.507	0.666
17	0.490	0.645
18	0.476	0.625
19	0.462	0.608
20	0.450	0.591
21	0.438	0.576
22	0.428	0.562
23	0.418	0.549
24	0.409	0.537
25	0.400	0.526
26	0.392	0.515
27	0.385	0.505
28	0.377	0.496
29	0.370	0.487
30	0.364	0.478

Answers for Selected Problems

Solutions are given for all numerical problems in the Testing Your Knowledge and Chapter Review Questions sections. For formulas and explanations, see the relevant sections of the text.

1

Testing Your Knowledge 1–1

2. **b.** From the sample of 600 to the population of all voters in the district.

Testing Your Knowledge 1–2

2. **a.** Type of feedback given.
   b. Duration of foot pronation.
   c. Creation of two equivalent groups and the manipulation of an independent variable.
   d. To determine if the pronation times differed more than expected by chance.

Testing Your Knowledge 1–3

2. **a.** To find if belief in paranormal phenomena and number of science courses taken are related.
   b. Belief in paranormal phenomena; number of science courses taken.

REVIEW QUESTIONS

1. **a.** To find if golf score is related to percentage of body fat.
   b. Percentage of body fat; average golf score.
2. **a.** Type of treatment.
   b. Body temperature.
   c. Creation of two equivalent groups and the manipulation of an independent variable.
   d. To find if body temperatures in the two groups differed by more than chance.
3. **b.** Percentage.

2

Testing Your Knowledge 2–1

2. Several examples: motivational level, locus of control, alertness, confidence, reliability, trustworthiness.
3. Nominal, ordinal, interval, ratio.
4. People are assigned to the same category although they do not possess the same amount of the variable being measured.
6. **b.** No, see text.

Testing Your Knowledge 2–2

2. **a.** Yes, the scale is interval; see text for characteristics.
   b. No.
   c. No.
3. **a.** Yes, the scale is ratio; see text for characteristics.
   b. Yes.
   c. Yes.

Testing Your Knowledge 2–3

2. **a.** Continuous.
   b. Continuous.
   c. Discrete.
   d. Continuous.
   e. Continuous.
   f. Discrete.
3. **a.** 152.35 to 152.45 cm.
   b. 17.25 to 17.35 sec.
   c. 3.5 to 4.5.
   d. 0.4365 to 0.4375 sec.
   e. 6.85 to 6.95 mm.
   f. 67.805 to 67.815 kg.
4. **a.** 27.4.
   b. 119.028.
   c. 1.44.
   d. 1263.7592.
   e. 0.4.

REVIEW QUESTIONS

1. Career orientation; ordinal scale.
2. Weight; ratio.
   a. 134.55 to 134.65 lbs.
   b. 127.6 lbs.
3. Emotional stability; rating scale—gray area between ordinal and interval scale.
   a. 7.5 to 8.5.
   b. No, it should be rounded to 5.8.
4. Amount of motivation; interval scale. Zero minutes of work does not necessarily correspond to zero motivation.
   a. 97.205 to 97.215 minutes.
   b. Three, or 88.052 minutes.
5. Interpersonal values; ordinal scale.
6. Behavioral interactions; nominal scale.

3

Testing Your Knowledge 3–1

2. a.

Score	Tally	f	rf	$\%f$	cf	crf	$c\%f$
19	/	1	.05	5	20	1.00	100
18		0	.00	0	19	.95	95
17		0	.00	0	19	.95	95
16		0	.00	0	19	.95	95
15	/	1	.05	5	19	.95	95
14	/	1	.05	5	18	.90	90
13	/	1	.05	5	17	.85	85
12	/	1	.05	5	16	.80	80
11	/	1	.05	5	15	.75	75
10	/	1	.05	5	14	.70	70
9	//	2	.10	10	13	.65	65
8	////	4	.20	20	11	.55	55
7		0	.00	0	7	.35	35
6	//	2	.10	10	7	.35	35
5	//	2	.10	10	5	.25	25
4	//	2	.10	10	3	.15	15
3	/	1	.05	5	1	.05	5

   b. Lowest = 3; highest = 19.
   c. 8.
   d. 55%.
   e. 3, 4, 5.

Testing Your Knowledge 3–2

2. 10 to 20.
4. 6.

5. 17.
9. a. 123.   d. 131.5.
   b. 131.   e. 125.5 to 128.5.
   c. 122.5.   f. 121.
10. a. See table on top of page 635.
    b. The large majority of stotting distances were 99 meters or less. Distances in the interval of 60 to 69 meters occurred most frequently. No distance was less than 10 meters or greater than 209 meters.
    c. 67.
    d. 60.4.

Testing Your Knowledge 3–3

1. a. See figures on top of page 636.
   b. The distributions are similar to those in 1a except that relative frequencies are portrayed on the ordinate.
   c. The majority of stotting distances were less than 104.5 meters. The most frequently occurring distances were in the interval of 64.5 meters. No distance was less than 9.5 meters or greater than 209.5 meters.

2.

Stem	Leaf
20	5
19	0
18	
17	
16	
15	4
14	0
13	
12	
11	
10	
9	11
8	133
7	022256
6	11234666778
5	04456789
4	237899
3	1377889
2	59
1	8

   a. 18 meters.
   b. 205 meters.
   c. 66 and 72 meters.

Table for Testing Your Knowledge 3–1, Problem 10.a.

Class Interval	Real Limits Lower	Upper	Midpoint of Class	Tally	f	rf	%f	cf	crf	c%f
200–209	199.5	209.5	204.5	/	1	.02	2	50	1.00	100
190–199	189.5	199.5	194.5	/	1	.02	2	49	.98	98
180–189	179.5	189.5	184.5		0	.00	0	48	.96	96
170–179	169.5	179.5	174.5		0	.00	0	48	.96	96
160–169	159.5	169.5	164.5		0	.00	0	48	.96	96
150–159	149.5	159.5	154.5	/	1	.02	2	48	.96	96
140–149	139.5	149.5	144.5	/	1	.02	2	47	.94	94
130–139	129.5	139.5	134.5		0	.00	0	46	.92	92
120–129	119.5	129.5	124.5		0	.00	0	46	.92	92
110–119	109.5	119.5	114.5		0	.00	0	46	.92	92
100–109	99.5	109.5	104.5		0	.00	0	46	.92	92
90–99	89.5	99.5	94.5	//	2	.04	4	46	.92	92
80–89	79.5	89.5	84.5	///	3	.06	6	44	.88	88
70–79	69.5	79.5	74.5	//////	6	.12	12	41	.82	82
60–69	59.5	69.5	64.5	///////////	11	.22	22	35	.70	70
50–59	49.5	59.5	54.5	////////	8	.16	16	24	.48	48
40–49	39.5	49.5	44.5	//////	6	.12	12	16	.32	32
30–39	29.5	39.5	34.5	///////	7	.14	14	10	.20	20
20–29	19.5	29.5	24.5	//	2	.04	4	3	.06	6
10–19	9.5	19.5	14.5	/	1	.02	2	1	.02	2

Testing Your Knowledge 3–4

2. **a.** symmetrical, unimodal.
   b. asymmetrical, positively skewed, unimodal.
   c. asymmetrical, positively skewed, bimodal.
   d. asymmetrical, negatively skewed, unimodal.

REVIEW QUESTIONS

1. **a.** Size of class interval = 20; class intervals start at stated limit of 220; first midpoint at 229.5; upper stated limit of last class interval = 499.
   b. 400 to 419; midpoint = 409.5; No, it is shorter.
   c. Value will be in interval 340 to 359.
   d. $X_{50} = 356.2$.
   e. $PR_{431} = 89$.
2. **a.** Size of class interval = 6; class intervals start at stated limit of 0; first midpoint

at 2.5; upper stated limit of last class interval = 65.
   b. 0 to 5.
   c. $X_{50} = 5.7$.

   d.

Stem	Leaf
*	
6 .	3
*	8
5 .	1
*	67
4 .	
*	7
3 .	
*	66
2 .	114
*	5778
1 .	0124
*	5555566666678899
0 .	00000000111122333344444

Lowest score = 0; highest score = 63.
Most frequently occurring score = 0.

Graphs for Testing Your Knowledge 3–3, Problem 1.a.

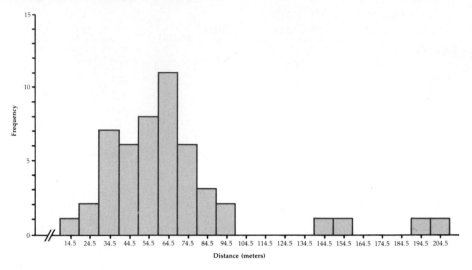

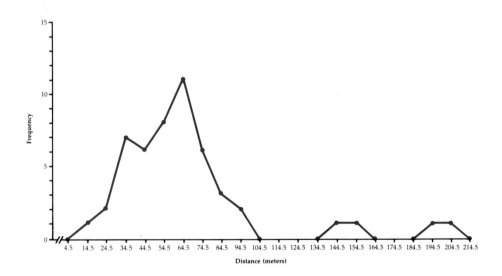

4

Testing Your Knowledge 4–1

  4. a. 49.
    b. Unimodal.
  5. a. 27.
    b. Unimodal.
  6. a. 24, 27, 49.
    b. Multimodal.

Testing Your Knowledge 4–2

  3. a. 46.
    b. 42.
    c. 46.

Testing Your Knowledge 4–3

  4. $\overline{X} = 88.0$.
    b. 262.

5. a. 41.0.
  b. 40.5.
  c. 39.4.

Testing Your Knowledge 4–4

2. a. Median.
  b. Mean.
  c. Mode.
  d. Mean.
3. Smaller than median.
4. Positively skewed.

REVIEW QUESTIONS

1. Negatively skewed; mean < median.
2. Positively skewed; mean > median.
3. Positively skewed; mean > median.
4. a. Mode = 38.
  Md = 38.
  $\overline{X}$ = 38.6.
  b. No—all measures of central tendency are about the same.
5. a. Mode = 28.
  Md = 29.
  $\overline{X}$ = 33.5.
  b. Positively skewed; mean is larger than the median.
6. a. Mode = 52.
  Md – 50.
  $\overline{X}$ = 46.7.
  b. Negatively skewed; mean is less than the median.
7. a. Mode = bimodal, 26, 52.
  Md = 40.
  $\overline{X}$ = 38.6.
  b. Approximately symmetrical.
  c. No, it is bimodal.
  d., e., Because the distribution is bimodal, neither the Md nor the $\overline{X}$ represents the typical score of a subject very well.

5

Testing Your Knowledge 5–1

2. Range = 44.
  IQR = 18.
  $SIQR$ = 9.

3. Range = 287 ms.
  IQR = 85 ms.
  $SIQR$ = 42.5 ms.

Testing Your Knowledge 5–2

2. a., b.

	Read by Themselves	Read by Teacher
$\overline{X}$	59.0	57.0
s	5.54	10.23
s^2	30.67	104.67

  c. Read by teacher group.

3. a.

	Male	Female
$\overline{X}$	15.6	7.0
s	7.41	2.58
s^2	54.93	6.68

  b. Males.

Testing Your Knowledge 5–3

1. a. Md, $SIQR$.
  b. Md, $SIQR$.
  c. $\overline{X}$, s.
  d. Md, $SIQR$.
  e. $\overline{X}$, s.
  f. Md, $SIQR$.

REVIEW QUESTIONS

1. a. Md = 50.
  $\overline{X}$ = 49.6.
  IQR = 10.
  s = 7.26.
  b. Both are equally good.
2. a. Md = 50.
  $\overline{X}$ = 49.4.
  IQR = 10.
  s = 11.56.
  b. Both are equally good.
  c. The IQR is not affected by scores in the tails of the distribution.

3. a. Range.
 b. IQR.
 c. SIQR.
 d. s^2.
 e. s.
 f. IQR.
 g. Range.
 h. s^2.
 i. s.
 j. SIQR.

6

Testing Your Knowledge 6–1

4. a. .3413.
 b. .4772.
 c. .4987.
 d. .3413.
 e. .4772.
 f. .4987.
 g. .8400.
 h. .9544.
 i. .9974.
 j. .1359.
 k. .1574.
 l. .0215.

Testing Your Knowledge 6–2

2.

	z	Area 0 to z	Area Beyond z
a.	+1.90	.4713	.0287
b.	−0.52	.1985	.3015
c.	+0.77	.2794	.2206
d.	−1.83	.4664	.0336
e.	+1.75	.4599	.0401
f.	−1.26	.3962	.1038

3. a. .0559.
 b. .1582.
 c. .3181.
 d. Approximately 59.7 to 85.5 (using $z = \pm1.65$).

Testing Your Knowledge 6–3

3. .0014.
4. .19.

5.

	z	p
a.	+1.90	.0287
b.	−0.52	.3015
c.	+0.77	.2206
d.	−1.83	.0336
e.	+1.75	.0401
f.	−1.26	.1038

6. a. .0793.
 b. .1887.
 c. .2685.

REVIEW QUESTIONS

3. a. .1587.
 b. .0228.
 c. .0038.
 d. .4082.
 e. .4525.
 f. Approximately 80.8 to 119.2.
 g. .6568.
 h. .0918.
 i. .0475.
 j. .0038.
4. .016.
5. a. .00033.
 b. .00019.
 c. .00022.
6. a. .0968.
 b. .0968.
 c. .8064.

7. a.

	Video Games	GPA
Alex	−0.34	−0.23
Lauren	0.00	−0.80
Yvonne	−1.37	+1.38
Laval	+1.19	+0.80
Bonnie	−0.85	+0.46
Jason	+1.37	−1.61

 b. That she is at the mean of the group for video-game playing.
 c. That she is 1.38 standard deviations above the mean GPA of the group.
 d. That the person's GPA is below the mean of the group.
 e. That the person's video-game playing-time is above the mean of the group.

7

Testing Your Knowledge 7–1

2.

	(a)	(b)
	Proportion	*Number*
Generalized Anxiety		
Disorder	0.27	27
Agoraphobia	0.23	23
Simple Phobia	0.19	19
Panic Disorder	0.22	22
Obsessive-Compulsive	0.09	9

Testing Your Knowledge 7–2

4. **a.** .6826.
   b. .1587.
   c. .0228.
   d. .0475.
   e. .4525.

Testing Your Knowledge 7–3

1. **a.** 9 seconds.
   b. 6 seconds.
   c. 3 seconds.
2. **a.** $s_{\overline{X}} = 2$.
   $s_{\overline{X}} = 3$.
   $s_{\overline{X}} = 4$.
   b. As s increases, $s_{\overline{X}}$ also increases.
3. Population A_2 because it has a larger value of σ.

Testing Your Knowledge 7–4

2. **a.** 73.
   b. 69.1 to 76.9.
   c. 67.8 to 78.2.
   d. 73.
   e. 71.0 to 75.0.
   f. 70.4 to 75.6.
   g. The value of $\sigma_{\overline{X}}$ becomes smaller as N increases.

Testing Your Knowledge 7–5

1. Biased; underestimates.
2. Unbiased.
3. Biased; underestimates.

REVIEW QUESTIONS

1. **a.** σ.   **c.** σ^2.
   b. μ.   **d.** $\sigma_{\overline{X}}$.
2. $N = 24$, because $\overline{X}$ is a consistent estimator.
3. Stratified; see text for explanation.
5. **a.** 9.0 cigarettes per day.
   b. 7.5 to 10.5 cigarettes per day.

8

Testing Your Knowledge 8–1

3. **a.** $H_0: \mu = 100$.
   $H_1: \mu \neq 100$.
   b. $H_0: \mu = 8.3$.
   $H_1: \mu \neq 8.3$.
   c. $H_0: \mu = 423$.
   $H_1: \mu \neq 423$.

4.

	z_{obs}	$p(z) \geq z_{obs}$
a.	−2.13	.0166
b.	−1.20	.1151
c.	+2.25	.0122
d.	−3.45	.0003

Testing Your Knowledge 8–2

3. Rejection region consists of values of z_{obs} more extreme than $z = -1.96$ or $+1.96$.

z_{obs}	**Falls into Rejection Region**	Decision
+3.21	yes	Reject H_0 Accept H_1
+1.43	no	Fail to reject H_0 Do not accept H_1
−2.65	yes	Reject H_0 Accept H_1
+2.58	yes	Reject H_0 Accept H_1
−2.36	yes	Reject H_0 Accept H_1
−0.63	no	Fail to reject H_0 Do not accept H_1
−3.01	yes	Reject H_0 Accept H_1

4. a. $z = (\overline{X} - \mu)/\sigma_{\overline{X}}$.
  b. See text.
  c. H_0: $\mu = 100$.
     H_1: $\mu \neq 100$.
  d. $\alpha = .05$.
  e. $z_{crit} = \pm 1.96$.
  f. Values of z_{obs} more extreme than
     $z = -1.96$ or $+1.96$.
  g. $z_{obs} = +2.45$.
  h. Reject H_0; accept H_1.
  i. The sample mean differs significantly from
     the population mean.

Testing Your Knowledge 8–3

3. Type I.
4. Type II.
5. Correct decision.
6. Correct decision.

REVIEW QUESTIONS

6. a. Reject H_0; accept H_1.
  b. Fail to reject H_0; do not accept H_1.
7. The sample mean differs significantly from
   the hypothesized population mean.
8. The sample mean does not differ significantly
   from the hypothesized population mean.
9. Rejection region consists of values of z_{obs}
   more extreme than $z = -2.58$ or $+2.58$.

z_{obs}	**Falls into Rejection Region**	**Decision**
+3.71	yes	Reject H_0 Accept H_1
−2.60	yes	Reject H_0 Accept H_1
+1.74	no	Fail to reject H_0 Do not accept H_1
−3.05	yes	Reject H_0 Accept H_1
−1.96	no	Fail to reject H_0 Do not accept H_1
+2.58	yes	Reject H_0 Accept H_1

10. $z_{obs} = -1.52$; nonsignificant; fail to reject H_0.
13. b. $p = \alpha$.
   c. A Type I error cannot occur if H_0
      is false.
14. b. No; see Table 8–2.

9

Testing Your Knowledge 9–1

3. a. 7.
  b. 6.
  c. 6.

4.

N	df
10	9
16	15
7	6
54	53
100	99
30	29

6. The distribution with 13 df.
7. When the $df = \infty$.

Testing Your Knowledge 9–2

1. a. H_0: $\mu = 493$.
      H_1: $\mu \neq 493$.
  b. H_0: $\mu = 36.1$.
      H_1: $\mu \neq 36.1$.

2.

df	α	t_{crit}
6	.05	2.447
17	.01	2.898
23	.05	2.069
32	.05	2.042
39	.05	2.042
75	.01	2.660
103	.05	2.000
256	.05	1.980

3.

t_{obs}	Falls into Rejection Region	Decision
+3.014	yes	Reject H_0 Accept H_1
−1.989	no	Fail to reject H_0 Do not accept H_1
−2.179	yes	Reject H_0 Accept H_1
+2.040	no	Fail to reject H_0 Do not accept H_1
−3.961	yes	Reject H_0 Accept H_1
+2.743	yes	Reject H_0 Accept H_1
−2.364	no	Fail to reject H_0 Do not accept H_1
+2.447	yes	Reject H_0 Accept H_1
−2.262	yes	Reject H_0 Accept H_1
+2.938	yes	Reject H_0 Accept H_1
−2.410	yes	Reject H_0 Accept H_1

5. a. $t = (\overline{X} - \mu)/s_{\overline{X}}$.
 b. See text.
 c. $H_0: \mu = 7$; $H_1: \mu \neq 7$.
 d. $\alpha = .05$.
 e. $t_{crit}(10) = 2.228$.
 f. Values of t_{obs} more extreme than −2.228 or +2.228.
 g. $t_{obs} = -4.98$.
 h. Reject H_0; accept H_1.
 i. The sample mean of 5.8 minutes differs significantly from the population mean of 7 minutes.

Testing Your Knowledge 9–3

1. a. 70.4 kg.
 b. 7.6 kg.
 c. One-sample t.
 d. $H_0: \mu = 75$ kg; $H_1: \mu \neq 75$ kg.
 e. 6.
 f. −1.482.
 g. 5.

h. ±2.571.
 i. Fail to reject H_0.
 j. Do not accept H_1.
 k. The sample mean does not differ significantly from the population mean.

2. a. 10.4 days.
 b. 2.3 days.
 c. One-sample t.
 d. $H_0: \mu = 8.7$ days; $H_1: \mu \neq 8.7$ days.
 e. 25.
 f. +3.696.
 g. 24.
 h. ±2.064.
 i. Reject H_0.
 j. Accept H_1.
 k. The sample mean differs significantly from the population mean; 10.4 days is significantly larger than the hypothesized mean of 8.7 days.

Testing Your Knowledge 9–4

1. 80.1 to 113.9 minutes.
2. 256.8 to 259.2 yards.

REVIEW QUESTIONS

2. The sample mean differs significantly from the hypothesized population mean.
3. The sample mean does not differ significantly from the hypothesized population mean.

4.

t_{obs}	Falls into Rejection Region	Decision
+3.713	yes	Reject H_0 Accept H_1
−2.615	no	Fail to reject H_0 Do not accept H_1
+2.794	yes	Reject H_0 Accept H_1
−3.058	yes	Reject H_0 Accept H_1
−1.960	no	Fail to reject H_0 Do not accept H_1
−2.368	no	Fail to reject H_0 Do not accept H_1

6. a. $t_{obs}(8) = -2.70$; significant at the .05 level; reject H_0, accept H_1.
  c. Yes.
  d. No.
  e. 6.82 to 7.72 hours; $\mu = 7.8$ is not included in this interval.

7. a. $t_{obs}(11) = +3.23$; significant at the .05 level; reject H_0, accept H_1.
  b. No, see Table 8–2.

10

Testing Your Knowledge 10–1

7. a. Extraneous variable = age; groups differ in average age as well as noise condition.
  b. Extraneous variable = experimenter's encouragement; groups differ in encouragement as well as noise condition.
  c. Extraneous variable = gender; groups differ in gender as well as noise condition.
  d. Extraneous variable = college major; groups differ in college major as well as noise condition.
  e. Extraneous variable = time of day when the experiment was conducted; groups differ in time of day as well as noise condition.

Testing Your Knowledge 10–2

8. a. 3.77.
  b. 3.56.
  c. 3.81.
  d. 2.25.

Testing Your Knowledge 10–3

5. See tables next column.
9. Problem 1
  a. H_0: $\mu_{A1} = \mu_{A2}$; H_1: $\mu_{A1} \neq \mu_{A2}$.
  b. $t_{obs}(34) = -3.66$.
  c. 34.
  d. 2.042.
  e. Values of t_{obs} more extreme than -2.042 or $+2.042$.
  f. Yes.
  g. Reject H_0; accept H_1.
  h. Different populations.

Tables for Testing Your Knowledge 10–3, Problem 5.

$\alpha = .05$

	df	t_{crit}	Falls into Rejection Region	Decision
a.	18	2.101	yes	Reject H_0 Accept H_1
b.	18	2.101	no	Fail to reject H_0 Do not accept H_1
c.	28	2.048	yes	Reject H_0 Accept H_1
d.	28	2.048	yes	Reject H_0 Accept H_1
e.	68	2.000	yes	Reject H_0 Accept H_1
f.	33	2.042	no	Fail to reject H_0 Do not accept H_1
g.	127	1.980	yes	Reject H_0 Accept H_1
h.	148	1.980	yes	Reject H_0 Accept H_1

$\alpha = .01$

	df	t_{crit}	Falls into Rejection Region	Decision
a.	18	2.878	no	Fail to reject H_0 Do not accept H_1
b.	18	2.878	no	Fail to reject H_0 Do not accept H_1
c.	28	2.763	no	Fail to reject H_0 Do not accept H_1
d.	28	2.763	yes	Reject H_0 Accept H_1
e.	68	2.660	yes	Reject H_0 Accept H_1
f.	33	2.750	no	Fail to reject H_0 Do not accept H_1
g.	127	2.617	no	Fail to reject H_0 Do not accept H_1
h.	148	2.617	no	Fail to reject H_0 Do not accept H_1

Testing Your Knowledge 10–3 (Cont.)

  i. Yes.

  j. Yes; the control group estimated a shorter time interval than the experimental group.

Problem 2

  a. $H_0: \mu_{A_1} = \mu_{A_2}; H_1: \mu_{A_1} \neq \mu_{A_2}$.

  b. $t_{obs}(28) = -1.74$.

  c. 28.

  d. 2.048.

  e. Values of t_{obs} more extreme than -2.048 or $+2.048$.

  f. No.

  g. Fail to reject H_0; do not accept H_1.

  h. There is no evidence that they are not from the same population.

  i. No; it is nonsignificant.

  j. No; the difference is treated as a chance difference.

Testing Your Knowledge 10–4

1. a. 2.
   b. 62.
   c. 79.7.
   d. 8.57.
   e. 73.0.
   f. 5.85.
   g. 3.60.
   h. 2.000.
   i. Reject H_0.
   j. Accept H_1.
   k. Statistically significant.
   l. The effect of the independent variable.

2. a. 2.
   b. 30.
   c. 22.78.
   d. 24.33.
   e. 0.80.
   f. 2.048.
   g. Fail to reject H_0.
   h. Do not accept H_1.
   i. Nonsignificant.
   j. Sampling error.

Testing Your Knowledge 10–5

6. a. Ex post facto; the independent variable of involvement in a residence hall disruption or not is an attribute independent variable.

  b. $t_{obs}(5398) = 25.00$, $p < .001$; the GPAs of the two groups differ significantly. The GPA of students involved in residence hall disruptions is significantly lower than the GPA of students not involved in disruptions.

REVIEW QUESTIONS

1. a. True experiment.
   b. True experiment.
   c. Ex post facto.
   d. Ex post facto.
   e. Both.
   f. Both.
   g. Both.
   h. Both.
   i. Both.
   j. Ex post facto.
   k. True experiment.

2. $t_{obs}(20) = -2.10$, $p \leq .05$. The mean blood pressure of the quiet group is significantly lower than that of the noise group.

3. $t_{obs}(20) = -0.91$, $p > .05$. The mean blood pressures of the two groups do not differ significantly.

4. $t_{obs}(28) = -0.43$, $p > .05$. Males and females do not differ significantly on the rated need for solitude.

11

Testing Your Knowledge 11–1

2. Only two groups may be compared at one time.

3. F.

4. $F = MS_A/MS_{Error}$.

6. $a = 4$; $n_A = 11$, $N = 44$.

10. $16 - 14.0 = (13.0 - 14.0) + (16 - 13.0)$.

Testing Your Knowledge 11–2

4. 150.
5. 24.1.
6. 80.
7. 25.
8. 10.
9. $df_A = 3$, $df_{Error} = 40$, $df_{Total} = 43$.

10.

Source	df	SS	MS	F
Factor A	1	24	24.0	6.00
Error	4	16	4.0	
Total	5	40		

11.

Source	df	SS	MS	F
Factor A	2	42	21.0	5.25
Error	6	24	4.0	
Total	8	66		

12. Table 1

Source	df	SS	MS	F
Factor A	1	50	50.0	5.00
Error	26	260	10.0	
Total	27	310		

a. 2.   **b.** 28.   **c.** 14.

Table 2

Source	df	SS	MS	F
Factor A	3	18	6.0	3.00
Error	76	152	2.0	
Total	79	170		

a. 4.   **b.** 80.   **c.** 20.

Testing Your Knowledge 11–3

6. Approximately 1.00.
7. It becomes > 1.00.
9. H_0: $\mu_{A_1} = \mu_{A_2}$; H_1: not H_0.
10. H_0: $\mu_{A_1} = \mu_{A_2} = \mu_{A_3} = \mu_{A_4}$; H_1: not H_0.
11. The independent variable has no effect.
12. The independent variable has an effect.
13. 0.
14. No upper limit.
15. See table top of next column.

Testing Your Knowledge 11–4

1. a. H_0: $\mu_{A_1} = \mu_{A_2}$; H_1: not H_0.
 b. $F_{obs}(1, 18) = 6.76$.
 c. $df_A = 1$, $df_{Error} = 18$.
 d. $F_{crit}(1, 18) = 4.41$.
 e. Values of $F_{obs} \geq 4.41$.

Table for Testing Your Knowledge 11–3, Problem 15.

F_{crit}	Falls into Rejection Region	Decision
a. 4.96	yes	Reject H_0 Accept H_1
b. 3.40	no	Fail to reject H_0 Do not accept H_1
c. 4.26	yes	Reject H_0 Accept H_1
d. 3.15	yes	Reject H_0 Accept H_1
e. 3.89	yes	Reject H_0 Accept H_1
f. 3.68	no	Fail to reject H_0 Do not accept H_1
g. 2.61	no	Fail to reject H_0 Do not accept H_1
h. 3.10	no	Fail to reject H_0 Do not accept H_1
i. 2.25	yes	Reject H_0 Accept H_1
j. 2.53	no	Fail to reject H_0 Do not accept H_1

f. Yes.
g. Reject H_0; accept H_1.
h. Different populations.
i. Yes.
j. They differ; the control group estimated a shorter time interval.
2. a. H_0: $\mu_{A_1} = \mu_{A_2} = \mu_{A_3}$; H_1: not H_0.
 b. $F_{obs}(2, 21) = 34.39$.
 c. $df_A = 2$, $df_{Error} = 21$.
 d. $F_{crit}(2, 21) = 3.47$.
 e. Values of $F_{obs} \geq 3.47$.
 f. Yes.
 g. Reject H_0; accept H_1.
 h. There is at least one mean from a different population.
 i. Yes; there is at least one significant difference among the means.
 j. Yes. The beard group had lower scores (thus greater rated masculinity) than either the bandana or control groups.

Testing Your Knowledge 11–5

1. a. 2.
   b. 62.
   c. 14.15.
   d. 4.00.
   e. Reject H_0.
   f. Accept H_1.
   g. Statistically significant.
   h. The effect of the independent variable.

2. a. 4.
   b. 40.
   c. 1.13.
   d. 2.92.
   e. Fail to reject H_0.
   f. Do not accept H_1.
   g. Nonsignificant.
   h. Sampling error.

Testing Your Knowledge 11–6

2. $F(1, 18) = 8.59$.
3. $t(22) = 3.00$.

REVIEW QUESTIONS

1. a. $F_{obs}(1, 30) = 25.01$, $p < .01$. The U.S. mean is significantly lower than the foreign mean.
2. a. $F_{obs}(2, 24) = 12.57$, $p < .01$.
   b. The throwing, catching mean appears to differ from both the none (A_1) and the soccer (A_2) means.
3. a. $F_{obs}(1, 20) = 4.41$, $p < .05$. The mean for the quiet group is significantly lower than the mean for the noise group.
   b. Yes, $t = \sqrt{F} = \sqrt{4.41} = 2.10$.
4. $a = 6$, $n_A = 7$, $N = 42$.
5. $df_A = 5$, $df_{Error} = 36$, $df_{Total} = 41$.
6. a. $\sum\limits_{j=1}^{5} \sum\limits_{i=1}^{12} (X_{ij} - \overline{X}_G)^2 = \sum\limits_{j=1}^{5} \sum\limits_{i=1}^{12} (\overline{X}_A - \overline{X}_G)^2$

$$+ \sum\limits_{j=1}^{5} \sum\limits_{i=1}^{12} (X_{ij} - \overline{X}_A)^2.$$

   b. $df_A = 4$, $df_{Error} = 55$, $df_{Total} = 59$.
   c. $H_0: \mu_{A_1} = \mu_{A_2} = \mu_{A_3} = \mu_{A_4} = \mu_{A_5}$; H_1: not H_0.
   d. $F_{crit}(4, 55) = 2.61$.
   e. Reject H_0; accept H_1.

7. Table 1

Source	df	SS	MS	F
Factor A	2	50	25.0	2.50
Error	27	270	10.0	
Total	29	320		

a. 3.
b. 30.
c. 10.
d. $F_{crit}(2, 27) = 3.35$; F_{obs} is nonsignificant.

Table 2

Source	df	SS	MS	F
Factor A	5	60	12.0	4.00
Error	72	216	3.0	
Total	77	276		

a. 6.
b. 78.
c. 13.
d. $F_{crit}(5, 72) = 2.37$; F_{obs} is statistically significant.

Table 3

Source	df	SS	MS	F
Factor A	3	45	15.0	3.00
Error	64	320	5.0	
Total	67	365		

a. 4.
b. 68.
c. 17.
d. $F_{crit}(3, 64) = 2.76$; F_{obs} is statistically significant.

12

Testing Your Knowledge 12–1

3. No. Only one pairwise comparison may be made.
4. $\overline{X}_{A_1} = \overline{X}_{A_2} < \overline{X}_{A_3}$.
5. $\overline{X}_{A_1} < \overline{X}_{A_2} > \overline{X}_{A_3}$; $\overline{X}_{A_1} = \overline{X}_{A_3}$.
6. $\overline{X}_{A_1} > \overline{X}_{A_2} < \overline{X}_{A_3}$; $\overline{X}_{A_1} = \overline{X}_{A_3}$.

7. $\bar{X}_{A_1} > \bar{X}_{A_2} > \bar{X}_{A_3}$.

8. f.

9. $\bar{X}_{A_1}$ vs. $\bar{X}_{A_2}$; $\bar{X}_{A_1}$ vs. $\bar{X}_{A_3}$; $\bar{X}_{A_1}$ vs. $\bar{X}_{A_4}$; $\bar{X}_{A_2}$ vs. $\bar{X}_{A_3}$; $\bar{X}_{A_2}$ vs. $\bar{X}_{A_4}$; $\bar{X}_{A_3}$ vs. $\bar{X}_{A_4}$.

Testing Your Knowledge 12–2

2. a.

Source	df	SS	MS	F
Type of model	2	526.750	263.375	4.81
Error	21	1150.875	54.804	
Total	23	1677.625		

b. H_0: $\mu_{A_1} = \mu_{A_2} = \mu_{A_3}$; H_1: not H_0.

c. $F_{crit}(2, 21) = 3.47$.

d. Values of $F_{obs} \geq 3.47$.

e. Yes.

f. Reject H_0; accept H_1.

g. There is at least one significant difference among the means.

h. A specific prediction was made prior to conducting the experiment.

i. 1, 21.

j. $F_{crit}(1, 21) = 4.32$.

k. $MS_{Error} = 54.804$.

l. $n_A = 8$.

m. $CD = 7.7$ seconds.

n. Any planned comparison equal to or greater than 7.7 seconds is statistically significant at the .05 level.

		Model		
		A_1 (32.9)	A_2 (36.0)	A_3 (44.0)
	A_1 (32.9)	—	3.1	11.1*
Model	A_2 (36.0)		—	8.0*
	A_3 (44.0)			—

q. H_0: $\mu_{A_1} = \mu_{A_3}$ Reject
  H_1: $\mu_{A_1} \neq \mu_{A_3}$ Accept
  H_0: $\mu_{A_2} = \mu_{A_3}$ Reject
  H_1: $\mu_{A_2} \neq \mu_{A_3}$ Accept

r. Panel *a*.

3. a. 3.

b. 27.

c. 4.39.

d. 3.40.

e. Reject H_0.

f. Accept H_1.

g. $F_{crit}(1, 24) = 4.26$.

h. 21.47.

i. 9.

k. 16.4 vs. 9.6 = 6.8; significant difference. 9.6 vs. 8.9; nonsignificant difference. The comparison of the 0.05-second retention interval against the 12-second retention interval was not planned.

Testing Your Knowledge 12–3

2. a.

Source	df	SS	MS	F
Group	3	7530.336	2510.112	36.15
Error	32	2222.219	69.444	
Total	35	9752.555		

b. H_0: $\mu_{A_1} = \mu_{A_2} = \mu_{A_3} = \mu_{A_4}$; H_1: not H_0.

c. $F_{crit}(3, 32) = 2.92$.

d. Values of $F_{obs} \geq 2.92$.

e. Yes.

f. Reject H_0; accept H_1.

g. There is at least one significant difference among the means.

h. No specific predictions were made about the expected relationship prior to conducting the experiment.

i. $q_k(4, 32) = 3.85$.

j. 69.444.

k. 9.

l. 10.7.

m., n.

		Group			
		A_1 (29.2)	A_2 (35.6)	A_3 (58.9)	A_4 (62.8)
	A_1 (29.2)	—	6.4	29.7*	33.6*
	A_2 (35.6)		—	23.3*	27.2*
Group	A_3 (58.9)			—	3.9
	A_4 (62.8)				—

o. The anxiety avoidance scores of normal weight (A_1) and dieters (A_2) do not differ. Both groups, however, have lower anxiety avoidance scores than either anorectic (A_3) or bulimic (A_4) individuals. The anorectic and bulimic groups do not differ from each other in anxiety avoidance.

p. $\mu_{A_1} = \mu_{A_2} < \mu_{A_3} = \mu_{A_4}$

REVIEW QUESTIONS

1. a. Tukey.
   b. Multiple F.
   c. Tukey.
2. $CD = 2.12$. No; the order is $\overline{X}_{A_1} < \overline{X}_{A_2} = \overline{X}_{A_3}$.
3. $CD = 4.6$; the theatrical beard group had lower ratings (thus higher rated masculinity) than either the bandana or nothing on the face group. The bandana and nothing on the face group did not differ on their ratings.
4. a. $MS_{Error} = 3.685$, $q_k(3, 24) = 3.53$, $n_A = 9$, Tukey $CD = 2.3$; using this CD, $\overline{X}_{A_1} = \overline{X}_{A_2}$, $\overline{X}_{A_1} < \overline{X}_{A_3}$, $\overline{X}_{A_2} = \overline{X}_{A_3}$.
   b. $F_{crit}(1, 24) = 4.26$, multiple F $CD = 1.9$; using this CD, $\overline{X}_{A_1} < \overline{X}_{A_2}$, $\overline{X}_{A_2} = \overline{X}_{A_3}$. This outcome is not in agreement with the predicted ordering.
   c. Because the Tukey test is used for post hoc comparisons, it employs a larger CD than the multiple F test.

13

Testing Your Knowledge 13–1

Testing Your Knowledge 13–2

7. $95.0 - 92.5 = (98.5 - 92.5) + (87.7 - 92.5) + (84.6 - 98.5 - 87.7 + 92.5) + (95.0 - 84.6)$.

Testing Your Knowledge 13–3

2. 240.
3. 43.7.
4. 54.4.
5. 59.2.
6. $df_A = 1$
   $df_B = 2$
   $df_{A \times B} = 2$
   $df_{Error} = 30$
   $df_{Total} = 35$.
7. $df_A = 2$
   $df_B = 1$
   $df_{A \times B} = 2$
   $df_{Error} = 72$
   $df_{Total} = 77$.
8. 79.
9. $MS_A = 14/1 = 14.0$
   $MS_B = 26/2 = 13.0$
   $MS_{A \times B} = 44/2 = 22.0$
   $MS_{Error} = 480/60 = 8.0$.

10. a.

Source	df	SS	MS	F
Factor A	1	108.00	108.00	27.00
Factor B	1	0.00	0.00	0.00
A × B	1	12.00	12.00	3.00
Error	8	32.00	4.00	
Total	11	152.00		

b. Because $\overline{X}_{B_1} = \overline{X}_{B_2}$, there is no main effect variation of factor B.

Testing Your Knowledge 13–1

2.

Design	Number of Independent Variables	Levels	Number of Subjects Needed
3 × 3	2	$A = 3$; $B = 3$	90
3 × 2	2	$A = 3$; $B = 2$	60
2 × 3	2	$A = 2$; $B = 3$	60
6 × 2	2	$A = 6$; $B = 2$	120
4 × 4	2	$A = 4$; $B = 4$	160
2 × 2 × 2	3	$A = 2$; $B = 2$; $C = 2$	80
2 × 4 × 3	3	$A = 2$; $B = 4$; $C = 3$	240
3 × 3 × 2	3	$A = 3$; $B = 3$; $C = 2$	180

3. See Tables 1 and 2 on top of page 648.

Tables for Testing Your Knowledge 13–1, Problem 3.

Table 1

			Factor A		Main Effect Means for Factor B
			A_1	A_2	
Factor B	B_1		13.3	20.2	16.8
	B_2		16.8	22.8	19.8
Main Effect Means for Factor A			15.1	21.5	$\overline{X}_G = 18.3$

Table 2

			Factor A		Main Effect Means for Factor B
			A_1	A_2	
Factor B	B_1		18.9	30.1	24.5
	B_2		31.3	33.9	32.6
Main Effect Means for Factor A			25.1	32.0	$\overline{X}_G = 28.5$

Testing Your Knowledge 13–3 (Cont.)

11. Table 1

Source	df	SS	MS	F
Factor A	2	32.0	16.0	2.00
Factor B	1	24.0	24.0	3.00
$A \times B$	2	24.0	12.0	1.50
Error	60	480.0	8.0	
Total	65	560.0		

a. 3.   **c.** 11.
b. 2.   **d.** 66.

Table 2

Source	df	SS	MS	F
Factor A	2	36.0	18.0	4.50
Factor B	4	24.0	6.0	1.50
$A \times B$	8	160.0	20.0	5.00
Error	210	840.0	4.0	
Total	224	1060.0		

a. 3.   **c.** 15.
b. 5.   **d.** 225.

Testing Your Knowledge 13–4

6. Becomes > 1.00.
7. Becomes > 1.00.

9.

F Ratio for	Statistical Hypotheses
Factor A	H_0: $\mu_{A_1} = \mu_{A_2}$ H_1: not H_0
Factor B	H_0: $\mu_{B_1} = \mu_{B_2} = \mu_{B_3} = \mu_{B_4}$ H_1: not H_0
$A \times B$	H_0: all $(\mu_{AB} - \mu_A - \mu_B + \mu_G) = 0$ H_1: not H_0

10.

F Ratio for	Statistical Hypotheses
Factor A	H_0: $\mu_{A_1} = \mu_{A_2} = \mu_{A_3}$ H_1: not H_0
Factor B	H_0: $\mu_{B_1} = \mu_{B_2}$ H_1: not H_0
$A \times B$	H_0: all $(\mu_{AB} - \mu_A - \mu_B + \mu_G) = 0$ H_1: not H_0

11. Table 1

Source	df	F_{obs}	F_{crit}	Falls into Rejection Region	Decision
Factor A	1	4.63	4.08	Yes	Reject H_0 Accept H_1
Factor B	3	2.11	2.84	No	Fail to reject H_0 Do not accept H_1
$A \times B$	3	3.97	2.84	Yes	Reject H_0 Accept H_1

Table 2

Source	df	F_{obs}	F_{crit}	Falls into Rejection Region	Decision
Factor A	3	1.42	2.68	No	Fail to reject H_0 Do not accept H_1
Factor B	2	3.51	3.07	Yes	Reject H_0 Accept H_1
$A \times B$	6	2.37	2.17	Yes	Reject H_0 Accept H_1

Testing Your Knowledge 13–5

2. Table 1
 a. Yes, the observed difference is statistically significant.
 b. No, the observed difference is not significant.
 c. No.
 d. Inductive teaching (A_1) leads to higher test scores than does deductive teaching (A_2).
 e. No effect.
 f. Yes; there is no interaction of A and B.
Table 2
 a. No, the observed difference is not significant.
 b. Yes, the observed difference is statistically significant.
 c. No.
 d. No effect.
 e. Quantitative material (B_1) leads to higher test scores than does qualitative material (B_2).
 f. Yes; there is no interaction of A and B.
Table 3
 a. Yes, the observed difference is statistically significant.

 b. Yes, the observed difference is statistically significant.
 c. No.
 d. Deductive teaching (A_2) leads to higher test scores than does inductive teaching (A_1).
 e. Quantitative material (B_1) leads to higher test scores than does qualitative material (B_2).
 f. Yes; there is no interaction of A and B.
Table 4
 a. No, the observed difference is not significant.
 b. No, the observed difference is not significant.
 c. Yes.
 d. It depends upon the type of material, factor B. For quantitative material (B_1), inductive teaching (A_1) leads to higher test scores. For qualitative material (B_2), deductive teaching (A_2) leads to higher test scores.
 e. It depends upon the type of teaching, factor A. For inductive teaching (A_1), quantitative material (B_1) leads to higher test scores. For deductive teaching (A_2),

qualitative material (B_2) leads to higher test scores.

f. No; the main effects indicate no overall effect of the independent variable; however, each independent variable does have an effect, but the effect of each independent variable depends upon the level of the other independent variable.

Figure 1

a. Yes, the observed difference is statistically significant.

b. No, the observed difference is not significant.

c. Yes.

d. It depends upon the type of material, factor B. For quantitative material (B_1), inductive teaching (A_1) leads to higher test scores. For qualitative material (B_2), the teaching methods do not differ from each other.

e. It depends upon the type of teaching, factor A. For inductive teaching (A_1), quantitative material (B_1) leads to higher test scores. For deductive teaching (A_2), there is no difference between the types of materials.

f. No; the main effect for factor A indicates an overall superiority for inductive teaching, but inductive teaching only leads to higher test scores with quantitative material. Thus, the overall main effect for factor A is an artifact of the interaction; it conveys no meaningful information about the effect of factor A on test scores.

Figure 2

a. No, the observed difference is not significant.

b. Yes, the observed difference is statistically significant.

c. Yes.

d. It depends upon the type of material, factor B. For qualitative material (B_2), deductive teaching (A_2) leads to higher test scores. For quantitative material (B_1), the teaching methods do not differ.

e. It depends upon the type of teaching, factor A. Both types of teaching lead to higher test scores for quantitative material, but the difference between quantitative and qualitative material is larger for inductive teaching than it is for deductive teaching.

f. Yes; the main effect for factor B indicates an overall superiority for quantitative material, and quantitative material leads to higher test scores for both types of teaching. The interaction, however, indicates that the difference between quantitative and qualitative material depends upon the type of teaching method.

Testing Your Knowledge 13–6

1. a. Analysis of variance summary.

Source	df	SS	MS	F
Locus of control (A)	1	704.125	704.125	1.15
Instructions (B)	1	1472.625	1472.625	2.41
A × B	1	46112.750	46112.750	75.39*
Error	20	12233.000	611.650	
Total	23	60522.500		

*$p < .05$

a. (1) No main effects for either variable.

a. (2) Significant interaction.

b. Because of the interaction, the nonsignificant main effects do not provide useful information for interpreting the outcome.

c. The effect of instructions depends upon the locus of control. For skill instructions, internal locus of control subjects spent more time on the task than did external locus of control subjects. For chance instructions, external locus of control subjects spent more time on the task than did internal locus of control subjects.

2. a. Analysis of variance summary.

Source	df	SS	MS	F
Instruction (A)	1	191.361	191.361	23.61*
Crime (B)	1	1667.361	1667.361	205.75*
A × B	1	210.250	210.250	25.94*
Error	32	259.333	8.104	
Total	35	2328.305		

*$p < .05$

a. (1) The main effect for factor A indicates that longer prison terms are assigned with filmed instructions. This main effect is artifactual, however. The main effect for factor B indicates that longer prison terms are assigned for a crime of rape. This main effect is meaningful and may be interpreted.

a. (2) Significant interaction.

b. The main effect for type of crime is meaningful, longer terms are assigned for rape under both normal and filmed instructions. The main effect for type of instruction is artifactual; there is no difference between the filmed and normal instructions for theft, but a longer term is assigned with filmed instruction for the crime of rape.

c. The interaction indicates that the effect of instruction depends upon the type of crime; there is no difference between the filmed and normal instructions for theft, but a longer term is assigned with filmed instruction for the crime of rape.

Testing Your Knowledge 13–7

1. a. 3.
   b. 2.
   c. 42.

   d.

	F_{crit}
A	3.32
B	4.17
$A \times B$	3.32

   e. Yes.
   f. Yes.
   g. No.

2. a. 2.
   b. 4.
   c. 96.

   d.

	F_{crit}
A	4.00
B	2.76
$A \times B$	2.76

   e. Yes.
   f. No.
   g. Yes.

REVIEW QUESTIONS

1. Analysis of variance summary.

Source	df	SS	MS	F
Eye contact (A)	1	24.500	24.500	0.76
Affect (B)	1	780.215	780.125	24.17*
$A \times B$	1	325.125	325.125	10.07*
Error	28	903.750	32.277	
Total	31	2033.500		

*$p < .05$

a. The observed difference between the eye-contact main effect means is nonsignificant.

b. Yes; there is a significant interaction of A and B. $CD = 5.8$. For positive affect conditions, the no eye-contact mean is significantly higher than the eye-contact mean. For negative affect conditions, the eye-contact condition means do not differ significantly.

c. The main effect for affect condition is artifactual; there is no significant difference between the affect conditions in the no eye-contact condition, but in the eye-contact condition, the negative affect cell mean is significantly higher than the positive affect cell mean.

2. Analysis of variance summary.

Source	df	SS	MS	F
Word size (A)	1	363.000	363.000	38.47*
Placement (B)	1	0.750	0.750	0.08
$A \times B$	1	10.083	10.083	1.07
Error	44	415.167	9.436	
Total	47	789.000		

*$p < .05$

a. The main effect for word size is statistically significant; the estimated percentage off the regular price was greater for large word size than for small.

b. The main effect for word placement is nonsignificant. There is no evidence that the main effect means for word placement differ.

c. No; there is no significant interaction.
d. The main effect for word size is meaningful. For both horizontal and diagonal placement, the large size leads to greater percentage reduction estimates.

3. Analysis of variance summary.

Source	df	SS	MS	F
Reading ability (A)	2	436.594	218.297	47.78*
Instruction (B)	1	60.168	60.168	13.17*
A × B	2	69.777	34.888	7.64*
Error	48	219.332	4.569	
Total	53	785.871		

$^*p < .05$

a., b. The $CD = 2.9$. For reading ability, the comparisons indicate that for control instruction conditions, the above average readers obtained the highest test score, the average readers the next highest score, and the below average readers the lowest score. For the questions instruction condition, the below average readers score was less than either the average or above average readers. The average and above average readers did not differ, however. For instruction condition, there was no significant difference between the control and questions instruction conditions for either the above average or average readers. For below average readers, however, the control condition mean was significantly less than the questions instruction condition mean.
c. Both main effects are artifactual.

4. Table 1

Source	df	SS	MS	F
Type of task (A)	3	15.00	5.00	2.50
Noise level (B)	2	16.00	8.00	4.00
A × B	6	36.00	6.00	3.00
Error	60	120.00	2.00	
Total	71	187.00		

a. 4.
b. 3.

c. 6.
d. 72.
e. F_{obs} for factor B and the A × B interaction are statistically significant.
f. Factor A: Fail to reject H_0
          Do not accept H_1
   Factor B: Reject H_0
          Accept H_1
   A × B: Reject H_0
          Accept H_1.

Table 2

Source	df	SS	MS	F
Training length (A)	4	40.00	10.00	0.50
Skill level (B)	3	120.00	40.00	2.00
A × B	12	960.00	80.00	4.00
Error	160	3200.00	20.00	
Total	179	4320.00		

a. 5.
b. 4.
c. 9.
d. 180.
e. F_{obs} for the A × B interaction is statistically significant.
f. Factor A: Fail to reject H_0
          Do not accept H_1
   Factor B: Fail to reject H_0
          Do not accept H_1
   A × B: Reject H_0
          Accept H_1.

14

Testing Your Knowledge 14–1

8. 199.9.
9. 33.3.
10. 23.3.
11. 95.5.
12. $df_A = 4$
    $df_S = 12$
    $df_{A \times S} = 48$
    $df_{Total} = 64$.
13. 59.
14. $MS_A = 11.0$
    $MS_S = 2.0$
    $MS_{A \times S} = 2.0$.

15. Table 1

Source	df	SS	MS	F
Factor A	4	48.0	12.0	6.00
Factor S	9	27.0	3.0	
$A \times S$	36	72.0	2.0	
Total	49	147.0		

a. 5.
b. 10.
c. 10.

Table 2

Source	df	SS	MS	F
Factor A	2	6.0	3.0	2.00
Factor S	12	36.0	3.0	
$A \times S$	24	36.0	1.5	
Total	38	78.0		

a. 3.
b. 13.
c. 13.

Testing Your Knowledge 14–2

4. $H_0: \mu_{A_1} = \mu_{A_2} = \mu_{A_3} = \mu_{A_4} = \mu_{A_5}$
$H_1:$ not H_0.

Testing Your Knowledge 14–3

1. a. F.
  b. see text.
  c. $H_0: \mu_{A_1} = \mu_{A_2} = \mu_{A_3}$
     $H_1:$ not H_0.
  d. $\alpha = .05$.
  e. $F_{crit}(2, 26) = 3.37$.
  f. Values of $F_{obs} \geq 3.37$.
  g. Summary table.

Source	df	SS	MS	F
Mouthrinse (A)	2	10.714	5.357	6.54*
Subjects (S)	13	51.143	3.934	
$A \times S$	26	21.286	0.819	
Total	41	83.143		

*$p < .05$

  h. Reject H_0; accept H_1.
  i. There is at least one significant difference among the means. Follow-up test: Tukey

$CD = 0.85$. The experimental mouthrinse group had lower plaque ratings than either the control or placebo groups. The control and placebo groups did not differ in their ratings.

2. Report 1
  a. 2.
  b. 19.
  c. 4.76.
  d. 4.41.
  e. Reject H_0.
  f. Accept H_1.
  g. Yes.
  Report 2
  a. 3.
  b. 12.
  c. 2.81.
  d. 3.44.
  e. Fail to reject H_0.
  f. Do not accept H_1.
  g. No.

REVIEW QUESTIONS

1. a. Summary table.

Source	df	SS	MS	F
Type word (A)	2	17.333	8.666	7.00*
Subjects (S)	7	16.667	2.381	
$A \times S$	14	17.333	1.238	
Total	23	51.333		

*$p < .05$

$CD = 1.5$. The mean for happy words is significantly greater than the mean for either neutral or sad words. The neutral and sad words means do not differ.

2. a. Summary table.

Source	df	SS	MS	F
Neckwear (A)	1	10.668	10.668	4.29
Subjects (S)	11	69.834	6.349	
$A \times S$	11	27.332	2.485	
Total	23	107.834		

F_{obs} is nonsignificant at the .05 level. There is no evidence that neckwear affected flicker fusion frequency.

b. $t_{obs}(11) = 2.07$.

c. Yes.

d. Same answers.

3. a. $\sum\limits_{j=1}^{5} \sum\limits_{i=1}^{12} (X_{ij} - \overline{X}_G)^2 =$

$$\sum\limits_{j=1}^{5} \sum\limits_{i=1}^{12} (\overline{X}_A - \overline{X}_G)^2 + \sum\limits_{j=1}^{5} \sum\limits_{i=1}^{12} (\overline{X}_S - \overline{X}_G)^2$$

$$+ \sum\limits_{j=1}^{5} \sum\limits_{i=1}^{12} (X_{ij} - \overline{X}_A - \overline{X}_S + \overline{X}_G)^2.$$

b. H_0: $\mu_{A_1} = \mu_{A_2} = \mu_{A_3} = \mu_{A_4} = \mu_{A_5}$

H_1: not H_0.

c. $df_A = 4$.

$df_S = 11$.

$df_{A \times S} = 44$.

$df_{Total} = 59$.

d. $F_{crit}(4, 44) = 2.61$.

e. Reject H_0; accept H_1.

f. There is at least one significant difference among the means. A follow-up test is necessary to locate the specific significant differences.

4. Table 1

Source	df	SS	MS	F
Factor A	2	22.0	11.0	2.00
Factor S	23	138.0	6.0	
$A \times S$	46	253.0	5.5	
Total	71	413.0		

a. 3.

b. 24.

c. 24.

d. No.

Table 2

Source	df	SS	MS	F
Factor A	5	60.0	12.0	3.00
Factor S	19	133.0	7.0	
$A \times S$	95	380.0	4.0	
Total	119	573.0		

a. 6.

b. 20.

c. 20.

d. Yes.

15

Testing Your Knowledge 15–1

3. a. t test for related groups or a one-factor within-subjects analysis of variance.

b. Chi square test.

c. t test for independent groups or a one-factor between-subjects analysis of variance.

d. Mann-Whitney U test.

e. Wilcoxon signed-ranks test.

4. Frequency scores.

5. Categories into which subjects may be placed.

6. Response categories.

10. See table top of page 655.

Testing Your Knowledge 15–2

1. $\chi^2_{obs}(2) = 0.168$; $\chi^2_{crit}(2) = 5.99$. This χ^2_{obs} is non-significant; there is no relationship between day of the week and time of day for cars passing red lights in this example.

Testing Your Knowledge 15–3

1. See middle table on page 655.

$U_{A_1} = 7$; $U_{A_2} = 9$.

a. U_{A_1}.

b. No.

2. $U_{A_1} = 7$; $U_{A_2} = 9$.

a. Yes.

4. U_{A_1} should be about equal to U_{A_2}.

5. They should differ considerably.

6.

	U_{crit}	Falls into Rejection Region	Decision
a.	0	No	H_0: Fail to reject H_1: Do not accept
b.	16	Yes	H_0: Reject H_1: Accept
c.	27	No	H_0: Fail to reject H_1: Do not accept
d.	22	Yes	H_0: Reject H_1: Accept
e.	56	Yes	H_0: Reject H_1: Accept
f.	87	No	H_0: Fail to reject H_1: Do not accept

Table for Testing Your Knowledge 15–1, Problem 10.

χ^2_{obs}	df	χ^2_{crit}	Falls into Rejection Region	Decisions
7.26	2	5.99	Yes	H_0: Reject H_1: Accept
8.33	4	9.49	No	H_0: Fail to reject H_1: Do not accept
15.51	8	15.5	Yes	H_0: Reject H_1: Accept
26.94	20	31.4	No	H_0: Fail to reject H_1: Do not accept

Table for Testing Your Knowledge 15–3, Problem 1.

Scores Ordered from Smallest to Largest	7	10	14	15	16	19	23	26
Group Identity	2	1	2	1	2	1	1	2
Rank	1	2	3	4	5	6	7	8
Number of Times an A_1 Score Precedes A_2 Scores		3		2		1	1	
Number of Times an A_2 Score Precedes A_1 Scores	4		3		2			

Testing Your Knowledge 15–4

1. Smaller $U = U_{A_1} = 54.5$. $U_{crit} = 41$. U_{A_1} does not fall into the rejection region. There is no evidence that the groups differ in their anxiety estimates.

Testing Your Knowledge 15–5

1. One-factor within-subjects design with two levels of the independent variable.
2. T = smaller sum of ranks.   3. See text.

4.

	T_{obs}	T_{crit}	Falls into Rejection Region	Decision
a.	2	4	Yes	H_0: Reject H_1: Accept
b.	9	8	No	H_0: Fail to reject H_1: Do not accept
c.	17	17	Yes	H_0: Reject H_1: Accept
d.	40	46	Yes	H_0: Reject H_1: Accept
e.	98	90	No	H_0: Fail to reject H_1: Do not accept

Testing Your Knowledge 15–6

1. $T_{obs}(14) = 27$; $T_{crit}(14) = 21$; T_{obs} is not statistically significant. The anxiety level did not change from game 1 to game 2 in this sample.

REVIEW QUESTIONS

1. a. $\chi^2_{obs}(1) = 1.23$, $p > .05$. The frequency of drop out is not related to gender.
   b. $\chi^2_{obs}(2) = 28.86$, $p < .05$. The frequency of drop out is related to the severity of the problem. A larger than expected number of individuals with mild problems drop out; fewer than expected individuals with severe problems drop out.
2. a. The uninteresting video condition scores are positively skewed.
   b. $\Sigma(-R) = 50$, $\Sigma(+R) = 5$; therefore $T_{obs}(10) = 5$, $p < .05$ ($N = 10$ because there is one zero difference). Reject H_0, the type of task affects yawning. The distributions of the number of yawns differ. More yawns occur with an uninteresting stimulus than with an interesting stumulus.
3. $U_{A_2} = 38.5$, $p > .05$. The distributions do not differ significantly.

4. $U_{A_2} = 44.5$, $p > .05$. The distributions do not differ significantly.
5. $T_{obs} = 3$, $p < .05$. The distributions differ significantly. Pitching speed is greater with the speed gun hidden for this sample of players.

16

Testing Your Knowledge 16–1

2. **a.** Correct decision.
   b. Type I error.
   c. Type II error.
   d. Correct decision.
3. 0.10.
4. 0.90.
6. Value of α; effect size; variability in the dependent variable; sample size.
7. Increases β, decreases power.
8. **a.** Small effect size.
   b. Large effect size.
   c. Large effect size.
9. Possibilities: college major, number of siblings.
10. **a.** Set 2.
    b. Set 2.
    c. Set 1.
11. Some possibilities: Give all subjects the same instructions and be sure all subjects understand the instruction; clarify how subjects should answer if they are not sure of a choice.
12. Sample 1.
13. $n_{A_1} = n_{A_2} = 20$.
14. $n_{A_1} = n_{A_2} = 29$.

Testing Your Knowledge 16–2

1. Value of α; effect size; variability in the dependent variable; sample size.
3. .7.
4. Small, $d = 0.2$; medium, $d = 0.5$; large, $d = 0.8$.
5. **a.** 0.44.
   b. 0.97.
   c. 0.21.
   d. 0.88.
   e. 0.08.
   f. 0.12.

6. **a.** About 15–16 subjects per group.
   b. 55.
   c. About 30 subjects per group.
   d. 250.
   e. 55.
   f. 150.
   g. 350.
7. **a.** 0.20.
   b. With 10 subjects per group, the test has a power of about 0.20. For an effect size of $d = 0.80$, the power is only about 0.44. Accordingly, even for an effect size of 0.80, the test had only about a 4 in 10 chance of detecting the effect of the independent variable.

Testing Your Knowledge 16–3

1. **a.** 0.42.
   b. 0.27.
   c. 0.19.
   d. 0.23.
   e. 0.08.
2. **a.** 0.23.
   b. 0.08.
   c. 0.06.
   d. 0.03.
   e. 0.11.
3. **a.** 0.26.
   b. 0.16.
   c. 0.31.
   d. 0.26.
   e. 0.28.
4. **a.** 0.703.
   b. 0.408.
   c. 0.505.
   d. 0.905.
   e. 2.000.

REVIEW QUESTIONS

1. **a.** $\eta^2 = 0.18$.
   b. $d = 0.937$.
   c. Large.
2. **a.** Power $= 0.08$ ($n_A = 15$).
   b. 0.28.
   c. 0.59.

3. Incorrect. The researcher found an effect of the independent variable, thus her test was powerful enough to detect the effect.
4. **a.** 65.
   b. 0.72.
   c. 0.80.
   d. 0.92.
   e. 0.05.

17

Testing Your Knowledge 17–1

2. **a.** Positive relationship.
   b. Less than perfect.
   c. Yes, although there would be some error in the prediction.
3. **a.** Negative relationship.
   b. Less than perfect.
   c. Because the scores are less strongly related in this example, there would be greater error than in the relationship of question 2. But, knowing the depression score allows better prediction of loneliness than can be achieved without knowing it.
4. **a.** Weak negative relationship.
   b. Less than perfect.
   c. No.

Testing Your Knowledge 17–2

4. The more sets of scores obtained, the larger the number of CP_{XY} values obtained. Thus, CF_{XY} increases with the number of sets of scores.
7. **a.** +2383.
   b. Positively related.
   c. $SS_X = 2294$, $SS_Y = 2520$.
   d. $r_{XY\,obs} = +0.991$.
8. **a.** −2133.
   b. Negatively related.
   c. $SS_X = 2294$, $SS_Y = 2418$.
   d. $r_{XY\,obs} = -0.906$.
9. **a.** −595.
   b. The minus sign indicates that if a relationship exists it will be negative.
   c. $SS_X = 3814$, $SS_Y = 1214$.
   d. $r_{XY\,obs} = -0.277$.

Testing Your Knowledge 17–3

2. H_0: $\rho_{XY} = 0$
   H_1: $\rho_{XY} \neq 0$

3.

| | | **Critical Value** | |
N	df	.05	.01
8	6	.707	.834
15	13	.514	.641
20	18	.444	.561
32	30	.349	.449
43	41	.304	.393
75	73	.232	.302

4. See table on top of page 658.
5. **a.** −0.550.
   b. $r_{crit}(10) = .576$; $r_{XY\,obs}$ is nonsignificant.
   c. There is no evidence for a relationship between absences and test scores for the population from which these scores were sampled.

Testing Your Knowledge 17–4

1. Reduce the value of $r_{XY\,obs}$.

2.

r_{XY}	r_{XY}^2
+0.12	.0144
−0.74	.5476
−0.59	.3481
−0.36	.1296
+0.23	.0529
+0.19	.0361

REVIEW QUESTIONS

1. **b.** Positive.
   c. $r_{XY\,obs} = +0.70$; $r_{crit}(10) = 0.576$; $r_{XY\,obs}$ is statistically significant.
   d. There is a positive relationship between golf score and percentage of body fat. The higher the percentage of body fat, the higher the golf score.
   e. $r_{XY}^2 = 0.49$.
2. **a.** $r_{XY\,obs} = -0.12$ for girls; $r_{crit}(51) = 0.273$; $r_{XY\,obs}$ is nonsignificant.
   $r_{XY\,obs} = +0.32$ for boys; $r_{crit}(40) = 0.304$; $r_{XY\,obs}$ is statistically significant.

Table for Testing Your Knowledge 17–3, Problem 4.

Statistical Hypotheses	Critical Value	Falls into Rejection Region	Decision
a. H_0: $\rho_{XY} = 0$ H_1: $\rho_{XY} \neq 0$	.576	yes	H_0: Reject H_1: Accept
b. H_0: $\rho_{XY} = 0$ H_1: $\rho_{XY} \neq 0$	.576	no	H_0: Fail to reject H_1: Do not accept
c. H_0: $\rho_{XY} = 0$ H_1: $\rho_{XY} \neq 0$	.444	yes	H_0: Reject H_1: Accept
d. H_0: $\rho_{XY} = 0$ H_1: $\rho_{XY} \neq 0$	.423	no	H_0: Fail to reject H_1: Do not accept
e. H_0: $\rho_{XY} = 0$ H_1: $\rho_{XY} \neq 0$	.232	yes	H_0: Reject H_1: Accept
f. H_0: $\rho_{XY} = 0$ H_1: $\rho_{XY} \neq 0$	.666	yes	H_0: Reject H_1: Accept

Review Questions (Cont.)

b. $r_{XY}^2 = 0.01$ for girls; $r_{XY}^2 = 0.10$ for boys.

c. There is no relationship for girls. For boys, the relationship is positive, taller boys obtain higher report card grades.

3. b. Positive.

c. $r_{XY\,obs} = +0.781$; $r_{crit}(8) = 0.632$; $r_{XY\,obs}$ is statistically significant.

d. They are positively related; the higher the midterm grade, the higher the final exam grade.

4. a. $r_{s\,obs} = +0.951$; $r_{crit}(12) = 0.591$; $r_{s\,obs}$ is statistically significant.

b. Popularity and physical attractiveness are positively related in the population from which the sample was drawn.

c. $r_{s\,obs} = -0.134$; $r_{crit}(14) = 0.545$; $r_{s\,obs}$ is nonsignificant.

d. There is no relationship between popularity and physical attractiveness in the population from which the sample was drawn.

18

Testing Your Knowledge 18–1

4. a. $b = +2$; $a = 0$; $Y = +2X$.

b. $b = -1$; $a = +2$; $Y = -1X + 2$.

c. $b = +1.5$; $a = +1$; $Y = +1.5X + 1$.

d. $b = -2$; $a = +4$; $Y = -2X + 4$.

Testing Your Knowledge 18–2

7. a. $Y' = +0.8X + 9$.

b.

X	Y'
60	57
65	61
80	73
85	77
90	81

8. a. $Y' = -1.4X + 23$.

b.

X	Y'
5	16.0
8	11.8
10	9.0
14	3.4
17	-0.8

c. $\overline{Y} = 7.6$. The regression line should thus pass through the points $X = 0$, $Y = 23$; $\overline{X} = 11$, $\overline{Y} = 7.6$.

Testing Your Knowledge 18–3

1. a. $+11.507$.

b. 202.215.

c. $Y' = 11.507X + 202.215$.

d. The regression line should pass through the points $X = 0$, $Y = 202.215$; $\overline{X} = 5.2$, $\overline{Y} = 261.7$.

e.

X	Y'
6	271.3
3	236.7
9	305.8
1	213.7
4	248.2
2	225.2
3	236.7
5	259.7
8	294.3
7	282.8
8	294.3
6	271.3

2. a. $b = -0.43$.
   b. $a = 24.6$.
   c. $Y' = -0.43X + 24.6$.
   d. 41 scans, $Y' = 7.0$.
   e. 18 scans, $Y' = 16.9$.

Testing Your Knowledge 18–4

3. a.

Person	Residual $(Y_i - Y'_i)$
1	−54.3
2	− 6.7
3	+ 9.2
4	+10.3
5	+22.8
6	−27.2
7	+19.3
8	+ 3.2
9	+26.7
10	+ 6.2
11	−29.3
12	+19.7

   b. 6824.43.
   c. 26.12.
   d. Yes; $s_{Y.X}$ is smaller than s_Y.
4. $s_{Y.X} = 2.49$; $s_Y = 4.47$. We are able to predict more accurately by using the scans rather than by simply predicting the value of $\overline{Y}$ for each bird.

REVIEW QUESTIONS

1. a. +0.884.
   b. +0.884.
   c. $Y' = 0.884X + 10.96$.
   d. 79.0.
   e. 5.52.
2. a. $Y' = -0.116X + 3.23$.
   b. 2.88.
   c. 2.64.
3. a. $Y' - -4.3X + 128$, where $X =$ number of cigarettes smoked per day.

   c.

Cigarettes per Day	Predicted Birth Weight (oz)
0	128.0
1	123.7
5	106.5
8	93.6
10	85.0
13	72.1
20	42.0

4. a. $Y' = 0.627X + 57.04$.

   b.

Golfer	Predicted Score
1	69.6
2	75.2
3	73.0
4	69.3
5	79.8
6	71.4
7	73.7
8	76.3
9	75.7
10	77.9
11	72.2
12	74.2

   d. Yes, the mean golf score, $\overline{Y}$, is 74.0. The predicted values for the extreme golf scores (e.g., 67, 68, 83) are closer to the mean than the actual scores. These predicted scores have regressed toward the mean.

References

Adams, J. M. (1986, November 11). Service jobs log best real earnings rise. *The Boston Globe*, p. 69.

Addison, W. E. (1986). Agonistic behavior in preschool children: A comparison of same-sex versus opposite-sex interactions. *Bulletin of the Psychonomic Society, 24*, 44–46.

Alberts-Corush, J., Firestone, P., & Goodman, J. T. (1986). Attention and impulsivity characteristics of the biological and adoptive parents of hyperactive and normal control children. *American Journal of Orthopsychiatry, 56*, 413–423.

Bausell, R. B. (1986). Health-seeking behaviors: Public versus public health perspectives. *Psychological Reports, 58*, 187–190.

Bellizzi, J. A., & Hite, R. E. (1987). Headline size and position influence on consumers' perception. *Perceptual and Motor Skills, 64*, 296–298.

Birth weight, secondary smoke linked. (1986, August 22). *The Boston Globe*, p. 83.

Black, J. A., & Champion, D. J. (1976). *Methods and issues in social research.* New York: Wiley.

Bond, C. F., Jr., & Anderson, E. L. (1987). The reluctance to transmit bad news: Private discomfort or public display? *Journal of Experimental Social Psychology, 23*, 176–187.

Boneau, C. A. (1961). A note on measurement scales and statistical tests. *American Psychologist, 16*, 260–261.

Borgia, G., & Gore, M. A. (1986). Feather stealing in the satin bowerbird (*Ptilonorhynchus violaceus*): Male competition and the quality of display. *Animal Behaviour, 34*, 727–738.

Bradley, J. V. (1980). Nonrobustness in classical tests on means and variances: A large-scale sampling study. *Bulletin of the Psychonomic Society, 15*, 275–278.

Bradley, J. V. (1984). The complexity of nonrobustness effects. *Bulletin of the Psychonomic Society, 22*, 250–253.

Bradley-Johnson, S., Graham, D. P., & Johnson, C. M. (1986). Token reinforcement on WISC-R performance for white, low-socioeconomic, upper and lower elementary-school-age students. *Journal of School Psychology, 24*, 73–79.

Brewer, J. K. (1987). A comment on the .05 level of significance: Franks and Huck (1986). *Research Quarterly for Exercise and Sport, 58*, 83–84.

Browning, J., & Dutton, D. (1986). Assessment of wife assault with the Conflict Tactics Scale: Using couple data to quantify the differential reporting effect. *Journal of Marriage and the Family, 48*, 375–379.

Buckalew, L. W., Daly, J. D., & Coffield, K. E. (1986). Relationship of initial class attendance and seating location to academic performance in psychology classes. *Bulletin of the Psychonomic Society, 24*, 63–64.

Caro, T. M. (1986). The functions of stotting in Thompson's gazelles: Some tests of the predictions. *Animal Behaviour, 34*, 663–684.

Carver, R. P. (1978). The case against statistical significance testing. *Harvard Educational Review, 48*, 378–399.

Champion, D. J. (1968). "Some observations on measurement and statistics": Comment. *Social Forces, 46*, 541.

Chances. (1985, December 31). *USA Today*, p. 4D.

Cipolli, C., & Galliani, I. (1987). Addiction time and intellectual impairment in heroin users. *Psychological Reports, 60*, 1099–1105.

Clarkson, P. M., James, R., Watkins, A., & Foley, P. (1986). The effect of augmented feedback on foot pronation during barre exercise in dance. *Research Quarterly for Exercise and Sport, 57*, 33–40.

Cohen, J. (1970). Approximate power and sample size determination for common one-sample and two-sample hypothesis tests. *Educational and Psychological Measurement, 30*, 811–831.

Cohen, J. (1977). *Statistical power analysis for the behavioral sciences* (Rev ed.). New York: Academic Press.

Cosmides, L. (1983). Invariance in the acoustic expression of emotion during speech. *Journal of Experimental Psychology: Human Performance and Perception, 9*, 864–881.

Coulter, R. G., Coulter, M. L., & Glover, J. A. (1984). Details and picture recall. *Bulletin of the Psychonomic Society, 22*, 327–329.

Craik, F. I. M., & Tulving, E. (1975). Depth of processing and the retention of words in episodic memory. *Journal of Experimental Psychology: General, 104*, 268–294.

Crews, D. J., Shirreffs, J. H., Thomas, G., Krahenbuhl, G. S., & Helfrich, H. M. (1986). Psychological and physiological attributes associated with performance of selected players of the Ladies Professional Golf Association tour. *Perceptual and Motor Skills, 63*, 235–238.

D'Alessio, M., & Zazzetta, A. (1986). Development of self-touching behavior in childhood. *Perceptual and Motor Skills, 63*, 243–253.

Davidson, J. D., & Templin, T. J. (1986). Determinants of success among professional golfers. *Research Quarterly for Exercise and Sport, 57*, 60–67.

Day, R. H., & Kasperczyk, R. T. (1984). The Morinaga misalignment effect with circular stimulus elements. *Bulletin of the Psychonomic Society, 22,* 193–196.

DiRenzo, G. J. (1986). Modal personality and values of medical students. *Psychological Reports, 58,* 33–34.

Doddridge, R., Schumm, W. R., & Bergen, M. B. (1987). Factors related to decline in preferred frequency of sexual intercourse among young couples. *Psychological Reports, 60,* 391–395.

Egli, E. A., & Meyers, L. S. (1984). The role of video game playing in adolescent life: Is there reason to be concerned? *Bulletin of the Psychonomic Society, 22,* 309–312.

Eisenman, R. (1987). Creativity, birth order, and risk taking. *Bulletin of the Psychonomic Society, 25,* 87–88.

Elgar, M. A., McKay, H., & Woon, P. (1986). Scanning, pecking and alarm flights in house sparrows. *Animal Behaviour, 34,* 1892–1894.

Emling, R. C., & Yankell, S. L. (1985). First clinical studies of a new prebrushing mouthrinse. *The Compendium of Continuing Education in Dentistry, 6,* 636–646.

Feaver, J., Mendl, M., & Bateson, P. (1986). A method for rating the individual distinctiveness of domestic cats. *Animal Behaviour, 34,* 1016–1025.

Franks, B. D., & Huck, S. W. (1986). Why does everyone use the .05 significance level? *Research Quarterly for Exercise and Sport, 57,* 245–249.

Franks, B. D., & Huck, S. W. (1987). Response to Armstrong, Brewer, and O'Brien and Israel. *Research Quarterly for Exercise and Sport, 58,* 87–89.

Gaito, J. (1977). Directional and nondirectional alternative hypotheses. *Bulletin of the Psychonomic Society, 9,* 371–372.

Gardner, P. L. (1975). Scales and statistics. *Review of Educational Research, 45,* 43–57.

Glass, G. V., & Stanley, J. C. (1970). *Statistical methods in education and psychology.* Englewood Cliffs, NJ: Prentice-Hall.

Good, L. R., & Good, K. C. (1973). An objective measure of the motive to avoid success. *Psychological Reports, 33,* 1009–1010.

Gormly, J., & Gormly, A. (1986). Social introversion and spatial abilities. *Bulletin of the Psychonomic Society, 24,* 273–274.

Gottesfeld, H., & Burke, E. (1986). Internal power, affiliation and self-fulfillment. *Psychological Reports, 59,* 303–306.

Gurnack, A. M., & Werbie, D. L. (1985). Characteristics of youths arrested for drunk driving in two Wisconsin counties 1981-1984. *Psychological Reports, 57,* 1271–1276.

Gustafson, R. (1987a). Alcohol and aggression: A test of an indirect measure of aggression. *Psychological Reports, 60,* 1241–1242.

Gustafson, R. (1987b). Alcohol and the acceptance of social influence: A preliminary study. *Psychological Reports, 60,* 488–490.

Gwartney-Gibbs, P. A. (1986). The institutionalization of premarital cohabitation: Estimates from marriage license applications, 1970 and 1980. *Journal of Marriage and the Family, 48,* 423–434.

Haffner, S. M., Stern, M. P., Hazuda, H. P., Pugh, J. A., & Patterson, J. K. (1986). Hyperinsulinemia in a population at high risk for non-insulin-dependent diabetes mellitus. *The New England Journal of Medicine, 315,* 220–224.

Haase, R. F., Waechter, D. M., & Solomon, G. S. (1982). How significant is a significant difference? Average effect size of research in counseling psychology. *Journal of Counseling Psychology, 29,* 58–65.

Hays, W. L. (1973). *Statistics for the social sciences* (2nd ed.). New York: Holt, Rinehart, & Winston.

Hicks, R. A., Hicks, G. J., Reyes, J. R., & Cheers, Y. (1983). Daily caffeine use and the sleep of college students. *Bulletin of the Psychonomic Society, 21,* 24–25.

Holliman, W. B., Soileau, G. A., Hubbard, J. M., & Stevens, J. (1986). Consent requirements and anxiety in university undergraduate students. *Psychological Reports, 59,* 175–178.

Homan, S. P., Topping, M., & Hall, B. W. (1986). Does teacher oral reading of test items affect the performance of students of varying reading ability? *Journal of Educational Research, 79,* 363–365.

Hughey, A. W. (1985). Further inquiry into the relationship between GPA and undesirable behavior in residence halls. *Psychological Reports, 56,* 510.

Hyde, J. S. (1981). How large are cognitive gender differences?: A meta-analysis using ω^2 and d. *American Psychologist, 36,* 892–901.

Ishee, J. H., & Titlow, L. W. (1986). Diurnal variations in physical performance. *Perceptual and Motor Skills, 63,* 835–838.

Jenkins, C. D., Zyzanski, S. J., & Rosenman, R. H. (1979). *Jenkins activity survey.* New York: The Psychological Corporation.

Keck, J. N., & Fiebert, M. S. (1986). Avoidance of anxiety and eating disorders. *Psychological Reports, 58,* 432–434.

Kennedy, J. J., & Bush, A. J. (1985). *An introduction to the design and analysis of experiments in behavioral research.* Lanham, MD: University Press of America.

Keppel, G. (1982). *Design and analysis: A researcher's handbook* (2nd ed.). Englewood Cliffs, NJ: Prentice-Hall.

Klintman, H. (1984). Original thinking and ambiguous figure reversal rates. *Bulletin of the Psychonomic Society, 22,* 129–131.

Kraft, R. N. (1987). Rules and strategies of visual narratives. *Perceptual and Motor Skills, 64,* 3–14.

Krantz, M. (1987). Physical attractiveness and popularity: A predictive study. *Psychological Reports, 60,* 723–726.

Labovitz, S. (1967). Some observations on measurement and statistics. *Social Forces, 46,* 151–160.

Langan, L. M., & Watkins, S. M. (1987). Pressure of menswear on the neck in relation to visual performance. *Human Factors, 29,* 67–71.

Lee, R. C. P. (1986). The role of male song in sex recognition in *Zaprionus tuberculatus* (Diptera, Drosophilidae). *Animal Behaviour, 34,* 641–648.

LeTourneau, J. E. (1976). Effects of training in design on magnitude of the Müller-Lyer illusion. *Perceptual and Motor Skills, 42,* 119–124.

Levy, P. F. (1983, June 7). Flog or shock all nonviolent criminals. *National Enquirer.*

Lhyle, K. G., & Kulhavy, R. W. (1987). Feedback processing and error correction. *Journal of Educational Psychology, 79,* 320–322.

Lindner, D., & Hynan, M. T. (1987). Perceived structure of abstract paintings as a function of structure of music listened to on initial viewing. *Bulletin of the Psychonomic Society, 25,* 44–46.

Linton, M., & Gallo, P. S., Jr. (1975). *The practical statistician: Simplified handbook of statistics.* Monterey, CA: Brooks/Cole.

Little, G. L., Bowers, R., & Little, L. H. (1987). Geophysical variables and behavior: XLII. Lack of relationship between moon phase and incidents of disruptive behavior in inmates with psychiatric problems. *Perceptual and Motor Skills, 64,* 1212.

McCarthy, P. R., & Betz, N. E. (1978). Differential effects of self-disclosing versus self-involving counselor statements. *Journal of Counseling Psychology, 25,* 251–256.

McCarthy, P. R., & Schmeck, R. R. (1982). Effects of teacher self-disclosure on student learning and perceptions of teacher. *College Student Journal, 16,* 45–49.

McCloskey, M., Washburn, A., & Felch, L. (1983). Intuitive physics: The straight-down belief and its origin. *Journal of Experimental Psychology: Learning, Memory, and Cognition, 9,* 636–649.

Marascuilo, L. A., & McSweeney, M. (1977). *Nonparametric and distribution-free methods for the social sciences.* Monterey, CA: Brooks/Cole.

Maynard, I. W., & Howe, B. L. (1987). Interrelations of trait and state anxiety with game performance of rugby players. *Perceptual and Motor Skills, 64,* 599–602.

Mehegan, D. (1985, October 17). Ya pays ya money and . . . . *The Boston Globe,* p. 2.

Meyer, G. E. (1986). Interactions of subjective contours with the Ponzo, Müller-Lyer, and vertical-horizontal illusions. *Bulletin of the Psychonomic Society, 24,* 39–40.

Miletic, A. (1986). The interpersonal values of parents of normal and learning disabled children. *Journal of Learning Disabilities, 19,* 362–367.

Mills, J., & Aronson, E. (1965). Opinion change as a function of the communicator's attractiveness and desire to influence. *Journal of Personality and Social Psychology, 1,* 173–177.

Mintz, L. B., & Betz, N. E. (1986). Sex differences in the nature, realism, and correlates of body image. *Sex Roles, 15,* 185–195.

Moore, A. J., & Breed, M. D. (1986). Mate assessment in a cockroach, *Nauphoeta cinerea. Animal Behaviour, 34,* 1160–1165.

Morrison, C., & Reeve, J. (1986). Effect of instructional units on the analysis of related and unrelated skills. *Perceptual and Motor Skills, 62,* 563–566.

Newburger, J. W., Takahashi, M., Burns, J. C., Beiser, A. S., Chung, K. J., Duffy, C. E., Glode, M. P., Mason, W. H., Reddy, V., Sanders, S. P., Shulman, S. T., Wiggins, J. W., Hicks, R. V., Fulton, D. R., Lewis, A. B., Leung, D. Y. M., Colton, T., Rosen, F. S., & Melish, M. E. (1986). The treatment of Kawasaki syndrome with intravenous gamma globulin. *The New England Journal of Medicine, 315,* 341–347.

O'Brien, E. J., & Wolford, C. R. (1982). Effect of delay in testing on retention of plausible versus bizarre mental images. *Journal of Experimental Psychology: Learning, Memory, and Cognition, 8,* 148–152.

O'Brien, K. F., & Israel, R. G. (1987). Response to: Why does everyone use the .05 level of significance? *Research Quarterly for Exercise and Sport, 58,* 85–86.

1 in 4 women agree they should be slapped. (1983, July 26). *National Enquirer.*

Ouellet, R., & Joshi, P. (1986). Loneliness in relation to depression and self-esteem. *Psychological Reports, 58,* 821–822.

Pedersen, D. M. (1979). Dimensions of privacy. *Perceptual and Motor Skills, 48,* 1291–1297.

Pederson, D. M. (1987). Sex differences in privacy preferences. *Perceptual and Motor Skills, 64,* 1239–1242.

Peterson, K. D., Simon, J. R., & Wang, J. (1986). Same-different reaction time to the sequential visual presentation of vowels and consonants. *Bulletin of the Psychonomic Society, 24,* 248–250.

Pfendler, C., & Widdel, H. (1986). Vigilance performance when using colour on electronic displays. *Perceptual and Motor Skills, 63,* 939–944.

Predebon, J. (1987). Familiar size and judgments of distance: Effects of response mode. *Bulletin of the Psychonomic Society, 25,* 244–246.

Provine, R. R., & Hamernik, H. B. (1986). Yawning: Effects of stimulus interest. *Bulletin of the Psychonomic Society, 24,* 437–438.

Reisberg, D. (1983). General mental resources and perceptual judgments. *Journal of Experimental Psychology: Human Performance and Perception, 9,* 966–979.

Riani, M., Tuccio, M. T., Borsellino, A., Radilová, J., & Radil, T. (1986). Perceptual ambiguity and stability of reversible figures. *Perceptual and Motor Skills, 63,* 191–205.

Roballey, T. C., McGreevy, C., Rongo, R. R., Schwantes, M. L., Steger, P. J., Wininger, M. A., & Gardner, E. B. (1985). The effect of music on eating behavior. *Bulletin of the Psychonomic Society, 23,* 221–222.

Rosen, B., & Mericle, M. F. (1979). Influence of strong versus weak fair employment policies and applicant's sex on selection decisions and salary recommendations in a management simulation. *Journal of Applied Psychology, 64,* 435–439.

Ross, J. L., Clifford, R. E., & Eisenman, R. (1987). Communication of sexual preferences in married couples. *Bulletin of the Psychonomic Society, 25,* 58–60.

Rotton, J., & Kelly, I. W. (1985). A scale for assessing belief in lunar effects: Reliability and concurrent validity. *Psychological Reports, 57,* 239–245.

Ruback, R. B., & Dabbs, J. M., Jr. (1986). Talkativeness and verbal aptitude: Perception and reality. *Bulletin of the Psychonomic Society, 24,* 423–426.

Rucci, A. J., & Tweney, R. D. (1980). Analysis of variance and the "second discipline" of scientific psychology: A historical account. *Psychological Bulletin, 87,* 166–184.

Schmid-Hempel, P. (1986). Do honeybees get tired? The effect of load weight on patch departure. *Animal Behaviour, 34,* 1243–1250.

Sechrest, L., & Yeaton, W. H. (1982). Magnitudes of experimental effects in social science research. *Evaluation Review, 6,* 579–600.

Senders, V. L. (1958). *Measurement and statistics.* New York: Oxford University Press.

Seretny, M. L., & Dean, R. S. (1986). Interspersed post passage questions and reading comprehension achievement. *Journal of Educational Psychology, 78,* 228–229.

Sherwood, J. V. (1987). Facilitative effects of gaze upon learning. *Perceptual and Motor Skills, 64,* 1275–1278.

Siegel, S. (1956). *Nonparametric statistics for the behavioral sciences.* New York: McGraw-Hill.

Siegel, S. F. (1986). Reduction of test anxiety using Pavlovian conditioning principles: A preliminary note. *Psychological Reports, 59,* 48–50.

Skinner, N. F. (1985). University grades and time of day instruction. *Bulletin of the Psychonomic Society, 23,* 67.

Spielberger, C. D. (1980). *Test anxiety inventory.* Palo Alto, CA: Consulting Psychologists Press.

Stahler, G. J., & Eisenman, R. (1987). Psychotherapy dropouts: Do they have poor psychological adjustment? *Bulletin of the Psychonomic Society, 25,* 198–200.

Thorndike, R. L. (1966). *Thorndike dimensions of temperament.* New York: The Psychological Corporation.

The way we are. (1985, December 31). *USA Today,* p. 4D.

Tismer, K. G. (1985). Sex and age differences in personal and global future time perspectives: A replication. *Perceptual and Motor Skills, 61,* 1007–1010.

Tobacyk, J., Miller, M. J., & Jones, G. (1984). Paranormal beliefs of high school students. *Psychological Reports, 55,* 255–261.

Tukey, J. W. (1977). *Exploratory data analysis.* Reading, MA: Addison-Wesley.

Verrillo, R. T. (1982). Absolute estimation of line length as a function of sex. *Bulletin of the Psychonomic Society, 19,* 334–335.

Villimez, C., Eisenberg, N., & Carroll, J. L. (1986). Sex differences in the relation of children's height and weight to academic performance and others' attributions of competence. *Sex Roles, 15,* 667–681.

Webster's ninth new collegiate dictionary. (1983). Springfield, MA: G. & C. Merriam.

Weinstein, L., & de Man, A. (1987). U.S. students do not know as much as foreign students about the world. *Bulletin of the Psychonomic Society, 25,* 202–203.

Weinstein, L., & Pickens, D. (1988). Emotions underlying obesity. *Bulletin of the Psychonomic Society, 26,* 50.

Weinstein, L., Prather, G. A., & de Man, A. F. (1987). College baseball pitchers' throwing velocities as a function of awareness of being clocked. *Perceptual and Motor Skills, 64,* 1185–1186.

Wellens, A. R. (1987). Heart-rate changes in response to shifts in interpersonal gaze from liked and disliked others. *Perceptual and Motor Skills, 64,* 595–598.

Wickens, D. D., & Cammarata, S. A. (1986). Response class interference in STM. *Bulletin of the Psychonomic Society, 24,* 266–268.

Wiehe, V. R. (1986). *Loco Parentis* and locus of control. *Psychological Reports, 59,* 169–170.

Wilcox, R. R. (1987). New designs in analysis of variance. *Annual Review of Psychology, 38,* 29–60.

Winch, R. F., & Campbell, D. T. (1969). Proof? No. Evidence? Yes. The significance of tests of significance. *American Sociologist, 4,* 140–143.

Windholz, G., & Diamant, L. (1974). Some personality traits of believers in extraordinary phenomena. *Bulletin of the Psychonomic Society, 3,* 125–126.

Wood, D. R. (1986). Self-perceived masculinity between bearded and nonbearded males. *Perceptual and Motor Skills, 62,* 769–770.

Yarnold, P. R., Grimm, L. G., & Mueser, K. T. (1986). Social conformity and the Type A behavior pattern. *Perceptual and Motor Skills, 62,* 99–104.

You are what you use. (1976, February 1). *Forbes,* p. 8.

Zusne, L. (1986–87). Some factors affecting the birthday-deathday phenomenon. *Omega, 17,* 9–26.

Name Index

Subject Index

Mean Squares

$$MS_A = SS_A/df_A$$
$$MS_B = SS_B/df_B$$
$$MS_{A \times B} = SS_{A \times B}/df_{A \times B}$$
$$MS_{Error} = SS_{Error}/df_{Error}$$

F Statistics

Source of Variation	F Ratio
Factor A	MS_A/MS_{Error}
Factor B	MS_B/MS_{Error}
Interaction of $A \times B$	$MS_{A \times B}/MS_{Error}$

One-Factor Within-Subjects Design

Sums of Squares

$$SS_{Total} = \sum_{j=1}^{a} \sum_{i=1}^{n_s} (X_{ij} - \overline{X}_G)^2$$

$$SS_A = \sum_{j=1}^{a} \sum_{i=1}^{n_s} (\overline{X}_A - \overline{X}_G)^2$$

$$SS_S = \sum_{j=1}^{a} \sum_{i=1}^{n_s} (\overline{X}_S - \overline{X}_G)^2$$

$$SS_{A \times S} = \sum_{j=1}^{a} \sum_{i=1}^{n_s} (X_{ij} - \overline{X}_A - \overline{X}_S + \overline{X}_G)^2$$

Degrees of Freedom

$$df_{Total} = N - 1$$
$$df_A = a - 1$$
$$df_S = n_S - 1$$
$$df_{A \times S} = (a - 1)(n_S - 1)$$

Mean Squares

$$MS_A = SS_A/df_A$$
$$MS_S = SS_S/df_S$$
$$MS_{A \times S} = SS_{A \times S}/df_{A \times S}$$

F Statistic

$$F = MS_A/MS_{A \times S}$$

MULTIPLE COMPARISON TESTS

Multiple F Test

$$CD = (\sqrt{2F_{crit}})(\sqrt{MS_{Error}/n_A})$$

Least Significant Difference Test

$$CD = (\sqrt{2})(t_{crit})(\sqrt{MS_{Error}/n_A})$$

Tukey Test

$$CD = q_k(\sqrt{MS_{Error}/n_A})$$

NONPARAMETRIC TESTS

Chi Square Test

$$\chi^2 = \sum_{k=1}^{c} \sum_{j=1}^{r} [(O_{jk} - E_{jk})^2/E_{jk}]$$

$$\text{Expected frequency of a cell} = \frac{\text{(Row marginal for cell)} \times \text{(column marginal for cell)}}{\text{Total number of responses}}$$

$$df = (r - 1)(c - 1)$$

Mann-Whitney U Test

$$U_{A_1} = n_{A_1}n_{A_2} + [n_{A_1}(n_{A_1} + 1)]/2 - \sum R_{A_1}$$

$$U_{A_2} = n_{A_1}n_{A_2} + [n_{A_2}(n_{A_2} + 1)]/2 - \sum R_{A_2}$$

or

$$U_{A_2} = n_{A_1}n_{A_2} - U_{A_1}$$

Wilcoxon Signed-Ranks Test

$$T = \text{smaller of } \sum(-R) \quad \text{or} \quad \sum(+R)$$

POWER AND STRENGTH OF EFFECT

Effect Size

$$d = (|\mu_{A_1} - \mu_{A_2}|)\sigma$$

Eta Squared

For t Test

$$\eta^2 = t_{obs}^2/(t_{obs}^2 + df)$$